New York City

Conner Gorry

D0011377

LONELY PLANET PUBLICATIONS
Melbourne • Oakland • London • Paris

New York City
3rd edition – November 2002
First published – September 1997

Published by
Lonely Planet Publications Pty Ltd ABN 36 005 607 983
90 Maribyrnong St, Footscray, Victoria 3011, Australia

Lonely Planet offices
Australia Locked Bag 1, Footscray, Victoria 3011
USA 150 Linden St, Oakland, CA 94607
UK 10a Spring Place, London NW5 3BH
France 1 rue du Dahomey, 75011 Paris

Photographs
Many of the images in this guide are available for licensing from
Lonely Planet Images.
w www.lonelyplanetimages.com

Front cover photograph
Times Square skyline, NYC, NY (Scott Gilchrist, Masterfile)

ISBN 1 74059 305 7

text & maps © Lonely Planet Publications Pty Ltd 2002
photos © photographers as indicated 2002

Printed through Colorcraft Ltd, Hong Kong
Printed in China

Contents – Text

3

4 Contents – Text

Contents – Maps

THINGS TO SEE & DO

EXCURSIONS

MAP SECTION

The Author

Conner Gorry

Conner spent her first six years on the stoops of Brooklyn's Park Slope when Mom put the family's future up for a vote (what was she thinking giving a 6-year-old suffrage?): stay in Brooklyn or move to the suburbs. The suburbs won 3 to 2 – damn democracy – but Conner was back in New York City within a decade. She received her BA from New York University and traveled a bunch before landing in California, where she received her MA from the Monterey Institute of International Studies. These days she lives, loves, writes, gains faith and discovers mysteries in Havana and El Bronx.

The first two editions of *New York City* were written by David Ellis. Over the past 15 years he has worked for publications such as *Time*, *People* and the *Wall Street Journal*. He has also worked on Lonely Planet's *New York, New Jersey & Pennsylvania* and LP *Out to Eat – London*.

FROM THE AUTHOR

The urban beat is distinct and while I've been known to jive to my own drummer, this project benefited from an entire cast of colorful characters. Making this book sing were, first and foremost, my sister Carolyn (the sweet-smart one) and my brother Brian who, though misguided about the Shrine to St Elizabeth Ann Seton, was an invaluable resource for the Downtown sections. Claudia Milne was a fount of knowledge about everything from Five Points to Flushing and she and Tom Naughton graciously ceded their couch to me on more than one Saturday night. Thanks guys! Scott 'Rockero' Goodman was, as always, an inspiration and Joseph Aguilar helped make the Uptown parts fabulous. Stephen Culp and Rob Muraskin were and remain my 'Village People.' A big *obrigado* to Stephen Walsh for his opinions on Manhattan's best cocktails and *muchas gracias* to Asli Pelit for her EV shopping and partying tips. Sandy Levinson was, once again, a wealth of insider information.

Finishing this project in Havana would not have been possible without the support of everyone at the Centro Memorial Martin Luther King, especially Gladys Ibarra, the IT Goddess. I'd also like to thank everyone at LP Oakland for their true grit (particularly Annette Olson and Suki Gear) and Melanie Dankel at LP Oz for her indomitable patience.

Finally, to Joel Suárez, with whom I share that rarest and most precious of dreams: 'nothing compares to you.'

This book is dedicated to the victims and families of September 11.

6

This Book

Conner Gorry wrote the third edition of *New York City*. The first and second editions were written by David Ellis.

FROM THE PUBLISHER

New York City 3 was produced at Lonely Planet's Melbourne office with invaluable assistance from LP's Oakland office. Editing was co-ordinated by Melanie Dankel with help from Peter Cruttenden, Susannah Farfor and Isabelle Young. Joelene Kowalski was the mapping queen with assistance from Piotr Czajkowski, Simon Tillema and Lachlan Ross. Design kudos to Cris Gibcus for a great looking book.

Thanks also to Kieran Grogan, Marcel Gaston, Suki Gear, Adriana Mammarella, Hilary Ericksen, Kerryn Burgess, Bruce Evans, Michelle Glynn, Alison Lyall, Gabrielle Green, Michele Posner, Ray Thomson, Mark Germanchis, Ryan Evans, Glenn Beanland, Gerard Walker and LPI. Extra big thanks to Helen Papadimitriou for all her help in chasing permissions.

Also, acknowledgment goes to Conner Gorry for writing a 'kick ass' book and bringing that true NY flavor to the project!

ACKNOWLEDGMENTS

Grateful acknowledgment is made for reproduction permission: MTA: New York City Subway Map © 2002 and Manhattan Bus Map © 2001

The EB White quote is reprinted by permission of International Creative Management, Inc. Copyright © 1948 by EB White.

The Minoru Yamasaki quote is from: Heyer, Paul. *Architects on Architecture: New Directions in America*. New York, Walker & Company, 1966.

Thanks

Many thanks to the travelers who used the last edition and wrote to us with helpful hints, useful advice and interesting anecdotes:

Tim Allen, Florian Ansorge, Arthur Armstrong, Jessie Attri, Victoria Ayres, Saeed Azam, Sandra Badelt, SM Baghdad, Cristiano Barberis, MG Bateman, Rosemary Behan, Matt Bellingham, Tim Bewer, Steven Bluestine, Christian Bosselmann, Harald Botha, Tammy Botsford, Margaret Boulos, Lesley Brett, Isabelle Broz, Ondine Bue, Katherine Burton, Matthew Caddock, Eileen M Cannaday, Birgitt Carlier, Emma Chadd, Niel Chivers, EM Clements, Toby Cox, Mark Davey, Kurt Davies, Alfonso DeGennaro, Dave Del Rocco, Tina Desai, Nancy Douglas, Fiona Eadie, Mike Earnest, June Egglestone, Madelaine Eisenlauer, Christina Eliason, Stephanie Engelsen, RA Escoffey, Curt Evans, Mike Evans, Yesim Evrensel, Zorana Fabrici, Jeff Fair, Chris Falkous, Alfredo Falvo, Bert Flower, Barbara Friedrich, Isabelle & Yves Gensane, Robert Gibson, Aaron Glazer, Jemma Golding, Joanne Goodwin, Kim Graham, Ronalie Green, Dina Hall, Paula Hanigan, Soren Mandrup Hansen, Helen Hardaker, Esther Hardiman, Hans Heerens, Patrick Hetherington, Peter & Joyce Hewitt, Andrew Hindmarch, Sarah Holland, Jamie Hunter, Miki Jablkowska, Markus Jakobsson, Rachel James, Polly Jantzen, Afton Johnston, Sade Jones, Patricia Kempf, Maia Kern, Iain Kimmins, Barbara Kingsman, Zoe Knights, Oscar Laforge, Sue Landy, Penny Lee, Adam Levy, Dave Lieberman, William Littleboy, Diego Marin, Annette Maudsley, Miranda B Maunsell, Nina Maynard, Phylip McConnon, Philip Michelbach, Adrian Millington, Chris Mirakian, Dodd Mohr, Lisa Motz-Storey, James Moult, J Munsee, Kaja Nyhuus, Steve Oades, Joanna Ogden, Camila Olaso, Louise O'Sullivan, Richard Owen, Ornella Panzera, Stuart Pattullo, Stefano Petroli, Mark W Pickens, Jonathan & Susan Powles, Marcelo Horacio Pozzo, Sian Regan, Graeme Reid, Laura Richter, Peter Riddell, Melanie Rieger, Lucy Roberts, Mees Roelofs, Mariette Rommers, Nicolas Rossier, Beth Ryan, Joanne Ryan, Nina Sander, Ginny Schug, Elizabeth Sercombe, Sarah Sheridan, Mirjam Skwortsow, Margot Smith, Maurice & Anne Smith, Tiffany Smith, Victoria Spackman, Vincent Stegman, Peter Steiner, Jo Taylor, Christy Themar, Diane Tider, Igor Tikhonov, Grahame Treasure, Marie Trimboli, Jenny Trott, Mike Vagianos, Jeroen Van Damme, Bodil van Dijk, Susanne van Iersel, Jef Van In, Bob Walter, T Watanabe, Julie Webb, Stephanie Weiss, Scott Weston, Martin White, Averil Williams, Paula Wilson, Roslyn Woods, Fenella Woodward, Rochelle Yeo, Greg Yeste, Andrew Young, Janey Young, Georges Zucka

Foreword

ABOUT LONELY PLANET GUIDEBOOKS

The story begins with a classic travel adventure: Tony and Maureen Wheeler's 1972 journey across Europe and Asia to Australia. There was no useful information about the overland trail then, so Tony and Maureen published the first Lonely Planet guidebook to meet a growing need.

From a kitchen table, Lonely Planet has grown to become the largest independent travel publisher in the world, with offices in Melbourne (Australia), Oakland (USA), London (UK) and Paris (France).

Today Lonely Planet guidebooks cover the globe. There is an ever-growing list of books and information in a variety of media. Some things haven't changed. The main aim is still to make it possible for adventurous travellers to get out there – to explore and better understand the world.

At Lonely Planet we believe travellers can make a positive contribution to the countries they visit – if they respect their host communities and spend their money wisely. Since 1986 a percentage of the income from each book has been donated to aid projects and human rights campaigns, and, more recently, to wildlife conservation.

> Although inclusion in a guidebook usually implies a recommendation we cannot list every good place. Exclusion does not necessarily imply criticism. In fact there are a number of reasons why we might exclude a place – sometimes it is simply inappropriate to encourage an influx of travellers.

UPDATES & READER FEEDBACK

Things change – prices go up, schedules change, good places go bad and bad places go bankrupt. Nothing stays the same. So, if you find things better or worse, recently opened or long-since closed, please tell us and help make the next edition even more accurate and useful.

Lonely Planet thoroughly updates each guidebook as often as possible – usually every two years, although for some destinations the gap can be longer. Between editions, up-to-date information is available in our free, quarterly *Planet Talk* newsletter and monthly email bulletin *Comet*. The *Scoop* section of our website covers news and current affairs relevant to travellers. Lastly, the *Thorn Tree* bulletin board and *Postcards* section carry unverified, but fascinating, reports from travellers.

Tell us about it! We genuinely value your feedback. A well-travelled team at Lonely Planet reads and acknowledges every email and letter we receive and ensures that every morsel of information finds its way to the relevant authors, editors and cartographers.

Everyone who writes to us will find their name listed in the next edition of the appropriate guidebook, and will receive the latest issue of *Comet* or *Planet Talk*. The very best contributions will be rewarded with a free guidebook.

We may edit, reproduce and incorporate your comments in Lonely Planet products such as guidebooks, websites and digital products, so let us know if you don't want your comments reproduced or your name acknowledged.

How to contact Lonely Planet:
Online: e talk2us@lonelyplanet.com.au, w www.lonelyplanet.com
Australia: Locked Bag 1, Footscray, Victoria 3011
UK: 10a Spring Place, London NW5 3BH
USA: 150 Linden St, Oakland, CA 94607

Introduction

If you need to be sold on the attractions and guiles of New York, you don't need a guidebook, you need a life. Hah! Just a little New York humor there to warm you up!!! Seriously, this city is jumping and thriving and, though tinged with sorrow around the miasmic southern edges, it is making the transition from requiem to recovery and renaissance with determination and grace. Such emotion, pride and creativity running so close to the surface means it's an excellent time to experience New York in ways that promise to be nothing short of marvelous.

Welcome to our kaleidoscopic whirlwind, that shape-shifting enchantress known to melt hard hearts and mold great minds, run ragged strong bodies and tenderize tough souls. Forever changing, evolving and innovating, the only truism about this grand and diverse city is that while the facades may change, the people never will – for good or ill! Here the diversity transcends race or religion or background: where there's black, there's white and an infinite spectrum of grays; peace coexists with violence; and billionaires tread upon the same avenues where huddled masses struggle to sleep. An innumerable variety of miniature universes coalesce in New York and herein lies the city's mystery and beauty: at any moment you could be thrown into an entirely separate orbit, with a different language, code of conduct or source of energy. As you travel from SoHo to Sugar Hill, and Lincoln Center to Wall St, this potential sense of discovery is tactile and real and what makes New York so damned exciting.

In a city that contains many of the world's cultures and languages, philosophies and habits within its diminutive borders, whatever flavor you seek, New York will deliver. More subtly, whatever state of mind you're in, this city will have you seeing it double. If you're rushed or impatient, trains will be frustratingly late, elevators will close in your face and the person ahead of you at the ATM will fumble with their PIN. If you're heady with love, you'll notice the stranger giving his seat to the expectant mom, the dandy banker helping a lost couple through the labyrinth of downtown alleys or a vendor proffering an apple to a guy pushing his life in a grocery cart.

Yet, despite the divergent and individual worlds floating in the New York cosmos, there's a common bond forged by the knowledge that we're all in this together. Let's face it: stinking garbage, stalled subways and near-fatal humidity don't discriminate, and to endure and enjoy this city, you'll have to embrace the very best and very worst it has to offer. The events of September 11 brought this into sharp focus, making it immediately clear to native, new, honorary and wannabe New Yorkers that our island, however great and powerful, is vulnerable and so are we. This city has always been long on character, and the inimitable, charitable, strong and loving face that has emerged since that morning will be evident to every repeat or virgin visitor, and each native-born son or daughter.

It all happens here in the Big Apple, where there's a *new* new thing daily, and so it will be when you turn up. Maybe it's a guerilla billboard campaign or an explosion of sexy, young designers setting Paris on its ear. It could be the latest hot sound or slang from the hood or controversial spoken word from marginalized punk squats. Unfortunately (or not, depending on your viewpoint), there's no guidebook that can bottle New York's brand of lightning. Admittedly, this particular guide's only goal is to train your city senses and urban radar so that you can sniff out that which intrigues, provokes, soothes or sates. Welcome to the city of dreams – yours and ours.

DALE BUCKTON

Facts about New York City

HISTORY
Native New Yorkers

Native Americans occupied the area now known as New York City more than 11,000 years before the first Europeans arrived. These early residents spoke a language called Munsee, common to the area all the way down to Delaware, and referred to themselves as the 'Lenape' (People) of the region. The Munsee language had several names for the island we call Manhattan, including Manahatouh (place of gathering bow wood), Menatay (the island) and, our personal favorite, Manahactanienk (place of general inebriation).

Through accounts and illustrations by early 16th-century settlers and artifacts culled from ancient settlements, archaeologists, anthropologists and historians have pieced together a picture of how the native Lenape lived. Essentially, they were a seminomadic hunting-and-gathering people who dwelled along the banks of the local waterways in the summer and moved inland to the woods during the colder months. Using bows and arrows, they hunted the plentiful small native game (turkey, rabbit, deer) and enjoyed shellfish (oysters mostly), berries and corn.

Some of the roadways in New York still follow the old Lenape paths – including Broadway, which bisects the island diagonally and continues all the way to Albany in one form or another.

European Arrival

Giovanni da Verrazano, a Florentine hired by the French to explore the American northeastern coast, hit these shores in 1524 (Verrazano's legacy endures through his eponymous narrows and the bridge between Staten Island and Brooklyn). Though history indicates a black Portuguese mariner named Esteban Gomez sailed part of the river two years later, no serious attempt was made to document the topography of the area or its peoples until September 1609. That's when English explorer Henry Hudson, on a mission to find the Northwest Passage, anchored *Halve Maen (Half Moon)* in the harbor for 10 days before continuing up the river. 'It is as beautiful a land as one can hope to tread upon,' reported Hudson.

RICHARD I'ANSON

The daily bustle of Fifth Avenue is emblematic of the city's energy

The Struggle to Control New York

By 1625, the first Dutch settlers were dispatched to establish a trading post they eventually called New Amsterdam, the seat of a much larger colony called New Netherland. Historians generally agree that the story about the purchase of the island from local tribes for goods worth 60 guilders ($24), while sounding apocryphal, may actually be true (though a more accurate exchange rate for the goods would be about $600 – still the quintessential New York bargain).

In 1647, a new governor and religious dogmatist named Peter Stuyvesant arrived to impose order on what the Dutch government considered an unruly colony (perhaps tipping the scales towards Manahactanienk, 'Place of General Inebriation,' as regards Manhattan's etymology!). His ban on alcohol and curtailment of religious freedoms – Jews and Quakers were particularly targeted – caused unrest among the settlers, and few regretted the bloodless takeover of New Amsterdam by the British in 1664.

Renamed New York, in honor of King Charles II's brother the Duke of York, the port town retained much of its Dutch character well into the mid-18th century. By that time, opposition to the excesses of British colonial rule had developed, and New Yorkers voiced their frustrations in John Peter Zenger's influential newspaper, the *Weekly Journal*. Though many New Yorkers resisted a war for independence, New York's Commons – where City Hall stands today – was the center of many anti-British protests. King George III's troops controlled New York for most of the Revolutionary War and took their time going home, finally withdrawing in 1783, a full two years after the fighting stopped. Many pivotal battlegrounds and war sites are memorialized throughout the boroughs and beyond, and will make fascinating explorations for history buffs.

Boom Years

By the time George Washington was sworn in as president of the new republic on the balcony of Wall St's Federal Hall in 1789, New York was a bustling seaport of 33,000 people. Still, the new US Congress abandoned the city after establishing the District of Columbia the following year and many people forget that New York, however briefly, was the first federal capital. The move was probably driven by the founding fathers' distaste for a city Thomas Jefferson regarded as a 'cloacina [sewer] of all the depravities of human nature,' which is, ironically, how some people describe modern Washington, DC!

New York boomed in the early 19th century, and by 1830 its population approached 250,000 (growing by a mind-boggling 750% in just 40 years), though it had no police force to speak of until the Civil War period in the 1860s. The Croton Aqueduct, completed in 1842 at a then-phenomenal cost of $12 million, brought 72 million gallons of fresh water to the city each day. This development not only improved public health conditions but finally allowed residents the opportunity to bathe regularly.

The years following the Union victory in the Civil War became a time of prosperity for both private and public figures. William Magear Tweed, the notorious 'Boss' of the city's Tammany Hall Democratic Organization, used public works projects to steal millions of dollars from the public treasury before being toppled from power, thanks in part to the public barbs of political cartoonist Thomas Nast; Tweed died in jail in 1878. Meanwhile, robber barons like railroad speculator Jay Gould were able to amass tax-free fortunes that approached $100 million.

Stirring the Melting Pot

A widening gap between the rich and poor, and interracial tensions made for episodic explosions among mid-19th-century New Yorkers. In July 1863, poor Irish immigrants went on a violent spree, ransacking factories, shutting down railroad lines, attacking policemen and burning draft offices. These 'draft riots' were sparked in large part by a provision that allowed wealthy men to pay $300 to avoid being conscripted to fight in the Civil War. Within days, the rioters turned their anger on black citizens, whom they considered to be the reason for the war (and incidentally, who were ineligible for the draft because they were not considered citizens) and their main competition for work. Disgracefully, more than 11 black men were lynched in the streets (some set afire after being hanged) and a black orphans' home was burned to the ground. A total of 105 died in the violence, ranking this as the deadliest urban riot to date.

Economic and racial tensions continued to fester as the city filled with different ethnic groups pouring in from Europe. New York City's population more than doubled, from 515,547 to 1,164,673, between 1850 and 1880, as southern blacks arrived in search of a better life and waves of poor immigrants from Ireland and Central Europe came seeking the storied 'streets of gold.' But for those tired, poor and huddled masses there was merely a life of manual labor and isolation at journey's end. Inevitably, a tenement culture developed, whereby the poorest New Yorkers worked in dangerous factories and lived in squalid apartment blocks.

The work of crusading journalist Jacob Riis, who chronicled how this 'other half' lived, shocked the city's middle class awake, leading to the establishment of an independent health board and a series of workplace reforms. Meanwhile, millionaires like Andrew Carnegie, John D Rockefeller and John Jacob Astor began pouring money into public works and created such major institutions as Carnegie Hall in 1891 and the New York Public Library in 1895.

By the late-19th century, New York's population was bursting beyond the city's official borders, giving rise to the consolidation movement. In an effort to accommodate all the new New Yorkers, residents of the neighboring and independent districts of Queens, Staten Island, the Bronx and financially strapped Brooklyn voted to become 'boroughs' of New York City in 1898. Indeed, throughout the great waves of immigration, one in four new arrivals settled in New York and, by 1905, four out of five of these were either immigrants or the children of immigrants.

Forging a new life in a new land is never without hardship and these New Yorkers beat an unprecedented path, embracing and defining freedoms unknown to them in their homelands. This was especially true as regards work and New York was a hotbed of unionizing efforts and activism at the beginning of the 20th century. In 1909, for example, more than 20,000 female workers went on strike in what remains the most massive work stoppage by women in US history. Still, this wasn't enough to change the ways of industrialist fat cats with undue influence in City Hall and workers continued to slave away in 'sweat shops' all over the city. On March 25, 1911, tragedy struck at the Triangle Shirtwaist Company when a fire broke out, furiously igniting bales of fabric and remnants littering the factory floor. Panic quickly spread and the workers – all women, mostly immigrants and some girls of just 14 years – crushed towards the doors only to find them locked. Bystanders watched as burning, screaming women jumped eight stories to their deaths and firefighters stood by impotently because their hoses only reached to the sixth floor. A total of 146 women died in the Triangle Shirtwaist Fire, which led to the creation of New York's Bureau of Fire Prevention and the International Ladies' Garment Workers' Union.

Still, then as now, the allure of the American dream continued to draw people and New York absorbed a second huge wave of European immigrants. Its population exploded once again, from just over three million in 1900 to seven million in 1930. During this period, horse-drawn trolleys were abandoned as a major network of elevated trains (els) made the city's outer reaches easily accessible. With a flat fare that continues today, the system of els and, later, subways, allowed New Yorkers of all means and hues to mingle and explore at will, a freedom that contributes to the great democratic feel of the city.

During the Great Depression in the 1930s, crusading mayor Fiorello La Guardia fought municipal corruption and expanded the social service network. Meanwhile, civic planner Robert Moses used his politically appointed position as a parks commissioner to wield power without the obligation of answering to voters.

Bite Me!

What's with the Big Apple moniker?' many of us have asked. There are no orchards here (never were) and there's nothing red and shiny in the big city but ubiquitous cop sirens, so what gives? For years, people thought that New York City was dubbed 'The Big Apple' by jazz musicians who regarded a gig in Harlem as patent proof that they had made it to the top. But Barry Popik, an amateur historian, did extensive research into the phrase and debunked that myth. He discovered that the term first appeared in the 1920s, when it was used by a writer named John FitzGerald, who reported on the horse races for the *Morning Telegraph*. Apparently, stable hands at a New Orleans racetrack called a trip to a New York racecourse 'the Big Apple' – or greatest reward – for any talented thoroughbred. The slang passed into popular usage long after the newspaper – and FitzGerald – went to the glue factory.

N.Y.C.

He used that influence to remake the city's landscape through public works projects and highways that glorified the car culture at the expense of public transportation. His schemes (which included the Triborough Bridge, Lincoln Center, several highways and Lower East Side projects) often destroyed entire neighborhoods and routed huge numbers of residents from their traditional neighborhoods. Moses-bashing is a bit of a sport among natives and others in the know, and if you hang around long enough, you're certain to get in a few jabs at this megalomaniac who created 416 miles of New York superhighway, yet never learned to drive himself.

Tailspin & Renewal

In 1945, New York emerged from WWII proud and ready for business. It was one of the rare world capitals undamaged by war, a major port, the center of culture and home of the burgeoning television industry. It seemed wholly appropriate that the headquarters for the fledgling United Nations should be located here.

But throughout the 1950s, the middle class began fleeing the city for the suburbs, and New York began a slow but steady decline. Also migrating were television production, manufacturing jobs and even the fabled Brooklyn Dodgers baseball team, who moved to the West Coast, as did their cross-town rivals, the New York Giants. Manufacturing plants shut down, and it was years before a service economy took hold and replaced heavy industry. Hardly a month went by without some city institution – be it a restaurant, famous nightclub, department store or architectural landmark – being shuttered, abandoned or razed.

By the 1970s, the unreliable, graffiti-pocked subway system became an internationally recognized symbol of New York's economic tailspin. Only a massive federal loan program rescued the city from impending bankruptcy. The summer of 1977 marked New York City's nadir. During those months, while the city was gripped by an infernal heat wave, a serial killer later dubbed 'Son of Sam' stalked and killed several young people. In the midst of it all, the city suffered a massive power outage (just days after a power company official stated that a wide-scale blackout was impossible). Throughout the night, thousands of rioters stole millions of dollars worth of store goods. Out of control and forbidding, New York had hit rock bottom.

Yet New York's prominence as a world financial center also provided a lifeline – the Twin Towers were finally completed in 1976, signaling in dramatic fashion that the worst of the economic woes were over. Culturally, the city began a minor revival right after 1977, with films being shot on the streets, Broadway musicals staging a comeback and the Yankees, the town's darling baseball franchise, winning back-to-back World Series. Yet the city faced an unanticipated health crisis in the form of AIDS and crack cocaine, and the latter released a frenzy of addiction and decrepitude unfathomable even by New York standards, leading to a spike in crime rates. Both issues taxed the city's already overextended welfare and law-enforcement resources.

FACTS ABOUT NYC

Gay & Lesbian New York

San Francisco's hubristic reputation notwithstanding, New York City has long been the true center of US gay culture. At least two neighborhoods – Chelsea and Greenwich Village – have become synonymous, in popular consciousness, with gay life. Gay and lesbian visitors should feel extremely comfortable (extending to public displays of affection) in these areas and practically anywhere else in the city.

At the beginning of the 20th century, gays and lesbians were widely known to tryst in hidden clubs around the Bowery. Later, gay men gathered in the theater district, while lesbians attended drag clubs in Harlem. After WWII, Greenwich Village (once the city's largest black neighborhood) became the city's prime gay enclave, though quiet clubs and bars could be found uptown – a trend that continues today.

Throughout the '50s, the police regularly arrested gays and lesbians on morals charges, leading to the establishment of the Mattachine Society, the country's largest gay political organization. At one time, it was illegal for women to dress in men's clothing and lesbians in drag were often arrested and transported to the Women's House of Detention on Sixth Ave and 8th St, now the site of the Jefferson Market public library. Gay men would gather in so-called tea houses in Times Square and cruise each other on the Midtown avenues well into the late '60s; high tea and cruising are trends still in fashion.

The signal moment of the modern gay rights movement occurred in New York on June 27, 1969. That night, the police launched a raid on the Stonewall Inn, a Christopher St men's bar. Its patrons were mourning the death of self-destructive singer Judy Garland, an icon for the gay community, and many angrily resisted the bust. Three nights of riots followed. The Stonewall rebellion and other protests led to the introduction in 1971 of the first bill designed to ban discrimination on the basis of sexual orientation. The controversial measure was finally passed by the city council in 1986, and seven years later gay couples won important legal protections when New York allowed the registration of 'domestic partnerships.' The September 11 terrorist attacks are providing another unexpected forum for the furtherance of gay rights, as widows of partners killed in the tragedy are suing for survivors' benefits.

Today, the Gay Pride parade, held on Fifth Ave on the last weekend of June, attracts visitors from around the world, and gay Greenwich Village has become a visitor destination. Local gay residents grumble that the area around Hudson and Christopher Sts is being ruined by day-tripping party-goers and tourists intent on getting a glimpse of gay life (though the cheesy, cheek-by-jowl bars crowding W 4th St and nearby Seventh Ave might be held just as responsible). Still, the overbearing tourist presence, plus outrageously expensive rents in the West Village, led to a massive gay exodus uptown to Chelsea. Clustered around Eighth Ave between 14th and 23rd Sts, Chelsea is New York's hottest gay neighborhood, with clubs, cafés, gyms and restaurants all flying the rainbow flag. Perhaps not coincidentally, many of the best and brightest galleries moved from SoHo to Chelsea around the same time as the queer diaspora.

You'll find lesbian clubs and restaurants on the 10 blocks of Hudson St, north of Houston St. There's also a thriving gay club scene in the East Village, along with a host of gay bars scattered Uptown. For more information, see Gay & Lesbian Venues in the Entertainment chapter.

ANGUS OBORN

N.Y.C.

These were the Ed Koch years, the colorful and opinionated three-term mayor who seemed to embody the New Yorker's ability to charm and irritate at the same time. During this time of anything-goes Reaganomics, the city regained much of its swagger as billions were made by 'yuppies' on Wall St (for more, see the movie). But in 1989, Koch was defeated in a Democratic primary election by David Dinkins, who became the city's first black mayor. Dinkins, consistently criticized for merely presiding over a city government in need of reform, was narrowly defeated for a second term by Republican Rudolph Giuliani, or Rudy or Hizzoner, as he was familiarly called.

A City Emergent

The Giuliani era, helped by the nationwide economic boom and a severe crackdown on 'quality-of-life' crimes (including busking, public drinking and prostitution), refashioned New York into a safer, beckoning, prosperous and clean-ish city. To be sure, during Mayor Giuliani's two-term reign the crime rate fell sharply, the subway remained efficient and cheap and, statistically speaking, New York became just about the safest big city in the US. Many mayors the world over have attempted to reshape their cities using Rudy's blueprint. By this time, New York was so dope, even former First Lady Hilary Rodham Clinton got in on the act, moving to a tony suburb and making a successful bid for a New York senatorial seat.

Of course, there's another side to the coin, which most tourists won't see and even some New Yorkers can't appreciate. Primarily, the gap between rich and poor has widened significantly, making New York hostile to the homeless and unwelcoming to the poor, young people, artists and outsiders. As the working classes become more marginalized, people are looking towards the boroughs as alternatives, meaning the colorful and cutting-edge subcultures for which New York is known are harder than ever to find on the island of Manhattan. Overall, New York's populace is becoming more homogenous, the retail outlets designed to serve them more generic and the feel of the city more parochial. Sure, Times Square feels as accessible as Tokyo or Topeka these days, but then how exactly does it distinguish itself from those cities?

September 11 & Beyond

The only particularly special thing about September 11, 2001 in New York was that it was the mayoral primary, the day when the door opened to usher Rudy Giuliani from City Hall: his two terms were up and the vote promised to be a dogfight between Democratic hopefuls Mark Green and Fernando Ferrar. The political PR spin machine was well into overdrive, with both candidates maneuvering for the lead when the clocked ticked to 8:46:26 and the north tower of the World Trade Center was hit by American Airlines Flight 11. By the time the south tower collapsed a little over an hour later, it was all too clear that this was no ordinary day, nor would the city ever be the same (for more on the those events and the aftermath, see the special section on 'September 11'). The primary was halted after nearly four hours of voting.

In the ensuing madness, it was unclear how the city would respond regarding the mayoral election (among many other much graver issues at the time) and there was even talk of tweaking New York laws to allow Mayor Giuliani to serve another term. Even his most acerbic critics lauded him with praise, marveling at his ability to marshal emergency forces, maintain calm, restore services and delegate authority. He quickly attained global hero status and was even knighted by Queen Elizabeth in October 2001.

The primaries were finally held on September 25, with neither Green nor Ferrar taking the required 40%, necessitating a runoff. On October 11, Mark Green won the Democratic primary by a hair, but lost to Republican Mike Bloomberg in general elections held on November 6. For more information, see the Government & Politics section later.

FACTS ABOUT NYC

GEOGRAPHY

New York City, a 309-sq-mi area, is largely made up of some 50 islands besides its most famous one, Manhattan. Some, like Cuban Ledge and Rat Island near City Island, are tiny apostrophes of land, while other islands are massive, like the borough of Staten Island, as well as Queens and Brooklyn, which together comprise the westernmost end of Long Island (a fact not made clear by maps of the city). In fact, only the borough of the Bronx is physically connected to the US continental mainland, though its official borders include the aforementioned fishing port of City Island. In all, New York City contains 6,374 miles of streets, over 500 miles of waterfront and 1700 parks.

The water gap between Brooklyn and Staten Island – the 'narrows' through which the first Europeans entered the area – serves as the entrance to New York Harbor, which is also accessible to ships from the north via Long Island Sound. Manhattan itself is bordered by two bodies of water: the Hudson River in the west and the East River in the east, both technically estuaries subject to tidal fluctuations.

CLIMATE

Books will usually tell you that New York's weather is 'temperate,' but the yearly averages do not convey the temperature extremes that can make life here a trial worthy of Dante. It's unbelievably, interminably hot and humid for days at a time in the summer, then glacially cold and windy in December, January and February, with the odd day of freakily warm weather thrown in.

Each year, about 45 inches of rain fall on New York City, with long wet stretches

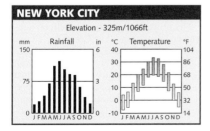

NEW YORK CITY

Elevation - 325m/1066ft

common in November and April. Snow and freezing ran fall almost exclusively from December to February, and the average total is about 30 inches, though major blizzards occur about once every four years when the city shuts down and takes on a special beauty to be coveted.

In winter, high winds and Canadian weather fronts can combine to drive temperatures well below the freezing mark of 32°F (which happens to be the mean daily temperature in January). These winds are especially strong on the West Side of Manhattan off the Hudson River, and local weather reports invariably estimate the windchill factor on these days.

In summer, the mean daily temperature is 77°F, and days can be comfortable until the humidity rises to between 60% and 90%. In general, temperatures tend to be a bit higher in Manhattan, because the heat is absorbed by concrete and asphalt. On particularly bad days, New Yorkers will complain that 'it's not the heat, it's the humidity' that's driving them to sweat-drenched distraction. In August it is not uncommon to have strings of days with the humidity hitting 99%. As they say in Spanish: *salsipuedes* (get out if you can).

ENVIRONMENT

In recent years, New York has come a long way in improving the quality of its air and waterways. Prior to these environmental changes, the city's docks suffered decades of decline while heavy shipping moved away from Manhattan to a 'superport' in New Jersey. But visitors will note that the city's narrow streets are anything but pristine, and its infrastructure is in desperate need of improvement (potholes riddle the streets, and flooding from century-old, cracked water mains are nearly a biweekly occurrence). The city also needs to find a new spot for its garbage now that Staten Island's dump has finally been closed.

The Hudson River used to be a dumping ground for 200 million gallons of sewage daily. But that changed with the opening of a new sewage treatment plant on W 125th St in 1986. The worst pollution actually came from two now-closed General Electric manufacturing facilities near Albany. These factories dumped PCBs (polychlorinated biphenyls) into the river and poisoned the fish supply. Today, it's actually possible to catch striped bass, blueback herring, yellow perch and blue crab in the Hudson, and health officials say they're safe to eat if you're so inclined.

The air quality in Lower Manhattan has been a topic of much heated debate since September 11, with the Environmental Protection Agency (EPA), City Hall, business interests and community groups all conducting independent tests in an effort to evaluate what exactly is floating around in the air down there. Interpreting the tests is especially difficult since there are no guidelines for certain airborne particles, though one Department of Labor report stated that all the dust that has settled since the collapse 'must be assumed to contain asbestos.' Indeed, an inordinate amount of emergency personnel have been diagnosed with what has been dubbed the 'World Trade Center cough' and residents are receiving 100% reimbursements from the Federal Emergency Management Agency (FEMA) for in-home industrial-strength air purifiers. Additionally, in March 2002, Senator Clinton and Mayor Bloomberg established the Lower Manhattan Air Quality Task Force, replete with lofty rhetoric and an air-quality hotline (☎ 212-221-8635).

Nevertheless, the average visitor shouldn't have any problems venturing south of Canal Street and will probably suffer more from the 24-hour noise pollution – car horns and alarms, sirens, jack hammers and trucks bedevil those accustomed to quieter corners of the world.

GOVERNMENT & POLITICS

New York has a long record of voting for the Democratic Party, though there are conservative pockets in the blue-collar sections of Queens and Brooklyn, and suburban Staten Island is almost exclusively Republican. Despite the Democratic tradition, socially liberal Republican reformers can be elected mayor, as proven by two-term mayor Rudolph Giuliani.

A former federal prosecutor, Giuliani was elected to City Hall on his second attempt in 1993, defeating the beleaguered David Dinkins. Giuliani shook up the city bureaucracy and took credit for the continuing drop in crime, but he was also known as a control freak who allowed his administrators little independence. He ran both the public schools' chancellor and the police chief out of town when they began garnering praise for good performances and threatened to diminish the mayor's own ability to take credit for innovations in the education system and law enforcement.

In 1997, Giuliani ran for re-election and won big, due to a combination of his genuinely decent record and the great weakness of his potential Democratic opponents. Law enforcement issues, however, came to plague Giuliani's administration, especially police brutality; the cases of Amadou Diallo and Abner Louima are just two of the most extreme and publicized failures of the NYPD in these years. Giuliani rarely took responsibility for his failures and this was made abundantly clear when he became the first outgoing mayor in New York history to block access to his administration's documents by refusing to deposit them with the Municipal Archives.

The mayoral election of 2001 was held in an atmosphere of turmoil and grief, and Mayor Bloomberg has a hard row to hoe indeed. He has come under fire for his severe fiscal policies that, at the time of writing, slashed the city budget by some $5 billion (with more likely to come); he maintains such Draconian measures are necessary following the irresponsible and profligate spending of the Giuliani administration. Still, his outsider status allows him to govern largely above the fray and his fiscal expertise inspires confidence among many New Yorkers who remain optimistic. Mayor Bloomberg's biggest bone is with the education system and he has been tussling mightily with parent-teacher groups and the Board of Education, which he wants to abolish. Bloomberg has continued Giuliani's crime crackdown with 'Operation Clean Sweep,' which has seen some 30,000 summons issued and 3500 arrests made for certain quality-of-life crimes, including public drinking and aggressive panhandling.

The city's political structure also includes five borough presidents, who have their own local staffs and smaller budgets for community-level works and patronage. Historically, these positions are held by career political hacks and/or mayoral candidates-in-waiting. The administration also includes a citywide comptroller (who serves as budget administrator and auditor) and a public advocate (who largely is concerned with consumer affairs).

New York also has a 51-member city council. These elected officials, who are paid over $70,000 a year, are meant to represent individual neighborhoods and serve as a check on mayoral power. In reality, however, city council members spend little time on their four-year jobs, and many of them are lawyers who conduct full-time legal practices.

ECONOMY

With a city budget of more than $42 billion annually, New York could stand alone as its own city-state. It is either the nation's leader or a major player in the worlds of finance, tourism, shipping and transportation, and is still a prestigious address for major US corporations and nearly all prominent foreign companies. Following the events of September 11, however, many big name corporations relocated offices from lower Manhattan and moved across the Hudson River to New Jersey or up north to Westchester. While no companies of note pulled up stakes all together, the security breach of September 11 awakened New York to potential future threats and many CEOs opted to spread their offices around the tri-state area rather than concentrate them on the southern tip of Manhattan.

With some 39 million visitors coming to New York in 2001, the importance of tourism to New York's financial health cannot be overstated and while that health is not exactly failing six months after the fact, the situation remains critical. An unprecedented local and domestic outpouring bolstered

hotel, theater, museum and retail receipts through March 2002, but those resources are finite, officials agree, and if foreign tourists don't start returning in significant numbers, New York could be in trouble.

Furthermore, estimates for lost revenue following the attacks were $750 million for the 2002 fiscal year and an injurious $1.3 billion for the 2003 fiscal year. Couple this with the fact that New York is facing the biggest budget gap since the 1970s (expected to grow to nearly $4.8 billion by 2003, despite painful cuts of nearly $5 billion at the time of writing) and the outlook remains bleak indeed. Downtown small businesses and neighborhoods, such as Harlem and Chinatown that relied heavily on tourist dollars, have been particularly hard hit with the drop-off. Chinatown's hardship is especially protracted as a full 10% of jobs lost in the three months following the attack were in that neighborhood.

Wall Street, where wealth is won and lost

POPULATION & PEOPLE

Approximately half of all New York state residents live in the New York City area, with the majority of those belonging to major ethnic groups. The latest census count (2000) indicates that some 35% of the population is 'white, non-Hispanic.' Blacks make up 24.5% of the population, and Asians or Pacific Islanders account for 9.8%. People of Latino origin (all races, though the largest groups in descending order were Puerto Ricans, Dominicans and Mexicans) comprise 27%; this was the first census in which Latinos registered as the largest minority group, though there are disputes as to the accuracy of this particular statistic because of the way the question was worded on the census.

Official estimates indicate that between the censuses of 1990 and 2000, New York City's population increased by 9.4% to eight million residents; of this total, some 1.2 million were immigrants. The fastest-growing immigrant groups in New York were Mexicans, who registered as three times their 1990 figures (from 61,722 to 186,872) and people from India whose numbers nearly doubled in the same decade from 94,590 to 170,899. Immigrants from China, Taiwan and Hong Kong continue to settle in Chinatown in large numbers, pushing the borders of that neighborhood north toward Little Italy and the East Village. Queens remains the country's most diverse county.

Some of the new subcultures may be here just temporarily. Some estimates suggest that more than 5000 young middle-class Japanese are currently living in the East Village. They've been attracted by the neighborhood's cutting-edge reputation and the fact that a cheap dollar takes the sting out of ever-increasing rent rates. Walking around the East Village, you'll see these young Japanese with their 'hip-hop' style and outrageous bleached Afros in a weird clash of retro styling.

Moreover, federal lotteries in the 1980s and '90s handed out a disproportionate number of resident visas to immigrants from Ireland and Poland. As a result, many Poles moved to the already established Eastern European neighborhoods of Williamsburg and Greenpoint in Brooklyn, while the Irish (who are basically everywhere) have added to their traditional stronghold in the Riverdale section of the Bronx.

Taken as a whole, New York City is a singular example of racial diversity. Visitors from abroad are often stunned at the variety of color in a single subway car and by the fact that they may be the only *gringo* in it. The city is home to the largest Chinese population in the US, along with the country's largest bloc of Asian Indians. On Labor Day, hundreds of thousands of Caribbean-born immigrants march, dance and party in Brooklyn's West Indian–American Day parade. New York City claims to have more Jews than anywhere but Israel, more native Greeks than anywhere outside of Athens, more native Russians than anywhere besides Moscow and perhaps more native Irish than anywhere outside of the British Isles. Differences in culture and undocumented immigration may make some of these boasts statistically unprovable, but a walk through several of the city's neighborhoods leaves the impression that the statement is probably not far off the mark.

African Americans

There are more than two million African Americans living in New York City. African slaves first arrived in New York in 1626, when it was still part of the Dutch colony of New Netherland. By the time the American colonies went to war with Britain, New York's black population numbered about 2000 (the majority from the West Indies), and slaves fought on both sides of the conflict in the hope of winning their freedom. (After the war, the state of New York freed those who fought in the local armed forces.) By the early 19th century, the abolitionist movement had been established in New York City, along with *Freedom's Journal*, the nation's first black newspaper. Although slavery was officially and completely abolished in 1841, voting rights were not bestowed on black males until well after the Civil War, in 1870. At the same time, black citizens found themselves losing economic ground to immigrants from Ireland and Eastern Europe.

By the early 20th century, migrating African Americans from the south triggered the development of Harlem in Upper Manhattan, helping to create a well-defined community with churches, black-owned businesses and nightclubs that welcomed whites from other neighborhoods. But the 'Harlem Renaissance' – as captured in writings by Langston Hughes and in photographs by James Van-DerZee – ended with the economic devastation of the Great Depression.

After WWII, the economic advancement of blacks again began to lag behind that of second- and third-generation white ethnic groups, but city officials did little to address the situation until riots broke out in Harlem in 1964 and again in 1968. As in many US cities, lower-income black residents were stuck in ugly, decaying housing projects, in the grip of crime, poverty and heroin addiction. By the 1970s, much of what was left of the black middle class had abandoned the city and followed earlier white residents in an exodus to the suburbs.

In 1994, the neighborhoods of Inwood, Washington Heights, and East, West and Central Harlem were collectively designated as the Upper Manhattan Empowerment Zone, which has since jump-started the economy with the opening of Harlem USA (a shopping and movie complex), added hundreds of jobs and brought many cultural events to upper Manhattan, signaling a new era for the area. After leaving the White House, even former president Clinton set up shop in the 'hood.

Latinos

Just under a third of New York City's 2.1 million Latino residents are of Puerto Rican descent. They began migrating here from the island in significant numbers during the Depression and began displacing Italians in East Harlem. Throughout the 1960s, political activism by 'Nuyoricans' led to increased recognition of their contribution to city life and to the establishment of several important cultural institutions, including the Museo del Barrio on Central Park's eastern edge and the Puerto Rican parade, which is one of the city's biggest fiestas.

Over the past 20 years, Latinos from many other countries have arrived in significant numbers, including Central Americans fleeing political unrest at home and Mexicans who immigrated from both Mexico and other parts within the US. Immigrants from Ecuador and Colombia have created new communities in Queens, and the Washington Heights neighborhood in Manhattan is home to many Dominicans and Salvadorans. New York is a very comfortable and welcoming city to Spanish speakers and even a halting *buenos días* will generate warm smiles.

Jewish People

The first Jewish people, a group of 23 refugees fleeing persecution in Brazil, came to New York in 1654, when it was still a Dutch colony. Jews have been an important part of the city's population and politics ever since. Until the early 20th century, most of this population lived in Manhattan's Lower East Side, and the neighborhood still retains its traditional character, even though most New Yorkers of Jewish background now live elsewhere. In Brooklyn, the neighborhoods of Crown Heights and Williamsburg are still home to large numbers of Orthodox Jews, and an influx of immigrants from the Soviet Union during the '80s added to their numbers. Today there are around 1.5 million Jews in New York City. They are the city's second-largest ethnic voting bloc, behind blacks, but are the most potent ethnic group politically because they vote in higher numbers.

Racial Tensions

Former mayor David Dinkins often spoke of New York City as a 'gorgeous mosaic' of differing peoples. But several well-publicized incidents have painted an uglier picture, largely because of a growing level of distrust between African Americans and other ethnic groups. In 1986, a black man confronted by a gang of white teens was beaten to death in Howard Beach, Brooklyn, leading city officials to promise a crackdown on bias crimes, or hate crimes.

Tensions between Jews and African Americans have resulted in two separate incidents that have rocked the city in recent years.

Martin Luther King: uniting politics & spirituality

When a black child was accidentally run over by a member of a Hasidic Jewish sect in Brooklyn's Crown Heights neighborhood during the summer of 1991, rumors spread that the girl had been refused treatment by a Jewish ambulance crew. During several days of rioting that followed, an innocent Hasidic man was murdered by an angry mob.

Mayor Guiliani's crackdown on crime seems to have resulted in increases in racial profiling and alleged episodes of police brutality or excessive force used against black New Yorkers. In one of the more publicized and controversial cases, a police officer was jailed for 30 years for assaulting a Haitian immigrant, Abner Louima; three others were acquitted. The NYPD also came under fire when more than 50 women were assaulted in Central Park after the Puerto Rican Day parade in 2000, when the police were criticized for not being vigilant enough to prevent the attacks.

But despite these well-publicized tragedies, millions of New Yorkers live and mingle together usually without incident, and visitors who skip visiting ethnic neighborhoods are missing the beauty of this cosmopolis.

ARTS
Dance

Since Isadora Duncan (1877–1927) introduced modern dance to New York audiences, the city has been home to most of the country's prominent companies and choreographers, including Martha Graham (1894–1991). Graham choreographed more than 140 dances and developed a new dance technique, still taught by her New York–based school, that emphasizes dramatic narrative.

The New York City Ballet was founded by Russian-born choreographer George Balanchine (1904–83) in 1948. The legendary talent combined traditional ballet and modern influences. Jerome Robbins (1918–1998), who took over from Balanchine in 1983, had previously collaborated with Leonard Bernstein on several of Broadway's biggest musicals, including *West Side Story* (1957).

Paul Taylor (born 1930) and Twyla Tharp (born 1942), two students of Martha Graham, borrow themes from popular culture. Taylor, who began with the Merce Cunningham Company, heads his own group; Tharp is now associated with the American Ballet Theater.

Alvin Ailey (1931–89) set up his Alvin Ailey American Dance Theater in 1958, giving new prominence to African American dancers performing contemporary works. His most famous work is *Revelations* (1960), a spiritually uplifting dance suite set to gospel music. Alvin Ailey is now headed by the phenomenal Judith Jamison. Mark Morris (born 1956) is a celebrated dancer and choreographer who formed his own dance group in 1988; the troupe performs original works, such as his reworking of *The Nutcracker* (called *The Hard Nut*) at the Brooklyn Academy of Music. The Dance Theater of Harlem, founded in Harlem by Arthur Mitchell in 1969, was the first major black classical company and appears regularly at Lincoln Center. Today, the Ailey, Graham and Taylor companies appear annually at City Center in Midtown, while Chelsea's Joyce Theater is the venue for the work of the Cunningham Company and newer groups.

For more information, see the Dance section of the Entertainment chapter.

Music

Classical New York is home to some of the foremost classical music and operatic institutions in the world. Lincoln Center for the Performing Arts is the venue for such prestigious organizations as the New York Philharmonic Orchestra, the Metropolitan Opera Company and the New York City Opera. The century-old Carnegie Hall is the famous venue for solo and orchestral performances.

For years, New York attracted foreign-born composers and conductors, often because the city was home to some of the finest recording facilities in the world. Gustav Mahler (1860–1911) served as musical director of the New York Philharmonic in the last years of his life, and Arturo Toscanini (1867–1957) achieved great fame in the US as head of the Philharmonic and the NBC Orchestra.

Though born and educated in Massachusetts, Leonard Bernstein (1918–90) built his career in New York and became the first major American-born classical conductor. He achieved fame in 1943, when he stepped in for the ailing Bruno Walter at the last minute and did such an expert job conducting the New York Philharmonic that he became the subject of a front page article in the next day's *New York Times*. Later, Bernstein became musical director of the Philharmonic while making frequent forays into popular music, most notably with the stage musicals *On the Town*, *Candide* and *West Side Story.*

John Cage (1912–92) moved from his native Los Angeles to New York in the 1940s and became known as the leading avant-garde composer, using atonal structures and even silence in his famous works. You can see some of his original scores at

The New York Sound

In the 1970s, the music industry moved west, following the migrations of the film and television industry before it. But as the songwriting geniuses from Tin Pan Alley settled in a sunnier climate, their complacency was reflected in their music: the 'adult-orientated rock' that dominated the airwaves. Independent record labels that made '60s protest music, or other rock that captured the energy of the streets, couldn't compete. Bebop jazz, which shook the city from the basements of Harlem to the clubs of 52nd St, died on the commercial and creative fronts, as fusion jazz challenged its supremacy.

But Gotham music was not dead, or even sleeping. In the late '70s, a new generation of black and Puerto Rican New Yorkers began creating innovative street music called rap, which expressed such controversial themes as conflicts between blacks and whites, struggles between inner-city youth and police, and rivalries among different street gangs. This gritty music gave rise to an urban subculture that became known as hip-hop, encompassing not only music but also fashion and graffiti art. Twenty years later, it's impossible to turn on a radio anywhere in the world and not hear music heavily influenced by the hip-hop sound generated in the New York streets of the '70s.

The hip-hop beat, the foundation of rap music, thumped to life around 1976 in the South Bronx, at the hands of a Bronx DJ known as Kool Herc. He's credited with discovering that playing two copies of the same record and repeating the 'breaks' over and over dramatically increased the dancing pleasure of his audience. (The break is the 'funkiest' snippet of a record, usually the point when percussion and bass meet up on a beat.) The so-called Grandmaster DJs of rap also began scratching LPs on turntables, creating a frenetic backdrop for the spoken-word lyrics that make up rap music.

When it started in the '70s, rap reacted against the upscale pretensions of disco, the most commercial music of the time. The Sugarhill Gang's 'Rapper's Delight' borrowed disco's perfect bass line from Chic's 'Good Times' to create the first international rap hit in 1979. And just as rappers tapped into mainstream music, mainstream bands soon began siphoning some energy from rap. The pop group Blondie was among the first to produce a crossover rap hit with 'Rapture,' which makes references to Bronx rappers Grandmaster Flash and Fab Five Freddie.

the Pierpont Morgan Library (see the Things to See & Do chapter).

Jazz Ragtime, the progenitor of jazz, was widely popular in New York during the early 20th century, thanks to Scott Joplin (1868–1917), whose 'Maple Leaf Rag' is a classic example of the form, and to the young Irving Berlin (1888–1989), whose 'Alexander's Ragtime Band' illustrates his Tin Pan Alley brand of ragtime.

After cities like Kansas City and New Orleans gave way to New York as the US jazz capital in the 1940s, every performer of note (and thousands of wannabes) headed to Manhattan to be discovered. Jazz became mainstream, moving from clubs to orchestral spaces, thanks to the works of George Gershwin (1898–1937) and Duke Ellington (1899–1974). (Ellington's famous recording 'Take the A Train' grew out of the first line of instructions he gave to composer Billy Strayhorn on how to get to his Harlem apartment.)

In the '40s, trumpeter Dizzy Gillespie (1917–93) and saxophonist Charlie Parker (1920–55) ushered in bebop, which quickly gave way to the freer expressions of trumpeter Miles Davis (1926–91) and Sonny Rollins (born 1929). Many old speakeasies of the '20s – particularly those on 52nd St – became jazz clubs in the post-WWII era.

In the early 1960s, jazz was caught in a struggle between structuralists and those seeking unfettered free expression. By the late '70s, jazz had become an expressive free-for-all, but a traditionalist movement has emerged in recent years, with trumpeter Wynton Marsalis and sax sensation Joshua Redman leading the way.

FACTS ABOUT NYC

The New York Sound

By the early '80s, technology forced a new wave of innovation in the hip-hop world, with disco drum machines and computer samplers gradually replacing record turntables and mixers. They've never been totally replaced, though – Funkmaster Flex still uses the 'wheels of steel' on his popular and influential weekly radio show.

The style of rap music also began to change in the '80s, as 'nu school' lyrical masterpieces exploded from the New York area. Some of the new stars included A Tribe Called Quest and De La Soul, both known for their gentler styles and the intelligent 'street poetry' in their songs. Public Enemy, which some critics consider to be the greatest rap music group ever, also reinvigorated the genre during the '80s, using its hard-edged sound to express strong views about race issues.

By the early '90s, 'gangsta' rap, a genre steeped in urban violence, had evolved into the most popular style of music in the hip-hop world. But the posturing of Los Angeles and New York 'gangsta crews' had deadly results, with the shooting deaths of the biggest hip-hop stars of the '90s, rivals Biggie Smalls and Tupac Shakur.

The subsequent decline of gangsta culture has led to the prominence of female performers such as Lil' Kim, who hails from Brooklyn, and Queen Latifah and Lauryn Hill, both of whom came out of the Newark, New Jersey, area. Some of their music expresses feminist themes or champions other socially conscious issues.

Today, there is a multitude of flourishing hip-hop clans outside New York, each with their own style and stars – but they can all trace their origins to the break masters in the South Bronx. In the city today, virtually every dance club's sound reflects this influence. See the Entertainment chapter for more information on venues.

Queen Latifah in da house

N.Y.C.

Today, Greenwich Village is still the site of many jazz clubs, including the 50-year-old Village Vanguard (see the Entertainment chapter), arguably the most famous jazz venue in the world. Each summer, the city hosts at least three major jazz festivals, and in 1996 Wynton Marsalis began the annual Jazz at Lincoln Center program, bringing dozens of major contemporary artists to the cultural mecca. Harlem has always played host to fierce jazz jams, with both local and visiting luminaries sitting in, and the tradition remains strong at places like the Lenox Lounge, St Nick's Pub and Showman's.

Rock, Folk & Punk Many pre-eminent figures in US popular music (including Bob Dylan and Jimi Hendrix) got their start elsewhere before heading to New York for validation and off-the-chart popularity. In fact, Alan Freed, the disc jockey credited with popularizing the term 'rock and roll,' was a Cleveland broadcaster who moved to New York to do a bit of his own chart busting.

By the '60s, New York became the rock-club capital of the world, with Jimi Hendrix making waves in clubs like Cafe Wha?, and Dylan heading a group of singers based in the club Folk City. By the '70s, homegrown alternative rock groups such as the Ramones and the New York Dolls were appearing at the now-defunct Max's Kansas City.

Certainly the most famous club of this era is CBGB, on the Bowery in the East Village. Though its initials stand for 'Country, Bluegrass and Blues,' CBGB became known as ground zero for the '70s punk and alternative movements. Talking Heads, The Police, Dead Kennedys and Black Flag are among the many groups that have appeared at CB's, as it's known colloquially, in the past 20 years.

Perhaps the most influential New York–based contemporary musician is Lou Reed (1943), one of the founders of the Velvet Underground. Reed's work with VU and his subsequent solo works ('Sweet Jane,' 'A Perfect Day') created an edgy, urban sound that's been echoed (but not bettered) by dozens of bands. He now lives in the West Village with his companion, singer Laurie Anderson.

Theater

New York theater is, to a large extent, US theater. The first theater district was centered on the area now known as Herald Square. It was the site of the first Metropolitan Opera House and many musical theaters.

Vaudeville, the US version of British musical comedy, was largely performed in venues around Times Square, which is today's center of 'legitimate theater.' (As opposed to 'illegitimate theater,' which, until Mayor Giuliani lowered the boom in the late '90s, was also centered on Times Square and included strip clubs, porn theaters and peep shows. You'll still find them hunkered down here and there if you look closely enough.) The first major theatrical impresario was Florenz Ziegfeld (1867–1932) who was best known for his 'Ziegfeld Follies,' featuring scantily clad female dancers. Performers like Buster Keaton, James Cagney, George Burns, the Marx Brothers and Al Jolson got their start in vaudeville, honing the talents that would make them famous in other media.

Alternative, experimental drama arose in New York City in the 1930s. The most prominent playwright of the era was Eugene O'Neill (1888–1953), whose works include *The Iceman Cometh* and the autobiographical *Long Day's Journey into Night*.

Today, Arthur Miller (born 1915) is the most powerful living American playwright. Besides his Pulitzer Prize–winning *Death of a Salesman*, his works include *A View from the Bridge* (1955) and *The Crucible* (1953), which dramatized the Salem witch trials, but indirectly commented on the anti-Communist fervor of McCarthyism. Miller continues to produce plays, and revivals of *The Crucible* and *The Man Who Had All The Luck* are currently up on Broadway.

CHERYL CONLON

There's no business like show business!

Alternative theater has produced some of the most prestigious American playwrights of recent decades, some of whose works have also shown on Broadway. Sam Shepard (born 1943) is known for his thought-provoking plays, including *Buried Child*.

August Wilson (born 1945), the country's best-known black playwright, found success on Broadway with *The Piano Lesson*, *Fences* and *Seven Guitars*, along with other works examining the African American experience. David Mamet (born 1947) has examined the seamier side of American life in plays like *Speed the Plow* and *American Buffalo*.

Neil Simon (born 1927), who got his start writing TV sketch comedy, is the modern playwright most closely associated with New York. His plays *The Odd Couple*, *Barefoot in the Park*, *Plaza Suite*, *Brighton Beach Memoirs* and *Biloxi Blues* have all been made into films. Simon not only has a Broadway theater named after him, but continues to produce hits: his recent production of *London Suite* was a case in point.

Musicals have always been a mainstay of New York theater, and the Tin Pan Alley composers George Gershwin (1898–1937) and Cole Porter (1893–1964) produced many of the most enduring works, such as *Porgy & Bess* and *Kiss Me Kate*, respectively. Stephen Sondheim (born 1930) has written popular and experimental Broadway fare, including the lyrics for *West Side Story* and the music and words for *A Funny Thing Happened on the Way to the Forum* and *Sunday in the Park with George*.

Recently, some Broadway productions have been trying to look more like off-Broadway shows, with relatively austere sets and offbeat themes. These 'alternative' musicals include *Chicago* and *Rent*, both of which have become major Broadway hits. Still, though, many of the 'serious' plays in New York come from London.

Painting

New York is as much about the business as creation of art, with many of the world's most important collectors, galleries and museums calling the city home. Nonetheless, it has long boasted an avant-garde art scene that periodically causes exciting controversies in the art world.

In 1913, for example, a young French painter named Marcel Duchamp (1887–1968) caused a sensation among the 300,000 people who attended the 1913 'Armory' show in New York (officially called the International Exhibition of Modern Art) and saw his *Nude Descending a Staircase* on display. Critics noted that the cubist painting didn't seem to portray a recognizable nude *or* a staircase. Duchamp responded that that was exactly the point, and thus the New York school of 'dada,' named after the French slang for hobbyhorse, began. Duchamp, fellow countryman Francis Picabia (1879–1953) and American Man Ray (1890–1976) led a dadaist group known for its antiwar attitudes and deconstructive art that sought to shock and offend. By the '20s, most of the dadaists had moved on, but the movement remained influential for the rest of the century.

In a more realist vein, the famous works of Edward Hopper (1882–1967) portray a New York of long nights and solitary citizens. *Night Hawks*, one of his signature works, focuses on late-night patrons at a coffee shop; it's displayed at the Art Institute in Chicago.

American art flourished after WWII with the emergence of a new school of painting called abstract expressionism, also known as the New York School. Simply defined, it combined the spontaneity of expression with abstract forms that were composed haphazardly. Abstract expressionism dominated world art until the mid-1980s, and two of its most famous exponents were Jackson Pollock (1912–56) and Willem de Kooning (1904–97). The Dutch painter Piet Mondrian (1872–1944) moved to New York in 1940 and used jazz music as his inspiration for a series of famous abstract works.

RINI KEAGY

Beginning in the 1950s, modern art began to borrow images and themes from popular culture. At Andy Warhol's Factory studio in New York, the artist and his sycophants commented on culture through many media. Warhol (1928–87) created the pop art movement, which encompassed mass-produced artworks, experimental films *(The Chelsea Girls)* and the monthly downtown magazine *Interview*. The '60s also saw the emergence of other modernist artists, such as Jasper Johns (born 1930) and Roy Lichtenstein (1923–97).

In the '80s, Warhol's legacy of the artist as celebrity spawned a host of well-known painters and illustrators whose work, to many critics, is somewhat questionable. But several of the artists/hustlers have broken out from the SoHo gallery scene to become internationally known, among them Julian Schnabel, Kenny Scharf and the late Keith Haring, who began his career as an underground graffiti artist.

Sculpture

The city's museums are filled with many examples of fine sculpture, as are the city's streets, plazas and atriums. Public sculpture has a strong tradition in New York, with works by such notables as Pablo Picasso, Jean Dubuffet, Louise Nevelson and others on display throughout the city. Sadly, the

World Trade Center plaza and lobbies were the setting for many important works lost on September 11.

Other public monuments have fared more favorably. Among them are a statue to George Washington in Union Square (1856), the Arch in Washington Square Park (1889), also dedicated to the first president, and the statue of colonial patriot Nathan Hale (1890) at City Hall Park. The Mall in Central Park features bronze portrayals of famous artists and statesmen (1876 to 1908), including Beethoven, Shakespeare and Robert Burns. Madison Square Park holds a number of statues of Union Army Civil War heroes, and at the Artist's Gate at Seventh Ave and Central Park South, there are several monuments to Latin American heroes, including the venerable José Martí. Certainly New York's creepiest public monument is the partially submerged Merchant Marine Memorial just south of Pier A in Battery Park City, which is also home to scores of public statues.

More-contemporary monuments can be found in the park at United Nations headquarters and all throughout ornate Rockefeller Center; these include Paul Manship's *Prometheus* (1934), overlooking the water fountain-skating rink, and Isamu Noguchi's *News* (1940), above the entrance to the Associated Press Building. Lincoln Center features Alexander Calder's *Le Guichet* (1963), at the New York Library for the Performing Arts, and Henry Moore's *Reclining Figure* (1965), in the reflecting pool in front of the Vivian Beaumont Theater.

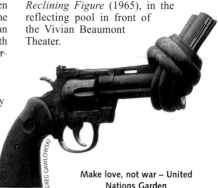

GREG GAWLOWSKI

Make love, not war – United Nations Garden

Photography

Photography developed as an art form at the end of the 19th century thanks to the work and influence of Alfred Stieglitz (1864–1946), who produced a number of images of New York City.

In the 1920s and '30s, Man Ray (1890–1976) became a leading figure in modernism's move away from traditional art forms, as he experimented with new techniques and surreal images. But Ray moved from New York after his dada years and settled in Paris.

The city's role as a publishing center provided many opportunities for photographers, particularly with the addition of advertising agencies, fashion companies and news-gathering organizations. Jacob Riis first exposed the depredations of late 19th-century New York tenement life (especially in the Five Points slum) in his book *How the Other Half Lives*. In later years, *Life* magazine was influential in the development of photojournalism. Among the most prominent photojournalists working in New York were the pioneering Margaret Bourke-White (1904–71), who was one of the first female photographers attached to the US armed forces, and Alfred Eisenstaedt (1898–1995), a portraitist and news photographer who took the famous image of a sailor kissing a nurse in Times Square at the end of WWII. Part paparazzi, part ambulance chaser and part photojournalist, Weegee (1899–1968) arrived early and often at grisly New York crime scenes with tips gleaned from his police radio. His gruesome, haunting images were collected in his book *Naked City*.

In more recent years, many photographers (including Richard Avedon, Herb Ritts and Annie Liebowitz) have become as famous for their commercial work as their more artistic endeavors. Others have forged careers with work that almost never reaches the general public. Prominent in this latter group are Nan Goldin, who charted the lives (and deaths) of her transvestite and junkie friends from the '70s to the present day, and Cindy Sherman, who specializes in conceptual series of photographs (such as those inspired by movie stills and crime scene photos).

Architecture

While many past treasures have been lost (like the much-lamented old Pennsylvania Station, which was demolished in the early 1960s), visitors to New York will nevertheless be able to explore the city's history in its architecture. In addition to the rich and varied architectural gems on the island of Manhattan, the outer boroughs are filled with some of the oldest buildings in the United States, from the 17th-century John Bowne House in Queens to the Williamsburg-like Richmond Town Restoration in Staten Island.

You'll discover grand architectural surprises in northern Manhattan, such as transplanted medieval monasteries at the Cloisters and the stunning yet infrequently visited Audubon Terrace, with its glowing, marble-faced Hispanic Society of America and the American Numismatic Society. Roosevelt Island features tumble-down Gothic ruins, and both Columbia University in Manhattan and Bronx Community College (New York University's former northern campus) boast imperial, beaux-arts campuses that put other schools to shame.

Probably the city's largest collection of significant buildings can be spied in the Lower Manhattan, Greenwich Village and Midtown areas. These structures range from the 18th- and 19th-century bohemian haunts of the Village to Midtown prewar skyscrapers like the Chrysler Building, and from the 19th-century cast-iron structures of SoHo to seminal modernist towers like the Seagram Building. There are even groundbreaking new structures to be found. Just walk down 57th St, east of Fifth Ave, and marvel at the new LVMH Tower, with its crystal-faceted facade by Pulitzer Prize–winning architect Christian de Portzamparc.

Whether you're into colonial, art deco, Romanesque revival, Moorish or French Gothic building design, you'll find wonderful examples here in New York. If architecture and building detail are your thing, learn to look *up* and tote a pair of binoculars, as some of the finest architectural craftsmanship, like the buildings themselves, reaches towards the sky.

FACTS ABOUT NYC

Stanford White's New York

Perusing a list of New York's most famous buildings, you would think no other architects were working at the turn of the century save for Stanford White, the most talented and colorful architect of the Gilded Age. His firm (McKim, Mead and White) created many of New York City's beaux-arts masterpieces, including the original Pennsylvania Station, built in 1911. Widely considered to be White's greatest creation, Penn Station was demolished in 1965 for a newer facility, over the protests of many prominent public figures, including modernist architect Philip Johnson.

Washington Square Arch

Once the elegant old train palace had been replaced by the ugly, inadequate and badly designed Penn Station/Madison Square Garden complex that now stands in Midtown Manhattan, public outcry forced the creation of the city's Landmarks Preservation Commission (which, incidentally, is playing a critical role in the preservation and restoration of Lower Manhattan since the September 11 attacks). Thanks to the laws protecting landmarks and to increased public awareness of the city's architectural treasures, other works by White – including the Player's Club on Gramercy Park, the Washington Square Arch and the Brooklyn Museum – will remain untouched by the wrecker's ball. In Chinatown, take note of the old **Bowery Savings Bank** *(130 Bowery)* building, designed in 1894 by White. The bank's Romanesque archway and vaulted gold-leaf interior are a tranquil juxtaposition to the mania of traffic and commerce that choke that corner of the Bowery and Grand St.

White himself met an ignominious end. A roué and spendthrift art collector, he was nearly bankrupt by 1905. When the coffers are empty, there's no consolation like sex, magic and intrigue, and White had all three during his wild affair with young married socialite Evelyn Nesbit. They often met for trysts in his apartment, located above an earlier version of Madison Square Garden and it was there, in the

Bowery Savings Bank

roof-garden restaurant, that White was shot and killed by Nesbit's jealous husband, Harry K Thaw. Subsequent revelations about the May to December romance during Thaw's trial damaged White's reputation and led a jury to declare Thaw not guilty by reason of insanity.

If New York architecture interests you at all, reference the *AIA Guide to New York City* (2000) by Norval White. It's the definitive text – written in a lively manner – on every building of import in all five boroughs.

N.Y.C.

SOCIETY & CONDUCT

Though being 'on' may be the New York style and all shades of black are always hip, there isn't any particular look you can adopt to fit in here. In the end, 'money talks and bullshit walks' as the New York saying goes and it doesn't matter what you look like as long as your money is green. The exception is if you're heading to a fine restaurant on the Upper East Side, where jacket and tie are required. A new trend in swanky hotel bars and exclusive lounges is to prohibit entrance to patrons in jeans and/or sneakers, so pack accordingly if this is your scene.

Yet even the most confident tourist can be marked as an outsider in dozens of tiny ways – by actually looking up at the buildings you pass (though this has changed since September 11 and now you see many locals greedily scanning the skyline so as to imprint it on their memory), or crossing the street at a corner instead of jaywalking and/or waiting for the light even when there's no oncoming traffic. Attempting to read the *New York Times* on a packed subway train without first folding it lengthwise and then in half is another dead giveaway. One thing you should never do is steal someone's cab by walking ahead of them to hail your own.

How many New Yorkers does it take to screw in a lightbulb? None of your fucking business! It's an old joke and, for the most part, it's now considered an old sterotype. Sure, fumble for your MetroCard at the turnstile during rush hour or walk slowly with a big umbrella in Midtown and you're going to piss off the natives and they're going to let you know it. But what surprises many visitors is the genuine friendliness and helpfulness of New Yorkers. Even during research for this book, in territories previously daunting and unknown, innumerable locals offered help, directions, tips and cautions. New Yorkers are a proud bunch (ever wonder why the 'I Love NY' campaign was always so successful?) and like to show their knowledge and expertise – a great resource for those new to the 'mean streets.'

RELIGION

New York City, often derided by 'religious' outsiders as some sort of modern-day Sodom, has more than 6000 places of worship – including Hindu and Buddhist temples and Jehovah's Witness kingdom halls.

Catholics are the single biggest religious group in New York City – about 44% of the population – and there are actually two dioceses here (one for Brooklyn and another for the rest of the city). Jews make up 12% of the population, and Baptists. Methodists, Lutherans, Presbyterians and Episcopalians total a combined 10%. About 8% of the population classifies itself as agnostic or nonbelieving.

Muslims have been part of the city's religious landscape since the late 1950s and now number more than 500,000. Most adherents follow the Sunni Islam tradition. In 1991, a huge new mosque opened at 96th St and Third Ave – a monument to the city's fastest-growing sect.

Afro-Caribbean religions (such as Santería), that blend Catholic and African belief systems, thrive in New York's Puerto Rican, Cuban and Haitian communities especially. Though official figures are hard to come by, adherents certainly number in the tens of thousands. Observant visitors will notice *botánicas* – stores offering medicinal remedies, icons, candles, and consultations – sprinkled throughout Harlem, the Bronx and parts of Brooklyn. Every so often, animal rights groups clash with practitioners due to the latter's belief in animal sacrifice.

PLEASE, NO GRAFFITI THIS IS A CHURCH

COREY WISE

LANGUAGE

American English has borrowed words from the languages of successive waves of immigrants who made New York City their point of arrival. From the Germans came words like 'hoodlum'; from Yiddish-speaking Jews, words like 'schmuck' (fool); from the Irish, words like 'galore.'

While you will immediately recognize the elongated vowels of New York City dwellers, the local accent (especially in Manhattan) sounds like a much milder version of the 'Noo Yawk Tawk' popularized in film and TV. Nevertheless, the New York accent grows stronger in the outer boroughs, provided the person you're speaking to was not born in another country! With a little practice, you'll be able to distinguish the heavy-tongued Brooklynite from the drawl of a Staten Island resident or the twang of a Queens native.

The city's huge Latino population has led to the emergence of Spanish as a semi-official second language. But so far, a Spanish-English hybrid has not developed for popular use, though everyone knows that *bodega* is slang for a corner convenience store, a corruption of the word for wine cellar.

It's easier to identify common phrases used, or at least recognized, by most New Yorkers, though even this is tricky because rap music is changing English in profound (but uncharted) ways. The meaning of phrases even changes between neighborhoods: asking for a 'regular' coffee in Midtown means you'll get it with milk and two sugars. The same request at a Wall St area shop will lead the server to throw three heaped spoonfuls of the sweet stuff in the cup, because that's the way the hyper stockbrokers and lawyers like it served.

September 11

The city, for the first time in its long history, is destructible. A single flight of planes no bigger than a wedge of geese can quickly end this island fantasy, burn the towers, crumble the bridges...the intimation of mortality is part of New York now...All dwellers in cities must live with the stubborn fact of annihilation; In New York the fact is somewhat more concentrated because of the concentration of the city itself, because of all the targets, New York has a certain clear priority. In the mind of whatever perverted dreamer might loose the lightning, New York must hold a steady, irresistible charm.

EB White, 1948

Dawn broke beautifully that Tuesday as city kids awoke nostalgic for summer and primary hopefuls made their final stump speeches for New York's mayoral election. News crews and pundits were already weighing in on which candidate would make it to the next round, while many New Yorkers were just glad to say adios to Rudy Giuliani. The polls had been open a couple of hours already when a commercial jet slammed into One World Trade Center. And the rest, as they say, is history.

But not quite. By definition, history means events in the past, and unfortunately, what happened that day will not go gently into the annals of the new millennium. Life changed for New Yorkers on September 11, 2001, and will never be the same in ways both large and small. While Senate investigators piece together what the Bush administration knew prior to the attacks and when, in New York the song remains the same: a requiem for a beloved city.

The World Trade Center (WTC) symbolized more than power and wealth and stood taller than two twins in the Downtown skyline. It showed the world that even when it had hit rock bottom and was riddled with crime, riots and financial dire straits, New York could marshal its forces and create something greater than the world had ever seen. Undoubtedly, again it shall be.

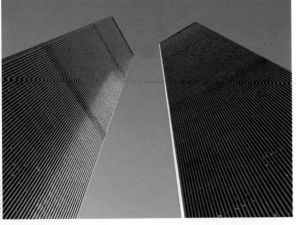

ANGUS OBORN

Title page & top: A stars and stripes tribute to emergency services personnel (photograph by Angus Oborn)

Left: Looking up to the tops of the former Twin Towers

THE BUILDINGS & THEIR BUILDER

Construction of the World Trade Center was conceived in 1962 when architect Minoru Yamasaki was contracted to build what he believed 'should… become a living representation of man's belief in humanity, his need for individual dignity, his belief in the cooperation of men and through his cooperation, his ability to find greatness.' Not everyone agreed with him (architects and urban planners cried 'foul!' while community groups balked at such a massive, some thought grotesque, project) and protests against the Twin Towers accompanied the construction. But build it he did and the first buildings opened in 1970. The ribbon cutting for the World Trade Center was held on April 4, 1973, and the last building in the complex was opened in 1988.

The plaza was modeled after St Marks Square in Venice and many observers have noted distinctly Islamic influences in the World Trade Center's layout and details. Interestingly, Yamasaki worked extensively in Saudi Arabia both before and after the WTC project, designing the King Fahd Dhahran Air Terminal and the Saudi Arabian Monetary headquarters, among other important buildings. The central plaza of the WTC drew comparisons to the courtyard of Mecca – with its fountains reminiscent of the holy spring and the clear demarcation of space. The Towers themselves, seen from below (a beautiful sight perhaps more inspiring than the much more familiar skyline view) were defined by their pointed arches which satisfied both form and function. This duality of purpose can be found throughout Islamic architecture and some have likened the Towers' facade to a *mashrabiya*, the dense, graceful filigree that defines the windows of mosques.

The Towers were not actually twins: Tower One stood 1368 ft tall, while Tower Two was 1362 ft tall (you'll find many sources citing different measurements, but these two are generally agreed upon); there were 110 floors in each. On clear days you could see 45 miles in each direction from the higher floors. The base length of each building was 400 ft, with a foundation 700-ft deep. There was more than nine million square feet of office space in the two buildings and around 40,000 workers passing through their doors each weekday. Those workers were shuttled to their offices via one of 104 passenger elevators within each building, which they might share with some of the estimated 10,000 tourists who visited the Towers every day.

The Center stood on a 16-acre plot, of which five acres were given over to the central plaza. In addition to the two Towers, there were ten major buildings in the immediate vicinity which collapsed following the attacks.

GREG GAWLOWSKI

Right: Damage done to nearby buildings

TV IS NOT REALITY

The footage is horrifying, but the reality is far worse and without parallel in the sanitized, virtual world of television, video games, Internet spam and Hollywood sputum. Throats didn't scald watching the Towers crumble on CNN and the eerie quiet and post-apocalyptic dust didn't blanket everything as network talking heads interpreted events. No matter how talented, no cinematographer could capture the new vista: the sickeningly permanent site looking south on Sixth Ave, over the water from New York Harbor, or across the way from Hoboken and Williamsburg. 'It's not there. It's not there,' stuttered one of New York's bravest from Engine 7, Ladder 1, the first company to arrive at the scene. And here we find ourselves six, nine, 12 months later or more, uttering the exact same thing, with equal disbelief.

The Viewing Platform Television is not reality and people from all corners are coming to New York to experience what their minds and hearts can't quite grasp in two dimensions. In an effort to accommodate all those coming to see what was and will be, a massive viewing platform was erected overlooking the site where workers toiled 24 hours a day, seven days a week for more than 235 days in order to wipe clean that soiled and spoiled space.

After many sleepless nights, teary days and conversations with New Yorkers of all stripes, I'm concluding that bearing witness to the tragedy – even long after the fact – is an effort to make it real: that human nature is such that we flock to disaster to pay our respects, mourn our innocence and try to understand what happened here. The viewing platform, the dramatic and comforting (but disconcerting) photographs of our old skyline and the sprawling vigils are attempts to provide a context and establish a connection that television fails to create, no matter how desperately it tries with its *Temptation Island–Survivor* reality claptrap. By the same token,

COREY WISE

Left: An old tourist information board close to the present-day viewing platform

I suppose this is also why not one single New Yorker in my circle visited the viewing platform: for them, having seen what no eyes should see, it's already way too real. A kinder, gentler reminder of our 'old' New York is the *Sphere* sculpture, recovered from the rubble of the World Trade Center Plaza and re-erected (albeit dinged and dented) in Battery Park; many people prefer to pay homage to our lost landscape by heading here.

The viewing platform, previously on the eastern edge of the site at Church St, eventually made way for a viewing area *(open 9am-9pm daily)* that runs alongside the southern boundary of the site from Broadway to Greenwich St. No tickets are necessary to access the area, just show up.

Onwards & Upwards The plans for rebuilding Downtown are complex, and made more so by the powerful emotional, political and financial forces coming to bear upon the disciplines of urban planning, public transportation, architecture and historic preservation. Save for the temporary memorial 'Tribute in Light' which shone into the sky like ephemeral towers between March and April, 2002, and the reconstruction of the PATH tunnel that once ran beneath the World Trade Center, no plans had been approved at the time of writing.

Indeed, the ethical question remains whether anything at all should be built atop what is a massive grave site (as of the beginning of May 2002, the remains of only 869 of a total 2843 victims had been recovered, though workers found 19,000 body parts). There is no doubt that rebuilding will occur, couched in terms of resiliency and democracy's triumph over terrorism. Above all, the question remains: Who should decide the future nature of the site?

Right: One of many makeshift memorials to September 11

JENNIFER STEFFEY

This last, dogged issue is being embraced wholeheartedly, with victims' families, preservationists, politicians, financiers and Downtown residents all adding their voices. One of the proposals is to replicate the Twin Towers, which has a certain appeal (a poll conducted in July 2002 showed that 48% of New York City residents preferred they be rebuilt exactly as they were). But this would discount the opportunity to make the site better, to improve what was always miserable traffic flow and streamline the public transportation there. Furthermore, there is still, and may always be, a question as to the structural integrity of the Towers (which had an interior steel 'skin' to make them more flexible instead of a steel 'skeleton' like other skyscrapers), precluding this option.

The rebuilding of Lower Manhattan is being called the 'largest urban redevelopment project in American history' and while the precise form this project will take is uncertain, six preliminary proposals were submitted in July 2002. From these proposals and several Town Hall meetings designed to incorporate public opinion, a final plan will be decided upon by the beginning of 2003.

Unfortunately, the requirements for the proposals were so strict (eg, 11 million sq ft of office space, another 600,000 sq ft of retail space and an 800-room hotel) that none of the original six were especially innovative or captivating, and most were remarkably similar. Mayor Bloomberg was disappointed with the submissions, calling them only 'a starting point', and many community activists lamented the fact that new housing did not figure in any of the proposals (though several buildings already flanking the site would be converted to residential units under most of the preliminary designs).

All the plans set aside a memorial park, some as big as two-thirds of the original 16-acre site, and a few of the designs incorporated the footprints of the fallen towers. Although these plans are considered preliminary, the designers agree that the final plan will definitely restore Greenwich St (this street terminated at the WTC, which was one of the greatest criticisms of the original site). An aesthetic element appearing in several of the designs are glass towers or 'beacons;' in more than one of the proposals, these glass structures would rise taller than the Twin Towers. While dissent and disappointment characterized the debate surrounding the six designs, planners agree that the final plan will likely incorporate aspects of all the original proposals.

Timeline

8:46am	9:02am	9:17am	9:21am
American Airlines Flight 11 crashes into One WTC (North Tower)	American Airlines Flight 175 crashes into Two WTC (South Tower)	Federal Aviation Administration (FAA) closes all New York area airports	Port Authority of NY & NJ closes all New York area bridges and tunnels, leaving innumerable commuters stranded on Manhattan

10:10am	10:28am	10:53am
United Airlines Flight 77 crashes in rural Pennsylvania	North Tower collapses	New York's mayoral primary elections are postponed

JON DAVISON

GREG GAWLOWSKI

Top: Battery Park and the old Manhattan skyline

Right: The Manhattan skyline, post September 11, viewed from the Staten Island ferry

Timeline

9:40am	9:43am	9:45am	9:59am
FAA halts all national air traffic for the first time in history	American Airlines Flight 77 crashes into the Pentagon	White House is evacuated	South Tower collapses

2:49pm		5:25pm
Mayor Giuliani announces that some subway and bus services have been restored; asked about the death toll he responds: 'I don't think we want to speculate about that – more than any of us can bear.'		Seven WTC collapses

New Yorker's State of Mind

It's six months to the day as I write this, but you wouldn't know it if the calendar and media weren't keeping track. In these days of sorrow and recovery, grief and regrouping, time refracts oddly here in New York, spinning along in a nonlinear way that makes its progress hard to grasp even as we tick off the days. All over the city, out to the boroughs and the suburbs beyond, vigils have taken root and grown – remembrance ceremonies and remittances to memorial funds are our humble offerings – and we welcome the daffodils pushing up in defiant rejuvenation. Even though we make motions to mimic these flowers, channeling springtime energy in a facsimile of the phoenix rising from the ashes, tears still erupt unexpectedly, Downtown still feels toxic, the altered skyline nauseates anew, and hanging over it all is a stunned incomprehension, most painfully among those who lost loved ones. I know this sounds melodramatic to anyone not living through it; give thanks.

Through this miasma, we're forced to search for a silver lining. Among the thunderclaps, we find proffered marriage proposals, buried hatchets, an explosion of creativity and art that gives form to our pain and a new-found respect, gratitude and awe for our firefighters, police officers and emergency personnel (a total of 403 uniformed officers were killed on September 11). The sanctity and brevity of life has dawned upon many and the kinship of peoples has deepened – certainly our connection with the rest of the war-torn globe has knit inextricably; even the national peace movement has been resuscitated. I feel inordinately fortunate that my sister and brother escaped physical harm that day, though watching it happen burned gruesome, abominable images on their eyes and minds. For those reading this who are mourning the death of friends and family, please forgive me for saying that we are lucky in one sense because it could have been much worse.

The inhumanity of September 11 shocked us from our stupor forcing us to take responsibility for this great cosmopolis and by extension, our world, to face its vulnerability and try and understand the causes of such an act. The seminal international city, New York, now truly belongs to all of us. Indeed, in the wake of the attacks, former mayor Rudy Giuliani proclaimed New York the 'capital of the world,' an assertion reinforced by the fact that 91 countries were represented among the 494 foreign nationals that died that day (accounting for 17% of total fatalities). Only time will tell what remains of this narrative and what will become of our protagonist, but between now and then, we'll have to hope for the best, brace ourselves for the worst and work together towards a new way. Forging a better reality and future: I hope this will be the legacy of that Tuesday.

Let the Healing Begin Still, my experience is singularly personal and one of the many lessons emerging from the attacks is that everyone has their own way of coping, with a different timeline, reasoning and flow.

Some folks can't even bear to venture south of Canal St, while others find solace at the site, visiting it to commune with the victims, augment the memorials and watch the progress and process there. Indeed, one

New Yorker's State of Mind

survey showed that 38% of New York residents have visited the World Trade Center site since September 11. As for denizens living near the awful mess, many have adopted a 'hell no, we won't go' attitude and refuse to leave their Downtown digs, while others have chosen to relocate in an effort to maintain what remains of their mental, spiritual and physical health. These are not easy choices and living with those decisions day after day is a challenge.

Some families have banded together to sue Osama Bin Laden, while others shun all media attention and entanglements in favor of a more private recovery. Of course, there is also anger, rage, guilt, vulnerability, denial and more in the mix. We are discovering that the spectrum of grief is infinitely varied and the healing process individual and complex.

The City of New York has thrown all its resources into the recovery effort and is making a public push to re-establish the mental and spiritual health of its population through Project Liberty. This program of the NYC Health Department encourages people to 'feel free to feel better' and staffs multiple toll-free numbers and counseling offices for those wishing to talk to someone about the anxiety, distress, sadness and depression that are lingering effects of the attacks. According to recent figures, 9.8% of people who sought counseling at city agencies were suffering from at least some symptoms of post-traumatic stress disorder (the figure increased to around 20% for those living south of Canal St).

One reaction seems universal, however. Since the collapse until this very day, New Yorkers scan the skyline greedily, naming the buildings aloud and etching their designs into their minds, should they awake one day and find these buildings gone: the Woolworth, Chrysler, Empire State, Dakota and others not as celebrated, but just as grand. They too, are proof that art, passion and sweet, symphonic melodies can be created through brick, mortar, glass and steel. They too, are the essence of our New York.

Conner Gorry

GREG GAWLOWSKI

Right: Memorials at the former World Trade Center site

Facts for the Visitor

WHEN TO GO

New York is a world-class, year-round destination, so there isn't really an 'off-season' when prices drop substantially. Winter airfare bargains are sometimes available, and many of the major hotels offer package deals for the slower months from January to mid-March.

If you're planning your trip solely on the weather, generally the nicest and most temperate time to visit is between mid-September and October (the latter affords memorable foliage), along with all of May (when New Yorkers emerge from their winter caves to greet the spring; at this time everyone is especially friendly and scantily clad) and early June. Unfortunately, as these months are popular with tourists, hotel prices are scaled accordingly. August in New York is notoriously awful, typified by hot, humid, sticky and cranky conditions, folks with the resources to do so get the hell out. At this time, you'll find things unusually quiet and uncrowded. What's more, the trying climatic conditions force a solidarity and camaraderie particular to New York's dog days of summer and even the greenest of tourists earn street cred by turning up and withstanding the hell that is August here.

ORIENTATION

Most of Manhattan is easy to navigate, thanks to a street plan imposed by a city planning commission in 1811. The plan covered the area north of Houston St and featured a grid system of 12 named or numbered avenues running the north-south length of the island, crossed by east-west numbered streets;

numbered streets go higher as you go north. (Walkers take note: 20 east-west numbered blocks equals approximately one mile. Also be warned when doing calculations that avenues – called cross-town blocks – are much longer than north-south blocks.)

Things get trickier south of 14th St, especially in the Lower Manhattan and Wall St area where the curvy lanes, cow paths and merchants' byways laid out by the Dutch and other early settlers still dominate and confuse. Lack of urban planning 'way back when' means you can actually stand at Wavery Place and Wavery Place in the West Village or at the nearby corner of W 4th and W 10th Sts. Here's a taxi tip for that screwy part of town: when cabbing it down to this area of the West Village, choose a major thoroughfare as your stated destination to avoid circling around at the behest of a dumbfounded driver, and walk from there.

Just above Washington Square, Fifth Ave serves as the general dividing line between the 'East Side' and the 'West Side.' Cross-street numbers begin there and grow higher toward each river, generally (but not exclusively) in 100-digit increments per block. Therefore, **Carnegie Hall** *(Map 6; 154 W 57th St)* is about 1½ blocks west of Fifth Ave.

Broadway is the only major avenue to cut diagonally across the island and up into the Bronx and is the remnant of old Native American paths.

MAPS

Lonely Planet publishes a pocket-size laminated map of New York City; it's available at all bookstores. You can also

NEIL SETCHFIELD

42

pick up free Downtown Manhattan maps in the lobby of any decent hotel. If you want to explore the city at large, buy a five-borough street atlas. Geographia and Hagstrom both publish paperback-size editions that sell for about $14.

Most subway stations in Manhattan have 'Passenger Information Centers' next to the token booth; these feature a wonderfully large-scale, detailed map of the surrounding neighborhood, with all points of interests clearly marked. Taking a look before heading above ground may save you from getting lost. A new handy, dandy item on the map market is a wallet-sized, laminated subway map ($2); the cards are available for each borough or with the whole system in teeny, tiny type.

You can buy maps at the **Hagstrom Map and Travel Center** (Map 6, #106; ☎ 212-398-1222; 57 W 43rd St • Map 3, #71; ☎ 212-785-5343; 125 Maiden Lane) and the **Rand McNally Travel Store** (Map 5, #50; ☎ 212-758-7488; 150 E 52nd St), between Lexington and Third Ave, which ships globes and atlases worldwide. Hagstrom produces a handy five-borough map and both stores sell colorful wall maps of Manhattan made by the Identity Map Company for $30. Though not practical for walking around the city, these detailed maps make great souvenirs.

TOURIST OFFICES

NYC & Company (also known as the Convention & Visitors Bureau) has a sleek, well-organized **Information Center** (Map 6, #20; brochures & reservations ☎ 212-397-8222, 800-692-8474; W www.nycvisit.com; 810 Seventh Ave at 53rd St; open 8:30am-6pm Mon-Fri, 9am-5pm Sat & Sun) in the Times Square area. You can pick up hundreds of brochures about cultural events here or use the hassle-free ATM. To speak directly with a multilingual counselor, call ☎ 212-484-1222.

The **Times Square Visitors Center** (Map 6, #53; W www.timessquarebid.org; 1560 Broadway; open 8am-8pm daily), between 46th and 47th Sts, is a great resource in the heart of Times Square with an ATM, free Internet access, public bathrooms, literature galore and the Broadway Ticket Center, which sells tickets to Broadway plays.

The **Big Apple Greeters Program** (☎ 212-669-8159, fax 212-669-3685; W www.bigapplegreeter.org) also offers special events information on its hotline. The program's 500 volunteers offer free, praiseworthy tours of lesser-known neighborhoods. Some greeters are multilingual and can accommodate foreign tourists; others specialize in helping the disabled. You must make reservations in advance. The website has links in French, German and Spanish.

The **New York State Travel Information Center** (Map 6, #20; ☎ 800-225-5697; 810 Seventh Ave at 53rd St) issues books that cover other areas upstate.

DOCUMENTS
Passports & Visas

Canadians must have proper proof of Canadian citizenship, such as a citizenship card with photo ID or a passport. Visitors from other countries must have a valid passport, and many visitors also require a US visa. Due to stricter visa regulations following September 11, foreigners needing visas to travel to the US should plan ahead.

However, there is a reciprocal visa-waiver program in which citizens of certain countries may enter the USA for stays of 90 days or less with a passport but without first obtaining a US visa. Currently these countries include Australia, Austria, Denmark, France, Germany, Ireland, Italy, Japan, Netherlands, New Zealand, Portugal, Singapore, Spain, Sweden, Switzerland and the UK. Under this program you must have a roundtrip ticket that is nonrefundable in the USA, and you will not be allowed to extend your stay beyond 90 days.

Other travelers will need to obtain a visa from a US consulate or embassy. In most countries, the process can be done by mail. To apply for a visa, your passport should be valid for at least six months longer than your intended stay, and you'll need to submit a recent photo (1½ inches square or 37mm x 37mm) with the application. Documents of financial stability and/or guarantees from a

US resident are sometimes required, particularly for those from developing nations.

Visa applicants may be required to 'demonstrate binding obligations' that will ensure their return home. Because of this requirement, those planning to travel through other countries before arriving in the USA are generally better off applying for their US visa while they are still in their home country – rather than after they're already on the road.

The Non-Immigrant Visitors Visa is the most common visa It is available in two forms, B1 for business purposes and B2 for tourism or visiting friends and relatives. The validity period for US visitor visas depends on what country you're from. The length of time you'll be allowed to stay in the USA is ultimately determined by US immigration authorities at the port of entry. If you're coming to the USA to work or study, you will probably need a different type of visa, and the company or institution where you're going to work should make the arrangements. Allow six months in advance for processing the application.

Non-US citizens with the HIV virus should know that they can be excluded from entry to the US.

Visa Extensions If you want, need or hope to stay in the USA beyond the date stamped on your passport, go to the **Immigration and Naturalization Service Office Information Branch** *(INS; Map 3; 3rd fl, 26 Federal Plaza)*, near Worth St, *before* the stamped date to apply for an extension. In these times of heightened security and scrutiny as regards all immigration issues, allowing your visa to expire prior to visiting the INS for an extension is not a bright idea; tend to your paperwork early and with deference.

Travel Insurance

No matter how you're traveling, make sure you take out travel insurance. This should cover not only medical expenses and luggage theft or loss, but also cancellations or delays in your travel arrangements, and worst-case scenarios such as medical treatment or evacuation. Coverage depends on your insurance and type of ticket, so read the fine print and ask your insurer to explain the finer points. When inquiring about insurance, make sure that the policy is for primary coverage and includes a 24-hour help line for emergencies.

Coverage usually costs between $80 and $150 for a 21-day trip, with surcharges for additional days running $3 to $5 extra for each day. **Travel Guard** *(☎ 800-826-1300)* is one of the better insurers available in the USA, offering comprehensive service. **Access America** *(☎ 800-284-8300)* offers similar options. The international student travel policies handled by **STA Travel** *(w www .statravel.com)* are usually pretty cheap.

Buy travel insurance as early as possible. If you buy it the week before you fly, you may find, for instance, that you're not covered for delays to your flight caused by strikes or industrial action that was in force before you took out the insurance.

Other Documents

You would be crazy to *want* to drive in New York, but if you *must*, you'll need a driver's license. Note that many companies in the US are reluctant to rent cars to drivers younger than 25. You may want to obtain an International Drivers Permit from your national automobile association before you leave for the USA.

Also, you have to carry your license with you if you intend to enter a bar, club or lounge, let alone actually purchase alcohol. By law, you must be 21 years of age to drink anywhere in the US, and bouncers fronting establishments selling alcohol became militant about demanding 'proof' of age under Giuliani. For reasons that escape us, these goons often won't accept a passport as adequate documentation.

Copies

All important documents (passport data and visa pages, credit cards, travel insurance policy, air tickets, driver's license etc) should be photocopied before you leave home. Leave one copy with someone at home and keep another with you, separate from the originals.

It's also a good idea to store details of your vital travel documents in Lonely Planet's free online Travel Vault in case you lose the photocopies or can't be bothered with them. Your password-protected Travel Vault is accessible online anywhere in the world – create it at **w** www.ekno .lonelyplanet.com.

EMBASSIES & CONSULATES
US Embassies & Consulates
US diplomatic offices around the world include the following:

Australia (☎ 02-6214-5600; **w** usembassy -australia.state.gov/index.html) 21 Moonah Pl, Yarralumla, ACT 2600

Canada (☎ 613-238-5335, **w** www.usembassy canada.gov) 490 Sussex Dr, PO Box 866, Station B, Ottawa, Ontario K1P 5T1

Denmark (☎ 3555-3144; **w** www.usembassy.dk) Dag Hammarskjölds Allé 24, 2100 Copenhagen

France (☎ 01 43 12 22 22; **w** www.amb-usa.fr) 2 Avenue Gabriel, 75382 Paris

Germany (☎ 30-8305-0; **w** www.usembassy.de) Neustädtische Kirchstrasse 4-5,10117 Berlin

India (☎ 11-419-8000, fax 11-419-0017) Shantipath, Chanakyapuri, 110021 New Delhi

Ireland (☎ 1-668-8777) 42 Elgin Rd, Ballsbridge, Dublin

Italy (☎ 06-46-741; **w** www.usembassy.it) Via Vittorio Veneto 119a, 00187 Rome

Japan (☎ 03-3224-5000; **w** usembassy.state .gov/tokyo) 10-5 Akasaka 1-chome, Minato-ku, Tokyo

Netherlands (☎ 70-310-9209; **w** www.usemb.nl) Lange Voorhout 102, 2514 EJ The Hague

New Zealand (☎ 04-462-6000; **w** usembassy .org.nz) 29 Fitzherbert Terrace, PO Box 1190, Thorndon, Wellington

Sweden (☎ 8-783-5300, fax 8-661-1964; **w** www .usis.usemb.se) Dag Hammarskjölds Väg 31, Se-115 89 Stockholm

Switzerland (☎ 031-357-7011, fax 031-357-7344; **w** www.us-embassy.ch) Jubilaums-strasse 93, 3001 Berne

Thailand (☎ 2-205-4000) 120–22 Wireless Rd, Bangkok 10330

UK (☎ 020-7499-9000; **w** www.usembassy .org.uk) 24 Grosvenor Square, London W1A 1AE

For other US diplomatic representation abroad, try the Web links at **w** usembassy .state.gov.

Consulates in New York City
The presence of the United Nations in New York City means that nearly every country in the world maintains diplomatic offices in Manhattan. Check the local *Yellow Pages* under Consulates for a complete listing. Some foreign consulates and consulate generals include the following:

Australia (Map 5, #90; ☎ 212-351-6500, fax 351-6501) 34th fl, 150 E 42nd St, New York, NY 10017

Belgium (Map 6, #19; ☎ 212-586-5110, fax 582-9657) 26th fl, 1330 Sixth Ave, New York, NY 10019

Brazil (Map 6, #51; ☎ 917-777-7777, fax 827-0225) 21st fl, 1185 Sixth Ave, New York, NY 10036-2601

Canada (Map 6, #38; ☎ 212-596-1628, fax 596-1793) 1251 Sixth Ave, New York, NY 10020-1175

France (Map 7, #76; ☎ 212-606-3680) 934 Fifth Ave, New York, NY 10021

Germany (Map 5, #55; ☎ 212-610-9700, fax 610-9702) 871 United Nations Plaza, New York, NY 10017

Ireland (Map 5, #59; ☎ 212-319-2555, fax 980-9475) 17th fl, 345 Park Ave, New York, NY 10154-0037

Italy (Map 5, #122; ☎ 212-737-9100, fax 249-4945) 690 Park Ave, New York, NY 10021

Netherlands (Map 6, #39; ☎ 212-246-1429, fax 333-3603; **w** www.cgny.org) 11th fl, 1 Rocke-feller Plaza, New York, NY 10020

New Zealand (Map 5, #58; ☎ 212-832-4038, fax 832-7602; **w** www.un.int/newzealand) Suite 1904, 780 Third Ave, New York, NY 10017

Spain (Map 5, #16; ☎ 212-355-4080, fax 644-3751; **w** www.spainconsul-ny.org) 150 E 58th St, New York, NY 10155

UK (Map 5, #51; ☎ 212-745-0200, fax 754-3062; **w** www.britainusa.com/ny) 845 Third Ave, New York, NY 10022

Your Own Embassy It's important to realize what your own embassy can and can't do to help you if you get into trouble. Generally speaking, it won't be much help in emergencies if the trouble you're in is remotely your own fault. Remember that you are bound by the laws of the country you are in. Your embassy will not be sympathetic if you end up in jail after committing a crime locally, even if such actions are legal in your own country.

In genuine emergencies, you might get some assistance, but only if other channels have been exhausted. If you need to get home urgently, a free ticket home is highly unlikely – the embassy would expect you to have insurance. If all your money and documents are stolen, it might assist you with getting a new passport, but a loan for onward travel is out of the question.

CUSTOMS

US customs allows each person over the age of 21 to bring 1 liter of liquor and 200 cigarettes duty-free into the USA (smokers take note: cigarettes cost around $7 a pack here in the big city, so take advantage of those duty-free shops). US citizens are allowed to import, duty-free, $400 worth of gifts from abroad, while non-US citizens are allowed to import $100 worth. If you're carrying more than $10,000 in US and foreign cash, traveler's checks, money orders and the like, you need to declare the excess amount. There is no legal restriction on the amount that may be imported, but undeclared sums in excess of $10,000 will probably be subject to investigation.

MONEY
Currency

The US dollar (familiarly called a 'buck') is divided into 100 cents (¢). Coins come in denominations of 1¢ (penny), 5¢ (nickel), 10¢ (dime), 25¢ (quarter) and the seldom seen 50¢ (half-dollar). Notes come in $1, $2, $5, $10, $20, $50 and $100 denominations (you'll be lucky to come across a $2 bill). A new, golden dollar coin, which was introduced in early 2000, features a picture of Sacagawea, the Native American guide who led the explorers Lewis and Clark on their expedition through the western United States. While striking, the new coins are prohibitively heavy and jingle conspicuously, alerting panhandlers to your well-heeled presence. These coins are often dispensed as change in ticket and stamp machines.

In recent years, the US treasury has redesigned the $5, $10, $20, $50 and $100 bills to foil counterfeiters. Yes, they're still that terrible drab green, but the portraits are pretty comical since the Presidential heads are all unnaturally huge. Most vendors are used to these bills by now (which circulate alongside the old), although you may encounter a few machines that still can't accept the 'new' $20 bill.

Exchange Rates

Exchange rates at press time were:

country	unit		US$
Australia	A1$	=	$0.56
Canada	C$1	=	$0.64
euro zone	€1	=	$0.95
Hong Kong	HK$1	=	$0.13
Japan	¥100	=	$0.80
New Zealand	NZ$1	=	$0.48
UK	£1	=	$1.50

Exchanging Money

Chase Manhattan Bank (Map 3, #69; ☎ 212-552-2222; 1 Chase Manhattan Plaza at William St, Lower Manhattan; foreign exchange open 8am-3:30pm Mon-Fri), between Liberty and Pine Sts, offers a commission-free foreign-currency exchange service. A **Midtown branch** (Map 5, #118; 349 Fifth Ave at 34th St), directly across the street from the Empire State Building, also offers foreign exchange during the same hours.

The main **American Express office** (Map 3, #59; ☎ 212-421-8240; World Financial Center, West & Vesey Sts; open 9am-5pm Mon-Fri • Map 3, #66; ☎ 212-693-1100; 111 Broadway • Map 6, #104; ☎ 212-687-3700; 1185 Sixth Ave at 47th St) has a reliable currency-exchange service, but there are long lines in the afternoon. Contact **American Express** (☎ 800-221-7282) for more locations.

Thomas Cook offers currency exchange at eight locations in the city, including the **Times Square office** (Map 6, #48; ☎ 212-265-6049; 1590 Broadway at 48th St; open 9am-7pm Mon-Sat, 9am-5pm Sun).

Chequepoint (Map 5, #6; ☎ 212-750-2400; 22 Central Park South; open 8am-8pm Mon-Sat, 9am-8pm Sun), between Fifth and Sixth Aves, offers less favorable rates.

Banks are normally open 9am to 4pm weekdays. **Chase Manhattan's** Chinatown branch, at the corner of Mott and Canal Sts, is open daily. Several other banks along Canal St also offer weekend hours.

Cash Despite having record-low crime rates, New York still has its share of ne'er-do-wells and it's not a good idea to flash (or carry) large amounts of cash. Set out with just what you'll need for the day and stash the rest in a safe place at your hotel (using credit or ATM cards when you need more; and you *will* need more). Keep some small bills at the ready for purchasing bagels, a slice or a canoli, and pocket change if you're prone to alms giving.

Be aware that NY vendors and cashiers typically balk at accepting bills in denominations of $50 or more, especially if they have to empty out their cash drawers making change for you. Instead, keep $20 bills on hand for smaller purchases.

Traveler's Checks These offer protection from theft or loss. Checks issued by American Express and Thomas Cook (see also Exchanging Money, earlier) are widely accepted, and both offer efficient replacement policies. Keeping a record of the check numbers and the checks you've used is vital when it comes to replacing lost checks. Keep this record in a separate place from the checks themselves.

Your life will be infinitely easier if you buy travel er's checks in US dollars. The savings you *might* make on exchange rates by carrying traveler's checks in a foreign currency don't make up for the hassle of exchanging them at banks and other facilities. Restaurants, hotels and most stores accept US-dollar traveler's checks as if they were cash, so if you're carrying traveler's checks in US dollars, the odds are you'll rarely have to use a bank or pay an exchange fee. Budget digs, dive bars and dirt cheap diners will likely stare in wonder at a traveler's check, so ask first if you intend to lay one on someone.

Bring most of the checks in large denominations. It's only toward the end of a trip that you may want to change a small check to make sure you aren't left holding too much local currency. Of course, traveler's checks are losing their popularity due to the explosion of ATMs (see following) and you may opt not to carry any at all.

ATMs Given the prevalence of Automated Teller Machines (ATMs) in New York City, you can easily draw cash directly from a home bank account, provided that your bank is linked with the Cirrus or Plus ATM networks. ATM fees for foreign banks are usually about $3 to $5; foreign-currency exchange commissions range from $5 to $7. Most New York banks are linked by the NYCE (New York Cash Exchange) system, and you can use local bank cards interchangeably at ATMs – for an extra fee if you're banking outside your system.

Credit & Debit Cards Major credit cards are accepted at hotels, restaurants, shops and car-rental agencies throughout New York. In fact, you'll find it hard to perform certain transactions, such as purchasing tickets to performances, without one. Besides, they're super-handy in emergencies.

Stack your deck with either a Visa or MasterCard, as these are the cards of choice here. Places that accept Visa and Master-Card are also likely to accept debit cards. Unlike a credit card, a debit card deducts payment directly from your checking or savings account. Instead of an interest rate, you're charged a minimal fee for the transaction. Be sure to check with your bank to confirm that your debit card will be accepted in other states or countries – debit cards from large commercial banks can often be used worldwide.

Carry copies of your credit card numbers separately from the cards. If your cards are lost or stolen, contact the company immediately. The following are toll-free numbers for the main credit card companies. Contact your bank if you lose your ATM card.

American Express	☎ 800-528-4800
Diners Club	☎ 800-234-6377
Discover	☎ 800-347-2683
MasterCard	☎ 800-826-2181
Visa	☎ 800-336-8472

FACTS FOR THE VISITOR

International Transfers Wiring money with a service such as Western Union is faster and easier than dealing with an international bank transfer. Western Union has over 100,000 agents worldwide, with outlets peppering the five boroughs; a $1000 transfer from anywhere in the world to the Big Apple costs $75 and takes a snappy 15 minutes. You can also transfer money at the offices of American Express and Thomas Cook. See Exchanging Money, previously, for the addresses of these companies' Manhattan branches.

You may save a few dollars by instructing your bank back home to send you a draft. Specify the city, bank and branch to which you want your money directed and make sure you get the details right. The procedure is easier if you've authorized someone back home to access your account.

Money sent by telegraphic transfer should reach you within a week; if it's coming by mail, allow at least two weeks. When it arrives, it will likely be converted into US dollars.

Security

Better safe than sorry is the guideline with any valuables here, especially cash and cards. Most hotels and hostels provide safekeeping, so you can leave your money there. Unless you must accessorize with the real thing, leave the good jewelry at home (a general rule of thumb for traveling in New York is to not bring anything you can't afford financially or, more importantly, emotionally, to lose). Carry your daily walking-around money somewhere inside your clothing (in a money belt, bra or socks) rather than in a handbag or an outside pocket. It helps to have money in several places, and don't walk around with your wallet in your back pocket – it's the petty thief's wet dream. Remember that just using a safety pin or twist tie to hold the zipper tags of a day-pack together can help prevent theft.

Costs

All price levels are catered for in New York City. With the very significant exception of housing and hotels, it's possible to live on the relative cheap here. Below are the average costs of consumer items:

Brewed coffee	$1.50
Bagel	$1
Beer	$5
Cigarettes	$7
Fruit	50¢ to $1
Pizza slice	$2
Soda	$1
Water	$1 to $1.75
Local call	25¢
Laundry	$3 a load at self-serve centers
Stamp	37¢

A Note on Prices

'Whatever the market will bear' is the old saying as far as price setting goes, and while many of us find New York prices unbearable, there are some 30 million visitors a year who seem to think otherwise. Museums and tourist attractions are now in the habit of raising prices in $5 increments rather than by just a dollar or two at a time like in the old days. Budgeting for a New York trip can mean financial hardship, especially if you want to sleep somewhere half decent or see a Broadway musical, where top prices have already reached $75 per seat.

Still, there are many ways to do this city on the cheap such as visiting museums with suggested donations, taking advantage of free attractions like tours of the Public Library or concerts in Central Park, taking the bus or subway everywhere (including to/from the airport) and using coupons. Food is one area where you can cut costs considerably: pizza parlors, Asian noodle shops and street vendors are all dirt-cheap places to eat. Also consider picnicking if the weather is nice or cooking in your room or hostel if that's a possibility. Die-hard foodies can save some money by eating out at the really fancy places at lunch rather than dinner or sticking to prix fixe menu options. And for those who come from countries with strong currencies, New York shopping still offers real opportunities for savings.

N.Y.C.

Tipping

Tipping is expected in restaurants, bars and better hotels, taxis and by hairdressers and baggage carriers. In restaurants, wait staff are paid less than the minimum wage and rely upon tips to make a living. Tip at least 15% unless the service is terrible, in which case a light tip will get your point across. Most New Yorkers either tip a straight up 20%, or just double the 8.25% sales tax. At bars, bartenders typically expect a $1 tip for every drink they serve (at preferred drinking spots, the old rule of fourth round free stands and decent tips help perpetuate that tradition). Never tip in fast-food, take-out or buffet-style restaurants where you serve yourself. And beware of restaurants that don't itemize the tax separately on a bill – it's a way to get you to tip on the tax amount as well.

Taxi drivers expect 10% and hairdressers 15% if their service is satisfactory. Baggage carriers (skycaps in airports, bellhops in hotels) receive $1 for the first bag and 50¢ for each additional bag. In first class and luxury hotels, tipping can reach ludicrous proportions – doormen, bellboys and parking attendants all expect to be tipped at least $1 for each service performed – including simply opening a taxi door for you. (Business travelers should tip the cleaning staff $5 a day.) However, it's OK to simply say 'thank you,' offer friendly banter or a quick joke in a situation where you could just as easily have done the task yourself.

Taxes & Refunds

Restaurants and retailers never include the tax in their prices, so beware of ordering the $4.99 lunch special when you only have $5 to your name. New York State imposes a sales tax of 7% on goods, most services and prepared foods. New York City imposes an additional 1.25% tax, bringing the total surcharge to 8.25%. Several categories of so-called 'luxury items,' including rental cars and dry-cleaning, carry an additional city surcharge of 5%, so you wind up paying an extra 13.25% in total for these services.

Hotel rooms in New York City are subject to a 13.25% tax, plus a flat $2-per-night occupancy tax. Believe it or not, that reflects a reduction in the previous hotel tax.

Since the US has no nationwide value added tax (VAT), there is no opportunity for foreign visitors to make 'tax-free' purchases. However, New York City has permanently suspended the sales tax on clothing items under $500, giving clothes horses a modest tax break.

POST & COMMUNICATIONS
Postal Rates

Rates for sending mail go up every few years, and with increasing frequency as of late it seems. With the latest increase, rates for first-class mail within the USA are 37¢ for letters up to 1oz (23¢ for each additional ounce) and 23¢ for postcards.

International airmail rates for a one ounce letter are 60¢ to Canada and Mexico and 80¢ elsewhere, plus 25¢ and 80¢ for each additional half-ounce. International postcard rates are 50¢ to Canada and Mexico and 70¢ elsewhere. Aerogrammes will cost you 70¢.

The cost for parcels being airmailed anywhere within the USA is $3.95 for up to two pounds, increasing by $1.25 per pound up to $7.70 for five pounds. For heavier items, rates differ according to the distance mailed. Books, periodicals and computer disks can be sent by a cheaper fourth-class rate. For whatever postal questions you may have, call ☎ 800-275-8777 or visit the website at W www.usps.com/welcome.htm.

Sending Mail

The **general post office** (Map 5; ☎ 212-967-8585; James A Foley Bldg, 380 W 33rd St 10001; open 24 hrs), at Eighth St, can help with postal requirements, as can the Rockefeller Center's **basement post office** (Map 5; ☎ 212-265-3854; 610 Fifth Ave at 49th St 10020; open 9:30am-5:30pm Mon-Fri).

The **Franklin D Roosevelt Station post office** (Map 5, #20; ☎ 212-330-5549; 909 Third Ave at 55th St 10022; open 9am-8pm Mon-Fri, 9am-4pm Sat) is open for most postal business at the hours specified here.

The **Cooper Station post office** (Map 4, #49; ☎ 212-254-1389; 93 Fourth Ave at 11th St 10003; open 8am-6pm, Mon-Wed & Fri, 8am-8pm Thur, 9am-4pm Sat) is the place to post in the Village.

Receiving Mail

If you plan on staying awhile, arranging a postal address before arriving is the best way to go. A good alternative is renting a post office box through one of the many branches of Mailboxes Etc stores scattered throughout the city or at one of the main branches of the US post office. Either offers post boxes for rent on a short- or long-term basis, though well-located post offices often have a waiting list.

General delivery *poste restante* mail is accepted at the general post office, provided it's marked 'General Delivery.' This method not recommended or reliable however.

Telephone

Phone numbers within the USA consist of a three-digit area code followed by a seven-digit local number. If you're calling long distance, dial 1 + the three-digit area code + the seven-digit number. If you're calling New York from abroad, the international country code for the USA is 1.

For local and national directory assistance, dial ☎ 411. To find a number in Manhattan from outside the US, call ☎ 1 + 212 + 555-1212. (These requests are charged as one-minute long-distance calls.)

In New York City, Manhattan phone numbers are in the 212 or 646 area code (although some businesses and cell phones take a 917 area code) and the four outer boroughs are in the 718 zone. No matter where you're calling within New York City, even if it's just across the street in the same area code, you must *always* dial the area code first.

All toll-free numbers are prefixed with an 800, 877 or 888 area code. Some toll-free numbers for local businesses or government offices only work within a limited region. But most toll-free phone numbers can be dialed from abroad – just be aware that you'll be connected at regular long distance rates, which could become a costly option if the line you're dialing regularly parks customers on hold.

Long-distance rates vary depending on the destination and the telephone company you're using – call the operator (☎ 0) for rate information. Don't ask the operator to put your call through, however, because operator-assisted calls are much more expensive than direct-dial calls. Generally, the cheapest times to call (60% discount) are nights (11pm to 8am), all day Saturday and 8am to 5pm Sunday. A 35% discount applies from 5pm to 11pm Sunday to Friday. Daytime calls (8am to 5pm Monday to Friday) are full-price calls within the USA.

International Calls To dial an international number directly, dial ☎ 011, then the country code, followed by the area code and the phone number. (To find the country code, check the phone book or dial ☎ 411 and ask for an international operator.) You may need to wait as long as 45 seconds for the ringing to start. International rates vary depending on the time of day and the destination. For example, the cheapest rates to London are available between 6pm and 7am, but if you're calling Sydney, the cheapest time is 3am to 2pm. Call the operator (☎ 0) for rates.

Hotel Phones In general, hotels (especially the ritzy ones) add a service charge of 50¢ to $1 for *every* call – even the toll-free variety – made from a room phone; they also levy hefty surcharges for long-distance calls. Public pay phones, which can be found in most lobbies, are always cheaper.

Pay Phones You can pump in quarters, use a phone credit or debit card or make collect calls from pay phones. There are thousands of pay telephones on the New York City streets, all with a seemingly different price scheme: many Verizon phones charge 50¢ for unlimited local calls, others charge 25¢ for three-minute local calls and still others demand $1 for calls anywhere in the US. On some pay phones in New York City, if you make a long-distance call with a credit card, you could end up with a whopping bill from an unscrupulous long-distance firm. Although it may seem inconsequential as you read this, it will drive you crazy once you're there: Park Ave has no pay phones.

Phone books are not provided at outdoor phone booths, so if you're unsure of a local address dial ☎ 411 (information, which is free) and ask for the location of the business. Tell the operator you are looking for an address. If you don't, the operator will immediately call up a computer message with only the telephone number and disconnect you.

Phone Cards A good long-distance alternative is phone debit cards, which allow you to pay in advance, with access through a toll-free 800 number. In amounts of $5, $10, $20 and $50, these are available from Western Union, machines in airports and train stations, some supermarkets and nearly every corner deli. Certain cards deliver better value depending on where you're calling (eg, New York Alliance is better for Brazil, while Payless is better for Ireland) and the purveyors of the cards can usually provide accurate information. The rates are generally unbeatable; for instance, a $10 New York Alliance card allows you 10 hours of chatting to Rio.

Lonely Planet's eKno Communication Card is aimed specifically at independent travelers and provides budget international calls, a range of messaging services, free email and travel information – for local calls, you're usually better off with a local card. You can join online at W www.ekno .lonelyplanet.com or by phone from New York City by dialing ☎ 800-707-0031. To use eKno from New York City once you have joined, dial ☎ 800-706-1333.

Check the eKno website for joining and access telephone numbers from other countries and updates on super budget local access numbers and new features.

When using phone credit cards in a public place, cover up the key pad to deter thieves from watching you punch in the numbers – they can and will memorize numbers and use your card to make phone calls to all corners of the earth. New York airports and the Port Authority Bus Terminal are notorious for this scam. Some newer pay phones (like those in Penn Station) provide shields at the telephone pad to prevent a stranger from viewing your number.

Fax
The copy-store chain **Kinko's** (Map 5, #47; ☎ 212-308-2679; 16 E 52nd St • Map 4, #50; ☎ 212-924-0802; 24 E 12th St • Map 8, #46; ☎ 212-316-3390; 2872 Broadway), with many locations in Manhattan, offers a 24-hour fax service in addition to its computer and photocopying services. (You can also have passport photographs taken at Kinko's.)

Village Copier (Map 4, #18; ☎ 212-924-3456; 20 E 13th St; open 24 hrs • Map 8, #41; ☎ 212-666-0600; 601 West 115th St & Broadway; open 10am-6pm daily) is a cheaper alternative and with other locations including the ones listed here.

Email & Internet Access
The **New York Public Library's main branch** (Map 7; ☎ 212-930-0800; E 42nd St at Fifth Ave) offers free half-hour Internet access, though there may be a wait in the afternoons; branches also have free access and usually no wait.

Log on at the Public Library

At cyber cafés all over the city, you can surf the Net for an hourly fee, which ranges from $5 to $12. Try the following places, all with their own vibe:

alt.coffee (Map 4, #109; ☎ 212-529-2233; 139 Avenue A; open 8am-'late' daily)
Cyber Cafe (Map 4, #184; ☎ 212-334-5140; 273 Lafayette St at Prince St; open 8:30am-10pm Mon-Fri, 11am-10pm Sat & Sun • Map 6, #43; ☎ 212-333-4109; 250 W 49th St; open 8am-11pm Mon-Fri, 11am-11pm Sat & Sun)
Cyberfeld's (Map 4, #18; ☎ 212-647-8830; 20 E 13th St; open 8am-3am Mon-Fri, noon-10pm Sat & Sun)
easyEverything (Map 6, #116; ☎ 212-398-0724, 234 W 42nd St; open 24 hrs) This is the cheapest place in town, starting at $1 an hour (surf here with the hordes)
Internet Cafe (Map 4, #124; ☎ 212-614-0747; 82 E 3rd St; open 11am-2am Mon-Sat, 11am-midnight Sun)
Time to Compute (Map 8, #27; ☎ 212-722-5700; 2029 Fifth Ave at 125th St; open 10am-7pm Mon-Fri, 10am-6pm Sat)

INTERNET RESOURCES

The World Wide Web is a rich resource for travelers. You can research your trip, hunt down bargain airfares, book hotels, check on weather conditions and chat with locals and other travelers about the best places to visit (or avoid).

There's no better place to start your Web explorations than the **Lonely Planet website** (**w** *www.lonelyplanet.com*). Here you'll find succinct summaries on traveling to most places on earth, postcards from other travelers and the Thorn Tree bulletin board, where you can ask questions before you go or dispense advice when you get back. You can also find travel news and updates for many of our most popular guidebooks, and the subWWWay section links you to the most useful travel resources elsewhere on the Web.

The following sites are particularly useful for finding out information about New York:

w **www.nycvisit.com** The NYC & Company (Convention & Visitors Bureau) site offers general tourist information
w **www.nytoday.com** New York Today, run by the *New York Times*, maintains entertainment, sports and restaurant listings, plus news articles and archives
w **www.chowhound.com** Chowhound, a *vox populi* site started by Web restaurant reviewer Jim Leff, offers feedback for eateries at all income levels. Navigating this site with all its cutesy terminology is a bit laborious – use its search engine if you're rushed
w **www.new-york-city-hotels.com** This site offers discounts, last-minute room bookings and direct links to the hotels
w **www.newyork.citysearch.com** Visit City Search for a comprehensive roundup of the city's happenings
w **www.nycsubway.org** NYC Subway is an unofficial site detailing the transit system, with everything from practical information to historical trivia
w **www.imar.com** Insider's Marketplace is *the* cool, insider site, listing guided New York 'experiences' from shopping with a fashion model to poetry slams with a Harlem wordsmith

In addition, almost every neighborhood has its own website. Not surprisingly, some are more helpful than others, but almost all of them offer discounts of some sort and could save you some change. Try these on for size:

w www.lowereastsideny.com
w www.tribeca.org
w www.downtownny.com
w www.littleitalynyc.com

ANGUS OBORN

BOOKS

Most books are published in different editions by different publishers in different countries. As a result, a book that's a hardcover rarity in one country may be readily available in another. Fortunately, bookstores and libraries can search by title or author, so your local biblio-outpost is the best place to find the following recommendations. Internet search engines, some of which allow you to purchase books online, are another good tool.

To find the books listed below, you can also head to any large New York bookstore – it will have a special section dedicated to tomes about the city. For a list of bookstores, see the Shopping chapter, later in the book.

For the Bookworm

Thousands of novels are set in New York, and you've probably read a few already. The following nonfiction choices will stuff your head full of city trivia. All can be obtained in whatever large New York bookstore you find yourself browsing.

- *Writing New York* (1998), edited by Phillip Lopate, offers the single best overview on the city's role in literature.

- *Gotham* (1998), by Edwin G Burrows and Mike Wallace, is the one book you'll need to read about the city. A magisterial but lively work, the first volume covers the city's history from prehistoric times to the consolidation of the five boroughs in 1898. A second volume chronicles greater New York City's first 100 years.

- *AIA Guide to New York City* (2000), by Norval White, is a classic work that chronicles almost every significant building throughout the five boroughs. A definitive, updated version was published by the American Institute of Architects in 2000.

- *The Encyclopedia of New York City* (1995), edited by Kenneth T Jackson, is a massive and entertaining array of facts and stories compiled by the distinguished Columbia University urban historian. Pictures and illustrations are included.

Lonely Planet

If you plan to go a little farther afield than New York City, pick up a copy of Lonely Planet's *New York, New Jersey & Pennsylvania*, which offers in-depth coverage of the region. For information on other US destinations, consult the *USA* guide.

History

Though it's a work of fiction rather than a straight history, Washington Irving's satirical *History of New York* (1809), published under the pseudonym of Dietrich Knickerbocker, includes glimpses of colonial-era New York. Those looking for a more historical perspective should seek out *Colonial New York* by historian Michael Kammen.

Irving Howe's *World of Our Fathers* offers a comprehensive look at the assimilation of Eastern European Jewish immigrants into late-19th century New York. If you're interested in the history of the East Village and Lower East Side, this is your book.

Luc Sante published two colorful works dealing with the grittier aspects of early 20th-century New York. *Low Life* dives into immigrant life in the tenements, while *Evidence* is an illustrated essay focusing on the mayhem of this world, accompanied by old police crime-scene photos. Disregard the pompous, superior tone that seeps through both.

The *WPA Guide to New York City*, published in 1939 as a Depression-era employment project for the city's writers (including John Cheever) and now back in print, offers a snapshot of a by-gone metropolis. This is a wonderful read for anyone who has lived in or explored the city in recent days.

Memoirs

EB White's essay *Here is New York* is a timeless and lyrical distillation of New York's essence. Written in 1949, it remains one of the most remarkable insights into the city's character, flaws and all.

Kafka Was the Rage by Anatole Broyard, the late book reviewer for the *New York Times*, offers a bittersweet look at life in Greenwich Village just after WWII, a time also recalled by journalist Dan Wakefield in *New York in the '50s*.

FACTS FOR THE VISITOR

Jack Kerouac's *Lonesome Traveler* focuses on his days in New York during the era of the Greenwich Village Beat writers, and the publishing of Allen Ginsberg's *Howl and Other Poems* in 1956 amid great controversy. A year later, Kerouac published his most famous work, *On the Road* (1957); as the story goes, Jack wrote the classic on a roll of teletype paper, in one sitting in the Chelsea Hotel.

The Andy Warhol Diaries (1990) is a bitchy and colorful account of the '70s nightclub culture by one of the most influential artists of the 20th century.

Literature
The publishing capital of the world has been featured in thousands of fictional books. Some of the following New York books have become classics in American literature.

O Henry, author of 'The Gift of the Magi' (1906), and F Scott Fitzgerald were archetypical New York writers whose short stories bring to life two distinctive social eras (the late-19th century and the Roaring '20s). Seek out Fitzgerald's *Tales of the Jazz Age* (1922), which includes 'The Diamond as Big as the Ritz,' and, of course, don't miss *The Great Gatsby* (1925).

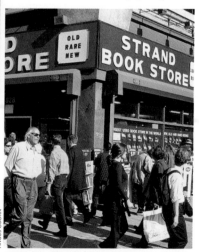

Eight miles of books – that's a whole lotta reading

Though largely an expatriate who lived in Europe for much of his life, American writer Henry James evokes New York upper class life before the Civil War in the novel *Washington Square* (1881). The row of houses then occupied by New York society still line the northern edge of Washington Square Park today.

James' contemporary Edith Wharton chronicles the Gilded Age of New York City in the Pulitzer Prize-winning *Age of Innocence* (1920) and in the collection *Old New York* (1924). Unfortunately, most of her New York – the original Metropolitan Opera House, the Metropolitan Museum of Art and the mansions of Fifth Ave's 'Millionaire's Row' – has disappeared or been altered beyond recognition.

JD Salinger's *Catcher in the Rye* (1951) has resonated with generations of angst-ridden youths through the misadventures of protagonist Holden Caulfield. The novel's events culminate at the Museum of Natural History and served as a tragic prop at the scene of John Lennon's murder at the Dakota (1 W 72nd St).

Of the many works by black artists set in New York, perhaps the most acclaimed is Ralph Ellison's *Invisible Man* (1952), a classic rumination on race and the USA. There is a strong tradition of black literature in New York; also see works by James Baldwin, Djuana Barnes and Langston Hughes.

EL Doctorow's works – including *Ragtime* (1975), *The Book of Daniel* (1971) and *World's Fair* (1985) – reflect on New York in its various eras, from turn-of-the-20th-century boomtown to Cold War ideological battleground. Mario Puzo's *The Godfather* (1969) describes the West Side's Hell's Kitchen neighborhood as it was in the years just after WWI.

Thomas Pynchon's debut novel *V* (1963) hops from the New York of the late 1950s to various points around the globe and illustrates the frentic philosophies of the young people who 'yo-yoed' their way through the city at the time.

Pynchon was the forerunner of those who ushered in a newer, more energetic style of writing in the '70s and '80s. Some authors adopted phantasmagoric or Gothic styles. Don DeLillo's *Great Jones Street* (1973) and Mark Helprin's *A Winter's Tale* (1983) are two prime examples of this disturbing new view of society. Paul Auster, who lives in Brooklyn's Park Slope section, has won many followers for his modern noir *New York Trilogy* (1990).

Jay McInerney was blessed, then cursed by his association with the yuppified early '80s, occasioned by his blockbuster first novel *Bright Lights, Big City* (1984). Tom Wolfe's *Bonfire of the Vanities* (1987) followed that up, offering a comic portrait of a city out of control and split along racial lines. Tama Janowitz, author of *Slaves of New York*, covers much the same ground and has enjoyed a life of literary celebrity. More recently, Michael Chabon's Pulitzer Prize–winning *The Amazing Adventure of Kavalier & Clay* (2001), takes a fantastic journey through a more innocent time in New York.

For an overview of the city in literature, pick up Shaun O'Connell's *Remarkable, Unspeakable, New York* (1995), a look at how American writers have regarded the metropolis over two centuries.

Children's Books

A singular destination for children, New York comes alive through the rich kiddy-lit set here. Any of the books in Kay Thompson's *Eloise* series will get kids into the swing of things or try Faith Ringgold's *Tar Beach*, the story of a Harlem girl who embarks on a flying adventure above the city. (Tar beach is city slang for a building rooftop as this is where urbanites take the summer sun.)

For the younger set, there's the all-time classic *Cricket in Times Square* by George Selden, charmingly illustrated by Garth Williams, or *The House on East 88th Street* in which Bernard Waber brings Lyle the Crocodile to life.

Mischievous types will get a thrill out of EL Konigsburg's *From the Mixed-up Files of Mrs. Basil E. Frankweiler* in which two kids hide out in the Metropolitan Museum after hours, causing all manner of trouble and hoopla.

FILMS

Just as it's nearly impossible to define the perfect New York book, there's almost no way to present a definitive list of films about the city. For years, New York movies were all shot on Hollywood soundstages, although actors sometimes came to the city for a few days to shoot exteriors (a sleight-of-hand practice used by several TV shows such as *NYPD Blue* and, most notoriously, *Seinfeld*).

That began to change substantially in the 1970s, when directors began striving for realism, and equipment became more mobile, making location shooting a less-expensive alternative to the studio. Today, it's common to stumble upon film shoots on the streets of New York – though some lower-budget films try to pass off various Canadian cities as the Big Apple; unfortunately, the natives among us can always tell. With a few noted exceptions, the following films listed were authentically set in New York and represent some sort of unique aspect of the city. They are all available on video.

On the Town (1949) stars Gene Kelly and Frank Sinatra as sailors on shore leave in New York City. Since Sinatra was soaring to unimagined, new heights of his bobby-soxer popularity at the time of filming and was mobbed wherever he went, director Stanley Donen would 'steal' a shot by setting up the cameras and sending the actors out at the last possible minute. It didn't always work – which is why you can spot hundreds of onlookers as Sinatra and Kelly sing 'New York, New York' in Rockefeller Center.

The first major noir film to make use of the city streets was *Naked City* (1948), which was loosely based on the crime photos of the famous newspaper photographer named Weegee, who also inspired the Joe Pesci film *The Public Eye* (1992).

The best black-and-white film ever shot in New York is the gritty *Sweet Smell of Success* (1957), starring Burt Lancaster as a ruthless gossip columnist (a thinly disguised Walter Winchell) and Tony Curtis as the desperate press agent he manipulates.

The cinematography, by the legendary James Wong Howe, captures the city's '50s nightclub scene perfectly.

West Side Story (1961) depicts love and gang rivalry in Hell's Kitchen and includes exterior shots of the tenements that were torn down to make way for the expansion of Lincoln Center.

A quintessential New York film, *The Taking of Pelham One, Two, Three* (1974) stars Walter Matthau as a beleaguered transit cop confronted with a subway hijacking. This cult classic, written by Peter Stone (the only writer to have won a Tony, an Oscar and an Emmy) includes a terrific twist in the last scene.

Three New York Film Directors

Along with literature, there is probably no other art form that captures history and reflects a people and its culture more honestly than film. New York has its share of extremely accomplished cinema, but the following three filmmakers are among the most talented ever to look through a camera.

Martin Scorcese

This quirky, nervous and visionary director is celebrated for bringing the darker side of New York to life. Born in Queens in 1942, Scorsese grew up on Elizabeth St in Manhattan's Little Italy. After working as an editor on the documentary *Woodstock* (1970), he made *Mean Streets* (1973), a drama about Little Italy – actually shot in the Bronx – with Robert De Niro and Harvey Keitel. Both actors became closely associated with Scorsese's films, starring together in *Taxi Driver* (1975), a critically acclaimed film about psychopaths in the East Village. De Niro won an Oscar for his performance in the instant classic *Raging Bull* (1980), a brutal biography of boxer Jake La Motta.

In recent years, Scorsese made *After Hours* (1985) that went almost directly to video, but is a brilliant distillation of the mid-1980s SoHo scene, and won praise for *Goodfellas* (1990), a true-life mob drama. Also garnering accolades was *The Age of Innocence* (1993), a detail-rich costume drama based on the Edith Wharton novel about 19th-century New York. Scorsese returned to New York's grittier underside in *Bringing Out The Dead* (1999), starring Nicholas Cage, and *Gangs of New York* (2002), a fictional account of Downtown's Five Points slum starring Leonardo DiCaprio, Daniel Day Lewis and Cameron Diaz. Lately, Scorsese has led the fight to preserve American film heritage through the restoration of classic films.

Woody Allen

As prominent and lauded as Scorcese, Woody Allen is unequaled among US filmmakers in enjoying so much control over his final product (though the younger Spike Lee is challenging Allen's position as all around auteur). Allen, who writes, directs and often stars in his own films, turns out motion pictures the way others produce short stories – about one per year, with more than 30 so far.

Born Allen Stewart Konigsberg in 1935 in Brooklyn, he began writing gags for TV comedians and landed a job on Sid Caesar's legendary *Your Show of Shows* in the mid-1950s. He then graduated to stand-up comedy, perfecting the now-familiar persona of a sex-obsessed, intellectual 'nebbish' who nonetheless gets the girl in the end. He made his Hollywood debut as an actor and screenwriter in *What's New Pussycat?* (1965) and followed that up a year later with *What's Up Tiger Lily?*, in which he

HAYDEN FOELL

N.Y.C.

A spot-on rendering of the mighty, but flighty, SoHo and TriBeCa scene (with plenty of insider skinny and dark humor according to director Martin Scorcese) is the eminently quotable *After Hours* (1985).

In recent years, foreign directors have traveled to New York to provide domestic audiences with a look at the city from an outsider's perspective. Wayne Wang's *Smoke* (1995) and *Blue in the Face* (1996) both star Harvey Keitel as a cigar-store owner in Brooklyn. In Ang Lee's bittersweet comedy *The Wedding Banquet* (1993), New York represents the land of sexual freedom for a Taiwanese gay man whose meddlesome parents arrive to supervise his 'marriage' to a woman.

Three New York Film Directors

dubbed comic dialogue onto a Japanese James Bond-style spy movie. While he was writing and directing the purely comic *Take the Money and Run* (1969), *Bananas* (1971) and *Sleeper* (1972), among others, he also began writing feisty comic essays for the *New Yorker* and had a Broadway hit in *Play It Again, Sam*. The play, in which his loser character gets advice from the ghost of Humphrey Bogart, became a hit movie in 1972.

But it was the classic *Annie Hall* (1975), one of the few comedies to ever win an Oscar for Best Picture, that forever established Allen's reputation as a comic artist. He followed it up with the serious drama *Interiors* (1978) and *Manhattan* (1979), an unabashed love letter to the city, beautifully shot in black and white.

His private and professional partnership with actress Mia Farrow produced a number of acclaimed films, including the Academy Award–winning *Hannah & Her Sisters* (1986). But Allen's affair with Soon-Yi Previn, Farrow's adopted daughter, led to a nasty breakup with Farrow in the early '90s.

Despite his controversial personal life, Allen still produces celebrated films. (Besides Farrow, his leading ladies have included Diane Keaton, Dianne Weist and Mira Sorvino.) In recent years, he has released *Mighty Aphrodite* (1995), *Deconstructing Harry* (1997), *Celebrity* (1998), *Sweet & Lowdown* (1999) and *Everyone Says I Love You* (1996), a quirky musical comedy that features Goldie Hawn, Alan Alda and Allen himself crooning famous love songs in New York, Paris and Venice. More recently, Allen won acclaim with *Curse of the Jade Scorpion* (2001) and debuted his new film *Hollywood Ending* at the 2002 Cannes Film Festival. In his spare time, Allen still plays clarinet in a traditional jazz band at Michael's Pub in Midtown most Monday nights and attends nearly every Knicks homegame.

Sidney Lumet

Born in 1924, Sidney Lumet represents an older, more idealistic New York liberal sensibility, one formulated in the '50s, when he got his start directing live TV drama. Even when most directors went into self-imposed sunny exile in Hollywood, Lumet preferred to shoot many of his films in the city. His first feature was *12 Angry Men* (1957) with Henry Fonda, a reprise of one of the best live TV dramas.

He went on to direct *Serpico* (1974), a true-life story of a policeman who exposed widespread department corruption; *Dog Day Afternoon* (1975), another true-life about a bank robber (played by Al Pacino) who has a bizarre scheme to get his lover money for a sex-change operation; and *Network* (1976), a stinging satire that foreshadowed the '90s era of junk talk shows on TV. Lumet has also proven his versatility as a director with the baroque costume melodrama *Murder on the Orient Express* (1974), set entirely in Europe. In all, his films – which in later years have included The *Verdict* (1982), *Q&A* (1990, shot in Spanish Harlem), *Night Falls on Manhattan* (1997) and *Gloria* (1999) – have garnered more than 50 Academy Award nominations.

Lumet still holds extensive preshoot rehearsals for his actors in the East Village, in a large room in the Ukrainian National Home on Second Ave between 8th and 9th Sts. He has written a wonderful treatise on his craft called *Making Movies*, essential reading for film buffs.

FACTS FOR THE VISITOR

N.Y.C.

HAYDEN FOELL

Spike Lee, doin' the right thing.

FACTS FOR THE VISITOR

In 1986, Spike Lee emerged as a major new New York filmmaker with *She's Gotta Have It* and followed it up with the controversial *Do The Right Thing* (1989), a film about racial tensions in Brooklyn. Since then, he's carved out a career that combines fine works like *Malcolm X* (1992) and *Clockers* (1995) with highly lucrative commercials for Nike. His 1999 feature, *Summer of Sam,* is a hard-driving portrayal of one of the city's worst years: the summer of 1977 when a serial killer stalked the city, a heat wave boiled citizens and a blackout inspired violent riots. For more about New York films, see the boxed text 'Three New York Film Directors.'

Documentaries

New York is nothing if not epic and no documentary captures that quite like Ric Burn's stellar, five-part *New York* series, produced for PBS in 2001. This mammoth work covers nearly 400 years of New York history. At the other end of the scale in both budget and scope is *The Cruise* (1998), a quirky, at times cranky, documentary spin through New York with a Grayline Tour guide.

NEWSPAPERS & MAGAZINES

Look up 'information overload' in any cheesy illustrated dictionary and you might see a picture of a well-stocked Manhattan newsstand. Whatever esteemed, offensive, informed, weird, alternative or esoteric periodicals you may crave, they can be found in one of these babies. On the local tip, there's really no single best source for listings – it depends what you're into: raves, readings, queer culture, high art, low budget; you get the picture. A few of the mainstays are listed here.

The *New York Times* (75¢, $3 Sunday) is still the nation's premier newspaper, with more foreign bureaus and reporters than any other publication in the world. Its Weekend section, published on Friday, is an invaluable guide to cultural events and its Metropolitan Diary in Monday's Metro section will give you a glimpse into witty, gritty New York. The Wall Street Journal ($1), published weekdays, is required reading for financial types.

The Goings on about Town section found in the *New Yorker* features weekly overviews of all the major art, theater, cinema, dance and music events. The *Village Voice* (distributed free each Wednesday) is well known for its mainstream nightlife listings, which are fast becoming eclipsed by its voluminous escort pages (what's up with that?!). It is also the city's best-known source for no-fee rental apartments and roommate situations. The *New York Press*, another free weekly, is worth checking out for local happenings. *New York* magazine offers thorough listings for its notoriously restaurant-obsessed readers. The *New York Observer*, a weekly newspaper for local politicos and society hounds, strives for quirky listings, with notices about literary readings and parties; it makes good café reading.

Time Out New York, published on Wednesday, has the same format as its London cousin, with the most comprehensive listings of any publication. *Where New York* is the best free monthly guide to mainstream city events. It's the most useful of the hotel freebies.

RADIO

The city boasts more than 100 radio stations, but most 'narrowcast' only one type of programming. For variety, head to the left-hand side of the dial where most college stations call home. On FM, classical music lovers turn to WNYC (93.9) and WQXR (96.3), which includes reviews and news reports from its owner. WBGO (88.3) carries National Public Radio in the morning and commercial-free jazz the rest of the day. WNEW (102.7), one of the nation's pioneering rock stations, abandoned the format in 1999 in favor of male-oriented (ie, silly and smutty) schlock talk. The best mixture of Top 40 pop and rock can be found on WHTZ (100.3). WBLS (107.5) is a premier spot for mainstream and light soul music, while WQHT (97.1) is known as 'Hot 97' for its hip-hop and rap programming.

Those seeking the widest musical variety will find it at WKCR (89.9), the Columbia station boasting the renowned Phil Schaap spinning jazz weekday mornings and the perennial favorite WFMU (91.1), broadcasting from beautiful Jersey City, NJ. WFDU (89.1), out of Farleigh Dickinson University, proudly features Across the Tracks, the world's greatest R&B and soul show from 1pm to 4pm weekdays.

On AM frequencies, talk and news rule. WCBS (880) and WINS (1010) carry news and weather updates and WNYC-AM (820) broadcasts National Public Radio programs. WABC (770) is a conservative pundit/radio-shrink outlet. WOR (710), one of the nation's oldest stations, carries a calmer type of talk, and WFAN (660) is home to 24-hour sports programming. Spanish speakers listen to WKDM (1380) and WADO (1280). WWRL (1660) is a talk station aimed at the city's black community.

TV

The flagship stations of all four major networks – NBC, CBS, ABC and FOX – are located in New York City and carry national prime-time fare in the evening. PBS can be found on channel 13.

Cable carries well-known networks like CNN, MTV and HBO. Channels dedicated to sports, culture, history and classic movies are also available. News broadcasts from Britain, Ireland, France, Mexico, Greece, Korea, Japan and Germany also appear on different Manhattan cable channels between 7pm and 11pm. Cable also carries dozens of local amateur programs on the 'public access' channels. The most (in)famous of them are essentially soft-core porn, carrying strip shows and ads for escort services.

PHOTOGRAPHY & VIDEO
Film & Equipment

Print film is widely available at supermarkets and discount drugstores (which offer the best prices). See the Shopping chapter for more on camera stores.

Drugstores are a good place to get your film processed cheaply (be sure to ask about any specials like free reprints). If you drop it off by noon, you can usually pick it up the next day or sooner. One-hour developing places are ubiquitous; reference the *Yellow Pages* under Photo Processing. Be prepared to pay double the overnight cost.

Video Systems

The USA uses the NTSC color TV standard, which is not compatible with other standards (PAL or Secam) used in Africa, Asia, Australia and Europe unless it is converted.

TIME

New York City is in the Eastern Standard Time (EST) zone – five hours behind Greenwich Mean Time, two hours ahead of Mountain Standard Time (including Denver, Colorado) and three hours ahead of Pacific Standard Time (San Francisco and Los Angeles, California). Almost all of the USA observes daylight-saving time: Clocks go forward one hour from the first Sunday in April to the last Saturday in October, when the clocks are turned back one hour. (It's easy to remember by the phrase 'spring ahead, fall back.') For the accurate time, call ☎ 212-976-1616.

ELECTRICITY

The USA uses 110V and 60 cycles, and plugs have two or three pins (two flat pins often with a round 'grounding' pin). Plugs with three pins don't fit into a two-hole socket, but adapters are available at hardware stores or drugstores.

WEIGHTS & MEASURES

Americans hate the metric system, and continue to resist it a full 25 years after it was supposed to be fully introduced.

Distances are in feet, yards and miles. Three feet equal one yard (.914m); 1760 yards, or 5280 feet, equal one mile. Dry weights are in ounces (oz), pounds (lb) and tons (16oz equal 1lb; 2000lb equal one ton), but liquid measures differ from dry measures. One pint equals 16 fluid oz; two pints equal one quart, a common measure for liquids like milk, which is also sold in half-gallons (two quarts) and gallons (four quarts). Gasoline is dispensed by the US gallon, which is about 20% less than the Imperial gallon. Pints and quarts are also 20% less than imperial ones. There is a conversion chart on the inside back cover of this book.

LAUNDRY

Self-serve laundries are virtually everywhere as most New Yorkers live in apartments without laundry facilities (excepting ritzy neighborhoods like the Upper East Side). The **Suds Cafe and Laundromat** (Map 4, #59; ☎ 212-741-2366; 141 W 10th St; open 7am-10pm daily), between Greenwich Ave and Waverly Place, has earned a reputation as a social scene.

Washing machines generally cost $1.50 for a 25-minute cycle; dryers are $1.50 for 30 minutes. (US washing machines run on far quicker cycles than their European counterparts.) Almost all laundries have change-making machines.

Many of these facilities also offer pick-up laundry services at a rate of about $1 per pound of clothing. Hotels charge very high prices for this service, so look for an outside laundry to save some change.

TOILETS

New York is downright hostile to the weak of bladder or bowels. The explosion in the homeless population in the 1970s (and the crackhead population in later years) led to the closure of subway facilities, and most places turn away nonpatrons from bathrooms. The city has also quietly abandoned its planned program to introduce Paris-style public toilets in the city (the lone soldier in City Hall Park notwithstanding). If you're desperate and discreet, you can try stealing into a crowded bar or restaurant, striding into a fast-food place or slipping into a branch library to use the bathroom. The toilets at Saks Fifth Avenue, Macy's, Bloomingdale's and other major department stores are other good bets (see the Shopping chapter for store locations).

LUGGAGE STORAGE

There are no public facilities that allow you to leave luggage at train stations or the airports (unless your bags have been delayed in flight, in which case the airline will hold onto them). All hotels will keep an eye on bags for guests, but take all items of value out beforehand – hotels will never assume responsibility for lost items or sticky fingers.

HEALTH

You don't need any special immunizations to visit the USA, and in New York your greatest health threat is heartburn from the ubiquitous dirt-water dogs, street vendor gyros and pepperoni slices you'll be tempted to feast upon. Still, you should have adequate travel insurance before hitting the road; See Travel Insurance, earlier in this chapter, for details.

Medical Services

If you have a medical emergency, call ☎ 911 for assistance (free from payphones). All hospital emergency rooms are obliged to receive sick visitors whether they can pay or not. However, showing up without insurance or money will virtually guarantee a long wait unless you are *in extremis*. One of New York's largest hospitals is the **New York University Medical Center** *(Map 5, #126; ☎ 212-263-5550; 462 First Ave)* near 33rd St. For the location of the hospital nearest you, look in the *Yellow Pages*.

New York is practically bursting with 24-hour 'pharmacies,' which are handy all-purpose stores with pharmaceutical counters. The main chains are **Duane Reade** *(Map 6, #3; ☎ 212-541-9708; cnr W 57th St & Broadway • Map 4, #78; ☎ 212-674-5357; 378 Sixth Ave & Waverly Pl)*, near the W 4th St subway entrance and **Rite Aid**.

For birth control and STD screening, travelers can go to **Planned Parenthood** *(Map 4, #129; appointments for all locations: ☎ 212-965-7000, 800-230-7526; W www.planned parenthood.com; 26 Bleecker St, Manhattan • Map 9, #23; 44 Court St, Brooklyn • Map 13; 349 E 149th St, the Bronx)*.

WOMEN TRAVELERS

In general, New York City is a pretty safe place for women travelers, including lesbians who will generally feel welcome. If you are unsure which areas are considered dicey, ask at your hotel or telephone the tourist office for advice; of course, other women are always a great source for the inside scoop. Given the almost historically low crime figures of late, the subway needn't be shunned by solo female travelers, though

it's wise to ride in the conductor's car (right in the middle of the train – look for the yellow off-hour waiting areas on subway platforms). If someone stares, behaves inappropriately or makes you uncomfortable, move to another part of the car or into a separate car altogether. You're far more likely to encounter obnoxious behavior on the street, where men may greet you with whistles and muttered 'compliments.' Any engagement amounts to encouragement – simply walk on.

If you're out late clubbing or at a venue farther afield, consider stashing away money for the cab fare home. If you're ever assaulted, call the **police** *(☎ 911)*. The **Violence Intervention Program** *(☎ 212-360-5090)* can provide support and assistance in English or Spanish.

GAY & LESBIAN TRAVELERS

New York is one of the most gay-friendly cities on earth, and several neighborhoods – particularly Greenwich Village and Chelsea in Manhattan and Jackson Heights in Queens – are largely gay and lesbian enclaves. Look for *The Blade*, a politically informed weekly on topics within the gay community at free boxes around town.

The **Gay and Lesbian Switchboard of NY Project** *(☎ 212-989-0999)* and the **Gay & Lesbian National Hotline** *(☎ 888-843-4564)* provide cultural and entertainment information, referrals and peer-counseling services. The hours for both are 6pm to 10pm weekdays and noon to 5pm Saturday. Both share the same website: W www.glnh.org.

The **Lesbian and Gay Community Services Center** *(Map 4, #12; ☎ 212-620-7310; W www.gaycenter.org; 208 W 13th St; open 9am-11pm daily)*, between Seventh and Greenwich Avenues, serves thousands of people each week, offering referrals, workshops, legal aid and fun social events. The center offers a free Visitor's Welcome Packet chock full of helpful stuff like an events calendar, *Gay Yellow Pages*, listings and the like.

Gay Men's Health Crisis *(Map 5, #136; ☎ 212-367-1000, 800-243-7692; W www.gmhc.org; 119 W 24th St)*, between Sixth and Seventh Aves, offers blood testing, health care for those with HIV, and a wide range of counseling services.

The **NYC Gay & Lesbian Anti-Violence Project** (Map 5, #101; ☎ 212-714-1184, hotline 212-714-1141; 240 W 35th St), between Seventh and Eighth Aves, has a 24-hour hotline.

For more information on gay life in the city, see the boxed text 'Gay & Lesbian New York' in the Facts about New York City chapter. Also, see the Gay & Lesbian Venues section in the Entertainment chapter.

DISABLED TRAVELERS

Federal laws guarantee that all government offices and facilities are available to the disabled. Most restaurant listings also note whether the location is accessible by wheelchair. For more information, contact the mayor's **Office for People with Disabilities** (☎ 212-788-2830).

Though things are improving slowly but surely, New York is still hard to navigate: streets are congested, street corners with ramps are often overcrowded with pedestrians and the general hustle and bustle is a drawback to anyone not operating at a breakneck pace. What's worse, subways are either on elevated tracks or deep below the ground and there are few elevators to access them (eg, of the nearly two dozen 6 train stops in Manhattan, there are a total of four elevators available for the disabled). For detailed information on system-wide wheelchair accessibility, call ☎ 718-596-8585. Traveling with a companion will make things easier and planning each day's logistics ahead of time should smooth the way.

Sath (Society for the Advancement of Travel for the Handicapped; Map 5, #119; ☎ 212-447-7284; e sathtravel@aol.com; Suite 610, 347 Fifth Ave, New York, NY 10016) provides information to travelers with disabilities who are Sath members. For membership information, call or write to the organization.

SENIOR TRAVELERS

Travelers who are 50 years of age or older (particularly those over 65) can often avail themselves of reduced transit fares and discount rates on hotels, drugstore prescriptions and museum admissions. New York restaurants don't generally offer age-specific discounts, but seniors are about the only class of person who can get a reduction in the $10 movie admission price.

Seniors over 65 with ID can obtain a free return-trip transfer slip when purchasing a token on the subway and there are substantial MetroCard discounts available for seniors; call ☎ 718-243-4999.

The country's most powerful elder organization is the **American Association of Retired Persons** (AARP; ☎ 800-424-3410; w www.aarp.org; 601 E St NW, Washington, DC 20049). It's a good resource for travel bargains and information. A one-year membership for US residents costs $12.50, but you can visit their website for free information.

NEW YORK CITY FOR CHILDREN

With its abundance of world-famous sites, tours and attractions, New York is a veritable wonderland for children. You'll find three museums dedicated to children (Children's Museum of Manhattan, Brooklyn Children's Museum and Staten Island Children's Museum) and many annual events that appeal to kids. The free publication 'Museums for Families,' available at tourist offices and information booths, is a detailed resource of interactive, age-specific and drop-in happenings around the city. You might also buy a copy of Christopher Maynard's Kids' New York, a guide crammed with funky facts, finds and trivia about the Big Apple.

Central Park and Prospect Park are a treasure for all ages and the classic carousels within the parks are tons of fun. Kids will also love the Central Park Zoo (officially named the Central Park Wildlife Center) and the more elaborate Bronx Zoo. The Big Apple Circus visits Lincoln Center each winter, and the Ringling Bros and Barnum & Bailey Circus takes over Madison Square Garden every May and June. A brand-new, beautiful carousel was also recently installed in Bryant Park, behind the New York Public Library. (Also see the boxed text 'What's a Kid to Do?')

What's a Kid to Do?

ANGUS OSBORN

It's hard to narrow down the many choices for kids, but here are a few good picks for the pint-size traveler. Assuming you've already put the Statue of Liberty, the Empire State Building and the Children's Museum of Manhattan on the 'to do' list, also check out what special events are happening when you're in town (for example, a few of the best circuses blow through town annually and the Fringe Festival each August features theater performances by kids, for kids). For more details on all of the following, see the individual headings in the Things to See & Do chapter.

Central Park

Horse-drawn carriages, rollerbladers, a children's zoo, six playgrounds and a famous carousel are just some of the reasons to spend an afternoon in New York's most famous open space. Also check out storytelling at the Hans Christian Andersen statue (11am Saturday) and the Marionette Theater in the Swedish Cottage.

New Victory Theater

This theater in the heart of Times Square is dedicated to children's plays and fun spectacles for the kiddies. If whatever is happening here doesn't grab you, head across the street to Madame Tussaud's Wax Museum.

South Street Seaport

Along with the tall ships and children's center here, head to the Seaport for kid-friendly food and fun entertainment like knife jugglers and sandcastle building.

Rockefeller Center at Christmas

Families can ice skate in the shadow of the center's huge Christmas tree, then take in the Radio City Music Hall Christmas show, a pricey spectacular.

Rose Center for Earth & Space

The American Museum of Natural History's fabulous new planetarium is an up-to-the-minute facility for the would-be space explorer. Teenagers tend to like the night-time laser rock shows.

Bronx Zoo

Visiting the oldest wildlife facility in the USA makes a journey to the Bronx worth it. But if that's too far with kids in tow, take in the much more manageable **Central Park Zoo**, right in Manhattan.

Circle Line

A classic New York delight, this boat trip around Manhattan is a perfect way to cool off on a hot summer day. (Also give the free **Staten Island ferry** a whirl.)

Coney Island

The Boardwalk, the beach, Astroland (and the Cyclone!), Deno's Wonder Wheel Amusement Park, the New York Aquarium, Brooklyn Cyclones baseball team and Nathan's hot dogs. 'Nuff said.

Chelsea Piers

There's something here for kids of all ages: bowling, batting cages, rock-climbing walls and year-round ice and roller skating.

N.Y.C.

UNIVERSITIES

New York is home to many world-class private universities and fine public colleges, including Columbia, New York (NYU) and Fordham Universities. There's also the New School for Social Research (which offers extensive evening adult classes), Cooper Union (New York's first free college) and the various colleges of the City University of New York (CUNY). These urban educational centers are not physically separated from the city – in fact, NYU's campus and dorm facilities are distributed throughout Greenwich Village (which some have come to refer to as 'NYU Village'). Columbia's main campus is on Broadway on Manhattan's Upper West Side. CUNY's City College campus at St Nicholas Terrace is significant for its neo-Gothic design and worth a visit.

Several world-class art schools also call New York City home, including the **Parson's School of Design** *(Map 4, #17; cnr Fifth Ave & 13th St)*, **School of Visual Arts** *(SVA; Map 5, #127; 209 E 23rd St)* and **Pratt** in Brooklyn.

LIBRARIES

The **New York Public Library** *(Map 5; main branch* ☎ *212-930-0830;* **w** *www.nypl.org; Fifth Ave at 42nd St • Map 7; Midtown Manhattan Annex* ☎ *212-340-0833; 455 Fifth Ave at 40th St • Map 4, #57; Jefferson Market branch* ☎ *212-243-4334; 425 Sixth Ave at W 10th St)* has 85 branches spread throughout Manhattan, the Bronx and Staten Island. The main branch is a research library and a stunning architectural attraction. Free tours are held at 11am and 2pm Monday to Saturday or check out the famous 3rd-floor reading room on your own. Periodicals, books, videos and CDs circulate at the Midtown Manhattan annex, directly across Fifth Ave, or at the Jefferson Market branch. For other branches, check the library's website.

Internet use is free throughout the New York public library system; patrons are entitled to 30 minutes per week and 10 printed pages free. Myriad interesting readings, concerts, children's activities, films and more are hosted by branch libraries; pick up a copy of the calendar listing 'Events' at any library.

CULTURAL CENTERS

New York City's major cultural centers include:

Alliance Française (Map 5; ☎ 212-355-6100; **w** www.fiaf.org) 22 E 60th St; with another branch (Map 3, #74; ☎ 212-809-2000) at 95 Wall St

Asia Society (Map 7, #86; ☎ 212-288-6400; **w** www.asiasociety.org) 725 Park Ave at 70th St

Center for Cuban Studies (Map 5, #158; ☎ 212-242-0559; **w** www.cubaupdate.org) 124 W 23rd St, between Sixth and Seventh Aves

Center for Jewish History (Map 5, #187; ☎ 212-294-8301; **w** www.cjh.org) 15 W 16th St, between Fifth and Sixth Aves

Czech Center (Map 7, #39; ☎ 212-288-0830; **w** www.czechcenter.com) 1109 Madison Ave at 83rd St

Goethe Institute (Map 7, #41; ☎ 212-439-8700) 1014 Fifth Ave, between 82nd and 83rd Sts

Hispanic Society of America (Map 8, #6; ☎ 212-926-2234; **w** www.hispanicsociety.org) 613 Broadway at W 155th St in Audubon Terrace

Italian Cultural Institute (Map 7, #85; ☎ 212-879-4242; **w** www.italcultny.org) 686 Park Ave

Japan Society (Map 5, #56; ☎ 212-832-1155; **w** www.japansociety.org) 333 E 47th St, between First and Second Aves

Scandinavia House (Map 5, #93; ☎ 212-879-9779) 58 Park Ave, between 37th and 38th Sts

Swiss Institute (Map 4, #249; ☎ 212-925-2035; **w** www.swissinstitute.net) 3rd fl, 495 Broadway, between Spring and Broome Sts

DANGERS & ANNOYANCES
Beggars

When asked why he robbed banks, criminal Willie Sutton replied, 'That's where the money is!' The same philosophy prompts panhandlers to set up shop at subway entrances, landmarks and street corners where tourists congregate. Requests for money come in dozens of forms, including appeals for a dubious support group ('I'm a member of the United Homeless Organization'), unsubtle appeals to tourist fear ('I don't want to hurt or rob anybody') or even guilt trips ('I know you won't help me because I'm black/poor/homeless...'). It's impossible to differentiate between those truly in need and someone on the hustle, and many assuage their guilt by giving. But few New Yorkers deny that money handed out even to genuinely destitute beggars will likely go to support a drug or alcohol habit rather than toward a meal or a room for the night. Giving or not is a personal choice, but you can't give to everyone or you'll go broke. If you're prone to handing out change, try to establish some criteria (eg, musicians/performers, moms with kids, women, veterans, etc) as to whom you'll help out before you're besieged by people hitting you up.

It is the nature of life in New York that even some once-decent efforts to help panhandlers have been corrupted, such as the selling of *Street News*, a homeless publication. At least a few subway beggars have taken to telling riders that the weather has prevented delivery of their copies or that they've nobly given their copies away to others. The upshot is that gullible listeners give these guys money anyway.

If you wish to give to a legitimate organization helping people in need, contact **Citymeals-on-Wheels** (☎ 212-687-1234), which reaches out to feed hundreds of hungry people each day.

Scams

A prominent scam that targets out-of-towners takes the form of a shoulder-shrugging appeal for help. This differs from outright panhandling in that the person asking for money makes no pretense of being impoverished. Instead, he or she approaches you with a sob story ('I just got locked out of my car and need money for a cab') and even promise to pay you back. Spare change isn't what these con artists are after – they're very persuasive in trying to get $5 or even $20 from you, with no intention of ever paying you back. When approached by anyone asking for money, remember that the person is asking a tourist for help because most locals (police included) are wise to scams.

In another frequent scam, hustlers set up three-card monte games – where 'players' try to pick the red card out of three shuffled on the top of a cardboard box. This variation on the shell game is widely known to be a no-win scam, but it's fun to watch; note that most of the other 'by-standers' are actually in on the graft. Yet enough people play along

(or get their wallets lifted while watching the proceedings) to make it a common sight on downtown streets during the weekends.

Drugs

There is drug activity in the far east of Alphabet City (Aves B, C and D), along Amsterdam Ave above 100th St and also in Washington Heights near the George Washington Bridge bus stop (this 'easy-on, easy-off' location has led many a carload of kids from Jersey to get busted here). All three neighborhoods have the attendant dangers of such places. Expect to be approached by drug dealers if you wander into any of these places, and avoid walking through them with any amount of cash at night. Despite the presence of NYU (or perhaps because of it!), Washington Square Park has long been the place to score pot and is the site of the annual Million Marijuana March (**W** www.cures-not-wars.org) on or around May 1.

Prostitution

New York's strip joints are unspectacular (topless only) and either sleazy and cheap (in Midtown) or sleazy and expensive (near Wall St); they're not havens for prostitution. The city also contains sex clubs that cater to Japanese businessmen and pricey escort services that meet the demand for prostitution.

In recent years, police have cracked down on street walkers, and instead of being on the stroll on Eleventh Ave near the Lincoln Tunnel, the women ply their risky trade from vans. Elsewhere, prostitutes approach visiting businessmen in public places, such as the stretch of Sixth Ave near Central Park South, the Bull and Bear pub at the Waldorf-Astoria and the lobby of the Grand Hyatt Hotel, one of the most open spots in the city for the hotel sex trade (perhaps because the hotel hosts many visiting professional athletic teams).

ESBIN ANDERSON PHOTOGRAPHY

FACTS FOR THE VISITOR

Emergency

For police, fire and ambulance calls, dial ☎ 911 – it's free from any phone. For non-emergencies, call the **police department** (☎ 212-374-5000; 7:30am-6pm Mon-Fri) – the number here will also direct you to the nearest station. All federal, state and city government offices appear in a special section in the white pages; the front of every phone book also contains a complete list of community organizations.

Here are some useful numbers:

Alcoholics Anonymous	☎ 212-647-1680
Dept of Health's AIDS Hotline	☎ 800-825-5448
Dept of Consumer Affairs	☎ 212-487-4444
Gay&Lesbian National Hotline	☎ 212-989-0999
Crime Victims Services	☎ 212-577-7777
Legal Aid Society	☎ 212-577-3300

LEGAL MATTERS

If you're arrested, you're allowed to remain silent. There is no legal reason to speak to a police officer if you don't wish, but never walk away from an officer until given permission. All persons who are arrested have the legal right to make one phone call. If you don't have a lawyer or family member to help you, call your consulate. The police will give you the number upon request.

Gone are the good old days when you could toke a joint or drink in public if your drink wore a 'dress' (a brown paper bag around a beer for example). These became 'quality of life' offenses under Giuliani's new New York and these days you party in public at your own risk. (Although Mayor Mike Bloomberg admitted to smoking pot *and* enjoying it, so maybe those laws will loosen a bit.) When polled as to what they missed most in the cleaner, safer New York, most folks offered some variation on the 'sitting on the stoop with a beer in summer' theme. Sigh.

In 1998, the city briefly tried to stop the strong New York tradition of 'jaywalking' – that is, crossing the street in the middle of the block – but the experiment fizzled fast. There are foot-traffic barriers in parts of Midtown that serve to keep people in line, but beyond that it's open season.

BUSINESS HOURS

You can shop in New York for almost anything seven days a week, with some exceptions. Stores are generally open 10am to 6pm Monday to Saturday, with big department stores open late on Thursday nights. Sunday shopping hours tend to be from noon to 6pm.

Bookstores and specialty shops often maintain regular night hours, and you'll find many 24-hour drugstores (Duane Reade, Rite Aid, Genovese) that sell pharmaceuticals and a variety of convenience items (toothpaste, candy, soft drinks and basic staples like milk and water). Indeed, whether it's bagels, Internet access, a car wash or a bowling lane, the axiom holds true: you can get anything at anytime in New York – sometimes you just need to know where to look.

In a barbaric holdover of the 'blue' laws, liquor stores are closed on Sunday throughout New York State. You can buy beer (but not wine) in stores after noon on Sunday.

Bakeries and clothing boutiques tend to be closed on Monday.

The right side of the law: Times Square police station

PUBLIC HOLIDAYS & SPECIAL EVENTS

Hardly a week goes by without a special event taking place in New York. In fact, some 50 officially recognized parades each year honor certain causes or ethnic groups. The city also hosts several hundred street fairs, most of which offer a rather unremarkable selection of fast food, house plants, athletic socks and cheap belts. You're bound to come across one as you stroll through town during the summer.

Fifth Ave shuts down several times a year for the major parades, including the granddaddy of all ethnic celebrations, the St Patrick's Day Parade on March 17.

On national public holidays (many of which are celebrated on Mondays), banks, schools and government offices (including post offices) shut down, and public transportation, museums and other services operate on a Sunday schedule. If a national holiday falls on Saturday, it's typically observed on Friday; if it falls on Sunday, it's observed on the following Monday.

For information on any of the events listed below, you can call **NYC & Company** *(New York Convention & Visitors Bureau;* ☎ *212-484-1222).*

January

New Year's Day The first day of the year is a national holiday. (See December for information on New Year's Eve festivities.)

Three Kings Parade Every January 5, El Museo del Barrio (☎ 212-831-7272) sponsors this parade, in which thousands of schoolchildren – along with camels, donkeys and sheep – make their way up Fifth Ave to 116th St, the heart of Spanish Harlem.

Winter Antiques Show At this show (☎ 718-292-7392; W www.winterantiquesshow.com), held mid-month at the Armory (Park Ave at 67th St), dealers peddle $30,000 couches and $15,000 tea services. The crowd includes many celebrities and everyday strollers who couldn't possibly afford the prices.

Martin Luther King Jr Day On the third Monday of the month, this national holiday celebrates the birthday of the civil rights leader.

Chinese New Year The date of the lunar new year varies from late January to early February each year, but the fireworks crackle in Chinatown for days before and after this holiday. Try to catch either the Lion or Dragon Dance Parades. Call ☎ 212-764-7241 for information.

February

Black History Month The Martin Luther King Jr national holiday (see January) serves as the unofficial kickoff to February's month-long celebration of African American history and culture. Call Harlem's Schomburg Center for Research in Black Culture (☎ 212-491-2200) for details.

Presidents' Day The third Monday of the month is a national holiday, celebrating the births of George Washington and Abraham Lincoln.

March

St Patrick's Day Parade For more than 200 years, the city's Irish population has honored their homeland's patron saint with this parade down Fifth Ave on March 17. In recent years, a gay Irish group has protested its exclusion from the parade with a demonstration at Fifth Ave and 42nd St.

Easter This Christian holiday falls on a Sunday in late March or early April. A wild parade takes place along Fifth Ave in Midtown, as New Yorkers don their best Easter bonnets.

April

Avignon Film Festival (☎ 212-355-6160) Hosted by the Alliance Française, it screens French, European and American independent films.

May

Ninth Avenue International Food Festival In mid-May, Ninth Ave between 42nd and 57th Sts teems with people gorging on ethnic fast food from stalls lining the avenue.

Fleet Week Near the end of the month, thousands of sailors from numerous nations descend on New York for this annual convocation of naval ships and air-rescue teams. Call the Intrepid Sea-Air-Space Museum (☎ 212-245-0072) for information.

Memorial Day The last Monday of the month is a national holiday honoring soldiers who died in past wars. It's also the unofficial kickoff of summer (the first day you can officially wear white without attracting the fashion police).

June

Restaurant Week Every June and November, many top restaurants, from Aquavit to Vong, participate in this event that gives diners a break: prix fixe meals cost whatever the year (eg, $20.03, $20.04 etc); reservations are typically not accepted.

Toyota Comedy Festival Comedians take to the stage of Carnegie Hall and at a host of clubs in early June. Call ☎ 888-338-6968 (information).

Bell Atlantic Jazz Festival This early June festival is co-sponsored by the Knitting Factory. Call ☎ 212-219-3006 or visit **W** www.jazzfest.com for information.

Puerto Rican Day Parade This is the one you've heard about: held the second Sunday in June along Fifth Ave from 44th to 86th Sts, this phat fiesta brings out tens of thousands to dance, eat and frolic *NYquina* style.

JVC Jazz Festival Nearly all the major concert halls in town are jumping with the top names in jazz from mid- to late-June. Call ☎ 212-501-1390 for information.

Museum Mile Festival On the second Tuesday in June, Fifth Ave from 86th to 104th Sts is closed to traffic from 6pm to 9pm, and all nine museums in the area open their doors for free. Call ☎ 212-606-2296 or visit **W** www.museummile festival.org for more information.

Buskers Festival A night of 'buskers' (street performers) highlights a series of free concerts and performances at the World Financial Center downtown. Call ☎ 212-945-0505 for details.

Celebrate Brooklyn This festival begins at the end of June, lasts the entire summer and includes concerts, Shakespearean plays and dance shows. Call ☎ 718-855-7882 or visit **W** www.brooklynx.org .

Shakespeare in Central Park The Public Theater (☎ 212-539-8750; **W** www.publictheater.org) sponsors popular outdoor performances of the Bard's work from late June to September in Central Park's Delacorte Theater. In the past, Michelle Pfeiffer, Denzel Washington and other major stars have appeared in the free productions.

Lesbian and Gay Pride Week On the last weekend of June, a huge parade flows down Fifth Ave from Midtown to Greenwich Village. Dance parties take place on the Hudson River piers, and clubs are hopping with the rainbow tribe. Call Heritage of Pride's bilingual English-Spanish information line at ☎ 212-807-7433 or visit the organizer's website at **W** www.nycpride.org.

July

Independence Day On July 4, Macy's (☎ 212-494-4495) sponsors its annual fireworks spectacular in the East River. Independence Day is a national holiday.

Lincoln Center Events Lincoln Center hosts an astounding number of events throughout the summer, many of them free, including Lincoln Center Out-of-Doors (☎ 212-875-5108), the Mostly Mozart concert series (☎ 212-875-5399) and the Lincoln Center Festival (☎ 212-875-5928), a biennial event that brings many international actors, singers and acrobats to New York for the first time.

Central Park Summerstage These mostly free musical performances (raucous!) and author readings (poignant!) are held en plein air at the Rumsey Playfield behind the park's bandshell from mid-June to mid-August. Call ☎ 212-360-2777 or see **W** www.summerstage.org for information.

Classic Movies in Bryant Park On Mondays in July and August, the park behind the New York Public Library hosts open-air film screenings – the first and still the best, when you can get a patch of grass. Call ☎ 212-768-4242 for information.

Outdoor Concerts Also in July and August, the New York Philharmonic (☎ 212-875-5709) and the Metropolitan Opera (☎ 212-362-6000) perform under the stars in Central Park, with other performances in parks in all the boroughs.

August

Harlem Week Throughout the month, the city's premier black neighborhood celebrates with festivities that culminate in the Harlem Jazz & Music Fest. Call ☎ 212-862-4777 (information).

Speaking out with passion during Gay Pride

COREY WISE

Fringe Festival This frenzy (more than 1200 performances!) stretches over two weeks in mid- to late-August in 20 locations. Call ☎ 212-420-8877 or see **w** www.fringenyc.org for full information.

September

Labor Day The first Monday of the month is a national holiday that honors American workers. It also marks the end of the summer tourist season. According to strict fashion etiquette, you don't wear white after today.

San Gennaro This 10-day festival honoring Naples' patron saint takes place in the second week in September in Little Italy; for more information see **w** www.littleitalynyc.com.

US Open Tennis Tournament This annual world-class event takes place in Flushing Meadows in Queens. Attracting the world's top tennis players, this two-week championship usually includes matches on Labor Day weekend. Call ☎ 888-673-6849 for information.

West Indian–American Day Parade On Labor Day, more than one million people take part in a parade along Eastern Parkway in Brooklyn, making this the single largest event of the year. Call ☎ 718-773-4052 for information.

All frocked up for the West Indian Day Parade

New York is Book Country Festival The literati take over NY in mid-September, with readings, talks and books sales, culminating in the Fifth Ave book fair between 48th and 57th Sts. Call ☎ 646-557-6625 or see **w** www.nyisbook country.com for details.

New York Film Festival This major event in the film world takes place at Lincoln Center's Walter Reade Theater, beginning in late September. For information, call ☎ 212-875-5600.

October

Columbus/Discoverer's Day The second Monday of the month is a national holiday.

Halloween Parade On October 31, this colorful and wild parade winds its way up Sixth Ave from Broome St, through Greenwich Village, and ending in a block party on Christopher St. Don a costume if you want in. See **w** www .halloween-nyc.com for details.

November

New York Marathon As the weather cools, the New York Road Runners Club (☎ 212-860-4455) sponsors this annual 26.2-mile road race, in which some 25,000 runners travel through all five boroughs on the first weekend in November.

Thanksgiving Day On this national holiday, Macy's (☎ 212-494-4495) sponsors its famous parade, a big event with huge balloons and floats that travel down Broadway from W 72nd St to Herald Square.

December

Rockefeller Center Christmas Tree Lighting At 7pm on the Tuesday after Thanksgiving, the big tree is fired up. The event features celebrity performances and an appearance by the Radio City Music Hall Rockettes. Call ☎ 212-632-3975.

Radio City Christmas Spectacular The high-kicking Rockettes are on display all month at the famous theater. Call ☎ 212-247-4777 for tickets.

Singing Christmas Tree Celebration At South St Seaport, dozens of costumed carolers perform several times a day, beginning just after Thanksgiving. Call ☎ 212-732-7678 for information.

Christmas Day December 25 is a national holiday.

New Year's Eve In addition to the annual New Year's Eve festivities in Times Square, the city's celebration features a five-mile midnight run in Central Park (☎ 212-860-4455), fireworks at the South St Seaport (☎ 212-732-7678) and First Night, a day-long festival of alcohol-free family events, including ballroom dancing in Grand Central Terminal's main concourse. Events run from 11am on December 31 to 1am New Year's Day. Call ☎ 212-883-2476 for details.

COREY WISE

FACTS FOR THE VISITOR

ACTIVITIES
Gyms

Some consider the massive **Chelsea Piers Complex** *(Map 5, #110; ☎ 212-336-6000; day pass $40; open 6am-11pm Mon-Fri, 7am-8pm Sat, 8am-8pm Sun)*, at the western end of 23rd St on the Hudson River, to be the best gym complex in the world. This huge facility includes a four-level driving range overlooking the river and an indoor ice-skating rink. A huge sports and fitness center contains a running track, swimming pool, workout center, sand for volleyball playing and a rock-climbing wall.

Other gyms all over the city offer day rates of $15 to $25. Many advertise in the *Village Voice*. One well-located, no-frills, gym to keep in mind is the **Gold's Gym** *(Map 6, #17; ☎ 212-307-7760; 250 W 54th St; day pass $25)*, between Seventh Ave and Broadway, with well-maintained machines.

All first-class hotels have at least a small room dedicated to fitness – call ahead or inquire when you reserve your room.

Running

The **New York Road Runner's Club** *(NYRRC; Map 7, #23; ☎ 212-860-4455; w www.nyrrc .org; 9 E 89th St)* organizes weekend runs all over the city, as well as the annual New York Marathon (see Public Holidays & Special Events, earlier). For more information, visit the NYRRC booth at the Engineer's Gate entrance to Central Park at E 90th St.

You'll find several good spots for solo runs in Manhattan. The 6-mile loop road around Central Park offers runners a respite from city traffic, since it's closed to cars from 10am to 3pm and 7pm to 10pm weekdays

and all weekend long. But if you don't want to jockey for space with rollerbladers and cyclists, try the soft, 1.6-mile path around the Jacqueline Kennedy Onassis Reservoir. You can also jog on the runner's pathway that begins along West St and runs beside the Hudson River from 23rd St all the way to Battery Park City; it passes a very pleasant stretch of public park and offers great views of the Jersey shoreline and the Statue of Liberty (though you'll be dodging skaters, strollers and cyclists down here). The Upper East Side boasts a path that runs along FDR Drive and the East River from 63rd St to about 115th St. If you're alone, it's not advisable to run farther north than 105th St, since the path isn't well lit beyond that point.

Cycling

If you hit the city's pockmarked streets, use a trail bike with wide wheels. Always wear a helmet and be alert so you don't get 'doored' by a passenger exiting a taxi. Dozens of cyclists die on New York City streets every year, so unless your urban skills are well honed, stick to the pastoral paths in Central or Prospect Park or along the Hudson River. And don't even think of peddling on sidewalks: it's illegal.

The **Five Borough Bicycle Club** *(☎ 212-932-2300 ext 115)* sponsors free or low-cost weekend trips to the outskirts of the city. For more information, visit the club's office at **Hostelling International-New York** *(Map 7, #5; 891 Amsterdam Ave at W 103rd St)*. The **New York Cycle Club** *(☎ 212-828-5711)* sponsors day trips and longer rides, and it offers printed guides to 65 of its

COREY WISE

New York boasts numerous spots for the avid jogger

members' favorite routes. Both of these organizations produce helpful newsletters.

Transportation Alternatives *(Map 5, #110;* ☎ *212-629-8080, fax 629-8334;* W *www .transalt.org; 12th fl, 115 W 30th St)*, which sponsors Bike Week NYC in May, has cycling maps available for download and acts as a clearinghouse for loads of cycle-related resources like your legal rights as a cyclist, antitheft tips and how to take your bike on public transportation.

Many places rent bicycles for the day, including **Sixth Ave Bicycles** *(Map 5, #197;* ☎ *212-255-5100; 545 Sixth Ave)* and **Manhattan Bicycle** *(Map 6, #24;* ☎ *212-262-0111; 791 Ninth Ave)*, between 52nd and 53rd, among other locations. **Frank's Bike Shop** *(Map 4, #223;* ☎ *212-533-6332; 533 Grand St)* is a neighborhood shop in the Lower East Side with a helpful staff and very low prices. Finally the name tells the story of **Central Park Bicycle Tours & Rentals** *(Map 7;* ☎ *212-541-8759; 2 Columbus Circle at 59th & Broadway)*.

In-Line Skating

Rollerblading is immensely popular in New York, and daredevil skaters with ripped bodies dart in and out of city traffic in warm weather. Central Park is the main place to show off your skills (or lack thereof); head to the mall that runs east of Sheep Meadow or in front of the bandshell. You can also skate on Central Park Dr, which is off-limits to cars from 10am to 3pm and 7pm to 10pm weekdays and all weekend long. Beginners will definitely want to lay off the wicked S-curve near E 106th St and Lasker Pool.

If you're just starting out, rent a pair from the nearby **Blades West** *(Map 7, #71;* ☎ *212-787-3911; 120 W 72nd St)* for $20 for 24 hours, and then ask a volunteer at the W 72nd St park entrance to show you how to stop. If you take the plunge and buy, go to Paragon Athletic Goods (see the Sporting Goods section of the Shopping chapter).

The look: an all important part of skating

Boating & Fishing

The city's western waterfront, now experiencing a major renaissance, has turned greener, thanks to the addition of the Battery Park Esplanade and Hudson River Park in Lower Manhattan. Part of a long-term, five-mile redevelopment project, the park already includes the **Downtown Boathouse** *(Map 3;* ☎ *646-613-0740;* W *www.downtownboat house.org; Pier 26)*, between Chambers and Canal St at the Hudson River, where you can take free kayaking lessons on weekends. Uptown, the 79th St Boathouse features a houseboat docking area and a nice restaurant, but few water sports activities are available for visitors.

You can actually fish for striped bass, porgies, flounder and more on the piers overlooking the Hudson River, but the river's history of chemical contamination makes eating the fish an unlikely proposition. For information on fishing the Hudson, contact the **Battery Park Conservancy** *(*☎ *212-267-9700;* W *www.bpcparks.org)*. For better fishing, head to City Island in the Bronx (see the Things to See & Do chapter).

You can learn to sail in Downtown Manhattan with the **North Cove Sailing School** *(Map 3, #65;* ☎ *800-532-5552; 393 South End Ave)* or head to the Chelsea Piers and sail with **Offshore Sailing School** *(Map 5, #140;* ☎ *800-221-4326;* W *www.chelseapiers.com/masail ing.htm; Pier 59)*; a three-hour sail is $195 per person.

COREY WISE

FACTS FOR THE VISITOR

Getting There & Away

Served by three major airports, two train terminals and a massive bus depot, New York City is the most important transportation hub in the northeastern USA.

AIR
Airports
Most international flights land at John F Kennedy International Airport (JFK), just 15 miles (but 90 minutes with any luck!) from Midtown in southeastern Queens. La Guardia Airport, eight miles from Midtown in northern Queens, serves domestic flights mostly, including air shuttles to Boston and Washington, DC.

Newark International Airport in New Jersey, 10 miles west of Manhattan, is the hub for Continental Airlines. Many major carriers use its new international arrivals terminal, and its new AirTrain means a quick transfer into Manhattan.

Warning
The information in this chapter is particularly vulnerable to change: prices for international travel are volatile, routes are introduced and canceled, schedules change, special deals come and go, and rules and visa requirements are amended. Airlines and governments seem to take a perverse pleasure in making price structures and regulations as complicated as possible. You should check directly with the airline or a travel agent to make sure you understand how a fare (and ticket you may buy) works. In addition, the travel industry is highly competitive and there are many lurks and perks.

The upshot of this is that you should get opinions, quotes and advice from as many airlines and travel agents as possible before you part with your hard-earned cash. The details given in this chapter should be regarded as pointers and are not a substitute for your own careful, up-to-date research.

The **Port Authority of New York & New Jersey** (W *www.panynj.gov*) operates all three airports and maintains a website with detailed information about each airport. **Flytecomm** (W *www.flytecomm.com/cgi-bin/trackflight*) tracks any domestic or Canadian flight, allowing you to check the status of scheduled arrivals and departures.

New security measures at all New York–area airports mean there is no curbside check-in; non-ticketed passengers are not allowed beyond the entrance doors; and there's no curbside parking. Passengers should arrive at least 90 minutes prior to domestic departures and a full two hours before international departures.

For information about getting to/from the airports, see the Getting Around chapter.

JFK International Airport This airport serves 35 million passengers a year. It's sprawling and unpopular – and its crowded international arrivals terminal rivals the chaos of London's Heathrow Airport. On the upside, the 'Train to the Plane' service on the Rockaway Beach A train trundles you from the airport to Manhattan for the price of a token.

Airlines used to build showcase terminals at JFK *(Map 1)*, and thus the airport grew to its uncoordinated state with no coherent plan. While some of the original airlines (Eastern, Pan Am) have disappeared, the terminals remain, linked by the JFK Expressway and a free shuttle bus. American Airlines, British Airways, Delta and United have their own terminals; most other airlines use the crowded International Arrivals Building.

To find out if the airport is closed in bad weather, call the **Airport information line** (☎ *718-244-4444*), as individual airlines may be reluctant to give specific information about flight delays over the phone.

Until the airport undergoes a much-needed renovation, set to be completed in 2005, it's best not to spend too much time there. JFK's duty-free shops, like those in most US cities,

The Verrazano Bridge

are good for cheap(er) cigarettes, but not much else – you can get more affordable alcohol, electronics and clothes in town.

La Guardia Airport For easy access, La Guardia Airport *(Map 12; ☎ 718-533-3400; W www.new-york-lga.com/index.html)* is more convenient than JFK. US Airways and the Delta Shuttle have their own terminals; all other airlines use the Central Terminal building in front of the parking garage.

La Guardia isn't equipped to accommodate wide-body jets, so cross-country or transatlantic flights can't land there. The airport mainly serves destinations in Canada and the northeastern USA.

Newark International Airport The best choice at the moment for foreign visitors, thanks to a new, well-organized international arrival terminal, is the Newark International Airport *(Map 1; ☎ 973-961-6000; W www.newarkairport.com)*. This airport's advantages include a large immigration hall that speeds passport checks and a monorail sys-

tem that links the terminals for quick transfers to domestic flights.

Moreover, flights to Newark are usually a bit cheaper because of the misplaced perception that the airport is less accessible than JFK – it is in *New Jersey* after all. One of the beauties of Newark however, is that you can get into Manhattan quickly by bus, or New Jersey Transit trains (see the Getting Around chapter for details).

Airline Offices

The following airlines have offices Downtown or at the airports:

Aer Lingus (Map 5, #25; ☎ 888-474-7424; W www.aerlingus.com) 509 Madison Ave

Aeromexico (Map 5, #4; ☎ 212-754-2140, 800-237-6639; W www.aeromexico.com) 37 W 57th St

Air Canada (Map 5, #68; ☎ 888-247-2262; W www.aircanada.ca) 15 W 50th St

Air France (Map 6, #12; ☎ 212-830-4000, 800-237-2747; W www.airfrance.com) 120 W 56th St

American Airlines (Map 5, #70; ☎ 800-433-7300; W www.aa.com) 18 W 49th St

British Airways (Map 5, #77; ☎ 800-247-9297; W www.british-airways.com) 530 Fifth Ave

Continental Airlines (Map 5, #84; ☎ 212-319-9494, 800-525-0280; W www.continental.com) 100 E 42nd St

Delta Air Lines (Map 5, #84; ☎ 800-221-1212; W www.delta.com) 100 E 42nd St

Japan Airlines (Map 1; ☎ 800-525-3663; W www.jal.co.jp) JFK International Airport

jetBlue (Map 1; ☎ 800-538-2583; W www.jetblue.com) JFK International Airport

KLM Royal Dutch Airlines (Map 5, #84; ☎ 800-374-7747; W www.klm.com) 2nd fl, 100 E 42nd St

Lufthansa (Map 5, #117; ☎ 800-645-3880; W www.lufthansa.com) 350 Fifth Ave, Ste 1421

Northwest Airlines (Map 5, #84; ☎ 800-225-2525; W www.nwa.com) 2nd fl, 100 E 42nd St

Qantas Airways (Map 5, #33; ☎ 800-227-4500; W www.qantas.com.au) 712 Fifth Ave

Singapore Airlines (Map 5, #9; ☎ 212-644-8801, 800-742-3333; W www.singaporeair.com) 55 E 59th St

United Airlines (Map 5, #84; ☎ 800-241-6522; W www.ual.com) 100 E 42nd St

US Airways (Map 5, #48; ☎ 800-428-4322; W www.usairways.com) 101 Park Ave

Virgin Atlantic (Map 1; ☎ 800-862-8621; W www.virgin.com) JFK International Airport

Buying Tickets

Plane tickets can take a ravenous bite from your budget and buying your passage can be a hassle, intimidating or both. Before you just walk into the nearest travel agent or airline office, do some research.

There are some rules of thumb for getting an economical ticket: Start the hunt early – some of the cheapest tickets and best deals must be purchased months in advance, and popular flights tend to sell out early. Be flexible: play with arrival and departure dates, arrival airports (remember there are three here) and stopovers. Consider a shorter trip, as airlines are no friend to long-term travelers, and ticket prices increase substantially once you surpass the 30-, 60- or 90-day mark. As always, some of the best information is available from travelers fresh from trips, so talk to them if possible.

Note that high season in NY runs from mid-June to mid-September (summer), and one week before and after Christmas. February, March and October through Thanksgiving (the fourth Thursday in November) serve as shoulder seasons, when prices drop slightly.

Of course, the Internet is a fabulous travel tool and a good place to start your research. For ballpark fare figures, try **Travelocity** (W www.travelocity.com) or **Expedia** (W www.expedia.com). The prominent online auction site **Priceline.com** (W www.priceline.com) offers deeply discounted tickets (we're talking like $150 across the Atlantic during high season in some cases!); you name the price you're willing to pay and the date you want to leave, and the search engine matches you with an available airline seat. *Caveat emptor*: The flight is nonchangeable and nonrefundable, and your credit card is billed immediately, as soon as a seat is located to match your price. Other websites offering discount tickets include **Orbitz** (W www.orbitz.com) and **Cheap Tickets** (W www.cheaptickets.com); **smarterliving** (W www.smarterliving.com) is a terrific clearinghouse for last-minute and discount airfare deals. Also, check the websites of individual airlines, which often list special offers available only online.

The professionals can usually ferret out good deals, especially with more complicated itineraries. **Council Travel** (Map 4, #83; ☎ 800-226-8624, reservations ☎ 212-254-2525; W www.counciltravel.com; 254 Greene St at E 8th St • Map 9; ☎ 212-666-4177; 895 Amsterdam Ave) and **STA Travel** (Map 4, #160; ☎ 800-777-0112, reservations ☎ 212-627-3111; W www.statravel.com; 10 Downing St), near Sixth Ave, offer some of the best rates, especially for students. Both agencies have multiple offices in Manhattan. You might also try the main **American Express office** (Map 3, #59; ☎ 212-421-8240; World Financial Center, West & Vesey Sts), which offers package deals.

Courier flights are a superb option for budget travelers with little baggage. Given its importance as a cargo port, New York is the best place in the USA to arrange courier flights around the globe. **Now Voyager** (☎ 212-459-1616) books courier flights and last-minute domestic specials. It's best to call their busy office after business hours to hear a comprehensive voice menu of locations and conditions. A good source for courier flights to Europe is **Air Tech** (☎ 212-219-7000). If you have the travel bug bad, consider joining a courier association: With a low annual fee, you receive a schedule of worldwide flights that let you jet between points like New York and Rio de Janeiro for as little as $325 roundtrip. Two reliable organizations include **Air Courier Association** (☎ 800-822-0888; W www.aircourier.org) and **International Association of Air Travel Couriers** (☎ 561-582-8320; W www.courier.org).

Some travel agencies known as 'consolidators' ('bucket shops' in the UK, see that section later) specialize in last-minute discount flights. See the Travel section of the Sunday *New York Times*, or the *Village Voice* for advertisements.

No matter where you shop for your ticket, find out the fare, route, duration of the journey and any restrictions on the ticket. Fares are in constant flux and some fares that include accommodations may be as cheap as roundtrip fares. Ask about discounts, as airlines often offer competitive low-season, student and senior citizens fares.

Once you have your ticket, write down its number, together with the flight number and other details, and keep the information somewhere separate. If the ticket is lost or stolen, this will help you get a replacement.

Visit USA Passes Most US carriers offer special deals for non-US citizens who book abroad. These passes usually come in the form of coupons – you use one for each leg of your flight. Ask a travel agent about these offers.

A typical Visit USA scheme is the one offered by American Airlines; this pass can be used with an international airline ticket from anywhere outside the USA except Canada. You must have your trip planned in advance and complete your travels within 60 days of the first domestic flight in the USA or 81 days after arrival in the USA, whichever comes first. During the high season, it costs around $540 for three coupons (minimum purchase; one coupon equals one flight), plus $115 for each additional coupon. Continental and Northwest Airlines offer similar deals. See Airline Offices, earlier, for contact information.

Round-the-World Tickets Round-the-World (RTW) tickets that include travel within the USA are popular and can be bargains. With a 14-day advance purchase and maximum flexibility, you should be able to net a fare for around UK£836, A$2244 or US$1200.

Official RTW tickets allow you to circumnavigate the globe by flying on the combined routes of two or more airlines. These tickets are typically valid for 12 months and require you travel in one general direction without backtracking. This means you can't fly in and out of the same airport twice, effectively putting half the world out of reach. Most airlines restrict the number of sectors that can be flown within the USA and Canada to four, and some airlines black out a few popular routes (like Honolulu to Tokyo). After you purchase your ticket, you can change the dates without penalty and add or delete stops for $25 to $75 each, depending on the carrier.

Major international airlines and partnerships, such as the Star Alliance and One World, offer RTW tickets through code-sharing flights on different routes and continents. It may be more time- and cost-efficient to price all the variations of your trip with a RTW specialist agent, rather than calling the airlines directly. US-based **Air Treks** (☎ 800-350-0612, 415-912-5600; W www.airtreks.com) and **Air Brokers** (☎ 800-883-3273, 415-397-1383; W www.airbrokers.com) have websites with helpful itinerary builders to get you started.

Travelers with Special Needs
If you have a special need – a broken leg, you're a vegan, are traveling with twin infants or have a flying phobia – let the airline know as soon as possible so that it can make arrangements to ensure an optimum travel experience. Remind them when you reconfirm your booking (at least 72 hours before departure) and again when you check in at the airport. Before you buy your ticket, it may be worth phoning several airlines to find out how they handle your particular needs.

Airports and airlines are usually quite accommodating to passengers in wheelchairs, but giving them advance warning increases your odds of a comfortable journey. Most major airports provide escorts from the check-in desk to the airplane if necessary, and most have ramps, lifts, accessible toilets and reachable phones. Aircraft toilets, on the other hand, are likely to present a problem; travelers should discuss this with the airline and, if necessary, with their doctor.

Guide dogs for the blind often have to travel in a specially pressurized baggage compartment with other animals, away from their owners, though smaller guide dogs may be admitted to the cabin. Guide dogs are not subject to quarantine as long as they have proof of being vaccinated against rabies.

Hearing-impaired travelers can ask for airport and in-flight announcements to be written down for them.

Children under two traditionally travel for 10% of the standard fare (or free, on some airlines) as long as they don't occupy a seat. (They don't get a baggage allowance, however.) 'Skycots' should be provided by the airline if requested in advance; these can fit a child weighing up to about 22lb. Children between two and 12 usually occupy a seat for half to two-thirds of the full fare, and they do get a baggage allowance.

Canada

Roundtrip fares to New York from Toronto start at around C$255 (US$160) on US Airways and Delta Air Lines. Fares from Montreal usually hover around C$239 (US$150).

The *Toronto Globe & Mail* and *Vancouver Sun* carry travel agency ads (including for consolidators); the magazine *Great Expeditions (PO Box 8000-411, Abbotsford, BC V2S 6H1)* is also useful. If you're looking for a reliable travel agency, try **Travel CUTS/Voyages Campus** (☎ 866-246-9762; W *www.travelcuts.com*), which has offices in all major cities.

UK & Ireland

In the winter, prices plummet on the crowded London to New York corridor – expect to get a roundtrip fare for about UK£245 (US$350), though price wars can bring the fare all the way down to UK£150 (US$215). In summer, the prices rise to UK£480 (US$694) and above for a roundtrip. Virgin Atlantic offers a standard, roundtrip, weekday, high-season fare for £543 (US$780), but cheaper advance-purchase tickets are available.

Aer Lingus offers direct flights from Shannon and Dublin to New York City, but because competition on flights from London is fiercer, it sometimes costs less to fly to London first. The best fare you'll find from Ireland is about €614 (US$540).

London is arguably the world's headquarters for bucket shops, which frequently place ads and can usually beat published airline fares. Two good, reliable agents for cheap tickets in the UK are **Trailfinders** (☎ 020-7938-3939; W *www.trailfinders.com; 194 Kensington High St, London)* and **STA Travel** (☎ 0870-1-600-599; W *www.statravel .co.uk; 117 Euston Rd, London)*. Trailfinders produces a lavishly illustrated brochure that includes airfare details.

Unregistered bucket shops are riskier, but sometimes cheaper. Be aware, though, that there are a few rogues who'll take your money and disappear, to reopen elsewhere a month or two later under a new name. If you feel suspicious, don't give the agents all the money at once – leave a deposit of 20% or so and pay the balance on receiving the ticket. If they insist on cash in advance, go elsewhere. Once you have the ticket, phone the airline to confirm that you are booked on the flight.

For special deals, check the adverts in magazines like *Time Out, TNT* and *City Limits*, plus the Sunday papers and *Exchange & Mart*.

Globetrotters Club (*BCM Roving, London WC1N 3XX;* W *www.globetrotters.co.uk*) publishes a newsletter called *Globe* that covers obscure destinations and contains ads for traveling companions; many of the Globe's features are available on the website.

Continental Europe

Though London is Europe's travel-discount capital, several other hubs make attractive departure cities, especially Amsterdam and Athens. Many travel agents in Europe have ties with STA Travel, which sells cheap tickets that can be changed free of charge (first change only). Council Travel also maintains partnerships with European travel agents.

In France, Council Travel works with **Usit Connect** (☎ 08-25-08-25-25; W *www.usit connect.fr; 85 Blvd St Michel, 75006 Paris)*. In Germany, Council Travel's counterpart is **Usit Connections** (☎ 89-38-838970; *Adalbert Strasse 32, Munich* • ☎ 69-97-129980; *Leipziger Strasse 1, Frankfurt)*. Usit has offices in 16 countries worldwide, plus 450 'service points' in scores of additional countries, including **Kilroy Travels** (☎ 31-20-524-5100; *Singel 413-415)* in Amsterdam.

In Athens, try **International Student & Youth Travel Service** (☎ 01-03-323-3767; *Nikis 11)*.

Australia & New Zealand

Qantas flies from Brisbane, Cairns, Melbourne and Sydney to New York (through Los Angeles) for A$3029 (US$1620), but

United serves the same route for A$2338 (US$1250). Hunt around, though, and you may be able to knock a couple of hundred dollars off that fare. The cheapest tickets require a 21-day advance purchase, a minimum stay of seven days and a maximum stay of 30 days. Flying with Air New Zealand can sometimes be a bargain, so check that out too.

In Australia and New Zealand, **STA Travel** *(main Australian office ☎ 03-8417-6911;* W *www.statravel.com.au; 260 Hoddle St, Abbotsford, Melbourne, Vic 3067 • main New Zealand office ☎ 09-0800-874-773, 309-0458;* W *www.statravel.co.nz; 182 Queen St, Auckland)* and **Flight Centre International** *(*W *www.flightcentre.com.au)* are major dealers in cheap airfares and they guarantee to beat any legitimate fare quote; also check the travel sections of the *Sydney Morning Herald* or Melbourne's *The Age*.

Asia

Japan Airlines, All Nippon Airlines and Northwest Airlines all offer nonstop flights from Tokyo to New York City. With a bit of flexibility, you can snag a very nice price of ¥120,078 (US$900). With most other airlines and/or departure cities, you will have to connect to New York through a US West Coast gateway such as Los Angeles, San Francisco or Seattle. The bonus with this scenario is that free stopovers in Honolulu are frequently included; ask.

Bangkok and Hong Kong are the discount plane ticket capitals of the region, but the trick is finding a reliable travel agent or bucket shop. Bangkok's Khao San Rd and Hong Kong's Nathan Rd in Tsimshatsui are full of agencies desperate to take your money, but be sure you're dealing with a straight shooter. A good way to find or check on a travel agent is to talk to other travelers or look it up in the phone book.

STA Travel has branches in Hong Kong, Tokyo, Singapore, Bangkok and Kuala Lumpur. Check their website W www.sta travel.com to locate the office nearest you.

If you're coming from South East Asia, it's a long flight to New York City (typically through Honolulu), but the region is serviced by Korean Air and Philippine Airlines.

DALE BUCKTON

Latin America & Caribbean

While there are some direct, and even nonstop, flights to New York City from Latin America (especially with individual countries' national carriers: eg, LANChile Airlines from Santiago de Chile, AeroMexico from various Mexican cities, and Varig from Rio de Janeiro or São Paulo), most flights go via Miami or Houston.

Continental Airlines dominates the region and offers flights from about 20 cities in Mexico, Central and South America, including Lima, San José, Guatemala City, Cancún and Mérida, to either their hub in Newark or Houston, from where there are connecting flights. Flights from Mexico City to New York are about US$500; from Guatemala City, you can get a fare for around US$600. Caracas is the cheapest hopping-off point in South America: flights through either Houston or Miami run around US$650.

There are some surprisingly good deals from the Caribbean if you hunt around. For example, Air Jamaica has daily direct services from Montego Bay or Kingston to JFK for as little as US$250 roundtrip.

BUS

All suburban and long-distance buses leave and depart from the **Port Authority Bus Terminal** *(Map 6; ☎ 212-564-8484; 41st St at Eighth Ave)*. Though Port Authority has much improved in recent years and it's not quite as rough as its reputation, it's likely you'll still be hassled by panhandlers looking for handouts or shady types offering to carry bags for tips. Watch your back and your luggage here.

Greyhound *(☎ 212-971-6300, 800-231-2222; W www.greyhound.com)* links New York with major cities across the country. **Peter Pan Trailways** *(☎ 800-343-9999; W www.peterpan-bus.com)* runs buses to the nearest major cities, including a daily express to Boston for $32 one way and $64 roundtrip, with a seven-day advance purchase.

Undoubtedly the sweetest deal to Boston, however, is with the reliable folks of **Fung Wah Transport Vans** *(Map 4, #233; ☎ 212-925-8889; 139 Canal St at the Bowery)*, with 10 departures a day between 7am and 10pm for $25 one way (dropping to $15 if you take the 4pm, 5pm or 7pm departure).

Short Line *(☎ 212-736-4700; W www.shortlinebus.com)* runs numerous buses to towns in northern New Jersey and up-state New York. **New Jersey Transit buses** *(☎ 973-762-5100, 800-772-3606; W www.njtransit.state.nj.us)* serve the entire Garden State, with direct service to Atlantic City for $17 to $22 one way.

Bus Passes

Greyhound's Ameripass is vital if you plan on doing a lot of bus traveling out of New York, as individual tickets will add up to way more than the pass price. During off-peak seasons, the pass costs $199/299/389 for seven/15/30 days of unlimited travel; passes purchased abroad are $184/274/364. During peak seasons, prices are slightly higher. Children under 11 travel for half-price. Students and seniors travel at a small discount. You can get on and off at any Greyhound terminal.

The International Ameripass can be purchased at overseas travel agencies or from the **Greyhound International Office** *(☎ 212-971-0492, 800-231-2222, fax 212-967-2239; open 8am-4pm Mon-Thur, 8am-7pm Fri, 9am-3pm Sat)* at the subway level of the Port Authority Bus Terminal.

TRAIN

Pennsylvania Station *(Penn Station; Map 5; 33rd St)*, between Seventh and Eighth Aves, is the departure point for all **Amtrak trains** *(☎ 212-582-6875, 800-872-7245; W www.amtrak.com)*, including the *Metroliner* service to Princeton, NJ, and Washington, DC. Note that the *Metroliner* is slightly faster than the *Northeast Direct* service to the same points, but the fare can be twice as high; the main advantage of the *Metroliner* is that you'll get a reserved seat. Basic service from New York to Washington, DC, costs $71; a *Metroliner* ticket costs $101. All fares vary based on the day of the week and the time you want to travel. Call Amtrak for information about special discount passes if you plan on traveling throughout the USA by train (which, while romantic, is an expensive proposition).

Long Island Rail Road *(LIRR; ☎ 718-217-5477)* serves several hundred thousand commuters each day, with services from Penn Station to points in Brooklyn, Queens and the suburbs of Long Island, including the North and South Fork resort areas. **New Jersey Transit** *(☎ 973-762-5100, 800-772-3606)* also operates trains from Penn Station, with service to the suburbs and the Jersey Shore.

The only train line that still departs from Grand Central Terminal, Park Ave at 42nd St, is the **Metro-North Railroad** *(☎ 212-532-4900; W www.mnr.org)*, which serves the northern city suburbs, Connecticut and the Hudson Valley.

CAR & MOTORCYCLE

If you're in a passenger car in New York that isn't a taxi, you should be armed with the Hagstrom five-borough map (see Maps in the Facts for the Visitor chapter) and a radio tuned to 1010 WINS, which broadcasts all the gnarly traffic details 'on the ones,' eg, 11, 21, 31 etc after the hour.

Needless to say, it's a nightmare to have a car in New York, but getting there is easy. I-95, which runs from Maine to Florida, cuts east to west through the city as the Cross Bronx Expressway (another nightmare, recognized locally as the worst roadway around). Outside of New York City, I-95 continues south as the New Jersey Turnpike; north as the Connecticut Turnpike. Via I-95, Boston is 194 miles to the north, Philadelphia 104 miles to the south and Washington, DC 235 miles south.

To reach the Long Island Expressway, take the Queens Midtown Tunnel out of Manhattan (an awful stretch of road often choked by traffic). Better is the Grand Central Parkway, right off the Triborough Bridge, which cuts through Queens on its way to Long Island. The 59th St Bridge takes you into Queens for free. Northern Blvd in Queens becomes Route 25A, which runs the northern length of Long Island.

Take the Lincoln or Holland Tunnels only if you must – they're a horror! If you're headed to central or northern Jersey, the George Washington Bridge (familiarly called the GWB) is the way to go. Once over the river, you'll want to connect with the New Jersey Turnpike, which runs roughly diagonally across the state to Philadelphia. The turnpike also connects to the Garden State Parkway (which travels to the Jersey Shore and Atlantic City). Leaving Manhattan by the Lincoln Tunnel also connects you (via Route 3) to the westbound I-80, which cuts through the middle of Pennsylvania. I-78, which goes to Harrisburg, PA, can be reached by taking the Holland Tunnel.

Highway speed limits in Connecticut and up-state New York are 65mph; in New Jersey, they remain 55mph except on certain interstate roads.

HITCHHIKING

Listen, anyone who would pick you up thumbing a ride in New York is going to be crazier than you – dangerous crazy, not just maverick, devil-may-care crazy. Because of this, Lonely Planet does not recommend hitchhiking. Travelers who do try to hitchhike should understand that they are taking a small but serious risk. People who hitch will be safer if they travel in pairs and let someone know where they are planning to go. Still, hitchhiking isn't common in the continental US and it's extremely rare to see anyone trying to thumb a ride, even at spots where it should theoretically be easy to do (the entrance to the Lincoln Tunnel, for example). No doubt you'll wait a long time for a lift.

BOAT

It's highly unusual for anyone to yacht their way into town, and those who do will find few ports ready to receive them – just an exclusive boat slip at the World Financial Center and a long-term slip at the 79th St Boathouse on the Upper West Side. Manhattan, on the whole, does not welcome the temporary tie-up of recreational boats.

Visiting boaters should contact **City Island Yacht** (☎ 718-885-2300), a full-service marina on City Island off the mainland of the Bronx.

ORGANIZED TOURS

The well-known West Coast firm **Green Tortoise Adventure Travel** (☎ 415-956-7500, 800-867-8647; W www.greentortoise .com; 494 Broadway, San Francisco, CA 94133) offers alternative bus transportation from San Francisco to New York, with stops at national parks, hot springs and other picturesque places en route. The trip crosses the country on either southern (14 days; $499, plus $131 for parks fees and food) or northern routes (12 days; $469, plus $121 for fees and food), depending on the seasonal weather. Lodging includes camping or sleeping on bunks on the bus. (Call ahead for information on current routes.) Like a hippie crash-pad on wheels, this is a fun and a cheap way to see the country and meet some cool people along the way.

N.Y.C.

Getting Around

Midtown is a nightmare any way you cut it and when it's crammed with horn-honking, teeth-gnashing, pissed-off New Yorkers all angling to get ahead with their two-ton weapons of steel, well, things can get ugly. Midday in Midtown is gridlock city, with entire avenues – primarily Lexington and Broadway – made impassable by double-parked trucks and traffic jams of unusual size. The subway is the fastest way to get where you're going and, contrary to popular belief, taking the subway is statistically safer than walking the streets in broad daylight.

Buses are largely a losing proposition (except north of Central Park when you need to get cross-town), especially during inclement weather, and the best overall plan is to use the subway until about 11pm or so and then switch to taxis late at night.

TO/FROM THE AIRPORT

Leave at least one hour's travel time to get to any of the three airports in the middle of the day.

The Port Authority of New York and New Jersey's **Air Ride Line** (☎ 800-247-7433; W www.panynj.gov) offers comprehensive information on ground transportation to and from all three airports, as does the website.

No matter what airport you fly into, there are several advantages to using a car service to get there. These hired cars (also known as 'black cars') are newer and larger than cabs, service is door-to-door, you can reserve a ride a day in advance and pay by credit card. If you ask for a 'price check' while ordering the taxi, the dispatcher can tell you the exact cost of the journey, which should run between $35 to $50,

depending on your departure point and destination. Two reliable services in Manhattan are **Tel Aviv** (☎ 212-777-7777) and **Carmel** (☎ 212-666-6666).

Shared minivan shuttles deliver you door-to-door and can save you quite a bit of money if you're willing to ride around while the driver drops off passengers all over town (some shuttles promise three stops or fewer). When you're ready to go back to the airport, taking one of these shuttles is a good alternative to hailing a taxi, especially if you're leaving town at rush hour; reserve a space *early*. **Gray Line** runs from all three airports to most major hotels in Manhattan and **SuperShuttle** travels from the airports to hotels and residences. See the individual airport headings for contact information, specific times, prices and locations for both services.

The New York Airport Service Express bus is a good middle ground and you can save $1 by booking online. Alternatively, purchase tickets at the **bus office** (Map 5; 125 Park Ave), between 41st and 42nd Sts, near Grand Central Terminal; see individual airport headings, below, for more information.

JFK Airport (Map 1)

Gray Line (☎ 212-315-3006, 800-451-0455; W www.grayline newyork.com) offers a minivan shuttle service to hotels in Manhattan located between 21st and 103rd Sts from all three New York–area airports. The fare is $14/19 from/to JFK; the roundtrip fare is $28. At the airport, the shuttle operates from 7am to 11:30pm, with hotel pickups from 5am to 9pm.

SuperShuttle (☎ 212-258-3826, 800-258-3826) serves hotels and residences in a wider area of Manhattan, from Battery Park at the tip of Lower Manhattan to 227th St. The fare is $15 to $19,

ANGUS OBORN

depending on the pickup or drop-off location. SuperShuttle runs 24 hours a day.

New York Airport Service Express buses (☎ 718-875-8200; Ⓦ www.nyairportservice .com) run to and from JFK every 15 to 30 minutes from 6am to 11pm daily. The fare is $13/23 for a one way/roundtrip. Buses leave from several locations: **Penn Station** (Map 5; 32nd St at Seventh Ave); **Port Authority Bus Terminal** (Map 6; 42nd St at Eighth Ave), look for the Airport Bus Center; and **Grand Central Terminal** (Map 5; Park Ave at 42nd St).

To reach JFK from Manhattan, you can also take the A train (Far Rockaway line) to the Howard Beach–JFK station (allow at least an hour), where you switch to a free yellow-and-blue bus for the 15-minute ride to the terminals. (You have to haul your luggage up and over several flights of stairs at the Howard Beach subway stop, but hey, it's the cheap way to JFK!)

The taxi fare is a flat rate of $35, plus tolls and tip, from JFK to any location in Manhattan. Be aware that this flat rate does *not* apply to trips out to the airport – you will pay for time spent in traffic.

The long-term parking lot at JFK costs $8 a day; short-term parking closer to the terminals costs $8 for four hours.

La Guardia Airport (Map 1)

Gray Line (☎ 212-315-3006, 800-451-0455; Ⓦ www.graylinenewyork.com) will take you to most major hotels in Manhattan; the one-way fare is $13/16 from/to La Guardia or $26 roundtrip. **SuperShuttle** (☎ 212-258-3826, 800-258-3826) offers a door-to-door shuttle service throughout the city and costs $15 to $19. Roundtrip tickets are slightly cheaper. See the JFK Airport section for schedule information.

New York Airport Service Express buses (☎ 718-875-8200) run to/from La Guardia airport every 15 to 30 minutes from 6:40am to 11pm every day. The bus picks up and drops off passengers at three different locations in Manhattan: Grand Central Terminal, Port Authority Bus Terminal and Penn Station. The fare is $10/17 one way/ roundtrip.

The **Delta Water Shuttle** (☎ 800-221-1212), operated by Delta Air Lines, leaves frequently for La Guardia from Pier 11 at South and Wall Sts and E 34th St on the East River. The placid trip takes 20 to 45 minutes, depending on where you board; the shuttle operates on the hour from 7:45am to 6:30pm weekdays. The fare is $15/25 one way/roundtrip.

If you're traveling light and have time to spare, there's some excellent public transportation out to La Guardia. Perhaps the best option is to grab the M60 bus ($1.50) anywhere along 125th street straight to the airport; subway lines A, B, C, D, 2, 3, 4, 5 and 6 to 125th St will put you right at the bus stop. Alternatively, you can ride the subway to the Roosevelt Ave–Jackson Heights or the 74th St–Broadway stops in Queens (two linked stations served by the E, F, G, R and 7 lines). You then take the Q33 bus to La Guardia main terminals or the Q47 bus to the Delta Shuttle's Marine Air Terminal. This journey takes well over an hour and costs two tokens ($3).

Taxis from La Guardia to Midtown cost $20 to $29, plus tip and roundtrip tolls.

Newark Airport (Map 1)

Gray Line (☎ 212-315-3006, 800-451-0455; Ⓦ www.graylinenewyork.com) and **Super-Shuttle** (☎ 212-258-3826, 800-258-3826) offer shuttle service to many locations in Manhattan (though Gray Line only goes to hotels). Gray Line's fares are $14/19 from/to Newark or $28 roundtrip. Super-Shuttle's prices range from $15 to $19 depending on where you're going. See the JFK Airport section, earlier, for schedule information.

Olympia Airport Express (☎ 212-964-6233) buses travel to Newark from three points in Manhattan: Penn Station (from 5am to 11pm daily), Grand Central Terminal (5am to 11pm daily) and Port Authority Bus Terminal (4:15am to 2:45am daily). The fare is $11. Prior to September 11, Olympia buses made the speedy 20-minute trip between Newark Airport and the World Trade Center, but had not reinstated the service at the time of writing; call Olympia for the latest.

NJ Transit (☎ 973-762-5100) introduced its new AirTrain system in 2001. This is a free monorail service leaving the airport every three minutes for the Newark International Airport Station, from where you can jump onto a NJ Transit train directly into New York's Penn Station ($11.15; 20 minutes) or points south in Jersey.

You can expect to pay around $45 for a taxi between the airport and Manhattan (including tolls and tip), depending on traffic and your destination.

BUS

City buses operate 24 hours a day, generally along avenues in a southerly or northerly direction, and cross-town along the major thoroughfares (including 34th, 42nd, 57th, 79th and 96th Sts).

Buses that begin and end in a certain borough are prefixed accordingly: ie, M5 for Manhattan, B39 for Brooklyn, Q32 for Queens, Bx29 for Bronx or S74 for Staten Island.

Bus maps for each borough are available at subway and train stations, and each well-marked bus stop has Guide-a-Ride maps showing the stops for each bus and nearby landmarks. Remember that some 'limited stop' buses along major routes pull over only every 10 blocks or so at major cross streets. 'Express' buses are generally for outer borough commuters and shouldn't be used for short trips; they cost about $5.

The regular bus fare is $1.50. You'll need exact change, a MetroCard or a token to board the bus, and if you plan on switching to a connecting route, you must ask for a transfer upon boarding (these are free and valid for two hours).

Drivers will be happy to tell you if their bus stops near a specific site, but don't try to chat them up unless you want to endure all manner of poisonous stares from crotchety riders around you. For safety's sake, you can request to be dropped off at any location along a bus route from 10pm to 5am – even if it's not a designated bus stop.

Slated to go into effect in September 2002, is the launch of The Connection, a fleet of electric buses connecting the east

PENELOPE RICHARDSON

and west sides of Downtown Manhattan. These pollutant-free buses will swing south around the tip of the island, allowing riders to get on and off at various stops en route.

For bus information, call ☎ 718-330-1234. Also see the boxed text 'Touring Manhattan on the Cheap – by Public Bus' in the Things to See & Do chapter.

TRAIN

New Jersey Path (Port Authority Trans-Hudson; ☎ 800-234-7284; W www.pathrail.com) trains are part of a separate-fare system that runs down the length of Sixth Ave, with stops at 34th, 23rd, 14th, 9th and Christopher Sts, en route to Hoboken, Jersey City and Newark. These reliable trains (called the 'Hudson Tubes' when they first opened) run every 15 minutes, and the fare is $1.50, payable in cash. These trains run 24 hours a day. Path service was seriously disrupted on September 11 when the entire line linking New Jersey and the World Trade Center was wiped out. A series of ferries have been launched by NY Waterway to offset the loss of that important link between Manhattan and New Jersey (see the Ferry section later in this chapter for details) and the new Downtown Path service should be up and running by late 2003, so stay tuned.

SUBWAY

Noisy, confusing, hot, crowded and not terribly user friendly, the 656 miles of NYC subway track can be intimidating at first. But dive in and you will soon learn its many virtues (not the least of which is you can get anywhere, almost anytime, in the five boroughs for $1.50) and be hooked like the natives. To soften the learning curve a bit, what follows is a bit of basic subway know-how gleaned from many sources and centuries of combined experience.

The New York subway (known colloquially as the 'train') is the fastest, most reliable way to get around town, and is safer than it has been in years. But before pushing through the turnstile, consider how far you have to go – a trip of 20 blocks or fewer is probably best traversed on foot, especially once you factor in your departure and arrival stations and how close they'll place you to your ultimate destination. During the day, resist the temptation to hop in a cab with the deluded hope that this will be faster than the train: gridlock, traffic lights, bike messengers, unforeseen mishaps and a whole host of other factors will conspire against you and you'll end up fuming in the back of the taxi watching the meter run away with abandon.

The subway experience is a must

Most major Manhattan attractions – especially those on the West Side and downtown – are easily accessible by several subway lines. Madison Square Garden, for example, is within four blocks' walking distance of three subway stations on 34th St; these stations serve a total of 12 different lines. Other areas, most notably the East and far–West Villages and the Upper East Side, are frustratingly removed from convenient subway stops.

Subway clerks sometimes seem to be irascible old coots afflicted with incurable ennui, but they are the single best source for information on how to get around. You're likely to get better treatment if you behave in a speedy manner and speak loudly and clearly into the microphone (clerks sit in bullet-proof glass booths) when engaging these folks. Remember also, that with so many train lines, transfer stations, service changes and convoluted connections, even lifelong New Yorkers don't know the whole system, so take heart that you're not alone!

Once you're in the flow and negotiating the system, use the maps. Entire system maps are located in every subway car; new-fangled, super-helpful linear maps in the middle of each car show the next stop and what transfers are available; and digital

Pay Your Fare!

Some time, in some bustling station, you'll likely hear a subway clerk yelling, 'Pay your fare! Pay your fare!' at swindlers hopping the turnstiles, and while this is the cheapest way to ride the rails, we can't recommend it. There are a few discount deals available for the subway, however you'll have to do a little figuring to find out which one is best for you.

The straight-up fare for one ride is $1.50, for which you buy tokens in subway stations. While tokens form a part of city lore and legacy that few New Yorkers are willing to relinquish completely, the fairly new and novel MetroCards are much more efficient, both in terms of time and money. The cards can be purchased at multilingual automated machines in many stations, at token booths or in convenience stores. MetroCards come in two varieties: Unlimited Ride and Pay-Per-Ride.

Unlimited Ride cards will be the best value for most travelers. If you're here for several days, consider the weekly Unlimited Ride card, which costs $17 and allows you as many rides as you can manage within seven days of purchase. The Fun Pass costs $4 and allows unlimited rides within 24 hours of purchase. These cards also deliver unlimited free bus transfers and are not beholden to the two-hour time limit of the other cards.

Pay-Per-Ride cards work as you might imagine: you have to pay $1.50 for each ride and cards accommodate anywhere from $3 to $80 worth. The bonus here is that if you put $15 or more on a card at one shot, you get a 10% reward (ie, a $15 card registers as $16.50, so you're getting 11 trips for the price of 10). This may work out better than the weekly unlimited card for people not planning on taking the subway on concurrent days.

MetroCards work for buses too, and provide free bus-to-bus, bus-to-subway and subway-to-bus transfers within two hours of swiping your card.

Travelers over age 65 or those with a disability qualify for massive MetroCard discounts (eg, a $17 unlimited weekly card is $8.50); call ☎ 718-243-4999 for information.

SUBWAY
SARDINES
Packed in Stagnant Air

HUGH D'ANDRADE

N.Y.C.

read-outs give you the time, train line and next station. The mistake most visitors make (other than getting turned around and taking a train in the opposite direction) is boarding an express train only to see it blow by the local stop they desired. The subway map delineates between local and express stops by representing local stops as black circles and express stops as white circles. (The back of this book contains official subway maps provided by the New York City Transit Authority.)

As for safety, standing in the middle of the platform – you'll see yellow signs designating this as the off-hour waiting area – will bring you to the conductor's car. Conductors may field quick questions if they feel like it, but information is generally better gleaned from the token clerks. Of course, watch your wallet on crowded trains and secure day packs with a safety pin.

If you're running for a train you simply must catch (and don't forget the old adage: 'never run for a train or a lover, there will always be another'), yelling 'hold the doors!' should do the trick. If you have a moment, check out some of the very good public art in New York's subway system (eg, there are terrific mosaics in the stations on the 1 line, and the multimillion dollar restoration of Times Square has brought some excellent installations to the tangle of tunnels, ramps and tracks there).

For subway schedules and other information, call ☎ 718-330-1234 or see W www .mta.info.

CAR

In New York, the cost, traffic and high incidence of thievery more than offsets any convenience having a car may offer. Making matters worse are Byzantine street-cleaning rules called 'alternate side of the street parking' that require you to move your car several times a week. Meanwhile, parking garages in Midtown are usually operated by the Kinney Corporation, whose near-monopoly in the garage industry means that parking a car will cost at least $30 a day during daylight hours.

You can find cheaper lots along West St in Chelsea, but even those $10 to $15 daily deals aren't a bargain after the city's phenomenal 18.25% parking tax is added. Using a hotel lot is no bargain either – Midtown hotels can charge $40 a day, even for their customers.

Rental

Hopefully, there is a special section of hell reserved for the people who set car-rental rates in New York. Though rental agencies advertise bargain rates for weekend or weeklong rentals, these deals are almost *always* blacked out in New York or can only be obtained in conjunction with a purchased airline ticket.

If you want to rent for a few days, book through your travel agent before leaving home. Without a reservation, a rental will cost at least $70 for a midsize car. And that's before extra charges like the 13.25% tax, the $15 'Collision Damage Waiver' (also known as 'Liability Damage Waiver' covering the value of the vehicle in case of an accident; some credit cards carry collision insurance, so check first) and other dubious charges like the $15 a day personal insurance coverage (which you don't need if you have medical coverage). All told, a rental car will cost about $100 a day – plus the option to prepay for a tank of gas to avoid filling up before you return; this costs $20, but it's worth it, due to the high price of gasoline in the city. With costs running well over $300 for a three-day weekend rental, you may be better off renting a car on a weekly basis to save money in the long run.

To rent a car, you need a valid driver's license and a major credit card. In March 1997, the New York State supreme court ruled that the nationwide policy of restricting rentals to drivers who are at least 25 years old was discriminatory. Though the major companies now must offer cars to younger renters, they are allowed to charge a higher rate and will no doubt make it prohibitively expensive for college-age consumers to take advantage of their new rights.

Call the agencies or visit their websites to inquire about office locations in the New York area and to troll for discounts:

Avis ☎ 800-331-1212; **w** www.avis.com
Budget ☎ 800-527-0700; **w** http://rent .drivebudget.com
Dollar ☎ 800-800-4000; **w** www.dollar.com
Hertz ☎ 800-654-3131; **w** www.hertz.com
Thrifty ☎ 800-367-2277; **w** www.thrifty.com

ANGUS OBORN

Gridlock in New York is not for the faint hearted

TAXI

Taxi drivers (familiarly called 'hacks') may drive like speed demons with a death wish, but most New York cabs are clean and, compared with those in most international destinations, pretty cheap.

Taxis cost $2 for the initial charge, plus 30¢ for every additional fifth of a mile (four blocks or so) and 20¢ a minute while stuck in traffic. There's an additional 50¢ surcharge for rides between 8pm and 6pm. Tampered meters turn over every 20 seconds or so while the cab is stopped in traffic or at a light, and if you notice it happening, don't hesitate to ask if it is 'running too fast.' If the driver apologizes a bit too energetically, be suspicious and try negotiating a lower fare than the meter. Tips are expected to run 10% to 15%, with a minimum of 50¢. If you feel ripped off, ask for a receipt and note the driver's license number. The city's **Taxi and Limousine Commission** (☎ 212-692-8294) is particularly aggressive, and the threat of a complaint puts the fear of god into some cabbies.

For hauls of 50 blocks or more, it's a good idea to instruct the driver to take a road well removed from Midtown traffic. Suggest the West Side Highway or Eleventh Ave if you hail a taxi west of Broadway; on the East Side, the best choice may be Second Ave (heading Downtown) or First Ave (Uptown), since you can hit a string of green lights in either direction. Dictating the taxi route is a near sport in New York and some cabbies don't take the two cents too kindly.

One thing worth knowing is that taxis are obliged to take you anywhere you want to go within the five boroughs, as well as to Newark Airport (though you must pay tolls each way). During rush hours, some drivers brazenly refuse fares from airport-bound customers (particularly during bad weather) because they can pick up easier fares in town. No matter where you're going, *do not* ask permission to get into the cab and don't negotiate a higher price for the trip above the metered fare. Simply hopping in and waiting for the driver to hit

Checkered History

For some 60 years, the tank-like checker cab was the toughest warrior on New York City's hard streets and appeared in many movies (including, appropriately enough, Martin Scorsese's *Taxi Driver*). The cabs sat higher off the street, making for a smoother ride, and offered a roomy interior and lift-up extra seats. Although checker cabs made up half the city's taxi fleet in the early 1970s, the Kalamazoo, Michigan, company that made them eventually went out of business, a victim of increased gas prices and regulations on pollution. By the early '90s, only 10 checkers were left in Manhattan. In July 1999, Earl Johnson, the very last checker cab driver, went into retirement and took his 1978 taxi off the streets. Johnson's cab, which he called Janie after an old girlfriend, went on the auction block at tony Sotheby's, and nostalgic bidders were undeterred by the fact that the taxi clocked up 994,050 miles and cost just $8000 new. The car, which the auction house described as having 'traditional New York exterior yellow livery with checker boarding' and 'interior black Naugahyde in good condition with one small repaired scratch to the upper portion of the back seat' – went to a private bidder for $134,500.

These days, cabs come in many varieties including sedans and mini-vans.

the meter before you tell them where you're going is usually a good tactic. If the cabbie refuses your business, threaten to report his/her license number to the Taxi and Limousine Commission. Even if this is an empty threat, the cab driver will take it seriously enough to relent.

Hailing a taxi is rarely like in the movies, where a hack pulls up just as you step to the curb. You'll know empty cabs by the lit light on the roof, which doesn't help during the day – especially around 4pm when many drivers end their shifts and it can be very tough time indeed to catch a cab.

Under no circumstances should you take an unlicensed taxi – these are by and large rip-off merchants who target tourists, usually at the airport arrival terminals. There's a trend lately for hailing 'black cars' – dark sedans that are not legally allowed to pick fares up on the street, but that are useful when taxis are hard to find.

FERRY

New Yorkers are rediscovering the convenience and pleasure of ferries, especially since the disruption of train services since September 11. **NY Waterway** (☎ 800-533-3779; ⓦ www.nywaterway.com) operates several important routes, including from Pier A near Battery Park City and Pier 11 at the foot of Wall St to Newport in Jersey City, Liberty State Park and Hoboken's Erie Lackawanna Train Terminal ($3, eight minutes). Ferries leave every six minutes during peak times and every 10 minutes or so all other times. The other popular ferry routes operated by NY Waterway are from

Pier 17 at the South St Seaport, E 34th St or E 90th St to Yankee and Shea Stadium during baseball season. With the wind in your hair and cocktails on deck, this is hands-down the best way to get to the game (adult/senior/child $16/13/12 round-trip to either venue).

NY Waterway also offers interesting trips if you want to escape the city for a day, including Hudson River cruises, and trips to the New Jersey and Long Island beaches (a good way to avoid traffic), as well as tours of riverside restaurants. Call for more information.

One of the most popular boat rides in New York is the free **Staten Island ferry** (☎ 718-815-2628). For details, see the Staten Island section of the Things to See & Do chapter.

Liberty Park Water Taxi (☎ 201-985-8000; ⓦ www.libertylandingmarina.com/taxi .htm) has daily services to the Liberty Science Center from Pier A in Battery Park City every 30 minutes (adult/senior/child $5/4/3). The little boats are zippy and painted like bright yellow checkered cabs.

BICYCLE

Cycling the New York City streets takes nerves of steel, precision maneuvering and just a touch of insanity if you aim to stay alive. For these reasons, we can't wholeheartedly recommend it for New York tenderfoots. Threading the needle between an opening car door and a zigzagging cab, weaving through crippling gridlock or bombing down one of the avenues should probably be left to the professionals, but if you're hell bent on biking, here's some well-placed advice.

Staten Island Ferry, refreshing, fun and free!

Cars will regard you as a nuisance and you'll have to ride defensively if you have any hopes of staying upright. Obey all traffic laws and wear a helmet. Always remain hyper-aware of parked cars pulling away from the curb, doors opening on all sides, cars cutting you off and clueless drivers in general. Wear a whistle or be ready to shout if confronted with any of the above circumstances. Don't lock up a bike on the street because chances are you'll return to find it long gone. Thieves can pick even some of the best Dutch bike locks here, so if you must lock up your steed on the street, do so only for short periods. Older, more ravaged bikes are as decent a thief deterrent as any.

Still, bicycle theft may be the least of your worries, compared with the fear for your life, and most travelers will want to stick to safe, sane traffic-free areas set aside for outdoor activities. Two recommended longer rides are across the Brooklyn Bridge to the Brooklyn Heights Promenade or Prospect Park, and bringing your bike on the Staten Island ferry and setting off for an adventure across the harbor. For information on recreational cycling in New York, see Activities in the Facts for the Visitor chapter.

WALKING

The best way to get around – especially in Manhattan – is with your own two feet. Alight from a subway near a cluster of major attractions (W 4th St, 34th St, Rockefeller Center, Canal St) and head out from there. Manhattan's Midtown grid pattern and prominent north-south avenues make it difficult to get badly lost. And don't be shy about asking for directions if you find yourself confused. Good areas for wandering include the East Village (especially for shopping), the Upper West Side for architecture, Chinatown if you're hungry, Chelsea for art and Flushing Queens for history.

The Things to See & Do chapter divides New York City into neighborhoods and offers some suggestions for self-guided walking tours.

Marching Orders

Traffic jams, kamikaze bike messengers and airborne garbage aside, New York is a fantastic pedestrian city, with myriad delights including cobblestone alleys, tree-lined promenades and secret pocket parks. But to make it in the mean streets of the concrete jungle without *seriously* pissing off the natives, you'll be well served to observe these few basic rules of pedestrian etiquette:

- On stairs and escalators, the right side is reserved for slow pokes, the left 'lane' is strictly for passing – keep right if you've got a hitch in your giddy up.
- Don't stop on street corners or at the foot of stairs to consult your map, thus impeding traffic flow; step aside, so you and others have more space to move.
- Umbrellas on crowded streets are a touchy subject. The best you can do is be aware of your spoke span and proximity to other people when inclement weather requires umbrella use.
- Cross against the light whenever it's safe to do so. In New York, if you can outrun any oncoming traffic, it's cool to cross.
- Jaywalking (crossing in the middle of the street rather than at the corners) is synonymous with New York, despite former Mayor Giuliani's attempt to legislate it to oblivion. You would have to be very unlucky indeed to be ticketed for this 'infraction' nowadays.
- No one takes the flashing 'Don't Walk' sign literally; it really means step lively (a die-hard New Yorker informs us that the sign flashes nine times before it holds steady – at which time you should heed it).
- Let people off the subway before boarding, stepping just beside the doors to allow them the maximum berth to disembark.
- If you're in front of me and mine, move.

N.Y.C.

ORGANIZED TOURS

Bus Tours

Gray Line *(Map 6, #9; ☎ 212-397-2620, 800-669-0051;* **W** *www.graylinenewyork.com; main bus terminal Eighth Ave & 54th St)* offers more than 29 different tours of the city from its main bus terminal, including a hop-on, hop-off loop of Manhattan. Tours range from $30 to $75 for adults and $25 to $55 for children, and some are offered in German, French, Italian or Spanish. Although these tours can offer a good overview of the city, there's always the chance you'll end up with a boring and/or challenged guide who knows far less about the city than some of the passengers. Also consider how much you want to do in a day – for many, the 8½-hour Manhattan Comprehensive tour is just too much. Gray Line also has Harlem Soul Food & Jazz tours ($95, including brunch) and Brooklyn Gospel tours ($39).

Boat Tours

More than one million people a year take the three-hour, 35-mile **Full Island Circle Line cruise** *(☎ 212-563-3200;* **W** *www.circleline .com; adult/senior/child $24/20/12)*, which leaves from Pier 83 at 42nd St on the Hudson River, from March to December. This is *the* tour to take, provided the weather is good and you can enjoy the waterside breezes on an outside deck. The quality of the narration depends on the enthusiasm of the guide; be sure to sit well away from the narrator if you'd like to avoid the inevitable 'where are you from?' banter.

In the summer, Circle Line also runs **Seaport Music Cruises** *(☎ 212-630-8888)*, which last about three hours. You can sway to blues on Tuesday night, rock and roll or classics and soul on Wednesday, enjoy some fine jazz on Thursday and shake your booty at a DJ dance party on Friday and Saturday. Prices range from $25 to $45; these fun cruises leave from Pier 16 at the Seaport.

World Yacht *(☎ 212-630-8100;* **W** *www .worldyacht.com)* offers well-regarded culinary cruises around Manhattan, replete with live music; these leave from Pier 81 at W 41st St. Reservations is a must and proper dress is required, and tickets range from $42 for a two-hour brunch (Sunday April to December) to $79 for a three-hour dinner (weekends January to March, daily April to December).

The ferry company **NY Waterway** *(☎ 800-533-3779;* **W** *www.nywaterway.com)* also offers two-hour island tours (adult/senior/child $24/19/12) and 90-minute harbor tours around the southern tip of Manhattan ($19/16/9), among other options. For an extra $2, you can rent a headset that transmits the tour in several foreign languages.

If you want the wind beneath your wings, try a two-hour schooner sail with **Schooner Adirondack** *(☎ 646-336-5270, 800-701-7245;* **W** *www.sail-nyc.com)*, leaving daily from Pier 62 at the Chelsea Piers (weekdays/weekends $30/35). They also have a sunset champagne tour for $40/45.

Walking Tours

Many companies and organizations conduct urban treks, and their phone lines offer detailed information on the latest schedules. **Big Onion Walking Tours** *(☎ 212-439-1090;* **W** *www.bigonion.com)*, established by two Columbia University history doctoral candidates, specializes in ethnic New York and offers an annual Christmas Day tour of the Jewish Lower East Side. Walks cost $12 for adults or $10 for seniors and students. Because all guides have advanced history degrees, these tours enhance the walking experience, though you can glean most of the history yourself from *The Big Onion Guide to New York City: Ten Historic Tours* (2002) by Seth Kamil, Eric Wakin and Kenneth T Jackson.

Foods of New York *(☎ 212-334-5070)* offers three-hour walking and tasting tours of SoHo and Greenwich Village food shops for $35; the price includes samples of the fare and vegetarians are welcome.

Greenwich Village Literary Pub Crawl *(☎ 212-613-5796;* **W** *www.geocities.com /newensemble/pubcrawl.html)* offers a 2½-hour tour of pubs where famous literati drank themselves to the grave – from Ernest Hemingway to Dylan Thomas. Tours cost $15, and reservations are highly recommended, though you may be able to jump on the tour by just showing up: Tours leave from the **White Horse Tavern** *(Map 4, #62; 567 Hudson St at 11th St)* 2pm Saturday.

To take some of the city's most comprehensive walking tours, contact the **92nd Street Y** *(☎ 212-996-1100; W www.92ndsty .org)*, the city's main Jewish cultural center. This group offers some 75 day tours, including Jewish Harlem, the Literary Bronx and If These Walls Could Talk: The Chelsea Hotel. Most tours range from $18 to $30, and you must make reservations in advance or pay a $5 on-site registration charge.

Radical Walking Tours *(☎ 718-492-0069; W http://he.net/~radtours/)* offers a dozen tours through radical political history. You can visit Black Panther landmarks in Harlem or learn about Stonewall in Greenwich Village. No reservations are required for the $10 tours. Also check out *Radical Walking Tours of New York City* (1999) by Bruce Kayton.

Adventures on a Shoestring *(☎ 212-265-2663)* charges $5 (the price has stayed the same for more than 30 years) for tours of historic houses, ethnic neighborhoods and other places of interest. Howard Goldberg, the founder/director/guide, will give you your money's worth.

New York Talks and Walks *(☎ 718-591-4741, 888-377-4455; W www.newyorktalk sandwalks.com)* features 20 historical tours, including Five Points and Ghosts of the City. Prices run around $12 for adults and $6 for children.

The **Municipal Art Society** *(MAS; ☎ 212-935-3960; W www.mas.org)* leads an array of weekly tours that focus on architecture, including a Grand Central Terminal tour that begins from the information booth at 12:30pm each Wednesday. Other tour themes include Indoor New York: the Stylish '50s, which visits interiors designed by IM Pei, Frank Lloyd Wright and Isamu Noguchi. Prices range from $12 to $15. (MAS walks are listed each week in the Spare Times section of the Friday *New York Times*.)

For information on walking tours in Harlem, see the boxed text 'To Tour or Not to Tour' in the Things to See & Do chapter.

Helicopter Tours

If you have some money to blow, try a helicopter tour. **Liberty Helicopter Tours** *(☎ 212-967-6464; W www.libertyhelicopters.com)* offers bird's-eye views of the city. Tours depart from two locations: W 30th St at Twelfth Ave in Midtown and Pier 6, on the East River near Whitehall St in Lower Manhattan. Tickets cost $49 to $155 depending on the length of the tour (five to 15 minutes).

Gray Line *(☎ 212-397-2620, 800-669-0051; W www.graylinenewyork.com)* also offers tours that depart from the heliport at W 30th St from 9am to 9pm daily and Pier 7 Downtown from 9am to 6pm Monday to Friday. All rides are 10 minutes long and cost $94.

Things to See & Do

Manhattan

For most visitors and residents alike, Manhattan (population 1.5 million) *is* New York City. Even residents of the outer boroughs refer to it as 'the city,' and if you mention you're going to Queens you might hear: 'Oh I've traveled internationally,' or: 'Do you have a visa?!' But with their ballparks, beaches, roller coasters and world-class museums, the Bronx, Brooklyn, Queens and Staten Island (which technically make up New York City along with Manhattan) each have their own special something. Take advantage of these 'foreign locales' and you'll be treated to secret delights that many locals aren't even hip to – yet.

The following sections in this chapter cover Manhattan neighborhood by neighborhood from south to north. While the neighborhoods have no official borders (and most are more a state of mind!), the extents run generally as follows.

Lower Manhattan encompasses the area below Canal St down to Battery Park, including the Civic Center (though no-one calls it this anymore), the Financial District and Tribeca, the 'TRIangle BElow CAnal St,' bordered by Canal St in the north, West St in the west, Chambers St in the south and Broadway in the east. To the east of Tribeca, Chinatown runs from Centre St east to the Manhattan Bridge, with Canal St and Chambers St as its northern and southern borders. Nearby, Little Italy is slowly being engulfed by Chinatown and now is almost an afterthought north of Canal St, between Lafayette St and the Bowery. Crouching in the shadows of the Brooklyn and Manhattan Bridges, just below Chinatown, is an area recently dubbed 'Two Bridges.'

The Lower East Side extends east of the Bowery to the East River. Houston St (pronounced **how**-ston) marks the northern boundary for both the Lower East Side and SoHo; the latter mingles with Little Italy around Lafayette St to the east. Between Houston St and 14th St to the north, Greenwich Village (or 'the Village') and the East Village cut a large swath through this part of the city. The Village proper surrounds Washington Square Park, where Fifth Ave begins; to the west, starting around Sixth Ave and stretching to the Hudson River, is the West Village. Sprinkled within this area are even smaller pockets, many of which have earned their own designations, such as the Meat Packing District (all the way west) and Alphabet City (all the way east).

North of the Village, Chelsea stretches from 14th to 23rd Sts, west of Sixth Ave. The area to the east of Sixth Ave includes the smaller neighborhoods of Union Square, Gramercy Park and the Flatiron District. Midtown generally refers to the cavernous commercial district running from 23rd St north to 61st St, it's an area that includes the Rockefeller Center, the Empire State Building, Times Square, the Broadway theater district, major hotels, Grand Central Terminal and the Port Authority Bus Terminal. The Upper East Side and Upper West Side include the areas above 61st St on either side of Central Park. Harlem begins above Central Park and runs from 110th to 142nd Sts, between Frederick Douglass Blvd in the west and the East River in the east. Between about W 110th and W 130th Sts west of Frederick Douglass Blvd is

Morningside Heights, site of Colombia University. Hamilton Heights and Sugar Hill begin above Harlem and give way to Washington Heights above W 153rd St.

Significant neighborhoods in the outer boroughs include Brooklyn Heights, Park Slope, Williamsburg and Brighton Beach in Brooklyn; Arthur Ave, Riverdale and City Island in the Bronx; and Astoria, Jackson Heights, Forest Hills and Flushing Meadows in Queens.

For more information on how to find your way around New York City, see Orientation in the Facts for the Visitor chapter. At the back of this book are detailed maps for all of the neighborhoods in Manhattan, as well as several of the outer boroughs.

The Best & Worst

Highs
- Central Park
- Skylines, new and old
- The subway
- Public art
- Pedestrian bridge crossings
- Restaurants and street food
- The Met, MoMA, Guggenheim and Whitney (in that order)
- Concerts, clubbing, cruising and other nightlife
- September 10

Lows
- Airborne, rotting and ubiquitous garbage
- August
- Lines for attractions and sites
- No public bathrooms
- Homelessness and poverty
- Sky-high prices
- September 11

DAVE LEWIS

N.Y.C.

LOWER MANHATTAN (MAP 3)

Home to the World Trade Center Site and Wall St, Lower Manhattan is associated in most people's minds with either terrorist tragedy or capitalist largesse-success. But head into this urban arroyo and you won't encounter memorials on every corner or streets paved with gold. Instead, you'll be treated to expansive parks, sweeping views and an unparalleled museum of architecture. Flanking these cramped, circuitous and sometimes confusing side streets and the grand avenue of Broadway, you'll find Federal homes, Greek Revival temples, Gothic churches, Renaissance *palazzos* and one of the finest collections of early 20th-century skyscrapers. Train your eyes skyward in this part of town, aided by binoculars if you're a big building and architecture fan, to fully appreciate all the masterful details.

After the Dutch finagled Manhattan from local Indians in the early 17th century, they protected their newly acquired turf with a fort and erected a wood-and-mud wall to keep out hostile Indians as well as the British. While no Dutch buildings from this period have survived, the paths and lanes mapped out by the engineer Cryn Fredericksz in 1625 have forever restrained and influenced every architect who ventured to build here.

Despite more than a century of British rule, very few buildings remain from that period, largely due to seven years of British military occupation during the Revolutionary War and major fires in 1776 and 1778 which devastated the area. By the end of the war, a quarter of the settled area – more than 1000 shops and homes – lay in burnt ruins. Only one building survives as an example of that era: St Paul's Chapel, which citizens saved from the flames. Miraculously, this blessed structure, which backs onto the former World Trade Center site, emerged unscathed from the terrorist attacks, and served as an oasis and bunkhouse for rescue workers and recovery crews during that time. The other buildings of note in this area date from the late 18th to early 20th centuries.

THINGS TO SEE & DO

Many buildings and attractions in this area are under extremely tight security these days, which generally means a low tolerance for loitering and gawking, especially if you look like you don't belong (this means you denim-clad backpackers!). Heightened security also means bag checks – sometimes using x-ray machines – and the closure of some sites to the public. At the time of writing, this included City Hall, the Statue of Liberty (the grounds remain open, but the statue itself is currently closed to visitors) and St Paul's Chapel (closed for structural and environmental reasons). These sites will all remain closed indefinitely.

The **Alliance for Downtown New York** (#67; ☎ 212-566-6700; W www.downtownny.com; 120 Broadway, Ste 3340) publishes maps and brochures and staffs the area from City Hall to Battery Park City with information crews who are handy with area information; look for the friendly folks wearing red vests.

GREG GAWLOWSKI

Lower Manhattan ferry terminal

Naming Neighbourhoods

Making up Manhattan is a bunch of small, self-sufficient neighborhoods, all with their own distinct flavors. To distinguish between here and there, our turf and yours, New Yorkers (and, more determinedly, real-estate agents) have devised various names for the different areas of the city. Sometimes they're purely geographical (the Lower East Side), ethnically descriptive (Chinatown) or just plain scary (Hell's Kitchen, which takes its name from a slum area dominated by Irish gangs in the 19th century). So off-putting was the last that developers and real-estate agents have started calling it Clinton.

Everyone has heard of Tribeca, an abbreviation for the area called 'TRIangle BElow CAnal St,' and SoHo, which describes the area south of Houston St. Nolita, a newish coinage, designates the area just NOrth of Little ITAly (which might just as well be called Littler Italy as it's shrinking so fast). Then there's the even newer NoHo (NOrth of HOuston St to Astor Pl and east from Mercer St to the Bowery), SoHa for 'SOuth of HArlem' and Nomad for 'NOrth of MADison Park,' that kind of no-man's land between the Flatiron District and Midtown proper, from around 26th to 34th Sts. It remains to be seen if these last two will actually make it into the vernacular or if they'll remain exiled to the real-estate listings.

The city's early Dutch occupation has left its mark on some street and neighborhood names. Harlem, for example, takes its name from Haarlem, a town in the Netherlands.

Some neighborhoods have long outgrown their designations. Few residents of Chelsea know their area was named after an 18th-century farm owned by a British army officer. Turtle Bay, a fashionable enclave surrounding the United Nations on the east side of Manhattan, took its name from a riverside cove that was drained in 1868.

THINGS TO SEE & DO

N.Y.C.

Lower Manhattan Walking Tour

Head down here on a weekday when the Monday-to-Friday activities of business, politics and the law are hopping and the streets are alive with work-abouts. This walk could take anything from three hours to an entire day, depending on how often you stop and the comfort of your footwear. Starting earlier is better (between 9am and 10am, say), but the Fulton St Fish Market is only on until about 8am. Lunchtime can be a real nightmare down here, so plan to break for a picnic or take a spin on the Staten Island Ferry between noon and 2pm to escape the crowds.

Lower Manhattan is served by 15 subway lines and nearly 20 stations, but for the purposes of this tour, it's best to take the Ⓜ 4, 5 or 6 trains to Brooklyn Bridge–City Hall, where the tour begins. These trains let you out either in City Hall Park or in the grand, domed waiting hall of the Municipal Building across the street.

Start at **City Hall**, across from the pedestrian approach to the Brooklyn Bridge (for details on City Hall, see the main entry later in the chapter). Directly behind City Hall stands **Tweed Courthouse** *(52 Chambers St)*, an inadvertent monument to late-19th-century municipal corruption. An estimated $10 million of the $14 million budget for this 1872 city courthouse wound up in the pockets of William Magear 'Boss' Tweed, the ruthless leader of the Democratic Party's Tammany Hall organization. At one point, Tweed's gang was filching about $1 million a month from the city treasury. In the end, the cost to build the courthouse was about twice what the US government paid for the Alaska Territory ($6.5 million) around the same time. The subsequent scandal over the building's price tag toppled Tweed from power – but left an architectural gem that boasts 28ft ceilings, stained-glass windows, cast-iron railings and neo-Renaissance pilasters. A lengthy $58 million restoration returning the gorgeous building to its original grandeur was finally completed in December 2001. Pitifully, the site *still* wasn't open to visitors at the time of writing because the city government was bickering over what to house there.

Nearby sits the former **Surrogate's Court** *(cnr Chambers & Centre Sts)*, a 1914 structure with a beaux-arts interior that deliberately mimics the style of Charles Garnier's Paris Opera House. The building is now home to New York City's official archival collection.

If you stroll north on Centre St, you'll reach **Foley Square**, a cluster of city, state and federal courthouses. The square was once the site of a pond called The Collect, on the shores of which sat notorious Five Points, New York's most debauched slum. Here gangs, prostitution, filth and disease festered, attracting the lens and pens of Jacob Riis and Charles Dickens. The Collect was filled by 1811 (the public-works project paid workers a nickel for each cartload of dirt they hauled off) and the slum razed.

The **US Courthouse** *(40 Centre St)*, on the east edge of Foley Square, plays host to high-profile organized-crime trials. A block north, the **New York County Courthouse** houses the state Supreme Court. Check out the lawyers holding noisy impromptu negotiations in its huge rotunda.

Top: Pier 17, the end of the tour (photograph by Michael Taylor)

LOWER MANHATTAN WALKING TOUR

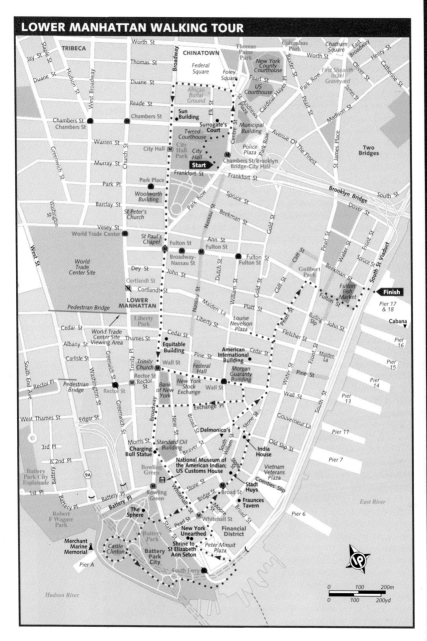

TRIBECA

CHINATOWN

Thomas Paine Park

Columbus Park

Chatham Square

Two Bridges

Worth St
Thomas St
Duane St
Reade St
Chambers St
Warren St
Murray St
Park Pl
Barclay St
Vesey St
Jay St
Staple St
Hudson St
West Broadway
Broadway
Federal Square
Foley Square
New York County Courthouse
US Courthouse
Pearl St
Park Row
Madison St
Henry St
Catherine St
Oliver St
James St
First Shearith Israel Graveyard

Chambers St
Duane St
Reade St
Chambers St

African Burial Ground
Sun Building
Tweed Courthouse
Surrogate's Court
Municipal Building
Police Plaza
St James Place

City Hall Park
City Hall

Start

Chambers St/Brooklyn Bridge-City Hall

Frankfort St
Frankfort St

Brooklyn Bridge

South St

Park Place
Woolworth Building
St Peter's Church
World Trade Center
St Paul's Chapel
Broadway-Nassau St

Park Row
Spruce St
Beekman St
Gold St
Dover St
Front St
South St Viaduct

World Trade Center Site

Dey St
Cortlandt St
Cortlandt St

Fulton St
Fulton St
Fulton St
Fulton St

Ann St
Fulton St

Nassau St
Dutch St
William St
Cliff St
Gold St
Pearl St
Water St
Front St
Spruce St

Guilbert Park
Beekman St
Fulton
Fulton St
Fulton Fish Market

Finish

Pier 17 & 18

Cabana

Pedestrian Bridge
LOWER MANHATTAN
Liberty Park

John St
Maiden La
Liberty St
Platt St
Louise Nevelson Plaza
Fletcher St
Burling Slip
John St

Pier 16

Cedar St
Albany St
Carlisle St

World Trade Center Site Viewing Area
Thames St
Cedar St
Equitable Building
Trinity Church
Wall St
Federal Hall

Pine St
American International Building
Morgan Guaranty Building
Cedar St
Pearl St
Front St
Water St
Maiden La
Pine St

Pier 15
Pier 14

West St
South End Ave
Washington St
Greenwich St
Trinity Pl
Rector St
Rector St
Rector St
Bank of New York
New York Stock Exchange
Wall St
Exchange Pl

Wall St
Water St
South St

Pier 13

Rector Pl
West Thames St
Edgar St

Broadway
New St
Broad St
Exchange Pl
Delmonico's
Stone St
William St
Old Slip St
Gouverneur La

Pier 11
Pier 7

3rd Pl
Battery Pl
2nd Pl

9A

Morris St
Charging Bull Statue
Standard Oil Building
Beaver St
South William St
India House
Vietnam Veterans Plaza

Battery Park City Esplanade
1st Pl
Battery Pl

Bowling Green
National Museum of the American Indian; US Customs House
Stone St
Bridge St
Broad St
Stadt Huys
Fraunces Tavern
Coenties Slip

Robert F Wagner Park
Battery Pl
Bowling Green
The Sphere

Whitehall St
State St
Pearl St
Moore St
Whitehall St
Financial District

Pier 6

Merchant Marine Memorial
Castle Clinton
Battery Park
Battery Park City

New York Unearthed
Shrine to St Elizabeth Ann Seton
Peter Minuit Plaza

East River

Pier A
South Ferry

Hudson River

VP

0   100   200m
0   100   200yd

Heading west on Duane St (in front of the US Courthouse) brings you to the **African Burial Ground**, a cemetery for the city's early black residents, the majority of whom were slaves. Unearthed in 1991, it was declared a National Historic Site, but not before protests by black activists and overruns by the project management team led to a firestorm of (largely negative) publicity, hindering the site's development. Artifacts still await their public debut and these days this archaeological site is a patch of grass behind a fence.

Turn left on Broadway and proceed two blocks to the **Sun Building**, at the corner of Chambers St. The *New York Sun* – one of many newspapers located here during the early 20th century – folded, but its clock and thermometer remain, promising that the publication 'shines for all.' As this book went to press, a new daily newspaper reviving the name *New York Sun* was launched.

Continuing down Broadway, you'll pass the City Hall complex again (from the west this time) and come to the **Woolworth Building** *(233 Broadway)*. When completed in 1913, it was the world's tallest building (792ft, 60 stories); it retained that title until 1929 when it was displaced by the Chrysler Building. Frank Woolworth, head of the famous discount-store chain, reputedly paid the $15 million cost of the building with nickels and dimes. The lobby of this so-called cathedral of commerce boasts a most distinguished interior, with stained glass ceilings, lots of gold leaf and painterly details, and gargoyles of the day's luminaries, including Woolworth counting his change.

Carrying on down Broadway will bring you to **St Paul's Chapel**, between Vesey and Fulton Sts. Designed in 1764 by Thomas McBean, the schist-and-brownstone chapel, modeled after St-Martin-in-the-Fields in London's Trafalgar Square, is one of the country's greatest Georgian structures and the last remaining colonial building in the area. When New York was (briefly) the nation's capital, President George Washington attended services in the chapel's airy interior, with its fluted Corinthian columns and Waterford chandeliers. His personal pew is still on display. This chapel is also known for its long-standing commitment to New York's poor and homeless. Check out the fine noontime concerts held here in summer. St Paul's is the site of myriad memorials to the victims of September 11 and provided a pocket of peace, sanity and safety for rescue crews. It was closed at the time of writing but was due to reopen sometime in the summer of 2002. This is also the northern edge of the World Trade Center viewing platform.

The **World Trade Center viewing platform** was erected in December 2001 to accommodate the tens of thousands of people who began flooding the area to get a look at history. A massive, plywood, one-block-square affair, the platform stretches from Fulton and Dey Sts in the north and south and from Broadway to Church St in the east and west. Looking over what was essentially a construction site is eerie, sad and disconcerting. Indeed, seeing the back of buildings never before visible, like the angular, glass facade of the Winter Garden, is like seeing your grandmother in her underwear – it's just wrong somehow. For information on obtaining the mandatory tickets (free) to the platform, see the special section 'September 11,' earlier in this book.

TOM SMALLMAN

Continuing south on Broadway, you'll come to the 41-story **Equitable Building** *(120 Broadway)*. When it opened in 1915, its sheer unapologetic bulk changed the shape of Manhattan – and world architecture – forever. At 1.2 million sq ft, it ranked as the largest office building on the planet. Its size created such an uproar that in 1916 New York enacted its first zoning laws, requiring building setbacks.

A block further down Broadway, you'll come upon **Trinity Church** (see the main entry, later in this chapter), one of the city's oldest surviving religious landmarks. When British-born Richard Upjohn built the brownstone church in 1846, its buttresses, finials and octagonal spire made it the tallest and most richly decorated building in the city. It's a beauty, especially when viewed from gently sloping Wall St to the southeast.

Wall St, which begins directly across from Trinity Church, stands at the site where early Dutch settlers constructed a northern barrier to protect New Amsterdam from attacks by Native Americans and the British. Today, Wall St is synonymous with world commerce. Check out the blazing red-and-gold art-deco lobby inside the **Bank of New York** *(1 Wall St)*, which serves as a distinctive monument to money. While abutting Wall St, the **New York Stock Exchange** (see the main entry, later in this chapter), the metaphorical center of Wall St, is officially located at 8 Broad St.

Across Wall St from the Stock Exchange is **Federal Hall**, the finest surviving example of classical architecture in Lower Manhattan. Designed by the influential architects Ithiel Town and Alexander Jackson Davis, the 1842 building is truly a temple to purity, with its eight Doric columns, two hefty porticos, two-story rotunda, circular colonnade and paneled dome. (For details on visiting Federal Hall, see later in this chapter.)

A block past Federal Hall stands the 1988 **Morgan Guaranty Building** *(60 Wall St)* whose sleek design symbolizes the financial successes and excesses of the 1980s. Look behind you up Wall St for photogenic views of Trinity Church. Inside the Morgan Guaranty Building is an atrium open to the public if you need a respite. For an added bonus, walk through the atrium to Pine St, where you'll see the art-deco **American International Building**, a whimsical, accomplished monument to the style.

From the Morgan Guaranty Building, turn right down Hanover St and make the next right on Exchange Place heading back to Broadway; turn left (south) there. As Broadway veers east and becomes Whitehall St, you'll be

Facing page: Woolworth Building

Right: Equitable Building

ANGUS OBORN

faced with the **Charging Bull statue**, a 7000lb beast that just appeared in this spot one day in 1989. Suspicious traders touch his flared nose for good luck. Also here is the **Standard Oil Building** (*26 Broadway*). One of many testaments to capitalism that line Broadway from St Paul's Chapel down to Battery Park, this curved edifice was built in 1922 by John D Rockefeller. On the second floor you'll find the small, super-specific **Museum of American Financial History** (☎ *212-908-4519; open 10am-4pm Tues-Sat*).

Continue down Whitehall St, past Bowling Green – the city's first public park – and you'll come upon the **Customs House**, completed in 1907. Architect Cass Gilbert's vast seven-story limestone building melds art and architecture in a tribute to the grandeur of trade. The four entrance statues by Daniel Chester represent the continents of commerce, Africa, Asia, Europe and North America, and the walls, doors, ceilings and floors are festooned with marine ornamentation (shells, sails, sea creatures etc). Dormers are galleon prows, and the glorious elliptical rotunda is a 135ft-long room encircled by Reginald Marsh's murals (added in 1937), portraying everything from the great explorers of America to Greta Garbo at an impromptu dockside press conference. It is simply one of the most sumptuous beaux-arts buildings ever built. Today, the Customs House is home to the **National Museum of the American Indian** (see the main entry, later in this chapter).

Turn right down Bridge St, which leads directly to **Battery Park** and **Castle Clinton**, a fortification built in 1811 to protect Manhattan from the British. Originally located 200yd offshore before landfill engulfed it, the imposing fortress, with 8ft-thick walls and a rusticated gate, once brimmed with 28 guns set in the embrasures. Its guns were never fired in anger, though, and in 1824 the government decommissioned the fort and turned it into Castle Garden, a concert hall resort that is said to have hosted up to 6000 people beneath a domed roof. Since then, it has also served as an immigration station and aquarium. Today, the castle is literally just a shell of its former self – the building is without a roof – but it houses the **ticket office** for the Statue of Liberty Ferry and the **NYC National Parks information booth** (*open 8:30am to 5pm daily*).

By circling the castle and then continuing southeast, you'll exit Battery Park at **Peter Minuit Plaza**, reputedly the site of the purchase of Manhattan for the equivalent of $24.

Turn right on State St and you'll be at the **Shrine to St Elizabeth Ann Seton** (America's first Roman Catholic saint). The lone survivor of a series of row houses that once hugged the shoreline (before landfill arrived), this Georgian home dates from 1793. A Federal-style western wing was added in 1806, reputedly by John McComb, the first New York–born architect of import. This section of the structure is enlivened with a curved porch and double colonnade of attenuated Doric and Ionic columns supposedly made from recycled ship masts.

Tucked just behind this building is **New York Unearthed** (*admission free; open noon-6pm Mon-Fri*), a rather interesting, albeit small, exhibition of historical items discovered by construction workers and archaeologists over the years. You may get lucky and spy some of the dirt diggers in action. Also, don't miss the cool gift shop.

ANGUS OSBORN

Make your first left onto Whitehall St and the first right onto Pearl St. Heading east up Pearl St will lead you to the historical block at Coenties Slip, a Dutch docking station that became a street as landfill extended the city further south. Near here, is the archaeological site of the **Stadt Huys**, the old Dutch City Hall, just across the street from the **Fraunces Tavern**. The current tavern (where you can still sup – see the Places to Eat chapter) is a 1907 renovation of the place where Washington gave his farewell address to Continental Army officers in 1783; for more information, see the Fraunces Tavern Museum heading, later in this chapter.

Continuing up Pearl St, you'll pass the **India House** *(1 Hanover Sq)*, a gorgeous pre–Civil War building that was once the Cotton Exchange and now houses two restaurants, including Bayard's (see the Places to Eat chapter). At the India House, make a left on Old Slip St. A short block later, at the crazy five-pointed corner of Beaver St (a name reflecting the trading activities of colonial New York) stands **Delmonico's**, part of the famous chain that created the American notion of 'dining out' in the 19th century and introduced the world to baked Alaska and lobster Newberg. This 1891 structure includes a marble portico supposedly bought in Pompeii. The storied restaurant is now a microbrewery and steak house.

Make a right on Beaver St and bear left on Pearl St when Beaver St ends. Walk three more blocks and turn left at Maiden Lane to take a brief detour to **Louise Nevelson Plaza**. You'll see a series of seven sculptures collectively entitled *Shadows and Flags* by the famous Russian American artist.

Back on Pearl St, proceed north several blocks to Fulton St. Make a right towards the East River and before you see it you'll start smelling the **Fulton Fish Market**, the city's wholesale seafood distribution point. Get here before 8am to see the frenetic before-dawn fish hawking. Fulton Fish Market is moving to Hunt's Point in the Bronx by the end of 2003. Nearby is the **South St Seaport** (see the main entry, later in the chapter). Arriving as night falls allows you to watch the sun set and the Brooklyn and Manhattan Bridges light up. The sight is worth the price of a drink at a bar or café with a good view (we like **Cabana** at Pier 17 or **Rise** at the Ritz Carlton in Battery Park – see the Places to Eat chapter and the boxed text 'Hotel Cocktails' in the Entertainment chapter, respectively). Alternatively, you can cross the bridge and gaze upon Manhattan from the Brooklyn Heights Promenade or from Fulton Landing near the River Cafe (see the Brooklyn Heights Walking Tour, later in this chapter).

Facing page: Be a Bully on Wall St

Right: Battery Park

KIM GRANT

City Hall

This hall (☎ 212-788-6871; Park Row; ⓜ 4, 5, 6 to Brooklyn Bridge-City Hall, J, M, Z to Chambers St), in placid City Hall Park facing the entrance to the Brooklyn Bridge, has been home to New York's government since 1812. In keeping with the half-baked civic planning that has often plagued large-scale New York projects, officials neglected to finish the building's northern side in marble, gambling that the city would not expand uptown. The mistake was finally rectified in 1954, completing a structure that architectural critic Ada Louise Huxtable has called a 'symbol of taste, excellence and quality not always matched by the policies inside.'

Highlights inside include the spot where Abraham Lincoln's coffin sat for a brief time in 1865. (Walk to the top of the staircase on the 2nd floor to view the historic site.) The Governor's Room, a reception area where the mayor entertains important guests, contains 12 portraits of the founding fathers by John Trumbull, George Washington's old writing table and other examples of Federal furniture, and the remnants of a flag flown at the first president's 1789 inaugural ceremony. If you peek into the City Council chambers, you might see lawmakers deliberating over the renaming of a city street in someone's honor – an activity that accounts for about 40% of all the bills passed by the 51-member body.

For generations, City Hall's steps had been a popular and visible site for political protests, but exercising free speech in this way was considered inappropriate or somehow distasteful by former mayor Giuliani who banned the practice. Citing security concerns, Mayor Bloomberg allows demonstrations here, as long as you get a permit first. The entire complex was closed to visitors following the September 11 attacks but may have reopened by the time you read this.

City Hall Park received a multimillion dollar facelift recently and its gas lamps, fountains, pretty landscaping, chess tables and benches make it a nice place to kick back for a spell.

Battery Park City

This 30-acre waterfront swath (ⓜ 4 or 5 train to Bowling Green) stretches along the Hudson River from Chambers St to Pier 1 on the southern tip of the island and encompasses Rockefeller Park, the Battery Park City Esplanade, Robert F Wagner Park and Battery Park. It's a fantastic getaway from Manhattan's madness, with glorious sunsets and Statue of Liberty views, and is a superb place to cycle, roller blade, play soccer, hit the jungle gym or just loll in the grass.

At the **Park House** (#38) near Rockefeller Park you can borrow pogo sticks, basketballs, jump ropes, board games or pools balls and a cue (for use on the outdoor tables gazing on Lady Liberty), free with identification. Kids will love the playgrounds and climbing on the laugh-out-loud funny sculptures by Tom Otterness. Speaking of sculptures, there are dozens sprinkled throughout this riverside area, which makes a peaceful stroll.

There are a range of free or low-fee walking tours, group swims, children's programming and classes on offer in these parks; for information you can contact the **Battery Park Conservancy** (☎ 212-267-9700; ⓦ www.bpcparks.org).

ANGUS OBORN

The serene surroundings of City Hall Park

World Financial Center This complex (☎ 212-945-0505; W www.worldfinancial center.com; West & Vesey Sts; M A, C, 4, 5 to Fulton St-Broadway Nassau), behind the former World Trade Center (WTC) site, stands on the landfill created by the excavation for the WTC's foundation. A group of four office towers surrounds the **Winter Garden**, a palm-filled, glass atrium that hosts free concerts during the summer and exclusive black-tie events year-round. This is a good place to head if the weather turns nasty as you can pass an hour or so in the shopping area and art gallery located next to the Winter Garden.

New York Stock Exchange

Though Wall St is the widely recognized symbol for US capitalism, the world's best-known stock exchange (☎ 212-656-5168; W www.nyse.com; 8 Broad St; M 1, 2, 4, 5 to Wall St, J, M, Z to Broad St) is actually on Broad St, not Wall St. More than 700,000 visitors a year used to pass behind the portentous Romanesque façade of the building, but the visitors' gallery overlooking the trading floor has been closed indefinitely in the wake of 9/11. Over one billion shares valued at around $44 billion change hands daily; an entire day of trading 10 years ago can be handled in just a half hour or less today. Cheers ring out if the market closes on a high note, groans and oaths abound on a down day.

The start (9.30am) and close (4pm) of the business day is signalled by ringing the bell on the trading floor – a tradition that was introduced in the 1870s when continuous trading was instituted.

Outside the exchange you'll see dozens of brokers dressed in color-coordinated trading jackets popping out for a quick cigarette or hot dog; the street scene outside is often more entertaining than the money swapping within.

Truly frantic buying and selling by red-faced traders screaming 'Sell! Sell!' goes on at the **New York Mercantile Exchange** (#60; ☎ 212-299-2499; W www.nymex.com; 1 North End Ave; M A, C, 4, 5 to Fulton St-Broadway Nassau), not far from Vesey St. This exchange deals in gold, gas and oil commodities, but not tourists just yet; they were trying to figure out how to accommodate visitors at the time of writing and it may or may not be open for drop-ins when you happen by. It's worth a try.

Federal Hall

Distinguished by a huge statue of George Washington, Federal Hall (☎ 212-825-6888; W www.nps.gov/feha; 26 Wall St; M 1, 2, 4, 5 to Wall St, J, M, Z to Broad St; museum open 9am-5pm Mon-Fri) stands on the site of New York's original City Hall, where the first US Congress convened and Washington took the oath of office on April 30, 1789, as the first US chief executive.

Following that structure's demolition in the early 19th century, the present Greek Revival building gradually rose in its place between 1834 and 1842. Considered to be one of the country's premier examples of classical architecture, it served as the US customs house until 1862. Today, the building contains a small museum dedicated to postcolonial New York. Free guided tours of the building leave at 11am and 3pm.

Federal Hall serves as the starting point for four self-guided Heritage Trail walking tours that explore the area's history in greater detail. Look for the wrought-iron maps and site descriptions that are sprinkled all over Lower Manhattan. Maps and an accompanying Junior Ranger Guide are available from the Alliance for Downtown New York.

New York Stock Exchange

GREG GAWLOWSKI

THINGS TO SEE & DO

National Museum of the American Indian

This museum (#86; ☎ 212-514-3700; W www.si.edu/nmai; 1 Bowling Green; ⓜ 4, 5 to Bowling Green; admission free; open 10am-5pm Fri-Wed, 10am-8pm Thur), an affiliate of the Smithsonian Institution, moved to the spectacular former US Customs House on Bowling Green in 1994. This is a grand space for the USA's leading museum on Native American art, established by oil heir George Gustav Heye in 1916. The facility's information center is in the former duties collection office, with computer banks located next to old wrought-iron teller booths.

The galleries are on the 2nd floor, beyond a vast rotunda featuring statues of famous navigators and murals celebrating shipping history. This museum does little to explain the history of Native Americans but instead concentrates its attention on Native American culture, boasting a million-item collection of crafts and everyday objects. Computer touchscreens feature insights into Native American life and beliefs, and working artists often offer explanations of their techniques. It has a good gift shop.

Although a similar museum was opened in Washington, DC, threatening to overshadow this facility, it's still worth a look (and you can't beat the free admission).

Trinity Church

This former Anglican parish church (☎ 212-602-0800; W www.trinitywallstreet.org; cnr Broadway & Wall St; ⓜ 1, 2, 4, 5 to Wall St, N, R to Rector St; open 8am-6pm Mon-Fri, 8am-4pm Sat, 7pm-4pm Sun, except lunchtime services) was founded by King William III in 1697 and once presided over several constituent chapels, including St Paul's Chapel, at the corner of Fulton St and Broadway. Its huge land holdings in Lower Manhattan made it the country's wealthiest and most influential church throughout the 18th century.

The current Trinity Church is the third structure on the site. Designed by English architect Richard Upjohn, this 1846 building helped to launch the picturesque neo-Gothic movement in America. At the time

Trinity Church in its third incarnation

KIM GRANT

of its construction, its 280ft bell tower made it the tallest building in New York City.

The long, dark interior of the church includes a beautiful stained-glass window over the altar. Trinity, like other Anglican churches in America, became part of the Episcopal faith following US independence from Britain. A pamphlet describing the parish's history is available for a small donation.

Trinity also hosts midday music concerts during the week. Call ☎ 212-602-0747 for a schedule.

Museum of Jewish Heritage

This facility (#90; ☎ 212-786-0820; W www .mjhnyc.org; 18 1st Pl, Battery Park City; ⓜ 4, 5 to Bowling Green; adult/senior & student $7/5; open 10am-5:45pm Sun-Wed, 10am-8pm Thur, 10am-5pm Fri, 10am-3pm Fri off season) explores all aspects of Jewish New York, from immigration to assimilation. Audio tours of the museum are available for $5. Just outside the museum you'll find a plaza that serves as New York City's Holocaust memorial.

Statue of Liberty

This monument *(Map 1; ☎ 212-363-3200; w www.nps.gov/stli)* is the most enduring symbol of New York City and, indeed, the New World. Modeled after the Colossus of Rhodes, the statue was the brainchild of political activist Edouard René Lefebvre de Laboulaye and sculptor Frédéric-Auguste Bartholdi. In 1865, the pair decided something monumental should be created to promote French republicanism, and Bartholdi dedicated most of the next 20 years to turning that dream into reality.

Once New York was chosen as the site for Lady Liberty and $250,000 was raised to cover costs, Bartholdi got busy creating his most famous sculpture, which included a metal skeleton by railway engineer Alexandre Gustave Eiffel. In 1883, poet Emma Lazarus published a poem called 'The New Colossus' as part of a fund-raising campaign for a statue pedestal. Her words have long since been associated with the monument: 'Give me your tired, your poor, / Your huddled masses yearning to breathe free, / The wretched refuse of your teeming shore, / Send these, the homeless, tempest-tost to me, / I lift my lamp beside the golden door!'. Ironically, these famous words were added to the base only in 1901, 17 years after the poet's death. On October 28, 1886, the 151ft *Liberty Enlightening the World* was finally unveiled in New York harbor.

By the 1980s, badly in need of restoration, more than $100 million was spent to shore up Lady Liberty for her centennial. The rotting copper skin required substantial work, and workers installed a new gold-plated torch, the third in the statue's history. The older stained-glass torch is now on display just inside the entrance to the staircase. The exhibition also shows how the statue has been exploited for commercial purposes.

Speaking of which, the **Statue of Liberty Ferry** *(☎ 212-269-5755; w www.statueof libertyferry.com)* – run by the Circle Line – has made more than a few dollars shuttling visitors to the statue and back. Well over four million people a year ride the boats to the Statue of Liberty and Ellis Island, while millions more take the boat ride just for the view of Manhattan, which surpasses the view from the statue itself. Since September 11, the statue, crown and museum have been closed to visitors and will remain so indefinitely, although the grounds are still open.

Although the ferry ride lasts only 15 minutes, a trip to both the Statue of Liberty and Ellis Island is an all-day affair. In the summer, you may wait up to an hour to embark on an 800-person ferry; if it reopens, the trek to the crown (a climb of 354 steps not for claustrophobics) takes three hours. Following the terrorist attacks, new security measures have been enacted (no backpacks, coolers or large parcels are permitted) and getting to the Statue of Liberty or Ellis Island now takes longer than ever.

The roundtrip ferry costs $8/6/3 for adult/senior/child. This price includes admission to both the Statue of Liberty and Ellis Island. Ferries depart from Battery Park (Ⓜ South Ferry, Bowling Green) every 30 minutes from 9am (8am in summer) to 5pm daily except Christmas. You'll find the **ticket office** *(Map 3, #92; Ⓜ 4, 5 to Bowling Green)* in Castle Clinton, the fort built in 1811 to defend Manhattan from the British – from the exit, cut diagonally south across Battery Park to reach Castle Clinton or go down Battery Pl to its terminus at the Hudson River and swing south around the edge of Battery Park. There is also a Statue of Liberty ferry service from Liberty State Park in New Jersey for US$8/6/3 adult/senior/child; call ☎ 201-435-9499 for information.

If the crowds are too much, try the nearby Staten Island ferry. It doesn't take you to the statue but provides a great view of it and Downtown Manhattan – best of all, it's free! (For details, see Staten Island later in this chapter.)

Ellis Island

Ferries to the Statue of Liberty make a second stop at Ellis Island *(Map 1)*, New York's main immigration station from 1892 until 1954. More than 12 million people passed through here before the island was abandoned; the record number of immigrants processed in one day was just under 12,000.

A $160-million restoration has turned the impressive red-brick main building into an **Immigration Museum** (☎ *212-363-3200)*, where you can explore the history of the island through a series of galleries. The exhibition begins at the Baggage Room and continues on to the 2nd-story rooms where medical inspections took place and foreign currency was exchanged.

The exhibits emphasize that, contrary to popular myth, most of the ship-borne immigrants were processed within eight hours and that conditions were generally clean and safe (especially for 1st- and 2nd-class passengers, who were processed on board; only immigrants from the steerage class were subjected to whatever conditions prevailed on Ellis Island). The 338ft-long Registry Room, with its beautiful vaulted tile ceiling, is where the polygamists, paupers, criminals and anarchists were turned around and sent back from where they came. Walking though the registry today – described as 'light and airy' in the museum literature – surely can't compare with the days when this room held 5000 confused and tired people waiting to be interviewed by immigration officers and inspected by doctors. The latter had literally seconds to diagnose a list of diseases; anyone with a contagious illness was rejected.

You can take a 50-minute audio tour of the facility for $6. But for an even more affecting take on history, pick up one of the phones in each display area and listen to the recorded memories of real Ellis Island immigrants, taped in the 1980s.

If you want still more, see *Embracing Freedom* (☎ *212-883-1986, ext 742; adult/senior & child over 14 yrs $3/2.50)*, a 30-minute play about the Ellis Island experience which shows five times a day on the half-hour from 10:30am to 3:30pm.

A free 30-minute film on the immigrant experience is also worth checking out, as is the exhibition on the influx of immigrants just before WWI.

Statue of Liberty ferry services run to Ellis Island daily (adult/senior/child $8/6/3). For ticket and schedule information, see under Statue of Liberty, earlier in this chapter.

KIM GRANT

The former immigration building: the first (and last) view of NYC for many immigrants

Fraunces Tavern Museum

This museum *(#83; ☎ 212-425-1778; 54 Pearl St; ⓜ 4, 5 to Bowling Green, 1, 2 to Wall St; adult/senior, student & child $3/2; open 10am-5pm Tues, Wed & Fri, 11am-5pm Thur & Sat)* sits in a block of historic structures that, along with nearby Stone St and the South St Seaport, comprise the best-preserved examples of early-18th-century New York. Fraunces Tavern recently re-opened as a restaurant (for more details, see the Places to Eat chapter).

On this site stood the Queen's Head Tavern, owned by Samuel Fraunces, who changed the name to Fraunces Tavern after the US victory in the Revolutionary War. It was in the 2nd-floor dining room on December 4, 1783, that George Washington bade farewell to the officers of the Continental Army after the British relinquished control of New York City. In the 19th century, the tavern was closed and the building fell into disuse. It was also damaged during several massive fires that swept through old downtown areas, destroying most colonial buildings and nearly all Dutch-built structures. In 1904, the Sons of the Revolution historical society bought the building and returned it to an approximation of its colonial-era look – an act believed to be the first major attempt at historical preservation in the USA. In 1975, the Fuerzas Armadas de Liberación Nacional, a radical group from Puerto Rico, detonated a bomb here, killing five people.

Just across the street from the tavern are the excavated remains of the old Dutch **Stadt Huys**, which served as New Amsterdam's administrative center, courthouse and jail from 1641 until the British takeover in 1664. This building, destroyed in 1699, was originally on the city's waterfront until landfill added a few more blocks to southern Manhattan. The excavation here between 1979 and 1980 was the city's first large-scale archaeological investigation, and it reaped many artifacts (including the privy and cistern remains displayed under Plexiglas).

Federal Reserve Bank

The only reason to visit the Federal Reserve Bank *(#68; ☎ 212-720-6130; 33 Liberty St;* ⓜ *J, M, Z to Fulton St-Broadway Nassau; admission free)*, near Nassau St, is to ogle the facility's high-security vault. Located 80ft below ground, more than 10,000 tons of gold reserves reside here. You'll only see a small part of that fortune, but you'll learn a lot about the US Federal Reserve System on the informative tour. You can also browse through an exhibition of coins and counterfeit currency. Reservations are required for the tour, which is held on the hour from 9:30am to 2:30pm Monday to Friday.

South Street Seaport

This 11-block enclave of shops, piers and sights *(☎ 212-732-7678;* ⓦ *www.southstseaport.org;* ⓜ *1, 2, 4, 5, J, M, Z to Fulton St-Broadway Nassau)* combines the best and worst in historic preservation. Pier 17, beyond the elevated FDR Dr, is a waterfront development project that is home to a number of shops and one recommended restaurant; there's also a rare public bathroom here. Clustered around the piers is a number of genuinely significant 18th- and 19th-century buildings dating from the heyday of this old East River ferry port, which fell into disuse with the building of the Brooklyn Bridge and the establishment of deepwater jetties on the Hudson River. The many pedestrian malls, historic tall ships and riverside locale make the seaport a picturesque destination or detour.

Schermerhorn Row, a block of old warehouses bordered by Fulton, Front and South Sts, contains novelty shops, upscale boutiques and the New York Yankees Clubhouse (where you can purchase fee-free tickets for the Bronx Bombers). Across the street, the **Fulton Market Building**, built in 1983 to reflect the red-brick style of its older neighbors, is a glorified fast-food court and shopping arcade.

The **South Street Seaport Museum** *(☎ 212-748-8600; adult/senior/student/child $6/5/4/3; open 10am-6pm Fri-Wed, 10am-8pm Thur Apr-Sept, 10am-5pm Wed-Mon Oct-Mar)* offers a glimpse of the seaport's history and a survey of the world's great ocean liners in its permanent exhibits. The museum operates several interesting sites in the 11-block area, including three galleries, an antique printing shop, a children's center, a maritime crafts center and historic ships.

Just south of Pier 17 stands a group of tall-masted sailing vessels, including the *Peking*, *Wavertree*, *Pioneer*, *Ambrose* and *Helen Mcallister*, currently being restored. The admission price to the museum includes access to these ships. You can also sail aboard the *Pioneer* (see Harbor Tours, following).

For more than 130 years, Pier 17 has been home to the **Fulton Fish Market**, where most of the city's restaurants get their fresh seafood. The open-air market is a perfect example of how this area maintains its old character while still catering to tourists. The fishmongers sling fish on the sidewalks and streets while spectators watch the nightly goings-on from midnight until 8am. This is no squeaky clean Seattle Pike's Market; the facility has always been entangled with local organized crime. A federal and city government crackdown on corruption led to months of labor unrest and a suspicious 1995 fire that destroyed part of the market. In 2001, Mayor Giuliani announced a deal that would move the Fulton Fish Market to Hunt's Point in the South Bronx; the move should be completed by the end of 2003.

Harbor Tours A booth on Pier 16 sells tickets for an hour-long excursion aboard the Circle Line's **Seaport Liberty Cruises** (☎ *212-563-3200;* W *www.circleline.com)* for $13/11/7 per adult/senior/child. Tours, which highlight Manhattan's maritime history, run at least four times a day from April to the end of November. Evening music cruises (☎ *212-630-8888)*, with the likes of Dr John and Popa Chubby, are also offered for $15 and up. From Pier 16, Circle Line also operates *The Beast*, a speedboat of obscene proportion and pace that careens around the harbor for 30 minutes; tickets cost $16/10 per adult/child.

New York Waterway (☎ *800-533-3779;* W *www.nywaterway.com)* offers 50-minute cruises from Pier 17 (adult/senior/child $11/10/6) and also offers direct water-taxi service to New York Yankees and New York Mets baseball games during the summer

(see Ferry in the Getting Around chapter for details).

Pioneer Sail (☎ *212-748-8786)* offers summer sailing trips on the East River, as well as lunch, sunset and late-night trips, daily except Monday; tickets cost $25/20/15 per adult/senior/child.

More sailing and cruising tours are listed under Boat Tours in the Getting Around chapter, earlier in this book.

Brooklyn Bridge

When the world's first steel suspension bridge (Ⓜ *4, 5, 6 to Brooklyn Bridge-City Hall)* opened in 1883, the 1596ft span between its two support towers was the longest in history. Although its construction was fraught with disaster, the bridge became a magnificent example of urban design, which inspired poets, writers and painters. Today, the Brooklyn Bridge continues to dazzle and many regard it as the most beautiful bridge in the world.

This East River suspension bridge was designed by the Prussian-born engineer John Roebling, who was knocked off a pier in Fulton Landing in June 1869; he died of tetanus poisoning before construction of the bridge began. His son Washington Roebling supervised construction of the bridge, which lasted 14 years, and managed to survive budget overruns and the deaths of 20 workers. The younger Roebling himself suffered from the bends while helping to excavate the riverbed for the bridge's western tower and remained bedridden for much of the project (his wife oversaw construction). There was one final tragedy to come in June 1883, when the bridge opened to pedestrian traffic. Someone in the crowd shouted, perhaps as a joke, that the bridge was collapsing into the river, setting off a mad rush in which 12 people were trampled to death.

The bridge entered its second century as strong and beautiful as ever, following an extensive renovation in the early 1980s. The pedestrian walkway that begins just east of City Hall affords a wonderful view of Lower Manhattan (albeit recently altered), and you can stop at observation points under the support towers to view brass panorama histories of the waterfront. Once you reach Brooklyn

The cathedral-like arches of the Brooklyn Bridge

THINGS TO SEE & DO

(about a 20-minute trek), you can bear left to Empire Fulton Ferry State Park or Cadman Plaza West, which runs alongside Middagh St in the heart of Brooklyn Heights. Bearing right brings you to Brooklyn's downtown area, which includes the ornate Brooklyn Borough Hall and the Brooklyn Heights Promenade (see the Brooklyn Heights Walking Tour, later in this chapter).

TRIBECA (MAP 3)

Prior to September 11, Tribeca (which stands for 'TRIangle BElow CAnal St,' with Broadway on the eastern side and Chambers St to the south) was the hottest neighborhood most visitors had never heard of. For those in the know, Tribeca meant huge lofts and tolerable (for New York) rents, world-class restaurants, historic bars and an emergent shopping and art scene, all with a neighborhood feel. In addition, Tribeca has amazing public transportation connections, few tourists (despite the presence of Robert De Niro's Tribeca Films production company and the home of the late John F Kennedy Jr) and even fewer of those ubiquitous chain stores that are overtaking the city. Thanks to community preservation efforts, there are four separate historic districts within Tribeca's boundaries.

As it borders the WTC site, Tribeca was rocked by the terrorist attacks and is still reeling. While residents retrenched and regrouped, filed for emergency aid, tried to salvage furnishings and installed air filters in their homes, theaters, small businesses such as liquor stores and locksmiths, restaurants and shops closed. Massive incentives designed to keep residents in the neighborhood (including cash disbursements from the Lower Manhattan Development Corporation, who pledged to split $225 million among residents who committed to remain in Tribeca for at least two years), small business loans, billions in federal money and reduced rent mean the neighborhood is on the rebound. Although it will never be the same, it's vital now more than ever that visitors come to this area to bear witness to Tribeca's rebirth.

A good way to get acquainted with the neighborhood is through the Tribeca Organization (W www.tribecaorganization.org).

Harrison Street Houses

Built between 1804 and 1828, the eight townhouses on the block of Harrison St (#37; ⓜ 1, 2 to Franklin St) immediately west of Greenwich St constitute the largest collection of Federal architecture left in the city. But they were not always neighbors:

six of them once stood two blocks away, on a stretch of Washington St that no longer exists. In the early 1970s, that area was the site of Washington Market, a wholesale fruit and vegetable equivalent of the Fulton Fish Market (see Lower Manhattan). But development of the waterfront (which resulted in the construction of Manhattan Community College and the Soviet-type concrete apartment complex that now looms over the townhouses) meant the market had to move uptown and the historic row of houses had to be relocated. Only the buildings at 31 and 33 Harrison St remain where they were originally constructed.

Clocktower Gallery

The PS1 Contemporary Art Center runs a free gallery space and studios known as the Clocktower Gallery (#28; ☎ 718-784-2084; ☒ www.ps1.org; 108 Leonard St; ☺ 1, 2 to Franklin St; open noon-6pm Wed-Sat), between Broadway and Lafayette St. It sits at the top of the ornate old headquarters of the New York Life Insurance Company (currently the headquarters of the New York City Probation Department and the Public Health and Hospitals Corporation). To get to the gallery, take the elevator to the 12th floor – which is as far as it goes – and ascend the staircase to the tower on the 13th floor.

The artists working in these studios are sponsored by the Institute for Contemporary Art, which funds the gallery. You can see their works in progress during the gallery's opening hours.

CHINATOWN & LITTLE ITALY (MAP 3)

Two of Manhattan's most dynamic ethnic enclaves, Chinatown and Little Italy, are just north of the Civic Center and the Financial District. Chinatown sprawls largely south of Canal St and east of Centre St to the Manhattan Bridge; over the years, however, it has steadily crept further east into the Lower East Side and north into Little Italy, which is a narrowing sliver extending north of Canal St.

Over 150,000 Chinese-speaking residents live in cramped tenements and crowded apartments in Chinatown, a community with its own unique rhythms and traditions. For example, some banks along Canal St keep Sunday hours, newsstands sell no fewer than six Chinese newspapers and illegal fireworks (the highlight of many a Chinese New Year's parade) are peddled openly. Stroll the streets for dinner fixings and you'll find live frogs a-swirl in a barrel, shark fins and exotic fruits and elixirs. Throughout the 1990s, Chinatown has attracted a growing number of Vietnamese immigrants, who have set up their own shops and opened inexpensive restaurants here.

In contrast, Little Italy's ethnic character has been largely diluted in the last 50 years. The area began as a strong Italian neighborhood (film director Martin Scorsese grew up on Elizabeth St), but in the mid-20th century, Little Italy suffered a large exodus, as many residents moved to the Cobble Hill section of Brooklyn and the city's suburbs. For that reason, few cultural sites and traditions remain. One exception is the raucous **Feast of San Gennaro** honoring the patron saint of Naples, which is held for 10 days starting in the second week of September. At this time, Mulberry St from Canal to Houston Sts is closed off to make room for the festival's games of chance, kiddie rides and enough food and wine to sate the Bacchus in all of us.

Heading west of Mulberry St towards Lafayette St and north towards Houston St, Little Italy begins to take on a more cosmopolitan character, with an overflow of SoHo-style shops, cafés and restaurants. This area is known as Nolita (for 'NOrth of Little ITAly') or NoHo (for 'NOrth of HOuston St,' where it extends into the East Village) even further north. It's essential to walk the streets immediately east of Broadway below Houston St to experience the flavor of this redeveloped neighborhood. However, as the chic boutiques, bakeries and intimate eateries continue to encroach, the historic ethnic character of Little Italy becomes even more of a distant memory.

To get to Chinatown or Little Italy, hop on the ☺ J, M, N, Q, R, W, Z, 6 to Canal St.

Chinatown & Little Italy Walking Tour

The length of this walking tour depends on your style. Some will zip through it in 90 minutes or less, but for those prone to poking around in odd shops, lingering over dim sum or delighting in chaotic street scenes, it could take two to three hours. Start your tour on bustling Canal St near Broadway. Right on the northeast corner here is **Pearl River Mart** (☎ 212-431-4770), a sprawling, two-floor emporium of every Chinese trinket imaginable, from paper lanterns to jade talismans. Walk south for a block to Cortlandt Alley, a perfectly preserved, three-block enclave of old sweatshops that Hollywood adores as a movie backdrop – if these walls could talk! On Walker St you'll find **Art in General** (☎ 212-219-0473; 79 Walker St), a nonprofit gallery exhibiting contemporary and un-conventional art in an airy two-floor space.

Snake your way left down Franklin, hook a right onto Lafayette, make another left on Leonard St and you'll emerge on Centre St, facing the **New York County Courthouse** (for more details on the courthouse, see the Lower Manhattan Walking Tour, earlier in this chapter). The stretch of Worth St (also known as 'Avenue of the Strongest,' named for New York's sanitation workers) leading to the corner of Columbus Park is the site of the infamous Five Points slum, which was razed in the early 1800s.

Turn left on Baxter St and hug the western edge of **Columbus Park**, one of New York's most intriguing public spaces. Here you'll see wizened men playing mah-jongg while a clutch of toughs scrutinizes their progress and places bets. On the northeastern corner, avian melodies pierce the air as residents treat their feathered friends to some sun, hanging their bamboo cages from tree limbs. The playground always buzzes with Asian dialects; a flower vendor whistles while he works. There are some terrific Thai and Vietnamese restaurants around the north end of the park if you're hungry (see Chinatown in the Places to Eat chapter).

If you can tear yourself away, continue north to Canal St. To the west is the shopping section, with its assortment of hardware and electrical-supply stores, and blocks of street vendors proffering phony designer clothing and bootleg videos. This is a great place to shop or just browse, but if you buy anything off the street, make sure it's something you can wear or check out on the spot – a hat, a book or a leather jacket.

Top: A warm welcome to Chinatown (photograph by Robert Reid)

Bottom: Columbus Park

109

The Chinese shopping district begins east of Baxter St, with stand after stand selling smelly stuff like fresh fish and durians, the infamously odiferous fruit banned from the subways of Singapore. Across Mott St is a strip full of Asian restaurants, but save your appetite, for soon you'll be among wall-to-wall classic Chinese restaurants and dim sum houses.

Turn right onto Mott St. The **Eastern States Buddhist Temple** (64B Mott St), in a storefront, is a shrine jam-packed with dozens of golden and porcelain Buddhas, many intricately carved. You can buy a fortune and watch the devout make offerings.

Continue south on Mott St and turn right on Bayard St. At the corner of Mulberry St, you'll come to the **Museum of Chinese in the Americas** (☎ 212-619-4785; ⓦ www.moca-nyc.org; 70 Mulberry St; suggested donation adult/senior & student $3/1; open noon-5pm Tues-Sat) on the 2nd floor of a former public school building. The museum offers walking tours, sponsors

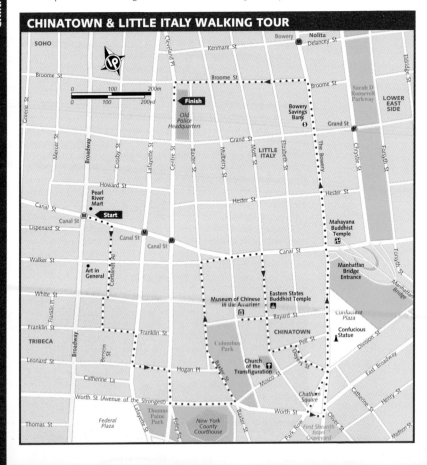

CHINATOWN & LITTLE ITALY WALKING TOUR

arts-and-crafts workshops and hosts exhibitions on the experiences of Chinese immigrants throughout the hemisphere. Crowding the sidewalks around the museum is some genuine Chinatown action: grey-whiskered musicians pluck their *san-hsien* (Chinese lutes), shrunken seers tell fortunes and sprightly men resole shoes.

Backtrack on Bayard St to Mott St and turn right. In another block is the **Church of the Transfiguration** *(29 Mott St)*. Though the building began as an Episcopal church in 1801, the Catholic incarnation of this church was founded by Cuban humanist, philosopher and priest Padre Felix Varela in 1827 to attend to the needs of poor Irish and Italian immigrants living in the neighborhood. The church got its first Chinese pastor in the 1970s and today holds services in Cantonese and Mandarin.

Turn left on Pell St, then bear right on Doyers St. Chinatown began in this small enclave in the 1870s, when Chinese railway workers, fed up with racial discrimination in the American West, moved to New York City in droves. During Chinese New Year celebrations in late January and early February, papier-mache dragons snake their way around this corner to a cacophony of firecrackers. There are several good places to eat tucked away in these sinuous alleys (see the Places to Eat chapter).

At the end of Doyers St, are several sites reflecting the neighborhood's ethnic history. At **Chatham Square**, public auctions took place to sell the goods of Irish debtors in the early 19th century. Nowadays, there's a monument to fallen Chinese American WWII soldiers and a wicked view of lower Manhattan. The **First Shearith Israel Graveyard** (150 yards south of the square on St James Pl) holds the remains of early Portuguese and Spanish immigrants and ranks as the oldest Jewish cemetery in the USA (dating to the 1680s).

Heading north up the Bowery, don't miss a sage-looking **Confucius** welcoming passersby into his plaza, beyond which is the grand but pollution-pocked entrance to the **Manhattan Bridge**. You can walk across the bridge to Williamsburg, or head into the **Mahayana Buddhist Temple** *(☎ 212-925-8787, 133 Canal St)*, where you'll be greeted by a gargantuan golden Buddha with a beatific smile. While you can't take photos of the profusion of flowers, incense and oranges on offer, $1 gets you a fortune which might predict that your 'probability of success is great.'

Two blocks north you'll find the **Bowery Savings Bank** *(130 Bowery at Grand St)*. The bank's Romanesque-inspired archway and vaulted gold-leaf interior

Right: No shortage of advertising in local Chinatown

ROBERT REID

ANGUS OBORN

offer a quiet respite from the bustling fruit stands and traffic. Stanford White, the most talented and colorful architect of the Gilded Age, designed the building in 1894.

Continue north on the Bowery one block to Broome St and turn left. In a little over four blocks, at the corner of Centre St, you'll reach the **Old Police Headquarters** (240 Centre St). Completed in 1909, this building overwhelms its neighbors and is a perfect example of why New York enacted its first zoning laws in 1916. In 1988, the structure became an apartment building.

Although the walking tour ends here, you can take in a couple more Little Italy sights by continuing north on Centre St, which merges into Lafayette St, for a few more blocks to Houston St. Near the corner of Lafayette and Houston Sts is the **Puck Building** (295-305 Lafayette St), home of the turn-of-the-century humor magazine. The stunning red-brick building has two gold-leaf statues of the portly Puck – one perches on a 3rd-floor shelf on the northeast corner, the other is at the Lafayette St entrance. It's a popular spot for magazine parties and film shoots.

If you turn right on Houston St, then right again on Mulberry St, you'll come to **Old St Patrick's Cathedral** (☎ 212-226-8075; 263 Mulberry St; services 5:30pm Sat, 9:30am & 12:30pm Sun). After a fire destroyed much of its exterior, Old St Pat's was undergoing a full restoration at the time of writing. This structure served as the city's first Roman Catholic cathedral from 1809 to 1878, before its more famous successor was built Uptown on Fifth Ave. The cathedral hosted the memorial mass for John F Kennedy Jr after his death in 1999. Sneak in for a peak at the displays of religious ephemera, the tumble-down graveyard or the funky gift shop.

KIM GRANT

Top: Puck me, what a building!

Bottom: Caffe Roma in the heart of Little Italy

LOWER EAST SIDE

In the early 20th century, half a million Jews from Eastern Europe streamed into the Lower East Side (LES), and today it remains one of New York's most desirable entry-level neighborhoods (read: It's relatively cheap). Lately, it's become a magnet for the bridge-and-tunnel crowd – suburbanites – who flood the area, hopping among the no-name bars and late-night lounges that pepper the four-block area on and around Ludlow St, which runs south from Houston St. Locals know to steer clear on Friday and Saturday nights.

Architecturally, this storied old tenement area still retains its hardscrabble character, with block after block of crumbling buildings. You can see why the early residents lamented that 'the sun was embarrassed to shine' on their benighted neighborhood.

But like Little Italy, the LES has lost much of its historic ethnic flavor. Only a small Jewish community and a handful of traditional businesses remain, but it's far from homogenous. Today, the LES is populated by youngsters experiencing city living for the first time, some holdout punks, painters, squatters and sculptors, and a good many 'lifers' holding onto rent-controlled apartments. Also, the Latino community is spilling over from Alphabet City, and Chinatown continues to colonize adjacent neighborhoods, making for a flavorful mix that is unique to the LES.

With its array of restaurants and nightlife, the LES ranks as one of New York City's hottest neighborhoods. In New York, to remain hot, high and mighty means to adapt, and in this sense the LES is mercurial, with cafés, shops, bars and lounges turning over constantly. Poke around and find what you like down here among the old classics and the New Wave.

While you're in the area, check out **East River Park** *(Map 3)*; it has just had a $4 million face-lift, which includes the 5000-seat amphitheater that hosts live music and other performances. Visit the **Lower East Side Visitors Center** *(Map 3; 261 Broome St)*, between Allan and Orchard Sts, to orient yourself in the neighborhood.

Orchard St (Map 4)

Bargain hunters prey upon the Orchard St Bargain District *(◍ F to Delancey St, J, M, Z to Essex St)*, a market area extending across Orchard, Ludlow and Essex Sts above Delancey St, which runs east to west. When the LES was still a largely Jewish neighborhood, Eastern European merchants set up pushcarts to sell their wares here.

Today, the 300-odd shops in this modern-day bazaar sell sporting goods, leather belts, hats and a wide array of 'designer fashions.' This is also a good area for scoring cheap 100% cotton socks and underwear. While the businesses are not exclusively owned by Orthodox Jews, they still close early on Friday afternoon and remain shuttered on Saturday in observance of the Sabbath. Serious shoppers should try bargaining to save some cash, although you're up against the world's best here, so don't get your hopes up.

There are some unique shopping experiences in this area, especially with regard to food. For all your unleavened-bread needs, check out **Streit's Matzoh Company** *(#221; ☎ 212-475-7000; 150 Rivington St; ◍ F to Delancey St, J, M, Z to Essex St)*.

KIM GRANT

THINGS TO SEE & DO

A bit off the beaten track, but worth the trek is **Essex Pickles** (#229; 25 Essex St; ⓓ F to East Broadway), where you can get sweet and sour pickles directly from the wooden barrels. Further north on Essex St, between Rivington and Delancey Sts, is the **Essex Street Retail Market** (#224; 120 Essex St; ⓓ F to Delancey St, J, M, Z to Essex St), a crowded warehouse of fruit vendors, fishmongers and *botánicas* (purveyors of candles, potions and other Santeria stuff). Take some nibbles at one of the dim-sum or Korean barbecue stalls inside.

Since 1937, **Economy Candy** (#220; ☎ 212-254-1531, 800-352-4544; ⓦ www .economycandy.com; 108 Rivington; ⓓ F to Delancey St, J, M, Z to Essex St), between Ludlow and Essex Sts, has been sating the city's sweet tooth at rock-bottom prices. Head straight here for anything hand-dipped in chocolate, Graham crackers, pretzels, jellies, a variety of Pez dispensers, Mary Janes, candy cigarettes and other classics, dried fruits, nuts, halvah by the pound and more. Head west a bit on Rivington St to **Toys in Babeland** (#218; ☎ 212-375-1701; 94 Rivington St; ⓓ F to Delancey St, J, M, Z to Essex St) for those adult cravings. Here you'll find a good selection of latex, vibrating, flared and leather treats, sold in a welcoming atmosphere.

Tenement Museum (Map 4)

This museum (#226, ☎ 212-431-0233; ⓦ www.tenement.org; 90 Orchard St at Broome St; ⓓ F to Delancey St, J, M, Z to Essex St; adult/senior & child $9/7; visitor center open 11am-5:30pm daily) puts the neighborhood's heartbreaking heritage on full display in several reconstructed tenements. The visitor center shows a video detailing the difficult life endured by the people who once lived in the surrounding buildings, which were more often than not without any running water or electricity. Museum visits are available only as part of scheduled tours (the price of which is included in the admission), so call ahead for the tour schedules.

The museum has recreated three turn-of-the-20th-century tenements, including one

owned by Lucas Glockner, a German-born tailor. This building, in which an estimated 10,000 people lived over 72 years, is accessible only by guided tour. The tours leave at 1pm, 1:30pm, 2pm, 2:30pm, 3pm and 4pm Tuesday through Friday and every half-hour from 11am to 4:30pm on the weekend. Other tenement tours include a visit to the late-19th century home and garment shop of the Levine family from Poland (held 1:20pm to 4pm Tuesday to Friday and 11:15am to 4:45pm Saturday and Sunday) and two immigrant dwellings from the great depressions of 1873 and 1929 (held 1pm to 3:40pm Tuesday to Friday, 11am to 4:30pm Saturday and Saturday).

On weekends, the museum also offers an interactive tour in which kids can dress up in period clothes and touch anything in the restored apartment (dating from around 1916) of a Sephardic Jewish family. This tour costs $8 for adults or $6 for seniors and children, and leaves on the hour between noon and 3pm. From April to December, the staff offer walking tours of the neighborhood (adult $9, senior and child $7). Tours leave at 1pm and 2:30pm on weekends.

Synagogues

Four hundred Orthodox synagogues once thrived here in the early 20th century, but few remain today. The **First Roumanian-American Congregation** (Map 4, #219; ☎ 212-673-2835; 89 Rivington St at Orchard St; ⓓ F to Delancey St, J, M, Z to Essex St) features a wonderfully ornate wooden sanctuary that can hold 1800 of the faithful, but membership has dwindled.

The landmark **Eldridge St Synagogue** (Map 3, #16; ☎ 212-219-0888; 12 Eldridge St; ⓓ F to East Broadway; adult/senior $5/3), between Canal and Division Sts, is another historic place of worship in an area that has been engulfed by Chinatown. This Moorish style synagogue faces one of the oldest surviving tenement blocks in New York City. Guided tours of the synagogue are available at 11:30am and 2:30pm Tuesday and Thursday or on the hour from 11am to 3pm Sunday.

SOHO (MAP 4)

This hip and trendy neighborhood has nothing to do with its London counterpart but instead takes its name from its geographical placement: SOuth of HOuston St. The rectangular area, graced by many cobblestone streets and grand buildings, extends as far south as Canal St and runs west from Broadway to West St.

No-one can satisfactorily explain why the street is pronounced '**how**-ston,' though it's presumed that this is the way a man named William Houstoun, who lived in the area, pronounced his surname. (Somewhere along the line the second 'u' in the spelling of the street was dropped.) No matter really, except out-of-towners are instantly pegged if they make this pronunciation gaffe.

SoHo is filled with block upon block of cast-iron industrial buildings (hence the neighborhood's nickname, Cast-Iron District) that date to the period just after the Civil War, when this was the city's leading commercial district. These multistory buildings housed linen, ribbon and clothing factories, which often featured showcase galleries at street level. But the area fell out of favor as retail businesses relocated uptown and manufacturing concerns moved out of the city. By the 1950s, the huge lofts and cheap rents attracted artists, misfits and other avant-garde types. Their political lobbying not only saved the neighborhood from destruction but assured that a 26-block area was declared a legally protected historic district in 1973. Unfortunately, the pioneers who were responsible for preserving the attractive district were pushed out by sky-high rents when SoHo became gentrified and attained hyper-fashionable status.

While many of the top galleries have hightailed it to Chelsea, today SoHo is a shopping mecca, with designer-clothing stores and shoe boutiques falling over each other for the same clientele. Still,

there are several museums and some good galleries keeping the flame lit (see the boxed text 'SoHo Hum?').

As you walk through fabulous SoHo, stop and look up – many of the buildings still have elaborately decorated flourishes on their upper floors. Some of the preserved structures here include the **Singer Building** *(#206; 561-563 Broadway)*, between Prince and Spring Sts, an attractive iron-and-brick structure that used to be the main warehouse for the famous sewing-machine company.

Above a fabric store and gourmet food shop, you can view what little is left of the marble facade of **St Nicholas Hotel** *(#248; 521-523 Broadway)*, between Spring and Broome Sts. This 1000-room luxury hotel was *the* place to stay when it opened in 1854. The hotel, which closed in 1880, also served as the headquarters of Abraham Lincoln's War Department during the Civil War.

Built in 1857, the **Haughwout Building** *(#246; 488 Broadway at Broome St)* was the first building to put to use the exotic steam elevator developed by Elisha Otis. Known as the 'Parthenon of Cast-Iron Architecture,' the Haughwout (pronounced **how**-out) is considered a rare structure for its two-sided design; look for the iron clock which sits on the Broadway-facing facade.

SoHo is mobbed with tourists shopping and gawking on weekends, when it can be annoyingly crowded. Weekdays are more real, when the traffic flow is dominated by 'gallerinas' and other assorted office and gallery workers. True to the clichés, you'll see a lot of black-on-black fashions worn by all the outrageously beautiful people here (where do they all come from and how did they get so good looking?).

ESBIN ANDERSON PHOTOGRAPHY

Museum for African Art

This museum (#188; ☎ 212-966-1313; W www.africanart.org; 593 Broadway at Houston St; ⬤ F, V, S to Broadway-Lafayette St, N, R to Prince St; adult/senior, student & child $5/2.50; open 10:30am-5:30pm Tues-Fri, noon-6pm Sat & Sun) is one of only two places in the USA dedicated solely to the works of African artists. Its collection concentrates on tribal crafts, musical instruments and depictions of spirituality. The interior was designed by Maya Lin, the young architect who first found fame with her stunning Vietnam Memorial in Washington, DC.

New Museum of Contemporary Art

This museum (#187; ☎ 212-219-1222; W www.newmuseum.org; 583 Broadway; ⬤ F, V, S to Broadway-Lafayette St, N, R to Prince St; adult/artist, senior & student/under 18 yrs $6/3/free; open noon-6pm Tues-Sun, noon-8pm Thur), between Houston and Prince Sts, is at the vanguard of the contemporary SoHo scene. Its mission is to give space to works created in the last decade, meaning you'll probably encounter artists you don't already know. Check out the new Media Z Lounge, with its digital, video and audio installations. There's also a fine bookstore here with an impressive selection of art reference titles and monographs.

New York City Fire Museum

Near Varick St, this museum (#262; ☎ 212-691-1303; W www.nycfiremuseum.org; 278 Spring St; ⬤ 1, 2 to Houston St, C, E to Spring St; suggested admission $3; open 10am-5pm Tues-Sun) occupies a grand old fire house dating to 1904. Inside, you'll find a well-maintained collection of gold horse-drawn fire-fighting carriages, along with modern-day red fire engines. Exhibits explain the development of the New York City fire-fighting system, which began with the 'bucket brigades.' All the colorful heavy equipment and the museum's particularly friendly staff make this a great place to bring children. The tone was somber here after September 11 – not surprising since the New York Fire Department lost 172 of their members in the attacks. Memorials and exhibits relating to that day may still be on display when you arrive.

SoHo Hum?

In 1996, art dealer Mary Boone, who launched the careers of Julian Schnabel, David Salle and Jean-Michel Basquiat, shocked the cultural elite by moving her powerhouse gallery from SoHo to 745 Fifth Ave. Boone, a pioneer in mixing art and commerce in the 1980s, claimed that the 'energy and focus of art has shifted uptown.' Skeptics blamed her move on her distaste for the cafés and shops that sprung up in SoHo, attracting crowds of tourists interested in looking at – but not buying – expensive art.

Boone immediately set a trend that's been followed by Paula Cooper, Jay Gorney and Matthew Marks, who moved their galleries north to Chelsea. But even if some of the contemporary heavyweights have moved on, a number of galleries still populate the streets of SoHo. These include the **Ward-Nasse Gallery** (Map 4, #197; ☎ 212-925-6951; 178 Prince St at Thompson St) which specializes in yet-to-be-discovered artists, the **Howard Greenberg Gallery** (Map 4, #201; ☎ 212-334-0010; 120 Wooster St at Prince St) and the adjacent **292 Gallery** (☎ 212-331-0010; 120 Wooster St at Prince St), both showing top-notch photography, and **The Drawing Center** (Map 4, #254; ☎ 212-219-2166; 35 Wooster St), between Broome and Grand Sts, a space dedicated entirely to the fine art of drawing.

For information on current exhibitions, pick up the free monthly NY/SoHo map in one of the Downtown galleries or scan the 'Goings on about Town' section in the New Yorker or the entertainment section of the Sunday New York Times. On the Internet, go to W www.artseensoho.com, which is useful for general gallery information.

Greenwich Village Rock Landmarks

Greenwich Village is a magical history tour as far as rock 'n' roll landmarks go and fans should pound the pavement to visit the haunts and houses of some of the genre's greatest.

In addition to checking out **Cafe Wha?** *(Map 4, #144; cnr MacDougal St & Minetta Lane)*, head over to 161 W 4th St, where Bob Dylan once lived and found inspiration for the song 'Positively 4th St.' He often performed (and reputedly smoked his first joint) at Gerdes Folk City, which originally stood at 11 W 4th St. Jimi Hendrix lived and recorded at the **Electric Lady Studios** *(Map 4, #79; 52 W 8th St at Sixth Ave)* and the studio is still laying down the tracks. Head a bit further east on 8th St to 96-98 St Mark's Pl between First Ave and Ave A to see the unmistakable facade featured on Led Zeppelin's monumental double album *Physical Graffiti*.

N.Y.C.

GREENWICH VILLAGE (MAP 4)

Roughly bordered by 14th St in the north and Houston St in the south, 'the Village' runs from Lafayette St all the way west to the Hudson River. Once a symbol for all things artistic, outlandish and Bohemian, this storied and popular neighborhood can look downright somnolent these days. But the student culture at New York University (NYU), which owns most of the village, especially around Washington Square Park, keeps things spicy and offbeat. In the area south of Washington Square Park (including Bleecker St, all the way west to Seventh Ave), you'll find an eclectic and crowded collection of cafés, shops and restaurants; beyond Seventh Ave is the West Village, a leafy, upscale neighborhood of winding streets and townhouses.

The Village's reputation as a creative enclave can be traced back to at least the early 1900s, when artists and writers moved in, and by the '40s the neighborhood became known as a gathering place for gays. In the '50s, the Village's coffee houses, bars and jazz clubs attracted scores of Bohemians, including the Beat poets, who adopted the neighborhood as their East Coast headquarters and listened to bebop and poetry throughout the Village. The area became an important incubator of American literature. Poet Allen Ginsberg lived here most of his life, and novelist Norman Mailer helped to found the influential *Village Voice* newspaper.

In the '60s, the neighborhood's rebellious spirit led to the birth of today's gay rights movement (see the boxed text 'Gay & Lesbian New York' in the Facts about New York City chapter). Today, many still think of Christopher St as the center of queer culture in New York. Crowds of gay men and lesbians continue to make pilgrimages to the Village in June for the annual Lesbian and Gay Pride Parade (see Public Holidays & Special Events in the Facts for the Visitor chapter).

George Segal's statues at Stonewall Place feel a little washed out.

THINGS TO SEE & DO

KIM GRANT

Greenwich Village Walking Tour

Plenty of companies offer guided walking tours of this neighbourhood – some focus on certain aspects of history, others provide a general overview – but they all come at a price. Here's one you can do free that should take about 90 minutes. Take the liberty of getting lost, as this is a wonderful area to let your feet and mind wander. To start the tour, take any of the following trains: Ⓜ A, C, E, F, V, S to W 4th St; Ⓜ N, R to 8th St–NYU; or the Ⓜ 6 to Astor Pl.

The best place to start any tour of the Village is the arch at **Washington Square Park** *(Fifth Ave at Washington Sq North)* – see the main entry, later in this chapter. On the eastern edge of the park, you can visit the site of the **Triangle Shirtwaist Fire** *(29 Washington Pl at Green St)*.

Heading south across the park brings you to **Judson Memorial Church** *(**W** www.judson.org; services 11am Sun)*, which graces the park's southern border. This yellow-brick Baptist church honors Adoniram Judson, an American missionary who served in Burma (Myanmar) in the early 19th century. The church continues to uphold a strong commitment to worldwide social causes. Designed by Stanford White, this National Historic Site features stained-glass windows by muralist John La Farge, who was born near the park, and a marble frontage by Augustus Saint-Gaudens. The adjoining tower, with its glorious park views, used to be NYU's finest residential dormitory. It was converted to offices several years ago.

As you exit the park, walk down Thompson St, past a series of chess shops where Village denizens meet to play the game for $2 an hour. At the intersection of Thompson and Bleecker Sts (Bleecker is Greenwich Village's main east-west thoroughfare), look up at the southwest corner to see the old sign for the legendary jazz club, the Village Gate, which relocated to Midtown some years back.

Turn right on Bleecker St and head west for two blocks, which will bring you to one of the old coffeehouses associated with New York's 1950s' beatnik culture: **Le Figaro** *(184 Bleecker St)*, which still features a weekend jazz brunch. You're better off just taking a look around Bleecker St and then turning right on MacDougal St, where you'll find a great cup of cappuccino at **Caffe Reggio** *(119 MacDougal St)*, which retains some old-world character thanks to its dark walls and massive trademark espresso machine. This is a veritable caffeinated ghetto, and you needn't take any advice: find one that looks to your liking and settle in.

Top & Bottom: Cafe culture in the Village

KIM GRANT

Double back half a block on MacDougal St to the corner of Minetta Lane, where you'll find **Minetta Tavern**, an old Village hang-out. This decent Italian restaurant is a great place to linger over a glass of wine. On the opposite side of Minetta Lane, you'll see **Cafe Wha?**, a legendary old club where Dylan and Hendrix once played. Its 'in' days are long past.

Walk down Minetta Lane and turn left onto Minetta St. You'll pass a block of 18th-century slums; like most of New York's debauched areas of yore, these have been transformed into what are now very desirable properties. The old Minetta Brook still runs under some of the ivy-covered row houses.

Cross Sixth Ave, bear right and walk up Bleecker St, past a three-block stretch full of record stores, leather shops, restaurants and great Italian pastry shops. This area has blossomed into a mini shopping district in recent years and is worth a browse.

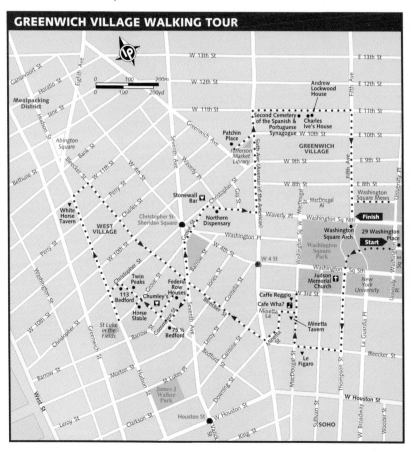

GREENWICH VILLAGE WALKING TOUR

Turn left onto Seventh Ave, walk half a block and make a quick right onto quiet Commerce St, then proceed one block to Bedford St. In these West Village alleys are some historic gems that conjure lottery-winning fantasies. At the corner of Commerce and Bedford Sts, you'll be standing just a few yards from **75½ Bedford St**, a quirky 9.5ft-wide house where poet Edna St Vincent Millay lived from 1923 to 1924. She penned the Pulitzer Prize–winning *Ballad of the Harp Weaver* here. (Incidentally, Cary Grant, John Barrymore and Margaret Mead also lived here at different times.) Next door, at 77 Bedford St, stands what is possibly the oldest house in the Village, a red-brick residence that was built in 1799.

Turn around and continue up Bedford St past Commerce St again. A short block beyond Commerce St, you might want to detour for a moment up Barrow St to check out the ivy-covered **Federal row houses** *(49 & 51 Barrow St)*, and then have a look at the block of six perfectly preserved, handsome red-brick residences on the west side of the street.

Head back to Bedford St; just beyond the corner of Bedford and Barrow Sts, you'll come to a spare wooden door – this is **Chumley's** *(86 Bedford St)*, a former speakeasy run by Lee Chumley, a socialist who poured tipples for many thirsty writers in the late 1920s. The bar's address is said to have inspired the slang phrase '86 it' – a shorthand imperative to get rid of something. Presumably this expression was whispered to patrons drinking alcohol just before a prohibition-era police raid began. Check out the side exit on Barrow St, which allowed a quick escape during raids.

A wonderful old horse stable from 1894 survives at 95 Bedford St, just past Chumley's. Before continuing further on Bedford, take a look down **Grove St** – a curved stretch of row houses that's been featured in several movies, including Woody Allen's *Annie Hall*. Back on Bedford St, note the early-19th-century home called **Twin Peaks** *(102 Bedford St)*; it got its name from the dual mock-Tudor tops that were added in the 1920s. The 1843 **Greek Revival residence** *(113 Bedford St)* used to belong to a local saloon keeper. Other buildings in this neighborhood sport detailed plaques noting who built them. Bedford St ends at Christopher St, the traditional center of New York gay life.

Turn left on Christopher St and walk one block to Hudson St. At this stage, you might want to turn left and take a small detour down Hudson St to check out the gardens at **St Luke in the Fields**, an Episcopal church and school. On weekends, the church holds rummage sales in the garden. Or you can take a break entirely by turning right on Hudson St and heading four blocks north to the storied **White Horse Tavern** *(☎ 212-989-3956; W 11th St)*, where you can enjoy a drink and a burger.

RICHARD I'ANSON

Left: Sullivan Street facade, the Village

Turn right on W 11th St and walk one block to Bleecker St, where you turn right again and proceed several blocks, past uninspiring shops of little note, to the corner of Bleecker and Seventh Ave; turn left here.

Head north one block on Seventh Ave to Grove St, where a right turn takes you to **Stonewall Place**, site of the 1969 gay rebellion (see the boxed text 'Gay & Lesbian New York' in the Facts about New York City chapter). The lifelike statue in the center is entitled *Gay Liberation* and has been cruised by many a drunk fella since its installation in 1992. The **Stonewall Bar** lies on the north side of Christopher St.

From Grove St, turn right on Waverly Pl and look for the oddly shaped **Northern Dispensary** *(165 Waverly Pl)*. The three-sided dispensary marks New York's strangest intersection: the corner of Waverly Pl and Waverly Pl! Built in 1831 to combat a cholera epidemic, the dispensary was New York's oldest public health facility until 1989, when it closed. This prime spot has often been pegged for redevelopment, but nothing has happened yet. Nearby Gay St was named long before the queer community took hold and was historically a black enclave.

Continue to Sixth Ave and turn left. Walk two blocks to the red-brick **Jefferson Market Library**. Built in 1876, this was the Women's Court (where nefarious ladies were tried and held) until 1932. The library's gardens are sometimes open to the public on weekends. Just behind the library is **Patchin Place** *(W 10th St)*, an enclosed courtyard with a block of flats where many luminaries once lived, including poet ee cummings (Edward Estlin Cummings), actor Marlon Brando, Theodore Dreiser and writer Djuana Barnes.

Double back to Sixth Ave, walk a block to W 11th St and head east. On the right, you'll find the tiny **Second Cemetery of the Spanish & Portuguese Synagogue**, which was used from 1805 to 1829. Continue along W 11th St and you'll pass by a series of traditional row houses, including builder **Andrew Lockwood's House** *(60 W 11th St)*, constructed in 1842 on a lot that was originally part of the larger Wouter Van Twiller farm in the Dutch colonial era. Next door was the home of composer **Charles Ives** *(70 W 11th St)*.

Turn right on Fifth Ave, and you'll be heading directly back toward the arch in Washington Square Park. Before you reach the end of Fifth Ave, wander up **Washington Square Mews**, a quiet, cobblestone street with old stables that now house NYU facilities. The gates are locked between 11pm and 7am daily.

Right: Jefferson Market Library

KIM GRANT

Washington Square Park

This park (⬤ *A, C, E, F, V, S to W 4th St, N, R to 8th St-NYU, 6 to Astor Pl*), like many public spaces in the city, began as a potter's field – a burial ground for the penniless. It also served as the site of public executions, meaning ne'er-do-wells were dead and buried in one fell swoop. The magnificent old tree near the northwestern corner of the park bears a plaque memorializing it as the 'Hangman's Elm,' though no-one is sure if it was actually used for executions. Note that the streets bounding the park are called Washington Square North, Washington Square South etc.

Though a welcoming and historically important oasis, Washington Square Park suffers from the usual urban ills: drug dealing, vandalism, rat infestation and panhandlers. Neighborhood activists have been trying to drum up support for a conservancy and $7 million restoration but as yet to no avail.

Dominating the tableau is the **Stanford White Arch** *(#81)*, colloquially known as Washington Square Arch, originally designed in wood to celebrate the centennial of George Washington's inauguration in 1889. The arch proved so popular that it was replaced in stone six years later and adorned with statues of the general in war and peace (the latter work is by A Stirling Calder, the father of artist Alexander Calder). Although string quartets played atop the arch as recently as 1991, the entire structure has been off limits since that year because of the danger of collapse.

In 1916, artist Marcel Duchamp climbed to the top of the arch by its internal stairway and declared the park the 'Free and Independent Republic of Washington Square.' These days, the anarchy takes place on the ground level, as comedians and buskers use the park's permanently dry fountain as a performance space. Every May 1, the **Marijuana March** takes over the park (see Public Holidays & Special Events in the Facts for the Visitor chapter).

Judson Memorial Church *(#141)* graces the park's south border. For more information on the church, see the Greenwich Village Walking Tour.

Judson Memorial Church

At 245 Greene St, on the park's eastern border, sits the building where the Triangle Shirtwaist Fire broke out on March 25, 1911. This sweatshop had locked its doors to prevent the young seamstresses from taking unauthorized breaks. The inferno killed 146 young women, many of whom jumped to their deaths from the upper floors (the fire department's ladders only extended to the 6th floor of the 10-floor building). Every year on March 25, the New York Fire Department holds a solemn ceremony in memory of the city's most deadly factory fire. Near here is **Grey Art Gallery** *(#82; ☎ 212-998-6780, 100 Washington Sq East; suggested admission $2.50; open 11am-6pm Tues, Thur & Fri)*, showing a wide spectrum of works, from classic watercolors to Cuban photographic retrospectives.

The row of townhouses at Washington Square North inspired *Washington Square*, Henry James' novel about late-19th-century social mores. James did not live here, as is popularly assumed, but he was born on the northeast corner of Washington Pl and Greene St in 1843.

Astor Place

This square (*E 8th St;* ⬤ *N, R to 8th St-NYU, 6 to Astor Pl*), between Third and Fourth Aves, is named after the Astor family, who built an early New York fortune on beaver trading and lived on **Colonnade Row** *(#86; 429-434 Lafayette St)*, just south of the

THINGS TO SEE & DO

ANGUS OBORN

square. Four of the original nine marble-faced Greek Revival residences on Lafayette St still exist, but have seen better days. Across the street, in the public library built by John Jacob Astor, stands the **Joseph Papp Public Theater** *(#89; 425 Lafayette St)*. When it went up in 1848, this building cost $500,000, a phenomenal sum then. The Public is now one of the city's most important cultural centers and presents the famous Shakespeare in the Park every summer (for more details, see Theater in the Entertainment chapter); also here is **Joe's Pub** *(#88; 435 Lafayette St)*, between Astor Place and E 4th St, a good place for a cocktail and cabaret.

Astor Place itself is dominated by the large brownstone **Cooper Union** *(#90)*, the public college founded by glue millionaire Peter Cooper in 1859. Just after its completion, Abraham Lincoln gave his 'Right Makes Might' speech in the Union's Great Hall condemning slavery. The fringed lectern he used still exists, but the auditorium is only open to the public for special events.

Right across the square, you'll see a symbol of the change happening in this now-gentrified neighborhood – the city's first Kmart, which opened in 1996. The following year, Irish rock band U2 kicked off its Rock Mart tour here and, despite initial protests from the neighborhood, the megastore seems to have won over lazy residents who enjoy the its convenience.

The cube sculpture entitled *Alamo*, in the middle of the square, is a popular spot for skate punks, anarchists and the occasional guerrilla art act. Get a group together and give it a whirl; with some powerful backs and legs you can set it spinning. The uptown subway entrance here is an exact replica of one of the first subway kiosks in the early 20th century.

Grace Church

This Gothic Revival Episcopal church *(#48; E 10th St; ⓜ N, R to 8th St-NYU, 6 to Astor Pl)*, two blocks north of Astor Pl, was made of marble quarried by prisoners at Sing Sing, the state penitentiary in the town of Ossining 30 miles up the Hudson River (which, legend

has it, is the origin of the expression 'being sent upriver'). After years of neglect, Grace Church has recently been cleaned up, and its floodlit white marble is an elegant night-time sight. The Broadway and 4th Ave views are completely different and it's worth checking it out from both vantage points.

James Renwick Jr designed the church, and many also credit him with creating **Renwick Triangle** *(#43; 112-128 E 10th St; ⓜ N, R to 8th St-NYU, 6 to Astor Pl)*, a stately cluster of brownstone Italianate houses one block to the east. This is one of New York's most pleasant residential pockets, especially considering its hectic East Village location. This same designer is responsible for the **Renwick Apartments** *(808 Broadway)* just north of Grace Church, which figured prominently in Claeb Carr's *The Alienist*.

Forbes Galleries

These galleries *(#16; ☎ 212-206-5549; 62 Fifth Ave at 12th St; ⓜ L, N, Q, R, W, 4, 5, 6 to Union Sq, F, V to 14th St; admission free; open 10am-4pm Tues-Sat)* house curios from the personal collection of the late publishing magnate Malcolm Forbes. The eclectic mix of objects on display include Fabergé eggs, models of ships, autographs and tin soldiers. Walking through here, you get the sense that the wily Forbes probably opened these public galleries as a way of giving his impulse purchases a tax-deductible status.

Merchant's House Museum

Little remains of the neighborhood that existed here before the tenement boom, but this museum *(#134; ☎ 212-777-1089; 29 E 4th St; ⓜ 6 to Bleecker St; adult/senior & student $5/3; open 1pm-5pm Thur-Mon)*, between Lafayette St and the Bowery, is a remarkably well-preserved example of how the business class lived. The house, dating from 1831, once belonged to drug importer Seabury Tredwell. His youngest daughter Gertrude lived here until her death in 1933, so its original furnishings were intact when it began life as a museum three years later. Period clothing and the fully equipped kitchen add to the historical allure.

EAST VILLAGE (MAP 4)

It's hard to encapsulate life in the East Village, a neighborhood that has swung wildly between hip and horrific, cutting-edge and cookie cutter (the Gap on St Marks Pl was almost too much to stomach; thankfully, it shut down recently, though it will surely reappear). Loose boundaries for the East Village (called the EV or sometimes the EVil) are from E 14th St south to E Houston St and from the East River west to Third Ave; some people consider Lafayette St or the Bowery as the dividing lines.

While the East Village takes its name from Greenwich Village, the two neighborhoods don't have much in common historically. Large farmland estates once stretched over this area, but as New York became more industrial and extended northward from Lower Manhattan in the late-19th century, urban development devoured the acreage. By the early 20th century, this region was considered the northern section of the Lower East Side, a poorer cousin to Greenwich Village. But it has come fully into its own over the last decade. The East Village is now completely gentrified, and the trend continues creeping east, to the once dangerous **Alphabet City**, which includes Aves A, B, C and D.

Good exploration grounds in the East Village include First and Second Aves between 14th and Houston Sts and St Mark's Pl from Third Ave to Tompkins Square Park. Among the vintage clothing stores, used-record shops, herbal apothecaries and gin joints, you can find virtually every type of cuisine here, including Italian, Polish, vegetarian, Indian, Lebanese, Japanese and Thai.

St Mark's-in-the-Bowery

This Episcopal church (*#39; ☎ 212-674-6377; 131 E 10th St at Second Ave; Ⓜ 6 to Astor Pl, L to Third Ave; open 10am-6pm Mon-Fri*) stands on the site of the farm, or *bouwerie*, owned by Dutch Governor Peter Stuyvesant, whose crypt lies under the grounds. The 1799 church, damaged by fire in 1978, has been restored. You can enjoy an interior view of its abstract stained-glass windows when the church is open to the public. This is also a cultural center, hosting poetry readings by the **Poetry Project** (*☎ 212-674-0910*) and dance performances by **Danspace** (*☎ 212-674-8194*).

The East Village – it may be gentrified, but it's still genuine

10th Street Baths

The waning of Eastern European traditions on the Lower East Side led to the closure of many old bathhouses in Manhattan, and the AIDS crisis ensured that most of these popular gay romping spots were shuttered as well. But the historic old Russian and Turkish steam baths (#34; ☎ 212-674-9250; ⓦ www.russianturkishbaths.com; 268 E 10th St; ⓜ L to First Ave, 6 to Astor Pl; daily/10 visits $22/150; open 11am-10pm Mon, Tues, Thur & Fri, 9am-10pm Wed, 7:30am-10pm Sat & Sun), between First Ave and Ave A, still remain. Since 1892, this spa for the lumpen proletariat has offered steam baths, an ice-cold plunge pool, sauna and sun deck. All-day access includes the use of lockers, locks, robes, towels and slippers. Extras such as Dead Sea salt scrubs ($30) and black-mud treatments ($38) are also available.

The baths are open to both men and women except between 9am and 2pm Wednesday (women only) and between 7:30am and 2pm Saturday (men only).

Tompkins Square Park

Long gone are this park's (ⓜ L to First Ave, 6 to Astor Pl) glory days, when the bandshell on the southern edge hosted impromptu concerts, protests and performances, and where genuine hardcore punks and anarchists gathered (as opposed to the suburban panhandlers of today who have little to protest but mom and dad's niggly rules). The turning point for this park was sparked by the razing of the bandshell and eviction of the squatters living in the 'tent city' within the park in 1991. That protest turned violent and the Tompkins Square Riot, as it came to be known, ushered in the new era of yuppies in the dog run, fashionistas lolling in the grass and undercover narcotics agents trying to pass as hippies or home boys and bust the same.

But enough with the nostalgia. Today, 16-acre Tompkins Square Park is still a good spot for a game of hoops, a chess challenge at one of the concrete tables or a guitar jam on a sunny day. Come here to mingle and play with a good cross section of locals.

East of Tompkins Square Park is **Alphabet City**, which technically includes all the avenues with letter designations. Traditionally a Puerto Rican barrio, young gringos and trendy international types started colonizing the area in the 1990s. Walk around and you'll find stretches of vintage-clothes shops and French bistros among the murals, graffiti and bodegas. The area is also dotted with **Green Thumb Gardens**, interesting urban artifacts, where small gardens (some with on-site shanties) serve as social clubs for neighborhood men. There are several on 8th St between Aves B and D. Walking around, you'll come across public sculpture gardens like Ken Kelaba's on 3rd St between Aves A and B.

The area east of Ave C can be dicey after dark.

CHELSEA (MAP 5)

North of Greenwich Village, Chelsea extends from 14th St north to 26th St and west from Broadway to the Hudson River. During the city's Gilded Age in the late-19th century, this was the dry goods and retail center, drawing well-heeled shoppers to its varied emporia. Closer to the Hudson River, you can still find plenty of old warehouses and many of the townhouses (especially those in the historic district) are beautifully restored. At the heart of the neighborhood, on Eighth Ave, there are scads of cafés, shops, gyms and restaurants, many flying the rainbow colors as a welcome beacon to its largely gay clientele. Further west, around 10th and 11th Aves, the Chelsea gallery scene has exploded, stealing much of SoHo's thunder (see the boxed text 'Chelsea Gallery Crawl' later in this chapter).

The **Chelsea Historic District** (ⓜ C, E to 23rd St), from W 20th to W 22nd Sts, between Eighth and Tenth Aves, is an urban gem. Leafy streets, refurbished Greek-Revival and Italianate townhouses and set-back buildings help create a spacious, welcoming atmosphere – something of an anachronism in crowded, chaotic New York City. The **General Theological Seminary** (#149; 175 Ninth Ave; ⓜ C, E to 23rd St; open noon-3pm Mon-Fri, 11am-3pm Sat), from 20th to 21st Sts, is a campus-cum-garden open to the public (both pious and not so!); access it through the Ninth Ave entrance.

The prime sight on noisy 23rd St is the **Chelsea Hotel** (#153; Ⓜ 1, 2, C, F to 23rd St), a red-brick hotel with ornate iron balconies and no fewer than seven plaques declaring its literary landmark status. Even before Sid murdered Nancy here, the hotel was famous as a hang-out for the likes of Mark Twain, Thomas Wolfe, Dylan Thomas and Arthur Miller. Jack Kerouac allegedly crafted *On the Road* during one marathon session at the Chelsea. Musicians have long favored the Chelsea, and it counts Leonard Cohen and Bob Dylan among its former guests. This is also where the fabulous Jean Reno and then little-known Natalie Portman got busy in *The Professional*.

A block east is the nonprofit **Cuban Art Space** (#158; ☎ 212-242-0559; Ⓦ www.cuban artspace.net; 124 W 23rd St; Ⓜ F, V, 1, 2 to 23rd St; donations welcome; open 11am-7pm

Tues-Sat), which boasts the largest collection of Cuban art outside the island (collectors should inquire about holdings on the 3rd floor). Openings are exciting affairs, often with live music, delicious nosh and the artists in the house. Admission is always free, but donations are gratefully accepted.

Chelsea Piers (#140; ☎ 212-336-6000; Ⓦ www.chelseapiers.com; Hudson River at end of 23rd St; Ⓜ 1, 2, C, E to 23rd St) cater to sporting types of all stripes – you can set out to hit a bucket of golf balls at the four-level driving range, ice skate in the complex's indoor rink or rent in-line skates to cruise along the Hudson River waterfront down to the Battery. There's a bowling alley, Hoop City for basketball, a sailing school for kids, batting cages, the works. Kayaks are let out free at the Downtown Boathouse just north of Pier 64. Though the Piers are somewhat cut off by the busy West Side Hwy, the wide array of attractions here brings in the crowds.

Chelsea Gallery Crawl

Sorry SoHo, Chelsea is New York's new gallery ghetto and has enough fabulous people with fashionable dogs to prove it. There are so many warehouses, store fronts and art spaces in the stretch between 20th and 27th Sts and Ninth and Eleventh Aves, you could spend a couple of afternoons here and not exhaust the fine, weird, derivative, accomplished and cutting-edge art on offer. Galleries are generally open 10am to 6pm Tuesday to Sunday and all but the nonprofit Dia Center for the Arts are free. The following are only a small selection of what's happening over here.

The block of 22nd St between Tenth and Eleventh Sts is wall-to-wall art. **Max Protetch** *(Map 5, #147;* ☎ *212-633-6999; 511 W 22nd St)* puts up innovative and intriguing shows in a small but well-designed space, and next door **303 Gallery** *(Map 5, #143;* ☎ *212-255-1121; 525 W 22nd St)* is also worth checking out. Across the street, the **Brent Sikkema Gallery** *(Map 5, #146;* ☎ *212-929-2262; 530 W 22nd St)* has shows to stir your intellect and the nearby **Yancey Richardson Gallery** *(Map 5, #141;* ☎ *212-343-1255, 3rd fl, 535 W 22nd St)* has long been a major player in the fine-photography field.

Dia Center for the Arts *(Map 5, #144;* ☎ *212-989-5566;* Ⓦ *www.diacenter.org; 548 W 22nd St; adults/seniors & students $6/3)* is a sprawling three-floor affair showing new works and hosting readings, screenings and lectures. This nonprofit center was one of the Chelsea trailblazers and also houses a terrific bookstore and a chill café.

One of the heavy hitters that colonized Chelsea early was the **Paula Cooper Gallery** *(Map 5, #142;* ☎ *212-255-1105; 521 W 21st St)*, between Tenth and Eleventh Aves, which represented the big art names, including one of my all-time favorites, Jonathan Borofsky. If you don't like what's up there, try the equally venerable **Miller Gallery** *(Map 5, #137;* ☎ *212-366-4774; 524 W 26th St)*, between Tenth and Eleventh Aves. If the weather isn't cooperating and you're itching for art, check out **Art 210** *(Map 5, #138; 210 Eleventh Ave)*, between 24th and 25th Sts, which has a dozen galleries in one building.

To get to this part of Chelsea, take Ⓜ C, E, 1 or 2 to 23rd St or the L to Eighth Ave and walk west.

UNION SQUARE (MAP 5)

This square *(cnr 14th St & Broadway;* ... **L, N, Q, R, W, 4, 5, 6 to 14th St-Union Sq)** originally served as one of New York City's first Uptown business districts, and throughout the mid-19th century it offered a convenient site for many workers' rallies and political protests. In fact its name has more prosaic origins: this was simply the 'union' of the old Bowery and Bloomingdale (now Broadway) roads. By the 1960s, this area was overrun by junkies and gigolos. But the '90s heralded a big revival, helped along by the arrival of the **Greenmarket Farmers' Market** *(open 8am-4pm Mon, Wed, Fri & Sat year-round)* held in the square. Today, Union Square, which underwent restoration work in 2002, hops with activity; its plethora of bars, and restaurants and the new Virgin Megastore make it a popular place to hang out night or day.

FLATIRON DISTRICT (MAP 5)

This neighborhood (Ⓜ *N, R, 6 to 23rd St)* takes its name from the **Flatiron Building** *(#163; intersection Broadway, Fifth Ave & 23rd St).* Built in 1902, the Flatiron Building (famously featured in a haunting 1905 photograph by Edward Steichen and best viewed from the island on 23rd St between Broadway and Fifth Ave) dominated this plaza when the district contained the city's prime stretch of retail and entertainment establishments. The Flatiron ranked as the world's tallest building until 1909, when it was overtaken by the nearby **Metropolitan Life Tower** *(#129; 24th St at Madison Ave),* which includes an impressive clock tower and golden top, illuminated in soothing hues at night.

Just above the Flatiron Building is **Madison Square Park**, which defined the northern reaches of Manhattan until the city's population exploded just after the Civil War. Madison Ave at 26th St was the site of the first and second **Madison Square Garden** arenas (1879 and 1890, respectively). The second, designed by Stanford White, was awe-inspiring: Moorish in design with several turrets and a tower, it held 8000 and was crowned by a gilded *Diana.* It was

The sun sets over the Flatiron Building

ANGUS OBORN

razed in 1925, a year after it hosted the Democratic National Convention.

The area of Fifth Ave just south of Madison Square used to be known as **Ladies' Mile**, back when stores such as B Altman's and Lord & Taylor catered to shoppers in the late 19th century. Macy's first store was also here. Present-day zoning laws have welcomed retail stores back to nearby Sixth Ave between 14th and 23rd Sts, and today you'll find the usual suspects, including Staples, Old Navy and Barnes & Noble.

For a 10-block radius, the Flatiron District, loaded with loft buildings and boutiques, does a good imitation of SoHo without the European pretensions, prices or crowds. There are some fine restaurants and a dance club or three hiding out up here, too.

GRAMERCY PARK (MAP 5)

This park (Ⓜ 6 to 23rd St) is one of New York's loveliest spaces, the kind of public garden area found in Paris and other European cities. While the botanical sentiment translated across the Atlantic, the socialist sense did not: when developers transformed the surrounding marsh into a city neighborhood in 1830, admission to the park was restricted to residents, and you still need a key to get in today. What's up with that?!

Gramercy Park is long on exclusivity – two other institutions with interesting architecture but restricted access are located here. **National Arts Club** (#169; ☎ 212-475-3424; 15 Gramercy Park South) boasts a beautiful, vaulted, stained-glass ceiling above its wooden bar. Calvert Vaux, who was one of the creators of Central Park, designed the building. The club holds art exhibitions (ranging from sculpture to photography) that are sometimes open to the public from 1pm to 5pm.

Players Club (#170; 16 Gramercy Park South; Ⓜ 6 to 23rd St) is an actors' hang-out created in 1888 by Shakespearean actor Edwin Booth (brother of Lincoln assassin John Wilkes Booth) and designed by Stanford White. It's closed to the public.

Fortunately, you *can* get inside **Pete's Tavern** and the **Old Town Bar and Grill**, two popular places riddled with history (see Bars & Lounges in the Entertainment chapter for more details).

Theodore Roosevelt's Birthplace

This National Historic Site (#165; ☎ 212-260-1616; Ⓦ www.nps.gov/thrb; 28 E 20th St; Ⓜ N, R, 6 to 23rd St; adult/child $3/free; open 9am-5pm daily), between Park Ave and Broadway, is a bit of a cheat, since the house where the 26th president was born was demolished in his lifetime. This building is simply a re-creation by his relatives, who joined it with another family residence next door. If you're interested in Roosevelt's extraordinary life, which has been somewhat overshadowed by the enduring legacy of his younger cousin Franklin, visit here, especially if you don't have the time to see his summer home in Long Island's Oyster Bay (see the Excursions chapter, later in this book). Included in the admission price are house tours, offered on the hour from 10am to 4pm.

MIDTOWN (MAP 5)

Home to many of the city's most popular attractions, you'll probably wind up spending plenty of time in New York's teeming Midtown area, which is a mixed blessing. It can be cold in both temperature (little sunlight reaches the shadowy streets below the skyscrapers) and temperament (most people are attending to the business of work rather than life) and is overwhelmingly crowded on weekdays. Very few people live in the center of Manhattan, with most apartment houses located east of Third Ave and west

Midtown's spectacular skyline

JEFF GREENBERG

THINGS TO SEE & DO

of Eighth Ave. Midtown isn't dangerous per se, but watch out for aggressive panhandlers and be savvy of your surroundings, belongings and orientation.

Hell's Kitchen

For years, the far west side of Midtown was a working-class district of tenements and food warehouses known as Hell's Kitchen, a neighborhood that predominantly attracted Italian and Irish immigrants, who drifted into gangs after arriving. *West Side Story* was set here. Hollywood films have often romanticized the district's gritty, criminal character, but by the 1960s, the population of junkies and prostitutes had made it a forbidding place that few cared to enter, including many movie directors.

In 1989, the construction of the **World Wide Plaza building** *(cnr W 50th St & Eighth Ave;* Ⓜ *C, E to 50th St)* was supposed to juice the area's revival. (The complex took over the site of the 1930s-era Madison Square Garden, which had been a parking lot in the interim.) Yet until the mid-1990s, Hell's Kitchen was largely unchanged. Eighth and Ninth Aves between 35th and 50th Sts was still the domain of wholesale food stores (not exactly big tourist attractions), and few buildings rose more than eight stories above the street.

But the economic boom of the late '90s seriously changed Hell's Kitchen and developers reverted to calling it Clinton, a name originating from the 1950s; locals are split on usage. A perfect link between the Upper West Side and Chelsea, the neighborhood exploded with nightspots and restaurants, as chefs eyed the large quantities of fresh food from nearby wholesalers and the large-ish spaces at cheap(er) rents. Moreover, many tourists began to filter into the neighborhood after glimpsing it on David Letterman's *Late Show*, taped at the **Ed Sullivan Theater** *(Map 6, #16; Broadway)* between 53rd and 54th Sts. Culturally, there's not much here but it's a great place to grab a meal away from the congested streets around Rockefeller Center or to start your day with a hearty plate of pancakes at a typical New York City diner.

Intrepid Sea-Air-Space Museum

At the western edge of Midtown, the Intrepid Sea-Air-Space Museum *(☎ 212-245-0072;* Ⓦ *www.intrepidmuseum.org; W 46th St;* Ⓜ *A, C, E to 42nd St; adult $13, senior, veteran & student $9, child under 12 $6; open 10am-5pm Tues-Sun)* sits on an aircraft carrier at Pier 86. The flight deck of the USS *Intrepid*, which served in WWII and Vietnam, features several fighter planes, and the pier area contains the Growler guided-missile submarine, an Apollo space capsule, Vietnam-era tanks and the 900ft destroyer *Edson*. The *Intrepid* is the nexus for the **Fleet Week** celebrations each May, when thousands of the world's sailors descend on Manhattan (for more details, see Public Holidays & Special Events in the Facts for the Visitor chapter). Free audio tours in French, German, Japanese, Russian and Spanish are available.

You can use your CityPass here; for more details on this pass, see the boxed text 'Museum Bargains,' later in this chapter.

Herald Square

This crowded convergence of Broadway, Sixth Ave and 34th St *(*Ⓜ *B, D, F, N, Q, R, V, W to 34th St-Herald Sq)* is best known as the home of **Macy's** *(#100)*, which for years (inaccurately) claimed to be the world's largest department store. The busy square doesn't offer much in the way of landmarks. Two indoor malls south of Macy's on Sixth Ave contain a boring array of shops.

Garment District

This district *(*Ⓜ *B, D, F, N, Q, R, V, W to 34th St-Herald Sq)*, where many New York fashion firms have their design offices, stands to the west of Herald Square, on Seventh Ave (known as 'Fashion Ave') from 34th St to Times Square. On weekdays, the side streets are packed with delivery trucks. Broadway between 23rd St and Herald Square is called the Accessories District because of the many ribbon and button shops that serve the city's fashion industry. These are trippy places with thousands of snaps, cinches and closures displayed among feathers, lace, sequins, rhinestones and hand-carved, painted and woven buttons.

Museum Bargains

New York can be damn expensive; if you're on the island of Manahattan reading this, you're already aware of the city's budget-busting ways. If you're feeling the pressure to maximize your fun while minimizing the impact on your wallet, take advantage of free nights (also called 'pay what you wish') at many museums around town. Remember also, that many museums have 'suggested' or 'requested' donation policies, which means you're not beholden to their suggestions or requests – offer a nickel and you're in. There are also several stellar free museums around town, including the **Hispanic Society of America**, **National Museum of the American Indian** and the branch of the **Whitney Museum of American Art** in the Philip Morris Building.

Here are some museums and their 'pay what you wish' schedules:

American Craft Museum:	6pm to 8pm Thursday
American Folk Art Museum:	6pm to 8pm Friday
American Museum of Natural History:	last hour daily
Brooklyn Botanic Garden:	before noon Monday to Saturday
Cooper-Hewitt National Design Museum:	5pm to 9pm Tuesday
Jewish Museum:	5pm to 8pm Thursday
Solomon R Guggenheim Museum:	6pm to 8pm Friday
Whitney Museum of American Art:	6pm to 9pm Friday

A terrific deal is the CityPass (**W** www.citypass.com). Good for nine days, the pass covers admission to the **Empire State Building** observatory, **American Museum of Natural History**, **Intrepid Sea-Air-Space Museum**, the **Circle Line**, **Whitney Museum of American Art** and **Guggenheim Museum**. The pass costs $38/31 per adult/youth aged 12 to 17; without the pass, you would pay $84/61.50 for admission to all these sites. As an added bonus, you can pick up the CityPass at the first attraction you visit.

N.Y.C.

Little Korea

Herald Square can become tiresome fast, so head for refueling at nearby Little Korea (**M** B, D, F, N, Q, R, V, W to 34th St-Herald Sq), a small enclave of Korean-owned shops that stretches from 31st to 36th Sts between Broadway and Fifth Ave. Over the past few years, this neighborhood has seen an explosion of restaurants serving Korean fare, with authentic Korean barbecues available around the clock at many of the all-night spots on 32nd St (for more details, see the boxed text 'Culinary Corners' in the Places to Eat chapter).

Empire State Building

Here's the real deal: New York's original symbol in the sky (**☎** 212-736-3100; **W** www.esbnyc.com; 350 Fifth Ave at 34th St; **M** B, D, F, N, Q, R, V, W to 34th St-Herald Sq) is a limestone classic built in just 410 days, or seven million man-hours, during the depths of the Depression at a cost of $41 million. Located on the site of the original Waldorf-Astoria Hotel, the 102-story, 1472ft (to the top of the antenna) Empire State Building opened in 1931 after the laying of 10 million bricks, installation of 6400 windows and setting of 328,000 sq ft of marble. The famous antenna was originally meant to be a mooring mast for zeppelins, but the Hindenberg disaster slammed the brakes on that plan. One airship accidentally met up with the building: a B25 crashed into the 79th floor on a foggy day in July 1945, killing 14 people.

Since 1976, the building's top 30 floors have been floodlit in seasonal and holiday colors (eg, green for St Patrick's Day in March, black for World AIDS Day on December 1, red and green for Christmas, pink for Gay Pride weekend in June; visit the website for each day's lighting scheme and meaning). This tradition has been copied by

Welcome to the Empire State Building

many other skyscrapers, notably the Metropolitan Life Tower at Madison Square Park and the Con Edison Tower near Union Square, lending elegance to the night sky.

The view from the Empire State Building is a dandy, but be prepared – the lines to get to the observation decks are notorious. Though getting there very early or very late will help you avoid delays, sunset is one of the most magical times to be up there because you can see the city don its night-time cloak in dusk's afterglow. Once up there, you can stay as long as you like. Coin-operated telescopes offer an up-close glimpse of the city, and diagrams map out the major sights.

The Empire State Building's **observatories** *(adult/senior & military/child under 12 $11/ 9/6; open 9:30am-midnight daily, last elevator 11:15pm)* are on the 86th and 102nd floors. You can use your CityPass here; for more information, see the boxed text 'Museum Bargains,' opposite.

Pierpont Morgan Library

The Pierpont Morgan Library *(#95; ☎ 212-685-0610; ｗ www.morganlibrary.org; 29 E 36th St; Ⓜ 6 to 33rd St; suggested admission adult/senior & student/child $8/6/free; open 10:30am-5pm Tues-Thur, 10:30am-8pm Fri, 10:30am-6pm Sat, noon-6pm Sun)*, near Madison Ave, is part of the 45-room mansion owned by steel magnate JP Morgan. His collection features a phenomenal array of manuscripts, tapestries and books (with no fewer than three Gutenberg Bibles), a study filled with Italian Renaissance artwork, a marble rotunda and the three-tiered East Room main library. The rotating art exhibitions here are top-notch.

A year-round program of lectures and concerts are held in the Garden Court, a lovely glass-enclosed space with a café and bookstore. The Pierpont Morgan Library definitely garners votes for best-kept New York secret.

New York Public Library

This epic library *(☎ 212-930-0800; ｗ www .nypl.org; 42nd St at Fifth Ave; Ⓜ S, 4, 5, 6 to Grand Central-42nd St, 7 to Fifth Ave; open 10am-6pm Mon & Thur-Sat, 11am-7:30pm Tues & Wed)* is a monument to learning, housed in a grand beaux-arts building, reflecting its big-money industrialist roots. When it was dedicated in 1911, New York's flagship library ranked as the largest marble structure ever built in the USA, with a vast 3rd-floor reading room designed to hold 500 patrons. This is not to mention the marble lions at the entrance, profligate use of gold leaf throughout, chandeliers, carved porticos and ceiling murals.

Today, this building, now called the Humanities and Social Sciences Library, is one of the best free attractions in the city. On a rainy day, hide away with a book in the airy reading room and admire the original Carr're and Hastings lamps, or stroll through the Exhibition Hall, which contains precious manuscripts by just about every author of note in the English language, including a 'fair copy' of the Declaration of Independence and a Gutenberg Bible. Interesting exhibitions also rotate through here. The free building tour is a bonanza of interesting tidbits; it leaves

RICHARD I'ANSON

THINGS TO SEE & DO

from the information desk at 11am and 2pm Monday to Saturday.

Just behind the library, **Bryant Park** offers a pleasant break in the middle of the day. Once overrun by drug dealers, the impressively restored park has become a popular sunbathing, wedding and picnic site. The brand new **carousel**, crafted in nearby Brooklyn, is sure to delight; rides cost $1.50. In summer, Bryant Park hosts a free **outdoor movie festival** (☎ 212-768-4242; W www .bryantpark.org) on Monday evening, but arrive early to stake your claim.

Grand Central Terminal

One of New York's most dramatic public spaces, Grand Central Terminal (42nd St at Park Ave; M S, 4, 5, 6, 7 to Grand Central-42nd St) evokes the romance of train travel at the turn of the 20th century, while enduring the bustle of present-day New York. Thanks to a lovingly tendered 1998 renovation, its interior remains as impressive as ever.

Completed in 1913, Grand Central Terminal (also called Grand Central Station) is another of New York's stunning beaux-arts buildings and boasts 75ft-high, glass-encased catwalks, with the constellations of the zodiac streaming across the vaulted ceiling backwards – the designer made a boo-boo. The balconies overlooking the main concourse afford an expansive view; perch yourself on one of these at around 6pm on a weekday to get a glimpse of the grace this terminal commands under pressure.

Today, Grand Central's underground electric tracks only serve commuter trains en route to northern suburbs and Connecticut.

But the old dame still merits a special trip for the fine dining, cool bars and occasional art exhibitions. See the Places to Eat and Entertainment chapters for more information.

The **Municipal Art Society** (☎ 212-935-3960; W www.mas.org) leads walks through Grand Central at 12:30pm every Wednesday; the suggested donation is $6. During the hour-long tour, you'll learn all kinds of stuff about the terminal, but the best perk is that you get to cross the glass catwalk high above the concourse. Tours meet at the passenger information booth in the middle of the terminal. Also in Grand Central is a tourist information booth, currency exchange and police post.

Across the street is a small branch of the Whitney Museum of American Art in the **Philip Morris Building** (☎ 212-878-2550; 120 Park Ave; admission free; open 11am-6pm Fri-Wed, 11am-7:30pm Thur).

Chrysler Building

The 1048ft Chrysler Building (Lexington Ave & 42nd St; M S, 4, 5, 6, 7 to Grand Central-42nd St), just across from Grand Central Terminal, briefly reigned as the tallest structure in the world until it was superseded by the Empire State Building a few months later. An art-deco masterpiece designed by William Van Allen in 1930, the building celebrates car culture, with gargoyles that resemble hood ornaments, amorphous block cars and thatched steel designs; binoculars are particularly handy for viewing these and other details unique to the Chrysler. The 200ft steel spire (known as the 'vertex'), constructed in secret, was raised through the

All aboard! Grand Central Terminal's main hall

ESBIN ANDERSON PHOTOGRAPHY

The dizzying heights of the Chrysler Building

false roof as a surprise crowning touch – which shocked and dismayed a competing architect who was hoping that his new Wall St building would turn out to be New York's tallest skyscraper at the time (it wasn't). Lit up at night, there are few more poignant symbols than the Chrysler Building.

Nestled at the top is the Cloud Club, a businessperson's club that closed years ago, and a private apartment built for Walter Chrysler, head of the company. For a long time, developers have been planning to convert part of the building into a hotel, but so far that remains a pipe dream.

Although the Chrysler Building has no restaurant or observation deck, wander inside to admire the elaborately veneered elevators (made from slices of Japanese ash, Oriental walnut and Cuban plum-pudding wood), the profusion of marble and the 1st floor's ceiling mural (purportedly the world's largest at 97ft by 100ft) depicting the promise of industry.

United Nations

The UN headquarters (☎ 212-963-8687; visitors' entrance cnr First Ave & 46th St; ⓜ S, 4, 5, 6, 7 to Grand Central-42nd St; adult/senior/student/child $8.50/7/6/5, child under 5 yrs not admitted; open 9:30am-4:45pm daily Mar-Dec, 9:30am-4:45pm Mon-Fri Jan & Feb) is technically on a slice of international territory overlooking the East River.

On a tour of the facility you'll see the General Assembly, where the annual autumn convocation of member nations takes place; the Security Council Chamber, where crisis management continues year-round; and the Economic & Social Council Chamber. A park south of the complex includes Henry Moore's *Reclining Figure* and several other sculptures with a peace theme.

English-language tours of the complex leave every 30 minutes; there are also limited tours in several other languages. Call ☎ 212-963-7539 for information. You may sometimes hear this area referred to as Turtle Bay, and though the turtles are long gone, there are some interesting architectural examples around here, especially among the permanent missions (such as Egypt's at 304 E 44th St between First and Second Aves and India's at 245 E 43rd St between Second and Third Aves).

Sutton Place

This place (ⓜ 4, 5, 6 to 59th St) encompasses several blocks of European-style luxury apartments that run parallel to First Ave from 54th to 59th Sts. The dead-end streets, which have pleasant benches looking out on the East River, served as the setting for Diane Keaton and Woody Allen's first date in the movie *Manhattan*. Under the 59th St Bridge (known as the Queensboro Bridge across the river), you'll see Sir Terence Conran's Bridgemarket, a collection of food stalls and restaurants in the arches of the bridge. This beautiful space features vaulted ceilings bejeweled with Gustavino tile, similar to those found in the Oyster Bar in Grand Central Terminal.

There's not much else in this area to recommend, though **PJ Clarke's** (cnr Third Ave & 55th St), an old bar from the 1890s, is still, after all these years, a good spot for a pint.

THINGS TO SEE & DO

Rockefeller Center

Built during the height of the Great Depression in the 1930s, the 22-acre Rockefeller Center complex (☎ 212-632-3975, w www.rockefellercenter.com; 48th-51st Sts; Ⓜ B, D, F, V to 47th-50th Sts/Rockefeller Center), between Fifth and Sixth Aves, gave jobs to 70,000 workers over nine years and was the first project to combine retail, entertainment and office space in what is often referred to as a 'city within a city.'

Perhaps most impressively, Rockefeller Center features commissioned works around the theme 'Man at the Crossroads Looks Uncertainly But Hopefully at the Future' by 30 great artists of the day. One great artist, however, was looking skeptically at the future. Mexican muralist Diego Rivera, persuaded to paint the lobby of the 70-story RCA Building (now the GE Building), was outraged, along with the rest of the art world, when the Rockefeller family rejected his painting for containing 'Communist imagery' – namely, the face of Lenin. The fresco was destroyed and replaced with a Jose Maria Sert work depicting the more 'acceptable' faces of Abraham Lincoln and Ralph Waldo Emerson.

Speaking from experience, even art neophytes will appreciate *Prometheus* overlooking the ice skating rink, *Atlas* doing his thing in front of the **International Building** (630 Fifth Ave), which has a wacky sculpture inset into its lobby walls, and *News* by Isamu Noguchi above the entrance to the **Associated Press Building** (45 Rockefeller Plaza). Anyone interested in artworks within the complex should pick up the Rockefeller Center Visitors Guide in the GE lobby, which describes many of them in detail.

Architectural details around the complex are varied. Note the tile work above the Sixth Ave entrance to the GE Building, the three flood-lit cameos along the side of Radio City Music Hall and the back-lit gilt and stained-glass entrance to the East River Savings Bank Building at 41 Rockefeller Plaza, immediately to the north of the skating rink.

Perhaps the best-known feature of Rockefeller Center is its gigantic Christmas tree, which overlooks the skating rink during the holidays. (This tradition dates back to the

Rockefeller Center at Christmas – a chilly treat

RICHARD I'ANSON

1930s when construction workers set up a small Christmas tree on the site.) The annual lighting of the Rockefeller Center Christmas tree on the Tuesday after Thanksgiving attracts thousands of visitors to the area and is something everyone should see once. The scene is too crowded to be believed, but skating at the **ice skating rink** (☎ 212-332-7654; Fifth Ave; adult/child $8.50/7 Mon-Fri, $11/7.50 Sat & Sun, skate rental $6; open 9am-10:30pm Mon-Thur, 8:30am-midnight Fri & Sat, 8:30am-10pm Sun, Nov-Apr), between 49th and 50th Sts, under the gaze of *Prometheus* is unforgettable.

The cluster of shops in Rockefeller Center is better than most, with outlets of the upscale cosmetic discounter Sephora, techie toy emporium Sharper Image and designer Tommy Hilfiger, among others.

Radio City Music Hall This 6000-seat art-deco movie palace (☎ 212-247-4777; w www.radiocity.com; 51st St at Sixth Ave; Ⓜ B, D, F, V to 47th-50th Sts/Rockefeller Center) had its interior declared a protected landmark and is looking fine, thanks to extensive renovation work in 1999. In a triumphant restoration, the velvet seats and furnishings were returned to the exact state they were in when the building opened in 1932. (Even the smoking rooms and toilets are elegant at the 'Showplace of the Nation.') Concerts here sell out quickly, and tickets to the annual Christmas spectacular featuring the hokey, but enjoyable Rockette dancers now cost up to $70. (Samuel 'Roxy' Rothafel, the man responsible for the high-kicking chorus line, declared that 'a visit to Radio City is as good as a month in the country.')

You can see the interior by taking a tour ($16/10 per adult/child); these leave every half-hour between 10am and 5pm Monday to Saturday and between 11am and 5pm on Sunday. Tickets are sold on a first-come, first-served basis.

NBC Studios The NBC television network (☎ 212-664-3700; ⓦ www.nbc.com; Ⓜ B, D, F, V to 47th-50th Sts/Rockefeller Center) has its headquarters in the 70-story GE Building, which looms over the Rockefeller Center ice-skating rink (the rink doubles as a café in the summer months). The *Today* show broadcasts live 7pm to 9am daily from a glass-enclosed street-level studio near the fountain.

Tours of the NBC studios leave from the lobby of the GE Building; they're offered from 8:30am to 5:30pm Monday to Saturday, 9:30am to 4:30pm Sunday, with extended hours during the holiday season in November and December. Tours cost $17.50 for adults, $15 for seniors or children aged six to 16; children under six are not admitted.

Tickets to show tapings (eg, *Saturday Night Live*, *Late Night with Conan O'Brien* etc) can be obtained by calling **NBC Show Tickets** (☎ 212-664-3056), 9am-5pm Monday to Friday. Plan well in advance if you want even a remote chance at tickets.

St Patrick's Cathedral

It's worth checking out this cathedral (☎ 212-753-2261; cnr 50th St & Fifth Ave; Ⓜ B, D, F, V to 47th-50th Sts/Rockefeller Center; open 6am-9pm daily), just across from Rockefeller Center, as this elaborate interpretation of French Gothic styles is a feather in the cap of the Roman Catholic church. The cathedral, built at a cost of nearly $2 million during the Civil War, originally didn't include the two front spires, which were added in 1888. Although it seats a modest 2400 worshippers, most of New York's 2.2 million faithful will have been inside at one time or another. While it may seem like each and every one is there when you show up, muddle through to see some of the exquisite details inside.

After you enter, walk by the eight small shrines along the side of the cathedral, past the shrine to **Nuestra Señora de Guadalupe** and the main altar to the quiet **Lady Chapel**, dedicated to the Virgin Mary. From here, you can see the handsome stained-glass **Rose Window** above the 7000-pipe church organ. A basement crypt behind the altar contains the coffins of every New York cardinal and the remains of Pierre Touissant, a champion of the poor and the first black American up for sainthood (he emigrated from Haiti).

Unfortunately, St Patrick's is not a place for restful contemplation because of the constant buzz from baseball-cap-wearing, video-taping, disrespectful visitors. It's also a regular protest site by gays who feel excluded by the church hierarchy. Since 1933, the exclusion of Irish gays from the St

Witness the French Gothic splendor of St Patrick's Cathedral

Patrick's Day Parade (an event not sponsored by the Catholic Church per se, but identified with Catholic traditionalists) has triggered protests near the cathedral every March.

Frequent masses take place on the weekend, and New York's archbishop presides over the service at 10:15am Sunday. Casual visitors are only allowed in between services.

Fifth Avenue

Immortalized in both film and song, Fifth Ave first developed its high-class reputation in the early 20th century, when a series of mansions on the avenue's uptown portion became known as Millionaire's Row. Today, the avenue's Midtown stretch still boasts upscale shops and hotels, including the garish, somehow endearing, **Plaza Hotel** (#7; Ⓜ N, R, W to Fifth Ave-59th St, F to 57th St) at Grand Army Plaza, overlooking Central Park and Fifth Ave. The historic institution doesn't have much of a grand lobby, but the stained-glass ceiling in the Palm Court is impressive. The fountain facing the hotel, with a statue of the Roman goddess Diana, is a good spot for a rest – provided you're not downwind from the horse-drawn carriages that line 59th St. Across the street, on the northwest corner of

Touring Manhattan on the Cheap – by Public Bus

SIMON BRACKEN

If you're interested in a guided bus tour of Manhattan, see Organized Tours in the Getting Around chapter. But if you'd rather not shell out the money (or listen to the prattle of a tour guide), you can make your own self-guided loop tour on the good old public bus. You can hop on and off as often you like to sightsee, returning by subway down Broadway. If you do opt for the public transportation tour, though, make sure to start in the morning, because traffic can turn this two-hour journey into a frustrating three-hour crawl.

For more details on most of the sights mentioned here, see the Chelsea, Midtown, Upper West Side and Washington Heights sections in this chapter.

Catch the Uptown-bound M5 bus anywhere along Sixth Ave above Houston St (Map 4; where the bus route begins). Be sure to board a 'limited stop' bus (weekdays only), which picks up passengers at several clearly marked spots, including W 3rd St and Sixth Ave, and then stops only at major cross streets (14th St, 23rd St etc), since you're taking the bus far Uptown. Buses do not take dollar bills, so you'll have to pay the $1.50 fare with a token, a MetroCard or exact change and ask for a transfer just in case you want to visit the Cloisters by switching to the M4 bus.

As the M5 continues up Sixth Ave, it travels first through **Chelsea** (Map 5), past Ladies' Mile, where fashionable women shopped for millinery and china in the late 19th century. Today, the old ornate buildings between 14th and 23rd Sts have been taken over by modern superstores (including Staples, Bed Bath & Beyond and Barnes & Noble).

The bus continues past **Herald Square** and Macy's department store and, to the right, the western edge of Bryant Park, located behind the main New York Public Library. In another six blocks, you'll travel by **Rockefeller Center**, including the GE Building and Radio City Music Hall, on your right at 50th St.

Turning left at 59th St, the bus skirts the southern end of Central Park before turning Uptown at **Columbus Circle**. This circle, with the statue of Christopher Columbus (built in 1892) as its centerpiece, is the closest thing New York has to a grand traffic circle in the European tradition.

As the bus continues up Broadway, you'll soon see **Lincoln Center** (Map 7) to your left between 62nd and 65th Sts. The white-marble complex houses the Metropolitan Opera, New York Philharmonic and the Julliard School of Music. At W 72nd St, the bus turns left and heads over to Riverside Dr, upper Manhattan's westernmost street, which is lined with block after block of well-kept

59th St and Fifth Ave, don't miss the outpost of the venerable used-book purveyor, **Strand Bookstore**.

Most of the heirs to the millionaire mansions on Fifth Ave above 59th St sold them for demolition or converted them to the cultural institutions that make up Museum Mile (see Upper East Side, later). The **Villard Houses** (Ⓜ B, D, F, V to 47th-50th Sts/ Rockefeller Center), on Madison Ave behind St Patrick's Cathedral, are a stunning exception. Financier Henry Villard built the six four-story townhouses in 1881 which flaunt artistic details by the likes of Tiffany, John LaFarge and Auguste Saint-Gaudens; the mansion was later owned by the Catholic church and then sold to a series of hotel magnates. If you have the cash and appropriate clothing, take a cocktail at the deluxe Villard Bar (see the Entertainment chapter) or a meal at Le Cirque 2000 (see Places to Eat).

While a number of the more exclusive boutiques have migrated to Madison Ave (see the Shopping chapter), several still line Fifth Ave above 50th St, including Cartier, Henri Bendel and Tiffany's. On 57th St nearby, you can shop at Burberry's, Hermès and Charivari, among several other designer boutiques.

Touring Manhattan on the Cheap – by Public Bus

apartment buildings. As the bus turns north, you'll see a statue of Eleanor Roosevelt that was dedicated in 1996 by Hillary Rodham Clinton.

Riverside Park looks downright elegant in beautiful weather, with its sloping hills and view of the cliffs of northern New Jersey. The park contains a number of monuments, including the 1902 **Soldiers' and Sailors' Monument** that honors those who served in the Civil War. At 89th St, turn to your left to note the monument's grand campanile. There's also a statue of **Joan of Arc** at 93rd St and you'll pass **Grant's Tomb** (Map 8; 120th St) and to the right of that, the magnificent **Riverside Church**, with its grand organ and bell-tower observation deck. (You might be tempted to alight here and explore, but a visit instead to Audubon Terrace, 35 blocks to the north, is highly recommended.)

The bus returns to Broadway at 135th St and heads north. At 155th St, you'll reach **Audubon Terrace**, which sits on the west side of the street. The former home of naturalist John James Audubon now contains two under-appreciated but inspirational museums: the American Numismatic Society and the Hispanic Society of America.

Provided you haven't hopped off the bus for any extended period of time, you can use your transfer at the George Washington Bridge bus station (Map 13) on Broadway between 178th and 179th Sts to take the M4 bus further Uptown (alternatively, you can hop off the bus entirely here and walk west to the Hudson River where you'll find the sweet **Little Red Lighthouse** standing in the shadow of the bridge stanchions). Like the M5, the M4 runs along Broadway until W 168th St, when it continues on Fort Washington Ave to the **Cloisters** in Fort Tryon Park. Since it opened in the 1930s, this spectacular museum has housed the Metropolitan Museum of Art's collection of medieval art, including parts of several medieval European monasteries. Nearby, on Broadway at 204th St, the 1783 **Dyckman House** is the last Dutch farmhouse to survive in Manhattan, although it's no longer sitting on a 28-acre farm.

If you took time out to see anything on the way, you'll want to take the subway back, using the A, C or 1 trains, depending on your location. To continue sightseeing from the bus, take the M4 back downtown; it travels south along Fort Washington Ave, then Broadway, cutting across to Fifth Ave at Central Park North (110th St) and continuing down to Midtown. (This will mean a separate fare.) The bus passes the **Museo del Barrio, Museum of the City of New York, New York Academy of Medicine, Guggenheim Museum** and **Metropolitan Museum of Art**.

The M4 then passes by Rockefeller Center's eastern edge and St Patrick's Cathedral. By this point, you're bound to be caught in traffic or just fed up with the bus, so hop off by the time it reaches the Empire State Building, on Fifth Ave at 34th St.

THINGS TO SEE & DO

N.Y.C.

Museum of Television & Radio

This couch potato's smorgasbord *(#40; ☎ 212-621-6800, w www.mtr.org; 25 W 52nd St; Ⓜ E, V to Fifth Ave-53rd St; adult/ senior & student/child $6/4/3; open noon-6pm Tues, Wed & Fri-Sun, noon-8pm Thur)*, between Fifth and Sixth Aves, contains a collection of more than 50,000 American TV and radio programs, all available from the museum's computer catalog with the click of a mouse. It's a great place to hang out when it's raining or when you're simply fed up with the real world. Nearly everybody checks out their favorite childhood TV programs and watches them on the museum's 90 consoles, but the radio-listening room is an unexpected pleasure. Your admission fee entitles you to two hours of uninterrupted audiovisual enjoyment. Special screenings are also held here.

Museum of Modern Art

This museum *(MoMA; #41; ☎ 212-708-9400; w www.moma.org; 11 W 53rd St; Ⓜ E, V to Fifth Ave-53rd St)*, between Fifth and Sixth Aves, is closed until 2005 while it expands to 630,000 sq ft (more than 50% more gallery space than it currently has available). In the meantime, MoMA QNS in Long Island City (see Long Island City in the Outer Boroughs later in this chapter for more details) will accommodate a meager portion of the museum's collection. Luckily, there are many attractions in this part of Queens and combining them with the relocated museum makes for a nice day trip.

American Craft Museum

Directly across the street from MoMA, the American Craft Museum *(#42; ☎ 212-956-3535; w www.americancraftmuseum.org; 40 W 53rd St; Ⓜ E, V to Fifth Ave-53rd St; adult/senior/child under 13 yrs $7.50/4/free; open 10am-6pm Tues, Wed, Fri-Sun, 10am-8pm Thur)*, between Fifth and Sixth Aves, displays innovative and traditional crafts in a spectacularly well designed and airy space. The museum is currently hosting a 10-year series of exhibitions that examines American craft-making, and you can view works from the eight identified periods of artisanship.

Across the street is the **American Folk Art Museum** *(#39; ☎ 212-265-1040; w www .folkartmusuem.org; 45 W 53rd St; Ⓜ E, V to Fifth Ave-53rd St; adult/student & senior $7.50/4; open 10am-6pm Tues-Thur, Sat & Sun, 10am-8pm Fri)* with a similar theme and a terrific gift shop.

Donnell Library Center

The Donnell branch *(#43; ☎ 212-621-0618; 20 W 53rd St; E, V to Fifth Ave-53rd St)* of the New York Public Library, across from MoMA, not only has excellent free jazz concerts, films and lectures, it's also home to the original Winnie-the-Pooh and crew given to Christopher Milne between 1920 and 1922, donated to the library in 1987. The gang's all here in a vitrine on the 2nd floor. Everyone's in pretty good shape, though Pooh looks like he could use some honey – he's a little wan.

ANGUS OBORN

MoMA Mia! How can you resist the Museum of Modern Art?

Times Square (Map 6)

Now enjoying a major renaissance, Times Square (N, Q, R, S, W, 1, 2, 3, 7 to Times Sq-42nd St) can once again trumpet its reputation as the 'Crossroads of the World.' Smack in the middle of Midtown Manhattan, this area around the intersection of Broadway and Seventh Ave has long been synonymous with gaudy billboards and glittery marquees – before the advent of TV, advertisers went after the largest audience possible by beaming their messages into the center of New York. With over 60 megabillboards and 40 miles of neon, it's startling how it always looks like daytime and, honestly, the wasted energy is hard to reconcile.

Once called Long Acre Square, the area took its present name from the famous newspaper, the *New York Times,* which is still located there. Also dubbed the 'Great White Way' after its brilliant lights, Times Square dimmed quite a bit in the 1960s, as once-proud movie palaces that had previously shown first-run films turned into 'triple X'

porn theaters. But in recent years, the city has reversed the area's fortunes by extending big tax breaks to businesses that relocated here (most notably Walt Disney) and legislating theaters to the hilt: under Mayor Giuliani an entertainment venue had to be at least 60% 'legitimate' theater to permit the other 40% to show or sell porn. Today, the square draws 27 million annual visitors, who spend something over $12 billion in Midtown.

The cacophony of color, zipping message boards (called 'zippers') and massive TV screens make Times Square seem like one big, blinding advertisement. Television networks such as ABC and MTV (you'll know the latter by the teens shrieking on the corner of 44th St and Broadway) have opened studios in Times Square, and major companies, including Virgin Megastore, have created commercial showcases. Several media conglomerates – among them German publisher Bertelsmann, Reuters and the US magazine group Condé Nast – have built headquarters in and around the square in recent years.

THINGS TO SEE & DO

Live from New York!

It seems like the television cameras are everywhere in these 'Reality TV' days, and New York has become *the* backdrop for network morning shows from 7am to 9am Monday to Friday. It all started when the *NBC Today* show debuted a windowed studio in Rockefeller Center. ABC then unveiled a **Good Morning America studio** *(cnr Broadway & W 44th St)* that overlooks Times Square. CBS's *The Early Show* followed suit with a ground-level studio in the General Motors Building on Fifth Ave across from the Plaza Hotel. MTV's US network overlooks Times Square, and the *David Letterman Late Show* features man-in-the-street gags near the Ed Sullivan Theater on Broadway near 53rd St.

If you'd rather sit in the studio audience of a TV show, you might be able to obtain free stand-by tickets on the same day as a show's taping (the advance tickets are usually snapped up months ahead by people who write to the show). **NBC** (☎ 212-664-3056; 30 Rockefeller Plaza, 49th St) distributes tickets from its offices. Line up for *Late Night with Conan O'Brien* at 9am Tuesday to Friday and *Saturday Night Live* at 9:15am on Saturday. For stand-by tickets to one of New York's most popular morning shows, *Live with Regis and Kathie Lee*, go to the show's **studio** *(cnr 67th St & Columbus Ave)* by 8am Monday to Friday. CBS sometimes offers stand-by tickets for the *Late Show*; call the network's **stand-by ticket line** (☎ 212-247-6497) at 11am. But don't get your hopes up, as the show's staff typically overbook the theater. If you do get a ticket, take identification (many shows require audience members to be 16 years of age or older), and something warm to wear to the taping – the studios are freezing.

Times Square also continues to serve as New York's official theater district, with dozens of Broadway and off-Broadway theaters located in an area that stretches from 41st to 54th Sts, between Sixth and Ninth Aves (see the Entertainment chapter).

Up to a million people gather in Times Square every New Year's Eve to see an illuminated Waterford Crystal ball descend from the roof of One Times Square at midnight. While this event garners international coverage, it lasts just 90 seconds and, frankly, is something of an anticlimax.

Times Square Visitors Center Sitting smack in the middle of the famous crossroads of Broadway and Seventh Ave, between 46th and 47th Sts, is the Times Square Visitors Center *(#53; ☎ 212-869-1890; ⓦ www.timessquarebid.org; 1560 Broadway; ⓜ N, Q, R, S, W, 1, 2, 3, 7 to Times Sq-42nd St; open 8am-8pm daily)*. More than one million visitors annually stop in to use the center's ATMs, video guides to the city and computer terminals with free Internet access. The center also offers free walking tours of the neighborhood at noon on Friday.

COREY WISE

Time flies at one of NYC's busiest squares

International Center of Photography

Recently consolidated at its expanded Midtown space, this center *(#105; ☎ 212-857-0000; ⓦ www.icp.org; 1133 Sixth Ave at 43rd St; ⓜ B, D, F, V to 42nd St, 7 to Fifth Ave; adult/senior & student $9/6; open 10am-5pm Tues-Thur, 10am-8pm Fri, 10am-6pm Sat & Sun)* remains the city's most important showcase for major photographers, especially photojournalists. Its past exhibitions have included work by Henri Cartier-Bresson, Man Ray, Matthew Brady, Weegee and Robert Capa, and have explored themes such as September 11 and the impact of AIDS.

UPPER WEST SIDE (MAP 7)

The Upper West Side begins as Broadway emerges from Midtown at Columbus Circle and ends at the southern border of Harlem, around 125th St. Many hotels ring Central Park, and many celebrities live in the massive apartment buildings that line Central Park West up to 96th St.

This neighborhood is an architectural wonderland, with everything from opulent mansions-turned-apartment buildings, such as **Dorilton** *(171 W 71st at Broadway)* and **Ansonia** *(2109 Broadway)*, to functional public buildings with succulent detail, such as the **McBurney School** *(#102; 63rd St)* off Central Park West and **Frederick Henry Cossitt Dormitory** *(#100; 64th St)* near Central Park West. Of course, almost every block up here sports gorgeous brownstones owned by the fiercely house-proud. On W 71st St, between Broadway and West End Ave, poets and dreamers will be inspired by **Septtuagesimo Uno** *(#68)* park; 'septtuagesimo' means 'seventy one' in Latin. A spaghetti-strand oasis of just 0.4 acres, you can sense past and future impromptu marriage proposals here.

Another great place to stroll up here is **Riverside Park** *(ⓜ 1, 2, 3, to 72nd St)*, which runs along the Hudson River from 72nd St to 125th St. Despite being underneath the traffic circle, the **79th Street Boat Basin** is a fine spot from which to watch the sunset, perhaps while sipping a margarita, available from the nearby bar/restaurant (eat your heart out Jimmy Buffet!).

Lincoln Center

The 16-acre Lincoln Center complex (☎ 212-546-2656; w www.lincolncenter.org; cnr Columbus Ave & Broadway; ⓜ 1, 2 to 66th St-Lincoln Center) includes seven large performance spaces built in the 1960s, which replaced a group of tenements that inspired the musical *West Side Story*. During the day, Lincoln Center presents a demure face, but at night the interiors fairly glow and sparkle with crystal chandeliers and the well heeled.

If you have even a shred of culture vulture in you, Lincoln Center is a must-see, since it contains the **Metropolitan Opera House**, adorned by two colorful lobby tapestries by Marc Chagall, and the **New York State Theater**, home of both the New York City Ballet and the New York City Opera, the low-cost and more daring alternative to the Met. The New York Philharmonic holds its season in **Avery Fisher Hall**.

The Lincoln Center Theater company performs at the 1000-seat **Vivian Beaumont Theater**, which also contains the smaller and more intimate **Mitzi Newhouse Theater**. To the right of the theaters stands the **New York Public Library for the Performing Arts** (☎ 212-870-1630), which houses the city's largest collection of recorded sound, video and books on film and theater.

The **Juilliard School of Music**, attached to the complex by a walkway over W 65th St, includes **Alice Tully Hall**, home to the Chamber Music Society of Lincoln Center, and the **Walter Reade Theater**, the city's most comfortable film-revival space and the major screening site of the New York Film Festival, held every September. On any given night, there are at least 10 performances happening throughout Lincoln Center.

Daily tours (☎ 212-875-5350) of the complex explore at least three of the theaters, which ones depend on production schedules. It's a good idea to call ahead for a space. Tours cost $10/8.50 for adults, $8.50 for students and seniors and $5 for children. They leave from the tour desk on the concourse level at 10:30am, 12:30pm, 2:30pm and 4:30pm daily. Another tour option ($16 for everyone; call ahead for times) visits the master piano-restorers of Klavierhaus.

Lavish lights at the Lincoln Center

ESBIN ANDERSON PHOTOGRAPHY

New-York Historical Society

As the antiquated, hyphenated name implies, the New-York Historical Society (☎ 212-873-3400; w www.nyhistory.org; 2 W 77th St at Central Park West; ⓜ B, C to 81st St-Museum of Natural History, 1, 2 to 79th St; suggested donation adult/senior & student $5/3; open 10am-5pm Tues-Sun) is the city's oldest museum, founded in 1804 to preserve the city's historical and cultural artifacts. It was also New York's only public art museum until the Metropolitan Museum of Art was founded in the late 19th century.

The New-York Historical Society has suffered severe financial problems in recent years and, lamentably, most visitors don't even notice it on their way to its neighbor institution, the American Museum of Natural History. This is pure oversight, because the collection here is as quirky and unique as New York itself; only here can you see 17th-century cowbells and baby rattles and the mounted wooden leg of Gouverneur Morris. The special events and lecture series are also full of surprises and worth investigating.

American Museum of Natural History

Founded in 1869, this museum (☎ 212-769-5000; w www.amnh.org; Central Park West at 79th St; ⓜ B, C to 81st St-Museum of Natural History, 1, 2 to 79th St; suggested admission adult/senior & student/child $10/7.50/6, last hr free daily; open 10am-5:45pm Sun-Thur, 10am-8:45pm Fri & Sat) began with a mastodon's tooth and a few thousand beetles; today, its collection includes more than 30

Ancient activities to keep the kids amused

million artifacts, interactive exhibits and loads of taxidermy. It's most famous for its three large **dinosaur halls**, which underwent a complete overhaul several years ago and reflect current knowledge on how these behemoths behaved. Enthusiastic guides roam the dinosaur halls ready to answer questions, and the 'please touch' displays allow kids to handle many items, including the skullcap of a pachycephulasaurus, a plant-eating dinosaur that roamed the earth 65 million years ago.

Other treasures in the permanent collection include the enormous (fake) blue whale that hangs from the ceiling above the Hall of Ocean Life and the Star of India sapphire in the Hall of Minerals and Gems. Newer exhibitions, such as the Hall of Biodiversity, feature a strong ecological slant, with a video display about the earth's habitats. The **Butterfly Conservancy** is a popular recurring exhibition, open from November to May, that features 600 butterflies from all over the world (admission is extra). The building itself is amazing: turn the corner to admire the 77th St facade.

The museum let its imagination go wild dreaming up the new **Rose Center for Earth & Space** (#45). The museum shot into the 21st century when the new center opened, the state-of-the-art, 3-D star show at the Hayden Planetarium is simply awesome. The big ball in the bigger glass box that contains the planetarium is a site to behold. It's called the Ecosphere and features hitech exhibitions tracing the development of the planet (rounding the ramps following the earth's creation and growth is a singular museum experience). Lasers and other special effects re-create the birth of the universe at the Big Bang Theater (the star and laser shows cost extra, but admission to the Rose Center is included with the basic museum price). The museum also has an IMAX theater.

The **live jazz** program called Starry Nights, which takes place in the Rose Center from 6pm to 8pm on Friday, is highly recommended. Tapas, drinks and top jazz acts are all included with museum admission at these weekly gigs.

You can use your CityPass here; for more details on the pass, see the boxed text 'Museum Bargains,' earlier in this chapter.

Children's Museum of Manhattan

This museum (#48; ☎ 212-721-1234; **w** www .cmom.org; 212 W 83rd St; **Ⓜ** 1, 2 to 86th St, B, C to 81st St-Museum of Natural History; adult & child over 1 yr/senior $6/3; open 10am-5pm Wed-Sun), near Amsterdam Ave, features discovery centers for toddlers, a postmodern media center, where technologically savvy kids can work in a TV studio, and the cutting-edge Inventor Center, where all the latest, cool tech stuff like digital imaging and scanners are made available. The museum also runs craft workshops on weekends and sponsors special exhibitions.

Both Brooklyn and Staten Island have affiliated children's museums. See those sections for more information.

MORNINGSIDE HEIGHTS
(MAP 8)
Cathedral of St John the Divine

This massive cathedral (☎ 212-316-7540; Amsterdam Ave at 112th St; ⓜ B, C, 1 to Cathedral Pkwy; open 7:30am-6pm daily) is the largest place of worship in the USA – and it's not done yet. When it's completed, the 601-ft long Episcopal cathedral should rank as the third-largest church in the world (after St Peter's Basilica in Rome, Italy, and Our Lady at Yamoussoukro in Côte d'Ivoire). Sadly, a fire broke out at St John the Divine a few years ago, irreparably damaging tapestries and other artifacts.

Though its cornerstone was laid in 1892, construction here is ongoing. Work has yet to begin on the stone tower on the left side of the west front and on the crossing tower above the pulpit. Other features shown on the church's cutaway floor plan near the front entrance, such as a Greek amphitheater, remain wistful visions.

Still, the cathedral is a flourishing place of worship and community activity, as well as the site of holiday concerts, lectures and memorial services for famous New Yorkers. There's even a Poet's Corner just to the left of the front entrance – though, unlike at Westminster Abbey in London, no-one is actually buried here. Also check out the altar designed and built by the late Keith Haring, a popular artist in the 1980s pop-art world.

Other points of interest are the whimsical **Children's Sculpture Garden** on the cathedral's south side and the **Biblical Garden**, planted with historically correct plants, around the back. An intriguing **Ecology Trail** wends its way through the cathedral and the grounds, tracing the four creation cycles (birth, life, death and re-birth) from a multicultural perspective.

Cathedral tours ($3 per person) are held at 11am Tuesday to Saturday and 1pm Sunday.

Columbia University

When Columbia University (☎ 212-854-1754; Broadway; ⓜ 1 to 116th St-Columbia University), between 114th and 121st Sts, and the affiliated Barnard College moved to this site in 1897, their founders chose a spot far removed from the downtown bustle. Today, the city has enveloped and moved beyond Columbia's gated campus, but the school's main courtyard, with its statue *Alma Mater* perched on the steps of the Low Library, is still a quiet place to take some sun and read a book. Hamilton Hall, in the southeast corner of the main square, was the famous site of a student takeover in 1968, and has seen periodic protests and plenty of wild student parties since then.

As befits a university setting, the surrounding neighborhood is filled with inexpensive restaurants, good bookstores and cafés. For a variety of eating options, see the Places to Eat chapter.

Riverside Church

Built by the Rockefeller family in 1930, Riverside Church (#38; ☎ 212-870-6700; 490 Riverside Dr at W 120th St; ⓜ 1 to 116th St-Columbia University; open 9am-4pm daily) is a Gothic beauty overlooking the Hudson River. In good weather, you can climb 355ft above the ground to the observation deck ($2) for expansive river views. The church rings its 74 carillon bells, the largest grouping in the world, with an extraordinary 20-ton bass bell (also the world's largest), at noon and 3pm on Sunday. Interdenominational services are held 10:45am on Sunday.

General US Grant National Memorial

Popularly known as Grant's Tomb (☎ 212-666-1640; Riverside Dr at W 122nd St; ⓜ 1 to 125th St; admission free; open 9am-5pm Wed-Sun), this landmark monument holds the remains of Civil War hero and president Ulysses S Grant and those of his wife, Julia. Completed in 1897 – 12 years after Grant's death – the granite structure cost $600,000 and is the largest mausoleum in the country. Though it plagiarizes Mausoleus' tomb at Halicarnassus, Grant's version doesn't qualify as one of the Seven Wonders of the World. Still, it's a marvel, inside and out. The building languished as a graffiti-scarred mess for years until the general's relatives shamed the National Park Service into cleaning it up by threatening to move his body elsewhere.

THINGS TO SEE & DO

CENTRAL PARK (MAP 7)

This 843-acre treasure (☎ 212-360-3444; w www.centralparknyc.org), right in the middle of Manhattan, is not to be missed. An oasis from the insanity, the downy lawns and meandering, wooded paths provide the bit of nature New Yorkers crave. There are acres of gardens, fathoms of freshwater ponds, miles of trails and innumerable secret pockets to explore here. While the park swarms with joggers, in-line skaters, musicians and tourists on warm weekends, there are quieter areas above 72nd St – recommended spots include the **Harlem Meer**, the **Lasker Rink & Pool** and the formal **Conservancy Gardens**. Meanwhile, winter exposes a different – though no less restorative – face of the park. Its sometimes scary reputation as a dark and menacing place (especially for women runners and parade-goers) is generally not justified; today the park ranks as one of the safest parts of the city.

Like the subway, Central Park is the great leveler. Created in the 1860s and '70s by Frederick Law Olmstead and Calvert Vaux on the marshy northern fringe of the city, the immense park was designed as a leisure space for all New Yorkers, regardless of color, class or creed. Olmstead (who also created Prospect Park in Brooklyn) was determined to keep foot and road traffic separate and cleverly designed the cross-town traverses so the two would not meet, which makes the park an especially rewarding pedestrian destination. That such a large expanse of prime real estate has survived intact for so long again proves that in the end, nothing eclipses the heart, soul and pride that forms the foundation of New York's greatness. Today, this 'people's park' is still one of the city's most popular attractions, beckoning throngs of New Yorkers with free outdoor concerts, a zoo and the famous annual Shakespeare in the Park productions (see Theater in the Entertainment chapter for more details).

When Central Park was first created, wealthy New Yorkers had their wish granted for a quiet place for carriage rides. Some traditions never die – although today most New Yorkers wouldn't be caught dead in a horse-drawn carriage. But tourists love them, despite the expense and the stench in the summer. Carriages line up along 59th St *(Central Park South;* Ⓜ *1, 9, A, B, C, D, E to 59th St-Columbus Circle)* and cost $35 for 20 minutes ($10 for every 15 minutes extra). Drivers expect tips.

For more information on outdoor activities in Central Park, see Activities in the Facts for the Visitor chapter.

Relax in the sunshine on the lawn of Central Park

NEIL SETCHFIELD

THINGS TO SEE & DO

Central Park Walking Tour

People come to the park for sheer recreational pleasure; unlike the streets of Downtown Manhattan, Central Park Dr, a 6-mile loop road, has a lane for cyclists, skaters and runners. Central Park Dr is closed to traffic from 10am to 3pm and 7pm to 10pm Monday to Thursday, and from 7pm on Friday to 6am Monday, which should offer your ears a break from Manhattan's ubiquitous noise pollution. You can't really get lost in Central Park, except in the Ramble (which is why it's so popular with cruising gays), but you should note that a wall encircles the entire park and you can only get in through designated 'gates' – breaks in the wall every five blocks or so.

A good walk in the park begins at the Columbus Circle entrance, at the park's southwest corner. (For descriptions of the memorial here, see the boxed text 'Central Park Statuary.') Pass through the **Merchants' Gate** up to **Sheep Meadow**, a wide green expanse that attracts sunbathers and Frisbee players. This is a great place for a picnic amid stellar skyline views. A pathway leading to the right takes you along the south side of the meadow to the enclosed **carousel**, which boasts some of the largest hand-carved horses in the country ($1 a ride).

Continue past the carousel along the 65th St pathway to the **Dairy**, overlooking Wollman Rink. The Dairy houses the park's **visitor center** *(open 10am-5pm daily summer, 10am-4pm winter)*, where you can pick up maps and information about park activities.

Across East Drive from the Dairy, you'll find the **Central Park Wildlife Center** *(☎ 212-861-6030; adult/senior/child 3-12 yrs $3.50/1.25/0.50; open 10am-5pm Mon-Fri, 10am-5:30pm Sat & Sun)*, a small zoo dating from the 1930s but renovated in 1988 to make the animals more comfortable.

Top: Fairy lights above Tavern on the Green (photograph by Kim Grant)

Bottom: Central Park in the Fall

ANGUS OBORN

Zoo residents include a lazy polar bear and several sea lions, whose frequent feedings delight children. Admission to the zoo includes entry to the **Tisch Children's Zoo**, a petting center for toddlers; it's across 65th St from the main zoo. At the entrance, don't miss the **Delacorte Clock**, a whimsical timepiece festooned with dancing bears, monkeys and other furry friends, who spin and hammer out the time every half-hour.

After the zoo, walk north on the path that parallels East Dr, cross the 65th St Transverse to a group of statues (including Christopher Columbus and William Shakespeare) that marks the beginning of **The Mall**, an elegant promenade lined with benches and a collection of 150 American elms. These trees, which have not suffered from the Dutch elm disease that destroyed most of the country's elms, are believed to be the largest surviving stand in the country.

At the north end of The Mall, you'll come to the **Naumburg Bandshell**. After years of disuse, the bandshell and the area immediately facing it are alive again with occasional performances and a DIY roller disco. Don't miss the **Pergola**, a wooden trestle festooned with wisteria, directly behind the bandshell. From here you'll see **Rumsey Playfield**, the site of the wildly popular and highly recommended **Central Park Summerstage** series (for more details, see Public Holidays & Special Events in the Facts for the Visitor chapter).

Continuing north of the bandshell and across the 72nd St Transverse brings you to **Bethesda Fountain**, a hippie hang-out in the 1960s (nattily depicted in the film *Hair*, which has many scenes set in the park). The fountain, with its *Angel of the Waters* sculpture at the center, has been restored and ranks as one of Central Park's most uplifting sights.

Continue on the path west of the fountain until you reach **Bow Bridge**, a special spot that will have you shouting 'I Love New York!' You can cross the bridge to **the Ramble**, a lush wooden expanse that serves as a decent bird-watching pocket and one of the city's most notorious gay cruising areas.

If you manage to emerge from the Ramble without being hopelessly turned around (no pun intended!), continue north to the 79th St Transverse. Right across the transverse, you'll find the 19th-century **Belvedere Castle** and the

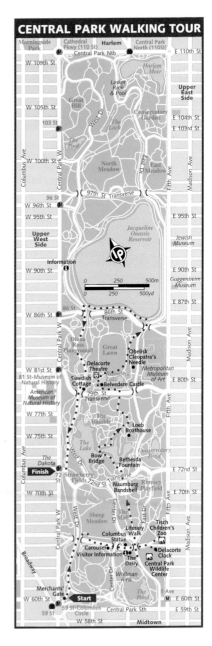

Delacorte Theater, where the Joseph Papp Public Theater holds free, popular, Shakespeare productions each summer.

Immediately beyond the theater is the appropriately named **Great Lawn**, where occasional free concerts take place, along with annual open-air performances by the New York Philharmonic and Metropolitan Opera in June and July. Rock and pop concerts used to be held here, but the lawn couldn't handle the audiences of 75,000, so these events have been banished to the **North Meadow** above 97th St.

RICK GERHARTER

If you walk to the north end of the Great Lawn and cross the 86th St Transverse, you'll come to the **Jacqueline Kennedy Onassis Reservoir**, named for the former first lady, who jogged here. A soft, 1.6-mile cinder path encircles the reservoir and draws a continual parade of runners. The **New York Road Runners Club** (☎ 212-860-4455), which sponsors regular runs through the park, operates an **information booth** (E 90th St & West Dr) near the reservoir entrance.

To wrap up the walking tour, return south on West Dr. At 79th St, you'll be treated to the **Swedish Cottage**, a sweet little chalet that is home to the **Marionette Theater** (☎ 212-988-9093; adult/child $5/4; performances 10:30am & noon Mon-Fri July & Aug, 10:30am & noon Tues-Fri, 1pm Sat Sept-June). Reservations are required for these well-attended professional performances. Continuing to the W 72nd St park entrance brings you to legendary **Strawberry Fields**, the three-acre landscape dedicated to the memory of John Lennon; it contains plants from more than 100 nations and motley offerings from fans. This spot was frequently visited by the former Beatle, who resided in the massive Dakota apartment building across the street, where he was fatally shot.

ANGUS OBORN

Top: Kids love Central Park

Bottom: Don't forget to bring your skates to the Wollman Rink

Central Park Statuary

Strolling through Central Park, an urban adventure slowly unfolds as you discover a secret copse on the shores of Harlem Meer or stumble across ladies and gentlemen in their best-pressed whites hurling balls over the well-groomed grass of a lawn-bowling field. However, one of the greatest surprises in Central Park are the statues, remarkable in number and detail, sprinkled liberally throughout its 843 acres.

Depending on where you enter the park, you might check out the **Maine Monument** (at the Merchants' Gate at Columbus Circle), a tribute to the sailors killed in the mysterious explosion in Havana Harbor in 1898 that sparked the Spanish American War. Alternatively, head further east to the Seventh Ave entrance to see statues of Latin America's greatest liberators, including **José Martí**, 'The Apostle of Cuban Independence' (history buffs will find Martí's proximity to the Maine Monument ironic, to say the least). Further east still, at the **Scholar's Gate** *(Fifth Ave at 60th St)* is a small plaza dedicated to Doris Chanin Freedman, the founder of the Public Art Fund, where you can see a new sculpture every six months.

While almost everyone is familiar with **Angel of the Waters** atop Bethesda Fountain, even those who know Central Park like the back of their hand may have overlooked the Falconer Statue, tucked away on a rise overlooking the 72nd St Transverse nearby. This 1875 bronze recreates the remarkable moment of flight, and the connection between master and charge is regal and palpable. Literary Walk, between Bethesda Fountain and the 65th St Traverse is lined with statues, including the requisite **Christopher Columbus** and literati such as **Robert Burns** and **Shakespeare**.

East and north of here is the Conservatory Water, where model sailboats drift lazily by and kids crawl over the giant toadstools of the **Alice in Wonderland** statue. Replete with Alice of flowing hair and dress, a dapper Mad Hatter and mischievous Cheshire Cat, this is a Central Park treasure and a favorite of kids of all ages. Nearby is the **Hans Christian Andersen** statue, where Saturday story hour (11am June to September) is an entertaining draw.

Heading north, check out **Cleopatra's Needle** on the hillock above 82nd St and East Dr. This obelisk was a gift from Egypt to the United States in 1877 for helping build the Suez Canal. Drop down to East Dr and look up to see the **crouching cat** sculpture, which is poised to pounce on unsuspecting in-line skaters.

At the northeastern extent of the park is the soaring **Duke Ellington** statue, depicting the man and his piano.

N.Y.C.

UPPER EAST SIDE (MAP 7)

The Upper East Side is home to New York's greatest concentration of cultural centers. While many refer to Fifth Ave above 57th St as Museum Mile, others use it as a punch line for the joke that goes: 'what's three miles long with an asshole every 18 ft?' A bit harsh perhaps, but this neighborhood *does* include many of the city's most exclusive hotels and residences. The side streets from Fifth Ave east to Third Ave between 57th and 86th Sts feature some stunning town houses and brownstones, and walking through this area at night offers opportunities to see how the other half lives – go ahead, peer inside those grand libraries and living rooms!

Roosevelt Island

New York's anomalous, planned neighborhood sits on a tiny island no wider than a football field in the middle of the East River between Manhattan and Queens. Once known as Blackwell's Island after the farming family who lived here, the city bought the island in 1828 and constructed several public hospitals and a mental hospital. In the 1970s, New York State built housing for 10,000 people along Roosevelt Island's Main Street, the island's only one. The planned area along the cobblestone roadway resembles an Olympic village or, as some observe more cynically, cookie-cutter college housing.

Zipping across the river via the three-minute aerial tram is a trip in itself and worth the stunning view of the East Side of Manhattan framed by the 59th St Bridge. Instead of heading straight back like most, however, bring a picnic or a bike, as this quiet island is conducive to lounging and cycling.

Trams from the **Roosevelt Island tramway station** (#126; ☎ 212-832-4543; cnr 60th St & Second Ave) leave every 15 minutes on the quarter-hour from 6am to 2am Sunday to Thursday, until 3:30am Friday and Saturday; the one-way fare is $1.50. Roosevelt Island has a subway station; from Manhattan, take the Q train during the day and the B train on nights and weekends. Just make sure that the train you board lists '21st St-Queensbridge' as its final destination.

Mount Vernon Hotel Museum & Garden

This 1799 carriage house, formerly known as the Abigail Adams Smith Museum (#130; ☎ 212-838-6878; 421 E 61st St; Ⓜ 4, 5, 6 to 59th St; adult/senior & student/child $4/3/ free; open 11am-4pm Tues-Sun), between First and York Aves, once belonged to a large riverside estate owned by the daughter of John Adams, the second US president. In the early part of the 19th century it became the Mount Vernon Hotel. House tours are included in the price of museum admission.

Temple Emanu-El

This temple (#112; ☎ 212-744-1400; Ⓦ www .emanuelnyc.org; 1 E 65th St at Fifth Ave; Ⓜ N, R, W to Fifth Ave-59th St; open 10am-5pm daily) is the world's largest reformed Jewish synagogue. Stop by for a look at its notable Byzantine and Middle Eastern architecture.

Frick Collection

The Frick Collection (#90; ☎ 212-288-0700; Ⓦ www.frick.org; 1 E 70th St at Fifth Ave; Ⓜ 6 to 68th St-Hunter College; adult/senior & student $10/5, child under 10 yrs not admitted; open 10am-6pm Tues-Sat, 1pm-6pm Sun) sits in a mansion built by businessman Henry Clay Frick in 1914, one of the many such residences that made up 'Millionaire's Row.' Most of these mansions proved too expensive for succeeding generations and were eventually destroyed, but the wily and very wealthy Frick, a Pittsburgh steel magnate, established a trust to open his private art collection as a museum.

It's a shame that the 2nd floor of the residence is not open for viewing, though the 12 rooms on the ground floor are grand enough and the garden beckons visitors. The Frick's Oval Room is graced by Jean-Antoine Houdon's stunning figure *Diana the Huntress*; the intimate museum also displays works by Titian and Vermeer, and portraits by Gilbert Stuart, El Greco, Goya, and John Constable. An audio tour is included in the price of admission and helps visitors to appreciate the art more fully; you can also dial up information on paintings and sculptures of your choosing on the ArtPhone.

THINGS TO SEE & DO

Whitney Museum of American Art

This museum (☎ 212-570-3600, 800-944-8639; W www.whitney.org; 945 Madison Ave at 75th St; ⓜ 6 to 77th St; adult/senior & student $10/8, child free, pay what you wish 6pm-9pm Fri; open 11am-6pm Tues-Thur & Sat & Sun, 1pm-9pm Fri) makes no secret of its mission to provoke and it starts with the brutalist structure housing the collection. Designed by Bauhaus architect Marcel Breur, the rocklike edifice is a fitting setting for the Whitney's style of cutting-edge American art. In recent years, high-profile exhibitions at MoMA and the Brooklyn Museum of Art have overshadowed the Whitney's efforts to display innovative work, but it continues to stage its famous Biennial (scheduled for 2004 and 2006), an ambitious survey of contemporary art that rarely fails to generate controversy – though the last Biennial was shocking only for its mediocrity.

Established in the 1930s by Gertrude Vanderbilt Whitney, who began a Greenwich Village salon for prominent artists, the collection features works by Edward Hopper, Jasper Johns, Georgia O'Keeffe, Jackson Pollock and Mark Rothko.

For information about the Whitney collection in the Philip Morris Building in Grand Central Terminal, see that section earlier in this chapter. You can use your CityPass at the Whitney; for more details about the pass, see the boxed text 'Museum Bargains,' earlier in this chapter.

Metropolitan Museum of Art

With more than five million visitors each year, the Metropolitan Museum of Art (☎ 212-535-7710; W www.metmuseum.org; Fifth Ave at 82nd St; ⓜ 4, 5, 6 to 86th St; suggested admission adult/senior & student $10/5, child free; open 9:30am-5:30pm Tues-Thur & Sun, 9:30am-9pm Fri & Sat) ranks as New York's most popular single-site tourist attraction, and it boasts one of the richest coffers in the arts world. The Met, as it's generally called, is virtually a self-contained cultural city-state, with two million individual objects in its collection and an annual budget of over $120 million. And, as the saying goes, the

There's so much to see at the Met

rich get richer – in 1999, the museum received a donated collection (worth $300 million) of modern masterpieces, including works by Picasso and Matisse.

Once inside the **Great Hall**, pick up a floor plan and head to the ticket booths, where you will find a list of exhibitions closed for the day, along with a line-up of special museum talks. The Met presents more than 30 special exhibitions and installations each year, and marked floor plans show you how to get to them. It's best to target exactly what you want to see and head there first, before museum fatigue sets in (usually after two hours). Then you can put the floor plan away and get lost trying to get back to the main hall. It's a virtual certainty that you'll stumble across something interesting along the way.

To the right of the Great Hall, an information desk offers guidance in several languages (these change depending on the volunteers) and audio tours of the special exhibitions ($5). The Met also offers free guided walking tours of museum highlights and specific galleries. Check the calendar, given away at the information desk, for the specific schedule. Families will want to see Inside the Museum: A Children's Guide to the Metropolitan Museum of Art and the kid-specific events calendar (both free at the information booth).

If you can't stand crowds, steer clear on a rainy Sunday afternoon in summer. But during horrible winter weather, you might find the 17-acre museum nearly deserted in the evening – a real New York experience.

DALE BUCKTON

THINGS TO SEE & DO

Permanent Galleries If you don't want to see anything in particular, then make a loop of the 1st floor before heading to the 2nd-floor painting galleries. Entering the Egyptian art section in the north wing, you'll pass the tomb of Pernebi (c. 2415 BC), as well as several mummies and incredibly well-preserved wall paintings, before you come to the **Temple of Dendur**. The temple, threatened with submersion during the building of the Aswan Dam, found a home in New York under this glass enclosure – if you look closely at its walls, you can see the graffiti etched by European visitors to the site in the 1820s. There are pretty Central Park vistas from here.

If you can't make it to Cooperstown, exit the gallery through the door behind the temple to behold the Met's collection of **baseball cards**, which includes the rarest and most expensive card in the world – a 1909 Honus Wagner worth some $200,000. Continue on to the left and you'll enter the **American Wing** of furniture and architecture, with a quiet, enclosed garden space that is a perennial favorite as a respite from the hordes. Several stained-glass works by Louis Comfort Tiffany frame the garden, as does an entire two-story facade of the Branch Bank of the US, preserved when the building was destroyed Downtown in the early 20th century.

After passing through the far door of the American Wing, you'll enter the gloomy galleries dedicated to **medieval art**. Turn right and walk across the European decorative arts section to the pyramid-like addition that houses the Robert Lehman Collection of **impressionist and modern art**, featuring several works by Renoir (including *Young Girl Bathing*), Georges Seurat and Pablo Picasso (including *Portrait of Gertrude Stein*). An unexpected bonus in this gallery is the rear terracotta facade of the original 1880 Met building, now completely encased by later additions and standing mutely on view as its own architectural artifact.

Continue on through the European decorative arts section and turn left into the Rockefeller Collection of arts of **Africa, Oceania and the Americas**, heading toward Fifth Ave. At the museum café (at the far end of the Rockefeller Collection) turn left and wander through the **Greek and Roman art** section. The museum has recently restored much of its Greek and Roman work, including the 2nd-floor Cypriot Gallery, which contains some of the finest pieces outside Cyprus.

Elsewhere on the 2nd floor, you'll see the Met's famous collection of **European paintings**, located in some of the museum's oldest galleries, beyond colonnaded entryways. The exhibition features works by every artist of note, including self-portraits by Rembrandt and Van Gogh and *Portrait of Juan de Parej* by Velázquez. An entire suite of rooms focuses on impressionist and postimpressionist art. The new collection of modern masters is housed on this level, as well as the photographs recently purchased by the Met, and the museum's exquisite musical instrument holdings. Also of interest up here are the treasures from Japan, China and Southeast Asia.

THINGS TO SEE & DO

GREG GAWLOWSKI

The ancient Egypt wing of the Metropolitan Museum of Art

Gracie Mansion

At 84th St and the East River, is **Carl Shurz Park**, a favorite spot for a placid riverside stroll or jog (a southbound path runs parallel to the Franklin D Roosevelt Dr until 63rd St). Within the park is Gracie Mansion (#33; ☎ 212-570-4751; 88th St; Ⓜ 4, 5, 6 to 86th St; open Wed late Mar-mid-Nov), the 1799 country residence where New York's mayors have always lived – except for Mr Bloomberg, who already had plush city digs when he landed the mayoral gig in 2002. You must call to reserve a tour slot. Tours take place at 10am, 11am, 1pm and 2pm on Wednesday.

Solomon R Guggenheim Museum

A sculpture in its own right, Frank Lloyd Wright's sweeping spiral building almost overshadows the collection of 20th-century art housed in this museum (☎ 212-423-3500; ⓦ www.guggenheim.org; 1071 Fifth Ave at 89th St; Ⓜ 4, 5, 6 to 86th St; adult/senior & student $15/12, child free, pay what you wish 6pm-8pm Fri; open 9am-6pm Sun-Wed, 9am-8pm Fri & Sat). Because of its unusual design, the building

sparked controversy during its construction in the 1950s, but today it's a distinctive landmark that architects fiddle with at their peril (though would it kill them to hire some contractors to deal with the peeling paint?!). An unpopular 1992 renovation added an adjoining 10-story tower that does indeed bear a striking resemblance to a toilet, just as the critics feared, despite being based on Wright's original drawings.

Inside, you can view some of the museum's 5000 permanent works (plus changing exhibitions) on a path that coincides with Wright's coiled design. Take the elevator to the top and wind your way down. The Guggenheim's collection includes works by Picasso, Chagall, Pollock and Kandinsky. In 1976, Justin Thannhauser's major donation of impressionist and modern works added paintings by Monet, Van Gogh and Degas. In 1992, the Robert Mapplethorpe Foundation gave 200 photographs to the museum, spurring curators to devote the 4th floor to photography exhibitions.

You can use your CityPass here; for more details on this pass, see the boxed text 'Museum Bargains,' earlier in this chapter.

JOHN BANAGAN

A long walk to the top – the Solomon R Guggenheim Museum

National Academy of Design

Cofounded by painter-inventor Samuel Morse, the National Academy of Design (#24; ☎ 212-369-4880; W www.nationalacad emy.org; 1083 Fifth Ave at 89th St; 🚇 4, 5, 6 to 86th St; adult/senior & student $8/4.50, child under 16 free; open noon-5pm Wed & Thur, 10am-6pm Fri, 10am-5pm Sat & Sun) includes a permanent collection of paintings and sculptures housed in yet another stunning beaux-arts mansion, featuring a marble foyer and spiral staircase. This gem was designed by Ogden Codman, who also designed the Breakers mansion in Newport, Rhode Island.

Cooper-Hewitt National Design Museum

This museum (#26; ☎ 212-849-8400; W www .si.edu/ndm; 2 E 91st St at Fifth Ave; 🚇 4, 5, 6 to 86th St; adult/senior & student $8/5, child free, admission free 5pm-9pm Tues; open 10am-9pm Tues, 10am-5pm Wed-Sat, noon-5pm Sun) sits in the 64-room mansion built by billionaire Andrew Carnegie in 1901 in what was, in those days, way Uptown. Within 20 years, the bucolic surroundings Carnegie craved disappeared as other wealthy men followed his lead and built palaces around him. Carnegie was an interesting character; an avid reader and generous philanthropist, he dedicated many libraries around the country and donated some $350 million in his lifetime. To learn more, hop on the 45-minute daily tour at noon or 2pm, which is included in the museum admission price.

Part of the Smithsonian Institution in Washington, this museum is a must for anyone interested in architecture, engineering, jewelry or textiles. Exhibitions have examined everything from advertising campaigns to Viennese blown glass. Even if none of this grabs you, the museum's garden and terrace are still worth a visit and the mansion is stunning.

Jewish Museum

This museum (☎ 212-423-3200; 1109 Fifth Ave at 92nd St; 🚇 6 to 96th St; adult/student & senior $8/5.50, child free, admission free 5pm-8pm Thur; open 10am-5:45pm Sun, 11am-5:45pm Mon-Wed, 11am-8pm Thur, 11am-3pm Fri) primarily features artwork examining 4000 years of Jewish ceremony and culture. Additionally, a wide array of children's activities (storytelling hour, arts and crafts workshops etc) is offered. The building, a 1908 banker's mansion, houses more than 30,000 items of Judaica.

The 2002 exhibition, entitled 'Mirroring Evil: Nazi Imagery/Recent Art', raised a tremendous din with such 'art' as a Lego concentration camp and a computer-altered image of a Holocaust victim going to the gas chamber while sipping a Diet Coke; protests and boycotts accompanied the opening of the exhibit.

You can use your CityPass here; for more details about the pass, see the boxed text 'Museum Bargains.'

New York Academy of Medicine

With over 700,000 catalogued works, New York Academy of Medicine (#10; ☎ 212-822-7200; W www.nyam.org; 1216 Fifth Ave at 103rd St; 🚇 6 to 103rd St; admission free; open 9am-5pm Mon-Fri) is the second-largest health library in the world (included in its holdings is the world's biggest cookbook collection). But skip all the books and head straight for the weird, yet fascinating, medical ephemera like the leper clapper (used by sufferers to warn a town of their arrival); a globule of the world's first penicillin culture; cupping glasses used in phlebotomy procedures; and George Washington's dentures.

Museum of the City of New York

It's too bad this museum (#9; ☎ 212-534-1672; W www.mcny.org; 1220 Fifth Ave; 🚇 6 to 103rd St; suggested donation adult/senior & student $7/4, family $12; open 10am-5pm Wed-Sat, noon-5pm Sun), between 103rd and 104th Sts, is being blocked from moving into the Tweed Courthouse, Downtown; at least that grand building would have brought in some folks to see the museum's hodgepodge collection. Alas, former mayor Giuliani promised them the space, but current mayor Bloomberg put the kibosh on the plan and the museum is in limbo.

Nevertheless, the Museum of the City of New York offers plenty of Internet-based

THINGS TO SEE & DO

historical resources and a decent scale-model of New Amsterdam shortly after the Dutch arrival. The notable 2nd-floor gallery includes entire rooms from demolished homes of New York grandees, an exhibition dedicated to Broadway musicals and a collection of antique doll houses, teddy bears and toys.

El Museo del Barrio

This museum (☎ 212-831-7272; 1230 Fifth Ave; ⓜ 6 to 103rd St; suggested admission adult/senior & student $5/3, child free; open 11am-5pm Wed-Sun), between 104th and 105th Sts, began in 1969 as a celebration of Puerto Rican art and culture and has since expanded its holdings to include the folk art of Latin America and Spain. Its galleries now feature pre-Columbian artifacts and a collection of more than 300 *santos*, hand-carved wooden saints in the Caribbean Catholic tradition. Interesting temporary exhibitions feature the work of local artists and themes such as contemporary Brazilian Art or the History of the Taínos. All signage and brochures are in both English and Spanish.

For over 25 years, the museum has held the **Three Kings Parade** every January 5, in which hundreds of schoolchildren, along with camels, donkeys and sheep, make their way up Fifth Ave to 116th St, the heart of the neighborhood. The parade starts at 10am from Fifth Ave at 106th St (call ☎ 212-831-7272 for information).

El Museo del Barrio is the best starting point for any exploration of Spanish Harlem (see under Harlem later in the chapter).

HARLEM (MAP 8)

From its origins as a 1920s black enclave until now, the heart of black culture has beat in Harlem. This neighborhood north of Central Park has been the setting for extraordinary accomplishments in art, music, dance, education and letters from the likes of Frederick Douglass, Paul Robeson, Thurgood Marshall, James Baldwin, Alvin Ailey, Billie Holiday, Jessie Jackson and just about any other African American luminary you can name.

Harlem gets a bad, scary rap because historically some bad, scary things have gone down here. Nearly half the neighborhood was burned to the ground during riots in the 1960s, crack cocaine devastated families and empowered gangs, and a downward economic spiral just made matters worse. Fortunately, that's old news and Harlem is undergoing a renaissance that is bringing jobs, pride and tourism back Uptown. Even former president Bill Clinton has staked a claim on 125th St, opening up his new offices here (to do exactly what, we're not sure, though there *is* a Krispy Kreme right close by to keep him occupied!).

There are two catalysts that have spurred Harlem's rebirth: the entire neighborhood was declared an Economic Redevelopment Zone in 1996 and tourists (mostly Japanese and European) have been flocking Uptown to check out the area's music and spiritual scene. While Harlem's development has attracted buckets of dollars, it has also brought Disney double-decker tour buses

Harlem kids in their Sunday best

VERONICA GARBUTT

To Tour or Not to Tour

Harlem has become a super-hot spot for visitors who are interested in exploring the roots of African American culture. Indeed, according to a survey conducted in 2000 by the Upper Manhattan Empowerment Zone Development Corp, 20% of respondents said they came to New York specifically to check out Harlem. Unfortunately, Harlem often gets a bad (and often erroneous) rap and many visitors are scared to walk the streets. Preying on these fears, bus companies have been doing a brisk business in overpriced guided tours to the neighborhood. One operator offers a $70 trip to Amateur Night at the Apollo, with dinner at an unspecified soul-food restaurant. Taking the subway yourself ($3 roundtrip), picking up a ticket at the Apollo box office (prices range from $7 to $20) and finding your own restaurant for a meal ($15 or less) represents a huge saving. Moreover, Harlem residents tend to give a better welcome to street-bound visitors than those who gawk at the neighborhood from the ersatz safety of a double-decker bus, as if they were on an urban safari.

Nevertheless, if you'd like some local insight into the neighborhood, a tour may be worthwhile, and there are some sensitive and informed outfits. **Harlem Spirituals** (☎ 212-391-0900; W www .harlemspirituals.com) offers several black heritage excursions for $15 to $90. **Harlem, Your Way!** (☎ 212-690-1687, 800-382-9363; W www.harlemyourwaytours.com) offers a wide array of bus and walking tours for $25 to $65. **Musical Feast of Harlem** (☎ 212-222-6059) offers Sunday morning tours of gospel services in local churches, with prices starting at $60 for adults, including lunch. **Big Onion Walking Tours** (☎ 212-439-1090; W www.bigonion.com) offers a very informative tour of historic Harlem for $12.

THINGS TO SEE & DO

N.Y.C.

and disrespectful crowds clamoring for pews at Sunday services. A balance has yet to be struck, and in the meantime everything is not coming up roses. Mom-and-pop stores are closing in the aftermath of the downturn in tourist revenue caused by September 11 and it's unclear how much local residents are benefiting from Harlem's new boom.

City officials have aggressively promoted Harlem to developers, with the **Harlem USA** (#34; 300 West 125th St) entertainment and retail complex acting as the jewel in the crown. It features a dance club, 12-screen cinema, a rooftop skating rink and an HMV store.

First-time visitors will probably be surprised to discover that Harlem is just one subway stop away from the Columbus Circle-59th St station. The trip on the A and D trains takes only five minutes, and both stop just one block from the Apollo Theater and two blocks from Malcolm X Blvd (Lenox Ave). The 2 and 3 trains from the West Side stop at 116th St, the site of Harlem Market, and at 125th St.

Despite its past reputation as a crime-ridden no-man's-land, today Harlem shouldn't cause you to exercise any more caution than you would anywhere else in New York.

Orientation

As you explore Harlem, you'll notice that the major avenues have been renamed in honor of prominent African Americans; however, many locals still call the streets by their original names, which makes finding your way around a little confusing. Eighth Ave (Central Park West) is Frederick Douglass Blvd. Seventh Ave is Adam Clayton Powell Jr Blvd, named for the controversial preacher who served in Congress during the 1960s. Lenox Ave has been renamed for the Nation of Islam leader Malcolm X. 125th St, the main avenue and site of many businesses, is also known as Martin Luther King Jr Blvd. Proper names have been used throughout this book.

Walking in Harlem can be really tiring as the sites are pretty spread out and subway stations are few and far between; up here the buses can be handier than the train.

Apollo Theater

The Apollo Theater (#32; ☎ 212-531-5337; 5253 W 125th St at Frederick Douglass Blvd; ⓜ A, B, C, D to 125th St) has been Harlem's leading space for political rallies and concerts since 1914. Virtually every major black artist of note in the 1930s and '40s performed here, including Duke Ellington and Charlie Parker. After a desultory spell as a movie theater and several years of darkness, the Apollo was bought in 1983 and revived as a live venue. It was renovated in 2002. The Apollo still holds its famous weekly Amateur Night, 'where stars are born and legends are made', at 7:30pm on Wednesday. Watching the crowd call for the 'executioner' to yank hapless performers from the stage is often the best part. On other nights, the Apollo hosts performances by established artists like Whitney Houston and comedian Chris Rock. Tours cost $10 person and leave at 11am, 1pm and 3pm Monday to Friday. Tour participants get to perform a number on the famed stage.

ESBIN ANDERSON PHOTOGRAPHY

Studio Museum in Harlem

This museum (#31; ☎ 212-864-4500; ⓦ www.studiomuseum.org; 144 W 125th St; ⓜ 2, 3 to 125th St; adult/senior & student $5/3, child $1; open noon-6pm Wed & Thur, noon-8pm Fri, 10am-6pm Sat & Sun), close to Adam Clayton Powell Jr Blvd, has been a leading benefactor and promoter of African American artists for nearly 30 years and provides working spaces for the up and coming. Its photography collection includes works by James VanDerZee, the master photographer who chronicled the Harlem renaissance of the 1920s and '30s.

Schomburg Center for Research in Black Culture

The nation's largest collection of documents, rare books, recordings and photographs relating to the African American

experience resides at this center (#21; ☎ 212-491-2200; 515 Malcolm X Blvd; ⓜ 2, 3 to 135th St; admission free; open noon-8pm Mon-Wed, 10am-6pm Thur-Sat, gallery spaces also open 1pm-5pm Sun), near W 135th St. Arthur Schomburg, who was born in Puerto Rica, started gathering works on black history during the early 20th century while becoming active in the movements for civil rights and Puerto Rican independence. His impressive collection was purchased by the Carnegie Foundation and eventually expanded and stored in this branch of the New York Public Library. Lectures and concerts are regularly held in the theater here.

Church Services

Harlem Sunday services, which are mostly Baptist, pack in the crowds with their deep spirituality and rocking gospel choirs. Unfortunately, the tour buses have been rolling in with their own crowds recently (some of the churches have side deals going with operators), which has resulted in a clash of cultures, with worshippers trying to get in touch with God and sightseers trying to snap the perfect photo. If you are heading to church this Sunday, take a look at the boxed text 'Church Comportment' for some basic tips on appropriate behavior. As the old saying goes, in Harlem 'there's a bar on every corner and a church on every block.' We've listed several churches here, but there are probably twice as many more in the immediate neighborhood, so instead of overwhelming the few we have space to mention, seek out your own – most church marquees proclaim 'all are welcome.' Services usually start at 11am.

Founded by an Ethiopian businessman, the **Abyssinian Baptist Church** (#19; ☎ 212-862-7474; 132 W 138th St; ⓜ 2, 3 to 135th St; services 9am & 11am Sun), near Adam Clayton Powell Jr Blvd called Odell Clark Pl, began as a Downtown institution but moved north to Harlem in 1923, mirroring the migration of the city's black population. Its charismatic pastor, Calvin O Butts III, is an important community activist whose support is sought by politicians of all parties. The church has a superb choir and the

Church Comportment

I'm the last heathen who should be throwing stones or doling advice on the finer points of church-going, but it seems some tourists among the throngs that have been swooping in on Sunday services lately are not showing the proper respect. So that the experience may be uplifting and joyous for everyone, here are some common-sense tips:

- Arrive early; in the case of Abyssinian, this means 30 to 60 minutes beforehand.
- Dress properly – parishioners will be in their Sunday best, pressed and proud; don't sully the scene by wearing jeans, sweatsuits, shorts or sneakers (unless they're clean, cool kicks).
- Don't get huffy and insistent if the church fills up and they can't let you in; usually they'll help you out, suggesting another service, but if not, wander around and find your own.
- As with any traveling experience, participating is way more dynamic and rewarding than simply observing. Participation could mean donating to the collection plate or singing, clapping or praying along.
- Ask about the church's photo policy (most won't let you shoot).
- Do not leave part way through the service.

N.Y.C.

THINGS TO SEE & DO

building is a beauty. Services are at 9am and 11am. Around the corner, **Mother African Methodist Episcopal Zion Church** (#20; ☎ 212-234-1545; 146 W 137th St; ⓜ 2, 3 to 135th St) usually takes the overflow from Abyssinian.

The **Canaan Baptist Church** (#50; ☎ 212-866-5711; 132 W 116th St; ⓜ 2, 3 to 116th St; services 10.45am Sun Oct-June, 10am July-Sept), near St Nicholas Ave, is perhaps Harlem's friendliest church.

As the churches mentioned above see a lot of traffic, you might try one of the following instead:

Baptist Temple (#56; ☎ 212-996-0334)
20 W 116th St
Metropolitan Baptist Church (#26; ☎ 212-663-8990) 151 W 128th St
St Paul Baptist Church (#24; ☎ 212-283-8174)
249 W 132nd St
Salem United Methodist Church (#25; ☎ 212-722-3969) 211 W 129th St
Second Providence Baptist Church (#55; ☎ 212-831-6751) 11 W 116th St

Harlem Market

Vendors at the semi-enclosed Harlem Market (#53; 116th St; ⓜ 2, 3 to 116th St; open 10am-5pm daily), between Malcolm X Blvd and Fifth Ave, do a brisk business selling tribal masks, oils, drums, traditional clothing and assorted African bric-a-brac. You can also get cheap clothing, leather goods, music cassettes and bootleg videos of films still in first-run theaters.

The market is operated by the **Malcolm Shabazz Mosque**, the former pulpit of Muslim orator Malcolm X.

Spanish Harlem

East of Harlem, Spanish Harlem (ⓜ 6 to 103rd, 110th or 116th Sts) extends from Fifth Ave to the East River, above 96th St. This is one of the biggest Latino communities (Puerto Rican, Dominican and Cuban mostly) in the city and proud of it: Puerto Rican flags fly from vans blaring salsa, men play dominos in front of ramshackle *casitas* (houses) in the community gardens and people hang out on stoops, shouting to their neighbors in Spanglish.

Interesting stops here include **El Museo del Barrio** (see the separate entry earlier in this chapter), **La Marqueta**, a colorful, ad-hoc collection of produce and meat stalls on Park Ave above 110th St, and Duke Ellington Circle, with a **statue** (#57) of the man and his piano, where Fifth Ave and Central Park North (also known as Tito Puente Way) converge.

HAMILTON HEIGHTS & SUGAR HILL (MAP 8)

This area, which extends north of Harlem from about 138th to 155th Sts west of Edgecombe Ave, is loaded with off-the-beaten path delights. One of the greatest ways to get to a Yankees game is to head east on 155th St and walk across the **Macombs Dam Bridge** (which is also the best way to get to Yankee Stadium from Manhattan by car). In the summer, die-hard basketball fiends will want to check out the legendary competitions at **Rucker Park** *(#4; 155th St at Harlem River;* Ⓜ *B, D to 155th St)*. Unfortunately, this can't be recommended without a local escort, as the tight-knit community up here doesn't readily welcome outsiders.

Architecture buffs will appreciate the **Bailey House** *(#11; 10 St Nicholas Pl at W 150th St;* Ⓜ *C to 155th St)*, former home of circus guru James A Bailey. Though it's now a funeral home, this 1880s, Gothic Revival mansion boasts granite facades and gabled roofs and is•worth a look. The building next door at 14 Nicholas Pl is another stroke of structural whimsy with its wooden shutters with flower details and cedar-shingled dome.

Striver's Row

Also known as the St Nicholas Historic District, Striver's Row *(cnr W 138th & 139th Sts;* Ⓜ *B, C to 135th St)*, just east of St Nicholas Park between Frederick Douglass and Adam Clayton Powell Jr Blvds, has prized row houses and apartments, many designed by Stanford White's firm in the 1890s. When whites moved out of the neighborhood, Harlem's black elite occupied the buildings, thus giving the area its colloquial name. This is one of the most visited blocks in Harlem, so discretion is the better part of valor, as the locals are a bit sick of all the tourists. Streetside plaques explain more of the area's history. Check out the alleyway signs advising visitors to 'walk their horses.'

Hamilton Grange

This was Alexander Hamilton's original country retreat *(#17;* ☎ *212-283-5154; 141st St at Convent Ave;* Ⓜ *A, B, C, D to 145th St; admission free; open 9am-5pm Fri-Sun)*.

When this Federal-style home was moved to this too-small spot from its original location, it had to be turned sidewise and squeezed to fit, so now the facade faces inward! The ink has just dried on an agreement to relocate it once and for all to a permanent site in St Nicholas Park, where it will be restored and reoriented to historic specifications.

Nearby, the **Hamilton Heights Historic District** runs along Convent Ave from the City College of New York campus (with its own architectural marvels; unfortunately they were under scaffolding at the time of writing) at 140th St to 145th St. This is one of the last remaining stretches of untouched limestone and brownstone townhouses in New York – it's gorgeous.

WASHINGTON HEIGHTS (MAP 8)

Near the northern tip of Manhattan (above 155th St), Washington Heights takes its name from the first US president, who set up a Continental Army fort here during the Revolutionary War. An isolated rural spot until the end of the 19th century, Washington Heights is attracting new blood as New Yorkers discover its affordable rents. Still, this neighborhood retains its Latino flavor, with a continual stream of Dominican immigrants settling here. Spanish comes in handy in the Heights.

Most visitors to Washington Heights come to see the handful of museums, particularly the Cloisters in Fort Tryon Park, a beautiful spot in warm weather. Free shuttle buses run between the area's museums between 11am and 5pm. (Call any one of the following museums to find out the schedule.)

Audubon Terrace

Naturalist John James Audubon once lived in Audubon Terrace *(Broadway at 155th St,* Ⓜ *1 to 157th St)*, which now houses three fantastic and free museums set in a delightful plaza.

The **American Numismatic Society** *(#7;* ☎ *212-234-3130; admission free; open 9am-4:30pm Tues-Fri)* owns a large permanent collection of coins, medals and paper money.

The **Hispanic Society of America** *(#6;* ☎ *212-926-2234;* ⓦ *www.hispanicsociety.org;*

admission free; open 10am-4:30pm Tues-Sat, 1pm-4pm Sun) is a treasure of Spanish, Portuguese and Latin American art housed in a two-level, ornately carved space hung with gold-and-silk tapestries. The society has a substantial collection of works by El Greco, Goya, Diego Velázquez, and the formidable Joaquín Sorolla y Bastida, and a library with over 25,000 volumes. Head upstairs for a bird's-eye view; all signage and brochures are bilingual in English and Spanish.

American Academy and Institute of Arts and Letters *(#7; ☎ 212-368-5900; admission free)* opens its bronze doors to the public several times a year for temporary exhibitions; call ahead for the schedule.

Morris-Jumel Mansion

Built in 1765, the columned Morris-Jumel Mansion *(#2; ☎ 212-923-8008; 65 Jumel Terrace at 160th St; ⓜ C to 163rd St-Amsterdam Ave; adult $3, senior, student & child over 9 yrs $2; open 10am-4pm Wed-Sun)*, east of St Nicholas Ave, served as George Washington's Continental Army headquarters. After the war, it returned to the Eliza Jumel who had a sordid past, not limited to being the second wife of vice president Aaron Burr. Rumor has it that Eliza's ghost still flits about the place. A designated landmark, the mansion's interior contains many of the original furnishings, including a 2nd-floor bed that reputedly belonged to Napoleon. The grounds are particularly attractive when the spring blossoms are out.

Leading east from St Nicholas Ave and 161st St to the mansion is lovely **Sylvan Terrace**, a cobblestone lane lined with wooden-shuttered row houses. Perpendicular to this street is **Jumel Terrace**, with some fine limestone houses; Paul Robeson once lived at No 16.

Down the block on the corner of 160th St is **555 Edgecombe Ave** *(#3)*. In addition to being the address of Jackie Robinson, Thurgood Marshall and Paul Robeson at one time or another, current resident Marjorie Eliot hosts convivial, free **jazz jams** in her home at Apt 3F *(☎ 212-781-6595)*; held at 4pm on Saturday and Sunday, open to the public and warmly recommended.

ANGUS OBORN

Enjoy the peace at The Cloisters

The Cloisters (Map 13)

Simply put, the Cloisters *(#1; ☎ 212-923-3700; ⓦ www.metmuseum.org; ⓜ A to 190th St; suggested admission adult/senior & student $10/5, child free; open 9:30am-4:45pm Tues-Sun Nov-Feb, 9:30am-5:15pm Tues-Sun Mar-Oct)*, in Fort Tryon Park overlooking the Hudson River, is one of the most peaceful places in the city to visit on a sunny day. Built in the 1930s, the museum incorporates fragments of old French and Spanish monasteries and houses the Metropolitan Museum of Art's collection of medieval frescos, tapestries and paintings. In summer, which is the best time to visit, concerts take place in the grounds, and more than 250 varieties of medieval flowers and herbs are on view.

Dyckman Farmhouse Museum (Map 13)

Built in 1784 on a 28-acre farm, the Dyckman House *(#2; ☎ 212-304-9422; 4881 Broadway at 204th St; ⓜ A to 207th St; admission $1; open 10am-4pm Tues-Sun)* is Manhattan's lone surviving Dutch farmhouse. Excavations of the property have turned up valuable clues about colonial life, and the museum includes period rooms and furniture, decorative arts, a half acre of gardens and an exhibition on the neighborhood's history.

To get to the Dyckman House, take the subway to the 207th St station and walk one block south – many people mistakenly get off one stop too soon at Dyckman St.

Outer Boroughs

THE BRONX (MAP 13)

The Bronx – a geographic area with a curious article before its name, like the Hague and the Yucatán – takes its name from the BroncK family, Dutch farmers who owned a huge chunk of the property here. They in turn gave their name to Bronck's River, which led to the derivation used today. In the street it's called 'The Boogie Down' and is the birthplace to famous New Yorkers, including J Lo, Puff Daddy and Colin Powell.

The Bronx, once a forest-like respite but now home to 1.3 million people, has long been a metaphor for urban decay – many know it only as the poverty-plagued and crime-ridden borough that gave birth to the disenfranchised voices of American rap music (see the boxed text 'The New York Sound' in the Facts about New York City chapter). But even the southwestern part of the Bronx – the area unofficially referred to as the South Bronx – doesn't quite live up to its reputation. Still, it's not a good place to wander on your own.

Although some sections of the lower Bronx, including Morrisania, are still blighted with abandoned buildings, the northern reaches of the borough feature areas like Fieldston, a community of Tudor homes occupied by some of the city's richest residents. The Bronx also boasts the quiet and isolated fishing community of City Island, as well as the 2764-acre Pelham Bay Park, the city's largest.

The only borough of New York City that is part of the US mainland, the Bronx begins northeast of Manhattan (across the Harlem River) and extends into upstate New York. The northern part of the borough gives way to the leafy suburbs of Westchester County.

The **Bronx Tourism Council** (☎ 718-590-3518; W www.ilovethebronx.com) offers a visitor's guide to the borough and keeps track of community events. The website is well designed and offers current calendar listings, links and event information. The **Bronx County Historical Society** (☎ 718-881-8900) sponsors weekend walking tours of various sites. Call for details.

Yankee Stadium

The Yankees call their legendary ballpark 'the most famous stadium since the Roman Coliseum.' Yankee Stadium (#18; ☎ 718-293-6000; W www.yankees.com; E 161st St &

Five Secret Pleasures of the Outer Boroughs

City Island in the Bronx

Thirteen miles from Midtown, this incongruous New England–style enclave offers opportunities for fishing and water sports.

Jacques Marchais Center of Tibetan Art

This quirky, tranquil Staten Island museum is worth the ferry trip on a sunny summer day or during its Tibetan cultural festival held in early October, when there are activities and performances to entertain both young and old.

Brighton Beach

A little bit of old mother Russia lives on the southeastern coast of Brooklyn, and the thrilling Cyclone roller coaster is a short stroll down the boardwalk in Coney Island.

Panorama of New York City

This incredibly detailed miniature representation of the city is a must-see at the Queens Museum of Art in Flushing.

The New York Yankees: Team of the Century

No team has loomed larger in American baseball history than the New York Yankees. The 'Bronx Bombers' are arguably one of the most famous sports team in the world (and the most successful team every other fan loves to hate), and their team logo, an interlocking 'NY' on a navy blue hat, has become an international symbol. You can find folks sporting Yankees caps in cities as diverse as London, Beijing, Havana and Cairo. Even the Yankees' ballpark has become famous; it's hosted a number of heavyweight title fights and masses celebrated by two popes (Pope Paul VI and John Paul II).

The Yankees' dynasty began in 1920, when the team picked up a pitcher named George Herman 'Babe' Ruth from the Boston Red Sox. Ruth's spectacular home-run hitting drew huge crowds, and he helped the Yankees win their first American League pennant in 1921 and their first World Series in 1923. When it was built in 1923, Yankee Stadium earned the nickname the 'House that Ruth Built' because it was partly designed to suit his hitting style and to fit the many fans who came just to see him.

In 1927, Babe Ruth hit 60 homers, which remained a record for a single season until 1961 (for an interesting, partially fictionalized, account of Roger Maris' bid to break Ruth's single season record, rent Billy Crystal's directorial debut, *61**). His career total of 714 home runs (659 for the Yankees) wasn't surpassed until Hank Aaron beat it in 1974.

This baseball team had a talent for attracting one major star after another from the 1920s to the '60s. Lou Gehrig, Joe DiMaggio and Mickey Mantle became popular cultural icons even to people who didn't follow baseball. Although the Yankees experienced an unfortunate shallow, fallow period during this author's formative fan years in the '80s, the team came roaring back at the end of the century, capturing four World Series victories from 1996 to 2000, and setting several records in the process. (When the Yankees won their 25th World Series title in 1999, it marked the team as the most successful baseball club of all time.) This success must be attributed to the star-studded roster, including superlative manager and native New Yorker Joe Torre. As if this wasn't enough drama for New York baseball fans, the 2000 World Series was a 'Subway Series' (the first since 1956), pitching the Yankees against the Mets, dividing families and office pools, neighbors and friends, and igniting the entire state with baseball fever. In 2001, the Yankees went to the World Series again, and ratcheted the drama meter up just a little higher when they fell to the Diamond-backs in the ninth inning of game seven.

Fever runs high at Yankee Stadium

ANGUS OBORN

THINGS TO SEE & DO

N.Y.C.

River Ave; **○** B, D, 4 to Yankee Stadium) hosts 81 home games from April to October (see the boxed text 'The New York Yankees: Team of the Century'). Gates open 90 minutes before night games on weekdays (two hours early on weekends) and if you have some time before the first pitch, take a stroll around **Monument Park**, behind left field, where plaques commemorate such baseball greats as Babe Ruth, Lou Gehrig, Mickey Mantle and Joe DiMaggio. The park closes 45 minutes before the game begins.

Tickets range from $15 to $42.50 and, since the Yanks kick ass, are usually hard to get hold of, but $8 bleacher seats are almost always available. This is because they are so far away, the runner may be out by the time you hear the bat thwocking the ball. There's also no shade and the section is so notoriously rowdy, they banned the sale of alcohol here; uniformed cops stand guard just in case. See Spectator Sports in the Entertainment chapter for how to purchase tickets.

You can also visit the dugout, the press room and the locker room during a guided tour of the ballpark (call **☎** 718-579-4531 for reservations). The hour-long tours take place between 10am and 4pm Monday to Friday and between 10am and noon Saturday when the team is on the road, or between 10am and noon Monday to Friday when the team is at home. Tours cost $10/5 per adult/senior and child. An expanded tour that also includes a short film costs $15/10.

Across the street from the stadium stand several bustling memorabilia shops and restaurants. **Stan's Sports Bar** gets particularly raucous when the Yankees play their rival, the Boston Red Sox.

Bronx Museum of the Arts

If you're headed to the ballpark, consider a quick detour to this museum (#17; **☎** 718-681-6000; **W** www.bxma.org; 1040 Grand Concourse at 165th St; **○** B, D, 4 to 161st St-Yankee Stadium, B, D to 167th St; adult/senior & student $3/2, admission free Wed; open noon-9pm Wed, noon-6pm Thur-Sun). The museum often shows the work of

young city artists, exhibiting lots of urban angst. The Grand Concourse, the Borough's largest avenue, is three blocks to the east of Yankee Stadium.

Hall of Fame for Great Americans

One of New York's most neglected sites is the Hall of Fame for Great Americans (#15; **☎** 718-220-6003; 183rd St at Sedgwick Ave; **○** 4 to 183rd St; admission free; open 10am-5pm daily) at Bronx Community College in University Heights. This outdoor colonnade, which overlooks the Hudson River, features bronze busts of more than 100 notables (the first 29 were crafted by Tiffany's studios).

The Hall of Fame languished in disrepair until a $3 million restoration spiffed things up in the mid-1980s. For years, the 620ft-long hall contained the bust of just one woman, suffragette Susan B Anthony, but now it also includes American Red Cross founder Clara Barton, astronomer Maria Mitchell and writer Harriet Beecher Stowe, among others. The men on display include George Washington, Ben Franklin and Alexander Graham Bell.

The neighborhood is rather out of the way, so if you visit the Hall of Fame, do so during the day, preferably when the college is in session.

New York Botanical Garden

This 250-acre garden (#4; **☎** 718-817-8700; **W** www.nybg.org; **○** B, D to Bedford Park Blvd; adult/senior & student $3/2, child $1; open 10am-6pm Tues-Sun Apr-Oct, 10am-4pm Nov-Mar & Mon holidays) features several beautiful gardens, 50 acres of primary forest and the restored Victorian **Enid A Haupt Conservatory**, a grand iron-and-glass edifice that is a New York City landmark. You can also stroll through an outdoor **rose garden**, just next to the conservatory, and a **rock garden** with a multitiered waterfall.

Metro-North trains (**☎** 212-532-4900; **W** www.mnr.org) leave hourly from Grand Central Terminal and stop right at the garden; the fare is $3.75 each way. You can also take the 4 train to Bedford Park Blvd and walk east down the hill seven blocks to the gate.

ANGUS OBORN

Grab a slice in Arthur Ave, the Little Italy of the Bronx

THINGS TO SEE & DO

Bronx Zoo

The Bronx Zoo (#10; ☎ 718-367-1010; W www.wcs.org; Ⓜ 2, 5 to Pelham Pkwy; adult/senior/child over 2 yrs $11/7/6, Wed free; open 10am-5pm Mon-Fri, 10am-5:30pm Sat & Sun summer, 10am-4:30pm daily winter, extended evening hours Thanksgiving-New Year), also known by its more politically correct title Bronx Wildlife Conservation Society, attracts more than two million visitors annually. Nearly 5000 animals live at the 265-acre facility, all in comfortable, naturalistic settings. It's best to visit the zoo in warm weather, since many of the outdoor rides close during the winter months and the animals retreat into shelter areas – which means that you'll be stuck touring the older buildings, where the reptiles and birds reside.

To see the usual array of lions, tigers and bears, take the Bengali Express, a 25-minute narrated monorail journey through the Wild Asia areas; it costs $2 and operates from May to October. The large Jungle World indoor exhibition (open year-round) re-creates the Asian tropics with 100 different species of animal and tropical plants. You'll either be delighted or terrified by the World of Darkness, where bats hover nearly unseen (but not unsmelled).

Liberty Lines Express (☎ 718-652-8400) charges $7 for a bus ride to the Bronx Zoo from Manhattan; buses pick up passengers along Madison Ave (at 26th, 47th, 54th, 63rd, 69th and 84th Sts). You can also drive to the zoo via the Bronx River Pkwy.

Arthur Avenue

Just south of Fordham University is Belmont, the Little Italy of the Bronx (Ⓜ B, D to Fordham Rd). More authentic than its Manhattan counterpart, even the ATM instructions are displayed in Italian here and the smell of baking bread will make you swoon. Arthur Ave in Belmont makes a good day trip for soaking up true Italian American culture; bring your appetite (for more information, see the Places to Eat chapter later).

Arthur Ave is the place to stock up on Italian provisions, including live chickens at the **Arthur Ave Poultry Market** (☎ 718-733-4006; 2356 Arthur Ave). The **Arthur Ave Retail Market** (2344 Arthur Ave) contains indoor food stalls, including **Mike & Sons**, (☎ 718-295-5033), a cheese shop with heartbreakingly tasty aged Parmesan and prosciutto. From a small street table, **Cosenza's fresh fish store** (☎ 718-364-8510; 2354 Arthur Ave) sells clams on the half-shell to pedestrians, while clerks at the **Calabria Pork Store** (☎ 718-367-5145; 2338 Arthur Ave) offer free samples of hot and sweet homemade sausages that age on racks along the ceiling. **Biancardi's** (☎ 718-733-4058; 2350 Arthur Ave) is an Italian butcher extraordinaire – look for the bunnies in the window. Most of the bread served in fine restaurants across the city comes from Arthur Ave. Try the **Arthur Avenue Baking Company** (2413 Arthur Ave) for freshly baked loaves.

The **Belmont Italian American Playhouse** (☎ *718-364-4700*, **w** *www.belmontplayhouse .org; 2384 Arthur Ave*) is the neighborhood's most lively performance spot. Its season of new theatrical works runs from April to December, and local authors and musicians perform year-round.

To reach Arthur Ave, take the Metro-North train (or the subway) from Grand Central to Fordham Rd and walk east 11 blocks; turn right at Arthur Avenue and continue south for three blocks.

City Island

Surely the oddest neighborhood in the Bronx is City Island, a 1.5-mile-long fishing community 15 miles from Midtown. Its numerous boat slips and three yacht clubs make City Island the place to go if you're interested in diving, sailing or fishing in Long Island Sound. Maritime buffs might also visit the **North Wind Environmental Center** (☎ *718-885-0777; City Island Ave*), a small museum that is home to Physty the Whale (we just like the name!).

All City Island's shops and seafood restaurants (there are dozens) are along City Island Ave, which runs the length of the island. On the short side streets, attractive clapboard houses overlook the surrounding water and there are terrific views of the Manhattan skyline.

As befits a seaside town, most activities here revolve around the water. If you're interested in fishing or sailing, head to the island's western side, home to all the main marinas. Boats offering fishing trips (as well as NY Harbor sightseeing tours and charters) include the **Riptide III** (☎ *718-885-0236*) and **Daybreak II** (☎ *718-409-9765*). Fishing trips cost $45/40/25 per adult/senior/child and last from 8:30am to 4:30pm; ask if the price includes bait and tackle.

To reach City Island, take the subway (line 6) to its terminus at Pelham Bay Park, then get on the Bx29 bus, which runs directly to City Island Ave.

If you're out this way, you might also like to visit **Pelham Bay Park**, which has miles of bike and hiking trails, a driving range and horseback riding. Nearby is **Orchard Beach**, a pretty stretch of sand once known as the 'Riviera of New York City.' Nowadays it hosts mobs of families escaping the summer swelter. To get here, you can take the Bx12 bus (in summer only); for more information, visit **w** *www.nyc.gov/parks*.

ANGUS OBORN

A traditional timber house on City Island

BROOKLYN (MAP 9)

Brooklyn is booming, baby! Pundits and scenemakers are calling this borough the 'new Manhattan' and, with the clubs, lounges, restaurants, art, history and architecture, it's almost true. The qualifier isn't meant as a zing to the considerable Brooklyn pride, but until there's a train to Red Hook, y'all can just lay down. There are 2.4 million Brooklynites out there, and the borough goes so far as to officially boast that 'one out of every seven famous people' in America was born in Brooklyn!

Brooklyn, officially called Kings County, derives its name from *breucklen*, the Dutch word for marshland. For most of its 350-year history, Brooklyn was a collection of farming villages, and its citizens joined greater New York City reluctantly. Even after the 1898 consolidation, the borough remained independent in spirit; citizens enjoyed Prospect Park (Brooklyn's own version of Central Park), followed the fortunes of the Brooklyn Dodgers baseball team and sun-worshipped at the ritzy resort hotels on Coney Island. But much of Brooklyn's separate city pretensions ended with the construction of the Brooklyn Bridge, forever linking it to Manhattan for better or worse. Furthermore, when the Dodgers – unforgivably – moved to the West Coast in 1957, it was the end of an era. Today, immigrants from the Caribbean, Eastern Europe and the former Soviet Union live in Brooklyn's inner neighborhoods, while Manhattan professionals have snapped up the old carriage houses and brownstones in the western part of the borough.

Information

Brooklyn Information & Culture (BRIC; #12; ☎ 718-855-7882; W www.brooklynx.org; 2nd floor, 647 Fulton St) issues a free calendar of events called *Meet Me in Brooklyn*. Copies are available at all Brooklyn cultural institutions. BRIC also has maps and other tourist information. *Brooklyn Bridge*, a monthly magazine available in shops and newsstands throughout the borough, offers a more extensive list of happenings. A number of free neighborhood newspapers also cover local events.

GERARD FRITZ / NOVASTOCK

The two bridges shine at night

For Internet access, try **PostNet** (#26; ☎ 718-852-0082; 41 Schermerhorn St) or **Mail Boxes, Etc** (#29; ☎ 718-246-6861; 138 Court St). Both are in Cobble Hill and are open daily.

New York Transit Museum

Appropriately enough, this museum (#24; ☎ 718-243-8601; W www.mta.nyc.ny.us/museum; cnr Boerum Pl & Schermerhorn St; Ⓜ 1, 2, 4, 5 to Borough Hall) resides in a decommissioned 1930s' subway station. Its exhibits include an impressive collection of subway cars from the transit system's first 100 years; most have their original advertisements still intact. Keep an eye peeled for the silver car used in the 1995 film *Money Train*, along with the model R-1, the vintage that inspired Duke Ellington's *Take the A Train*. You'll also see the 1947 R-11 model, which featured 'germicidal' lighting designed to sterilize tunnel air; this model was discontinued amid fears that the lights would also sterilize subway conductors!

The museum was closed for a major renovation in 2002; it's due to reopen in 2003.

THINGS TO SEE & DO

Brooklyn Heights Walking Tour

This neighborhood of brownstones, mansions and landmark churches near the mouth of the East River developed as a ferry departure point for Lower Manhattan in the early 19th century and is now a fashionable address. There's a stunning view of Manhattan's new skyline from the promenade, framed at the bottom by the metalstorage warehouses along the waterfront – it's an interesting contrast. This walking tour should take around 90 minutes, but adjust your time accordingly if you walk across the Brooklyn Bridge, shop a bit or take pit stops for beers, pastries or lunch.

The best way to approach Brooklyn is on foot. This walking tour begins in Lower Manhattan, at the entrance to the Brooklyn Bridge. After a 20-minute walk across the bridge (look back for picture-perfect vistas of the Municipal and Woolworth Buildings), bear right on the bridge's pedestrian walkway (bearing left will dump you in Dumbo – see that heading, later). This puts you on Adams St, from where you head south one long block to begin this tour in **Columbus Park**. A patch of concrete with benches, this park has a **Columbus statue** by Emma Stebbins, the sculptor who crafted *Angel of the Waters* in Central Park.

At the southern end of Columbus Park is the landmark 1848 **Brooklyn Borough Hall** (☎ 718-875-4047; 209 Joralemon St; open 9am-5pm Mon-Fri); a free tour of the historic facility takes place at 1pm on Tuesday. On the tour, you'll see the massive central rotunda, marble entrance hall and beaux-arts-style courtroom.

Bearing west from Columbus Park along Montague St, you'll come to Clinton St. Turn right and walk one block to Pierrepont (pronounced **pier-pont**) St, site of the **Brooklyn Historical Society** (☎ 718-624-0890; w www.brooklynhistory.org; 128 Pierrepont St; open noon-5pm Tues-Sat). This beautiful landmark building was completely renovated in 2002 and houses a library, museum and auditorium. You can surf the society's digitized collection of 31,000 photographs and prints in the 2nd-floor library. The society also leads walking tours; call ☎ 718-222-4111.

Make a left heading south on Henry St and you'll come to Montague St, the main avenue for cafés, bars and shops. Make a right here, refuel with a cup of coffee and head to **Heights Books** (☎ 718-624-4876; 109 Montague St) to browse some high-quality, low-priced used books.

ANGUS OBORN

Top: The Brooklyn Bridge (photograph by Angus Oborn)

Bottom: Squeeze a little shopping in at Court Street, Brooklyn

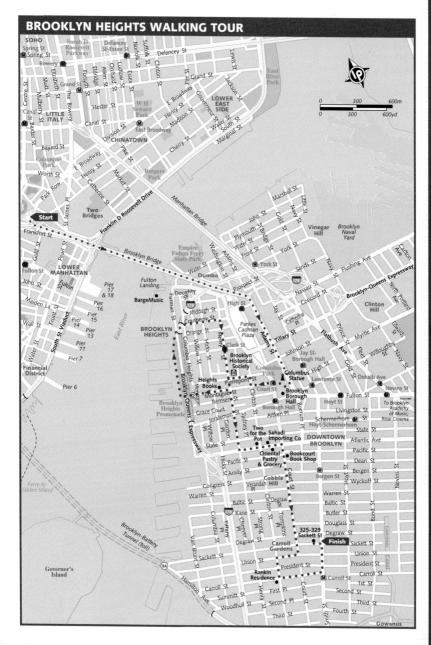

BROOKLYN HEIGHTS WALKING TOUR

Proceed several blocks east to the waterfront promenade at the end of the street. From here you can turn right and continue along the promenade to **Fulton Landing**, the old ferry dock at the base of the Brooklyn Bridge. Most Manhattan-bound ferries departed from here before the bridge loomed overhead. Now classical music concerts take place on **BargeMusic** (☎ 718-624-4061), a magical place to check out an all-Brahms repertoire or a Mozart concerto; tickets cost $20 to $40, and concerts are held from Thursday to Sunday. This is the perfect spot to watch the sun set beyond Manhattan.

At the end of the promenade, bear right under the Brooklyn Queens Expressway (BQE) until Cranberry St; this brings you to the heart of the Brooklyn Heights Historic District, designated in 1965, with row upon row of Italianate and Greek Revival town houses. Note the old wooden-frame houses around the intersection of Middagh and Henry Sts.

Turn right on Henry St and continue uphill to Atlantic Ave, a busy thoroughfare crowded with spice shops, Muslim bookstores and an array of restaurants. The wholesale broker **Sahadi Importing Co** (☎ 718-624-4550; 187-189 Atlantic Ave; open to 7pm Mon-Sat) sells dried fruits and nuts all over the country, and it's worth stopping in to pick up some tasty snacks. For more exotic spices in a less hectic atmosphere, head across the street to **Oriental Pastry & Grocery** (☎ 718-875-7687; 170 Atlantic Ave; open until 8:30pm daily). **Two for the Pot** (☎ 718-855-8173; 200 Clinton St) is around the corner, with a fantastic selection of coffee beans.

Walking two blocks east on Atlantic Ave brings you to **Court St**. From here, turn right to reach the Italian enclave turned hip hood of Cobble Hill. Court St features a good mix of pastry shops, pizza joints, bars and cafés, with brownstone residences on the surrounding streets.

Meander south on Court St for 11 blocks, stopping in at the fine **Bookcourt Book Shop** (☎ 718-875-3677; 163 Court St at Dean St). At Union St, turn right and walk west one block to Clinton St, to see the red-brick Greek Revival **Rankin Residence** on the southwest corner. Now a funeral home, this 1840

ANGUS OBORN

mansion was once the only house on a large farm with a view of New York Harbor. It sits today in the middle of the **Carroll Gardens Historic District**, a well-preserved neighborhood of brick and brownstone houses, most with little front yards, dating from the mid-to late-19th century.

Heading south for two blocks brings you to Carroll St, make a left turn here and head east to Smith St, which is reminiscent of the East Village with its boutiques, funky cafés and hipster eateries. You could spend an entire day strolling this stretch (see the Places to Eat and Shopping chapters for some good ideas). Don't miss the **brick row-houses** with their intricate ironwork at 325–329 Sackett St just west of Smith St.

Left: Brownstone buildings in Brooklyn Heights

Dumbo (Map 9)

Down Under the Manhattan Bridge Overpass (Dumbo) is fast becoming a destination neighborhood. Here, you'll find art galleries, cafés and a burgeoning music scene in a 10-block area that boasts more than 700 working artists. If you're in town in late October, be sure to check out the **Dumbo Arts Center's** (#2; ☎ 718-624-3772; W www.dumboartscenter.org; 30 Washington St; Ⓜ A, C to High St, F to York St) Art Under the Bridge Festival, where neighborhood artists strut their stuff.

St Ann's Warehouse (#4; ☎ 718-858-2424; 38 Water St; Ⓜ A, C to High St, F to York St) is a cool performance place hosting the even cooler rocker Joe Strummer, the Wooster Group theater troupe and other creative artists. Down the block is **Jacques Torres Chocolate** (#3; ☎ 718-875-9772; W www.mrchocolate.com; 66 Water St), a little piece of heaven disguised as a chocolate factory and two-table café. Run here, do not walk, for the most velvety and innovative chocolates ever crafted: we dare you to disagree. The shop does a brisk Internet and phone-order business ($10 for ¼ pound or $20 for ½ pound, plus shipping).

See if you can walk to the water's edge at nearby **Empire Fulton Ferry State Park** before diving into your chocolates.

Brooklyn Academy of Music

The oldest concert center in the USA, the Brooklyn Academy of Music (BAM; ☎ 718-636-4100; W www.bam.org; 30 Lafayette Ave; Ⓜ M, N, Q, R, W, 1, 2, 4 to Atlantic Ave), between Ashland Pl and St Felix St, has hosted such notable events as Enrico Caruso's final performance. Today, it continues to feature first-rate arts programs, including performances by visiting international opera companies and the resident Mark Morris dance troupe. The complex contains the **Majestic Theater**, the **Brooklyn Opera House** and the **Rose Cinema** (☎ 718-623-2770), the first outer-borough movie house dedicated to independent and foreign films.

BAM is easily accessible by public transport or you can reserve a spot on the BAM-bus, which leaves from the **Philip Morris Building** (120 Park Ave at E 42nd St) in Manhattan, an hour before most performances; on the return trip, it makes numerous Manhattan stops. The roundtrip fare is $10 ($8 for students). For reservations, contact BAM at least 24 hours in advance.

BAM was undergoing a massive multiyear, multimillion dollar renovation at the time of writing, which was to include the creation of a 'cultural district' block around the complex; hopefully this innovative proposal will come off.

Williamsburg (Map 1)

This neighborhood (Ⓜ L to Bedford Ave), located just over the namesake Williamsburg Bridge in northern Brooklyn, is on the up. Considered the new East Village, Williamsburg has scores of bars and restaurants that are drawing crowds and convincing even the most chronic Manhattanites of the wonders across the bridge (for information on eating and drinking in Williamsburg, see the Places to Eat and Entertainment chapters). Traditionally it's an Orthodox Jewish community – and a living embodiment of what Manhattan's Lower East Side was in the early 20th century – over the years Williamsburg has diversified and now includes Italians, Latinos and Polish residents. The newest immigrants to Williamsburg, are the struggling writers, artists and musicians who are taking advantage of the cheap(er) rents and large lofts. This makes for a vibrant mix; take an afternoon stroll across the Williamsburg Bridge to discover what's happening over here.

A college-campus atmosphere prevails along Bedford St, where locals looking for apartment shares post signs on mini 'democracy walls'. The area around the **Pratt Art School** (DeKalb Ave) is a popular pub crawl spot (perhaps due to its reputation for welcoming underage drinkers). Waterfront Weekly is the free publication covering Williamsburg and Greenpoint and is a good source of information on current doings. Keep your eyes peeled for open-studio events and street fairs, which are common affairs in the warmer months and make a terrific warmup to the sunset views you get from Kent Ave along the waterfront.

THINGS TO SEE & DO

Brooklyn Brewery Since 1988, the Brooklyn Brewery has made its award-winning Brooklyn Lager under contract at breweries outside the borough. But the beer came home to Brooklyn in 1996 with the opening of a microbrewery in Williamsburg *(☎ 718-486-7422; ⓦ www.brooklynbrewery.com; 79 N 11th St; ⓜ L to Bedford Ave)*. Housed in a series of buildings that once made up the Hecla Ironworks factory (the firm that made the structural supports for the Waldorf-Astoria Hotel), the brewery has become a Williamsburg institution and the beer a local favorite.

In the tasting room, you'll find a display of historical beer bottles and monthly specials. Happy hour takes place every Friday and Saturday between 6pm and 10pm and is a terrific time out with $3 pints and live music. In addition, the brewery also features live music and entertainment many nights of the week (see the web site for an events calendar). On Saturday, the brewery offers free tours, (including tastings), from noon to 5pm. The tours often fill up during the summer, so call ahead if you're keen to join in.

Prospect Park (Map 10)

This park *(ⓜ 1, 2 to Grand Army Plaza, Q, S to Prospect Park, F to 15th St-Prospect Park)* was created in 1866. This 526-acre Brooklyn masterwork by Frederick Law Olmsted and Calvert Vaux (the same duo who designed Central Park) may be their greatest achievement. Though less crowded than its more famous Manhattan sister space, **Prospect Park** *(☎ 718-965-8951; ⓦ www.prospectpark.org)* offers many of the same activities along its broad meadows, including ice skating at the **Kate Wollman Rink** *(#29; ☎ 718-287-6431; adult/senior & child $1/2, skate rental $3.50; open daily Oct-early Mar)*. You can catch music, dance and other live entertainment at the **bandshell** during the Celebrate Brooklyn! festival held during summer; call ☎ 718-855-7882 for information.

Like Central Park, there's also a **carousel** (rides $0.50), which operates Thursday to Sunday, and a small **zoo** *(#27; ☎ 718-399-7339; adult/child $2.50/0.50; open 10am-5pm daily)*, with a teeny pool where the sea lions turn depressingly tight half circles; try

and catch feeding times at 11:30am, 2pm and 4pm. Kids will also enjoy the **Lefferts Homestead Children's Historic House Museum** *(#28; ☎ 718-789-2822; open 1pm-4pm Thur & Fri, 1pm-5pm Sat & Sun Apr Nov)*. For information on other activities, including park walks and art exhibitions, visit the boathouse or call the events hotline *(☎ 718-965-8999)*.

Grand Army Plaza *(cnr Eastern Pkwy & Flatbush Ave; ⓜ 1, 2 Grand Army Plaza)* stands at the northwest entrance to the park. Its 80ft **Soldiers' and Sailors' Monument** *(#5)*, constructed in 1892, commemorates the Union army's triumph during the Civil War. In the summer, a gallery in the arch displays work by local artists and the observation deck just below the bronze chariot offers a view of the park. A small **farmer's market** is also held here very weekend.

New York City's only **structure honoring President John F Kennedy** *(#6)* stands in a small fountain park just to the north of the Grand Army arch. The immense art-deco **Brooklyn Public Library** *(#3)* faces the arch on its south side.

From noon to 6pm Saturday and Sunday year-round, a free hourly trolley service makes a loop from Prospect Park to points of interest around the Brooklyn Museum of Art, including the park zoo

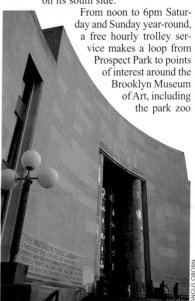

Brooklyn Public Library

ANGUS OBORN

and ice rink, Brooklyn Botanic Garden and the Brooklyn library. Ask at the museum's information desk (see Brooklyn Museum of Art, later in this chapter).

Park Slope (Map 10)

This rectangular-shaped residential neighborhood (**◐** F to 7th Ave-Park Slope) sits immediately west of Prospect Park, and most of its shops and restaurants lie along the 18 blocks of Seventh Ave between the two subway stations at 9th St and Park Pl. A smattering of writers live here, including novelist Paul Auster, so there's a healthy literary atmosphere. Take advantage of it by visiting one of the many neighborhood bookshops, such as the terrific **Community Bookstore** (#18; ☎ 718-783-3075; 143 Seventh Ave at Carroll St), which puts on readings by noted authors on a regular basis. Visit the small café.

You can get online at several cool places in this connected area. Try **Microchip Cafe** (#16; ☎ 718-499-4259; 175 Seventh Ave) or the slightly cheaper **Computer Café** (#26; ☎ 718-788-4745; 435 Seventh Ave).

Park Slope has some good shopping. For vintage everything, try **Hooti Couture** (#7; ☎ 718-857-1977; 179 Berkeley Pl) near Seventh Ave. The best place for used CDs and LPs, plus the latest local music happenings is **Holy Cow!** (#23; ☎ 718-788-3631; 422 9th St) between Sixth and Seventh Ave. Among the many chill places to take a coffee are **Ozzie's** (#9; ☎ 718-398-6695; 57 7th Ave), near Lincoln Pl, or the **Tea Lounge** (#24; ☎ 718-768-4966; 350 Seventh Ave), near the corner of 10th St, with cozy couches and chess sets; it transforms into a wine bar at night.

Grand Prospect Hall This banquet hall (#25; ☎ 718-788-0777; **W** www.grandprospect.com; 263 Prospect Ave), between Fifth and Sixth Aves, is a palatial riot of gold leaf and pastel overlay, crystal chandeliers and other spangly things. In the works for over 20 years, the restoration of this banquet hall is worth a peek for its over-the-top tacky factor alone – check out the preposterous gold-leaf toilets. Movie directors like the place; films shot here include *Prizzi's Honor* and *Cotton Club*.

Brooklyn Museum of Art Were it located anywhere else, this museum (#19; ☎ 718-638-5000; **W** www.brooklynart.org; 200 Eastern Pkwy; **◐** 1, 2 to Eastern Pkwy-Brooklyn Museum; suggested admission adult/senior & student $6/3, child free; open 10am-5pm Wed-Fri, 11am-6pm Sat & Sun), near Washington Ave, would be considered a premier arts institution. Even though it's overshadowed by the Met in Manhattan, this museum, with 1.5 million pieces, is the second biggest in the country and very much worth a visit. It's never really crowded, even on Sunday, and you can take a day exploring its collection and visiting the nearby Brooklyn Botanic Garden and Brooklyn Children's Museum.

The museum was thrown into a publicity maelstrom in 1999 when it sponsored an exhibition of young British artists, including Chris Ofili, who uses elephant dung in his paintings. Once Mayor Giuliani attacked Ofili's shit-smeared Virgin Mary portrait, the newshounds jumped on it, giving the museum (and the mayor) a lot of press.

For those turned off by cutting-edge art, the museum showcases plenty of more traditional exhibitions as well. The permanent galleries feature African, Islamic and Asian art, with colorful Egyptian cartonnages (mummy casings) and funerary figurines on display in the modern 3rd-floor galleries. The 4th floor, which overlooks a tiled court crowned by a skylight, contains period rooms, including a reconstruction of the Jan Schenck House, a 17th-century Dutch settlement in Brooklyn. On the 5th floor, the colonial portraiture on display includes a famous Gilbert Stuart painting of Washington. You'll also find a collection of 58 Auguste Rodin sculptures nearby.

Brooklyn Botanic Garden The 52-acre botanical garden (☎ 718-623-7200; **W** www.bbg.org; 1000 Washington Ave; **◐** 1, 2 to Eastern Pkwy-Brooklyn Museum, Q, S to Prospect Park; adult/senior & student $3/1.50, child under 16 free; open 8am-6pm Tues-Fri, 10am-6pm Sat, Sun & holidays Apr-Sept, 8am-4:30pm Tues-Fri, 10am-4:30pm Sat, Sun & holidays Oct-March), near Eastern

Pkwy, features more than 12,000 different plants in its 15 gardens. The fanciful Celebrity Path, with slate steps, honors nearly 150 famous Brooklynites (Mary Tyler Moore and Spike Lee among them), and the Fragrance Garden makes for a wonderful walk. The Discovery Garden is a hands-on floral playground for kids and the nearby Children's Garden has been tended by little hands since 1914.

If you're around in the last part of April, don't miss the **Sakuri Matsuri** (Cherry Blossom Festival) that heralds the blooming of the garden's 45 varieties of cherry trees. The garden also boasts the biggest and oldest collection of bonsai trees in the USA.

Brooklyn Children's Museum The hands-on Brooklyn Children's Museum (☎ 718-735-4400; W www.brooklynkids.org; 145 Brooklyn Ave at St Marks Ave; ◑ 1 to Kingston Ave; suggested donation $4; open 10am-5pm Mon, Wed, Fri-Sun Apr-Sept, 2pm-5pm Wed-Fri, 10am-5pm Sat & Sun Oct-Mar) emphasizes art, music and ethnic culture. Founded in 1899, this forerunner of all children's museums features a world playground that celebrates different cultures and a greenhouse designed to teach kids about environmental preservation. Each June, the museum holds a balloon festival of custom-made balloons from around the world. It also hosts frequent cultural events.

Coney Island (Map 1)

A trip down memory lane Americana-style, Coney Island (◑ F, Q, W to Coney Island-Stillwell Ave) once thrived as a bustling showplace where sweating city dwellers came to take the sea air and enjoy the fun house and bumper cars in the Dreamland amusement park before WWI. These days, folks come to scrappy but endearing Coney Island for the baseball, roller coaster, aquarium, boardwalk and beach. As it's only about 60 minutes from the city, Coney Island makes a fun day trip. If you take the Q train, make sure it's the round variety, not the diamond one, which terminates at Brighton Beach.

As you emerge from the colorfully decrepit subway station, you'll see a 24-hour

A windy day on the Coney Island Boardwalk

coffee shop right in the middle of the station, where hard-bitten patrons sit at a counter top hunched over their meals. Pass through the doors to Surf Ave, and you'll see Russian residents picking up odd tools and electronic equipment at **flea-market** stalls along the street. The sellers drive a hard bargain, but you can find interesting housewares and funky old Russian frocks for cheap here.

You probably saw the original **Nathan's Famous** (1310 Surf Ave at Stillwell Ave; open 8am-6pm daily) sign from the subway and you're highly encouraged to test one of these tasties, though you might want to wait until after you ride the Cyclone. These folks have been selling hot dogs here since 1916 and the $2 dog with mustard and sauerkraut is a killer (incidentally, the hot dog was invented in Coney Island in 1874). There are public bathrooms around the back.

Walking down Stillwell Ave towards the beach and boardwalk, you'll come to several entertaining attractions, including a **go-cart track** ($5), **climbing wall** ($5) and a **batting range** ($2 for 14 balls). On Sunday between November and April, you can watch the truly demented members of Coney Island's **Polar Bear Club** shock their systems alive with an icy romp in the surf. They take the plunge rain or shine at 1pm.

Three blocks south of the subway station is KeySpan Park, the 7500-seat home to the brand new **Brooklyn Cyclones** (☎ 718-449-8497; W *www.brooklyncyclones.com; cnr Surf Ave & 17th St)* baseball team. This Mets minor-league team plays each summer and games are great, cheap family fun.

Several blocks in the other direction on Surf Ave is the **Coney Island Sideshow** (☎ 718-372-5159; 1208 Surf Ave at 12th St; admission $5; open noon-sunset Sat & Sun Sept-May, noon-sunset Wed-Sun June-Aug), a small museum and freak show where you can see snake charmers, tattooed ladies, sword-swallowers and fire eaters.

Coney Island's 70-year-old wooden **Cyclone** (1000 Surf Ave at Dewey Albert Pl; 1st/subsequent rides $5/4; open daily year-round weather permitting) roller coaster attracts crowds in summer, but tourists desert the area after Labor Day (the first Monday in September) – the best time to get a front seat on this hair-raising, rickety beast. The first clickety clackety climb and near-vertical drop will turn your knees to rubber and by the time you slam round the last bend at almost 60 miles an hour, you'll know why enthusiasts consider this one of the world's greatest coasters. Try to convince the ticket seller to go for his first ride.

Along the boardwalk, you'll see two relics of Coney Island's past glory: the bright-red parachute jump, relocated here from the 1939 World's Fair in Queens, and the ivy-covered **Thunderbolt** roller coaster, which operated from 1925 to 1983 and is older than the more famous Cyclone in the Astroland Amusement Park, just up the boardwalk. Also here is **Deno's Wonder Wheel Amusement Park** (☎ 718-372-2592), with it's photogenic, neon Wonder Wheel affording terrific topside views and scads of kiddie rides ($2/15 for one/10 rides).

The annual **Mermaid Parade**, held each year on the weekend nearest the summer solstice, is a raucous, scantily clad affair when mermaid wannabes take to the streets. For more information, call ☎ 718-372-5159 or visit W www.coneyislandusa.com.

New York Aquarium The New York Aquarium (☎ 718-265-3400; Ⓜ F, Q to W 8th St-NY Aquarium; adult/senior & child $11/7; open 10am-5pm Mon-Fri, last tickets 4:15pm, 10am-5:30pm Sat & Sun, last tickets 4:45pm), along the Coney Island boardwalk, is now officially called the Aquarium for Wildlife Conservation. We still call it fun and perfect for the wee ones.

At the touch pool, kids can handle starfish and other diminutive forms of sea life, and the small amphitheater features Sea World–style dolphin shows several times daily. Most kids love viewing whales, otters and sea lions from the outside railing overlooking their tanks or from the observation windows that afford views of the animals' underwater habitats. Don't miss Wendell and Cass, a pair of male black-footed penguins that Aquarium officials just discovered were gay, after eight years together. You can spend the better part of a day at the aquarium viewing its 10,000 specimens of marine life.

THINGS TO SEE & DO

Coney Island – dare you to ride on the Cyclone

CHRISTOPHER GROENHOUT

Brighton Beach

There's more than a little bit of Russia to be found in Little Odessa by the Sea, or Brighton Beach (**Ⓜ** Q *to Brighton Beach*), just a five-minute walk north on the boardwalk from the New York Aquarium. Home to the largest group of Russian emigrés in the USA, this community features a full array of Russian shops, bakeries and restaurants along Brighton Beach Ave, which runs parallel to the boardwalk one block off the beach.

Although police have uncovered money-laundering schemes run by the Russian mafia in Brighton Beach, you don't have to worry about crime on the street – just about the only criminal behavior you'll observe are the babushkas selling illegal prescription medicine Moscow-style on the street corner.

This community is so tight, someone who doesn't speak Russian will stick out like a sore thumb, but the shopkeepers are friendly to outsiders, a category that includes Brooklynites from any other neighborhood.

For more information on doings here, contact the **Brighton Neighborhood Organization** (**☎** *718-891-0800; 1121 Brighton Beach Ave*) or the **Brighton Beach Business Improvement District** (**☎** *718-934-1908;* **W** *www.brightonbeachbid.com*).

Rockaway Park

For a quick urban getaway, head to the end of the line on the A train to Broad Channel and change to the Shuttle to 116th St and **Rockaway Park Beach**. This terrific beach with nice water is quieter and less crowded than Coney Island and though the train ride is about the same (under an hour from the Village or Chelsea), the scenery kicks ass. For most of the way the train is elevated, which is a delight in itself after so much below-ground travel and once you hit the Gateway National Recreation Area and Jamaica Bay, your troubles will start melting away and you'll forget you're in New York. This neighborhood is a close-knit Italian and Irish enclave and the further you venture south on Beach Channel Dr and Rockaway Pt Blvd, the more evident it will become that you're a day-tripper.

QUEENS

Manhattan has the fame. Brooklyn has the pride. The Bronx has the attitude. Staten Island, well, at least Staten Island has big hair and a big dump. But, Queens, poor Queens, what has this borough got? We're here to tell you that Queens can be glorious, offering some of the area's richest history, zaniest attractions and finest art (MoMA is here temporarily until 2005). It's also New York's largest borough (282 sq miles, with over 2.2 million residents) and the most ethnically diverse spot in the USA (more than 100 minority groups are represented). Immigrants from all over the world come to settle in Queens and for visitors that means an international mix of food, music and festivals.

The **Queens Council on the Arts** (**☎** *718-647-3377;* **W** *www.queenscouncilarts.org*) is a clearinghouse for community cultural events; in keeping with the borough's multicultural demographics, it provides information in English, Spanish, Korean and Chinese.

There are several art institutions spread throughout Astoria and Long Island City in the eastern part of Queens, and MoMA runs a free shuttle bus called **Queens ArtLink** (**☎** *718-6708-9750;* **W** *www.queensartlink.org*) connecting them all. It leaves from MoMA Midtown (53rd St between Fifth and Sixth Aves) and stops at PS 1 Contemporary Art Center, Isamu Noguchi Garden Museum, MoMA QNS, Socrates Sculpture Park and the American Museum for the Moving Image. Call for schedules (MoMA was in total flux at the time of writing).

Astoria (Map 11)

Named after millionaire fur merchant John Jacob Astor, the area of eastern Queens known as Astoria (**Ⓜ** N, W *to Broadway, R, V, G to Steinway St*) began as a mid-19th-century ferry depot, but it soon developed into a neighborhood of factories. Since the 1950s, the Greeks have been moving to Astoria and it's now the biggest Greek community in the country (opa!). Although there are pockets of the original German and Italian settlers, and some more recent Eastern European immigrants living here, you wouldn't know it among all the Greek bakeries, deli-

Ride on the International Express

The phrase 'National Historic Trail' may bring to mind the Oregon Trail or the Trail of Tears, but probably not the No 7 subway line, which cuts through the heart of Queens and is known as the International Express. But the US government has designated it as just that, since the burgundy-colored subway trains pass through the long-time immigrant neighborhoods of Woodside, Jackson Heights and Corona in the middle of Queens. It's a terrific ride, with some spectacular sights, sounds and smells and though the city is planning to phase out the distinctive 'Red bird' cars by 2003, it still makes for an interesting ride.

These areas, with their cheap rents and direct subway connection to Midtown Manhattan, have attracted an international array of residents from Ireland, Uruguay, Panama, Korea, China, Vietnam and many other countries. The area is such a phenomenal mix of cultures and colors, Atlanta Braves buffoon John Rocker made racist comments about No 7 train riders, many of whom take the train not only home, but also out to Shea Stadium to catch Mets' games.

In Manhattan, board the No 7 subway at Grand Central Terminal or Times Square. About five minutes from the city, the No 7 goes above ground, offering spectacular views of the Midtown Manhattan skyline and the 59th St Bridge to the north. Keep your eyes peeled for the riot of graffiti spread across a complex of industrial buildings out the northern-facing windows (if you want to see the spectacular spray paint art in more detail, alight at the 45 Rd-Court House Square station).

If you're headed for Woodside, home to one of the city's oldest Irish neighborhoods, get off at 46th St-Bliss St, 52nd St-Lincoln Ave or 61st-Woodside. To visit Jackson Heights, get off at 74th St-Broadway (where you'll find Filipino, Korean and Indian communities) or 82nd St-Jackson Heights (if you're looking for some South American spots). The Junction Blvd station marks the dividing line between Jackson Heights and Corona; here, several Latino communities exist side by side, including Cuban, Bolivian and Dominican communities. In Corona (disembark at 103rd St-Corona Plaza) you'll find a large group of Mexicans, as well as Muslims from Pakistan and India.

You won't get lost if you keep Roosevelt Ave, which runs directly under the elevated train tracks for the final third of the line, as a reference point. The journey from Manhattan to the very end of the line at Main St-Flushing takes about 35 minutes.

The Queens Council on the Arts offers information on the sites along the International Express. Call ☎ 718-647-3377 or send $1 for postage to the organization at 1 Forest Park at Oakridge, Woodhaven, NY 11421. You can also stop by and pick up a free guide at the council's main office, which also offers other cultural information.

N.Y.C.

THINGS TO SEE & DO

catessens and diners. A great place to eat heartily among hearty folks, Astoria is also the birthplace of Hellman's Mayonnaise.

If you're desperate for email, head to **Cyber Station Café** (#3; ☎ 718-777-5900; 2nd floor, 22-55 31st St; open daily), under the subway tracks.

American Museum of the Moving Image The American Museum of the Moving Image (#16; ☎ 718-784-0077; W www.ammi.org; 35th Ave at 36th St; ❻ R, V, G to Steinway St; adult/senior & student $8.50/5.50, child $4.50; open noon-5pm Tues-Fri,

11am-6pm Sat & Sun) stands right in the middle of the **Kaufman Astoria Studios** (#15; W www.kaufmanastoria.com) complex. A number of movies and TV shows have been shot at this 75-year-old film-production center, including the Marx Brothers' Coconuts, Glengarry Glen Ross and television's Cosby Show.

Though the studios are closed to the public, the museum has over 90,000 items, interactive galleries, video games and computer installations relating to the TV industry. Galleries display the make-up and costumes from films like The Exorcist, as well as sets from the 1987 movie *The Glass Menagerie*, directed by Paul Newman, and the popular TV series *Seinfeld* (fans will appreciate such artifacts as Jerry's infamous 'puffy shirt')

The museum also holds interesting film retrospectives year-round, with several movies screened daily in a small theater built by conceptual artist Red Grooms, who was inspired by the Egyptian-themed movie palaces of the 1930s. For first-run flicks, you can head across the street to the **United Artists cinema** *(#17)*.

Socrates Sculpture Park

Where Broadway meets Vernon Blvd near the East River, you'll find the **Socrates Sculpture Park** *(#8; ☎ 718-956-1819; Ⓜ N, W to Broadway; admission free; open 10am-dusk year-round)*, an open-air public space on a former illegal waste dump, with terrific views. The local artists' work on display, including the five-wind chimes along the shoreline, have a stark industrial look to them, in keeping with the park's location right next to a steel company.

Long Island City (Map 11)

This is another of those cool New York pockets easily overlooked by locals, but Long Island City (LIC) will be known before long, because it has so much going for it: it's only 10 minutes from Midtown on the No 7 train, MoMA just moved to temporary digs here (joining several art spaces that have long called LIC home), the views of the Manhattan skyline are to die for and the elevated subway, graffiti and bustling diners imbue it with that old-school New York feel missing elsewhere.

For one of the best collections of **graffiti** left anywhere in New York, get off the No 7 train at the 45 Rd-Court House Square stop and walk parallel to the tracks (southeast) for half a block to Davis St. Admire the murals blanketing the walls on the right, but continue to the cluster of industrial buildings just a bit further on for some dazzling displays of this public art form that, while not dying, lacks for canvas since former mayor Giuliani enacted his quality-of-life laws. You might also check out the nearby **New York Supreme Court** *(#20; ☎ 718-520-3933;*

25-10 Court Sq; Ⓜ G to Long Island City-Court Sq, 7 to 45 Rd-Court House Sq); it's not only a fine beaux-art specimen, it's also where murderess Ruth Snyder was handed down her death sentence. She became the first woman ever killed by the state.

PS 1 Contemporary Art Center Fledgling no more, the former nonprofit art space PS 1 *(#22; ☎ 718-784-2084; Ⓦ www.ps1.org; 22-25 Jackson Ave at 46th Ave; Ⓜ E, F, V to 23rd St-Ely Ave, G to Long Island City-Court House Sq, 7 to 45th Rd-Court House Sq; suggested admission adult/child under 21 $5/2; open noon-6pm Wed-Sun)* merged with MoMA a few years ago. With its sprawling galleries spread over five floors, outdoor installation spaces and commitment to new artists and their work (no matter how controversial), PS 1 far outstrips the Modern in its modernity.

Isamu Noguchi Garden Museum It seems a lot of the museums in this area are in transition these days and the Isamu Noguchi Garden Museum *(#18; ☎ 718-204-7088; 36-01 43rd Ave; Ⓜ E, F, V to 23rd St-Ely Ave, G to Long Island City-Court House Sq, 7 to 45th Rd-Court House Sq; adult/senior & student $4/2; open 10am-5pm Wed-Fri, 11am-6pm Sat & Sun)*, near 36th St, is no exception. Having moved from its permanent home along the East River in Astoria, this facility now holds only a fraction of the work by this Japanese-American sculptor, who died in 1988.

MoMA QNS It's still unclear exactly what works will make the jump across the river from MoMA Midtown to MoMA QNS *(#19; ☎ 212-708-9400, Ⓦ www.moma.org; 45-20 33rd St; Ⓜ E, F, V to 23rd St-Ely Ave, G to Long Island City-Court House Sq, 7 to 45th Rd-Court House Sq)*, near Queens Blvd. What is clear, however, is that the Swing-line stapler factory, converted by the museum, has about 25% of the gallery space of the former Midtown location and officials expect fewer than half the annual visitors. A mix of the permanent collection and special exhibitions will be displayed here.

The museum runs the free QueensArtlink shuttle to their Queens facility and several other art spaces nearby (see under Queens earlier in this chapter).

Flushing (Map 12)

Historians and Mets fans have been hip to it all along, but the world-at-large should know that Flushing is fabulous! So what if it takes ages to get there? Simply put, Flushing is a bustling, homely neighborhood harboring secrets and history. It's where 17th-century Quakers met clandestinely, successfully resisting Dutch governor Peter Stuyvesant's religious persecution. The once-forested village was also the site of the first commercial nursery in the USA; it served as a stop on the underground railroad, helping escaped slaves to freedom; and was the hometown of Lewis Latimer, Thomas Edison's head draftsman and only black colleague. Additionally, many jazz greats called Flushing home, including Dizzie Gillespie and Billie Holiday.

Despite these auspicious beginnings, Flushing (**Ⓜ** 7 to Flushing-Main St) eventually became an urban eyesore, home to a huge commercial ash heap (mentioned in F Scott Fitzgerald's The Great Gatsby) and a hunk of junkyards. Before the World's Fair of 1939, this area reverted into parkland again, but much of the neighborhood is chock-a-block with 99¢ stores, 24-hour diners and municipal offices.

In the 1980s, Flushing attracted a massive influx of Korean and Chinese immigrants. Along the commercial strips, almost everything is in Korean, making it feel more like some residential neighborhood in Seoul. Like everywhere in New York City, the many immigrant groups here coexist peacefully for the most part.

Flushing's center is at the corner of Roosevelt Ave, which runs east-west, and Main St, which runs north-south; these two streets meet at the subway exit.

Flushing Meadows–Corona Park & Shea Stadium One of the greatest attractions out here (and making it worth the 45-minute subway ride from Manhattan, in our opinion), is Flushing Meadows–Corona Park (**Ⓜ** 7 to 111th St or Willets Point-Shea Stadium). The site of the spectacular 1939 and 1964 World's Fair, this 1255-acre park is dominated by the exquisite, stainless steel **Unisphere** (#19) globe – at 120ft tall and 380 tons, it's the world's biggest. You can rent bikes, golf clubs or paddle boats here, and in winter you can skate in the **World's Fair Ice Rink** (☎ 718-271-1996).

Sports fans will dig the world-class arenas, including **Shea Stadium**, the ballpark of the New York Mets (see Spectator Sports in the Entertainment chapter), and the **USTA National Tennis Center**, home of the premier US Open tournament every fall (see Public Holidays & Special Events in the Facts for the Visitor chapter). The 'pick-up' soccer games here, with many Latino ringers from nearby Corona, are near legendary.

Adding to this park's allure are several abandoned World's Fair pavilions peppering the otherwise tidy landscaped grounds; the two towers rising in the distance were the spaceships in Men in Black.

New York Hall of Science This former World's Fair pavilion (#22; ☎ 718-699-0005; **Ⓦ** www.nyhallsci.org; **Ⓜ** 7 to 111th St; adult/child $7.50/5; open 9:30am-2pm Mon, 9:30am-5pm Tues-Sun), which resembles a Stalin-era concrete block, houses a children's museum dedicated to technology. **Kidpower,** outside the museum, is perhaps the coolest playground ever; it's free with museum admission.

Queens Museum of Art The former New York City building from the 1939 World's Fair has been completely renovated and turned into the Queens Museum of Art (#20; ☎ 718-592-5555; **Ⓦ** www.queensmuse .org; **Ⓜ** 7 to 111th St; adult/senior & child $5/2.50; open 10am-5pm Tues-Fri, noon-5pm Sat & Sun). The building also hosted the first sessions of the UN before the body moved into its permanent quarters on Manhattan's East Side; a gallery here explains the history of those early peace-making meetings. The rotating exhibitions here are interesting and high quality.

Everyone should see the incredible **Panorama of New York City**. This 9335-sq-ft model of all five boroughs debuted at the 1964 World's Fair, where visitors marveled at its details, reproduced at a scale of 1200:1 (100 ft = 1 inch).

Today, we're still marveling at the teeny, detailed 895,000 structures re-creating New York City in miniature. A glass-bottom observation deck encircles the panorama, and every 15 minutes, the cycle of dawn and dusk are simulated, prompting thousands of tiny lights to flicker across the metropolis. The panorama was last updated in 1992 and has been altered and augmented to account for the September 11 attacks, but you should go see it for yourself.

The Queens Museum of Art recently received the green light to undertake a major expansion project, but when they'll have the greenbacks to make it a reality is unclear.

Adjacent to the museum is **Queens Theatre in the Park** (#21; ☎ 718-760-0064; W www.queenstheatre.org), which hosts top-notch dance, drama and music performances.

Flushing Council on Culture & the Arts Housed in the historic Flushing Town Hall, the council (#2; ☎ 718-463-7700; W www.flushingtownhall.org; 137-35 Northern Blvd; ◑ 7 to Main St-Flushing; adult/ senior & student $3/2, child $1; open 9am-5pm Mon-Fri, noon-5pm Sat & Sun) houses a contemporary art museum and historical gallery. Built in 1864, this Romanesque Revival building also hosts a year-round series of jazz, world music and classical concerts. The council runs free weekend trolleys to several historical sites around Flushing and to the botanical gardens and Flushing Meadows–Corona Park; also ask about their $15 **Queens Jazz Trail** trolley tours (or ask them for the map and do it on your own!).

Queens Botanical Gardens This 40-acre botanical garden (#17; ☎ 718-886-3800; W www.queensbotanical.org; 43-50 Main St; ◑ 7 to Main St-Flushing; admission free; open 8am-4:30pm Tues-Sun Nov-Mar, 8am-6pm Tues-Fri, 8am-7pm Sat & Sun Apr-Oct)

includes a variety of non-native flora. The expansive meadows are great for a picnic and the sinewy pathways are perfect for cycling. On weekends, a trolley ($1) runs between the botanical garden and Flushing Meadows–Corona Park.

Flushing Cemetery This sprawling graveyard (◑ 7 to Main St-Flushing), at the intersection of 46th Ave and 164th St, houses many famous remains. Jazz buffs will want to visit the graves of Johnny Hodges (section 11, division D, plot 519), Dizzie Gillespie (section 31, unmarked grave 1252) and Louis Armstrong (section 9, division A, plot 12B). Satchmo fans shouldn't miss the Louis Armstrong Archives (☎ 718-997-3670; W www.satchmo.net; 65-30 Kissena Blvd) on the Queens College campus.

STATEN ISLAND (MAP 1)

Residents of the 'forgotten borough' of Staten Island have long entertained fantasies of secession from greater New York City and have voted to cut loose, but have yet to actually go through with it. Its tiny population of 443,728 – largely white, middle-class and Republican – has historically had little clout in what is a predominately Democratic New York City. Most politicians have made little secret of their disdain for this suburban tract of land close to the New Jersey shoreline. What's worse, the borough is home to the city's largest garbage dump. (The dump, called Fresh Kills, was finally closed in 2001, but had to be reopened to accommodate rubble and refuse being shifted from the World Trade Center.) And the gray, dirty waterfront near the ferry terminal doesn't help the borough's image.

Staten Island came into its own when railway magnate Cornelius Vanderbilt established a ferry service between the island and the port of New York in the 19th century. For more than 100 years, Staten Island remained a quiet outpost for the wealthy, who built large estates among the verdant farmlands. But large-scale development finally got under way in the 1960s, after the construction of the Verrazano Narrows

Bridge forged a land link with the rest of New York City. Still, mention Staten Island and most other New Yorkers think of the ferry, the starting point of the New York City Marathon, the dump and heavy accents. Of course, there's more to Staten Island than just that, and it's worth a day trip.

The **Staten Island Chamber of Commerce** (☎ 718-727-1900; 130 Bay St), near Victory Blvd, provides information on cultural events and attractions. Pick up a copy of the *Staten Island Advance* (Ⓦ www .silive.com/advance) for coverage of local news and events. The website is jam-packed with information and updated daily.

Twenty-one bus routes converge on the St George Ferry Terminal in Staten Island; from there, you can pick up buses to all the major sites. The buses are coordinated to leave within minutes of the ferry's arrival.

Staten Island Ferry

One of New York's greatest bargains, the free ferry (☎ 718-815-2628) takes 70,000 passengers each day on the 25-minute, 6-mile journey from Lower Manhattan to Staten Island. The ferry departs on the half-hour, 24 hours daily. Republican former mayor Giuliani abolished the 50¢ roundtrip fare during his first term, winning him points with other New Yorkers and even more votes from heavily Republican Staten Island.

If crowds don't float your boat and the expense of a Circle Line or similar tour to the Statue of Liberty and Ellis Island doesn't appeal, try this. The journey takes you within half a mile of both Ellis and Statue of Liberty Islands, and the view of Manhattan and Brooklyn Heights is breathtaking. It's best to pack up a lunch or snack before heading out to the ferry, since the places to eat in the outdated South Ferry Terminal and the concession on the boat serve generic, grease-laden grub. This roundtrip is a beautiful way to watch the sunset or moonrise.

Only the most brutal weather will keep the ferries in their slips. Ferries carrying cars operate from early morning until 11:30pm ($3 per vehicle each way; bicycles free); call to confirm schedules. In Manhattan, you'll find the ferry terminal at the bottom of Whitehall St, just east of Battery Park.

Snug Harbor Cultural Center

The Snug Harbor Cultural Center (☎ 718-448-2500, Ⓦ www.snug-harbor.com; 1000 Richmond Terrace) is situated on an old retirement complex built between 1831 and 1917 for about 1000 sailors. The group of five buildings just inside the north gate features some of the finest small-scale Greek Revival architecture left in the USA. Don't miss the Great Hall and the Veterans Memorial Chapel nearby, both of which have impressive interiors.

In 1976, the city took control of the run-down 83-acre site, which overlooks the oil tankers and container ships docking in New Jersey, and restored it as a complex for the borough's cultural institutions. You can easily spend a day exploring the attractions housed in the several buildings here, including the **Staten Island Botanical Garden** (☎ 718-273-8200; Ⓦ www.sibg.org), which has surprises like an entirely white garden

Lady Liberty stands tall (view from the Staten Island ferry)

and a 'secret garden' with a hedge maze and miniature castle, and the **Staten Island Children's Museum** (☎ 718-273 2060; admission $5; open noon-5pm Tues-Sun Sepl-May, 11am-5pm Tues-Sun June-Aug), which specializes in hands-on science and nature exhibitions. A free tour of the 28 landmark buildings on the site leaves from the visitor center at 2pm Saturday and Sunday.

You can reach the Snug Harbor Cultural Center by taking the S40 bus 2 miles west from the ferry terminal.

Jacques Marchais Center of Tibetan Art

Home to the largest collection of Tibetan art outside China, the Jacques Marchais Center (☎ 718-987-3500; Ⓦ www.tibetanmuseum .com; 338 Lighthouse Ave; adult/senior & student $5/3; child $2; open 1pm-5pm Wed-Fri Dec-Mar, 1pm-5pm Wed-Sun Apr-Nov) was built by art dealer Edna Koblentz, who collected the artworks under an alias that did not betray her gender. The center opened to the public in 1947, a year before her death.

The unusual objects on display include a number of golden sculptures and religious objects made from human bone. Just about the only authentic thing missing from the center, built in Tibetan temple style, is the smell of yak butter. In the early part of October, the museum holds its annual weekend-long Tibetan cultural festival among the stone Buddhas in the outdoor garden. Visit the website to learn about the frequent special events hosted here, including lectures, films and workshops, many of which are free.

Colorful prayer flags at the Tibetan Art Center

To get to the center, take the S74 bus along Richmond Rd for 30 minutes and ask the driver to let you off at Lighthouse Ave. The museum sits at the top of a hill and offers pretty views over the island.

Wright Residence

There's a bonus in store for those who make the trek out to the Jacques Marchais Center. Just across Lighthouse Ave from the museum sits the only private home that famed architect Frank Lloyd Wright ever built in New York City. Look for the low-slung, cliffside residence (called Crimson Beech for the copper beech that once stood on the property; the one there at present is a replacement after the original fell in a storm) at 48 Manor Court, constructed in 1959. Don't knock on the door, though – people still live here.

Historic Richmond Town

The village of Richmond (☎ 718-351-1611; Ⓦ www.historicrichmondtown.org; 441 Clarke Ave at St Patrick's Pl; adult/child over 5 yrs $4/2.50; open 1pm-5pm Wed-Sun Sept-June, extended hours July & Aug) once served as the county seat of Staten Island, and 11 original buildings still stand in what is now a borough preservation project maintained by the Staten Island Historical Society.

Historic Richmond Town includes the 300-year-old redwood **Voorlezer's House**, which is believed to be the oldest surviving school building in the country. In the 1960s, other historic structures were moved here from around the island in an ambitious attempt to protect local history; there are now 40 buildings collected on the property. Begin your exploration of the 100-acre site at the village courthouse, which serves as a visitor center. Every hour, a guide conducts tours beginning at the courthouse. You'll find a historical museum in the former county clerk's office.

Visit Historic Richmond Town in warm weather, when you can enjoy the surrounding landscape along Richmond Creek. During the summer season, volunteers dressed in period garb roam the grounds and describe 17th-century rural colonial life.

You can reach the historic town by taking the S74 bus from the ferry to Richmond Ave and St Patrick's Pl, a journey of about 35 minutes.

Greenbelt Nature Walks

The 2500-acre Greenbelt environmental preserve (☎ 718-667-2165; 200 Nevada Ave) in the middle of Staten Island encompasses several parks with five different ecosystems, including swamp areas and freshwater wetlands. It's one of New York City's unexplored natural treasures, offering some spectacular walks not far from the bustle of Downtown Manhattan. The 28 miles of trails should suit both casual walkers and aggressive hikers. Bird-watchers can track 60 different species of birds here.

The **High Rock Park** section of the Greenbelt includes six trails through hardwood forest, as well as three gardens. To get there, take the S74 bus from the ferry to Rockland Ave, walk up Rockland and bear right at Nevada Ave to the park entrance.

The **William T Davis Wildlife Refuge** once housed the wells that gave Staten Islanders their drinking water; today, it's a sanctuary for migrating birds and the site of the Greenbelt Native Plant Center. To reach the refuge walking trails, take the S62 or S92 buses from the ferry along Victory Blvd to Travis Ave.

THINGS TO SEE & DO

Places to Stay

It's been tough-going filling the more than 70,000 hotel rooms in New York since September 11 and while prior to that date the average room went for around $265 a day, there are some super deals floating around now. As the New York tourist industry and government officials are making a concerted effort to revitalize Lower Manhattan, it's worth checking the hotels south of Canal St (especially for weekend stays) for some extremely attractive deals. For the very budget-minded, however, the New York housing picture is still pretty bleak: a clean, safe room with private bath will cost you around $100.

Still, there are ways to do New York on the cheap, even where places to stay are concerned. Of course, couch surfing with friends and family is always a good way to go, but let's face it: fish and houseguests start to stink after three days, especially considering the size of the average New York apartment. If you can't or won't shell out at least $100 a night, consider staying at a hostel, one of the Ys (see the boxed text 'Playing & Staying at the Y') or joining **Servas** (Map 3, #62; ☎ 212-267-0252, fax 267-0292; W www.usservas.org; 11 John St, Suite 105, NY 10038; annual membership $65), an innovative worldwide program whereby members stay in approved host homes (there are around 140 in the tri-state area) for two-night stays, free of charge. Call or visit the website for application and program details.

Having a reservation in hand at least for your first night is a good idea. Book a room as soon as you know your itinerary and reconfirm a day or two before your arrival. If you do come to New York on the fly and with a limited budget, pick a few inexpensive places and turn up well before noon on the day you want to stay.

Beware of cheapie hotels that request full payment in advance. This policy is usually in response to fleeing customers who bug out after a night or two, and the payment policy could be a ploy to keep you there. Insist on paying only for the first night; that way you can always split without losing money.

Except where noted, rates quoted in this book do not include city taxes, which are a steep 13.25% plus a $2-per-night room charge. Prices fluctuate slightly depending on the season.

HOSTELS

For more detailed information on many of the hostels listed here, visit the website: W www.hostels.com/us.ny.ny .html, which has links to the hostels' own sites and listings of more hostels than space here allows.

Chelsea (Map 5)

Chelsea International Hostel (#152; ☎ 212-647-0010, fax 727-7289; W www.chelseahostel.com; 251 W 20th St; Ⓜ 1 to 18th St, C, E to 23rd St; dorm beds/private rooms $25/60) is between Seventh and Eighth Aves. A festive, international scene defines this hostel, where the back patio serves as party central. Bunk rooms sleep four to six and there are also private rooms. Amenities include communal kitchens and laundry facilities. You must show your passport when you check in (but you don't have to be a foreigner to stay here) and there's a two-week maximum stay.

Chelsea Center Hostel (#106; ☎ 212-643-0214; W www.chelseacenterhostel.com; 313 W 29th St; Ⓜ 1 to 28th St, A, C, E to 34th St-Penn Station; dorm beds $25), near Eighth Ave, is more cramped but quieter than the Chelsea International. It has 18 beds. The same folks also run a 25-bed **hostel** (427 E 12th St) between First Ave and Ave A; the prices are the same, but you must book through the 29th St location.

KIM GRANT

Playing & Staying at the Y

As the old ditty goes, 'it's fun to stay at the Y-M-C-A,' and while we're quite sure the Village People were referring to a different kind of fun back there in the swinging '70s, the Y of today is a great, safe and affordable place to stay. The rooms are generally spare and generic, like your typical dorm room, but as a bonus each outpost has its own programming, which might include classes, tours, gym facilities, lectures or even a swimming pool. Be aware, however, that this is still New York and no matter where you go in this great city, you'll always encounter some freaks, and the Ys are no different. Here's a breakdown of Y facilities in Manhattan:

92nd St Y de Hirsch Residence *(Map 7, #30; ☎ 212-415-5650, 888-699-6844, fax 415-5578; 4th floor, 1395 Lexington Ave;* Ⓜ *6 to 96th St; shared single day/month $35/845, private single $50/1045),* between 91st and 92nd Sts, is a big facility with sophisticated and well-organized programming. Rooms here have lots of closet space (with locks) and shared bathroom, kitchen and laundry facilities; lectures and use of the fitness center are included in the price. The lectures, performances, readings and other events put up by the 92nd St Y are of the highest quality. Reservations are essential here.

Vanderbilt Y *(Map 5, #57; ☎ 212-756-9600, fax 752-0210; 224 W 47th St;* Ⓜ *4, 5, 6, 7 to Grand Central; singles/doubles $85/95, doubles with bath $134, quads $129),* between Second and Third Aves, is a bit more expensive, but the location is great. All rooms have color TV and air-conditioning. The quad rooms come with two bunk beds. Luggage storage is available and there's a full gym facility, with pools, sauna, basketball courts, the works.

West Side Y *(Map 7, #101; ☎ 212-787-4400, fax 875-1334; 5 W 63rd St;* Ⓜ *A, B, C, D, 1, 2 to 59th St-Columbus Circle; singles/doubles $80/90, with bath $110/130),* off Central Park West, has a fantastic location near Central Park and over 500 tidy rooms. Still, reservations are a good idea.

McBurney YMCA *(Map 5, #154; ☎ 212-741-9210, fax 741-0012;* Ⓦ *http://ymcanyc.com; 215 W 23rd St;* Ⓜ *C, E, 1, 2 to 23rd St),* between Seventh and Eighth Aves, doesn't have a residence, but they have decent pool and gym facilities, lectures and classes.

N.Y.C.

PLACES TO STAY

Chelsea Star Hotel *(#107; ☎ 212-244-7827, 877-827-6969, fax 279-9018;* Ⓦ *www .starhotelny.com; 300 W 30th St at Eighth Ave;* Ⓜ *1 to 28th St, A, C, E to 34th St-Penn Station; dorm beds $30, private theme rooms from $70)* is a classic European-style hostel with a twist: private rooms come done up in different flavors, such as Star Trek, Absolutely Fabulous etc. This budget place is wickedly popular with good reason, as there's a little patio, Internet access, bike and Rollerblade rental and a mixed, friendly crowd. If you can't get in here, try the Manhattan Inn across the street (see Midtown under Hotels later in this chapter), which has a more subdued atmosphere, but is still good value.

Gershwin Hotel *(#132; ☎ 212-545-8000; fax 684-5546;* Ⓦ *www.gershwinhotel.com; 7 E 27th St;* Ⓜ *6 to 28th St; dorm beds $35, private rooms from $99)* is near Fifth Ave. Just

four blocks north of the Flatiron Building, this popular and funky spot (half youth hostel, half hotel) is buzzing with original artwork, touring bands and other fabulousness. In some ways, it feels more bohemian than the more historic, classic and pricey Chelsea Hotel (see Chelsea, Gramercy Park & Flatiron District under Hotels, later in this chapter), and because young travelers dig it so much beds can be hard to come by. Reservations and reconfirmations are a must.

ANGUS OBORN

Book ahead for the hip Gershwin Hotel

Times Square (Map 6)

Big Apple Hostel (#81; ☎ 212-302-2603, fax 302-2605; W www.bigapplehostel.com; 119 W 45th St; ⓂN, R, S, 1, 2, 3, 7 to Times Sq 42nd St; dorm beds/private rooms $33/90; open 24 hrs), between Sixth and Seventh Aves, is a clean, spare place just off Times Square. Rates are for rooms with shared bath, and include access to the kitchen, laundry room and cute backyard and barbecue.

Upper West & East Sides (Map 7)

Hostelling International-New York (#5; ☎ 212-932-2300, fax 932-2574; W www.hinewyork.org; 891 Amsterdam Ave; Ⓜ1 to 103rd St; dorm beds $29-35, nonmembers extra $3, family rooms with/without bath $135/120; open 24 hrs) is near W 103rd St. With clean, safe and air-conditioned rooms, the dorm beds at HI-New York go fast in the summer (book ahead!). This is your best option if you hit town at an ungodly hour.

Rooms with fewer beds cost more. This HI also has some family rooms sleeping four; there is no member discount for these rooms.

Central Park Hostel (#8; ☎ 212-678-0491; W www.centralparkhostel.com; 19 W 103rd St; ⓂB, C to 103rd St; dorm beds $25, private rooms $75), between Central Park West and Manhattan Ave, is a new hostel option with a terrific location and clean rooms.

International Student Center (#22; ☎ 212-787-7706; 38 W 88th St; ⓂB, C to 86th St; dorm beds $20), also Uptown near Central Park West, accommodates non-US residents aged 18 to 30.

Park View Hotel (#2; ☎ 212-369-3340; 55 Central Park North; ⓂB, C to 110th St; dorm beds/private rooms $22/75), near Lenox Ave overlooking Central Park, has the killer location and nice price for simple dorm beds in a cool setting. Even if you take a private room you can use the rooftop deck and communal kitchen.

Gay-Friendly Hotels & Inns

Several hotels cater almost exclusively to the queer crowd (but are still welcoming to het travelers), and you'll find the bulk of them in SoHo, Greenwich Village and Chelsea. Be sure to make reservations at least a month in advance for these popular gay-friendly spots.

In Greenwich Village, try **Incentra Village** and the **Washington Square Hotel** (for more on both of these, see Greenwich Village and East Village under Hotels, later in this chapter). The **East Village B&B** (Map 4, #116; ☎ 212-260-1865; 252 E 7th St), a hot spot for lesbians, was being renovated at the time of writing but will surely be back up and better than ever by the time you read this.

Fast eclipsing Greenwich Village as the city's prime gay neighborhood, Chelsea contains a number of accommodations where gay and lesbian travelers should feel particularly comfortable. The awfully friendly **Chelsea Pines Inn** (Map 5, #200; ☎ 212-929-1023, 888-546-2700, fax 620-5646; W www.chelseapinesinn.com; 317 W 14th St; rooms from $99), between Eighth and Ninth Aves, is terrific value, and the comfortable **Colonial House Inn** (Map 5, #150; ☎ 212-243-9669, 800-689-3779; W www.colonialhouseinn.com; 318 W 22nd St; rooms from $90), between Eighth and Ninth Aves, is a popular option. The famous **Chelsea Hotel** (see Chelsea, Flatiron District & Gramercy Park under Hotels) is a pricier option. Closer to Midtown, **Grand Union** (Map 5, #120; ☎ 212-683-5890; 34 E 32nd St; rooms from $125), between Park and Madison Aves, offers comfortable but generic accommodations.

For more information, contact the **Lesbian & Gay Community Services Center** (Map 4, #12; ☎ 212-620-7310; W www.gaycenter.org; 208 W 13th St) or see the comprehensive **Out & About Newsletter** (☎ 800-929-2268, W www.outandabout.com), which provides information about gay-friendly hotels in New York City, as well as restaurants, clubs, gyms and shops. Their website is a veritable treasure trove of useful information for gay travelers.

Harlem (Map 8)

Sugar Hill International House (#13; ☎ 212-926-7030, fax 283-0108; 722 St Nicholas Ave; Ⓜ B, C to 145th St; dorm beds $25) is a reliable place. It has a sister hostel, **Blue Rabbit** (#13; ☎ 212-491-3892; 730 St Nicholas Ave), just down the block. Together they offer a total of 60 dorm beds in two renovated limestone homes that date back to the 19th century. Both places are unsigned.

Brooklyn (Map 9)

New York Connection (☎ 718-386-5539; Ⓦ www.hostel.com/hostelnytravel; 197 Humboldt St; dorm beds $15-18), in Williamsburg, comes highly recommended by readers for its good value, international crowd and emphasis on community-building among travelers.

B&BS & APARTMENTS

Many bed and breakfasts in New York are exclusive affairs, serving as hideaways for the super rich, famous, beautiful and/or neurotic. For this reason, many have no signs out front and reservations are essential. A basic list of New York B&Bs with their contact information can be found at the **B&B Locator website** (Ⓦ www.bnb-locator.com/NewYork/newyork.htm), but it offers no details on the properties.

Broadway Inn (Map 6, #72; ☎ 212-997-9200; Ⓦ www.broadwayinn.com; 264 W 46th St; Ⓜ N, R, S, 1, 2, 3, 7 to Times Sq; rooms $119-199), near Eighth Ave, might have the rates of a hotel, but it has the convivial feeling of a B&B. Breakfast is included in the price, making this a popular choice in the Times Square area.

Inn at Irving Place (Map 5, #172; ☎ 212-533-4600; 56 Irving Pl at E 17th St; Ⓜ L, N, R, 4, 5, 6 to 14th St-Union Sq; rooms from $325) is a charming 11-room townhouse a few blocks south of Gramercy Park. Its location, ambience and reputation for romance (all the rooms have fireplaces and beds craving more action than sleep) mean it's often booked.

Inn New York City (Map 7, #67; ☎ 212-580-1900, fax 580-4437; 266 W 71st St; Ⓜ 1, 2, 3 to 72nd St; rooms $295-575), near West End Ave, features four beautifully ap-

pointed suites in an elaborate and well-regarded town house. Poverty sucks, eh?

Le Refuge Inn (Map 13, #7; ☎ 718-885-2478, fax 885-1519; Ⓦ www.lerefugeinn.com; 620 City Island Ave; singles/doubles weekdays $65/85, weekends $130/170, suites $140/280), on City Island in the Bronx, is housed in a 19th-century home and run by French chef Pierre Saint-Denis. Rates include breakfast and you can savor a fireside Provençal dinner here as well.

Bed and Breakfast on the Park (Map 10, #21; ☎ 718-499-6115, fax 499-1385; Ⓦ www.bbnyc.com; 113 Prospect Park West; Ⓜ F to 7th Ave-Park Slope; rooms $125-300), between 6th and 7th Sts, is a fantastically romantic getaway and Brooklyn's premier B&B. It's in a gorgeous brownstone overlooking Prospect Park. Rates include breakfast in the formal dining room.

As with many aspects of city life lately, the Brooklyn B&B scene is perhaps richer, with more options (certainly more affordable ones) than Manhattan's. **Fund for the Borough of Brooklyn** (☎ 718-855-7882; fax 802-9095; Ⓦ www.brooklynx.org) publishes a list of Brooklyn B&Bs.

Rental Services

Several rival companies vie for the B&B reservations business, many proffering 'outlaw' digs in B&Bs not registered with the city or any organization. Rooms cost around the same as those at the cheapest hotels – about $75 to $120 a night – but the value (such as decor, personalized service, kitchen use etc) far exceeds what you'll get in most hotels. Ask about reduced rates for monthly studio and apartment rentals. A two-night stay and deposit are usually required.

Though you're not calling the B&B directly when you contact one of these services, jump right in and quiz them about the degree of contact you'll have with the host, what the neighborhood is like or what attractions are nearby. You may hear the terms 'hosted' and 'unhosted' bandied about; the hosted variety is most like traditional B&B-style accommodations in a private home with hosts who can offer advice on the city and who may actually serve breakfast (but don't count on it). Unhosted accommodations are typically vacant apartments that locals rent out while they're not using them. (The tight hotel market in New York has given birth to a cottage industry, of sorts, with enterprising New Yorkers turning into part-time innkeepers.)

Urban Ventures (☎ 212-594-5650, fax 947-9320; W www.nyurbanventures.com; rooms $80-125) has 600 rooms in its registry.

CitySonnet (☎ 212-614-3034, fax 425-920-2384; W www.westvillagebb.com; hosted rooms from $80, lofts from $100, studios from $135) rents hosted rooms or unhosted apartments and lofts, many in the hippest Downtown locations.

Manhattan Lodgings (☎ 212-677-7616, fax 253-9395; W www.manhattanlodgings.com; hosted studios from $105, B&Bs $90-135, 1-bedroom apartments $110-190, 2 bedrooms $190-350) has a selection of studio, one-bedroom and two-bedroom apartments, plus hosted B&B facilities.

City Lights Bed and Breakfast (☎ 212-737-7049, fax 535-2755; singles from $95, apartments up to $200) lists nearly 400 private apartments in Manhattan and Brooklyn. It can also offer unhosted rooms.

Gamut Realty Group (☎ 212-879-4229, 800-437-8353; W www.gamutnyc.com; studios from $125, 1-bedroom apartments from $150, weekly rates $800-1450) handles a number of short- and long-term apartment rentals from Herald Square north.

A Hospitality Company (☎ 212-965-1102, 800-987-1235, fax 965-1149; W www.hospitalityco.com; studios from $99, 1-bedroom apartments from $125) rents fully furnished apartments with amenities like data ports, cable TV and fully equipped kitchens in whatever neighborhood might float your boat. Its website is available in six languages.

HOTELS
Lower Manhattan & Tribeca (Map 3)

Most hotels below Canal St cater to the business set, so they usually offer very attractive weekend deals. The drawback is that this part of the city (particularly below Chambers St) is comatose on Saturday and Sunday, when food and taxis can be difficult to drum up.

Best Western Seaport Inn (#52; ☎ 212-766-6600, 800-468-3569, fax 766-6615; 33 Peck Slip; ⓜ A, C, 2, 3, 4, 5 to Fulton St-Broadway Nassau; singles $179), between Front and Water Sts, sits in the shadow of the Brooklyn Bridge at the edge of the South St Seaport. Try for a terrace room with a view; rates include continental breakfast.

Seaport Suites (#72; ☎/fax 212-742-0003, 877-777-8483; 129 Front St; ⓜ 1, 2 to Wall St; rooms/suites from $209/229) has pretty pedestrian decor, but its large, one-bedroom suites sleep four ($249) and are great for families. The full kitchen in most rooms are good for budget-minded folks; rates are $100 cheaper on weekends.

Regent Wall Street (#75; ☎ 212-845-8600, 800-545-4000, fax 845-8601; W www.regent hotels.com; 55 Wall St; Ⓜ 1 to Wall St; rooms weekends/weekdays from $245/395) is in an 1842 Greek Revival landmark building and boasts a Wedgewood-paneled lobby and Italian marble ballroom floors. The rooms might be described as executive delicious; if you're spending this much, go for a terrace loft suite with views of Trinity Church.

Wall Street Inn (#80; ☎ 212-747-1500, 800-695-8284, fax 747-1900; 9 South William St at Broad St; Ⓜ N, R to Whitehall St, J, M, Z to Broad St; doubles from $150) is a smaller, more personal option in Lower Manhattan. There's an on-site fitness center and all rates include breakfast.

Millennium Hilton (#61; reservations ☎ 800-445-8667; 55 Church St), across from the World Trade Center site, is due to reopen by 2003; call the Hilton toll-free reservation line for the latest developments.

Cosmopolitan Hotel (#43; ☎ 212-566-1900, 888-895-9400, fax 566-6909; W www .cosmohotel.com; 95 West Broadway; Ⓜ 1, 2, 3 to Chambers St; doubles $119-149), near Chambers St, was renovated and booming before September 11, whereupon it became a haven for rescue workers and clean-up crews. This place maintains its cheap prices and clean rooms and is a great option in a prime Tribeca location.

Tribeca Grand Hotel (#7; ☎ 212-519-6600, 877-519-6600, fax 519-6700; W www.tribe cagrand.com; 2 Sixth Ave; Ⓜ 1, 2 to Franklin St; rooms $259-549, suites $549-999), at the triangle of White, Church and Walker Sts, is quintessentially New York: expensive, exclusive and the place to be seen. Skip the disastrous website and call the toll-free reservations line.

SoHo, Chinatown, & Lower East Side (Map 4)

SoHo Grand Hotel (#258; ☎ 212-965-3000, 800-965-3000, fax 965-3200; W www.soho grand.com; 310 West Broadway; Ⓜ A, C, E to

Canal St; doubles $259-499) is brought to you by the same real-estate-savvy folks responsible for the Tribeca Grand. The outside is totally nondescript, but inside the 367 rooms feature cool, clean lines in that urban chic way that's all the rage these days.

60 Thompson (#253; ☎ 212-431-0400, 877-431-0400; W www.60thompson.com; 60 Thompson St; Ⓜ C, E to Spring St; rooms from $275), between Spring and Broome Sts, is another snazzy boutique hotel distinguished by its terrific SoHo location, gorgeous rooftop terrace with views and intimate courtyard. The Thom restaurant here is also a winner (see the Places to Eat chapter).

Holiday Inn Downtown (#244; ☎ 212-966-8898; fax 966-3933; W www.holidayinn -nyc.com; 138 Lafayette St; Ⓜ J, M, N, R, Z, 6 to Canal St; doubles from $149), between Canal and Howard Sts, is in a hectic Chinatown location. The rooms are standard chain-motel fare.

World Hotel (#232; ☎ 212-226-5522, fax 219-9498; 101 Bowery; Ⓜ B, D, S, Q to Grand St, J, M to Bowery; doubles with/without bath $85/60), between Grand and Hester Sts, is a strict budget place – it most closely resembles a Chinese-run hotel in Southeast Asia, odiferous hallways and all. This fairly clean, transient place has 130 tiny rooms. You'll find several other closet-like 'hotels' near here, but they're flophouses and best avoided.

Pioneer Hotel (#236; ☎ 212-226-1482, 800-737-0702, fax 226-3525; W www.pion eerhotel.com; 341 Broome St; Ⓜ B, D, S, Q to Grand St, J, M to Bowery; rooms from $70), near the Bowery, is a good-value place on the fringes of Chinatown. The basic rooms have sinks and TVs. Rates are slightly higher in summer and for $10 more you can upgrade to bigger, nicer rooms with a window.

Off SoHo Suites (#212; ☎ 212-979-9815, 800-633-7646, fax 279-9801; W www.off soho.com; 11 Rivington St; Ⓜ F, V to Second Ave, J, M to Bowery; rooms/suites $99/149), between Chrystie St and the Bowery on the Lower East Side, is a good deal (ignore the nausea-inducing interior decoration). Suites have kitchenettes and there's a 10% discount for stays of a week or more, so there's substantial value to be had here. It's also a great location, straddling Chinatown and the Lower East Side.

Howard Johnson Express Inn *(#170; ☎ 212-358-8844, fax 473-3500; W www .hojo.com; 135 E Houston; ◍ F, V to Second Ave; singles $129-139, doubles $159-169)*, on the corner of Forsyth St, is the newest place to stay in the heart of the action-packed Lower East Side. With the amenities you would expect in a chain, it's not a bad choice to put up the parents.

Greenwich Village & East Village (Map 4)

A number of hotels and inns downtown cater to gay travelers; for more information, see the boxed text 'Gay-Friendly Hotels & Inns,' earlier in this chapter.

Incentra Village *(#8; ☎ 212-206-0007, fax 604-0625; 32 Eighth Ave; ◍ A, C, E to 14th St, L to Eighth Ave; rooms from $169)*, near W 12th St, is a charming 12-room inn that is booked solid every weekend, partly due to its popularity with queer travelers popping into town for some fun. This quiet place has a lovely parlor and fireplaces and/or kitchenettes in some rooms.

Larchmont Hotel *(#52; ☎ 212-989-9333, fax 989-9496; W www.larchmonthotel.com; 27 W 11th St; ◍ F, V to 14th St; singles $70-80, doubles $90-100)* is more like a cozy inn than a hotel, with shared baths and communal kitchens. The hotel's 52 rooms include sinks and perks such as robes and slippers. What's more, the Larchmont is on a beautiful, leafy Fifth Ave block. As you might imagine, it fills up fast.

Washington Square Hotel *(#80; ☎ 212-777-9515, 800-222-0418, fax 979-8373; W www.washingtonsquarehotel.com; 103 Waverly Pl; ◍ A, C, E, F, S, V to W 4th St; singles/doubles from $126/148)*, between MacDougal St and Sixth Ave, has such a good reputation for its price and location (right off Washington Square Park) that it's hard to get a reservation. Continental breakfast is included in the price.

St Marks Hotel *(#92; ☎ 212-674-2192, fax 420-0854; 2 St Marks Pl at Third Ave; ◍ 6 to Astor Pl; singles/doubles from $80/90)*

is the classic, rough-around-the-edges East Village place. Of course, the block is noisy (request an interior room if noise pollution piques your ire) and some rooms are rented by the hour, so you might want to avert your eyes now and then.

Chelsea, Gramercy Park & Flatiron District (Map 5)

Chelsea Savoy Hotel *(#155; ☎ 212-929-9353, fax 741-6309; 204 W 23rd St; ◍ 1 to 23rd St; rooms $99-195)*, near Seventh Ave, is a lower-priced option on the same block as the Chelsea Hotel.

Chelsea Inn *(#193; ☎ 212-645-8989, 800-640-6469; 46 W 17th St; ◍ L, N, R, 4, 5, 6 to 14th St-Union Sq; doubles without/with bath $129/169, suite $199)*, between Fifth and Sixth Aves, are adjoining town houses, well located for clubbing and art crawls in Chelsea. This is a clean and popular spot.

Chelsea Hotel *(#153; ☎ 212-243-3700, fax 675-5531; 222 W 23rd St; ◍ 1 to 23rd St; rooms from $135)*, between Seventh and Eighth Aves, is a literary and cultural landmark brimming with New York nostalgia and art by past and present residents. The list of noteworthy guests and residents is long, from Dylan Thomas and Bob Dylan to Arthur Miller and Arthur C Clarke. This is also where Sid Vicious killed Nancy Spungen and where *The Professional* was filmed. The cheapest rooms have shared bath and the most expensive suites ($385) have a separate living room, dining area and kitchen; every room is different and there are a range of prices and options – chat with the friendly staff to find something right for you.

Union Square Inn *(#176; ☎ 212-614-0500, fax 614-0512; W www.unionsquareinn .com; 209 E 14th St; ◍ L to Third Ave; doubles $99-129)*, off Third Ave, is a quiet and clean place despite being on a loud, slightly skanky block. Rooms are tiny but functional, with TV, phone and bath. Prices are about $40 more during high season.

Hotel 17 *(#173; ☎ 212-475-2845, fax 677-8178; 225 E 17th St; ◍ N, Q, R, 4, 5, 6 to 14th St-Union Sq, L to Third Ave; singles/doubles/ triples $70/87/110)*, between Second and Third Aves, is a popular queer-friendly

Gramercy Park choice with shared baths throughout. Unfortunately, this friendly place has earned a reputation for overbooking, so reconfirm to be safe.

W New York – Union Square (#181; ☎ 212-253-9119, 877-946-8357, fax 253-9229; W www.whotels.com; 201 Park Ave South; Ⓜ L, N, Q, R, 4, 5, 6 to 14th St-Union Sq; rooms from $319), on the corner of E 17th St, demands a black wardrobe and a platinum credit card. Like all the W hotels, everything is top of the line, comfortable and classy here, but reserve early if you want to stay at this ultra popular place. The W has several Manhattan outposts, including the **W New York – Tuscany** (#92; 120 E 39th St at Lexington Ave) and **W New York – Times Square** (Map 6, #57; 1567 Broadway at 47th St); call the toll-free number (☎ 877-946-8357) or visit the website for more details.

Gramercy Park Hotel (#168; ☎ 212-475-4320, 800-221-4083, fax 505-0535; W www.thegramercyparkhotel.com; 2 Lexington Ave; Ⓜ 6 to 23rd St; singles/doubles/1-bedroom suites from $150/160/200), on the corner of E 21st St, is a New York institution overlooking Gramercy Park (guests receive a key to the private garden haven). The bar off the lobby is a must (see the 'Hotel Cocktails' boxed text in the Entertainment chapter).

Gramercy Park Hotel

MICHELLE BENNETT

Madison Hotel (#131; ☎ 212-532-7373, 800-962-3476, fax 686-0092; 21 E 27th St; Ⓜ 6 to 28th St; doubles from $99), between Madison and Fifth Aves, is a less desirable but cheap and acceptable option if you can't get into the fun and funky Gershwin Hotel nearby (see under Hostels, earlier in this chapter). No matter what the desk clerk demands, don't pay for your entire stay in advance. Continue trying to book a room at the Gershwin for subsequent nights.

Park Ave south of Grand Central Terminal is crowded with reasonably priced places of forgettable composition.

Midtown (Map 5)
Budget & Mid-Range There are several budget and moderately priced places near Herald Square and Murray Hill (a bit further east) which are convenient to Penn and Grand Central stations. While these aren't luxury digs, you should be comfortable at any of these places.

Herald Square Hotel (#114; ☎ 212-279-4017, 800-727-1888; 19 W 31st St; Ⓜ B, D, F, N, Q, R, V, W to 34th St-Herald Sq; doubles without/with bath $60/85), between Broadway and Fifth Ave, is a simple place with small rooms and fair value for the price.

Murray Hill Inn (#124; ☎ 212-683-6900, 888-996-6376, fax 545-0103; W www.murrayhillinn.com; 143 E 30th St; Ⓜ 6 to 33rd St; doubles without/with bath $60/99), between Lexington and Third Aves, is a safe, good-value place in an area with unseemly tendencies. This hotel also extends a super bargain: A private room with two bunk beds and shared bath for $50.

Hotel 31 (#123; ☎ 212-685-3060, fax 532-1232; 120 E 31st St; Ⓜ B, D, F, N, Q, R, V, W to 34th St-Herald Sq; doubles with/ without bath $85/60 low season), between Park Ave South and Lexington Ave, is a short stroll from the Empire State Building. It offers teeny, but comfortable rooms in an 80-year-old building. Rates climb by about $25 in peak season.

Manhattan Inn (#105; ☎ 212-629-9612, fax 629-9613; W www.manhattaninn.com; 303 W 30th St; Ⓜ A, C, E to 34th St-Penn Station; doubles $89), between Eighth and Ninth

PLACES TO STAY

Aves, is a real New York bargain. Rooms are tidy, with private bath and DirectTV, air-conditioning and continental breakfast.

Wolcott Hotel (#115; ☎ 212-268-2900; 4 W 31st St; ⓜ B, D, F, N, Q, R, V, W to 34th St-Herald Sq; doubles from $120), near Fifth Ave, is a 280-room beaux-arts hotel designed by John Duncan, the architect of Grant's Tomb.

ThirtyThirty (#121; ☎ 212-689-1900, fax 689-0023; ⓦ www.thirtythirty-ny.com; 30 E 30th St; ⓜ 6 to 33rd St; rooms $125-175), between Park and Madison Aves, is part of the Citylife hotel group, known for its stylized, cozy digs at comfortable prices.

Hotel Metro (#99; ☎ 212-947-2500, 800-356-3870, fax 279-1310; 45 W 35th St; ⓜ B, D, F, N, Q, R, V, W to 34th St-Herald Sq; doubles/suites $155/210), between Fifth and Sixth Aves, combines 1930s' art deco (its lobby features movie posters from Hollywood's golden era) with the comfort of a gentlemen's club in its attractive lounge and library area. Upstairs you'll find rather plain rooms, but the price, location (near the Morgan Library, Madison Square Garden and Penn Station) and friendly staff make this 160-room hotel a worthy choice.

The Mansfield (#76; ☎ 212-944-6050, 877-847-4444, fax 764-4477; ⓦ www.mansfield hotel.com; 12 W 44th St; ⓜ B, D, F, V to 42nd St, 4, 5, 6, 7 to Grand Central; rooms/suites $149/179), between Fifth and Sixth Aves, is a 1904 building renovated according to historic specifications and is a great deal in an excellent location. Everything is top of the line, from the EO bath products to the Belgian linens. The M Bar here has a fabulous domed glass-and-lead ceiling.

Clarion Hotel (#79; ☎ 212-447-1500, 800-252-7466, fax 213-0972; ⓦ www.clarion fifthave.com; 3 E 40th St; ⓜ 4, 5, 6, 7 to Grand Central; rooms $149-199), between Fifth and Madison Aves, is just around the corner from the New York Public Library. The 186-room business hotel discounts its regular rates on weekends, when occupancy drops.

Pickwick Arms Hotel (#52; ☎ 212-355-0300, 800-742-5945, fax 755-5029; 230 E 51st St; ⓜ 6 to 51st St, E, F to Lexington Ave; rooms from $129), between Second and Third Aves, has frayed furnishings and some

rooms sharing a bath, but is popular with European budget travelers nonetheless.

Salisbury Hotel (Map 6, #5; ☎ 212-246-1300, 888-692-5757, fax 977-7752; ⓦ www .nycsalisbury.com; 123 W 57th St; ⓜ N, R, Q, W to 57th St; rooms from $139), between Sixth and Seventh Aves, is well located for high-brow or low-brow entertainment, whatever you're craving. Discounts are extended to nearby spas and a health and racquet club.

Westpark Hotel (Map 6, #1; ☎ 212-445-0200, 866-937-8727, fax 246-3131; ⓦ www .westparkhotel.com; 308 W 58th St; ⓜ A, B, C, D, 1, 2 to 59th St-Columbus Circle; rooms/ suites from $109/180), between Eighth and Ninth Aves, is near Central Park and popular for its individually decorated rooms, complimentary breakfast, cocktail hour, DVD library and international feel.

Top End Rates at most of the expensive Midtown hotels start at $200 but fluctuate greatly according to seasonal demand – they often go up, but they don't usually fall below that mark.

Morgan's (#94; ☎ 212-686-0300, 800-334-3408, fax 779-8352; ⓦ www.ianschra gerhotels.com; 237 Madison Ave; ⓜ 4, 5, 6, 7 to Grand Central; doubles from $325), between 37th and 38th Sts, is one of Mr Schrager's creations and attracts the young, rich and well groomed to its beautiful, well-appointed rooms. The hotel's Morgan Bar and restaurant sensation Asia de Cuba are all the rage (see the Places to Eat chapter for details). Visit their website for promotions.

Royalton (Map 6, #107; ☎ 212-869-4400, 800-635-9013, fax 869-8965; ⓦ www.ian schragerhotels.com; 44 W 44th St; ⓜ B, D, F, V to 42nd St, 4, 5, 6, 7 to Grand Central; doubles from $365), between Fifth and Sixth Aves, is another of Ian Schrager's places and is done up in typical city chic. The rooms are glorious, featuring deep bathtubs, fireplaces and down comforters. The restaurant and lobby lounge can be annoyingly loud and crowded, however.

Algonquin (Map 6, #82; ☎ 212-840-6800, 800-555-8000, fax 944-1419; 59 W 44th St; ⓜ B, D, F, V, to 42nd St, 4, 5, 6, 7 to Grand Central; rooms $149-349), between Fifth and

Life rushes by the Peninsula Hotel

Sixth Aves, is the storied classic of Algonquin Round Table fame. It still attracts visitors with its upscale wood and chintz decor, plus amenities such as a 24-hour fitness center, though rooms can be cramped. Don't miss the beautiful lobby dating from 1902.

The Iroquois (#75; ☎ 212-840-3080, 800-332-7220, fax 398-1754; 49 W 44th St; Ⓜ B, D, F, V to 42nd St, 4, 5, 6, 7 to Grand Central; standard rooms $325-345, suites $550-625), between Fifth and Sixth Aves, is a 1920s' era hotel that has undergone a complete renovation that spared no detail. James Dean lived here from 1950 to 1953 and the James Dean Lounge is a cool spot for a cocktail.

Waldorf-Astoria (#61; ☎ 212-355-3000, 800-925-3673; Ⓦ www.waldorfastoria.com; 301 Park Ave; Ⓜ 6 to 51st St, E, F to Lexington Ave; standard rooms $205-495, weekend specials about $200), between 49th and 50th Sts, needs no introduction. The legendary hotel – now part of the Hilton chain – has an elegant lobby (surprisingly not as grand as you might hope, though do check out the bathrooms) and restaurants and bars that charge prices befitting the Waldorf's reputation. Middle-aged executives frequent the smoky Bull & Bear restaurant and the Cocktail Terrace above the lobby is a fine place to sip a Manhattan to the strains of piano ditties.

Warwick (Map 6, #14; ☎ 212-247-2700, 800-223-4099, fax 247-2725; Ⓦ www.warwickhotels.com; 65 W 54th St; Ⓜ B, D, F, V to 47th-50th Sts/Rockefeller Center; rooms $295-370, suites $500-900), near Sixth Ave, is a classic Midtown hotel near Rockefeller Center. It has been renovated in recent years and offers 400-plus rooms that count as spacious by Manhattan standards.

Peninsula (#34; ☎ 212-956-2888, 800-262-9467, fax 903-3949; 700 Fifth Ave at 55th St; Ⓜ E, F to Fifth Ave; doubles from $560) dates back to 1904, making it one of the oldest surviving grand hotels in Midtown. The totally renovated hotel includes a sprawling spa and athletic club; the pool is almost big enough for laps.

Four Seasons (#49; ☎ 212-758-5700, 800-487-3769, fax 758-5711; Ⓦ www.fourseasons.com/newyorkfs/index.html; 57 E 57th St at Park Ave; Ⓜ N, R, W to Fifth Ave; weekend rates from $535, suites around $2500) was designed by IM Pei. This limestone monolith has 52 floors, all full of spacious rooms that don't come cheap.

Plaza Hotel (#7; ☎ 212-759-3000, 800-527-4727, fax 759-3167; Ⓔ newyork@fairmont.com; 768 Fifth Ave; Ⓜ N, R, W to Fifth Ave; rooms from $350), between 58th and 59th Sts, is the home of the famous Oak Bar. The Plaza has attracted some high-profile customers, including none other than the Beatles, Cary Grant and Grace Kelly. Suites are decadent affairs costing up to $15,000.

For information on hotels above 59th St, see the Upper West Side and Upper East Side sections, later in this chapter.

PLACES TO STAY

Times Square & Theater District (Map 6)

Budget & Mid-Range With nearly 700 rooms, **Hotel Carter** (#113; ☎ 212-944-6000, 800-553-3415, fax 398-8541; 250 W 43rd St; doubles from $95; ⓜ N, Q, R, S, W, 1, 2, 3, 7 to Times Sq), between Seventh and Eighth Aves, is the place to try if you need a room at short notice. This old hotel has a dark past: In the summer of 1999, a front-desk clerk died after a fellow employee stabbed him.

Milford Plaza (#94; ☎ 212-869-3600, 800-221-2690, fax 944-8357; ⓦ www.milford plaza.com; 270 W 45th St; ⓜ N, Q, R, S, W, 1, 2, 3, 7 to Times Sq; doubles $135-240), near Eighth Ave, is a glittery, bustling 1300-room property owned by the Ramada chain. It's an OK choice for inexpensive, standard rooms in a good location, but it's jam-packed with tour-bus ejecta.

Portland Square Hotel (#52; ☎ 212-382-0600, 800-388-8988, fax 382-0684; ⓦ www .portlandsquarehotel.com; 132 W 47th St; ⓜ B, D, F, V to 47th-50th Sts/Rockefeller Center; singles/doubles $65/75 singles/doubles/ triples/quads with bath $110/125/150/ 160), between Sixth and Seventh Aves, is just steps away from the heart of Times Square. This renovated, clean and family-owned hotel is good value, especially if you're in a group.

Hotel Edison (#59; ☎ 212-840-5000, 800-637-7070, fax 596-6850; ⓦ www.edison hotelnyc.com; 228 W 47th St; ⓜ 1, 2 to 50th St, N, R, W to 49th Sts; singles/doubles/triples $150/170/185), between Broadway and Eighth Ave, was once a high-class spot for Broadway stars. The Edison caters to tourists now (witness the cheesy decor), though theater people still hang out in its coffee shop.

Days Hotel Midtown (#44; ☎ 212-581-7000, 800-325-2525, fax 974-0291; 790 Eighth Ave at W 48th St; ⓜ N, Q, R, S, W, 1, 2, 3, 7 to Times Sq; rooms $99-399) offers bland but cheap rooms; the price varies depending on season and availability.

Ameritania Hotel (#15; ☎ 212-247-5000, 800-664-6835, fax 247-3313; ⓦ www.nyc hotels.net; 230 W 54th St at Broadway; ⓜ B, D, E to Seventh Ave; rooms from $125) is near the Ed Sullivan Theater, where David Letterman's *Late Show* is taped. The clientele is a great mix of upscale folks mingling to piped-in hip hop in the lobby (also see the Twist bar here). Though the rooms were renovated recently, they retain a charming scruffiness. Check the website for discounts, which can drop the price of a basic room as low as $99.

Top End With the generic, top-end hotels around Times Square (ⓜ N, Q, R, S, W, 1, 2, 3, 7 to Times Sq) charging $200 or more a night, you're paying for location, location, location. They include the **Marriott Marquis** (#77; ☎ 212-398-1900, 800-843-4898; 1535 Broadway), between 45th and 46th Sts; **Novotel** (#29; ☎ 212-315-0100, 800-668-6835, fax 765-5333; 226 W 52nd St), near Broadway, which is more international and features a terrace and Café Nicole with views and a solarium; and the luxurious **Doubletree Guest Suites** (#55; ☎ 212-719-1600, 800-222-8733, fax 921-5212; cnr Seventh Ave & 47th St).

Paramount (#60; ☎ 212-764-5500, 800-225-7474, fax 354-5237; ⓦ www.ianschrager hotels.com; 235 W 46th St; ⓜ 1, 2 to 50th St; rooms from $250), between Broadway and Eighth Ave, is trying really hard to win the character contest; painfully mismatched chairs and rotary phones in the lobby are just the start. Still, it's staffed by gracious folk and the stylized rooms are super comfortable. The hotel houses the Whiskey Bar (for more details, see the boxed text 'Hotel Cocktails' in the Entertainment chapter).

Casablanca Hotel (#102; ☎ 212-869-1212, 888-922-7225, fax 391-7585; ⓦ www .casablancahotel.com; 147 W 43rd St; ⓜ N, Q, R S, W, 1, 2, 3, 7 to Times Sq; standard/deluxe rooms $265/295, suites $375), just east of Times Square, is a low-key, high-class 48-room place done out in North African motifs. Complimentary breakfast, all-day snacks and espresso, free wine and appetizers (weekdays only), plus fresh flowers and plushy robes are nice touches

Upper West Side (Map 7)

You'll find a good selection of mid-range hotels in this part of town, most charging between $90 and $200. Also see the Hostels section earlier in this chapter for some super cheapies.

Hotel Olcott (#72; ☎ 212-877-4200; 27 W 72nd St; Ⓜ B, C to 72nd St; doubles from $130), between Columbus Ave and Central Park West, is well located steps away from the W 72nd St entrance to Central Park. It's good value if you can get a room; book early.

Mayflower (#105; ☎ 212-265-0060, 800-223-4164, fax 265-0227; ⓦ www.mayflower hotel.com; 15 Central Park West; Ⓜ A, B, C, D, 1, 2 to 59th St-Columbus Circle; rooms from $189), near W 61st St, is slightly stodgy, but you can't beat the location facing Central Park. Check the Sunday *New York Times* for special offers.

Amsterdam Inn (#61; ☎ 212-579-7500, fax 579-6127; ⓦ www.amsterdaminn.com; 340 Amsterdam Ave; Ⓜ 1, 2, 3 to 72nd St; singles with shared/private bath $75/115, doubles $95/115), at 76th St, has 25 renovated rooms with air-conditioning in a five-story building.

On The Ave (#59; ☎ 212-362-1100, 800-509-7598, fax 787-9521; ⓦ www.stayinny .com; 2178 Broadway; Ⓜ 1, 2 to 79th St; rooms $175-235), near W 77th St, is another Citylife property boasting warm earth tones and stainless steel and marble baths in sunny rooms hung with original artwork.

Excelsior Hotel (#46; ☎ 212-362-9200, fax 580-3792; ⓦ www.excelsiorhotelny.com; 45 W 81st St; Ⓜ B, C to 81st St-Museum of Natural History; doubles from $129, 1-bedroom suites from $240), near Columbus Ave, is an old, 169-room place that overlooks the American Museum of Natural History.

Newtown (#15; ☎ 212-678-6500; ⓦ www .newyorkhotel.com; 2528 Broadway; Ⓜ 1, 2, 3 to 96th St; doubles from $85, suites with kitchenette from $140), between 94th and 95th Sts, has 96 rooms and offers a more intimate alternative to the big West Side hotels.

Astor on the Park (#4; ☎ 212-866-1880, fax 316-9555; ⓦ www.nychotels.com; 465 Central Park West; Ⓜ B, C to 103rd St; rooms Sun-Wed/Thur-Sat $100/135), between 106th and 107th Sts, is a clean friendly place with simple rooms, some overlooking Central Park.

Upper East Side (Map 7)

Some of New York's most elegant and expensive hotels are near Fifth and Madison Aves on the Upper East Side.

The Bentley (#131; ☎ 212-644-6000, 888-664-6835; ⓦ www.nychotels.com; 500 E 62nd St; Ⓜ F to Lexington Ave/63rd St; rooms/suites from $135/235), near York Ave, is a chic boutique hotel with some of New York's most spectacular views. If you don't stay, at least grab a cocktail at the rooftop restaurant (see the boxed text 'Hotel Cocktails' in the Entertainment chapter).

Lowell Hotel (#120; ☎ 212-838-1400, fax 605-6808, 800-221-4444; 28 E 63rd St; Ⓜ F to Lexington Ave/63rd St; doubles from $495), between Park and Madison Aves, is intimate and quiet and one of New York's hot-spot hotels, favored by super celebrities, including Brad Pitt and Madonna. More important, most rooms have kitchenettes and/or fireplaces and terraces.

Gracie Inn (#34; ☎ 212-628-1700, 800-404-2252, fax 628-6420; 502 E 81st St; Ⓜ 4, 5, 6 to 86th St; doubles from $159), a 12-room hotel between York and East End Aves, offers a cheaper alternative. This undiscovered country-style inn is near the East River. Rates include a good breakfast.

Franklin (#36; ☎ 212-369-1000, 877-847-4444, fax 369-8000; 164 E 87th St; Ⓜ 4, 5, 6 to 86th St; standard/superior rooms $275/295), between Third and Lexington Aves, is a friendly hotel with 48 rooms featuring fine linens, fresh flowers and similar perks.

Hotel Wales (#29; ☎ 212-876-6000, 877-847-4444, fax 860-7000; ⓦ www.waleshotel .com; 1295 Madison Ave at 92nd St; Ⓜ 6 to 96th St; rooms from $169) is a century-old place that was returned to its former glory a few years ago. It has 100 rooms and rates include a continental breakfast you can take on the lovely terrace. Don't miss the provocative Puss in Boots canvasses in the lobby.

Brooklyn (Map 9)

New York Marriott Brooklyn (#19; ☎ 718-246-7000, 800-436-3759, fax 246-0563; 333 Adams St; Ⓜ M, N, R to Lawrence St, A, C, F to Jay St-Borough Hall; rooms from $259) is between Tillary and Willoughby Sts. Brooklyn's only full-service hotel has what you would expect from a Marriott: a restaurant, health club, lounge and business services. Prices drop substantially on weekends.

PLACES TO STAY

Places to Eat

This book could easily be titled 15,000 Fabulous Places to Eat in New York City. In fact, you could eat out every night for 46 years without exhausting your restaurant options here. New York's dining spectrum is simply awesome, from sumptuous and snooty to greasy spoon dirt cheap; gourmands galloping through the Big Apple will not want for toothsome fare. There are some general rules of thumb, however.

While every neighborhood can boast a $3 breakfast special, most can also serve up the flipside, with fancy 'in' places, celebrity chefs or old-money classics that come with commiserate price tags. Don't be shy about asking wait staff about the cost of dishes (they rarely, if ever, tell you the price of the daily specials as they reel them off) and also consult them about portion size, ingredients and recommendations (sometimes they'll dish attitude, but they're slaving for tips, so usually not). To save some cents, check out tasting menus or prix fixe options in higher-end places – these can be a real bargain. Another bargain are bar menus: many upscale restaurants (eg, Odeon, Café de Bruxelles and Gramercy Tavern) have more affordable, but just as tasty, food available at the bar. Lunchtime offers opportunities to dine at restaurants that might be out of reach otherwise, so keep your eyes peeled for lunch specials no matter what your budget may be. Wine is generally sold at an incredibly expensive mark-up at restaurants so don't be shocked if that bottle of Merlot costs as much as

your meal (places allowing you to bring your own wine in are obviously a different story).

If you're on a super strict budget, you've come to the right place. You can grab a gyro, hot dog, pretzel, fresh fruit or soup from street vendors (skip those tasty smelling roasted nuts; they're never as good as the aroma). Ethnic food (Chinese, Middle Eastern, Indian, Turkish, Japanese, Korean etc) is usually a decent bet for cheap eats as well.

Devoted foodies will spend a lot of money eating in New York because it's futile to try to resist such feastable fare. But do your research: there are too many restaurants in New York relying on reputation, chic clientele, celebrity ownership or fashionable decor instead of what you're putting to your lips. there are also scads of mediocre places serving middle-of-the-road food at gourmet prices – avoid these at all costs. The best research tool is the ever-popular and annually updated *Zagat Survey*, available all over the city. Restaurant reviews also appear weekly in *Time Out* and *New York* magazine and in the Weekend section of Friday's *New York Times*.

This book might also be titled 2055 Fabulous Places to Take a Cocktail in New York City; here drinking is not a way to pass the time, as much as a way of life and style. Cocktails before dinner is a fantastic way to kick off the night (not to mention the preferred way to wrap it up), so please see the Bars & Lounges section of the Entertainment chapter.

HUGH D'ANDRADE

Five-Star Dining at Two-Star Prices

Most budget travelers can't even consider eating at the temples of New York cuisine, many of which keep out the hoi polloi by charging $50 and up per person for a meal. But the big-city aristocracy must have begun to bore New York's elite restaurateurs, who started opening their dining rooms to the common people in a stunning democratic move called 'Restaurant Week.' Held for one week in February and one week in June each year (and after September 11, again in November in an effort to raise quick revenue), Restaurant Week offers elaborate three-course lunches for the price of the year (eg, $20.03, $20.04 etc). More than 85 restaurants participate, including such premier spots as Tavern on the Green, Aquavit and Union Pacific. True foodies travel to the city just for this event, then spend each Restaurant Week dashing around town with a well-thumbed Zagat's guide in hand. Many places won't accept reservations during Restaurant Week, but it's worth calling to ask if you want to dine somewhere special. Be warned however, that some places cut corners at this time, for example substituting less exquisite produce and game for their usual top notch stuff, passing off ready-made salads and delivering slack or chilly service. For more information, visit the website W www.newyork.citysearch.com and search for Restaurant Week.

N.Y.C.

LOWER MANHATTAN (MAP 3)

While food is hard to find here after the workers go home and the streets are rolled up, the lunch offerings are varied. For really cheap eats, check out the 'roach coaches' (cafeterias on wheels) that line Front St and sell everything from fried chicken to burritos.

Pearl Palace (#84; ☎ 212-482-0771; 60 Pearl St; M N, R to Whitehall St; lunch buffet $7; open 24 hrs), near Broad St, is a no-frills Indian restaurant catering to the workabouts from nearby Wall St and environs. The bargain all-you-can-eat buffet lunch (11am to 2:30pm weekdays) includes a salad bar.

Cabana (#54; ☎ 212-406-1155; 89 South Street Seaport; M 1, 2, 4, 5, J, M, Z to Fulton St-Broadway Nassau; appetizers $4-11, entrees $13-19), at Pier 17, heralds the debut of fine food in the Seaport, finally. They bill their menu as 'nuevo Latino,' which means wholesome, tasty food using ingredients like plantains, chiles, rice, beans and jerk spices. Portions are generous and the view across New York Harbor is unsurpassed – come for a cocktail at sunset.

Radio Mexico (#53; ☎ 212-791-5416, fax 267-9564; 259 Front St; M 4, 5, 6 to Brooklyn Bridge-City Hall; appetizers $3.95-5.95, entrees $5.95-11.95), near Dover St under the Brooklyn Bridge, is a festive joint serving huge burritos, tacos etc. The $2.50 margaritas are a steal (4:30pm to 6:30pm weekdays).

Jeremy's (#51; ☎ 212-964-3537; 254 Front St; M 4, 5, 6 to Brooklyn Bridge-City Hall; appetizers $1.95-3.95, burgers $3-4.95), at Dover St, is the type of place that defies description. Passing through the door, you're blasted by stale beer and fried fish and chips ($6.95) and greeted by all manner of bras and unmentionables hanging from every available rafter. Here, construction workers, prim secretaries, fishmongers and musicians sidle up to the wooden tables and roll up their sleeves to dig in. Pints start at $2.75, which is a great way to wash down a half dozen oysters ($9.50).

Bridge Café (#50; ☎ 212-227-3344; 279 Water St at Dover St; M 4, 5, 6 to Brooklyn Bridge-City Hall; pasta, meat & seafood entrees around $16) is worth the detour if you can afford to spend a few more bucks. This homey haven is underneath the Brooklyn Bridge. Certified as the oldest pub in the city, the restaurant offers an extensive wine list.

Fraunces Tavern (#83; ☎ 212-968-1776, 797-1776; 54 Pearl St; M N, R to Whitehall St; sandwiches $16, entrees $22-32; open 11:30am-9pm Mon-Sat), corner of Broad St, transports diners from Wall St to Williamsburg: This building hosted George Washington's farewell address (more notable than the expensive food). A better bang for the buck is **Bayard's** (#78; ☎ 212-514-9454; 1 Hanover Sq), between Pearl and Stone Sts, in the India House, which was the old Cotton Exchange.

PLACES TO EAT

TRIBECA (MAP 3)

People are playing it down, but Tribeca has been in a spot of trouble since September 11. Restaurants are quietly closing or moving away and while the neighborhood will no doubt regain its platinum status, you should eat and play here now. In an effort to stem the bleeding, many of the restaurants below formed a coalition called the Tribeca Organization following the attacks and slashed prices, in some cases up to 25%. Still, it remains to be seen which places will survive.

Bubby's *(#33; ☎ 212-219-0666; 120 Hudson St at N Moore St; ❶ 1, 2 to Franklin St; salads $8.95-9.95, entrees $10-16; open 8am-10pm Mon, 8am-11pm Tues-Thur, 8am-midnight Fri & Sat, 8am-10pm Sun)* is an old Tribeca standby (especially for brunch – check out what one local calls 'the best bloody Mary I've ever had in my life!'). At lunch and dinner, the big, breezy restaurant dishes healthy salads, sandwiches, pastas and what might be New York's best burger. This is a good place for vegetarians (lots of meat-free entrees) and kids (crayons free to all diners).

Walker's *(#31; ☎ 212-941-0142; 16 N Moore St at Varick St; ❶ 1, 2 to Franklin St)* is a dark watering hole serving tasty, gussied up standards like turkey sandwiches and burgers for under $10. A laid-back, homey feel pervades the three dining rooms and the poetry-bedecked bathrooms are worth a thought or chuckle. Sunday may be the best time to visit: between noon and 4pm there's a reasonable brunch and live jazz combos (no cover) at 8pm.

Obeca Li *(#40; ☎ 212-393-9887; 62 Thomas St; ❶ A, C, 1, 2 to Chambers St; open 6pm-11pm Tues-Thur, 6pm-midnight Fri & Sat)*, between Church St and West Broadway, serves up a pan-Asian menu in a phenomenal and sprawling space. Sake fans will delight in their classic choices, plus sake martinis which are all the rage.

Yaffa's *(#36; ☎ 212-274-9403; 363 Greenwich St; ❶ 1, 2 to Franklin St)*, corner of Harrison St, is a laid-back place with Middle Eastern ambiance where you can fill up for $10 or less. Try the handmade merguez sausages or the favorite Mediterranean platter, which has ample samples of the usual (hummus, taboule, olives etc). In the back is **Yaffa's Tea Room** where you can sip the steeped stuff in luxe couches.

Odeon *(#11; ☎ 212-233-0507; 145 West Broadway; ❶ A, C, 1, 2 to Chambers St; dinner entrees $16-30; open until at least 2am Sun-Thur, 3am Fri & Sat)*, between Duane and Thomas Sts, burns with the energy and panache that typifies uber New York: the food is classy without being fussy (try the grilled duck special or croque monsieur – a fancy grilled ham and cheese), the staff is on the ball, the drinks are strong and the kitchen is open until the wee hours. The atmosphere is refreshingly attitude-free, which is doubly impressing considering Odeon's origins as the seminal see and be seen bistro.

Bouley Bakery *(#39; ☎ 212-694-2525; 120 West Broadway; ❶ A, C, 1, 2 to Chambers St)*, near Duane St, is the type of place where mere mortals can only get as close as the glass window, fogging it up with hot, hungry breath. You can try and get a reservation at David Bouley's hot spot or just pop in to the bakery for some of New York's best bread or an excellent soup or pastry.

Capsouto Frères *(#1; ☎ 212-966-4900; 451 Washington St; ❶ 1, 2 to Canal St)*, near Watts St, is a fine French bistro with a superlative prix fixe lunch ($20), where you might get a fluffy soufflé and decadent duck pâté to start, followed by a roast chicken entree and rounded out with a crème brulle for dessert.

Montrachet *(#5; ☎ 212-219-2777; 239 West Broadway; ❶ 1, 2 to Franklin St; appetizers $12-17, entrees $25-30)*, near the intersection of Vesey and West Sts, was the first outpost in the Brothers Nieporent dining empire (now including Nobu and Tribeca Grill, among many others). Here you'll find a French menu spiked with Asian and home-style twists: try the sliced beef with soy and enoki mushrooms ($15) or the braised rabbit with olives and bacon ($25). The lunchtime prix fixe ($30/46) is a bargain and the wine list is exceptional.

Chanterelle *(#35; ☎ 212-966-6960, fax 966-6143; 2 Harrison St; ❶ 1, 2 to Franklin St; prix fixe lunch $38, prix-fixe dinner tasting menu $95)* is near Hudson St. Its changing menu often features a heavenly grilled seafood sausage, and pulls flavors from France, Morocco and the Mediterranean (there's also an encyclopedic wine list). Finish off your dinner with the sublime cheese platter. Make reservations weeks or months in advance at this romantic French restaurant.

NoBu (#34; ☎ 212-219-0500; 105 Hudson St; 1, 2 to Franklin St; appetizers $8-20, entrees $22-25), on the corner of Franklin St, is almost nauseatingly trendy. Nobu's tasting menu *(omakase)*, is a multicourse chef's choice for $70, and while some swear it's worth the price, you might be just as sated in one of the much cheaper sushi restaurants on E 9th St off Third Ave (see the 'Culinary Corners' boxed text, later). You might try **Next Door Nobu** (☎ 212-334-4445) if your heart is set on eating here; they don't take reservations and serve up much the same pricey raw fish.

For a quick wholesome snack, head to **Bell Bates Natural Foods** (#42; ☎ 212-267-4300; 97 Reade St; A, C, 1, 2 to Chambers St), between Church and West Broadway, a neighborhood institution and formidable health food purveyor, especially since it upgraded to this space some years back.

CHINATOWN (MAP 3)

You may have been to other Chinatowns around the world, but the New York version, with streets and alleys crammed with all manner of Asian restaurants, street vendors and fish markets, is almost overwhelming. Most Chinatown restaurants (including those listed here) offer bargain meals, with appetizers for around $5 and entrees for $10 or less.

To reach any of the following spots, take the subway to the Canal St stations at Broadway, Lafayette or Centre Sts (J, M, N, Q, R, W, Z, 6 to Canal St).

Vegetarian Paradise 3 (#22; ☎ 212-406-2896; 33 Mott St; appetizers, rice & soup dishes $2-6.95, entrees $7.50-10.95; open 11am-10pm Mon-Thur, 11am-11pm Fri-Sun), near Pell St, specializes in faux meat. From ham to lamb, vegetarians will drool over the amazingly well done 'meats' here; they also boast a huge selection of soups and fresh juices.

Vegetarian Dim Sum House (#20; ☎ 212-577-7176, fax 577-2008; 24 Pell St) has all the mock meats of the others, plus an extensive dim sum menu with everything under $2.

House of Vegetarian (#14; ☎ 212-226-6572; 68 Mott St), near Bayard St, is related to Vegetarian Dim Sum House and does similar faux meats. Here, nothing costs more than $10; cash only.

Hee Win Lai (#21; ☎ 212-285-8686; 28-30 Pell St), near Doyers St, serves up cheap and tasty (though some of it unidentifiable to the uninitiated!) dim sum at communal tables packed with locals. Two people can stuff themselves for under $15.

Joe's Shanghai (#19; ☎ 212-233-8888, fax 233-0278; ⓦ www.joesshanghai.com; 9 Pell St; appetizers $2.95-4.95, entrees $9.95-13.95; open 11am-11:15pm daily) is an old favorite serving classic Chinese standbys like sesame chicken, beef with broccoli and shrimp lo mein at slightly higher prices than other places around here.

ROBERT REID

Locals peek at the Peking ducks in Chinatown

In recent years, a number of Vietnamese restaurants have also found a home in Chinatown:

Nha Trang *(#10, ☎ 212-233-5948; 87 Baxter St; open 10am-10pm daily)*, near Bayard St, attracts a lunchtime crowd of cops, jurors and lawyers from the nearby courthouses. Stick to basic classics like salt-and-pepper shrimp and you'll spend less than $10 or try a steaming bowl of *pho* (beef soup) for $3.75. For a legal speedball, chase your meal with the super-rich and delicious Vietnamese-style coffee ($1.50).

New Pasteur *(#11; ☎ 212-608-3656; 85 Baxter St)*, near Bayard St, is next door to Nha Trang, and serves such a similar menu, they must share a printer to cut costs.

Pho Viet Huong *(#9; ☎ 212-233-8988; 73 Mulberry St; appetizers $3.50-5, entrees $8.50-12.50)*, near Canal St, has a terrific menu, belying the cheesy decor and little bamboo courtyard theme. The Vietnamese clay-pot curries and fondues arrive burbling, and the vegetables come crispy and glistening.

Thailand Restaurant *(#12; ☎ 212-349-3132; 106 Bayard St; appetizers $4.95-7.50, entrees $7.95-9.95)*, between Baxter and Mulberry Sts, proffers authentic, filling dishes rivaling the best Bangkok street vendors, including the particularly good spicy vegetarian soup for two and the picante pad thai.

Nice Restaurant *(#17; ☎ 212-406-9510, fax 571-6827; 35 East Broadway)*, between Catherine and Market Sts, offers fancy Hong Kong–style food in a distinctly local atmosphere (ask for the English menu!). There smiling matrons circle the room with dim sum carts cooling their offerings in Chinese; it's okay to look before you order.

LITTLE ITALY (MAP 4)

Generally, you'll want to avoid the places in Little Italy that post snazzy waiters at the door trying to drum up business.

During the summer, the two blocks of Mulberry St, north of Canal St, close to traffic so that the restaurants here can set up outdoor tables. Most of the places offering al fresco dining offer entrees for $15 and under, and if you stick with pasta, you can't go far wrong. Scrutinize your bill though: Some Little Italy restaurants tack on a bit of a 'vig' – a 25% service charge scam that waiters will occasionally try out on unsuspecting tourists.

Benito One *(#239; ☎ 212-226-9171; 174 Mulberry St; ❷ 6 to Spring St, J, M to Bowery; appetizers $7.50-10, pasta dishes $7-10; open 11am-11pm Sun-Fri, 11am-midnight Sat)*, between Grand and Broome Sts, is a local institution. Benito One bills itself as the neighborhood's last authentic Italian restaurant, but some folks prefer **Benito Two** *(#240)* just across the street. Entrees range from basic spaghetti ($7) to a grilled seafood plate with shrimp, mussels and clams ($24).

Lombardi's *(#210; ☎ 212-941-7994, fax 941-4159; 32 Spring St; ❷ 6 to Spring St; pizza $11.50-13.50, extras from $3; open 11:30am-11pm Mon-Thur, 11:30am-midnight Fri & Sat)* is between Mott and Mulberry Sts. It is indisputably New York's oldest and perhaps most legendary, pizza joint. Established in 1905, this brick-oven pizzeria serves only pies and huge calzones, delicious half-moon pillows of dough stuffed with ricotta cheese and herbs. The fresh mushroom pie comes with three different types of fungi.

Caffe Roma *(#238; ☎ 212-226-8413; 385 Broome St; ❷ 6 to Spring St, J, M to Bowery)*, near Mulberry St, is by far the best spot to cool your heels for a spell. Here you can take cannoli and espresso in a lazy, tin-ceilinged setting after a Chinatown meal or SoHo shopping spree.

Many of the old eateries in this neighborhood now cater almost exclusively to tourists, which means that you'll probably pay more than you should. These include **Vincent's** *(#243; ☎ 212-226-8133, fax 226-0713; 119 Mott St; ❷ J, M to Bowery, S to Grand St)*, on the corner Hester St, which has a decent prix-fixe lunch for $21, and the cheaper **Puglia** *(#242; ☎ 212-226-8912; 189 Hester St; ❷ J, M to Canal St, S to Grand St)*, between Mulberry and Mott Sts, with its raucous singing (audience participation!) and huge crowds.

LOWER EAST SIDE (MAP 4)

Katz's Deli *(#175; ☎ 212-254-2246; 205 E Houston St at Ludlow St;* Ⓜ *F, V to Second Ave)* was where the pastrami sent Meg Ryan into a tizz of a faux climax in *When Harry Met Sally*, but we prefer the kosher dill pickles and chocolate egg creams for titilating the taste buds. Regardless of what flavors you favor, head here for a classic New York deli experience.

Yonah Shimmel Bakery *(#171; ☎ 212-477-2858; 137 E Houston St;* Ⓜ *F, V to Second Ave)*, between Eldridge and Forsyth Sts, has been selling knishes, bagels and bialys for 92 years and knows how it's done: there are no fewer than eight varieties of potato and five types of cheese knish on offer. Pull up a chair and kibbitz with the locals.

Bereket *(#174; ☎ 212-475-7700; 187 E Houston St at Orchard St;* Ⓜ *F, V to Second Ave; kebabs $5, daily specials $7.50; open 24 hrs)* serves Turkish kebabs and a good selection of vegetarian dishes all day, every day, making it popular with Turkish hacks, club kids and poor slobs stuck working the graveyard shift.

Among the two hottest new places (with reason, thankfully) are **71 Clinton Fresh Foods** *(#222; ☎ 212-614-6960; 71 Clinton St;* Ⓜ *F to Delancey St, J, M, Z to Essex St)*, between Rivington and Stanton Sts, which made a quick name for itself through its fresh, innovative and reasonably priced fare (look for original chef Wylie Dufresne's WD50, due to open down the block at 50 Clinton St) and **Paladar** *(#216; ☎ 212-473-3535; 161 Ludlow St;* Ⓜ *F to Delancey St, J, M Z to Essex St)*, at Stanton St, which combines tropical flavors in revolutionary ways thanks to chef Aaron Sanchez. What's more, the kitchen stays open until 2am from Thursday to Saturday.

SOHO (MAP 4)

Gourmet Garage *(#252; ☎ 212-941-5850; 453 Broome St at Mercer St;* Ⓜ *A, C, E to Canal St • #70; ☎ 212-699-5980; 117 Seventh Ave at 10th St • Map 7, #128; ☎ 212-535-6271; 301 E 64th St • Map 7, #11; ☎ 212-663-0656; 2567 Broadway at 96th St)* is good for picnic creations or if you have a kitchen

Bagels to go

ANGUS OBORN

in your hostel. An olive bar, perky fruits and veggies, a large cheese and pâté selection, plus breads and a variety of upscale prepared foods await.

Ben's Famous Pizza *(#198; ☎ 212-966-4494; 177 Spring St;* Ⓜ *C, E to Spring St; open 11am-11:30pm Mon-Wed, 11am-12:30am Thur-Sat, noon-10:30pm Sun)*, corner of Thompson St, does a very respectable slice ($2), though whether this is NY's best slice as some natives claim is debatable. The Italian ices are the shit, however.

Lupe's East LA Kitchen *(#261; ☎ 212-966-1326; 110 Sixth Ave;* Ⓜ *A, C, E to Canal St; appetizers $3.95-4.25, entrees $7.50-10.25; open 11:30am-11pm Sun-Tues, 11:30am-midnight Wed-Sat)*, between Watts and Broome Sts, serves up nice-sized burritos and enchilada plates and is a popular neighborhood hang-out.

Souen *(#195; ☎ 212-807-7421; 219 Sixth Ave at Prince St;* Ⓜ *C, E to Spring St; appetizers $7.50-8, entrees $10-11; open 11am-11pm Mon-Fri, 10am-11pm Sat, 10am-10pm Sun)* is the city's longtime purveyor of macrobiotic and creative vegetarian fare (including fish). They have a terrific salad selection ($3.50-7.50).

Spring St Natural *(#208; ☎ 212-966-0290, fax 966-4254; 62 Spring St;* Ⓜ *6 to Spring St; appetizers $6.25-7.25, entrees $9-16.25)*, near the corner of Lafayette St, is a large bright place reminiscent of a cafeteria, except here the food is good. Choose from many vegetarian selections (pastas, stir-fries and salads), plus healthy fish and organic chicken dishes.

PLACES TO EAT

Fanelli's Café (#203; ☎ 212-226-9412; 94 Prince St at Mercer St; N, R to Prince St; appetizers $5.50-7.50, entrees $9.95 12.95; open 10am-2am Sun-Thur, 10am-3pm Fri & Sat) is the grizzled old timer of the neighborhood, predating all the artists, landmark committees and gentrification. Fanelli's is New York's second-oldest restaurant, established in 1872, and was once a speakeasy. The dark, smoky bar features a pressed-tin ceiling and a century-old dining room full of tables covered in red checkered cloths.

Soup Kiosk (#204; ☎ 212-254-1417, cnr Prince & Mercer Sts; N, R to Mercer St; small soups $4.45-5.90, large $5.75-7.75; open 11am-6pm daily) is adjacent to Fanelli's Café, but unaffiliated. Seven different soups are ladled out here daily, from mussel chowder to carrot ginger. There are always vegetarian and vegan options.

Lucky Strike (#256; ☎ 212-941-0479; 59 Grand St; A, C, E, 1, 2 to Canal St; appetizers $5.50-8.50, entrees $16-21; open noon-2am Sun-Thur, noon-4am Fri & Sat), between West Broadway and Wooster, serves moderately priced French bistro fare to young trendsetters. The menu is nothing special, but the place is popular for its nightly DJs and late-night kitchen hours.

Balthazar (#207; ☎ 212-965-1414; www .balthazarny.com; 80 Spring St; 6 to Spring St; dishes $17.50-27; open noon-1am Sun-Wed, noon-2am Thur-Sat) is between Broadway and Crosby St. The world should be over this bistro already, but somehow it retains its superstar status, making dinner and brunch reservations hard to wrangle. Still, nobodies like us can land a table for lunch or early dinner (or drop in late at night). The menu features oysters from the raw bar, a nice grilled brook trout and meatier options like roasted pork chops or free range chicken.

Kitchen Club (#181; ☎ 212-274-0025; 30 Prince St at Mott St; N, R to Prince St; appetizers $5.50-10.50, entrees $19-24; open noon-3:30pm & 6pm-11:30pm Tues-Fri, 6pm-11:30pm Sat & Sun) is an intimate eatery in Nolita, where owner-chef Marja Samson works in full view of diners. She's a bit eccentric – if a worm were to inch its way across your salad, she would respond with a lecture on the wonders of organic foods. Try the mushroom dumplings or a Bento box dinner.

Mekong (#266; ☎ 212-343-8169; 44 Prince St; N, R to Prince St; appetizers $4.95-6.95, entrees $7.95-13.95), located at the corner of Mott St, is a solid Vietnamese restaurant with a warm interior and decent bar scene. Vegetarians will find plenty to choose from here.

Raoul's (#196; ☎ 212-966-3518; 180 Prince St; C, E to Spring St; appetizers $12-17, entrees $17-28), between Sullivan and Thompson Sts, is a dark, cramped bistro at the crossroads of SoHo and Paris – replete with the prices you might expect. The garden dining here is a bonus.

Pão! (#264; ☎ 212-334-5464; 322 Spring St; C, E to Spring St; entrees around $20), at Greenwich, is a bit farther afield and not cheap, but is worth it for the scrumptious, homestyle Portuguese fare. Catch a beer at The Ear Inn afterwards (see Bars & Lounges in the Entertainment chapter).

Test your 'star power' at this superstar restaurant

WEST VILLAGE (MAP 4)

Paticceria Bruno (#151; ☎ 212-242-4959; 245 Bleecker St; ◐ A, C, E, F, V, S to W 4th St), near Cornelia St, is a good place to soothe your sweet tooth with some chocolates and a cappuccino.

Cones (#153; ☎ 212-414-1795; 272 Bleecker St; ◐ A, C, E, F, V, S to W 4th St; double scoop $3) is between Seventh Ave South and Jones St. Self-proclaimed 'ice cream artisans' practice their craft here, where the Italian-style ice creams and sorbets offer a great respite from the summer heat.

Grange Hall (#155; ☎ 212-924-5246; 50 Commerce St; ◐ 1, 2 to Christopher St-Sheridan Sq; breakfast & lunch $4.75-8.25, dinner $14.50-22.50), a block off Bedford St, is the modern incarnation of an old neighborhood speakeasy, which was called the Blue Mill. The renovated tavern-restaurant features hearty meals like stuffed brook trout and a sirloin big enough to choke a horse. Organic vegetables and roasted potatoes round out the meal. It's a loud, but comfortable and friendly local place – a great spot to take a drink at the bar.

Chow (#71; ☎ 212-633-2212, 230 West 4th St; ◐ 1, 2 to Christopher St; appetizers $7-10, entrees $14-21), on the corner of W 10th St, is making its name with big portions, a gregarious atmosphere and a fresh, creative menu. Don't miss the baby clams in sake broth ($10). The filling and tasty house Chow selections ($14-16) change daily. You can smoke here, there's a womb of a back dining room and staff don't hustle you off the tables; check the bathroom for a stoner moment.

Little Havana (#149; ☎ 212-255-2212; 30 Cornelia St; ◐ A, C, E, F, V, S to W 4th St; dishes $14-16), between Bleecker and W 4th Sts, is a tiny Village gem serving earthy and filling but still delicate dishes in a cozy setting. Try the first-rate tamales or the spicy roast pork with *tomatillo* sauce.

Pó (#150; ☎ 212-645-2189; 31 Cornelia St; ◐ A, C, E, F, V, S to W 4th St; appetizers $8-9, 1st course $12.50-14, 2nd course $16-18), between Bleecker and W 4th Sts, is the small, spare home to renowned chef Mario Batali. The contemporary Italian coming from his kitchen is to swoon for; take advantage of the six-course dinner tasting menu ($35) and you'll have to be rolled from the table. Reservations are compulsory.

Do Hwa (#158; ☎ 212-414-2815; 55 Carmine St; ◐ 1, 2 to Houston St; appetizers $6-8, entrees $16-22) is near the corner of Bedford St, between Sixth and Seventh Aves. Quentin Tarantino's investment in Do Hwa has no doubt helped to boost the popularity of this Korean barbecue spot in the heart of the Village. Harvey Keitel, Wesley Snipes and Uma Thurman have stopped by for a taste of the flavorful beef ribs and kimchi in the spare Asian dining room. Entrees can often feed two and the restaurant has DJs spinning nightly.

El Faro (#7; ☎ 212-929-8210, fax 929-8295; 823 Greenwich St; ◐ A, C, E to 14th St, L to Eighth Ave; entrees $16-23), on the corner of Horatio St, is a classic old Spanish restaurant that's quiet during the week but impossibly crowded on Friday and Saturday nights. The decor hasn't changed in 20 years, nor have the waiters. Choose from no fewer than four types of paella – one order feeds two.

Café de Bruxelles (#11; ☎ 212-206-1830; 118 Greenwich Ave; ◐ A, C, E to 14th St, L to Eighth Ave), at Horatio St, is a cozy neighborhood institution serving up killer value and ambiance. There are over two dozen Belgian beers, mussels in 15 different varieties ($15.50 and big enough for two; we slobber over the Au Vert spiked with cilantro) and a killer bar menu. Perch here to save some dollars and better appreciate the swarthy weekend bartender.

Florent (#6; ☎ 212-989-5779; 69 Gansevoort St; ◐ A, C, E to 14th St, L to Eighth Ave; open 9am-5am Mon-Fri, 24 hrs Fri-Sun), between Greenwich and Washington Sts, colonized the meatpacking district in the far West Village many moons ago. This bustling spot draws clubbers at all hours with its hangar steak, burgers and breakfast selections. Try the praiseworthy blood sausage or pork chops. On the weekend closest to July 14th, Florent takes over Gansevoort St for an open-air Bastille Day celebration. The cartographic jewels gracing the walls must be some of New York's most original art.

PLACES TO EAT

Old Homestead *(Map 5, #201; ☎ 212-242-9040, fax 727-1637; 56 Ninth Ave;*  *A, C, E to 14th St, L to Eighth Ave; raw bar $1.60-5.50, steaks $25-35, prix-fixe dinner $42),* on the corner of Little West 12th St, was serving up juicy steaks back in the days when the meatpacking district was still full of slaughterhouses and she-males turning tricks in minivans. These days the 'king of beef' has loads of competition, but still does a wicked porterhouse, sirloin and prime rib.

The perfect way to relax and recharge

ANGUS OBORN

GREENWICH VILLAGE (MAP 4)

French Roast *(#55; ☎ 212-533-2233; 458 Sixth Ave at W 11th St;* 🚇 *L to Sixth Ave, F, V to 14th St; breakfast $6.75-9.50, lunch $6.75-11.50, dinner $6.75-15.50; open 24 hrs)* is yet another French-style bistro; this one is distinguished by its airy dining room and 24/7 hours.

Sammy's Noodle Shop *(#56; ☎ 212-924-6688; 453-461 Sixth Ave;* 🚇 *L to Sixth Ave, F, V to 14th St; lunch specials $4.95, noodle dishes under $8.25),* near W 11th St, is a noodle shop that sprawls over several storefronts. Passersby can watch the homemade noodles being prepared.

Rocco *(#165; ☎ 212-677-0590; 181 Thompson St;* 🚇 *1, 2 to Houston St; appetizers $7-10, entrees from $14; open noon-11pm daily),* between Bleecker and Houston Sts, is a colorful place loved by all and certainly worth the few extra dollars. Here the friendly and attentive wait staff will be happy to provide your favorite dish even if it's not on the menu. This gathering place for local Village eccentrics has been around for 60 years.

Tomoe Sushi *(#166; ☎ 212-777-9346; 172 Thompson St;* 🚇 *1, 2 to Houston St; full sushi meal $15-25),* between Bleecker and W Houston Sts, is a wildly popular sushi spot that always seems to have a line (perhaps because the sushi here is reputed to be New York's best).

Two places that are 'all hat and no cattle' as the Texan saying goes, but that will do in a pinch are **Caffe Lure** *(#164; ☎ 212-473-2642; 169 Sullivan St;* 🚇 *1, 2 to Houston St),* between Bleecker and W Houston Sts, where you should stick to the wood burning oven pizzas and **Bar Six** *(#14; ☎ 212-691-1363;* 502 *Sixth Ave;* 🚇 *L to Sixth Ave, F, V to 14th St),* between 12th and 13th Sts. The latter is crowded by hipster wannabes dining on mediocre, pricey fare, but the kitchen does stay open until 2am every night (until 3am on Friday and Saturday), so that's something.

EAST VILLAGE & ALPHABET CITY (MAP 4)

Delis, diners, lunch counters and cafés are all crammed happily together in these neighborhoods and you should have no problem finding places for a cheap, yummy fill up.

Internet Café *(#124; ☎ 212-614-0747; 82 E 3rd St;* 🚇 *F, V to Second Ave),* between First and Second Aves, is a cute place to get online and have a bite to the strains of live jazz. Another option in this 'hood for java and email is **Lalita Java** *(#119; ☎ 212-228-8448; 210 E 3rd St;* 🚇 *St; F, V to Second Ave),* between Aves B and C.

Cafe Pick Me Up *(#35; ☎ 212-673-7231; 145 Ave A;* 🚇 *6 to Astor Pl),* corner of 9th St, is a lively local place with terrific espresso and people watching – smokers head here.

Veselka *(#37; ☎ 212-228-9682; 144 Second Ave;* 🚇 *6 to Astor Pl, N, R to 8th St-NYU; open 24 hrs),* on the corner of 9th St, is a Ukrainian diner with a strong local following. Stick to one of the seven homemade soups ($2.75/3.50 cup/bowl) to avoid any disappointment.

Culinary Corners

Manhattan is full of neighborhoods and pockets where one type of ethnic cuisine predominates. Beyond the famous Little Italy and Chinatown, some of these lesser-known areas offer exotic culinary adventures for bargain rates.

Little India

Since the late 1970s, almost two dozen Indian restaurants have popped up on E 6th St between Second and First Aves. (According to the old joke, all the restaurants share the same kitchen.) At one time, these spots all drew crowds on weekend nights, but as Indian restaurants have spread throughout town (and the Indian population has shifted to the Jackson Heights section of Queens), these eateries have hit slower times. They now engage in a mad war for lunch business, with many offering four- and five-course meals, including a beverage, for as little as $5. **Rose of India** *(Map 4, #100;* ☎ *212-533-5011; 308 E 6th St)* is an all-time favorite for its kitschy, spangly decor and birthday surprises (be sure to mention it's your special day). Another good one over here is **Windows on India** *(Map 4, #101;* ☎ *212-477-5956; 344 E 6th St)* which has more atmosphere than most. In general, the restaurants offering live Indian music and/or a wine list wind up being more expensive than their alcohol-free counterparts. Arrive at the dry places with your own store-bought beer. Despite the block's 'Little India' nickname, most of the immigrants who operate shops here actually hail from Bangladesh.

Little Korea

Korean-owned fashion and accessories shops fill the streets near Herald Square, with food shops and restaurants clustered between Broadway and Fifth Ave from 31st to 36th Sts (also known as Little Seoul or Kimchi Alley for the pickled vegetables accompanying each meal). Strung along 32nd St are scads of eateries good for a cheap fill-up no matter the time of day and night (most places are open 24/7). Korean barbecue (meat cooked at your table on gas or coal-fired grills) is a tasty treat and a fun, communal experience. **Mandoo Bar** *(Map 5, #116;* ☎ *212-279-3075; 2 W 32nd St)* is a sleek place where you can choose from many varieties of fried or steamed *mandoo* (Korean dumplings) which they wrap up right in the storefront window.

Kum Gang San *(Map 5, #113;* ☎ *212-967-0909; 49 W 32nd St)*, is a garish place with good Korean BBQ; the $6.95 lunch special is a steal. Another tacky place popular with Koreans and others in the know is **Kang Suh** *(Map 5, #111;* ☎ *212-564-6845; 1250 Broadway)* entrance on 32nd St.

Little Tokyo

In the East Village, the two-block stretch of E 9th St between First and Third Aves has become a gathering spot for young Japanese who've moved to the neighborhood over the past few years. Excellent sushi restaurants line the street.

Hasaki *(Map 4, #42;* ☎ *212-473-3327; 210 E 9th St)*, between Second and Third Aves, has the best reputation. Try there first, but if you find a long wait, head across the street to **Sharaku** *(Map 4, #40;* ☎ *212-598-0403; 14 Stuyvesant St)*, near E 9th St, where you'll find plenty of tables and a large menu featuring many Japanese specialties aside from sushi.

KOREAN FOOD

PLACES TO EAT

ANGUS OBORN

N.Y.C.

Grab some classic food at a kosher landmark

Second Ave Deli (#38; ☎ 212-677-0606; 156 Second Ave; Ⓜ 6 to Astor Pl, N, R to 8th St-NYU; open 7am-midnight Sun-Thur, 7am-3am Fri & Sat), on the corner of E 10th St, is one of the last great Jewish delis in this part of New York (along with Katz's; see the Lower East Side section earlier). Head here for your hot pastrami or matzo ball soup.

B&H Dairy (#95; ☎ 212-505-8065; 127 Second Ave; Ⓜ 6 to Astor Pl, N, R to 8th St-NYU), between St Marks Place and 7th St, is a classic lunch counter with some of the most authentic New York food and 'tude around. Everything is homemade, fresh and vegetarian, including the six types of soups on offer daily and lovely loaves of challah. Grab a stool before 11am daily for the $3.50 breakfast special. Carnivores prefer **Stage Restaurant** (Map 4, #96; 128 Second Ave), across the street with a similar atmosphere.

Yaffa (#107; ☎ 212-677-9001; 97 St Mark's Pl; Ⓜ 6 to Astor Pl, N, R to 8th St-NYU; pastas & salads $5.95-8.25, seafood dishes $10.25; open 24 hrs), between First Ave and Ave A, serves up reliable fare in two eclectic spaces, including a back patio (where you can smoke). The Yaffa salad ($5.95) and the chicken dijon ($8.25) win repeated praise.

Benny's Burritos (#110; ☎ 212-254-2054; 93 Ave A; Ⓜ 6 to Astor Pl • #10; 113 Greenwich Ave), near 6th St, might disappoint taquería-savvy Californians, but the super-filling burritos and enchiladas ($8 and under, with plenty of options for vegetarians) are good value. (You'll find a larger and more crowded Benny's in the West Village.)

Sidewalk Bar & Restaurant (#111; ☎ 212-473-7373; 94 Ave A; Ⓜ 6 to Astor Pl; burgers, salads & sandwiches under $8.50; open 8am-5am Sun-Thur, 24 hrs Fri & Sat), on the corner of 6th St, is a neighborhood favorite with art bedecked walls, a good beer selection, pool tables, solid food and live music nightly (never a cover). In addition to more casual fare like burritos ($6), they do a decent steak au poivre ($15).

Two Boots (#122; ☎ 212-505-2276; 37 Ave A; Ⓜ F, V to Second Ave • Map 4, #61; ☎ 212-633-9096; 201 W 11th St at Seventh Ave) is so-called for the cuisines of Italy and Louisiana that it mixes so well. Some New Yorkers consider the cornmeal crust pizza here ($6.25/10.25/13.75 small/medium/large) the best in the city, but while it's good, it's not *that* good. The po' boy sandwiches ($7.95 to $9.25) are extraordinary however, and this is a very kid-friendly place.

Stromboli's Pizza (#104; ☎ 212-673-3691; 83 St Marks Pl; Ⓜ 6 to Astor Pl, N, R to 8th St-NYU; slice $1.75), on the corner of First Ave, *was* the best slice (with perfectly thin crust, dynamic sauce and just the right amount of cheese and grease), until the research for this book uncovered Patsy's Pizzeria (see the Spanish Harlem section).

Mama's Food Shop (#121; ☎ 212-777-4425; 200 E 3rd St; F, V to Second Ave; open 11am-10:30pm Mon-Sat), between Aves A and B, serves cheap and big portions of simple food in a homey setting, typifying what can be great about this neighborhood. There are tons of daily veggie options that make a meal (like broccoli with roasted garlic or honey glazed sweet potatoes; $5 each) and meat delights too (fried, grilled or roasted chicken is $8). Across the street is **StepMama** (#120; ☎ 212-228-2663; 199 E 3rd St; open 11am-10pm Mon-Sat), serving yummy sandwiches ($3 to 7) and soups ($3/7 pint/quart).

Casa Adela (#117; ☎ 212-473-1882, 66 Ave C; Ⓜ F, V to Second Ave), between 4th and 5th Sts, is the standard bearer for the *Puertorriqueño* flavors that once dominated this area. All the old favorites are here: roasted chicken ($6.75), *bacalao* (salt cod) smothered in vegetables ($8) and *batidas* (fruit shakes) from mango to guanabana ($3). There's also a $1.10 toast and coffee breakfast special.

Lucky Cheng's (#123; ☎ 212-473-0516; 24 First Ave; Ⓜ F, V to Second Ave; appetizers $6-9, entrees $14-19), between 1st and 2nd Sts, is a gimmicky place where drag-queen

ANGUS OBORN

PLACES TO EAT

waitresses serve up so-so Asian fusion food. But hey, you don't go to strip clubs for the cocktails and you don't come here for the food. Reservations are required, even if they're not always respected.

Cyclo (#25; ☎ 212-673-3975; 203 First Ave; ❶ L to First Ave; entrees $9-15), between 12th and 13th Sts, is a renowned Vietnamese restaurant that serves some tasty *pho* and spring rolls, among other authentic Asian dishes.

Lanza's (#32; ☎ 212-674-7014, fax 674-6181; 168 First Ave; ❶ 6 to Astor Pl, L to First Ave; 5-course Italian dinner $18.95) is between 10th and 11th Sts. With its pressed-tin ceilings and faded paintings, Lanza's will take you back to an earlier time. Its five-course Italian dinner includes a selection of delicious desserts.

DeRobertis (#31; ☎ 212-674-7137; 176 First Ave; ❶ 6 to Astor Pl, L to First Ave), between 10th and 11th Sts, is a *pasticceria* (bakery) that's been in business since 1904. Here is a good spot for an espresso and pastry, served up by Italian matrons shuffling around in bedroom slippers.

Time Cafe (#137; ☎ 212-533-7000; 380 Lafayette St; ❶ 6 to Bleecker St; appetizers $5-8.50, entrees $11-18), on the corner of E 3rd St (Great Jones St), is a pleasant surprise: a trendy nightspot that actually serves tasty organic food (though the cavernous dining room can get too full and wreak havoc on noise level and service). The varied menu includes everything from grilled brook trout to grilled portobellos. Entrees range from $11.50 for a smoked chicken pizza to $22 for Black Angus steak. You can eat outside under umbrellas or join the indoor hubbub. One of the real treats here is **Fez**, under Time Cafe (see Jazz in the Entertainment chapter for more).

Astor Restaurant & Lounge (#128; ☎ 212-253-8644; 316 Bowery at Bleecker St; ❶ 6 to Bleecker St; entrees under $20) is a sleek bistro with plentiful wood trim and enormous mirrors. It has a great airy dining room fashioned from an old warehouse. Downstairs, the colorful lounge features a Moroccan theme, with candles and festive tiles. This place may be too popular for its own good.

CHELSEA, FLATIRON DISTRICT & GRAMERCY PARK (MAP 5)

Chelsea is New York's newest gourmet ghetto, with a stunning variety of dining options for all budgets. The Flatiron District, Gramercy Park and Union Square have also heated up as of late; foodies with their taste buds set on one of the hotter places should definitely make reservations, especially on weekends.

Budget

Big Cup Tea & Coffee House (#151; ☎ 212-206-0059; 228 Eighth Ave; ❶ C, E to 23rd St), between 21st and 22nd St in the heart of Chelsea, is a perky, beautiful-boy meeting place. It does a mean biscotti ($1.50).

Chelsea Market (#203; ☎ 212-243-6005; 75 Ninth Ave; ❶ A, C, E to 14th St, L to Eighth Ave; 7:30am-10pm Mon-Fri, 8am-8pm Sat & Sun), between 15th and 16th Sts, is an indoor emporium housing dozens of shops, including the veritable land of fruit and veggie plenty that is **Manhattan Fruit Exchange** (☎ 212-243-6005); **Fat Witch Bakery** (☎ 212-807-1335) with blue ribbon brownies; and **Amy's Breads** (☎ 212-462-4338), baking heavenly breads and sticky buns (check out the $1.50 to $2.50 breakfast specials). There are tables and chairs here for taking a load off and noshing, occasional live music and dance performances.

Uncle Moe's Burrito & Taco Shop (#191; ☎ 212-727-9400; 14 W 19th St; ❶ F, V to 23rd St; tacos $2.75-3.75, burritos $5-7; open 11:30am-9:30pm Mon-Fri, noon-7pm Sat), between Fifth and Sixth Aves, can hang with the best Mission taquerías; indeed, the psychedelic Fillmore posters make it feel remarkably like good old San Francisco.

Republic (#185; ☎ 212-627-7168; 37 Union Sq West; ❶ L, N, Q, R, W, 4, 5, 6 to Union Sq; appetizers $3-5, broth noodles $6-8, noodle or rice dishes $7-9), between 16th and 17th Sts, is a terrific noodle house and one hell of a bargain. Start with a salmon sashimi salad or coconut-crusted shrimp for a few bucks and move on to a tofu udon soup or spinach noodles with soy lime sauce. The restaurant's big, airy space gives diners slurping room; you can smoke up front.

MICHELLE BENNETT

Empire Diner (#148; ☎ 212-243-2736; 210 Tenth Ave; C, E to 23rd St; sandwiches $6.95-10.95, entrees $11.95-13.50; open 24 hrs), between 22nd and 23rd Sts, packs them in with its always open policy and fabulous people watching (though why anyone would want to choke on exhaust fumes while dining en plein air at this corner is a puzzlement; yet, the pavement tables are always taken).

Mid-Range & Top End

Union Square Cafe (#188; ☎ 212-243-4020, fax 627-2673; 21 E 16th St; L, N, Q, R, W, 4, 5, 6 to 14th St-Union Sq; appetizers $9.75-15, entrees $12.50-19.50), between Fifth Ave and Union Square West, is a neighborhood hottie and considered one of New York's best. This famous eatery features fine American cuisine, top-flight service and a reasonably priced menu. The yellow-fin burger comes recommended and the desserts and accompanying wines are exquisite.

L'Acajou (#162; ☎ 212-645-1706; 53 W 19th St; F, V to 23rd St), near Sixth Ave, is the grand pappy of the Chelsea restaurant scene and that's a good thing: the Alsatian fare here is hearty (duck and foie gras figure prominently) and the atmosphere convivial, especially at the old mahogany bar up front. The bar menu includes a nice steak au poivre ($18) and a decadent pâté maison ($7.50). The full menu is a few dollars more.

Coffee Shop (#186; ☎ 212-243-7969; 29 Union Sq West; L, N, Q, R, W, 4, 5, 6 to Union Sq; open 7am-6am daily) is a Brazilian meets American place, meaning it doesn't really do either cuisine justice. Still, the late night hours, reasonable prices, pavement tables, live music and downstairs lounge keep it on the hit parade.

Tabla (#130; ☎ 212-889-0667; 11 Madison Ave at 25th St; N, 6 to 23rd St; prix-fixe fancy/ultrafancy/custom dinner $65/75/88) is a fusion Indian restaurant bursting with refreshing combinations like shrimp stuffed skate with green mango ($25). If you can't get a reservation in this divinely appointed place, head to their much more casual **Bread Bar** on the ground floor, where soups, breads and a selection of street food costs between $4 to $9. The summer pavement tables here are a nice bonus.

Gramercy Tavern (#166; ☎ 212-477-0777; 42 E 20th St; L, N, Q, R, W, 4, 5, 6 to 14th St-Union Sq; appetizers $13-15, entrees $21-25, prix fixe dinner $80), between Park Ave South and Broadway, is another super star on the restaurant scene. Though it can be tough to get a table here (reserve early), you can always dine at the more casual and affordable bar up front.

Union Pacific (#167; ☎ 212-995-8500; 111 E 22nd St; 6 to 23rd St; prix-fixe lunch/pre-theater/dinner $20/45/65), between Park Ave South and Lexington Ave, provides a sublime dining experience, though with offerings like pickled veal tongue with braised escarole, it might be a bit too creative for some (we hear the curried blowfish with nightshade and pumpkin confit is to die for!). The wall of falling water and deep hues in the dining room provide unforgettable ambiance.

PLACES TO EAT

The Classics

In a town with balls-to-the-wall cultural monuments like the Metropolitan Museum of Art and Carnegie Hall, it's surprising that a handful of restaurants have managed to become major landmarks in their own right. People now make pilgrimages to famous spots like Tavern on the Green more for the experience of eating there than for the food itself (though in this day and age, restaurants are realizing that if they live by the tourist dollar, they die by it and are again paying attention to culinary details). Still, a memorable meal at one of these famous places makes a good story for the folks back home, even if the food doesn't taste quite as exotic as the great kimchi and mung-bean pancakes you had in Little Korea. Be prepared for big bills at these celebrated standbys (consider dining here at lunch or during Restaurant Week to save some money; also, the prix-fixe options are usually a righteous deal).

Four Seasons
This premier spot *(Map 5, #49; ☎ 212-754-9494; 99 E 52nd St; ⑩ 6 to 51st St)*, between Park and Lexington Aves in Midtown, features luxurious Continental cuisine in a gold-colored dining room. The menu offers lots of fresh seafood, a selection of entrees for two to share and seasonal specialties such as a springtime dish of shad and roe with shallots, spring peas and bacon. The prix-fixe pre-theater and lunch options for $55 will give you a very good idea of what this kitchen turns out.

Le Cirque 2000
Filled with fine crystal and china settings lightened up by a beautiful vaulted mosaic ceiling and stained-glass windows partially obscured by reams of colorful bunting, this elegant spot in the historic Villard Houses at the Palace Hotel *(Map 5, #65; ☎ 212-303-7788; 455 Madison Ave; ⑩ 6 to 51st St)*, between 50th and 51st Sts, features a nightly 'classic' as well as a menu full of innovative, serious cuisine like tripe à l'Armagnac. The five-course tasting menu ($90) will leave you fat and happy.

21
The classic spot for ladies (and their lovers) who lunch, this club-like place *(Map 5, #44; ☎ 212-582-7200; 21 W 52nd St; ⑩ E, V to Fifth Ave-53rd St)*, between Fifth and Sixth Aves in Midtown, serves traditional fare and flaming desserts to business people and tourists sprawled in leather banquettes. Try the amazingly affordable prix fixe pre-theater menu for $33; proper attire required.

Tavern on the Green
The most profitable restaurant in the USA, Tavern on the Green *(Map 7, #93; ☎ 212-873-3200; Central Park West at W 67th St; ⑩ B, C to 72nd St)*, on the Upper West Side, pulls in an astounding $34 million annually bilked from 500,000 visitors. Despite a new chef in 1999 and some positive reviews, it's still largely a tourist trap – and an expensive one, at that. Skip the food and head straight for the back garden and take a cocktail amid the whimsical topiaries. If you must dine, try the prix-fixe lunch ($20 to $28) or the pre-theater ($27 to $33) menus.

Erin Corrigan

N.Y.C.

MIDTOWN (MAP 5)

Midtown can be a culinary disappointment, with too many soup and salad places catering to office workers, if you don't know what to look for. The new **dining concourse** downstairs in Grand Central Terminal is a welcome addition to the Midtown dining scene (where you can get everything from curried tofu to blueberry cheesecake), as is the upstairs **Grand Central Market** with its fine meats, cheeses, chocolates and seafood.

Pan Bagnat (Map 6, #13; ☎ 212-765-7575; 54 W 55th St; ❶ B, Q to 57th St, E, V to Fifth Ave-53rd St; open 7am-6:30pm Mon-Fri, 8am-4pm Sat), between Fifth and Sixth Aves, has coffee, wonderful pastries ($1.60 to $3.50) and gorgeous cakes and tarts ($24 to $47). They also do fresh baguette sandwiches.

La Bonne Soupe (#38; ☎ 212-586-7650; 48 W 55th St; ❶ F to 57th St, E, F to Fifth Ave; soups $13.95) is a sweet, little bistro with checked tablecloths where you'll rub elbows with other diners on a busy Friday night. The soups are a meal in themselves, coming with bread, salad and dessert. There's also a selection of salads ($11.50) and fondue (chocolate/cheese/bourguignonne $8.75/15.95/19.25).

Soup Kitchen International (Map 6, #8; ☎ 212-757-7730; 259A W 55th St; ❶ B, D, E to Seventh Ave; closed summer) is between Eighth and Ninth Aves. Writing about soup in a 100°F swelter is tough, except when it comes to this place, which serves up tasty chicken chili and other yummy soups. The abrasive owner, Al Yeganeh, was nicknamed the 'Soup Nazi' by the *Seinfeld* crew and they're not far off: Don't dawdle or daydream here, instead figure out what you want before reaching the head of the line. Beware of the idiosyncratic hours.

Carnegie Deli (Map 6, #10; ☎ 212-757-2245, 800-334-5606; 854 Seventh Ave; ❶ B, D, E to Seventh Ave), on the corner of W 55th St, packs them in, although why tourists adore this place remains a mystery – maybe it's the star endorsements plastering the walls or the stream of film crews shooting here. The food comes in enormous portions, but the prices match; expect to pay $11 for a pastrami sandwich bigger than your head.

Café St Bart's (#60; ☎ 212-888-2664; 109 E 50th St; ❶ 6 to 51st St; appetizers $6-9, lunch entrees $12-17), on the corner of Park Ave, is housed in the Romanesque St Bartholomew's and is a pleasant spot for a break from the Midtown madness. You can grab a sandwich or a fancy wild salmon with cranberry chutney (especially nice on a Friday afternoon when live jazz wafts about) or just bring a bag lunch and snag a courtyard table.

Vong (#21; ☎ 212-486-9592; 200 E 54th St; ❶ E, V to Lexington Ave-53rd St; prix-fixe lunch menu $28; open lunch noon-2:30pm Mon-Fri, dinner 6pm-11pm Mon-Thur, 5:30pm-11pm Fri, 5:30pm-11:30pm Sat, 5:30pm-10pm Sun), on the southeast corner of Third Ave, combines French and Thai cuisine in such unusual dishes as duck breast in a silky tamarind-sesame sauce and honey-ginger seared squab. The elegant setting here brings to mind the Bangkok hotel, where chef Jean-Georges Vongerichten learned some of his craft (for the latest coming from Vongerichten's creative kitchen, see Upper West Side, later). Slackers take note: no jeans and/or sneakers allowed.

Asia de Cuba (#94; ☎ 212-726-7755; 237 Madison Ave; ❶ 6 to 33rd St), in Morgan's between 37th and 38th Sts, is another Midtown hottie. Folks dig this place for its communal seating (request an upstairs table if you want your own space), warm atmosphere, generous portions and combination of flavors that defies categorization. Here, avocados meet Thai spices and papaya collides with peanut sauce atop sliced beef, charred tuna or crispy noodles.

Michael's (#37; ☎ 212-767-0555, fax 581-6778; 24 W 55th St; ❶ F to 57th St; appetizers $12-18, entrees $25-35, chef's tasting menu $90), between Fifth and Sixth Aves, is a classy, upscale place with modern art on the walls and a light and airy dining room with garden views. The cuisine here is fresh, California style: the wild poached salmon ($29) or steak in a Shiraz veal sauce ($35) standout. There's also a fixed-price pre-theater menu.

Michael Jordan's Steakhouse (#85; ☎ 212-655-2300; 23 Vanderbilt Ave at 43rd St; ❶ S, 4, 5, 6, 7 to Grand Central-42nd St;

steaks around $30) sits smack in the middle of Grand Central Terminal, on the west balcony overlooking the concourse and is a nice surprise: the steaks are sumptuous, the setting grand and you can purchase and smoke cigars while having a cocktail at the bar. Yet another reason to 'like Mike.'

Oyster Bar *(#85; ☎ 212-490-6650; open 11:30am-9:30pm Mon-Fri, noon-9:30pm Sat; Ⓜ S, 4, 5, 6, 7 to Grand Central-42nd St)* is in the Grand Central Terminal. What a place: the vaulted ceilings of Gustavino tile, the tireless oyster shuckers, the smoky saloon (cigars sold here) and the mouthwatering, handwritten menu are what this place has been all about since 1913. At least two dozen types of oyster are available daily, from fat Long Island bluepoints ($1.45 each) to teeny, tasty California kumamotos ($2.25 each). Also check out the 75 wines by the glass, panroasts (from $9.95) that are so savory they're criminal, and the total New Yawk atmosphere.

Aquavit *(#36; ☎ 212-307-7311; 13 W 54th St; Ⓜ B, D, F, V to Rockefeller Center, E, V to Fifth Ave-53rd St; tasting menu $58)*, between Fifth and Sixth Aves, serves as a fine example of how to combine sublime cuisine with memorable atmosphere: a stunning six-story glass atrium, complete with a silent waterfall, encloses the main dining room, where you can dine on roast duck with foie gras and mango sauce or mustard-crusted rack of lamb. Appetizers appearing on the tasting menu include an artful three smoked salmon sampler.

Hell's Kitchen (Map 5)

Munson Diner *(#2; ☎ 212-246-0964; 600 W 49th St at Eleventh Ave; Ⓜ C, E to 50th St)*, where the waitresses call you 'Hon,' must be one of the most authentic greasy spoons in the city. Cab drivers favor this place after hours.

Landmark Tavern *(#3; ☎ 212-757-8595; 626 Eleventh Ave; Ⓜ A, C, E to 42nd St; entrees from $18)*, on the corner of 46th St, is more a restaurant than a bar and serves the best fish and chips in the city and the world's best Irish soda bread, warm and

---

Take a Taste of the Melting Pot

The stretch of Ninth Ave from W 38th to 40th Sts may be unique in the city, as it offers at least 12 different types of food within three blocks. The many recent immigrants who work as cab drivers or pushcart vendors like to frequent the area after their shifts, which has led to a profusion of international and graveyard-shift eateries. Along the avenue, or just off it, you'll have your pick of Italian, Indian, Chinese, West African, Haitian, Filipino, Pakistani, Mexican, Cuban or Cajun cuisine.

The area's mainstays include the **Cupcake Cafe** *(Map 6, #122; ☎ 212-465-1530, 522 Ninth Ave)*, on the southeast corner of W 39th St, which makes specialty wedding cakes and cupcakes slathered in a butter cream frosting to die for. It's not 'international,' but it's justly famous locally for its pastries. Across the street in the Supreme Macaroni Company building, the pasta restaurant **Guido's** *(Map 6, #124; ☎ 212-564-8074; 511 Ninth Ave)* offers a taste of Italy, as does **Manganaro's** *(Map 5, #102; ☎ 212-563-5331; 488 Ninth Ave)*, near W 38th St, a wood-floored Italian grocery that serves cheap pasta dishes and heroes for about $5 in a bright, bustling dining room.

For authentic Mexican (including real, hot salsa, BBQ goat and fruit shakes called *batidos*) try **El Ranchero Mexicano** *(Map 5, #103; ☎ 212-868-7780; 507 Ninth Ave)*, at the corner of W 38th St. Up the street a bit is **Jam's Jamaican** *(Map 6, #123; ☎ 212-967-0730, 518 Ninth Ave)*, between W 38th and 39th Sts, where you can get anything and everything (well, almost) jerked. A little farther afield, **Bali Nusa Indah** *(Map 6, #68; ☎ 212-974-1875, 651 Ninth Ave; Ⓜ N, Q, R, S, W, 1, 2, 3, 7 to Times Sq-42nd St)*, between W 45th and 46th Sts, specializes in Javanese-Malaysian food such as the classic *rendang* (a type of curry), *ayam opor* (coconut chicken curry), *sambals* (chile relish) and *otak otak* (spiced coconut fish cake steamed in a banana leaf). The $5.95 lunch special is a winner.

PLACES TO EAT

fresh from the oven. This 1868 structure once housed the tavern owner's family (see the 2nd-floor living room); this means that you can enjoy your steak and grilled fish in a historic setting, complete with fireplace and period furniture. But don't expect a cramped, dull replica of bygone days. This spacious eatery buzzes with the energy of modern-day Manhattan.

Bricco *(Map 6, #7; ☎ 212-245-7160; 304 West 56th St; ⓜ A, B, C, D, 1, 2 to 59th St-Columbus Circle; appetizers $6.95-8, pasta $11-14.50, meats $13.95-22.95)*, on the corner of Eighth Ave, stands out in this neighborhood for its reasonable prices, high-quality service and great Italian-inspired fare. Fresh ravioli stuffed with crabmeat is a house specialty, but the pasta primavera and other vegetable choices make Bricco a good choice for herbivores, too.

TIMES SQUARE & THEATER DISTRICT (MAP 6)

Hamburger joints and mid-range ethnic restaurants fill up the side streets off Times Square. The quality of these places varies widely, so you might stick to the basics. Ninth Ave is especially rich for international food choices.

Mee Noodle Shop *(#23; ☎ 212-765-2929; 795 Ninth Ave; ⓜ 1, 2 to 50th St; most dishes $6-9 • Map 5, #53; 922 Second Ave at E 49th St • Map 4, #26; 219 First Ave at E 13th St)*, near W 53rd St, is a star in the city's cheap Chinese constellation. Mee Noodle Shop serves a hearty bowl of broth, noodles and meat dishes for just $6 and in a jiffy. (You can find the same offerings at Mee's other locations.)

Island Burgers and Shakes *(#25; ☎ 212-307-7934; 766 Ninth Ave; ⓜ C, E to 50th St)*, between W 51st and 52nd Sts, specializes in *churascos*, juicy chicken breast sandwiches that come in over 50 different varieties for under $8.

Stage Deli *(#18; ☎ 212-245-7850; 834 Seventh Ave; ⓜ B, D, E to Seventh Ave; diner fare $5-12;*

open 6:30am-1:30am daily), between W 53rd and W 54th Sts, is popular with tourists, but also late-night noshing locals. Silly names, like the Calista Flockhart Salad Platter (note author refraining from eating-disorder jokes!) and the John Stamos (who?) Greek Salad, are either charming or not, depending on your disposition.

Basilica *(#65; ☎ 212-489-0051; 676 Ninth Ave; ⓜ A, C, E to 42nd St; appetizers $4.45-8.95, homemade pastas $6.95-10.95, pre-theater special $20.95; open 3:30pm-midnight daily)*, between W 46th and 47th Sts, offers a great, four-course Italian pre-theater menu, which includes a bottle of wine.

Zen Palate *(#66; ☎ 212-582-1669; 663 Ninth Ave; ⓜ A, C, E to 42nd St; dishes $6.50-8.50 • Map 5, #180; ☎ 212-614-9291; 34 Union Sq East at 16th St • Map 7, #60; ☎ 212-501-7768; 2170 Broadway)* serves an exclusively vegetarian menu of Asian-inspired dishes (read: oodles of noodles and tons of tofu) and is a good spot for some quick, cheap nourishment.

Restaurant Row Officially the block of W 46th St between Eighth and Ninth Aves, Restaurant Row generally refers to almost all the restaurants west of Times Square. To reach any of the following places, take the subway (ⓜ N, Q, R, S, W, 1, 2, 3, 7) to Times Square-42nd St. Most restaurants in this area keep 'theater hours,' opening for pre-matinee meals at around 11:45am

Wednesday, Saturday and Sunday and closing until around 5pm when they reopen for dinner.

Joshua Tree (#69; ☎ 212-489-1920; 366 W 46th St; sandwiches $7-9, pastas $9-12, steaks $15-18; open 11:30am-4am daily), between Eighth and Ninth Aves, is a casual bar and restaurant catering to a younger crowd. The beer selection is good, the lighting candle-lit and the kitchen stays open late.

Joe Allen (#70; ☎ 212-581-6464; 326 W 46th St; appetizers $6-10, salads $12-15, entrees $15-22), between Eighth and Ninth Aves, does simple food with flair, like a gigantic chicken salad ($15) or pan-roasted sole ($22). The brick walls of the dining room reverberate loudly when it's crowded, which is almost every night. It's impossible to get a table for dinner without a reservation unless you wait until the theater starts at 8pm.

Orso (#71; ☎ 212-489-7212; 322 W 46th St; entrees about $20-24), also run by Joe Allen, traffics in more expensive and esoteric Tuscan food like roasted quail stuffed with sausage and walnuts ($24) and calfs' liver with pine nuts ($20). It's popular with theatergoers and the kitchen stays open until 11:45pm.

Barbetta (#63; ☎ 212-246-9171; 321 W 46th St; pre-theater menu $45) is steeped in history, from its townhouse digs once belonging to the Astor's, to the fact that it has been family owned and operated since 1906. The baroque dining room, serene garden and impeccable service (not to mention their Piemonte specialties like Crespelle alla Savoiarda, a vegetable- and cheese-filled crepe with veal essence, and liberal use of high-quality ingredients like white truffles) will no doubt keep it around for another century.

Hourglass Tavern (#64; ☎ 212-265-2060; 373 W 46th St; daily specials $15.75), between Eighth and Ninth Aves, the same one featured in John Grisham's novel *The Firm*, is a quaint, close place squeezed onto two floors. While specials like filet mignon (was that really a filet cut?!) and swordfish steak with asparagus and potatoes are filling, James Beard isn't visiting anytime soon.

UPPER WEST SIDE (MAP 7)

This area of town has a surprisingly good selection of places to eat and gorge, from upscale markets and vegetarian spots to bohemian cafés and serious seafood joints.

Budget

Zabar's (#54; ☎ 212-787-2000; 2245 Broadway at W 80th St; ⓜ 1, 2 to 79th St), the city's most classic food emporium, offers very good prices on smoked salmon, cheeses and other gourmet items. Slicing salmon is something of an art form here – experienced slicers earn up to $80,000 a year!

Fairway Market (#63; ☎ 212-595-1888; 2127 Broadway; ⓜ 1, 2, 3 to 72nd St), between W 74th and 75th Sts, is a gigantic covered market selling cheeses, super-fresh produce and prepared salads at rock-bottom prices.

H&H Bagels (#55; ☎ 212-595-8000, fax 799-6765; 2239 Broadway at 80th St; ⓜ 1, 2 to 79th St • #35; ☎ 212-734-7441, fax 535-6791; 1551 Second Ave; open 24 hrs) are considered by many to be New York's finest bagels (yes they'll ship!).

Zanny's Cafef (#3; ☎ 212-316-6849; 975 Columbus Ave; ⓜ B, C to Cathedral Parkway-110th St; open 6am-8pm Mon-Fri, 7am-8pm Sat, 9am-9pm Sun), between 107th and 108th Sts, is a welcoming, neighborhood café in an area largely limited to coffee that comes in blue and white 'We Are Happy to Serve You' cups.

Empire Szechuan (#64; ☎ 212-496-8460; 251 W 72nd St; ⓜ 1, 2, 3 to 72nd St • #95; ☎ 212-496-8778; 193 Columbus Ave; ⓜ 1, 2, 3, 9 to 72nd St; dishes around $7.95) has a reliable Chinese selection, with two Upper West Side locations and others sprinkled around the city; **The Village outpost** (☎ 212-691-1535; 15 Greenwich Ave), between Sixth Ave & West 10th St, is especially good. These bustling places serve generally healthy fare.

Tibet Shambala (#51; ☎ 212-721-1270; 488 Amsterdam Ave; ⓜ 1, 2 to 86th St; soups & salads $3.50-7.95, entrees $7.95-10.95), between 83rd and 84th Sts, features a menu split evenly between meat and vegetarian dishes.

Ayurveda Café (#14; ☎ 212-932-2400; 706 Amsterdam Ave at 94th St; ⓜ 1, 2, 3 to 96th St; prix-fixe lunch/dinner $6.95/10.95;

open 11:30am-11:30pm daily) has an all-vegetarian menu that delivers the six flavors essential to an ayurvedic diet: sweet, sour, salty, bitter, pungent and astringent. Check out their daily tea powwow ($1) from 4pm to 5:30pm, which sometimes features readings or guest speakers.

Quintessence (#21; ☎ 212-501-9700, fax 501-0900; 566 Amsterdam Ave; ❶ 1, 2 to 86th St; open 11:30am-11pm daily • Map 4, #33; ☎ 646-654-1823, fax 654-1804; 263 E 10th St; appetizers $6.50-8, entrees $9-15) serves 100% organic vegetarian fare that will delight even hardcore carnivores with its well-balanced flavors and textures. Try the vegetable bonanza that is the 'Buddha bowl' custom-built for you ($8 to start, making additions like marinated portobello mushrooms or pine nuts for $1 to $2).

Cafe Lalo (#49; ☎ 212-496-6031; 201 W 83rd St; ❶ 1, 2 to 86th St), between Amsterdam and Broadway is a neighborhood hotspot. Here you can wile away a rainy afternoon reading dozens of newspapers and magazines – or just the 14-page menu of expensive pastries; the lines are out the door for the daily brunch.

Cafe con Leche (#13; ☎ 212-678-7000; 726 Amsterdam Ave; ❶ 1, 2, 3 to 96th St; entrees $7.95-10.50), between 95th and 96th Sts, serves up authentic Latin American fare – rice, beans and plantains accompanying all manner of beef, chicken and seafood dishes – in a casual, kid-friendly atmosphere. The feisty paella feeds two.

Mid-Range & Top End

Ruby Foo's (#58; ☎ 212-724-6700; 2182 Broadway; ❶ 1, 2 to 79th St • Map 6, #37; ☎ 212-489-5600; 1626 Broadway; entrees $10-20) is where dim sum and sushi collide in dramatic, larger-than-life fashion. Ruby Foo's is a campy, red-and-black Asian theme park that seats 400. The pan-Asian menu ranges from baby back ribs with black bean sauce to a tangy green papaya salad.

Cafe Luxembourg (#69; ☎ 212-873-7411, fax 721-6854; 200 W 70th St; ❶ 1, 2, 3 to 72nd St; 1st course $10-13, 2nd course $18-26), between Amsterdam and West End Aves, attracts pre-performance crowds from

Lincoln Center with its French-inspired food, including cassoulet, escargots and interesting salads. You'll need an advance reservation for the restaurant, but may be able to sneak into the less formal café (first course $8 to $11, second course $11 to $15).

Dock's Oyster Bar & Seafood Grill (#20; ☎ 212-724-5588, fax 769-3514; 2427 Broadway; ❶ 1, 2 to 86th St; • Map 5, #91; ☎ 212-986-8080, fax 490-8551; 633 Third Ave at 40th St) is a quintessential New York seafood place: loud, bustling and full of happy diners feasting on fresh tidbits from the sea. A fish or steak entree will cost you at least $25, but check out the Sunday and Monday New England clambake (two 1lb lobsters, salad, dessert and coffee, all for $28).

Carmine's (#19; ☎ 212-721-5493; 2450 Broadway; ❶ 1, 2 to 86th St; pastas lunch $10.50-12.50, dinner $17.50-20.50; open 11:30am-11pm Sun-Thur, 11:30am-midnight Fri & Sat), near 90th St, is a zoolike Italian restaurant loved by big crowds. It serves huge, community-style pasta that can serve several people or try one of the heroes ($7.50 to $9.50).

Café des Artistes (#94; ☎ 212-877-3500; W www.cafedesartistesnyc.com; 1 W 67th St; ❶ B, C to 72nd St; entrees $22-29, fixed-price dinner $37.50), between Central Park West and Columbus Ave, is a romantic eatery (thanks in no small part to the famous mural of naked, romping nymphs) that has witnessed innumerable marriage proposals over the years, plus a few appearances by former President Bill Clinton. Though some believe

MICHAEL TAYLOR

Visit Carmine's for authentic Italian food

The Restaurant Reservations Game

Theoretically, New York is a town where everyone's born equal, provided they can make the rent. But equality ends at the door of a hot restaurant. These snobby eateries might not have bouncers, but they hardly shy at turning 'nobodies' away, especially at peak times.

To get yourself a table at seriously popular restaurants like the Union Square Cafe, Tabla and Picoline, you must make reservations a month in advance for Friday or Saturday night. But at least these places pride themselves on providing the same standard of service to all customers. Others, hungry for celebrity clientele and the publicity that goes with them, will likely treat you with disdain (tourists are especially easy prey for haughty hosts). These offenders include the overpriced sushi den Nobu, the too hot to handle Rao's in Spanish Harlem and the neo-Parisian SoHo café Balthazar. Indeed, both Nobu and Balthazar are notorious for never answering their listed telephone lines, and the latter eatery has been accused of having a 'secret' phone line available only to a select group of 3,000 of the beautiful people.

The only advice we can give for the super-hot restaurants is to call at least a month in advance for a table, try for a weeknight and offer to take a table at 10pm or later (you could also try for a 5:30pm reservation but who can eat dinner at that hour?!).

N.Y.C.

this place rests on its laurels, meaty entrees (like osso bucco served with fettuccine) are high quality, there are several vegetarian options (including a 5-course tasting menu) and the quail eggs are free at the bar! Men must wear jackets after 6pm and at no time will people wearing jeans, sneakers or shorts be admitted.

Picholine (#99; ☎ 212-724-8585; 35 W 64th St; ❶ 1, 2 to 66th St-Lincoln Center; 2-/3-course fixed-price dinner $57/63), near Central Park West, offers first-rate Mediterranean-influenced cuisine that sets celebrities to slavering (symbolized by the lines out the door). It's one of the few restaurants in the city to maintain an after-dinner cheese course, with cheeses kept in a special cellar on the premises. House specialties include the Moroccan lamb with vegetable couscous and lobster bisque.

Jean-Georges (#104; ☎ 212-299-3900; 1 Central Park West; ❶ A, B, C, D, 1, 2 to 59th St-Columbus Circle), between 60th and 61st Sts, in the Trump International Hotel, is the newest taste sensation from the mind and heart of chef Jean-Georges Vongerichten. You can easily spend a few hundred dollars here for dinner and drinks for two, so come hungry for the game birds, fresh seafood and tender meats turned out with style by this celebrity chef.

UPPER EAST SIDE (MAP 7)

Although this neighborhood tends to be tony, you'll find dozens of moderately priced restaurants along Second and Third Aves between 60th and 86th Sts; many of these offer lunch specials for under $10.

Lexington Candy Shop (#38; ☎ 212-288-0057; 1226 Lexington Ave at E 83rd St; ❶ 4, 5, 6 to 86th St) is a picture-perfect lunch spot complete with an old-fashioned soda fountain. Here, school kids suck up malteds while neighborhood folks nurse a coffee or a famed fresh lemonade. Best of all, this place sells burgers and other classic diner fare at reasonable prices in one of the city's most expensive neighborhoods.

Cafe Greco (#82; ☎ 212-737-4300; 1390 Second Ave; ❶ 6 to 68th St-Hunter College; entrees $12.95-23.95; open noon-4pm & 5pm-11pm daily), between E 71st and 72nd Sts, serves decent Greek fare (try the fresh fish entrees, like swordfish and flounder, both about $15) and also offers a reasonable three-course fixed-price menu and weekend brunch choices.

Favia Lite (#127; ☎ 212-223-9115; 1140 Second Ave at E 60th St; ❶ 4, 5, 6 to 59th St, N, R to Lexington Ave) is a health-oriented, Italian restaurant that serves surprisingly tasty pasta entrees, considering the low calorie and fat content for every menu item.

ANGUS OBORN

The only way to start the day!

The large grilled chicken pizza costs $15, with skim-milk or soy mozzarella available at no extra charge.

Many small, wood-paneled restaurants with a French flavor line Madison Ave north of 60th St and several nearby side streets. Places to find a bit of Paris (including pricey entrees in the $20 to $30 range and a well-dressed clientele) are the see-and-be-seen **La Goulue** (#117; ☎ 212-988-8169; 746 Madison Ave; Ⓜ F to Lexington Ave-63rd St), between 64th and 65th Sts, and **Madame Romaine de Lyon** (#123; ☎ 212-758-2422; 132 E 61st St; Ⓜ N, R, W to Lexington Ave-59th St), between Lexington and Park Aves. At either place, you can enjoy a moderately priced meal by sticking to the appetizers or by ordering lighter fare like crepes or omelettes (Madame Romaine features hundreds of varieties).

Park View Restaurant at the Boathouse (#75; ☎ 212-517-2233; E 72nd St at Park Dr North; Ⓜ 6 to 77th St; dinner entrees under $30), within Central Park, occupies a romantic, picturesque spot overlooking the lake and crooning gondoliers, but if the way to anyone's heart is through their stomach, Cupid has left the building. Maybe take a cake and espresso after a picnic, but skip the main event here.

HARLEM (MAP 8)

Justifiably famous for its soul food (battered, fried and blackened everything with loads of hearty greens accompanying), travelers will need to bring an appetite to Harlem tables, as a few dollars buys a feast. There's also a good selection of West African, Caribbean and even bistro fare uptown.

Manna's Restaurant Too (#23; ☎ 212-234-4488; 486 Malcom X Blvd; Ⓜ 2, 3 to 135th St), between 133rd and 134th Sts, is a terrific example of the food bargains to be had up here: Sidle up to their sprawling buffets (one hot, the other cold) and load up on ribs, collard greens and corn bread for $3.99 per pound. This is a good place for soul food newbies, as you can see all the dishes on offer (even if you can't name them!).

Pan Pan (#22; ☎ 212-926-4900; 500 Malcolm X Blvd; Ⓜ 2, 3 to 135th St), corner of 135th St, has spicy Jamaican meat patties or a coffee-and-bagel breakfast for $1. This place does a brisk business in southern fried chicken ($3.50/6.75 for half/whole chicken), especially on Sunday when after-church crowds fill the stools.

M&G Diner (#36; ☎ 212-864-7326; 383 W 125th St; Ⓜ A, B, C, D to 125th St; breakfast $3.50-8.50, lunch & dinner $9.75-12.25; open 8:45am-11:30am Fri & Sat, 24 hrs Sun-Thur), near Morningside Ave, just a short stroll from the Apollo Theater, has a terrific old-school atmosphere with locals bent over their missals and huge plates of eggs with salmon croquettes ($8.50) or fried pork chops ($10).

Slice of Harlem II (#29; ☎ 212-426-7400; 308 Malcolm X Blvd; Ⓜ 2, 3 to 125th St; pizza slice $1.75; open 6:30am-10pm Mon-Thur, 6:30am-midnight Fri & Sat, noon-10pm Sun), between 125th and 126th Sts, serves up terrific brick oven pizza with every topping imaginable. Their stromboli, stuffed with meat and cheese or veggies ($4) is another good bet. Sharing this space is the popular **Bayou** (☎ 212-426-3800), serving classic Creole cuisine like blackened catfish and po' boys ($5.95 to $8.95).

Amy Ruth's Restaurant (#51; ☎ 212-280-8779, fax 280-3109; 114 W 116th St; Ⓜ 2, 3 to 116th St; waffles $4.95-8.95, meat entrees

$9.50-16.95), between Malcolm X Blvd and Adam Clayton Powell Jr Blvd, is another good soul food place specializing in waffles: chocolate, strawberry, blueberry, smothered in sauteed apples – you name it, they've got it. Only 100% pure maple syrup would do these babies justice and Amy Ruth's is proud to provide it.

Sylvia's *(#28; ☎ 212-996-0660; 328 Malcolm X Blvd; ◍ 2, 3 to 125th St; entrees $8-16.50, Sunday gospel brunch $16)*, between W 126th and 127th Sts, has all but cornered the soul-food market literally and figuratively (the famous restaurant now occupies three adjacent storefronts and seats 450). Finger-licking good specials like oxtails or meatloaf come with side options including collard greens and black-eyed peas ($8.75 to $9.25). Entrees are generous. On Sunday, you can feast on an array of food at the rousing Sunday gospel brunch, but go with a reservation.

Hamilton Heights & Sugar Hill

Mom's Eatery *(#14; 513 W 145th St)*, between Broadway and Amsterdam, is a no-nonsense Caribbean place serving cheap, filling meals loaded with carbs. Fatten up here on some jerk chicken, fried plantains and rice and beans.

Charles' Southern Style Kitchen *(#10; ☎ 212-926-4313; 2839 Frederick Douglass Blvd; ◍ A, B, C, D to 145th St; lunch/dinner buffet $6.99/9.99)* is located between W 151st and 152nd Sts in the Sugar Hill area. It has the best fried chicken in Harlem – the batter is pure perfection. You also can't go wrong with the salmon cakes and the macaroni and cheese. Bring a voracious appetite to the all-you-can-eat buffet, which is an astounding bargain.

Copeland's *(#16; ☎ 212-234-2357; 547 W 145th St; ◍ 1 to 145th St; appetizers $4.50-6.50, entrees $8.95-17.50, all-you-can-eat jazz buffet $14.95)* is between Broadway and Amsterdam Ave. Like Sylvia's, Copeland's also has a popular Sunday gospel brunch (make reservations a month ahead), with offerings like chitterlings vinaigrette. There's also an all-you-can-eat jazz buffet (4:30pm to 10:30pm Tuesday to Thursday).

Spanish Harlem

Though Spanish Harlem loses a lot of its charm the farther east you head, there are some good restaurants in these parts.

Rao's Restaurant *(#61; ☎ 212-722-6709; 455 E 114th St; ◍ 6 to 116th St; open Mon-Fri)* is near First Ave in the old Italian enclave of East Harlem. The tiny Rao's (pronounced **ray**-o's) contains only 12 tables, which makes it next to impossible to score a reservation here unless you're Martin Scorsese or another of Rao's favorite patrons. Rao's only offers one seating weekdays and there's no menu, but don't worry, you won't be disappointed. A full-course authentic Italian meal will cost you over $50.

Patsy's Pizzeria *(#60; ☎ 212-534-9783; 2291 First Ave; ◍ 6 to 116th St; slice/pizza $1.50/$10; open 11am-midnight daily)*, between E 117th and 118th Sts, pioneered the use of coal-fired ovens in the 1930s and aw hell, might as well just say it: This is New York's best slice (sorry Stromboli's). Paper thin and bowing from the grease, the cheese is perfectly distributed over a layer of rich sauce and though they're larger than your average slice, you might just gobble down two. A nephew of the original owner, Patsy Grimaldi, now runs Patsy Grimaldi's Pizzeria in Brooklyn (see later in this chapter). There are four outlets around Manhattan as well, but none do slices like the uptown original.

Emily's *(#58; ☎ 212-996-1212, fax 996-5844; 1325 Fifth Ave at 111th St; ◍ 6 to 110th St; appetizers $6.25-9, entrees $9.95-16.50; open 11am-midnight Mon-Wed & Sun, 11am-3am Fri & Sat)* is a big place serving up lots of southern hospitality. Grilled catfish, chicken wings and strong doses of Jack Daniels dominate the menu. Wednesday at Emily's means raucous karaoke.

Morrone's Bakery *(#59; ☎ 212-722-2972; 324 E 116th St; ◍ 6 to 116th St)*, between First and Second Aves, sells gorgeous loaves of peasant bread.

Morningside Heights

Columbia and its charges have colonized much of this part of Manhattan and you'll stumble across many cafés, diners and bars in your wanderings, most are cheap and open late – a double bonus. For more on restaurants up here, see the Columbia University heading in the Things To See & Do chapter.

Ollie's Noodle Shop & Grille (*#10;* ☎ *212-932-3300, fax 749-0811; 2957 Broadway;* Ⓜ *1 to 116th St; noodles $5.50-7.95, entrees $7.50-9.50; open 11am-1:45am Mon-Fri, 11:30am-1:45am Sat, 11:30am-midnight Sun*), on the corner of 116th St, is a solid place with hundreds of plates to choose from, including all manner of traditional Chinese fare like chicken with cashews, special noodle dishes, and even burgers and pasta.

Tomo Sushi & Sake Bar (*#48;* ☎ *212-665-2916, fax 665-2917; 2850 Broadway;* Ⓜ *1 to Cathedral Parkway-110th St; open noon-11:30pm Mon-Sat, noon-11pm Sun*), between Cathedral Parkway and 111th St, is the place to go for sushi and hand rolls ($3 to $8.75), sashimi ($2 to $4.50) and noodle soups ($6.95 to $8.75), not to mention sake shots.

Terrace in the Sky (*#39;* ☎ *212-666-9490; 400 W 119th;* Ⓜ *1 to 116th St-Columbia University; open dinner only*), off Amsterdam Ave, is a French-fusion restaurant distinguished by 16th-floor views that will make you weep or at least go weak in the knees. While it ain't cheap (figure on $50 per person before wine), memories like these are priceless.

Tom's Restaurant (*#45;* ☎ *212-864-6137; 2880 Broadway at W 112th St*), also called Tom's Diner, an ordinary place, shot to psuedo-stardom once the exterior started appearing regularly as the hangout for TV's *Seinfeld* crew. Disputes rage as to whether this is the place Suzanne Vega sings about, but the majority agree Ms Vega was sipping coffee in a Tom's in Brooklyn, not up here.

If you'd like to eavesdrop on the crisis-driven student chatter while waiting for your espresso, try one of the many cafés, including the landmark **Hungarian Pastry Shop** (*#49;* ☎ *212-866-4230; 1030 Amsterdam Ave*), near W 111th St. The **West End** (*#43;* ☎ *212-662-8830; 2911 Broadway*), between W 113th and 114th Sts, is no longer a breeding ground for intellectuals as it was in Beat poet Allen Ginsberg's day, but you can still find inexpensive food and decent jazz there on weekend nights; the kitchen is open until 2am.

THE BRONX (MAP 13)

The Bronx's most famous culinary neighborhood is Belmont, an Italian enclave centered around Arthur Ave, just south of Fordham University. It helps not to be rushed here as almost all the restaurants sport lines out the door. To get to any of these places on or around Arthur Ave, take the 4 train to Fordham Road.

Some of the restaurants in this eight-block neighborhood have been in business since WWI, including **Mario's** (*#13;* ☎ *718-584-1188; 2342 Arthur Ave; appetizers $6.25-8.75, pastas $10-12*), serving robust Neapolitan food, and **Ann & Tony's** (*#11;* ☎ *718-933-1469; 2407 Arthur Ave*), a family-style Neapolitan restaurant with pasta specials for $12 or less.

Dominick's (*#12;* ☎ *718-733-2807; 2335 Arthur Ave; closed Tue*) packs in the hordes at cramped, communal tables with the requisite red-and-white checkered tablecloths. Spaghetti with meatballs, lasagne, *fra diavlo,* all the classics are here, but don't be surprised if you have to wait an hour to sample them: the wait here is notorious and they shunt waiting diners into a bar so as to make a little more money off you. Dinner will cost around $20 per person, less the bar tab.

Roberto's Restaurant (*#14;* ☎ *718-733-2868; 632 E 186th St; appetizers $8-14, pasta $13-18*) also features long wait times, but is worth it for the friendly service, warm atmosphere and delicious Italian dishes like artichoke stuffed ravioli or scallops, shrimp and clams served over linguine. Best of all, there are pavement tables and they don't hustle you to eat and run once you're seated. Don't be surprised if the chef pops out from the kitchen for a chat.

Rhodes Restaurant (*#8;* ☎ *718-885-1538; 288 City Island Ave; open to 3am daily*), in City Island, is a local hangout serving standard pub specials and burgers for under $10.

Tony's Pier (*#9;* ☎ *718-885-1424; 1 City Island Ave; dinner $9-12; open noon-11:30pm Mon-Thur, noon-1am Fri & Sat, noon-midnight Sun*), at the farthest end of City Island Avenue, is a trip. Navigate the bilingual English-Spanish signs festooning the place, pass the bar (pick up your piña colada in a plastic cup with paper umbrella here) and wiggle into line at the fried-food counter (calamari, porgies, clams, snapper and more) or raw bar. It's (barely) controlled chaos, but the vistas from the end of the pier are killer and the party goes late on hot summer nights.

Jimmy's Bronx Café (☎ 718-329-2000; 281 W Fordham Rd; cover $20), at the Major Deegan Expressway, is *the* place to heat it up with the hotties to New York's steamiest Latin rhythms. This is an all in one club, with a sports bar, restaurant and catering hall on the premises, but you'll want to go to The Patio (after 1am is when to hit it) where the likes of J Lo, Derek Jeter and LL Cool J have all had a spin. A strict dress code is enforced: No sneakers, hats or construction boots.

For detailed information on getting to these neighborhoods on public transportation, see the Bronx in the Things to See & Do chapter.

BROOKLYN
Brooklyn Heights (Map 9)
Brooklyn is up and coming in so many ways and culinary endeavors are no exception.

Cousin's Café (#40; ☎ 718-596-3514; 160 Court St; ⓜ F, G to Bergen St; bar menu $6.95-9.95, dinner menu $10.95-14.95), between Pacific and Amity Sts, is your standard pub (10 beers on tap) with the usual grub. On weekend nights, Cousin's hosts live jazz combos.

Sam's Restaurant (#42; ☎ 718-596-3458; 238 Court St; ⓜ F, G to Bergen St; pasta $7.50-10.50, pizzas $10-12; open noon-10:30pm daily), between Baltic and Kane Sts, is a no-nonsense place which probably hasn't changed in 50 years (witness the recommendation that 'if your wife can't cook, don't divorce her – eat at Sam's'). Try a classic Italian hero ($5 to $6.25).

Osaka (#44; ☎ 718-643-0044; 272 Court St; ⓜ F, G to Carroll St; open noon-3pm & 5pm-10:45pm daily), near Douglass St, is a good spot to pop in for some sushi or sashimi ($1.75 to $4.50 à la carte). Grab the window seat.

Court Pastry (#45; ☎ 718-875-4820; 298 Court St; ⓜ F, G to Carroll St), near DeGraw

St, is a good place for dessert, where the famously filling pastries include the cream-filled lobster tail.

Patsy Grimaldi's Pizzeria (#6; ☎ 718-858-4300; 19 Old Fulton St; ⓜ A, C to High St; open 11:30am-11pm Mon-Thur, 11:30-midnight Fri, noon-midnight Sat, noon-11pm Sun), between Front and Water Sts at Fulton Landing, offers cheap, tasty pizza prepared by one of the descendants of the pioneering Manhattan pizza maker (see Patsy's Pizzeria in the Harlem section). Like his uncle before him, Patsy Grimaldi uses a coal-fired oven to produce a crispy crust on his super pies. This friendly family place makes a great stop for kids.

Henry St Ale House (#10; ☎ 718-522-4801; 62 Henry St; ⓜ A, C to High St, 1, 2 to Clark St), between Orange and Cranberry Sts, is a microbrewery pouring over a dozen local suds, which make a good accompaniment to the cheap sandwiches and burgers (around $8).

Noodle Pudding (#8; ☎ 718-625-3737; 38 Henry St; ⓜ A, C to High St, 1, 2 to Clark St; appetizers $4.95-8.50, entrees $9-13.75; open 5:30pm-10:30pm Tues-Thur, 5:30pm-11pm Fri & Sat, 5pm-10pm Sun), between Middagh and Cranberry Sts, is a local favorite serving classic Italian fare in a super friendly atmosphere. The menu changes daily; cash only.

Teresa's (#12; ☎ 718-797-3996; 80 Montague St; ⓜ 1, 2 to Clark St; dishes $3-8.95; open 7am-11pm daily), near Hicks St, has zero atmosphere, but no matter because the reason to come to this classic Polish diner is the food. Try the borscht, *kielbasa* or goulash, but don't miss the *pierogis*.

Hale & Hearty Soups (#14; ☎ 718-596-5600; 32 Court St; ⓜ M, N, R, 1, 2, 4, 5 to Court St-Borough Hall) is part of the chain that has made its name by living up to its name. There are a dozen soups daily ($2.75/3.50/4.50 small/medium/large), plus a filling soup and sandwich/salad combo ($5.99 to $7.29).

Queen (#25; ☎ 718-596-5954, fax 254-9247; 84 Court St; ⓜ M, N, R, 1, 2, 4, 5 to Court St-Borough Hall) has been cranking out reliable Italian food for over 40 years and is a good bet for finer dining in the Borough Hall area. You can either mix and match a variety of fresh pastas and homemade sauces ($9 to $15) or choose from classic sandwiches like veal or meatball parmigiana ($7.25).

Damascus Breads & Pastry *(#30; ☎ 718-625-7070; 195 Atlantic Ave; Ⓜ M, N, R, 1, 2, 4, 5 to Court St-Borough Hall; open 7am-7pm daily)*, between Court and Clinton Sts, has a dizzying array of pita and pastries sure to go straight to your hips, plus a dozen types of meat, vegetable and cheese pies – individual pillows of flaky dough surrounding warm, tasty fillings ($1.50).

Fountain Cafe *(#32; ☎ 718-624-6764, fax 422-0997; 183 Atlantic Ave; Ⓜ M, N, R, 1, 2, 4, 5 to Court St-Borough Hall; veggie fare $5.50-7.95, meat dishes $4.65-9.95; open 11am-10:30pm Mon-Thur, 11am-11pm Fri & Sat)* is a favorite Middle Eastern place on the Atlantic Ave strip. There are lots of vegetarian choices here like hummus and felafel, but also plenty for meat eaters like shawerma and kebabs. Round out your meal with one of the several types of fresh squeezed juice ($2.75 to $3.75).

La Bouillabaisse *(#35; ☎ 718-522-8275; 145 Atlantic Ave; Ⓜ M, N, R, 1, 2, 4, 5 to Court St-Borough Hall; appetizers $5.95-7.95, entrees $12.95-20.95)*, between Henry and Clinton Sts, offers its signature dish and other French fare, which often attract lines out the door. This enveloping bistro is so cozy you can smell the treasures being whipped up in the kitchen. Check it out during lunch to save some $$.

Junior's *(#20; ☎ 718-852-5257, fax 260-9849, open 6:30am 12:30am, Sun-Fri, Sat 6:30am-2am; 386 Flatbush Ave Extension at DeKalb Ave; M, N, Q, R to DeKalb Ave; burgers & sandwiches $6.75-9.50)* is not far from the Brooklyn Academy of Music. It serves some of New York's best cheesecake ($4.25 to $5.25), along with other high-calorie pleasures such as an enormous burger that weighs in at more than half a pound.

Gage & Tollner *(#22; ☎ 718-875-5181; 372 Fulton St at Smith St; Ⓜ M, N, R to Lawrence St; prix-fixe lunch $20, appetizers $8.95-12.95, entrees $18.95-25.95)*, established in 1879, is one of New York's oldest restaurants. A meal here doesn't come cheap, but you're paying for both the romantic, gaslight atmosphere and the solid seafood fare, which includes huge clams and crab cakes.

River Cafe *(#5; ☎ 718-522-5200; 1 Water St; Ⓜ A, C to High St; prix fixe dinner menu $70)*, near Old Fulton St at Fulton Landing, is a famous romantic restaurant which gazes upon Downtown Manhattan (that's enough to make you lose your appetite these days). Still, it's a wonderful riverside setting and an amazing splurge (there's a six-course tasting menu for $90 and several caviar services $60 to $75). You can save a bit by taking a cocktail or supping on lighter fare in the Terrace Room; note that gentlemen must wear jackets in the main dining room after 5pm.

Park Slope (Map 10)

For a do-it-yourself meal, try the empanadas ($1.50) at **Lopez Bakery** *(#13; ☎ 718-832-5690; 423 5th Ave; Ⓜ M, N, R, F to 4th Ave-Ninth St; open 24 hrs)* or any of the healthy, wholesome stuff sold at **Back to the Land** *(#17; ☎ 718-768-5654; 142 7th Ave; Ⓜ 1, 2 to Grand Army Plaza; open 9am-9pm daily)*, between Carroll and Garfield Sts, a neighborhood institution since 1971.

Lemongrass Grill *(#8; ☎ 718-399-7100; 61A 7th Ave; Ⓜ 1, 2 to Grand Army Plaza; appetizers $3.95-6.95, entrees $7.95-12.95)*, between Lincoln and Berkeley Places, is a popular place serving spicy and generous Thai dishes (many meatless).

Dizzy's *(#22; ☎ 718-499-1966; 511 Ninth St; Ⓜ F to 7th Ave-Park Slope; open 7am-10pm Mon-Thur, 9am-11pm Fri & Sat, 9am-10pm Sun)*, corner of 8th Ave, is a hot, hipster lunch and brunch place sporting frayed, classic diner decor and welcoming pavement tables. Everything from egg and cheese on a roll ($1.95) to homemade soups ($3.95/4.95 cup/bowl) are available and the cinnamon and spiced french toast stuffed with chocolate ($7.50) garners rave reviews; cash only.

Park Slope Brewing Co *(#14; ☎ 718-788-1756; 356 6th Ave at 5th St; Ⓜ F to 7th Ave-Park Slope; appetizers $3.50-7.95, entrees $7.50-11.95; kitchen open 4pm-10:30pm Sun-Thur, 11am-11:30pm Fri & Sat)* serves hearty pub grub from chili to crabcakes and local brews. There's always a cool, mixed crowd here getting playful at the pool table, dart board and pinball machines.

Chip Shop *(#12; ☎ 718-832-7701; 383 5th Ave; ◍ M, N, R, F to Ninth St; fish & chips $7-9)* serves up some 'bloody lovely' fish and chips. You can also get bangers and mash ($9) or baked beans on toast here ($5) and wash it all down with one of nine beers on tap ($4 to $5).

Two Boots Brooklyn *(#15; ☎ 718-499-3253; 514 Second St; ◍ 1, 2 to Grand Army Plaza; appetizers $5.25-7.95, entrees $9.95-16.95; open 5pm-midnight Sun-Thur, noon-midnight Fri & Sat)*, between 7th and 8th Aves, is as fun as always. The cuisine is part Big Easy, part Italy and the atmosphere is pure carnival. Little kids love this place and big kids dig the bar.

The Minnow *(#23; ☎ 718-832-5500; 442 Ninth St; ◍ M, N, R, F to 4th Ave-Ninth St)* is an all seafood place (save room for dessert as the fairer half of the husband-wife team that owns the place is a pastry chef) and one of Park Slope's best restaurants. It's not surprising then, that the staff is often overwhelmed on weekends.

HUGH D'ANDRADE

Eastern Parkway (Map 10)
Tom's Restaurant *(#2; ☎ 718-636-9738; 782 Washington Ave; ◍ 1, 2 to Eastern Pkwy-Brooklyn Museum)*, on the corner of Sterling Pl, is a legendary place that has survived for 65 years by keeping it basic and hearty. Head straight for the egg creams, burgers and good old, greasy-spoon breakfasts.

Coney Island (Map 1)
There are a couple of good places to eat out here, but of course, the number one recommendation is a hotdog straight from the famous Nathan's grill (see Coney Island in the Things to See & Do chapter for details).

Totonno's *(☎ 718-372-8606; 1524 Neptune Ave; ◍ F, Q, W to Coney Island-Stillwell Ave;* open noon-10:30pm Wed-Sun), two blocks away from the boardwalk, is one of the city's best and oldest brick-oven pizza restaurants.

Gargiulo's *(☎ 718-266-4891; 2911 W 15th St; ◍ F, Q, W to Coney Island-Stillwell Ave; dishes around $15)* is a noisy family-style place that first attracted crowds with a huge Styrofoam octopus, reputedly stolen from the aquarium. Unfortunately, it's gone now, but people still come for the filling southern Italian dishes.

Brighton Beach (Map 1)
Brighton Beach has had a massive influx of Soviet emigrés over the years and several raucous nightclub-restaurants offer elaborate floor shows to accommodate their desires. Drinking, dancing and debauchery until dawn pretty much sums it up: Think Vegas with free flowing vodka. To get to any of these places, take the Q train to Brighton Beach.

Winter Garden *(☎ 718-934-6666; 3152 Brighton at 6th St; prix-fixe dinner $40; open 11am-midnight daily)*, on the boardwalk, attracts Muscovites with a prix-fixe dinner, including two shots of vodka and a live nightclub act of music and dancing.

National *(☎ 718-646-1225; 273 Brighton Beach Ave; dinner & show $55 plus 10% service charge)* has a completely over-the-top variety show and dinner on Friday, Saturday and Sunday nights, well oiled by carafes of vodka.

Primorski *(☎ 718-891-3111; 282 Brighton Beach Ave; set menu weekdays/weekends $22/25)* offers a cheaper set menu than at the National – but if you lose track of the vodka consumption, the bill is sure to balloon. As with Winter Garden and National, the price of your dinner includes the nightclub act, and if you don't fancy the Russian dinner, expect to pay extra for a 'French' version. Primorski is open '11 to never: I open 11 in the morning, who knows what time I close?'

The bakeries on Brighton Beach Ave sell fantastic dark Russian sourdough bread for $2 a loaf.

Williamsburg & Greenpoint (Map 1)

Planet Thailand (☎ 718-599-5758; 133 N 7th St; ⓤ L to Bedford Ave; most entrees $10-12; open 11:30am-1am daily), corner of Berry St in northern Williamsburg, started as a phenomenal Thai place, but now serves sushi and Korean BBQ. It's still wicked popular – the two full bars and DJs nightly see to that.

Thai Cafe (☎ 718-383-3560; 925 Manhattan Ave; G to Greenpoint Ave; appetizers $2.95-3.95, salads $6.50-7.25, entrees $5.95-7.50; open 11:30am-10:30pm Mon-Wed, 11:30am-11pm Thur-Sat, 1pm-11pm Sun), corner of Kent in Greenpoint, picks up where Planet Thailand leaves off. It kitchen cranks out fresh, well-prepared staples like *pad Thai* and chicken with chili and basil. The atmosphere is laid back and the portions large.

Peter Luger Steakhouse (☎ 718-387-7400; 178 Broadway; ⓤ J, M, Z to Marcy Ave; dinner & wine per person from $50), between Bedford and Driggs Aves, is New York's most famous steak house, but some leave asking why? On a good day, the Porterhouse is juicy and the creamed spinach perfect. Peter Luger's takes cash only.

QUEENS
Astoria (Map 11)

Astoria is a culinary marvel: of course, there are Greeks moving about everywhere among clouds of blue smoke, but you can also get Mexican, Czech, Afghan and other ethnic food in this mixed neighborhood.

Broadway Natural (#9; ☎ 718-545-1100; 30-11 Broadway; ⓤ N, W to Broadway), near 31st St, whips up 65 different types of vegetable and fruit juices fresh to order ($3 to $4.25). Enjoy one of their combinations like apple-pear-mango, or make up your own.

Angelo's Food Emporium (#2; ☎ 718-278-0705; 31-27 Ditmars Blvd; N, W to Astoria-Ditmars Blvd), between 31st and 32nd St, is a great stop for picnickers. Here you can choose from mountains of olive varieties, fresh bread, dried fruits and many types of cookies, all nicely priced.

Uncle George's (#12; ☎ 718-626-0593; 33-19 Broadway; ⓤ N to Broadway, R, V, G to Steinway St; everything $3-12; open 24

hrs), between 33rd and 34th Sts, is where unabashed diners blow you kisses, baby lambs turn on a spit and roasted goat heads give you the hairy eyeball. Rabbit, barbecued pork and red snapper are available here. Try the *tzatziki*, or the roasted lemon potatoes ($3).

Zygo's Taverna (#4; ☎ 718-728-7070; 22-55 31st St; ⓤ N, W to Astoria-Ditmars Blvd; open 11am-midnight daily), near 23rd Ave, is a terrific family place with Christmas lights in June and photos of the clan covering the walls. Come here for succulent gyros ($4) and classic tidbits like *skordalia* (garlic and potato spread) and *taramosalata* (caviar roe, olive oil and lemon juice) for $4.50 each.

Omonia Cafe (#10; ☎ 718-274-6650; 32-20 Broadway; ⓤ N to Broadway, R, V, G to Steinway St; pastries $3.75-4.75), between 32nd and 33rd Sts, is a smoky and sleek patisserie where you'll hear children beseeching their *yaya* for a baklava and you might think you're back in Greece. For something more substantial, try a salad or spanakopita ($4.50 to $8.50) and a demitasse of ouzo from the full bar. Still, for our money, **Kolonaki** (#11; ☎ 718-932-8222; 33-02 Broadway), between 33rd and 34th Sts, is the best pastry place on this strip.

Elias Corner (#6; ☎ 718-932-1510; 24-02 31st St at 24th Ave ; ⓤ N, W to Astoria Blvd), near Hoyt Ave North, is more expensive and out-of-the-way, but merits a special trip for its floppingly fresh grilled fish and bracing retsina, a potent Greek wine. There is no menu at this moderately priced, cash-only, seafood-only spot; you get what was caught fresh early that morning.

Court Square Diner (#21; ☎ 718-392-1222, 45-30 23rd St, G to Long Island City-Court Sq, 7 to 45 Rd-Court House Sq; open 24 hrs) Is a rock-solid place with killer grilled cheese sandwiches and other classic diner food.

Jackson Heights (Map 1)

Tacos Mexico (☎ 718-899-5800; 88-12 Roosevelt Ave; ⓤ 7 to 90th St), near Elbertson St, is a minichain, fast-food joint offering the usual tacos, enchiladas and the like. The handmade salsa and tortilla chips are a bonus.

Local market stalls are a great place to purchase fresh produce.

Jackson Diner (☎ 718-672-1232; 37-47 74th St; ❿ E, F, R, V, G to Jackson Heights-Roosevelt Ave, 7 to 74th St-Broadway; entrees $8-17), between 37th and Roosevelt Aves, is considered by many to be the city's best South-Indian restaurant. This coffee shop turned festive charmer is famous for its *masala dosa* (crepe with potato, onion and peas) and *seekh kabab* (a long sausage made of tender lamb). Check out the buffet spread at lunchtime ($6/7.95 weekdays/weekends).

La Porteña (☎ 718-458-8111; 74-25 37th Ave; ❿ E, F, R, V, G to Jackson Hts-Roosevelt Ave, 7 to 74th St; entrees $13-18), between 74th and 75th Sts, around the corner from the Jackson Diner, offers a spicy taste of Argentina, serving Buenos Aires–style barbecue entrees prepared in the storefront window. Meals come to the table with *chimichurri*, a garlic-laden oil and vinegar sauce.

Chibcha (☎ 718-429-9033; 79-05 Roosevelt Ave; ❿ 7 to 82nd St-Jackson Hts), between 78th and 79th Sts, is a restaurant-nightclub frequented by the Colombian population in this neighborhood, who dance the night away to salsa (11pm Friday and Saturday). It also offers what one critic dubbed the 'cardiac special,' a sampler of grilled sausages, beef, cracked pork skin topped with an egg, plus plantains, rice and beans ($10.50).

Inti Raymi (☎ 718-424-1938; 86-14 37th Ave; ❿ 7 to 90th St-Elmhurst Ave; open Thur-Sun), between 86th and 87th Sts, serves Peruvian specialties like grilled cow's heart ($8) and does seafood particularly well. Try the ceviche and bring a bottle to wash it down.

Corona (Map 12)

Several Latin American communities mix and mingle between Jackson Heights and Corona, so you'll find a strong Latino influence in the cuisine.

Broadway Sandwich Shop (☎ 718-898-4088; 96-01 Roosevelt Ave; ❿ 7 to Junction Blvd), near Junction Blvd, serves garlicky Cuban pork sandwiches (under $5) and strong as love *café con leche*, which makes it worth the trip out to Queens.

Quisqueya Restaurant (☎ 718-478-0704; 97-03 Roosevelt Ave), near 97th St, a block from the Broadway Sandwich Shop, offers sweet plantain plates and Dominican specialties like young goat stew for $8.

La Espiga (#24; ☎ 718-779-7898; 42-13 102nd St; ❿ 7 to 103rd St) is near 42nd Ave. Tomas Gonzalez offers a taste of Mexico at this combination bakery, taco bar, restaurant and grocery store. People line up for the fresh tortillas (2lb for $1), made several times a day.

Lemon Ice King of Corona (#25; ☎ 718-699-5133; 52-02 108th St; ❿ 7 to 103rd St; open year-round), near Corona Ave, would have to be the king of homemade ices. The signature flavor has chunks of lemon and is the perfect refresher to go for on a hot summer day. The Lemon Ice King is about a mile from the subway. Walk south on 104th St to Corona Ave, turn left and walk two blocks to 52nd Ave. Alternatively, grab an ice after a stroll through Flushing Meadows Corona Park and then head up to the 7 train at 111th St.

Flushing (Map 12)

If you're craving Asian, Flushing is the place. Here you'll find Chinese, Japanese and Vietnamese, all at reasonable prices; most entrees at the following spots cost less than $10, although whole-fish dishes at seafood restaurants usually fall in the $10 to $15 range. To reach any of these places, take the No 7 subway all the way to the last stop at Main St.

Joe's Shanghai (#10; ☎ 718-539-3838; 136-21 37th Ave; appetizers $1.95-5.95, entrees $7.95-13.95; open 11am-10pm Sun-Thur, 11am-10:30pm Fri & Sat), near Main St, is known for its steaming bowls of handmade dumplings and noodle dishes, but also serves more esoteric items such as raw drunken crab ($7).

Shanghai Tide (#13; ☎ 718-661-0900; 135-20 40th Rd; dim sum $1.50-4.95, dishes $6.95-15.95), between Roosevelt and 41st Aves, has hundreds of menu items to choose from, including a separate Szechuan menu ($3.95 to $9.95). The Family Meal is a bargain, letting you pick three entrees for $16.95.

KB Garden (#9; ☎ 718-961-9088; 136-28 39th Ave; dishes $3-8) is the place to head for a dim sum feast; it also does à la carte, from sweet-and-sour chicken ($8.95) to shark fin soup ($65).

Kum Gang San (#5; ☎ 718-461-0909; 138-28 Northern Blvd; dishes $8.95-17.95; open 24 hrs), between Union and Bowne Sts, are the same folks with the Little Korea outpost (see the boxed text 'Culinary Corners,' earlier in this chapter). This branch has a little garden and wall of water, the usual Korean BBQ and a smattering of Japanese dishes.

Tay Do (#14; ☎ 718-762-1223; 135-29 40th Rd; appetizers $2.95-6.95, entrees $3.95-10.95), right under the Long Island Railroad stop, has over 20 varieties of pho, plus fun stuff like frogs legs.

Pho Bang (#15; ☎ 718-939-5520; 41-07 Kissena Blvd; open 10am-10pm daily • Map 3, #4; ☎ 212-966-3797; 157 Mott St • Map 3, #24; ☎ 212-587-0870; 6 Chatham Sq) is the king of pho, with over two dozen varieties ($4.25 to $6.25). Though they have more substantial entrees, a bowl of pho is a meal in itself. There are two branches of Pho Bang in Chinatown.

Two good places to take exotic elixirs, shakes and teas are **Sweet 'n Tart Café** (#11; ☎ 718-661-3380; 136-11 38th Ave; open 9am-midnight daily) and **Sago Tea Café** (#12; ☎ 718-353-2899; 39-02 Main St).

STATEN ISLAND (MAP 1)

Things are bleak and unattractive near the ferry terminal, but if you venture a little farther, you'll find some worthwhile dining spots.

Sidestreet Saloon (☎ 718-448-6868; 11 Schuyler St), just a few minutes' walk from the ferry, is a popular lunch spot for workers from the borough courthouse across the street. Look for lotsa pasta here.

Cargo Cafe (☎ 718-876-0539; 120 Bay St at Slossen Terrace), three blocks east of the ferry terminal, serves up recommended meat and seafood specials in a gregarious atmosphere.

The Rare Olive (☎ 718-273-5100; 981 Bay St; lunch entrees about $7, dinner from $13, lobster $23) serves an interesting combination of Italian and southern Creole food. There's a full bar here.

Bocelli (☎ 718-420-6150; 1250 Hylan Blvd; appetizers $8.50-12, pastas $12.95-14.95, entrees $12.95-23.95) is a neighborhood stalwart serving the regular pasta primavera and veal fra diavolo, but also has some surprises like tangy shrimp, lobster and scallop kababs in lime marinade.

Entertainment

No single source could possibly list everything going down in the city, but the weekly *Time Out* does its damnedest. For high-culture events, check out the Sunday and Friday editions of the *New York Times*, as well as *New York* magazine and the *New Yorker*. Dance clubs and smaller music venues take out numerous ads in free weeklies like the *Village Voice* and *New York Press*. Clubbers should look for *Flyer*, a pocket-sized, monthly freebie, at bars, lounges and clubs with a day-by-day break down of parties.

The **Department of Cultural Affairs** (☎ 212-643-7770) has a hotline that lists events and concerts at major museums and other cultural institutions. You can also call **NYC On Stage** (☎ 212-768-1818), a 24-hour information line that publicizes music and dance events.

THEATER

The heart of Broadway runs right through Times Square, which has long served as the center of New York's theater world – both legitimate and lascivious. 'Legitimate' is the term used by municipal officials to distinguish dramas and musicals from the porn houses that populated the area until Rudy Giuliani introduced his heavy legislation. However, the preponderance of overblown Andrew Lloyd Weber spectaculars (including *Cats*, *Phantom of the Opera*, *Miss Saigon*) and film spin-offs from Disney (eg, *The Lion King* and *Beauty and the Beast*) cast doubt on the term legitimate for what's been up on Broadway recently.

Then along came innovative, musical works such as *Rent* and more recently, *Urinetown*, *Proof* and *Contact*. Repackaged movie hits like *The Producers*, *The Graduate* and *The Full Monty* have taken the town by storm, redeeming and legitimizing the theater scene a bit as well. A few classic revivals (including *The Iceman Cometh, The Crucible* and *Death of a Salesman*) starring big-name film actors, started attracting burgeoning, enthusiastic crowds to Broadway and revived musicals garnered acclaim too, including *Oklahoma*, *Chicago* and *Cabaret*.

All this has added up to a great era of success for Broadway, which was threatened following the September 11 attacks when tourist revenues plummeted and receipts for Broadway shows, museums, restaurants and hotels took a huge hit. While some shows closed under the immediate pressure of empty houses, other casts and crews agreed to take pay cuts and suspensions and a massive local campaign was launched to fill seats. The response was so overwhelmingly positive that six months after the attacks, a consortium of theaters returned $1 million in relief donations. Nowadays, Broadway is booming, as any peek at the ABC listings (daily in the *New York Times* Arts & Leisure section) makes clear.

Theater buffs should definitely investigate what is happening downtown or Off Broadway (see that section later), as some of the freshest, most accomplished stage work is happening far south of the renowned Times Square.

'Showplace of the Nation,' New York's famous Radio City Music Hall

Broadway Theaters

In general, 'Broadway' productions are staged in the large theaters surrounding Times Square. Some of the major venues include the following, but if you're searching for a particular Broadway theater not listed here, consult Map 6 in the map section at the back of this book. You can reach all of these theaters via **subway** (◐ *N, Q, R, S, W, 1, 2, 3, 7 to Times Sq-42nd St*). To purchase tickets for the spots listed below, see Tickets, later.

Eugene O'Neill Theater *(Map 6, #42; ☎ 212-239-6200; 230 W 49th St)*, between Broadway and Eighth Ave, has staged top theatrical productions like Neil Simon's *A Thousand Clowns* and *Prisoner of Second Avenue*. Its production of Arthur Miller's *Death of a Salesman* earned rave reviews and its staging of *The Full Monty* is wildly popular. The pleasant theater seats 1100.

Majestic Theater *(Map 6, #92; 247 W 44th St)*, near Eighth Ave, is arguably Broadway's best theatre. In the past, the Majestic has staged the blockbuster musicals *Carousel*, *South Pacific* and *Camelot* with Julie Andrews. Its legendary current production, *Phantom of the Opera*, opened in January 1988 and may play until the sky falls down. Most of the 1600 seats here offer good views.

COREY WISE

Broadway, NY's theatrical heartland

New Amsterdam Theatre *(Map 6, #118; ☎ 212-282-2900; 214 W 42nd St)*, near Seventh Ave, is a 1771-seat jewel. This theater was rescued from decrepitude by the Disney corporation, which stages upbeat, kid-friendly productions like *The Lion King* here. The lobby, rest rooms and auditorium are lavish, but the seating is a bit cramped.

Winter Garden Theatre *(Map 6, #31; ☎ 212-239-6200; 1634 Broadway)* finally dropped the curtain on *Cats* in September 2000 after an unbelievable 18-year run. The theater recently emerged from the darkness with *Mamma Mia!*, an over-the-top musical extravaganza celebrating the music of Swedish super group ABBA.

New Victory Theater *(Map 6, #111; ☎ 212-362-4000; 209 W 42nd St)* is another former triple-X gem that has been rescued from the wrecking ball and refurbished; it now produces theater exclusively for children.

Off-Broadway Theaters

'Off Broadway' usually refers to shows performed in smaller spaces (200 seats or fewer) elsewhere in town, although you'll find some in the Times Square area. 'Off-off Broadway' events include readings, experimental and cutting-edge performances and improvisations held in spaces with fewer than 100 seats. Some of the world's best theater happens in these more intimate venues: recent notable productions have included Eve Ensler's *The Vagina Monologues*, the Pulitzer Prize–winning *Wit* and the airborne, trippy *De La Guarda*.

A big business in itself, off-Broadway theater now attracts four million people a year. Some prominent spots include the following.

Circle in the Square Theater *(Map 6, #32; ☎ 212-307-2705; 1633 Broadway at 50th St; ◐ 1, 2 to 50th St)* staged groundbreaking productions like Eugene O'Neill's *The Iceman Cometh* at its original 159 Bleecker St premises. The company takes an active role in New York's thespian scene, training new actors at its theater school.

Joseph Papp Public Theater *(Map 4, #89; ☎ 212-260-2400; ⓦ www.publictheater.org; 425 Lafayette St; ◐ N, R to 8th St-NYU, 6 to Astor Pl)*, between E 4th St and Astor Place in Greenwich Village, presents its famous and fabulous Shakespeare in the Park productions at Central Park's Delacorte Theater every summer. Meryl Streep, Robert DeNiro, Kevin Kline and many other stars have performed at the Public, one of the city's most important cultural centers.

Performing Garage (Map 4, #255; ☎ 212-853-9623; 33 Wooster St; ⓜ A, C, E to Canal St), between Broome and Grand Sts, was founded in the '60s and remains one of the most consistent of the avant-garde performance spaces. It's home to the Wooster Group, whose members have included Willem Dafoe, Spalding Gray and Steve Buscemi.

PS 122 (Map 4, #36; ☎ 212-477-5288; ⓦ www.ps122.org; 150 First Ave; ⓜ N, R to 8th St-NYU, 6 to Astor Pl), near E 9th St in the East Village, has been committed to fostering new artists and their far-out ideas since its inception in 1979. Its two stages have hosted such performers as Meredith Monk, Eric Bogosian and the Blue Man Group.

Astor Place Theatre (Map 4, #87; ☎ 212-254-4370; 434 Lafayette St; ⓜ N, R to 8th St-NYU, 6 to Astor Pl), between W 4th St and Astor Place, is on the map because of the phenomenal Blue Man Group (ⓦ www.blueman.com), a trio of bald, blue guys who get wild and wooly with all manner of props and paint while poking fun at the art mob mentality. Audience participation is required (whether you like it or not!).

Daryl Roth Theatre (Map 5, #179; ☎ 212-239-6200; 20 Union Sq East; ⓜ L, N, Q, R, W, 4, 5, 6 to 14th St-Union Sq), at 15th St, is another theater hosting sold-out shows thanks to the innovative work of its presenting company: De La Guarda (ⓦ www.dlgsite.com) is a high-flying team of Argentines exploring the energy and ecstasy of dancing and prancing while soaring above the crowds standing below. They like to get the audience involved.

Jean Cocteau Repertory (Map 4, #130; ☎ 212-677-0600; 330 Bowery; ⓜ F, V to Second Ave), on the corner of E 2nd St, puts up consistently good revival classics, often with a twist. This is a comfortable theater that's been going strong for years.

PS 122 – always staging the unexpected

ANGUS OBORN

Todo Con Nada Show World (Map 6, #114; ☎ 212-586-7829; 675 Eighth Ave at 42nd St; ⓜ A, C, E to 42nd St) is a response to Rudy Giuliani's Draconian legislation designed to clean up Times Square: Under Hizzoner's mandate, porn theaters that dedicated at least 60% of their space to 'legitimate' theater could still give over 40% of their space to less lofty productions. This innovative collaboration between Todo Con Nada, an established theater company, and Show World, a video-porn purveyor, has been a smash success. Here, high-quality and original productions are held in three theaters (complete with the mirrored ceilings, red flocked wallpaper and cabaret thrusts that once hosted strippers). Don't miss the freaky clown scene upstairs before entering the theaters.

Tickets

Broadway Line (☎ 212-302-4111; ⓦ www.broadway.org) provides descriptions of plays and musicals both on and off the Great White Way; you can use it to obtain information on ticket prices and to make credit card purchases.

Telecharge (☎ 212-239-6200, 800-432-7250) sells tickets for most Broadway and off-Broadway shows (though there's a per-ticket surcharge). To buy same-day standing-room tickets for sold-out shows, contact theaters directly. For $10 to $15, you'll get great views and sore feet (but you can always scope out vacant seats at intermission).

When venturing to the theater, it's important to know where to sit given the seating configuration of each individual house and the desireability of some seats over others.

Discount Tickets In Times Square, **TKTS booth** (Map 6, #56; ☎ 212-768-1818; Broadway & W 47th St) sells same-day tickets to Broadway and off-Broadway musicals and dramas. Tickets sell at either 25% or 50% off regular box-office rates, plus a $3 service charge per ticket. The booth's electric marquee lists available shows; availability depends on the popularity of the show you're looking to see. (Before you go, check out the Friday New York Times and Time Out to make selections, but you'll have to be flexible.)

On Wednesday and Saturday, matinee tickets go on sale at 10am, and on Sunday the windows open at 11am for afternoon performances. Evening tickets go on sale at 3pm daily, and a line begins to form up to an hour before the booth opens. Note that TKTS accepts cash or traveler's checks only. There's a smaller, less crowded **TKTS outlet** at Bowling Green Park Plaza in Lower Manhattan, in front of the National Museum of the American Indian; it maintains the same hours.

BARS & LOUNGES

Lounges started cropping up here like fungi under cow patties following a hard rain once Rudy Giuliani resurrected New York's arcane cabaret laws. These laws dictated that bars could not have music (except for a jukebox), unless the establishment had a cabaret license – a difficult piece of red tape to wrangle for an already existing bar. This had several effects: some places just shut down, other places moved to Brooklyn and then there were lounges. At these living room-cum-bars, DJs spin tunes (circumventing the cabaret bureaucratic horseshit), drinks are copious and cigar smokers are welcome. Every lounge has a different vibe set by the music, lighting, secret nooks, plush furnishings and clientele and there are always new ones cropping up, so ask around town if this is your scene. The usual neighborhood stereotypes apply to lounges too: Chelsea is mostly gay, the East Village and Lower East Side are edgier than most other places, SoHo more arty and Uptown more moneyed.

Some people don't like lounges though. They can be too much of a scene, loud, expensive and crowded. If this is you, no doubt you'll want to investigate the seedy, dive bar atmosphere which New York serves up deftly. A proper listing of New York City's best bars could fill an entire book, but here's a highly selective list of bars that stay open until 2am most nights (though bars are legally allowed to stay open until 4am and most do). For more details, see the subjective (in a good way) reviews collected at the New York City Beer Guide website: **w** www.nycbeer.org/drink ing.html.

Long gone are the days when underage drinkers could discover and uncover their alcohol tolerance and tendencies in New York's drinking dens. In today's New York, everyone (even 40-year-olds!) is required to present picture identification at bars and lounges before purchasing drinks and sometimes even before stepping through the door.

Lower Manhattan (Map 3)

Remy Lounge (#76, ☎ 212-267-4646; 104 Greenwich St; ❶ N, R to Rector St), between Carlisle and Rector Sts, is loco with salsa and other tropical rhythms heating up the dance floor nightly. DJs also play plenty of reggae and R&B at this two-level lounge. Dress to impress as they say; call to be added to the guest list.

Two of the best, but very different, bars down at Manhattan's tip are **Rise** at the Ritz-Carlton in Battery Park (see the 'Hotel Cocktails' boxed text) and the bar at **Cabana** (#54) at the South St Seaport (see Places to Eat for details).

Hotel Cocktails

Some of the most luxe interiors, breathtaking vistas and high-class atmospheres are tucked away in the bars, cocktail lounges and lobbies of New York City's hotels. 'You get what you pay for' holds true here and you will have to shell out some serious dough to take advantage of the ambiance imbuing these places (beers usually start at around $10, cocktails at about $14). Also, come appropriately dressed as most enforce a dress code. Here are some of the best on offer.

KIM GRANT

For history, check out the **Blue Bar** (Map 6, #82; 59 W 44th St), at the Algonquin Hotel between Fifth and Sixth Aves, with its old money, smoke-filled air or the **Oak Room**, which hosts the world's greatest cabaret acts. Another classic is the Hotel Elysee's **Monkey Bar** (Map 5, #27; 60 E 54th St), between Fifth and Madison Aves, which opened in 1936 and is still pouring its signature cocktails under the gaze of a zany monkey mural. Carlyle Hotel's **Bemelmen's Bar** (Map 7, #78; 35 E 76th St), between Madison and Park Aves, is a whimsical old place in the famed Carlyle Hotel named after the creator of *Madeline* (the bar is covered with his murals). If you're over here and have the money and the appropriate attire, catch Bobby Short or another fabulous crooner at the hotel's **Cafe Carlyle**. Finally, the famed **Nat King Cole Bar** (Map 5, #28; 2 E 55th St), at the St Regis Hotel between Fifth and Madison Aves, has an exquisite Maxfield Parrish mural and strong cocktails to delight your senses as you smoke a fine cigar.

For views, the new **Rise bar and terrace** (Map 3, #89; 14th fl, 2 West St at 1st Pl), in the Ritz-Carlton, is sublime, with its panoramic New York Harbor vistas taking in the Verrazano Narrows Bridge, the Statue of Liberty and gorgeous sunsets. As a bonus, the appetizers and bar snacks are quite tasty. The **lobby lounge** here is also a treat, with a Brazilian duet on piano and guitar, oversized, fluffy chairs and cigar smoking. **The View** (Map 6, #77; 1535 Broadway at 45th St), in the Marriott Marquis, is a revolving rooftop affair soaring above Times Square. Dodge the tourists in the so-so restaurant and head straight to the bar for the uber-urban sights. Heading east between 49th and 50th Sts at First Ave, **Top of the Tower** (Map 5, #54; 26th fl, 3 Mitchell Pl), at the Beekman Tower Hotel near 49th St, delivers the bird's eye of the East Side, including the Chrysler Building, the United Nations and across the East River to the retro Pepsi sign done up in neon script. **Penthouse B** (Map 7, #131; 500 E 62nd St at York Ave), at The Bentley, also takes in sweeping 360° views across the East River.

For chic, boutique appeal, check out the delicious **Villard Bar & Lounge** (Map 5, #64; 455 Madison Ave at 50th St), in the Palace Hotel, with its deep maroon velvet everything, 24-karat gold-leaf details, mahogany and marble, all done up in Louis XIV style. Have a cigar or a tête-à-tête here in one of the many secret nooks. **44** (Map 6, #107; 44 W 44th), at the Royalton between Fifth and Sixth Aves, is one of those places where they try to throw down NY bitchy attitude, but it doesn't matter, the martinis are so divine (skip the lobby lounging and check out the tiny bar just to the right of the entrance). In the same see-and-be-seen vein is **Whiskey Bar** (Map 6, #60; 245 W 46th), at Paramount between Broadway and Eighth Ave, which is actually an interesting spot to check out the junkies on laptops and rock stars on the skids. The **UnderBar** (Map 5, #181; 201 Park Ave South at E 17th St), in the W New York-Union Square, is another luscious place with velvet upholstery and curtains for discretion. If the out-of-towner, too-cool-for-school attitude gets to be too much, slip around back to the lower key two-floor hotel lounge.

Tribeca (Map 3)

Bubble Lounge (#30; ☎ 212-431-3433; 228 West Broadway; ◐ 1, 2 to Franklin St), between White and Franklin Sts, is patronized by well-heeled Wall St types getting giddy on 280 varieties of champagne and sparkling wine. It's the place to drop $2000 on a bottle of champagne, but you can also order bubbly by the glass for around $8.

Raccoon Lodge (#44; ☎ 212-776-9656; 59 Warren St; ◐ A, C, 1, 2, to Chambers St), between Church and West Broadway, has the best drinking atmosphere of any Tribeca bar – the hooch is strong, the popcorn free and the fire place and pool table are unbeatable on any given winter night. After work is a little stiff with suits, but as the evening progresses the neighborhood and biker regulars come out.

Liquor Store Bar (#6; ☎ 212-226-7121; 235 West Broadway; ◐ A, C, E to Canal St), at White St, is a popular night-time hang-out in a Federal-style building that its owners proudly claim has been in continuous commercial use since 1804. Big windows and outdoor tables offer plenty of people watching. The bar takes its name from a previous business at the same site; locals, inspired by the furry animals often seen scampering down the street, call it the Rat Bar.

Lower East Side (Map 4)

Ludlow St and environs used to be a dingy, fringe neighborhood populated by old timers and pre-curve newcomers until the early '90s when the entire area exploded with bars, lounges, restaurants and live-music clubs. Now it's a convenient and popular spot for a pub crawl as there is so much variety of scene in a condensed area. There are many more places than space here allows – ask or walk around to get an idea of what's happening down here.

Barramundi (#217; ☎ 212-529-6900; 147 Ludlow St; ◐ F, J, M, Z to Delancey St), between Stanton and Rivington Sts, is an Australian-owned arty place featuring convivial booths, reasonably priced drinks and a lovely shady garden.

Orchard Bar (#179; ☎ 212-673-5350; 200 Orchard St; ◐ F, V to Second Ave), between Stanton and E Houston Sts, is an unmarked place populated by mostly drunk, mostly beautiful urbanites kicking back on the banquettes and grooving to DJs spinning deep house and techno-type beats.

Two other cool places enthusiastically recommended are **Lolita** (#227; ☎ 212-966-7223; 266 Broome St; ◐ S to Grand St, F, J, M, Z to Delancey St), at Allen St, and **Motor City Bar** (#225; ☎ 212-358-1595; 127 Ludlow St; ◐ F, J, M, Z to Delancey St), near Delancey St.

SoHo (Map 4)

The Ear Inn (#265; ☎ 212-226-9060; 326 Spring St; ◐ C, E to Spring St) is between Greenwich and Washington Sts, a block from the Hudson River. It sits in the old James Brown House (the James Brown who was an aide to George Washington, not Soul Brother No 1), which dates back to 1817. This is a great old dive, with patrons ranging from sanitation workers and office dweebs to bikers and poets. The bar menu features a great shepherd's pie.

Cafe Noir (#259; ☎ 212-431-7910; 32 Grand St; ◐ A, C, E to Canal St), at Thompson St, has North African and Mediterranean-inspired appetizers which you can munch while watching the passing SoHo parade from the open-air bar railing.

Sweet & Vicious (#211; ☎ 212-334-7915; 5 Spring St; ◐ J, M to Bowery), between Elizabeth and Bowery, is a wide-open bar with hardwood floors and hardass benches that will leave your butt sore if you don't get up and shake your thang to the good music played here.

Pravda (#185; ☎ 212-226-4944; 281 Lafayette St; ◐ F, V, S to Broadway-Lafayette St) is between Prince and Houston Sts. Pravda tried to remain on the down low, but lines out the door leaked the secret to the entire city. If you dress hep enough and look sufficiently intense, you'll make it past the gatekeepers and enter clouds of cigar smoke in this mock Eastern European speakeasy. The martinis make all the hassle worth it, though; the two-page vodka list includes Canada's Inferno Pepper and a homegrown Rain Organic.

Greenwich Village (Map 4)

Bowlmor Lanes *(#19; ☎ 212-255-8188; 110 University Pl; ⓜ L, N, Q, R, W, 4, 5, 6 to 14th St-Union Sq)* is between E 12th and 13th Sts. While not technically a lounge, bowling falls under that 21st-century hip rubric and the in-crowd has embraced this place. The disco soundtrack and glow-in-the-dark bowling (Monday nights) produce a retro atmosphere worthy of a club (as do visits by Julia Roberts and other celebrities). You can throw strikes until 4am Friday and Saturday nights here.

B Bar *(#132; ☎ 212-475-2220; 40 E 4th St; ⓜ 6 to Bleecker St)*, at Bowery, packs in a mixed, moneyed crowd, especially on hot summer nights when the outdoor patio provides sweet relief. Tuesdays at B Bar mean the notorious Beige party, for which the fabulously queer only need apply (although super fly women in the company of similarly stellar men *might* be admitted).

Swift's Hibernian Lounge *(#133; ☎ 212-260-3600; 34 E 4th St; ⓜ 6 to Bleecker St)*, near the Bowery, is a wildly popular bar with live folk music and fine pints of Guinness. Church pews and candles complete the Irish atmosphere here and the musicians cozy up to their audience, since they can't perform on the nonexistent stage.

West Village (Map 4)

Corner Bistro *(#9; ☎ 212-242-9502; 331 W 4th St; ⓜ 1, 2 to Christopher St-Sheridan Sq)*, between Jane St and W 12th St, is a famous bar from the bygone beat era where you can eat charred hamburgers until 2am at carved wooden tables. Some consider the enormous, half-pound bistro burger with bacon and onions the best in the city.

Blind Tiger Ale House *(#65; ☎ 212-675-3848; 518 Hudson St; ⓜ 1, 2 to Christopher St-Sheridan Sq)* is between W 10th and Christopher Sts. Gregarious and without pretension, this place may be the single best place to sample an array of interesting beer; happy hour is until 8pm daily.

Bar d'O *(#159; ☎ 212-627-1580; 29 Bedford St; ⓜ 1, 2 to Houston St)*, near Downing St, is a smoky retro lounge that features drag acts several nights a week (cover charge is usually $3 to $7). It attracts a chic mixed crowd of gays and straights, except on Monday which is lesbian night.

Chumley's *(#154; ☎ 212-675-4449; 86 Bedford St; ⓜ 1, 2 to Christopher St-Sheridan Sq)*, between Grove and Barrow Sts, is a hard-to-find, storied speakeasy that serves decent pub grub along with 11 beers on tap (for more on the history of this place, see the Greenwich Village Walking Tour in the Things to See & Do chapter). Look for the unmarked brown door in a white wall.

East Village & Alphabet City (Map 4)

The Scratcher *(#131; ☎ 212-477-0030; 209 E 5th St; ⓜ 6 to Astor Pl)*, near Third Ave, attracts a large Irish clientele because it looks like a true Dublin pub. It's a quiet place to sip coffee and read the newspaper during the day but a crowded and raucous spot at night.

McSorley's Old Ale House *(#93; ☎ 212-473-9148; 15 E 7th St; ⓜ 6 to Astor Pl)*, between Second and Third Aves, predates the Civil War and bears the dubious distinction of resisting the modern age: it barred women from its doors until the 1970s. This stodgy old bar often served as a setting for Joseph Mitchell's well-known *New Yorker* short stories, but these days it's mostly tourists and stale beer pouring out from this cramped place.

Vazac's *(#112; ☎ 212-473-8840; 108 Ave B at E 7th St; ⓜ L to First Ave, 6 to Astor Pl)* is a local favorite at the southeast end of Tompkins Square Park, with sticky floors, a horseshoe-shaped bar and plenty of pinball for the restless. Also called 7B's, it's been featured in a number of films, including *The Verdict* and *Crocodile Dundee*.

Tribe *(#103; ☎ 212-979-8965; St Marks Pl at First Ave; ⓜ 6 to Astor Pl)* tells you everything you need to know about today's hip EV. Formerly the storied old St Marks Bar & Grill, this place now features a DJ, dance-floor lighting and pricey pints.

WCOU Radio *(#102; 115 First Ave at E 7th St; ⓜ 6 to Astor Pl)* is the place to go if you're tired of the trendy East Village scene. This low-key hang-out bears a slight resemblance to a bathroom, thanks to the old tiles on the floor. Sit in the window and watch life pass by to the soundtrack of the cool jukebox.

Baraza (#111; ☎ 212-539-0811; 133 Ave C), between 8th and 9th Sts, is a relative new-comer to the bar and lounge scene, though you wouldn't know it by the ready, steady crowds. They flock to this place for the hot, tropical rhythms and late-night delights.

Other local places we like over this way include: **Plant** (#118; ☎ 212-375-9066; 217 E 3rd St), between Aves B and C, for the hipster scene and **Zum Schneider** (#115, ☎ 212-598-1098; 107-109 Ave C at 7th St) or **Esperanto** (#113, ☎ 212-505-6559; 145 Ave C at 9th St) for something a little more international.

Union Square (Map 5)

Pete's Tavern (#171; ☎ 212-473-7676; 129 E 18th St; ❶ L, N, Q, R, W, 4, 5, 6 to 14th St-Union Sq) is a dark, atmospheric watering hole near Irving Pl. You can get a respectable burger and beer here for around $12 (for more on the history of this place, see the Grammercy Park section of the Things to See & Do chapter).

Old Town Bar and Grill (#183; ☎ 212-529-6732; 45 E 18th St; ❶ L, N, Q, R, W, 4, 5, 6 to 14th St-Union Sq) is between Broadway and Park Ave and bears some similarity to Pete's Tavern for its hard drinking, local tenor.

The East Village: Still the One

The East Village – particularly the area on and around St Marks Place and Tompkins Square Park – has long been known as New York's prototypical fringe neighborhood. Against all gentrifying odds, the EV has always attracted down-at-the-heels characters, including junkies, recently homeless suburban outcasts and outré artists such as Beat poet Allen Ginsberg and eccentric English dandy Quentin Crisp. Enriching this eclectic mix is the close-knit Eastern European community which has long and strong East Village roots. In the '70s and '80s, it served as ground zero of the US punk movement: the infamous nightclub CBGB, on the Bowery, helped to launch the careers of such famous bands as Talking Heads, Blondie and the Ramones. By the late '80s, Tompkins Square became a stomping ground (literally) for local punks and anarchists. They congregated at the late, much-lamented **Coney Island High** (St Marks Pl), a barn-like bar and performance space, or at the still-thriving **7B's** (also known as Vazac's; see the Bars & Lounges section).

But by the early '90s, the mean streets of the East Village began a rapid, stunning transformation which extended even into the notorious Alphabet City (Aves A, B, C and D) and the Lower East Side around Ludlow St. The change started with a resurgence in cutting-edge nightlife. A number of groundbreaking cafés opened near Tompkins Square, including **Cafe Siné** (St Marks Pl), a literary-musical hang-out that became a magnet for Irish-born immigrants, including doomed folk singer Jeff Buckley. (It's closed now.) When the Gap opened on St Mark's Place and Second Ave, New Yorkers asked what is this world coming to? (It, too, is closed now.)

The East Village continued its rise with the refurbishment of once-wrecked apartment buildings in an area that stretched from E 2nd to E 13th Sts east of Third Ave. Funky places like the Guinness-dispensing Irish bars **Swift's Hibernian Lounge** and **The Scratcher** (see the Bars & Lounges section) sprang up in the area, pre-empting drunk hang-outs like the **Village Idiot**, **Bar 81** and **Sophie's** (though local bar flies will never ditch and switch).

The natural progression of the East Village led to the establishment of Internet cafés and more upscale venues that attracted celebrities but served up an attitude and pretty lousy food. Still, there's some grunge life left in the East Village: **Continental** (see the Rock section) attracts a heavily pierced crowd with its live rock bands, **Brownie's** rocks out nightly and CBGBs will hopefully never die.

These days, even the side streets off Aves B and C are hopping with lounges that stay open to 2am nightly. It's yours to explore – check out the listings in *Paper*, the Downtown magazine, for more information.

Belmont Lounge *(#178; ☎ 212-533-0009; 117 E 15th St; Ⓜ L, N, Q, R, W, 4, 5, 6 to 14th St-Union Sq)*, near Irving Place, is a trendy stop with plenty of nooky nooks. You can stargaze in the garden or nosh your way through the night, picking from a selection of sandwiches, salads and appetizers (the kitchen is open until 2am).

Beauty Bar *(#174; ☎ 212-539-1389; 231 E 14th St; Ⓜ L to Third Ave)*, between Second and Third Aves, was the beginning of the end for the truly hip East Village for many people: suburbanites and tourists sipping martinis under old hairdryers is the gimmick here.

Midtown & Times Square

Campbell Apartment *(Map 5, #86; ☎ 212-953-0409; 15 Vanderbilt Ave; Ⓜ S, 4, 5, 6, 7 to Grand Central)* is accessible from Grand Central (take the elevator beside the Oyster Bar or the stairs to the West Balcony and head out the doors to the left) and is a sublime spot for a cocktail. This used to be the apartment of a landed railroad magnate and has the velvet, mahogany and murals to prove it. Cigars are welcome, but sneakers and jeans are not.

Rainbow Room *(Map 5; ☎ 212-632-5100; 30 Rockefeller Plaza; Ⓜ B, D, F, V to 47th-50th Sts/Rockefeller Center)* is at the Rainbow Grill, on the 65th floor of the GE Building. While drinks here don't come cheap (that Ketel One martini will be $15, thank you very much), this ranks as one of the most romantic spots in New York as the views (including a bird's eye of the Empire State) are dreamy. The Rainbow Room is open Friday nights and some Saturdays for dinner and dancing; jackets and reservations are required.

Rudy's Bar & Grill *(Map 6, #97; ☎ 212-974-9169; 627 Ninth Ave; Ⓜ A, C, E to 42nd St)*, between 44th and 45th Sts, practically glories in its reputation as a spot for sots. Wash down that $2 pint o' piss with free hotdogs and you'll no doubt be hooked like the rest of us.

Film Center Cafe *(Map 6, #96; ☎ 212-262-2525; 635 Ninth Ave; Ⓜ A, C, E to 42nd St)*, between 44th and 45th Sts, is a lively local place with an unlimited champagne brunch ($9.95) on weekends, a raw bar and stiff drinks. The kitchen is open until 4am – what more could you want?

McHale's Bar & Cafe *(Map 6, #62; ☎ 212-997-8885; 750 Eighth Ave at 46th St; Ⓜ A, C, E to 42nd St)* has been a hang-out for old guys, actors and wannabes for years. It's a down-to-earth spot with decent pub grub and burgers, all for under $9. Look for McHale's great neon sign, which should take you back at least a half-dozen decades.

Mercury Bar *(Map 6, #67; ☎ 212-262-7755; 659 Ninth Ave; Ⓜ A, C, E to 42nd St)* is between 45th and 46th Sts. A sleek new spot in an up-and-coming West Side neighborhood near Port Authority, the Mercury packs in patrons on Thursday and Friday nights, or whenever a major sporting event plays on the two gigantic TVs here; otherwise the televised pabulum is a major nuisance.

British Open *(Map 5, #17; ☎ 212-355-8467; 320 E 59th St; Ⓜ 4, 5, 6 to 59th St)* is between First and Second Aves. In a city packed with Irish pubs, the British Open, in the shadow of the Queensboro Bridge, fills the sports bar niche; come here for football, cricket and golf on the television.

GREG ELMS

The Manhattan skyline sparkles at night

Upper West Side (Map 7)

Raccoon Lodge (#50; ☎ 212-874-9984; 480 Amsterdam Ave; ⓜ 1, 2 to 86th St), on the corner of 83rd St, is as cool as its Downtown counterpart (see the Tribeca section earlier). Here you'll mingle with Romanian Olympians, Wisconsin prophets, local bikers and honorable men from Jamaica. There's a rocking jukebox, pool table and groovy bartenders to boot.

The Evelyn (#57; ☎ 212-724-5145; 380 Columbus Ave at 78th St; ⓜ 1, 2 to 79th St), a roomy, cellar-level space with plenty of couches, includes a classy cigar lounge and a martini list with more options than the dinner menu. A laid-back crowd frequents this spot during the week but is shoved aside by hobnobbing students on the weekend.

Dublin House (#56; ☎ 212-874-9528; 225 W 79th St; ⓜ 1, 2 to 79th St), between Broadway and Amsterdam Ave, is an old-school Irish bar that shouldn't be remarkable but is, thanks to the odd combination of old men and undergrads who patronize the place.

The Parlour (#52; ☎ 212-580-8923, 86th St; ⓜ 1, 2 to 79th St), between Broadway and West End Ave, is another good place from across the pond, where there's almost always a soccer game on and clutches of hard-drinking Scots in kilts.

Saints (#1; ☎ 212-961-0599; 992 Amsterdam Ave; ⓜ 1 to Cathedral Parkway-110th St), between Broadway and Amsterdam Ave, is a quiet spot that welcomes a mixed crowd, though it's a predominantly gay bar.

Broadway Dive (#7; ☎ 212-865-2662; 2662 Broadway; ⓜ 1 to 103rd St), between 101st and 102nd Sts, is just that, with sticky floors and a dart board. Or you might try the affiliated **Dive Bar** (#12; ☎ 212-749-4358, 732 Amsterdam Ave; ⓜ 1, 2, 3 to 96th St), between 95th and 96th Sts, which is a little more upscale, but not much.

Upper East Side (Map 7)

Subway Inn (#125; ☎ 212-223-8929; 143 E 60th St; ⓜ 4, 5, 6 to 59th St), between Lexington and Third Aves, is a classic old-geezer watering hole with cheap drinks and loads of authenticity, right down to the barmen's white shirts and thin black ties.

Mark Hotel (#80; ☎ 212-744-4300; ⓦ www.themarkhotel.com; 25 E 77th St; ⓜ 6 to 77th St; open until 1am daily) is between Madison and Fifth Aves. The quiet lounge at this hotel epitomizes Upper East Side elegance.

Kinsale Tavern (#31; ☎ 212-348-4370; 1672 Third Ave; ⓜ 6 to 96th St), between 93rd and 94th Sts, is a classic pub/sports bar that attracts rugby and soccer fanatics with its live-satellite broadcasts of European matches. This place features more than 20 beers on tap and you can smoke while enjoying the terrific $4.95 burger and fries special.

Brooklyn (Map 9)

Lauded as the 'new Manhattan,' Brooklyn is not *all* that, but it does manage to steal plenty of the Big Apple's thunder. The bar and club scene is especially fertile across the bridges.

Waterfront Ale House (#34; ☎ 718-522-3794; 155 Atlantic Ave; ⓜ M, N, R, 1, 2, 4, 5 to Court St-Borough Hall), in Cobble Hill, has cheap pints and pub grub (chili, chicken wings etc). They have 15 beers on tap and hundreds of different bottled choices. The bar features live music at night, and 'happy hour' runs from 4pm to 7pm.

Last Exit (#36; ☎ 718-222-9198; 136 Atlantic Ave; ⓜ M, N, R, 1, 2, 4, 5 to Court St-Borough Hall), also in Cobble Hill, is Atlantic Ave's contribution to the lounge craze; lizards like the fact that it's open until 4am daily.

Henry's End (#9; ☎ 718-834-1776; 44 Henry St; ⓜ A, C to High St, 1, 2 to Clark St), between Cranberry and Middagh Sts in Brooklyn Heights, has a terrific international beer selection ($5 to $8 pints) and lots of greasy bar food.

Bar Tabac (#41; ☎ 718-923-0918; 128 Smith St; ⓜ F, G to Bergen St), on the corner of Dean St in Carroll Gardens, is a cool place with an en plein air feel thanks to the French doors opening onto the sidewalk. There are pool and foosball tables here for gamers.

The Bar (#50; ☎ 718-246-9050; 280 Smith St; ⓜ F, G to Carroll St), at the corner of Sackett St in Carroll Gardens, is a cozy watering hole with a colorful interior and big windows to watch the passersby.

Excelsior *(Map 10, #11; ☎ 718-832-1599; 390 5th Ave; ⑩ F to 7th Ave)*, between Sixth and Seventh Sts in Park Slope, strikes that difficult balance between dive and destination by being cool, but not desperately so. It's a queer friendly place with a nice outside space in the back.

Great Lakes *(Map 10, #10; ☎ 718-499-3710; 284 5th Ave; ⑩ M, N, R to Union St)*, at First St in Park Slope, is a favorite local dive.

CLUBS

Like a chameleon, the New York club scene is constantly changing and defies all attempts to pin down what's hot and what's not. For the up-to-the-minute news on clubs, check out the monthly magazine *Paper* (ⓦ www.papermag.com), which costs $3.50 at newsstands. The publication also offers the very latest listings at its website. You should also keep an eye out for club and band flyers on walls and billboards while trolling the East Village – sometimes that's the best way to find out about clubs that don't have phones or advertise. Also look for the freebie *Flyer* in bars and clubs, which has good listings of New York's famous roving parties and raves that hop, skip and jump between different venues.

Don't even think about going to any of these places before 11pm, even on a weeknight; things don't truly pick up until 1am or later.

Tribeca & SoHo (Map 4)

Vinyl *(Map 3; #2; ☎ 212-343-1379; 6 Hubert St; ⑩ 1, 2 to Canal St; cover varies)* is between Hudson and Greenwich Sts in Tribeca. Vinyl hosts a raging, alcohol-free dance party called Body and Soul, from 4pm to midnight on Sunday (early hours mean you can still go out, even though it's a school night!). This popular event attracts a diverse crowd, getting its groove on to house music. Check out this hot spot during the week as well.

Double Happiness *(#237; ☎ 212-941-1282; 173 Mott St; ⑩ J, M, N, Q, R, W, Z, 6 to Canal St)*, between Broome and Grand Sts on the Chinatown fringe, is a cavernous basement retreat that remains in with the in crowd. Mingle, chat and lounge in the early hours and shake your money maker to house music later in the evening.

Culture Club *(#194; ☎ 212-243-1999; 179 Varick St; ⑩ 1, 2 to Houston St; cover $15)* is between King and Charlton Sts. Despite the name, you won't find much culture here, as this club spins '80s tunes for bridge and tunnel bachelorette parties.

Naked Lunch *(#260; ☎ 212-343-0828; 17 Thompson St at Grand St; ⑩ A, C, E, 1, 2 to Canal St; cover free-$5)*, in SoHo, is primarily a bar, but can erupt into a jamming dance party on a good night, with a mellower atmosphere than the hard-core nightclubs. The DJ mixes a good dose of hits with house and while the scene is pretty laid-back, sneakers won't cut it.

West Village & Lower East Side (Map 4)

Baktun *(#1; ☎ 212-206-1590; 418 W 14th St; ⑩ A, C, E to 14th St, L to Eighth Ave; cover $5-10)*, between Ninth Ave and Washington St, is a trippy space playing everything from underground to house to electronic. Friday night usually features a house party, while drum 'n' bass performances happen on Saturday. Monday nights are free and feature the heavy hitting, deep sounds of the Tronic Treatment party.

The Cooler *(#2; ☎ 212-229-0785; 416 W 14th St; ⑩ A, C, E to 14th St, L to Eighth Ave; cover usually $8-15)* is between Ninth Ave and Washington St. This used to be a meat locker in New York's meatpacking district but now hosts punk, rock, electronica, surf, indie rock, reggae, and hip-hop happenings. The Monday night 'free series' is a great opportunity to catch local bands *gratis*. Other nights there are better-known bands (commanding bigger covers).

Sapphire *(#173; ☎ 212-777-5153; 249 Eldridge St; ⑩ F, V to Second Ave)*, at E Houston, has survived the crowds of the mid-'90s Ludlow St boom with its hip factor intact. Come here for some steamy dancing on a tight dance floor.

Chelsea (Map 5)

Centro-Fly (#160; ☎ 212-627-7770; 45 W 21st St; Ⓜ F, V, N, R to 23rd St; cover $10-20), between Fifth and Sixth Aves, is still hopping with the hipsters, especially the GBH party, which is the place to be on Friday (visit Ⓦ www.gbh.tv for access to their reduced admission guest list). The club has different vibes in different rooms – head on back and chill to rock and new wave in Tapioca or get down to hip hop in Pinky (and attune your star radar while flitting about).

Roxy (#145; ☎ 212-627-0404; 515 W 18th St; Ⓜ A, C, E to 14th St, L to Eighth Ave; cover varies), between Tenth and Eleventh Aves, keeps the good times rolling with free-wheeling Tuesday and Wednesday roller disco. Gather a group for maximum boogey (though it can get crowded – grab a booth). Saturday is a good night to get wild to the hard house and dance tunes spinning at this old school club.

Twirl (#157; ☎ 212-691-7685; 208 W 23rd St; Ⓜ C, E, 1, 2 to 23rd St; cover up to $25), between Seventh and Eighth Aves, offers plenty of space for hard-core clubbers to strut their stuff and little niches replete with curtains for loungers to mingle and ??? This chic and trendy Chelsea hot spot plays house music and hosts special events.

True (#164; ☎ 212-254-6117; 28 E 23rd St; Ⓜ N, R, 6 to 23rd St) is between Madison Ave and Park Ave South north of Union Square. This intimate one-room dance club attracts an eclectic, older crowd that swings from the campy, kitschy Friday night party hosted by the ubiquitous Mistress Formika to the fetishy, heavy, leather Wednesday night party (the straighter dressed the arrow, the higher the cover charge).

Midtown & Times Square

Float (Map 6, #28; ☎ 212-581-0055; 240 W 52nd St; Ⓜ B, D, E to Seventh Ave, 1, 2 to 50th St; cover $15-25) is between Eighth Ave and Broadway in the Times Square area. After all this time, Float is still a popular scene among the beautiful and famous; maybe it's the lighted runway on the dance floor and leather-strutting, caged dancing

Life in the fast lane

JON DAVISON

girls. If you're worthy enough to enter (dress your best), be on the lookout for Leonardo di Caprio, Ben Affleck and the like on the 3rd floor, reserved for those with the right stuff.

Exit (Map 5, #1; ☎ 212-582-8282; 610 W 56th St; Ⓜ A, B, C, D, 1, 2 to Columbus Circle; cover $25), between Eleventh and Twelfth Aves in Midtown, is the four-floor multiplex king of all clubs (with none other than DJ Junior Vasquez stepping up to the decks once in a while). You'll get lost in the maze of theme rooms on every floor, each equipped with leopard-patterned sofas and its own DJ playing specialty music. Whatever music you're craving, it's in there somewhere. Also check out the roof garden.

Brooklyn (Map 9)

Some of the most happening parties are going down in Brooklyn these days.

Lunatarium (#1; ☎ 718-813-8404; Ⓦ www .lunatarium.com; 10 Jay St; Ⓜ F to York St, A, C to High St; cover usually $10-20), near John St in Dumbo, is open late at night. This is a good spot for its mixed crowd and house DJs spinning classic sounds like Run DMC in a gigantic warehouse space; this place also hosts funky special events like full moon parties.

Halcyon *(#46; ☎ 718-260-9299; 227 Smith St; Ⓜ F, G to Bergen St; cover free-$7)*, in Carroll Gardens, is a good concept well executed. Here you can connect on your iMac, browse and buy grooving vinyl or take a beer in the back patio, all in a funky, graffiti-tagged atmosphere among friendly locals. At night the place transforms into a dance party – try the drum 'n' bass fest on Friday or the Hangover Helper party on Sunday noon-7pm.

Luxx *(☎ 718-599-1000; 256 Grand St; Ⓜ G to Metropolitan Ave, L to Lorimer St; cover usually $5-10)*, between Roebling St and Driggs Ave in Williamsburg, hosts the block buster Berliniamsburg (a mouthful of a nickname for Williamsburg) party on Saturday. The crowd here is big, happy and largely queer.

Galapagos *(☎ 718-782-5188; 70 N 6th St; Ⓜ G to Broadway)*, between Kent and Wythe Aves, also in Williamsburg is an art and music performance space putting up hip-hop events and concerts that are often free. Oh yeah, there's a heavy aqua-interior in keeping with the archipelago theme.

No turtles, but plenty of free entertainment

GAY & LESBIAN VENUES

For a list of gay clubs and bars catering to every taste, pick up the free sheets *HX/Homo Xtra* (which has listings for her also) and *Next*, available at most restaurants and bars.

On the whole, gay drinking places tend to cater to men, but most popular gay dance clubs welcome women of all persuasions – a great trait of NY's unstraight. Most mainstream clubs (see Clubs, earlier) feature gay nights either weekly or monthly, and you're likely to find mixed crowds everywhere you go. Predominantly gay venues populate Chelsea and Greenwich Village, the traditional heart of the gay community, but things have spilled out all over town as of late.

The **Saint at Large** *(☎ 212-674-8541;* Ⓦ *www.saintatlarge.com)* brain trust was responsible for some of New York's most groundbreaking, booty shaking queer parties in the decade past and now puts on several blow out events each year, including the Black Party. This annual night of heavy frolicking for leather-clad men and their chained charges takes place each March (tickets $90), when thousands of disciplinarians and their disciples flock to the city. The entire weekend around this and other Saint at Large parties are studded with similarly themed events.

For the ladies, the longest running, most popular party is the Clit Club, now hosted at **Flamingo** *(Map 4, #24; ☎ 212-533-2861; 219 Second Ave; Ⓜ L to Third Ave)*, between 13th and 14th Streets.

SoHo & The West Village (Map 4)

Don Hill's *(#263; ☎ 212-219-2850; 511 Greenwich St; Ⓜ C, E to Spring St)*, near Spring St, is where live soul and pop give way to trashy transvestite parties with go-go boys, drag shows and anything goes.

The **Lure** *(#3; ☎ 212-741-3919; 409 W 13th St; Ⓜ A, C, E to 14th St, L to Eighth Ave)*, near Ninth Ave, is a leather bar with all kinds of enforcement efforts, including a dress code: leather, latex, denim or uniform. The particularly naughty entertainment on Wednesday night might include body painting, piercing, tattooing and other stuff Mom shouldn't know about.

ANGUS OBORN

Hell (#5; ☎ 212-727-1666; 59 Gansevoort St; Ⓜ A, C, E to 14th St, L to Eighth Ave), between Greenwich and Washington Sts, is a fiendish, yet friendly crowd. Check out a weeknight when the locals outnumber the rubberneckers and there's happy grooving in this club's deep, red depths.

Monster (#69; ☎ 212-924-3558; 80 Grove St; Ⓜ 1, 2 to Christopher St-Sheridan Sq), at the corner of W 4th St, is a gay old place. Downstairs picante go-go boys gyrate round the dance floor, while upstairs the better-heeled harangue the piano man to play their favorite *Cabaret* tunes.

Henrietta Hudson (#156; ☎ 212-924-3347; 438 Hudson St; Ⓜ 1, 2 to Christopher St-Sheridan Sq; open to 4am nightly), near Morton St, is a spacious lesbian dive bar where you can play pool or dance to DJ music into the wee hours. The club recently launched its Back Room Booty Friday night party with go-go girls.

Rubyfruit (#64; ☎ 212-929-3343; 531 Hudson St; Ⓜ 1, 2 to Christopher St-Sheridan Sq), near W 10th St, is a civilized spot with a welcoming regular crowd frequented by older lesbians. Weekend entertainment runs from piano-bar schmaltz to '50s bebop. Dinner is served every night (stick to the parlor menu and save the budget for drinks).

Crazy Nanny's (#157; ☎ 212-929-8356; 21 Seventh Ave; Ⓜ 1, 2 to Houston St), near Leroy St, brings out the wild women to play tournament pool on Monday, karaoke on Wednesday and Sunday and a drag show on Thursday. This brash bar gets crowded and rowdy on weekends.

Marie's Crisis (#68; ☎ 212-243-9323; 59 Grove St; Ⓜ 1, 2 to Christopher St-Sheridan Sq), near Seventh Ave, caters mostly to the older fellas and their charges. This wonderful tavern features piano playing and loud renditions of show tunes that often involve the vocal stylings of everyone in the place – all of them, most out of tune.

East Village (Map 4)

The Cock (#28; ☎ 212-777-6254; 188 Ave A; Ⓜ L to First Ave), near E 12th St, is just this side of sleazy in a queenie rock 'n' roll kinda way – leather-clad boys with props, that kind of thing. This boozy, cruisey club with a back room hosts wild Saturday night through-the-roof parties with DJs and drag queens.

Urge (#125; ☎ 212-533-5757; 32 Second Ave; Ⓜ F, V to Second Ave; open until 4am daily), near E 2nd St, is a new club bringing a bit of fashionable Chelsea to the artsy East Village and mixing them up in a fun, lounge atmosphere for the guys, though women are welcome.

Meow Mix (#177; ☎ 212-254-0688; 269 E Houston St; Ⓜ F, V to Second Ave), between Clinton and Suffolk Sts, is a prime lesbian hang-out in the East Village that's been going strong for years. It attracts a youthful crowd with live indie girl rock. Happy hours, open jams and DJs all help to get the joint moving and grooving. Men are welcome, but usually have to pay a bit extra to get in.

Chelsea (Map 5)

SBNY (#194; ☎ 212-691-0073; 50 W 17th St at Sixth Ave; Ⓜ L to Sixth Ave, F, V to 14th St) is the same old Splash Bar, despite the new name. It's still boy-man chic, cruisey, fun and boozy, though with a bigger, better dance floor. The two-for-one happy hour before 8pm daily is a good deal.

Barracuda (#156; ☎ 212-645-8613; 275 W 22nd St; Ⓜ C, E, 1, 2 to 23rd St), between Seventh and Eighth Aves, is ruby red and beckoning (there's no sign, but look for the glowing red globes). Barracuda is dimly lit up front; for your more intimate exchanges there's a smoky back lounge where you can sink into the chairs and chat for a while. Ladies are welcome here.

xl (#202; ☎ 212-995-1400; 357 W 16th St; Ⓜ A, C, E to 14th St, L to Eighth Ave), between Eighth and Ninth Aves, is a new, hi-tech Chelsea favorite with the handsome set. Don't miss the bathroom, though you might miss the subtle signage; look for the velvet ropes.

ROCK

Once in awhile 'super groups' and superstar singers play smaller venues in the big city, but you have to keep your ears real close to the ground to be able to procure such a platinum ticket. What you will catch without a worry are up-and-coming artists and lesser-known bands, many of whom know how to put on a better show in intimate venues than big-name stars who play one huge concert after another. Two fantastic venues outside New York City for rock, pop and soul acts are **Jones Beach** (summer only) and the **Stephen Talkhouse**, both on Long Island (see the Excursions chapter for details).

Mercury Lounge (Map 4, #176; ☎ 212-260-4700; 217 E Houston St; ◐ F, V to Second Ave; cover usually $10-15), near Essex St on the Lower East Side, sometimes turns up big names (eg, Lou Reed or John Popper), but almost always has something worth hearing. This intimate, comfy venue with tables and ample dance space facing the riser stage, has a quality sound system – a great combination for the local and touring indie groups and their audience.

Arlene Grocery (Map 4, #215; ☎ 212-358-1633; 95 Stanton St; ◐ F, V to Second Ave), near Orchard St, is a convenience-store-turned-club that was just pre-curve enough of the LES's '90s explosion to entitle it to a snooty vibe. The one-room hothouse incubates local talent, with great live shows for free every night; the beer is cheap too.

Bowery Ballroom (Map 4, #231; ☎ 212-533-2111; 6 Delancey St; ◐ J, M to Bowery; tickets $12-20), at Bowery, is a terrific venue. The size, sound and feel are all just right for seeing acts like Jonathan Richman, They Might Be Giants, Low and other bands demanding audience attention.

Luna Lounge (Map 4, #178; ☎ 212-260-2323; 171 Ludlow St; ◐ F, V to Second Ave), near Stanton St on the Lower East Side, hosts garage bands, local musicians and up-and-coming indie darlings in its small back room. Since there's never a cover charge at this mellow bar, it's worth poking your head in to check out the night's act.

Bottom Line (Map 4, #140; ☎ 212-228-6300; 15 W 4th St; ◐ 6 to Astor Pl) is near Mercer St in the Village. All sorts of live acts (from big-ish to bygone) perform in this huge cabaret-style music hall. There are usually two sets a night at 7:30pm and 10:30pm by whatever artist or group is on the bill.

CBGB (Map 4, #127; ☎ 212-982-4052; 315 Bowery; ◐ 6 to Bleecker St), between E 1st and 2nd Sts in the East Village, is still going strong after nearly three decades. The name stands for 'Country, Bluegrass and Blues,' but since the mid '70s, the place has heard more rock than anything else. Some of the luminaries who've sweated through legendary sets here include Debbie Harry, Talking Heads and the B52s. Today, the bands experiment with rock, Motown, thrash and everything in between. Also here is **CBGBs Downstairs Lounge**, with quality jazz on Sunday ($7 to $10).

Brownie's (Map 4, #30; ☎ 212-420-8392; 169 Avenue A; ◐ L to First Ave, 6 to Astor Pl; cover $5-20), between 10th and 11th Sts, is the torchbearer of cutting edge rock 'n' roll in the East Village. From legends like the Bush Tetras to the newest indie acts, you can see it here.

Continental (Map 4, #45; ☎ 212-529-6924; 25 Third Ave; ◐ N, R to 8th St-NYU, 6 to Astor Pl), off St Marks Pl, is famous for its cheap drink specials and unannounced gigs by the likes of Iggy Pop and Jakob Dylan. This club built its following by not charging a cover for quality rock 'n roll and this is oftentimes the case still.

Irving Plaza (Map 5, #177; recorded info ☎ 212-777-1224; 17 Irving Pl; ◐ L, N, Q, R, W, 4, 5, 6 to Union Sq), near E 15th St in the Union Square area, is probably the best club of its size hosting mainstream indie acts like Cracker and Pavement. You might also catch smoother stuff here like the John Scofield Band or, at the other end of the spectrum, Tesla.

Madison Square Garden (Map 5; ☎ 212-465-6741, Ⓦ www.thegarden.com; Seventh Ave at W 33rd St; ◐ 1, 2, 3 to 34th St-Penn Station), above Penn Station in Midtown is known as 'the world's most famous arena' and seeing blue-chip rock, pop and rap here, with 19,000 other energized fans, is unforgettable and worth the ticket prices.

Radio City Music Hall *(Map 5; ☎ 212-247-4777; Sixth Ave at W 51st St; ⓜ B, D, F, V to 47th-50th Sts-Rockefeller Center)*, in Midtown, hosts the likes of Los Van Van from Havana and PJ Harvey from the British sticks, while the **Beacon Theater** *(Map 7, #62; ☎ 212-496-7070; 2124 Broadway; ⓜ 1, 2, 3 to 72nd St)* on the Upper West Side between W 74th and 75th Sts has the same sort of vibe, but usually hosts stuff deeper in the pocket like George Clinton and the Parliament Funkadelic or the Funky Meters. Either venue can deliver a treat of a show, though theater seating in both often inhibits dancing.

JAZZ & BLUES

The West Village is a veritable jazz ghetto, with many clubs offering long jams, cheap cover charges and a hot buffet of all flavors of jazz. Uptown is still the granddaddy of jazz joints though, so old-school enthusiasts might want to hop the 1 or 9 up to Harlem.

Knitting Factory *(Map 3, #29; ☎ 212-219-3055; 74 Leonard St; ⓜ 1, 2 to Franklin St)*, between Church St and Broadway in Tribeca, has a long and influential history in the realm of New York jazz, folk and experimental music, spoken word and performance. Its four performance spaces host all manner of music, from cosmic space jazz to Tokyo shock rock and the occasional traditional gig (the Preservation Hall Jazz Band has taken the stage here), plus rock and hip-hop. Listen to bands on the main floor or the balcony or lounge in the bar downstairs.

ANGUS OBORN

The one thing you won't find here is wool!

Chicago B.L.U.E.S *(Map 4, #4; ☎ 212-924-9755; 73 Eighth Ave at W 14th St; ⓜ A, C, E to 14th St, L to Eighth Ave)* is a venue in the West Village that hosts visiting blues masters nightly. The up-and-coming also perform at this none-too-flashy club, and if you've got a harmonica in your pocket, you can jump in for Monday night's blues jam.

Village Vanguard *(Map 4, #60; ☎ 212-255-4037; 178 Seventh Ave at W 11th St; ⓜ 1, 2 to Christopher St-Sheridan Sq; cover $15-20)*, a basement-level venue in the West Village, may be the world's most prestigious jazz club; it has hosted literally every major star of the past 50 years. There's a two-drink minimum.

Sweet Basil in the West Village shut its doors in April 2001, but look for this venerable club's new incarnation as **Sweet Rhythms**.

Smalls *(Map 4, #72; ☎ 212-929-7565; 183 W 10th St; ⓜ 1, 2 to Christopher St-Sheridan Sq; cover Mon-Fri/Sat $10/20)* is a sliver of a lit doorway near Seventh Ave that's easy to miss, but don't. This place hosts smoking 10½-hour jazz marathons every night from 10pm to 8:30am. Descend the stairs and grab a couch, pop whatever beverage of choice you've brought along (Small's has no liquor license, meaning it's all ages, adding to the nice mix on stage and in the audience) and sit back for quality jazz, from straight ahead to far out.

Blue Note *(Map 4, #147; ☎ 212-475-8592; 131 W 3rd St; ⓜ A, C, E, F, V, S to W 4th St)*, near Sixth Ave in the Village, is by far the most famous (and expensive) jazz club. You might pay as much as $60 to hear big stars play short sets for a throng of tourists here.

55 Bar *(Map 4, #73; ☎ 212-929-9883; 55 Christopher St; ⓜ 1, 2 to Christopher St-Sheridan Sq; cover $3-15)*, near Seventh Ave, is an authentic smoky West Village joint, hosting jazz, blues and fusion nightly, with performances by first-rate artists-in-residence and stars just passing through. Cover charges range from next-to-nothing to about $15 (but that includes two drinks).

Fez *(Map 4, #138; ☎ 212-533-2680; 380 Lafayette St; ⓜ 6 to Bleecker St)*, near E 3rd St, is below the Time Cafe, in the East Village.

It hosts the popular Mingus Big Band ($18 cover) every Thursday. On other nights you can catch drag shows, readings of novels in progress or rock concerts.

Iridium *(Map 6, #30; ☎ 212-582-2121; 1650 Broadway;* Ⓜ *1, 2 to 50th St)*, on the corner of W 51st St, just moved to this location from up Lincoln Center way. The tables are really tight, but the sound is good and the sight lines fairly clear. High-quality, big-ticket traditional jazz acts play two sets a night from Sunday to Thursday, and three sets on weekends. Monday night is reserved for the talented and hilarious Les Paul trio, as it has for the past several decades. There's also a Sunday jazz brunch here ($18.95).

Cleopatra's Needle *(Map 7, #18; ☎ 212-769-6969; 2485 Broadway;* Ⓜ *1, 2, 3 to 96th St)*, between W 92nd and 93rd Sts, is a great addition to the Uptown jazz scene. Late-night and open-mic jams are a hallmark and the music goes until 4am. Some of the best band views are from the bar, where you can take a pint on tap and nosh on Mediterranean-influenced fare; there's never a cover, but mind the $10 drink and/or food minimum.

Lenox Lounge *(Map 8, #30; ☎ 212-427-0253; 288 Malcolm X Blvd;* Ⓜ *2, 3 to 125th St; cover $5-20)* is between W 124th and 125th Sts. The Lounge is an old favorite of local jazz cats and has recently blipped onto the radar of farther flung enthusiasts (especially Japanese transplants and visitors). Don't miss the luxe Zebra Room in the back.

St Nick's Pub *(Map 8, #12; ☎ 212-283-9728; 773 St Nicholas Ave;* Ⓜ *A, B, C, D to 145th St)*, at 149th St, is an amazing place to hear the raw jazz created by musicians for musicians. Monday nights feature an open jam until 12:30am when axe- and horn-toting tourists take up the creative gauntlet. Later in the evening, big-name jazz cats come from their bigger gigs around town, keeping it real and live here at the Pub.

Showman's *(Map 8, #35; ☎ 212-864-8941; 375 W 125th St;* Ⓜ *A, B, C, D to 125th St)*, between Morningside and St Nicholas Aves, features jazz combos and R&B vocalists. There are three nightly shows weekdays, two on weekends.

Small by name, big on jazz

Lickety Split *(Map 8, #18; ☎ 212-283-9093; 2361 Adam Clayton Powell Jr Blvd;* Ⓜ *2, 3 to 135th St)*, near W 139th St, specializes in Caribbean bands.

FOLK & WORLD MUSIC

Fast Folk Cafe *(Map 3, #32; ☎ 212-274-1636; 41 N Moore St;* Ⓜ *1, 2 to Franklin St)*, between Varick and Hudson Sts in Tribeca, features acoustic music every weekend.

SOBs *(Map 4, #193; ☎ 212-243-4940; 204 Varick St;* Ⓜ *1, 2 to Houston St)* is between King and Houston Sts on the SoHo fringe. SOBs stands for Sounds of Brazil, but this spot isn't limited to samba: you can shake it to Afro-Cuban music, salsa and reggae, both live and on the turntable. SOBs hosts dinner shows nightly but it doesn't really start jumping until 2am.

World Music Institute *(☎ 212-545-7536;* Ⓦ *www.worldmusicinstitute.org)* brings Algerian folk singers, Brazilian chanteuses, Zairean congo players and other international artists to various venues around town.

Back Fence *(Map 4, #163; ☎ 212-475-9221; 155 Bleecker St;* Ⓜ *A, C, E, F, V, S to W 4th St)*, between MacDougal and Sullivan Sts, is a laid-back venue in the center of Greenwich Village. It offers folk and blues during the week, classic rock on weekends. Plenty of college students congregate here.

CLASSICAL MUSIC

New York Philharmonic (Map 7; ☎ 212-875-5000; ⓦ www.newyorkphilharmonic.org; ⓜ 1, 2 to 66th St-Lincoln Center; tickets $15-70) was getting rave reviews under the direction of German-born conductor Kurt Masur, but after 11 seasons, he conducted his final performance in 2002. You can still expect the highest standards here at the classic repertoire that continues to define the Philharmonic. Tickets can be purchased through **Center Charge** (☎ 212-721-6500). All concerts take place at Lincoln Center's **Avery Fisher Hall** (Map 7; 10 Lincoln Center Plaza, Broadway at W 64th St).

Chamber Music Society of Lincoln Center (Map 7; ☎ 212-875-5050; ⓜ 1, 2 to 66th St-Lincoln Center) ranks as the foremost chamber music ensemble in the country. Its main concert season takes place in early autumn at Lincoln Center's **Alice Tully Hall** (Map 7; ☎ 212-721-6500), which is also home to the American Symphony Orchestra and the Little Orchestra Society.

Carnegie Hall (Map 6; ☎ 212-247-7800; ⓦ www.carnegiehall.org; 154 W 57th St at Seventh Ave; ⓜ N, R, Q, W to 57th St; tickets for nonsubscription events from $12) hosts visiting philharmonics and the New York Pops orchestra. Since 1891, the historic performance hall has hosted the likes of Tchaikovsky, Mahler and Prokofiev.

Symphony Space (Map 7, #16; ☎ 212-864-5400; 2537 Broadway at W 95th St; ⓜ 1, 2, 3 to 96th St), has just had a major facelift and is drawing crowds to its new, innovative environs. Not limited to classical music, the Symphony Space is fostering a 'multi-culti' persona by also presenting hip hop, jazz, world music and dance performances. There's also a healthy dose of children's programming here, much of it free.

The city's more intimate venues for classical music include the **Merkin Concert Hall** (Map 7, #98; ☎ 212-501-3330; 129 W 67th St; ⓜ 1, 2 to 66th St-Lincoln Center), between Broadway and Amsterdam Ave on the Upper West Side, which seats 451; and **Town Hall** (Map 6, #103; ☎ 212-840-2824; ⓦ www.the-townhall-nyc.org; 123 W 43rd St; ⓜ B, D, F, V to 42nd St), near Sixth Ave in Times Square.

OPERA

Metropolitan Opera (Map 7; ☎ 212-362-6000; ⓦ www.metopera.org; ⓜ 1, 2 to 66th St Lincoln Center; tickets for center orchestra seats from $155, upper balcony seats $55, standing-room tickets $12-16), New York's premier opera company, offers a spectacular mixture of classics and premieres. It's nearly impossible to get into the first few performances of operas that feature such big stars as Jessye Norman and Plácido Domingo, but once the B-team moves in, tickets become available. The season runs from September to April in the company's namesake **Metropolitan Opera House** (Map 7; cnr W 64th St & Amsterdam Ave). Standing-room tickets are one of NY's greatest bargains. They go on sale at 10am on Saturday for the following week's performances. For a season schedule, visit the website.

New York City Opera (Map 7; ☎ 212-870-5630; ⓦ www.nycopera.com; ⓜ 1, 2 to 66th St-Lincoln Center; tickets from $25) is a more daring and lower-cost company that performs new works, neglected operas and revitalized old standards in the Philip Johnson–designed **New York State Theater** (Map 7; ☎ 212-870-5570) at Lincoln Center. The split season runs for a few weeks in early autumn and again in early to late spring.

DANCE

New York is home to more than half a dozen world-famous dance companies. For season schedules of the following companies, visit their websites.

New York City Ballet (☎ 212-870-5570; ⓦ www.nycballet.com; ⓜ 1, 2 to 66th St-Lincoln Center), established by Lincoln Kirstein and George Balanchine in 1948, features a varied season of premieres and revivals, always including a production of The Nutcracker during the Christmas holidays. The company performs at the 2755-seat **New York State Theater** (Map 7; Broadway at W 63rd St; tickets $28-66), in Lincoln Center on the Upper West Side. Student-rush tickets ($10) are made available online and at the box office on the day of the performance; you must be under 29 and a full-time high school or university student. For more information call the student-rush hotline (☎ 212-870-7766).

American Ballet Theatre *(Map 7; ☎ 212-477-3030; ⓦ www.abt.org; ⓜ 1, 2 to 66th St-Lincoln Center; tickets $20-125)* presents its largely classical season during the late spring and summer at the **Metropolitan Opera House** *(Map 7)* at Lincoln Center.

City Center *(Map 6, #11; ☎ 212-581-1212; ⓦ www.citycenter.org; 131 W 55th St; ⓜ N, R, Q, W to 57th St)*, between Sixth and Seventh Aves in Midtown, hosts the energized and original **Alvin Ailey American Dance Theater** *(☎ 212-767-0590; ⓦ www .alvinailey.org)* every December, plus a steady stream of engagements by renowned companies like the premier classical company, the **Dance Theatre of Harlem** *(Map 8, #9; ☎ 212-690-2800; ⓦ www.dancetheatre ofharlem.org; 466 W 152nd St; ⓜ C to 155th St)*, between Amsterdam and Convent Aves, and **American Ballet Theatre** (see above). The box office is on 55th St between Sixth and Seventh Aves.

Joyce Theater *(Map 5, #199; ☎ 212-242-0800; ⓦ www.joyce.org; 175 Eighth Ave at W 19th St; ⓜ A, C, E to 14th St, L to Eighth Ave; tickets around $35)*, an offbeat, intimate venue in Chelsea, offers noncommercial companies the chance to shine. The Merce Cunningham and Pilabolus dance companies make annual appearances at this renovated cinema, which seats 470.

CINEMAS

Cinemophiles can sate any and all cravings here in New York, from the latest Japanese animation import to versions of saucy European films banned elsewhere in the US. While it might seem strange to come to New York City to go to the movies, a lot of New Yorkers consider film to be just as evolved an art form as opera or Broadway drama. Besides, nothing beats an air-conditioned movie theater in the thick of the dog days of summer here, which have been known to perpetuate murderous tendencies.

Even though movie tickets cost at least $10, long lines on evenings and weekends are not uncommon – bearing testament to New Yorkers' devotion to film and just how much disposable income is flying around here; unfortunately, the 'bargain matinee' known in the rest of the country is virtually unheard of in New York, though some art houses still show double features. Most first-run films sell out a half hour early on date nights (Friday and Saturday). You're likely to have to stand in one line to buy a ticket and another to get into the theater, but you can avoid one of these lines (or sold out showings) by calling ☎ 212-777-FILM (3456) or visiting ⓦ www.moviefone.com and prepaying for the movie of your choice for an additional $1-per-ticket charge.

Independent & Revival Theaters

Film Forum *(Map 4, #192; ☎ 212-727-8110; 209 W Houston St; ⓜ 1, 2 to Houston St)*, between Varick St and Sixth Ave, is a three-screen cinema in SoHo featuring independent films, revivals and career retrospectives.

Angelika Film Center *(Map 4, #168; ☎ 212-995-2000; 18 W Houston St; ⓜ F, V, S, to Broadway-Lafayette St)*, near Mercer St in the Village, specializes in foreign and independent films and is often crowded for it. The roomy café here serves gourmet sweet treats. If you've time to kill before the screening, check out the Stanford White–designed beaux-arts building that houses Angelika. Called the Cable Building (the miles of cable here moved the country's first and last cable cars ever installed), it features a dainty oval window and caryatids on its Broadway facade.

Screening Room *(Map 3, #3; ☎ 212-334-2100; 54 Varick St; ⓜ 1, 2 to Canal St)*, on the corner of Laight, is a cozy place to take your honey for a movie and a meal at the attached restaurant. Programming includes funky first runs, art flicks and the occasional classic.

Anthology Film Archives *(Map 4, #126; ☎ 212-505-5181; 32 Second Ave; ⓜ F, V to Second Ave)*, near E 2nd St in the East Village, screens low-budget European and fringe works, plus revives classics such as *From Here to Eternity* and puts on festivals like the 'World of Werner.' Ticket prices are just $8/5 for adult/student and senior.

Walter Reade Theater *(Map 7; ☎ 212-875-5600; 165 W 65th St; ⓜ 1, 2 to 66th*

St-Lincoln Center), at Lincoln Center, boasts wide, screening room–style seats. The New York Film Festival take place here every September. At other times of the year, you can see independent films, career retrospectives and themed series.

Lincoln Plaza Cinemas *(Map 7, #103;* ☎ *212-757-2280; Broadway;* Ⓜ *A, B, C, D, 1, 2 to 59th St-Columbus Circle)*, near W 62nd St, is a six-screen venue that is the place to go for artsy independent films on the Upper West Side.

Other places worth checking out for various independent and foreign films include: The **Leonard Nimoy Thalia** *(Map 7 #16;* ☎ *212-864-1414; 2537 Broadway;* Ⓜ *1, 2, 3 to 96th St)*, at Symphony Space on the corner of W 95th St, which screens quality double features ($9); **Cinema Classics** *(Map 4, #27;* ☎ *212-677-5368; 332 E 12th St;* Ⓜ *L to First Ave)*, between First Ave and Ave A, where you can catch the likes of *Modern Times* or the *Manchurian Candidate* for a mere $6; and the oldie but goodie **Cinema**

Village *(Map 4, #51;* ☎ *212-924-3363; 22 E 12th St;* Ⓜ *L, N, Q, R, W, 4, 5, 6 to 14th St-Union Sq)*, between Fifth Ave and University Place.

Chain & Mainstream Theaters

Landmark Sunshine Cinemas *(Map 4, #172;* ☎ *212-358-7709; 143 East Houston St;* Ⓜ *F, V to Second Ave)*, next to Yonah Shimmel Bakery on the Lower East Side, shows foreign and mainstream art films and is a welcome addition to the neighborhood.

Loews 42nd St E–Walk Theater *(Map 6, #112;* ☎ *212-505-6397; 42nd St;* Ⓜ *N, Q, R, S, W, 1, 2, 3, 7 to Times Sq)*, between Broadway and Eighth Ave, is a massive, 13-screen theater in Times Square. This theater dishes all the latest Hollywood pabulum in state-of-the-art facilities.

Sony Theaters Lincoln Square *(Map 7, #96;* ☎ *212-336-5000; Broadway & W 68th St;* Ⓜ *1, 2, 3 to 72nd St)*, on the Upper West Side, includes a 3D Imax theater and 12 large screens that play first-run features.

Culture Fixes in the Outer Boroughs

If you should find yourself a bridge or tunnel away from Carnegie Hall and Lincoln Center, don't despair. Brooklyn boasts its own array of classical music offerings. The prime spot for high culture in the outer boroughs is the **Brooklyn Academy of Music** *(Map 9;* ☎ *718-636-4100;* Ⓦ *www .bam.org; 30 Lafayette Ave;* Ⓜ *M, N, Q, R, W, 1, 2, 4 to Atlantic Ave)* which hosts concerts, operas, dances and plays year-round in the Majestic Theater and the Brooklyn Opera House. The shows here range from formal Shakespeare productions to avant-garde music concerts. The Rose Cinema is also here, showing art flicks. For a schedule of events, visit the website.

Most definitely try **St Ann's Warehouse** *(Map 9, #4;* ☎ *718-858-2424; 38 Water St;* Ⓜ *A, C to High St, F to York St)*, in Dumbo, which features cutting-edge music, drama and dance performances for about $25.

The chamber and classical music program **Bargemusic** *(*☎ *718-624-4061;* Ⓜ *A, C to High St)*, at Fulton Landing, takes place on a floating barge in the East River during the summer.

The **Brooklyn Center for the Performing Arts** *(Map 1;* ☎ *718-951-4500;* Ⓦ *www.brooklyn center.com; 2900 Campus Rd;* Ⓜ *2, 5 to Brooklyn College-Flatbush Ave; tickets $20-30)*, at Hillel Place on the Brooklyn College campus, hosts music headliners like Santana and Luciano Pavarotti and dance performances by the likes of the Paul Taylor Dance Company.

With the temporary relocation (until 2005) of MoMA to Long Island City in Queens, this area is the newest culture vulture destination. Not only can you see some of the world's greatest modern art at MoMA QNS, you can get a sculpture fix at the Isamu Noguchi Garden Museum, see some truly avant garde works at PS 1 Contemporary Art Center or take a picnic at the en plein air Socrates Sculpture Park close by (see the Things to See & Do chapter for details).

Sony also operates other multiplexes throughout Manhattan, as does **Cineplex Odeon** (☎ 212-505-2463).

Brooklyn (Map 9)

Rose Cinema (☎ 718-623-2770; 30 Lafayette Ave; Ⓜ Q, 1, 2, 4, 5 to Atlantic Ave), in Fort Greene at the Brooklyn Academy of Music, shows independent and foreign films.

Brooklyn Heights Cinemas (#11; ☎ 718-369-0838; cnr Henry & Orange Sts; Ⓜ A, C to High St, 1, 2 to Clark St), shows better offbeat films and has a bar-cum-café.

For first run and mainstream films, check out **United Artists Cinema** (#27; cnr State & Court Sts), in Cobble Hill, or **Clearview Cobble Hill Cinemas** (#43; ☎ 718-596-9113; cnr Court & Butler Sts), also in Cobble Hill. You can take the M, N, R, 1, 2, 4 or 5 train to Court St-Borough Hall for either of these.

COMEDY CLUBS

Surf Reality (Map 4, #214; ☎ 212-673-4182; 2nd fl, 172 Allen St; Ⓜ F, V to Second Ave; tickets from $3) is between Stanton and Rivington Sts. This comedy cave has wild and wooly nightly shows – none of your Mama's hahas here. Sunday night is open mic.

Luna Lounge (Map 4, #178; ☎ 212-260-2323; Ⓦ www.lunalounge.com; 171 Ludlow St; Ⓜ F, V to Second Ave) is near Stanton St. Edgier comedians like Janeane Garofalo and Colin Quinn try out their stuff at this venue's free Monday night Eating It comedy showcase. But you never know who you'll see, since the comedians aren't announced ahead of time. (On other nights of the week, the Luna Lounge features live music. See Rock, earlier in the chapter.)

Comedy Cellar (Map 4, #143; ☎ 212-254-3480; Ⓦ www.comedycellar.com; 117 MacDougal St; Ⓜ A, C, E, F, V, S to W 4th St; tickets $10-12), between 3rd and Bleecker Sts, is a long-established basement club in Greenwich Village featuring mainstream material. This spot showcases high-profile comics (eg, Jon Lovitz and Jon Stewart), a number of whom like to make surprise visits. Drop-ins are of the star-studded variety, including Robin Williams, Jerry Seinfeld and Chris Rock. There's a two-drink minimum.

Caroline's on Broadway (Map 6, #36; ☎ 212-757-4100; 1626 Broadway; Ⓜ N, R W, to 49th St, 1, 2 to 50th St; tickets weekdays/weekends from $15/17), near W 50th St, is a big and bright venue on Broadway in Times Square. Comedy specials are frequently filmed here, reflected by the caliber of the talent. There's a two-drink minimum.

Chicago City Limits (Map 7, #129; ☎ 212-888-5233; 1105 First Ave at E 61st St; Ⓜ N, R, W to Lexington Ave, 4, 5, 6 to 59th St; tickets $20, with college ID $15), on the Upper East Side, features a comedy revue that has performed over 7500 shows and is acclaimed for its improvisational comedy style.

SPECTATOR SPORTS
Baseball

The first baseball game ever played took place in Hoboken, across the Hudson River, and despite the grumbling of uppity Bo Sox fans, New York *is* a baseball town. While the rest of the world (and especially Mets fans) loves to hate the world champion Yankees, the baseball scene here delivers no matter who you root for (Go Yanks!). Tickets can be hard to score, but since there are a combined 162 regular season home games (April to October) between the Mets and the Yankees, chances are you can catch a game. Face value ticket prices range from $8 to $55, but you'll incur usurious 'processing' fees if you buy them anywhere but at the stadium (the exception is the Yankee Clubhouse at the South St Seaport). A good place to hunt for tickets is Craig's List (Ⓦ www.craigslist .com), where locals unload their unwanted seats, sometimes quite cheaply.

New York Mets (Map 12; ☎ 718-507-8499; Ⓦ www.mets.com; Ⓜ 7 to Willets Point-Shea Stadium), a National League team, play in windswept old **Shea Stadium** (Map 12) in Flushing Meadows, Queens; it's a 40-minute journey by subway from Midtown.

New York Yankees (Map 13, #18; ☎ 718-293-6000; Ⓦ www.yankees.com; Ⓜ B, D, 4 to 161st St-Yankee Stadium), an American League team, play at their legendary namesake stadium in the South Bronx, just 15 minutes from Midtown by subway.

ANGUS OBORN

You can't visit New York without watching a Mets versus Yankees game

The two crosstown rivals play a limited number of regular season inter-league games and of course, every New Yorker always prays for another Subway Series, when the two teams meet in the World Series – as they did for the first time since 1956 in 2000. Night games usually start at 7:30pm, while day games begin at 1pm. (For more on the stadiums, see the Queens and Bronx sections of the Things to See & Do chapter.)

The newest team in New York baseball is the **Brooklyn Cyclones** (Map 1; ☎ 718-449-8497, Ⓦ www.brooklyncyclones.com; Ⓜ F, Q, W to Stillwell Ave), the Mets farm team that plays summer ball in a brand new stadium on Surf Ave in Coney Island. Tickets top out at $10.

Basketball & Hockey

New York's high-profile basketball and hockey teams play in the famous 19,000-seat **Madison Square Garden** (Map 5; Seventh Ave at 33rd St; Ⓜ 1, 2, 3 to 34th St-Penn Station) from early fall until early summer. The NBA **New York Knicks** (☎ 212-465-6741) and the NHL **New York Rangers** (☎ 212-465-6741) sell a huge number of season tickets, so visitors must buy individual game tickets through TicketMaster, Madison Square Garden or deal with the many scalpers who converge on the area on game nights.

Buying tickets from scalpers used to be a wicked expensive proposition, but since the Knicks suck big time as of late (Oh, Coach Van Gundy, come back!!), you can sidle up to the Garden ten minutes before tip time and score $100 seats for $30 in many instances. No matter the team, when dealing with scalpers, the best strategy is to wait until after the 7:30pm game time, when prices drop. For big games, you'll pay a premium on tickets that already have a face value of $200 or more. A note of warning: Scalping is technically illegal and you'll want to inspect your tickets carefully to avoid getting scammed.

While New York teams swirl in the toilet, New Jersey franchises are on the ascendancy. The NBA **New Jersey Nets** (☎ 800-765-6387; Ⓦ www.nba.com/nets; tickets $10-80) and the NHL **New Jersey Devils** (☎ 800-653-3845; Ⓦ www.newjerseydevils.com) play at **Continental Airlines Arena** in the **Meadowlands Sports Complex** (Route 120, East Rutherford); both of these teams roared into the 2002 postseason. Though it's a bear to get out to Jersey, the games are usually exciting. You can buy tickets for both through TicketMaster (☎ 212-307-7171; Ⓦ www.ticketmaster.com). To reach the complex, take the NJ Turnpike to the Meadowlands exit (exit 16W). Public buses also run from the Port Authority Bus Terminal in Midtown ($6.50/8 roundtrip if purchased at the ticket window/on the bus).

We love Title IX (the legislation that commanded collegiate sports programs to pour as many resources into women's sports as men's) and we love the WNBA. While women's professional basketball is an entirely different bird from men's (and takes some getting used to), the **New York Liberty** (☎ 212-465-6741) is a hot ticket. Come catch the women hooping it up from Memorial Day to Labor Day at Madison Square Garden.

Football

Ironically, New York's two football teams both play home games in New Jersey. The **New York Giants** (☎ 201-935-8111, tickets 201-935-8222; W www.giants.com) and the **New York Jets** (☎ 516-560-8200) share New Jersey's **Meadowlands Sports Complex** (Route 120, East Rutherford) from August to December; they play on alternate weekends, but tickets are expensive and scarce. In reality, football is better on TV, but if you want the hot breath of rabid fans breathing down your neck on third down, try scalping tickets on game day or visit W www.craigslist.com.

Tennis

USTA National Tennis Center (Map 12, #18; ☎ 718-760-6200; ⑩ 7 to Willets Point-Shea Stadium), in Flushing Meadows–Corona Park in Queens, is the venue for the **US Open** (W www.usopen.org), the year's final Grand Slam event, which takes place over two weeks at the end of August (often including Labor Day weekend). Corporations buy up blocks of seats for the Open, so you might have to resort to scalpers for tickets to the big matches. As you approach the main court (Arthur Ashe Stadium), you'll find a gauntlet of hawkers offering tickets at outrageous prices. For early-round or doubles matches, try the box office.

The USTA rents out courts to amateurs year-round for $25 an hour and up. With the exception of US Open weeks, you play on the same courts the pros use for practise.

Horse Racing

Aqueduct Racetrack (☎ 718-641-4700; ⑩ A to Aqueduct), in Brooklyn, hosts the winter racing season (November to May). When Off Track Betting (OTB) offices were established in the 1970s, turnstile figures at racetracks in the New York area plummeted. Now the 'Sport of Kings' is the sport of cigar-smoking retirees.

Belmont Park (☎ 718-641-4700), just beyond the Queens border in Nassau County, is the venue for the Belmont Stakes, the third leg of thoroughbred racing's Triple Crown, which takes place in early June. A special **Long Island Rail Road train** (☎ 718-217-5477; W www.lirr.org) leaves Penn Station for Belmont several times each racing day and costs $9.50 roundtrip.

Meadowlands Racetrack (☎ 201-935-8500; Route 120, East Rutherford), in New Jersey, features harness racing from late December to August and thoroughbred racing from Labor Day to early December.

Shopping

If you can't get it in New York, you probably can't get it, period. Virtually all neighborhoods in the city have retail stores of some kind or other, from big-name emporiums to quirky little. If you're here to shop, you can spend days browsing and window-shopping, from the fanciest Fifth Avenue boutiques to thrift stores on the Lower East Side.

WHAT TO BUY
Antiques

Despite a price-fixing scandal between the world's two biggest auction houses in 2000, both Christie's and Sotheby's continue to rake in the dough through their lucrative online and live auctions. Friday's edition of the *New York Times* contains announcements about exhibitions of sale items.

Christie's *(Map 5;* ☎ *212-636-2000;* W *www.christies.com; 20 Rockefeller Plaza at W 49th St, Midtown),* between Fifth and Sixth Aves, holds top-level auctions. This premier auction house has sold items that once belonged to John F Kennedy, Marilyn Monroe and Frank Sinatra.

Sotheby's *(Map 7, #83;* ☎ *212-606-7000;* W *www.sothebys.com; 1334 York Ave, Upper East Side),* near E 72nd St, specializes in paintings and fine furniture.

Park Ave Armory *(Map 7, #114; Park Ave at E 67th St)* holds frequent antiques shows.

Browsers should head to the antique-furniture stores on 59th St between Second and Third Aves. You'll find more stores on Broadway just below Union Square and along E 12th St in the East Village.

Annex Antique Fair & Flea Market *(Map 5, #133;* ☎ *212-243-5343; 107-111 W 25th St at Sixth Ave;* ⓜ *F, V, 1, 2, 3 to 23rd St; admission $1; open 10am-6pm Sat & Sun)* is an outdoor emporium with more than 700 dealers, offering a generally high-quality selection of pocket watches and estate jewelry, used cameras and one-of-a-kind items like gumball machines. You can hover on the fence to see if there's anything you like before paying to get in. The popularity of the market has spurred the creation of the **Garage Antique Fair** *(Map 5, #135; 112 W 25th St;* ⓜ *F, V, 1, 2, 3 to 23rd St),* between

RICHARD I'ANSON

A chess set for patriots, Thompson Street, Greenwich Village

Sixth and Seventh Aves, as well as other markets in empty parking lots nearby; these markets are free and are open from dawn to dusk on Saturday and Sunday.

Chelsea Antiques Building (Map 5, #134; ☎ 212-929-0909; 110 W 25th St, Chelsea; Ⓜ F, V, 1, 2, 3 to 23rd St; open 10am-6pm daily), between Sixth and Seventh Aves, features 1st-edition books, furniture, lighting fixtures and other items at indoor stalls. Any of these places are great for passing a lazy weekend day.

Beauty Products

Sephora (Map 5, #67; ☎ 212-245-1633; 636 Fifth Ave; Ⓜ B, D, F, V to 47-50th Sts/Rockefeller Center • Map 6, #78; ☎ 212-944-6789; 1500 Broadway; Ⓜ 1, 2 to 50th St), between 50th and 51st Sts, is the mother lode of high-quality cosmetics, all sold at a nice discount. Come here to shop and browse in a comfortable atmosphere for all your favorite Clinique, Lancôme products and more. There are seven branches sprinkled around town.

Kiehl's (Map 4, #23; ☎ 212-677-3171, 800-543-4571; 109 Third Ave; Ⓜ N, Q, R, W, 4, 5, 6, to 14th St-Union Sq, L to Third Ave), between E 13th and 14th Sts, is a unique pharmacy in the East Village that has been selling organic skin-care products since 1851 (among its bestsellers is Kiehl's Musk Oil, which it invented in the 1800s). Cosmetics giant L'Oréal bought Kiehl's in mid-2000 for a reported $100 million, but the company promises it will not alter the nature of this shop, including its reputation for personal service, generous sample sizes and its strict no-advertising policy. They've stayed true to their word and you can still come here for the best moisturizers, masks and emollients or to admire the late owner's eccentric collection of antique Harley-Davidson motorcycles.

Books

General Between Fifth and Sixth Aves, **Gotham Book Mart** (Map 5, #72; ☎ 212-719-4448; 41 W 47th St; Ⓜ B, D, F, V to 47-50th Sts/Rockefeller Center) has been in business since 1920, but is due to move

from its current digs by the end of 2002. This premier book purveyor is packed with the highest quality reads, accompanied by impressively knowledgeable staff. Its trademark shingle (a copy; the original was stolen in the '60s) declares that 'wise men fish here,' and poets WH Auden and Marianne Moore have both dangled a line. Check out the gallery, which has terrific rotating exhibits from the likes of Edward Gorey.

Shakespeare & Co (Map 4, #84; ☎ 212-529-1330; 716 Broadway, Greenwich Village • Map 3, #85; ☎ 212-742-7025; 1 Whitehall St, Lower Manhattan • Map 5, #128; ☎ 212-220-5199; 137 E 23rd St • Map 7, #84; ☎ 212-580-7800; 939 Lexington Ave, Upper East Side) has several pleasant Manhattan shops that offer an assortment of general-interest and academic selections. Its Greenwich Village store, across the street from New York University's Tisch film school, features a large selection of theater and film books and scripts.

Three Lives (Map 4, #74; ☎ 212-741-2069; 154 W 10th St; Ⓜ 1, 2 to Christopher St/Sheridan Sq), between Waverly Pl and Seventh Ave, is a Greenwich Village institution and a paragon of independent bookselling. Three Lives stocks a good number of biographies and top-notch mainstream selections; the wall-to-wall wooden shelves lend the place a comfy feel and it's staffed by friendly, informed and helpful people.

St Marks Bookshop (Map 4, #44; ☎ 212-260-7853; 31 Third Ave; Ⓜ 6 to Astor Pl; open 10am-midnight Mon-Sat, 11am-midnight Sun), between E 8th and 9th Sts, is a lovely big bookshop in the East Village that specializes in political literature, poetry and academic journals. It has become a popular neighborhood stop.

Rizzoli (Map 4, #190; ☎ 212-674-1616; 454 West Broadway, SoHo; Ⓜ N, R to Prince St • Map 5, #5; ☎ 212-759-2424; 31 W 57th St, Midtown; Ⓜ F to 57th St) is a handsome store selling great art, architecture and design books (as well as general interest books) in two upscale shops. Check out **Untitled** (Map 4, #191; ☎ 212-982-2088; 159 Prince St), around the corner from Rizzoli's

SoHo store, for a mind-boggling selection of rare, vintage and quirky postcards.

Barnes & Noble (Map 5, #189; ☎ 212-675-5500; 105 Fifth Ave at 18th St; ◍ N, R to 23rd St • Map 5, #182; ☎ 212-253-0810; 33 E 17th St, Union Sq; ◍ L, N, Q, R, W, 4, 5, 6 to 14 St-Union Sq • Map 4, #85; ☎ 212-420-1322; 4 Astor Pl; ◍ 6 to Astor Pl • Map 5, #159; ☎ 212-727-1227; 675 Sixth Ave, Chelsea; ◍ F, V to 23rd St • Map 7, #53; ☎ 212-362-8835; 2289 Broadway at W 82nd St, Upper West Side; ◍ 1, 2 to 72nd St • Map 9, #28; ☎ 718-246-4996; 106 Court St, Cobble Hill; ◍ M, N, R, 1, 2, 4, 5 to Court St/Borough Hall) has several 'superstores' located throughout New York City, including the chain's main store at Fifth Ave. Each store features more than 200,000 titles, a music department, comfortable seating and a café where patrons can read magazines for free.

Borders (Map 5, #125; ☎ 212-481-2913; 550 Second Ave at E 32nd St, Midtown • Map 5, #14; ☎ 212-980-6785; 461 Park Ave, Midtown) rivals Barnes & Noble in breadth of titles, setting and atmosphere. It has several other locations.

Travel Near Canal St, **Traveler's Choice** (Map 4, #257; ☎ 212-941-1535; 2 Wooster St, SoHo) sells guides, phrasebooks, dictionaries, maps and travel accessories – everything to inspire you to stay on the road.

The Complete Traveller (Map 5, #96; ☎ 212-685-9007; 199 Madison Ave at W 35th St, Midtown; ◍ 6 to 33rd St) offers an intriguing selection of 1st editions and old Baedeker guides, plus newer titles and some maps.

Hagstrom Map & Travel Center (Map 6, #106; ☎ 212-398-1222; 57 W 43rd St; ◍ S, 4, 5, 6, 7 to Grand Central Terminal • Map 3, #71; ☎ 212-785-5343; 125 Maiden Lane; ◍ 1, 2 to Wall St) carries a wide assortment of maps and travel guides.

Civilized Traveler (Map 7, #97; ☎ 212-875-0306; 2003 Broadway; ◍ 1, 2 to 66th St-Lincoln Center • Map 7, #115; ☎ 212-288-9190; 864 Lexington Ave; ◍ 6 to 68th St) is another good place to stock up on travel guides and literature.

Gay & Lesbian Every decent bookstore, even the chains, now includes a gay and lesbian department, some quite good; check out the Barnes & Noble outlets in Chelsea and Astor Place.

Creative Visions/Gay Pleasures (Map 4, #63; ☎ 212-255-5756; 548 Hudson St; ◍ 1, 2 to Christopher St/Sheridan Sq), between Perry and Charles Sts in the Village, has gay titles galore and stocks magazines and all the entertainment weeklies.

Oscar Wilde Memorial Bookshop (Map 4, #76; ☎ 212-255-8097; 15 Christopher St; ◍ 1, 2 to Christopher St/Sheridan Sq), New York's oldest gay-and-lesbian bookshop, is between Sixth and Seventh Aves in the Village. This small place is floor to ceiling queer literature, and sells rainbow flags and other souvenirs.

Blue Stockings (Map 4, #213; ☎ 212-777-6028; 172 Allen St; ◍ F, V to Second Ave), between Stanton and Rivington Sts, is an independent bookstore owned by women and strong on dyke lit and crit. This gathering spot has a café and puts on special events such as live music, lesbian sewing circles and poetry readings.

Specialty Titles Near Broadway, on the Upper West Side, **Applause Books** (Map 7, #70; ☎ 212-496-7511; 211 W 71st St; ◍ 1, 2, 3 to 72nd St) for screenplays and film essays.

Drama Bookshop (Map 6, #121; ☎ 212-944-0595; 250 W 40th St; ◍ A, C, E to 42nd St), between Eighth and Ninth Aves, features the city's largest selection of plays and musical scores. The recent move to this new space means more room for browsing and leafing through the treasures it holds.

Books of Wonder (Map 5, #192; ☎ 212-989-3270; 16 W 18th St; ◍ L to Sixth Ave, F, V to 14th St, Chelsea), between Fifth and Sixth Aves, is a fun-loving place that carries children's titles and young-adult fiction.

East-West Books (Map 4, #15; ☎ 212-243-5994; 78 Fifth Ave), between E 13th and 14th Sts, is the place to go for a wide array of titles on Buddhism, Asian philosophies and general spirituality.

Mysterious Bookshop (Map 6, #6; ☎ 212-765-0900; 129 W 56th St, Midtown), between

Sixth and Seventh Aves, will appeal to whodunnit lovers. This place has an extensive collection of signed copies and 1st editions.

Murder Ink *(Map 7, #17; ☎ 212-362-8905; 2486 Broadway, Upper West Side; ❻ 1, 2, 3 to 96th St)*, between W 92nd and 93rd Sts, is another spot for mystery fans. Sharing the same welcoming space is **Ivy's Books** *(Map 7, #17; ☎ 212-362-8905; 2488 Broadway)*, with a broad selection of quality new and used books.

Urban Center Books *(Map 5, #62; ☎ 212-935-3592; 457 Madison Ave at E 51st St; ❻ 6 to 51st St)* is an impressive shop in the courtyard of the historic Villard Houses, selling all manner of architecture books.

Used Books Just south of Houston St, **Used Book Café** *(Map 4, #186; ☎ 212-334-3324; 126 Crosby St; ❻ F, V, S to Broadway-Lafayette St)* is a great used-bookstore to camp out in with an espresso and to read, write or work. It crawls with locals on the weekends, but brave the throngs to shop and browse through over 45,000 used, rare and new titles; proceeds benefit Housing Works, a charitable organization serving New York City's HIV-positive and AIDS homeless community.

Strand Bookstore *(Map 4, #21; ☎ 212-473-1452; 828 Broadway)*, near E 12th St, is a well-loved New York institution in the Village that is hard to navigate but delivers on its promise of eight miles of used books and review copies. They always have scads of sale books. Also check out their **en plein air outlet** *(Map 5; cnr Fifth Ave & 59th St)* at the Grand Army Plaza entrance to Central Park.

The Argosy *(Map 5, #15; ☎ 212-753-4455; 116 E 59th St, Midtown)*, between Park and Lexington Aves, features estate sales, rare prints, autographs, old maps, art monographs, classics and other eclectic books on a variety of topics.

Heights Books *(Map 9, #13; ☎ 718-624-4876; 109 Montague St; ❻ M, N, R to Court St, 1, 2 to Clark St)* makes for some tight browsing as floor space is given over to shelves rather than aisles, but they have tons of good used books at attractive prices.

Cameras

New York's camera prices are hard to beat, but make sure you know what you want before sallying forth, as stellar service is not usually included in the price. Indeed, some camera stores (in Midtown especially) have earned reputations for 'bait and switch' tactics, so if you go in to buy a Canon lens and the salesperson begins offering a cheaper, generic alternative that's supposedly better, beware.

B&H Photo-Video *(Map 5, #104; ☎ 212-444-6344, 800-606-6969; ⓦ www.bhphotovideo.com; 420 Ninth Ave, Midtown; ❻ A, C, E to 34 St-Penn Station; open Sun-Fri)*, between W 33rd and 34th Sts, is New York's most popular camera store, though it suffers mightily from zoo-like crowding and a pay-first, pick-up-second bureaucracy. It does a brisk business with international clients, thanks to its linguistically adept staff, who speak 15 languages all told. You definitely should know what you want before heading in here.

Ken Hansen Photo *(Map 5, #26; ☎ 212-317-0923; Suite 1901, 509 Madison Ave at W 53rd St, Midtown)* specializes in Leicas and other top-end equipment and is a favorite with professionals. Don't hesitate to come here even if you need a lot of guidance; the salespeople are most helpful.

Cigars

While you can't get the world's finest cigars in New York (the US government's Trading with the Enemy Act prohibits the sale of Cuban cigars), there are many fine tobacconists selling close approximations. Whether you're looking for a $2 tiparillo or a pricey Punch, take advantage of the many smoking bars throughout the city; in addition, many cigar shops have their own on-site smoking lounges.

Barclay-Rex *(Map 3, #81; ☎ 212-962-3355; 75 Broad St at William St; ❻ J, M, Z to Broad St, N, R to Whitehall St • Map 5, #89; ☎ 212-888-1015; 570 Lexington Ave; ❻ 6 to 51st St • Map 5, #83; ☎ 212-692-9680; 70 E 42nd St; ❻ S, 4, 5, 6, 7 to Grand Central-42nd St)* has a decent selection, if at slightly inflated prices.

Sanchez Cigars (Map 5, #108; ☎ 212-239-8861; 265 W 30th St), between Seventh and Eighth Aves, is a tiny, atmospheric shop where you can watch the extended family hand-roll cigars from Cuban seed. Singles are as cheap as $1 here.

J&R Cigar Emporium (Map 5, #73; ☎ 212-997-2777; 562 Fifth Ave at 46th St; Ⓜ S, 4, 5, 6, 7 to Grand Central-42nd St) carries all the top bands at reasonable prices, plus a variety of accessories, including cutters, humidors, cigar ashtrays and lighters.

Nat Sherman (Map 5, #78; ☎ 212-764-5000, 800-692-4427; 500 Fifth Ave at 42nd St; Ⓜ S, 4, 5, 6, 7 to Grand Central-42nd St) sells all the usual cigars, plus its own brand. You can relax and smoke in the lovely upstairs lounge which has comfy chairs and windows overlooking Fifth Ave. Don't miss the cavernous walk-in humidor with esoteric cigars, and the individual humidors made from the parquet floor of the old Madison Square Garden.

Davidoff of Geneva (Map 5, #24; ☎ 212-751-9060; 535 Madison Ave; Ⓜ E, V to Fifth Ave-53rd St, 6 to 51st St), near E 54th St, sells fancy cigars, pipes, tobacco and accessories at fancy prices.

Recycled & Retro

The East Village is crawling with all manner of fashion wonks, wannabes, tragedies and trendsetters and you can bet they're shopping locally. There are scores of thrift stores, vintage boutiques and used-clothing emporiums sprinkled throughout this part of town and even further south and east into the Lower East Side. Most places down this way don't open until 11am or even later, so catch a nice brunch somewhere first.

Of course, there isn't room here to mention all the cool places, and there is a slew of stores clustered along 9th St between First Ave and Ave A and more on Ludlow St between Houston and Delancey Sts that you might want to hit. Consider starting at the **Salvation Army** (cnr Delancey & Allen Sts), where you'll have to sift through the dross to dig out some pinstripe flares or patent-leather unmentionables, but be patient; this place is a gold mine. Here are some other suggestions:

Resurrection (Map 4, #105; ☎ 212-228-0063; 123 E 7th St; Ⓜ 6 to Astor Pl • Map 4, #209; ☎ 212-625-1374; 217 Mott St; Ⓜ 6 to Spring St) sells sweet vintage clothing heavy on the paisley, fringe and velvet flavors.

Rue St Denis Vintage Clothes (Map 4, #29; ☎ 212-260-3388; 174 Avenue B; Ⓜ L to First Ave) is a big place, with talented buyers; this is high-quality vintage thrift.

Rags-A-Go-Go (Map 4, #108; ☎ 212-254-4771; 119 St Marks Pl; Ⓜ N, R to 8 St-NYU, 6 to Astor Pl • Map 4, #13; ☎ 646-486-4011; 218 W 14th St; Ⓜ A, C, E, L, 1, 2, 3 to 14th St) is the real deal for the really thrifty; take your time to pick through the huge holdings here.

Physical Graffiti (Map 4, #106; ☎ 212-477-7334; 96 St Marks Pl; Ⓜ N, R to 8th St-NYU, 6 to Astor Pl), between First Ave and Ave A, sells funky and hip used clothing and accessories; the two buildings here were used for the cover of Led Zeppelin's album of the same name.

Amarcord (Map 4, #99; ☎ 212-614-7133; 84 E 7th St; Ⓜ N, R to 8th St-NYU, 6 to Astor Pl), between First and Second Aves, peddles high-quality (and highly seasonal) vintage clothing for women.

Tokio 7 (Map 4, #98; ☎ 212-353-8443; 64 E 7th St; Ⓜ N, R to 8th St, 6 to Astor Pl), between First and Second Aves, is the high-holy hip-consignment place with designer labels for men and women. It's impressive, with good prices and a great men's selection, from sneakers to suits.

N.Y.C.

Clothing

The Garment District is jam-packed with shops selling off-brand clothing at wholesale prices, mainly on W 37th St between Eighth and Ninth Aves. For funky vintage and used togs, head to the East Village (see the boxed text 'Recycled & Retro' for suggestions). This neighborhood also pops with eponymous shops belonging to young clothing designers trying to make a name for themselves in the big, bad world of New York fashion; this is the logical area to hit for a weekend shopping outing.

Amy Downs *(Map 5, #175; ☎ 212-358-8756; 227 E 14th St; ◍ L to Second Ave)*, between Second and Third Aves, specializes in original and inspired (yet fully functional) women's hats.

Stüssy *(Map 4, #189; ☎ 212-274-8855; 140 Wooster St; ◍ F, V, S to Broadway-Lafayette)*, between Houston and Prince Sts, is the bee's knees with the stylish skate crowd, who flock here for the baggy shorts, saggy pants, dope hats and more.

For jeans, a lot of people like **Canal Jean Company** *(Map 4, #247; ☎ 212-226-1130; 504 Broadway, SoHo; ◍ 6 to Spring St)*, between Spring and Broome Sts, for the gigantic selection and so-so prices.

Urban Outfitters *(Map 4, #169; ☎ 212-475-0009; 628 Broadway; ◍ 6 to Bleecker St • Map 7, #66; ☎ 212-721-5900; 2081 Broadway at W 72nd St; ◍ 1, 2, 3 to 72nd St)* once reigned as the hip new-and-used store *du jour*, but has lost a little something with expansion. Still, it's better than Gap and the rest.

Dave's New York *(Map 5, #196; ☎ 212-989-6444; 581 Sixth Ave, Chelsea; ◍ 1, 2 to 18th St)*, between W 16th and 17th Sts, has $35 Levi's flying out the door. This is also the place to come for construction boots, Carhart and other rugged wear.

Century 21 *(Map 3, #63; ☎ 212- 227-9092; 22 Cortlandt St; ◍ 1, 2 to Chambers St; open 7:45am-8pm Mon-Wed, Fri, 7:45am-8:30pm Thur, 10am-8pm Sat, 11am-7pm Sun)*, between Church St and Broadway, has legendary bargains and is the darling of savvy New York shoppers. It offers deep discounts on designer clothing (including Armani shirts and Donna Karan dresses), perfume, sportswear and accessories, and boasts a selection of menswear as extensive as the women's department. Century 21 accommodates the early-bird Wall St crowd during the week. This store is located across from the World Trade Center site, and the city rejoiced when it finally reopened in March 2002.

Brooklyn has been rivaling Manhattan in all realms of late, and couturiers and fashion boutiques are right in the mix. There's some terrific window-shopping along Smith St from Carroll Gardens to Cobble Hill (take the F or G train to Carroll St), where you can spend a day strolling and browsing, perhaps taking a break for a cocktail or snack at one of the many bars and restaurants on this strip.

Habit *(Map 9, #47; ☎ 718-923-0303; 231 Smith St)*, near Douglass St, stocks racks of sassy and swank ladies' apparel that will tempt even the most prosaic shoppers. Bring big bucks, though, as this little boutique isn't cheap (apart from the clever accessories, which are reasonably priced).

Crush *(Map 9, #48; ☎ 718-852-7626; 244 Smith St at Douglass St)* is packed with vintage cocktail dresses for those of tiny waists, Hello Kitty camisole sets for those of juvenile tastes, and clothes boasting Brooklyn pride (F train T-shirts, for example). You can also accessorize with a leopard flask, sequin poodle purse and other cool kitsch here.

flirt *(Map 9, #49; ☎ 718-858-7931; 252 Smith St)*, between DeGraw and Douglass Sts, is a cooperative of local designers, who keep this shop chock full of funky, original dresses. Come here for a little coquette number that you can be sure no-one else will be wearing to the big bash.

NEIL SETCHFIELD

SHOPPING

Computers & Electronics

J&R Music & Computer World *(Map 3, #55; ☎ 212-238-9100; 15 Park Row; Ⓜ A, C, J, M, Z, 1, 2, 4, 5 to Fulton St-Broadway Nassau)*, between Ann and Beekman Sts, is a massive outfit in Lower Manhattan offering a good selection at reasonable prices but the service is spotty at best. Avoid shopping here on busy weekends.

CompUSA *(Map 5, #98; ☎ 212-764-6224; 420 Fifth Ave, Midtown)*, between 37th and 38th Sts, features aisles of computer software and a good range of printers.

Staples *(Map 6, #120; ☎ 212-944-6744, 1075 Sixth Ave)*, between W 40th and 41st Sts in the Times Square area, sells computer peripherals, printers and office supplies at decent prices. This is one of those chains that seems to have colonized every block; check the phone book for more locations.

If you're looking for light electronics, such as extension cords and plugs, head to the stores that line Canal St between Sixth Ave and the Bowery. Avoid buying anything that requires a warranty here, including cameras and stereo equipment, as a lot of the stuff has 'fallen off the truck' (ie, is stolen or is otherwise floating in the grey market abyss) and *never* buy a phone or video camera from a roving street vendor – the equipment won't work or the box will be empty.

Jewelry

Groups of cooperative stalls sell discount diamonds, pearls and other jewelry in the so-called Diamond District on W 47th St between Fifth and Sixth Aves. The vendors here know how to look pained while offering you the 'best deal, my friend' – even though they're making a fat profit. Still, this is usually a win-win situation, as you're getting the goods at far better prices than you could ever hope for in a regular shop. Since Orthodox Jews own many of the stores, the street shuts down early Fridays and is closed weekends.

You'll find a similar cluster of Chinese-owned jewelry shops in Chinatown (though far fewer than there used to be before September 11), with the greatest concentration near the intersection of the Bowery and Canal St. These are open weekends.

ANGUS OBORN

Skip breakfast and have the real deal at Tiffany's

Cartier *(Map 5, #46; ☎ 212-753-0111; 653 Fifth Ave; Ⓜ E, V to Fifth Ave/53rd St • Map 7, #89; ☎ 212-472-6400; 828 Madison Ave at 69th St; Ⓜ 6 to 68th St)* is one of the biggest names in the business for first-rate jewelry. It sells eye-popping rocks set in rings, watches, glasses, bags and brooches.

Tiffany & Co *(Map 5, #29; ☎ 212-755-8000; 727 Fifth Ave at 57th St; Ⓜ F to 57th St)* needs no introduction. This famous jeweler has won many hearts with its fine watches, rings, necklaces and more. Check out the really swanky stuff in the window, but then head inside for some affordable signature stationery, a key ring or handkerchiefs – all come in the unmistakable baby-blue box.

Kitchenware

It might seem odd to buy cookware and other ho-hum domestic bric-a-brac in New York, but you can really beat department-store and catalog prices on items such as espresso machines, Kitchenaids, Cuisinarts, chef knives, pepper mills and even pizza peels (the wooden paddles that slide pizzas into the oven) by shopping the restaurant supply stores lining the Bowery just below Houston St. Be warned, though, that some of these places are closed on Saturday.

Bari *(Map 4, #180; ☎ 212-925-3845; 240 Bowery; ◑ F to Second Ave; open daily)* is between Houston and Stanton Sts.

Zabar's *(Map 7, #54; ☎ 212-787-2000, 800-697-6301; 2245 Broadway at W 80th St; ◑ 1, 2 to 79th St)* is a gourmet emporium that is not only famous for its food but also for its large 2nd-floor kitchenware department. Here you'll find some very good prices on items such as espresso machines.

Music & Video

New At its huge main store, **Tower Records** *(Map 4, #139; ☎ 212-505-1500; 692 Broadway at 4th St; ◑ 6 to Bleecker St)* offers a wide selection of music but specializes in rock and soul. You can purchase concert tickets at the TicketMaster outlet here. Down the block, you could also check out **Tower Video** *(Map 4, #135; ☎ 212-505-1166; 383 Lafayette St at W 4th St)* and their discount record outlet across the street.

HMV *(Map 5, #74; ☎ 212-681-6700; 565 Fifth Ave at 46th St, Midtown; ◑ B, D, F, V, to 47-50th Sts/Rockefeller Center • Map 7, #37; ☎ 212-348-0800; 1280 Lexington Ave at E 86th St, Upper East Side; ◑ 4, 5, 6 to 86th St • Map 8, #34; ☎ 212-932-9619; 300 W 125th St at Frederick Douglass Blvd, Harlem; ◑ A, B, C, D to 125th St)* is running roughshod over the chain-store music business, with its wide selection, open floor plans and well-located stores. Prices, however, are less than great.

Virgin Megastore *(Map 6, #79; ☎ 212-921-1020; 1540 Broadway; ◑ N, Q, R, S, W, 1, 2, 3, 7 to Times Sq-42nd St • Map 4, #20; ☎ 212-598-4666; 52 E 14th St at Broadway in Union Sq; ◑ L, N, Q, R, W, 4, 5, 6 to 14th St-Union Sq)* is a massive store that possibly edges out both Tower and HMV for selection and certainly has the best service of the three. This sprawling store has plenty of top-of-the-pops, plus a decent selection of dance, jazz, classical and progressive CDs.

Colony *(Map 6, #35; ☎ 212-265-2050; 1619 Broadway at 49th St; ◑ N, R, W to 49th St, 1, 2 to 50th St; open until 1am daily)* has been going strong for over half a century. Head here for rare, unusual or simply run-of-the-mill music. Colony specializes in sheet and karaoke music.

Discount, Used & Rare If you've spent years searching for that elusive Seven Shades of Brown LP or need to unload old CDs, New York City is the place. There are loads of stores around St Mark's Pl, Third Ave and Bleecker St between Sullivan and Christopher Sts that make a business of buying and selling used music. Head to these areas to trade up.

Route 66 Records *(Map 4, #146; ☎ 212-533-2345; 99 MacDougal St; ◑ A, C, E, F, V, S to W 4th St)*, between Bleecker St and W 3rd St, is decent for discount CDs (less than $10), as well as bootlegs and imports.

Norman's Sound & Vision *(Map 4, #91; ☎ 212-473-6599; 67 Cooper Sq on Third Ave; ◑ N, R, to 8 St-NYU, 6 to Astor Pl)* is a Village fave. Here you can buy, trade and sell CDs, videos and DVDs. What's more, the prices are just right, the service is friendly and laid-back and the selection covers it all, with particularly good world music, jazz and blues sections.

Other Music *(Map 4, #136; ☎ 212-477-8150; 15 E 4th St; ◑ 6 to Bleecker St)*, between Broadway and Lafayette St, brazenly opened right across the street from the main Tower Records outlet, but it thrives thanks to its informed selection of offbeat lounge, psychedelic, electronica and indie label CDs.

Kim's Video & Music *(Mondo Kim's; Map 4, #41; ☎ 212-598-9985; 6 St Mark's Pl; ◑ N, R to 8th St-NYU, 6 to Astor Pl • Map 4, #167; ☎ 212-260-1010; 144 Bleecker St at Laguardia Pl; ◑ 6 to Bleecker St • Map 4, #66; 350 Bleecker St at 10th St; ◑ 1, 2 to Christopher St-Sheridan Sq • Map 8, #44; Broadway, Morningside Heights)* is an independent chain that started operating in the Village but is slowly starting to spread its wings. Head here for fringe, bootleg and anarchist-type stuff, including magazines, books and videos.

Footlight Records *(Map 4, #22; ☎ 212-533-1572; 113 E 12th St; ◑ N, R to 8 St-NYU, 6 to Astor Pl)* is between Third and Fourth Aves. Drama queens adore Footlight for its magnificent collection of out-of-print vinyl, Broadway show scores and foreign movie soundtracks.

Academy Records & CDs *(Map 5, #190; ☎ 212-242-3000; 12 W 18th St; ⓜ N, R, 6 to 23rd St)*, just west of Fifth Ave, is jam-packed daily with folks going through the $1.50 bargain bins looking for good vinyl, and poking through the reasonably priced rock, jazz and classical LPs. Academy also sells quality used CDs and videos.

Gryphon Records *(Map 7, #65; ☎ 212-874-1588; 233 W 72nd St; ⓜ 1, 2, 3 to 72nd St)*, off Broadway, is what New York is all about; pass through the doors of what is seemingly a private residence and you'll be confronted with a veritable firetrap of vinyl treasures and some very intense, fedora-doffing clients silently browsing the largely classical collection. Consult the professionals here for that rare or out-of-print classical LP.

NYCD *(Map 7, #47; ☎ 212-724-4466; 426 Amsterdam Ave; ⓜ 1, 2 to 79th St)*, between W 80th and 81st Sts, runs a permanent special whereby if you buy four CDs, you get the fifth free.

Musical Instruments

Gear heads and guitar junkies know the place to go to satisfy all their material desires is W 48th St between Sixth and Seventh Aves (to get there, take the ⓜ N, R, W to 49th St or B, D, F, V to 47-50th Sts/Rockefeller Center). Here you'll find legendary music shops, luthiers and retail outlets, including **Manny's Music** *(Map 6, #49; ☎ 212-819-0576, 800-448-8478; 156 W 48th St)* and **Sam Ash Music** *(Map 6, #40; ☎ 212-719-2299; 163 W 48th St)*. Both sell just about anything you can play, new and used. Many of the purveyors of better instruments are in 2nd-floor shops, with big windows packed with their specialty, such as horns, strings or woodwinds, so don't forget to look up.

Matt Umanov *(Map 4, #152; ☎ 212-675-2157; 273 Bleecker St; ⓜ A, C, E, F, V, S to W 4th St, 1, 2 to Christopher St-Sheridan Sq)*, between Jones and Cornelia Sts, is a guitar lover's wet dream with its rare Martin's, Gibson's and steel guitars. But you'll definitely have to pay the price for one of these beauties.

Shoes & Handbags

Street vendors sell affordable knockoffs of Coach bags and leather backpacks in numerous spots around the Village, including along Broadway just above Houston St, on Bleecker St and on W 4th St immediately off Sixth Ave. We're told that only professionals can tell the difference between a good fake and the real thing, so feel free to indulge.

If you simply must have the authentic item, check out **The Coach Store** *(Map 5, #13; ☎ 212-754-0041; 595 Madison Ave; ⓜ 4, 5, 6 to 59th St)*, near 57th St, or **kate spade** *(Map 4, #251; ☎ 212-274-1991; 454 Broome St, SoHo; ⓜ 6 to Spring St)* at the corner of Mercer St.

The Village Scandal *(Map 4, #94; ☎ 212-460-9358; 19 E 7th St)*, between Second and Third Aves, has a terrific selection of quirky hats, handbags and accessories.

Fab 208 *(Map 4, #97; ☎ 212-673-7581; 77 E 7th St; ⓜ N, R to 8th St-NYU, 6 to Astor Pl)*, between First and Second Aves, has a good selection of used high-fashion handbags, shoes and cowboy boots (especially for 'ladies' with larger than usual feet). The handmade original women's line created by the husband-and-wife team who own the place is worth a special stop.

Fans of Doc Martens and other shit kickers should head straight to the stretch of W 8th St running between Sixth Ave and Broadway, where approximately 30 shoe stores offer reasonable prices on work shoes, sneakers and construction boots. For great hiking shoes, check out the shops on Broadway in the five or six blocks immediately above and below the intersection with Houston St. Also scan the advertisements in the *Village Voice* for various other specials.

Suarez New York *(Map 5, #22; ☎ 212-753-3758; 450 Park Ave; ⓜ 4, 5, 6 to 59th St)*, between 56th and 57th Sts, sells Chanel, Hermès and Veneta copies so accomplished no-one will know your feet aren't clad in the real thing. The prices are fair.

For more elegant shoes, head to SoHo, where you'll find higher-priced shoe shops among the clothing boutiques.

Sporting Goods

Paragon Athletic Goods *(Map 5, #184;* ☎ *212-255-8036; 867 Broadway;* Ⓜ *L, N, Q, R, W 4, 5, 6 to 14 St-Union Sq)*, just off Union Square between E 17th and 18th Sts, offers a comprehensive selection of sports merchandise, with better prices than the chain stores. Particularly popular for its end-of-season sales on tennis rackets and running shoes, Paragon also boasts the best selection of in-line skates in the city and helpful staff.

Tent & Trails *(Map 3, #56;* ☎ *212-227-1760, 800-237-1760; 21 Park Pl;* Ⓜ *1, 2 to Park Pl)*, between Broadway and Church St, is a fantastic outdoor outfitter with top-of-the-line gear to satisfy even the most extreme enthusiasts.

NBA Store *(Map 5, #45;* ☎ *212-515-6221; 666 Fifth Ave at 52nd St;* Ⓜ *E, V to Fifth Ave-53rd St)* carries some cager gear, franchise jerseys and basketballs but mainly has steeply marked-up memorabilia. One bonus is that you can shoot hoops here.

Toys

FAO Schwarz *(Map 5, #10;* ☎ *212-644-9400; 767 Fifth Ave;* Ⓜ *F to 57th St, N, R, W to Fifth Ave/59th St)*, between 58th and 59th Sts, is famous for its cutting-edge (critics cry 'rip-off!') toys and jostling, jubilant crowds. During the holidays, you'll know the place by the lines out the door (the wait rarely exceeds 30 minutes, if you must check it out). The trippy, kitschy Barbie salon here is worth the wait.

Toys for kids and kids-at-heart

Enchanted Forest *(Map 4, #250;* ☎ *212-925-6677; 85 Mercer St, SoHo)*, between Broome and Spring Sts, is a smaller store that is a delightful spot where you can avoid brand-name toys and commercial tie-ins (such as action figures from movies and things that go beep with batteries). It specializes in teddy bears, hand puppets and other toys to ignite children's imagination.

Warner Bros Studio Store *(Map 6, #108;* ☎ *212-840-4040; 1 Times Sq;* Ⓜ *N, Q, R, S, W, 1, 2, 3, 7 to Times Sq-42nd St)* has all manner of stuffed and blow-moulded Sylvesters, Bugs Bunnies and other Warner Bros creations. Not for kids only, it also sells animation cels for $2500 and up. This most profitable of NYC retail outlets had to move to bigger digs recently, but can still feel crowded.

Disney Store *(Map 5, #31;* ☎ *212-702-0702; 711 Fifth Ave;* Ⓜ *E, V to Fifth Ave-53rd St)* is near 55th St. A visit to the Disney Store will probably include some glad-handing with Mickey Mouse and other life-size Disney characters as you browse three floors of merchandise.

WHERE TO SHOP

You can break the bank ˙shopping New York–style, but to save some pennies, check out discount stores such as **Daffy's**, **Strawberries** and **H & M**; these places have multiple branches throughout the city and stock steeply discounted designer togs. The Lazar Shopping website (Ⓦ www.lazarshopping.com) will delight the fashion-conscious crowd with its list of sample sales (updated weekly), shopping tips and bargain secrets. Also see the weekly *Time Out* for current sample sales – the cheapest way to snag some chic clothing and shoes.

At the time of writing, the SoHo Partnership was offering the SoHo & Tribeca Shopping Card, which provides up to 20% discounts at 200 area businesses; call ☎ 212-877-764-6746 to get yours. A similar deal called the Go East Card was being offered by the Lower East Side Business Improvement District; call ☎ 888-825-8374 or visit Ⓦ www.lowereastsideny.com to receive one.

Department Stores

Bergdorf Goodman (*Map 5, #8;* ☎ *212-753-7300; 754 Fifth Ave;* Ⓜ *N, R, W to Fifth Ave, F to 57th St*), between 57th and 58th Sts, is an elegant store that's a favorite with well-heeled suburbanites, Upper East Side dowagers and out-of-towners looking for classy gifts in prestige wrapping to take home. Bergdorf's features first-rate jewelry and couture collections, plus attentive staff and great sales.

Bloomingdale's (*Map 7, #124;* ☎ *212-705-2000; cnr E 59th St & Lexington Ave;* Ⓜ *4, 5, 6 to 59th St*) is loved and despised by many, depending on where their philosophy lies. Bloomies, as it's known colloquially, can be overpriced and full of cranky staff, but, to be fair, it has a good selection of high-quality goods and the clothing sales are redeeming. In recent years, snappy young designers have reinvigorated the apparel department. The 1st-floor perfume section has some of the most bizarre marketing tactics ever – you'll be accosted by dozens of automaton types trying to spray you with the latest scent while intoning the sales pitch. Gas mask anyone?

Henri Bendel (*Map 5, #35;* ☎ *212-247-1100; 712 Fifth Ave at 56th St;* Ⓜ *E, V to Fifth Ave-53rd St, N, R, W to Fifth Ave-59th St*) is a pricey department store specializing in curious, stylish clothing, cosmetics and accessories from newly established and flavor-of-the-moment designers. Don't miss the original Lalique windows here.

Bloomingdales, a New York institution

Lord & Taylor (*Map 5, #97;* ☎ *212-391-3344; 424 Fifth Ave, Midtown;* Ⓜ *7 to Fifth Ave, B, D, F, V to 42nd St*), between 38th and 39th Sts, has 10 floors of mostly conservative, matronly fashion. This place also offers a good selection of swimwear. Over all, this is a pleasant place to shop as the salespeople refrain from pressuring you, even in the cosmetics department.

Macy's (*Map 5, #100;* ☎ *212-695-4400; 151 W 34th St at Broadway;* Ⓜ *B, D, F, N, Q, R, V, W to 34th St-Herald Sq*) may not be the world's largest store, but it is certainly massive. Most New Yorkers have an affectionate regard for the multistoried emporium, in large part because of its sponsorship of a spring flower show, a fireworks festival on July 4 and its annual Thanksgiving Day Parade. Though Macy's has experienced financial problems in recent years, the store's stock hasn't diminished, and it continues to hold its famous Wednesday One Day Sales.

Saks Fifth Ave (*Map 5, #66;* ☎ *212-753-4000; 611 Fifth Ave at 50th St, Midtown;* Ⓜ *B, D, F, V to 47-50th Sts/Rockefeller Center*) is famous for its January sale. It boasts a vast user-friendly ground-floor space and helpful staff. Saks only sells men's and women's fashion items.

Takashimaya (*Map 5, #32;* ☎ *212-350-0100; 693 Fifth Ave;* Ⓜ *E, V to Fifth Ave-53rd St*) is near 55th St. The Japanese owners have brought elegant Eastern style to this stunning store, which sells furniture, clothing, homewares and more from all over the world. In keeping with its well-tuned aesthetic, this place concentrates on high-quality craftsmanship and gorgeous packaging. Even if you don't buy, browse through the ground-floor floral department. The Teabox in the basement features a relaxing afternoon tea.

Madison Avenue

The funkiest boutiques are in SoHo, Nolita or the Lower East Side, but Madison Ave has kept the *haute* in *couture* for decades. Strolling from Midtown to the Upper East Side along Madison Ave equals a Parisian experience, as designers try to outdo each other in their showplace stores. You'll encounter fewer crowds on Sunday, but you won't be able to drop in on any of the avenue's first-rate art galleries, which are closed that day.

Walking north on Madison Ave from 42nd St, you'll pass the following shops.

Brooks Brothers *(Map 5, #81; ☎ 212-682-8800; 346 Madison Ave; Ⓜ S, 4, 5, 6, 7 to 42nd St-Grand Central)*, near E 44th St, is a legendary outfit selling conservative clothing and formal wear for men; it also includes a smaller women's clothing department. Their baker's dozen of cotton handkerchiefs for $25 is a steal. Look for the brand new **Ann Taylor** that's due to open across the street.

Lederer de Paris *(Map 5, #63; ☎ 212-355-5515; 457 Madison Ave; Ⓜ 6 to 51st St)*, near E 51st St, sells fine leather goods and diaries from France.

Calvin Klein *(Map 5, #12; ☎ 212-292-9000; 654 Madison Ave; Ⓜ 4, 5, 6 to 59th St)*, between E 60th and 61st Sts, is a study in elegance by the media-savvy designer.

Barney's *(Map 5, #11; ☎ 212-826-8900; 660 Madison Ave; Ⓜ 4, 5, 6 to 59th St)*, between E 60th and 61st Sts, has become famous for treating potential customers as too fat, too poor and, in the men's department, too straight. Barney's is expensive, but you can scoop up some fine fashion at more comfortable prices at **Co-Op Barney's** *(Map 5, #198; ☎ 212-593-7800; 236 W 18th St; Ⓜ 1, 2 to 18th St)*, between Seventh and Eighth Aves, or wait for their warehouse sale, which is held February and August.

Sherry-Lehman *(Map 7, #122; ☎ 212-838-7500; 679 Madison Ave; Ⓜ 4, 5, 6 to 59th St)*, between E 61st and 62nd Sts, is a world-class wine-and-spirits store with reasonable prices.

Givenchy *(Map 7, #118; ☎ 212-772-1040; 710 Madison Ave; Ⓜ F to Lexington Ave-63rd St, 4, 5, 6 to 59th St)*, near E 63rd St, features traditional French suits and accessories.

Waterford-Wedgwood Store *(Map 7, #119; ☎ 212-759-0500; 713 Madison Ave; Ⓜ F to Lexington Ave-63rd St, 4, 5, 6 to 59th St)*, between E 63rd and 64th Sts, is one of Madison Ave's premier shops for fine china and blown glass. These are the folks responsible for the crystal ball lowered from One Times Square every New Year's Eve.

Valentino *(Map 7, #116; ☎ 212-772-6969; 747 Madison Ave; Ⓜ F to Lexington Ave-63rd St, 4, 5, 6 to 59th St)*, between E 64th and 65th Sts, displays the creations of one of the world's best-known designers and couturier to the stars.

Giorgio Armani *(Map 7, #113; ☎ 212-988-9191; 760 Madison Ave; Ⓜ F to Lexington Ave-63rd St, 4, 5, 6 to 59th St)* is between E 65th and 66th Sts. This massive store shows that the world-famous designer can't bear to be outdone by anyone. Armani's gorgeous clothes fill four just as gorgeous floors.

Prada *(Map 7, #88; ☎ 212-327-4200; 841 Madison Ave; Ⓜ 6 to 68th St • Map 4, #205; 575 Broadway at Prince St • Map 5; 724 Fifth Ave • Map 5, #23; 45 E 57th St • Prada Sport; Map 4, #200; 116 Wooster St)* showcases the Milan company's expensive and trendy offerings. The shoes start at $300.

Polo/Ralph Lauren *(Map 7, #87; ☎ 212-606-2100; 867 Madison Ave; Ⓜ 6 to 68th St)*, near E 72nd St, is housed in an old mansion. You've seen the advertisements, now come see the real thing.

Bang & Olufsen *(Map 7, #77; ☎ 212-879-6161; 952 Madison Ave; Ⓜ 6 to 77th St)*, near E 75th St, sells the most expensive and best-designed electronic equipment in the world. The desk consoles are sublime, sexy and somewhat affordable. Oh yeah, they sound good too.

Vera Wang *(Map 7, #79; ☎ 212-628-3400; 991 Madison Ave; Ⓜ 6 to 77th St)*, near E 77th St, offers bridal gear and a ready-to-wear line for New York's high society. You need an appointment to try on this stylish attire.

Missoni Boutique *(Map 7, #81; ☎ 212-517-9339; 1009 Madison Ave; Ⓜ 6 to 68th St)*, near E 78th St, features the popular Italian designer's trendy and expensive knitwear.

SHOPPING

N.Y.C.

Excursions

New York State

If you're in New York City for any length of time, you'll likely start looking for tranquility and a spot of green beyond the five boroughs before you start screaming 'I can't take it anymore!' (especially in summer). Luckily, the bucolic serenity of New York State and even (dare I say it?) New Jersey, is just a short drive or train ride away from the madding crowds. The quickest way to recharge your Big Apple battery is to hop a ferry to the beaches of Sandy Hook or catch a train to the Jersey Shore. Fun in the sun also beckons from Jones Beach and Fire Island, and if you have a car, you can venture all the way out to the Hamptons or the wineries on the 'Forks' of Long Island. North and west of the city, Hudson Valley is simply gorgeous, with long wooded stretches dotted with the old mansions of New York's robber barons. While not all the suggested excursions here are accessible by public transportation, a train, bus or boat can usually get you pretty close and cyclists have especially good opportunities to explore the enchanted territory outside the city.

LONG ISLAND
pop 2,753,913
The largest island in the US (120 miles from end to end) begins with Brooklyn (Kings County) and Queens (Queens County) on the western shore. New York City then gives way to the suburban housing, strip malls and working-class heroes in neighboring Nassau County (where you might also hear reference to the north and south shores; the north is the ritzy part). The terrain becomes flatter, less crowded and more exclusive in rural Suffolk County, which comprises the eastern end of the island. Suffolk County itself contains two peninsulas – commonly called the North and South Forks – divided by Peconic Bay.

Long Island (colloquially called Strong Island or, alternatively, The Rock) began as a series of whaling and fishing ports, as well as an exclusive outpost for the ultrarich, who built estates along the secluded coves on the north shore. In the years following WWII, Nassau County became increasingly more populated as thousands of middle-class families moved to the suburbs. Many of them migrated to infamous Levittown, built in 1947 in the center of Nassau County. This seminal planned community was laid out with thousands of cookie-cut, low-cost homes on huge tracts near major highways and railway lines leading into Manhattan. Named after its developer (Levit & Sons), the town attracted 55,000 residents (many of them returning war veterans with their new brides in tow) and became the model for innumerable similar, boring suburban communities across the country.

In Suffolk County, economic development patterns were geographically reversed. The

Mashomack Nature Preserve is a peaceful sanctuary away from the crowds

EXCURSIONS

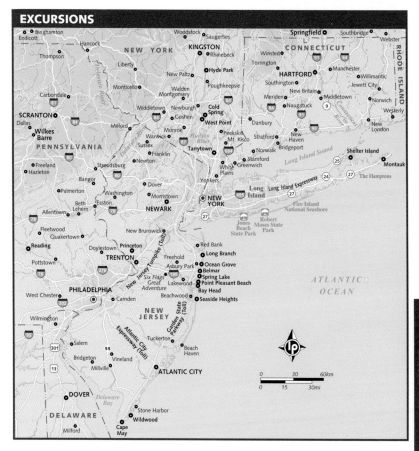

North Fork is home to salaried workers and small farm owners, while the South Fork is dominated by several upscale villages (Hampton Bays, Southampton, Bridgehampton, East Hampton and Amagansett), known collectively as the Hamptons. Actors, writers, entertainment executives and capitalist types gather in the Hamptons to schmooze away the summer season on private estates and in expensive restaurants.

For most visitors, a trip to Long Island means a trip to the beach, whether the destination is crowded Jones Beach, quiet Shelter Island or the showy Hamptons enclaves.

All are within easy reach via public transportation, which is the best option for summer weekends when traffic jams are particularly hellish. However, if you're interested in exploring Long Island's historic mansions or sampling wine in the vineyards of the North Fork, it's best to have a car. If you do have wheels, a nice junket out this way would take in Sag Harbor and Shelter Island on the South Fork, returning to the city via the wineries stretched out along the North Fork. With an added extra day you can also hit Montauk for some beach combing, camping or cycling.

Information

The **Long Island Convention and Visitors Bureau** (☎ *516-951-3440, ext 660, 877-368-6654 ext 660;* **w** *www.licvb.com*) publishes a free travel guide. You can obtain maps, restaurant listings and lodging guides from the local chambers of commerce:

East Hampton ☎ 631-324-0362;
  w www.easthamptonchamber.com
Greenport ☎ 631-477-1383;
  w www.greenport.com
Montauk ☎ 631-668-2428;
  w montaukchamber.com

Parks Information ☎ 516-669-1000;
  w www.nysparks.com
Shelter Island ☎ 631-749-0399;
  w www.onisland.com/si/chamber
Southampton ☎ 631-283-0402;
  w www.southamptonchamber.com

Getting There & Away

Bus The **Hampton Jitney** (☎ *631-283-4600, 800-936-0440; $25/44 one way/roundtrip*) leaves several times daily for Long Island's South Fork from three locations on the East Side of Manhattan, including 41st St between Lexington and Third Aves. **Sunrise**

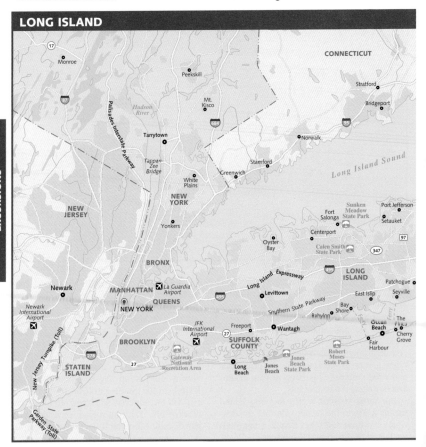

LONG ISLAND

Coach Lines (☎ 800-527-7709, 516-477-1200; $15/29 one way/roundtrip), which travels to the North Fork, picks up passengers at 44th St and Third Ave in Midtown Manhattan. The drivers usually pretty savvy and know ways of circumventing summer weekend traffic, which makes riding these buses a good alternative to driving a car in sometimes maddening traffic.

A number of private bus companies serve points within Long Island. Call ☎ 516-766-6722 for information on transportation in Nassau County; for Suffolk County, call ☎ 631-360-5700.

Train The **Long Island Rail Road** (LIRR; ☎ 516-822-5477, 718-217-5477; Ⓦ www.lirr.org) carries 275,000 passengers daily to 134 stations throughout Long Island from New York City's Penn Station. Trips to the farthest points on the railroad – Greenport in the North Fork and Montauk in the South Fork – cost $10.25/15.25 off peak/peak one way. In the summer, the LIRR offers roundtrip deals to the south shore beaches.

Car The Long Island Expressway (I-495, also known as the LIE) cuts through the center of the island and ends by joining two

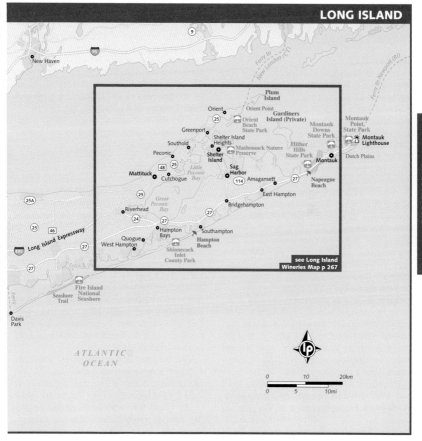

LONG ISLAND

EXCURSIONS

smaller roads. The older Route 25 (also known as the Jericho Turnpike) runs roughly parallel to I 495, then continues to the end of the North Fork at Orient Point. Route 27 (also known as the Sunrise Hwy) runs along the bottom of Long Island from the Brooklyn border, eventually becoming the Montauk Hwy, and ends up at the tip of the South Fork at Montauk Point. A trip to the end of Long Island takes at least three hours, but on weekends, traffic jams can turn it into a six-hour ordeal; consult 1010 WINS radio for the latest traffic updates. The LIE is simply horrendous (especially due to the 'LIE effect,' where there's bumper to bumper traffic for no discernible reason at all), and makes a very good argument for taking public transportation out here.

Oyster Bay

Driving through tony, secluded Oyster Bay may take you back to the gilded days of the robber barons and hot nights of the Jazz Age. Just one hour from New York City, this quiet, waterside village is a refuge for the rich, from presidents to magnates; the hills gazing upon the water are dotted with million-dollar residences built a tasteful distance from one another and landscaping to make Martha Stewart drool. In 1885, Theodore Roosevelt built a 23-room mansion on **Sagamore Hill** (☎ 631-922-4447; adult $5, senior & child free; open 9am-5pm daily May-Sept, 9am-5pm Wed-Sun Oct-Apr), which eventually served as the summer White House during his tenure in office from 1901–09. In this dark Victorian mansion, Roosevelt brokered an end to the Russo–Japanese War, for which he won the Nobel peace prize.

Though he was also the first chief executive to concern himself with land conservation, he was a man of his times and animal rights activists will grow pale at the many mounted heads, antlers and leopard skins on display, along with the inkwell made from a rhinoceros foot.

Roosevelt died at Sagamore Hill in 1919 and was buried in a cemetery a mile away. A red-brick Georgian house on the grounds houses his gold Nobel medal. Later occupied by Theodore Roosevelt Jr, the home

now holds a museum that charts the 26th president's political career. Tours of the Roosevelt home leave on the hour.

To get to Sagamore Hill, take the 41N exit from the LIE to Route 106, turn right on E Main St and follow the signs on Cove Neck Rd.

In nearby Centerport, the **Vanderbilt Mansion and Planetarium** (☎ 631-854-5579; w www.vanderbiltmuseum.org; Route 25A, 180 Little Neck Rd; adult/senior/child $8/6/5, planetarium laser show $7/5/4; open noon-5pm Tues-Sun) once belonged to Willie Vanderbilt, one of the last major heirs to the Staten Island family railroad fortune. Willie was one of those super-rich eccentric types and spent most of his life – and considerable savings – collecting sea creatures and curiosities from the South Pacific and Egypt, many of which are on display at his former estate, also known as Eagle's Nest. The **planetarium** (☎ 631-854-5555), added to the grounds in 1971, features a 60-foot 'Sky Theater' and telescope. The mansion is now owned by Nassau County, which holds community events on the 43-acre, beautifully landscaped site.

Jones Beach

Jones Beach (☎ 631-785-1600) might be the most crowded public beach in the world. Though it's always mobbed, the sand and water at this 6.5-mile beach are generally clean, and it makes an enjoyable respite from the city heat. If you're at all spoiled by beaches of the Caribbean, Mediterranean or Pacific variety, however, prepare yourself for a shockingly different experience with greased up bodies laying cheek by jowl, music blaring from boom boxes and lots of overweight and overbearing city folks getting their ya-yas out. Nevertheless, this is an excellent spot to check out Fourth of July fireworks extravaganzas.

The summer **concert series** (☎ 516-221-1000; w www.jonesbeach.com) here is one of the best venues in the tri-state area – at least for the location, if not the sound. Head to the beach for some fun, sun and grooving sounds from Lenny Kravitz, Jewel, Green Day and the like.

The LIRR offers $14 roundtrips from Penn Station in the city to the Freeport station on Long Island; the trip takes less than 40 minutes and includes a shuttle bus to Jones Beach.

Fire Island

Robert Moses State Park (☎ 631-669-0449; W www.nysparks.state.ny.us), which lies at the westernmost end of the **Fire Island National Seashore** (☎ 631-289-4810; W www .nps.gov/fiis), is the only Fire Island spot that's car accessible. Because it's so easy to reach (count on about 90 minutes' drive time from Manhattan, barring any significant traffic snarls), the park attracts the same kinds of crowds as neighboring Jones Beach. Still, its long stretch of soft sand makes for some good walking (there are guided walking tours from May 15 to October 11) and, if you've got the motivation, you can stroll away from the worst of the crowds.

The rest of Fire Island is a cluster of villages accessible only by ferry from three points on mainland Long Island (see Getting There & Away, later). The two hot vacation spots are Ocean Beach (for the hep, college crowd) and The Pines. Though the tourist board tries to play it down, Fire Island in general, and The Pines specifically, is probably the country's leading gay resort area and the cute and chic beach houses here are often rented way ahead of time by groups of fabulous gay men looking to entwine and unwind with a gorgeous sunset backdrop. The scene tends to get a little wild on summer weekends.

Places to Stay & Eat Because Fire Island is a protected national park, you won't find many places to stay here, so it's best to make this spot a day trip. But if you're determined to stay overnight, try the following (plan well in advance to snag a spot at these coveted camp sites).

Heckscher Park (☎ 631-581-4433; Southern State Parkway; sites $15; open May-Sept) has camping spots in East Islip, at the end of the Southern State Parkway.

Watch Hill (☎ 631-289-9336; dune campsites $20), on Fire Island, is across the inlet

from Patchogue (pronounced **patch**-oog) on the mainland; to get there, take the **Davis Park Ferry** (☎ 631-475-1665). The dune campgrounds are only accessible on foot or by boat and you have to enter a lottery for a site (start trying at least nine months in advance).

The Ocean Beach area, halfway between Robert Moses State Park and Cherry Grove, contains a few hotels:

Houser Hotel on the Bay (☎ 631-583-8900; East Bay Walk; rooms weekdays/weekends $50/75; open May-Sept) has 12 rooms with shared shower.

Ocean Beach Hotel (☎ 631-583-9600; rooms to $225; open May-Sept) has 21 rooms and offers many weekend and holiday package deals.

Four Seasons Bed & Breakfast (☎ 631-583-8295; 468 Dehnhoff Walk) has nice touches like a weekend, family-style BBQ, nice continental breakfast and a no-small-children policy. Two-day (required) stays on weekends cost $300 for a double; all other times it's $125 per night.

Where you eat will largely depend on what town you're lounging in. While the majority of places are in Ocean Beach, you can find decent food all over Fire Island and the bar/club scene is especially rich in The Pines and Cherry Grove. If you're after some action any night of the week, head to the latter's **Ice Palace** (☎ 631-597-6600; Ocean Walk) where the Sunday Tea Dances, terrific drag shows and indoor/outdoor pool are hot cruising spots.

Rachel's Bakery & Restaurant (☎ 631-583-5953; Bay Walk) is one of Fire Island's favorite breakfast spots, though you can get lunch, dinner and any manner of pastries here too.

China Beach (☎ 631-583-0200; Bay Walk) is the place to go if you're hankering for Chinese food. They also cover that other craving: Sushi. Both genres are done justice here.

The Island Mermaid (☎ 631-583-8088; Bay Walk) won't take the honors for hip spot of the year, but you can head here for wonderful sea views from the dining deck and disco-dancing nights. The menu tries to make everyone happy with its mosaic of seafood, pasta and meat dishes.

Getting There & Away The three ferry terminals are all close to the Bay Shore, Sayville and Patchogue LIRR stations. The ferry season runs from early May to November. Trips take about 20 minutes and cost an average of $15/7 for adult/child roundtrip, with discount season passes available. Most ferry departures are timed to coincide with the scheduled arrivals of trains from New York City.

Fire Island Ferry Service (☎ 631-665-3600; w www.Pagelinx.com/sayvferry/fip.shtml; 7am-5pm Sept-Apr, 7am-9pm May-Sept) runs from Bay Shore to Saltaire, Fair Harbor and Ocean Beach. **Sayville Ferry Service** (☎ 631-589-0810) runs from Sayville to Cherry Grove and the Pines. **Davis Park Ferry Company** (☎ 631-475-1665) travels from Patchogue to Davis Park and Watch Hill.

To get to Robert Moses State Park by car, take exit 53 off the LIE and travel south across the Moses Causeway.

The Hamptons

Prominent artists, musicians and writers have long sought refuge and inspiration in the beautiful beaches and rustic Cape Cod–style homes in the Hamptons, but the easy-money '80s brought a stampede of showier summertime visitors who made fast fortunes in the fashion industry and on Wall St. In recent years, the Hamptons have become an even more desirable destination, as West Coast entertainment moguls purchased large homes here, following in the footsteps of Steven Spielberg. The dot-com madness brought even more nouveau rich who snapped up or built McMansions on this part of the island and year-round residents seem annoyed and amused in equal measures by the show – a love-hate relationship that's common to any tourist hot spot from Martha's Vineyard to Monterey.

If you're celebrity-obsessed, you're better off heading to the Hamptons than standing in line at Planet Hollywood in New York City. Eccentricity is flaunted like a newborn baby in these parts and to get a glimpse of some bizarre doings Hampton-style, rent the truly weird film *Grey Gardens*, a documentary about the batty old aunt of Jaqueline Kennedy Onassis.

Many of the attractions, restaurants and hotels situated in the Hamptons close during the last week in October and remain shuttered until late April. B&B prices drop – and traffic jams along the Montauk Hwy disappear – about two weeks after Labor Day, which makes it a terrific time to venture out this way. The fall foliage on these further extents of Long Island also make this a flamboyant, memorable time to visit; the colors reach their peak around the first week in October.

Southampton Although Southampton village doesn't have half the flash of its neighbors to the east, it's a pleasant place to spend an afternoon in search of history and art. The nightlife ain't bad either. Pick up maps and brochures about the town at the **Southampton Chamber of Commerce office** (631-283-0402; w www.southampton chamber.com; 76 Main St), squeezed among a group of high-priced artsy-crafty shops and decent restaurants.

Just a few steps away from the chamber office is the **Halsey Homestead** (☎ 631-283-3527; admission $2; open 11am-5pm Tues-Sun June-Sept or by appointment), a saltbox house built in 1648, eight years after the first of the European settlers arrived in the area. The gardens make a pretty retreat.

The **Parrish Art Museum** (☎ 631-283-2118; w www.thehamptons.com; 25 Jobs Lane; suggested admission $4; open 11am-5pm Mon-Thur & Sat, 1pm-5pm Sun) is just a short walk from Main St. It has been open to the public since 1898, and its gallery features the work of major artists like the late Roy Lichtenstein, who owned a nearby house and studio.

Sag Harbor This old whaling town, seven miles north of Bridgehampton on Peconic Bay, is far less beach-oriented than the other Hampton towns. There are bunches of historic homes and points of interests here and you can pick up an historic walking tour map at the **Windmill Information Center** (☎ 631-692-4664) on Long Wharf at the end of Main St. The full tour is about an hour long and takes in 20 historic homes, monuments and churches, including the **Customs House** (*cnr Main & Garden Sts*) which has been restored to its original state in meticulous detail. There are also several cemeteries and old Indian sites in Sag Harbor dating from the 1800s that the curious might want to check out.

The **Whaling Museum** (*☎ 631-725-0770; Main St; adult/child $3/1; open 10am-5pm Mon-Sat, 1pm-5pm Sun May-Sept*), in a Greek Revival building just west of the shops on Main St, celebrates Sag Harbor's history.

Sag Harbor is manageable and quaint, meaning parking can be hell; stash the wheels somewhere outside of town and hike or bike in if you can.

East Hampton & Amagansett The heart of trendy Long Island beats in East Hampton, where you can shop at the Coach leather store and attend readings and art exhibitions at the **Guild Hall** (*☎ 631-324-0806*). This is the Long Island enclave where you're most likely to have brushes with greatness (eg, celebrity sightings, drive-by mansion fantasies etc). Drive or bike down Main Beach along Ocean Ave to espy the larger saltbox estates with water views. You can see some other grand (private) houses by turning right at Lily Pond Lane and peeking through the breaks in the high shrubbery.

Amagansett is basically an extension of East Hampton, and can be distinguished by the huge flagpole in the center of Montauk Hwy.

Places to Stay In the Hamptons, there's virtually no price difference between places calling themselves B&Bs and smaller inns – most have rates well over $150 a night in high season. Each chamber of commerce website (see earlier for addresses) lists area accommodation options. You might also try an independent service such as the **Bed & Breakfast Reservation Service of South Hampton** (*☎ 631-287-0902*), which handles properties throughout the Hamptons.

Mill House Inn (*☎ 631-324-9766; w www.millhouseinn.com; 31 N Main St; rooms from*

$200), a renovated property in East Hampton run by Dan and Katherine Hartnett, offers eight rooms (the prices are the same regardless of the season).

Sea Breeze Inn (*☎ 631-267-3692; 30 Atlantic Ave; rooms $60-140*), in Amagansett, has been run by the Fariel family since 1957. It's just a block away from the LIRR station and its 12 rooms (some with shared bath) are all clean. Weekly discounts are available.

American Hotel (*☎ 631-725-3535; Main St; rooms weeknights/weekends $195/325*), in Sag Harbor, has eight rooms. The ground-floor restaurant and bar attract weekending media types from Manhattan.

Places to Eat It's easier to find reasonably priced places to eat than reasonably priced lodging in the Hamptons. Relatively inexpensive **seafood stands** line Route 27 near Napeague Beach (between Amagansett and Montauk); these serve fish sandwiches, fresh steamers and fried clams for $10 or less during the summer.

The most popular spots are the **Lobster Roll** (*☎ 631-267-3740*), with its distinctive 'Lunch' sign and delicious namesakes, and the **Clam Bar** (*☎ 631-267-6348*), which also does a brisk business selling T-shirts to its BMW- and Mercedes-driving clientele.

Cyril's Fish House, (*☎ 631-267-7993*), a restaurant started by an ex-Marine with a handlebar mustache and loose tongue, serves an excellent sesame shrimp meal and might be the best of the bunch on this strip.

Laundry (*☎ 631-324-3199; 31 Race Lane; appetizers & raw bar $10-24, fish entrees $18-24*), one block from the LIRR station in East Hampton, was among the first celebrity-spotting restaurants to open in the Hamptons. There's less attitude here than in other places, and the food – generally fresh fish entrees – is quite good. They make a mean chowder and there's always a veggie entree option.

Maidstone Arms (*☎ 631-324-5006; 207 Main St*) is the most elegant and expensive restaurant in East Hampton, though the four-course, prix-fixe dinner including wine is only $40.

Entertainment In East Hampton, **Stephen Talkhouse** (☎ 631-267-3117; 161 Main St; tickets $10-100) is simply amazing for its line-up and reputation; recent appearances included Hank Williams, The Samples, Suzanne Vega, AWB – the list goes on. In addition, both Billy Joel and James Taylor have popped into this 25-year-old concert venue on nonperformance nights.

Rowdy Hall (☎ 631-324-8555; 10 Main St), also in East Hampton, is a microbrewery that gets crowded during the summer.

Southampton Publick House (☎ 631-283-2800; 40 Bowden Sq), in Southampton, is a microbrewery serving 40 signature beers and lagers.

Montauk

Montauk, where beach bumming and fishing are a way of life, is a long, flat 13-mile drive from Amagansett along Route 27. With little of the glitz and ostentation of its Hampton neighbors, Montauk makes a great getaway, especially if you're into hiking, cycling or fishing. Cyclists, especially, will dig the challenging Old Montauk Hwy route (peel off to the right from Route 27), an undulating road that overlooks the ocean and passes by several resorts. Take care here, however, as this road is spaghetti thin and pocked with blind spots. Another good **cycling route** is from the Old Montauk Hwy to the Montauk Lighthouse. It's a healthy five-mile ride, with

---

Long Island Wineries

Today there are 16 full-scale wineries on the North Fork and three on the South Fork of Long Island, plus 50 vineyards that take up a collective 2000 acres of land. Long Island seems to have perfected the art of making white wine, but its reds lag behind because the soil and climate aren't conducive to those heartier grapes (though the Schneider Vineyard specializes in reds). Judge for yourself by visiting a few wineries – the vintners are more than happy to pour out a few free glasses of their product.

You'll find most of the major wineries in the North Fork on Route 25. Just look for the distinctive green 'wine trail' road signs that crop up past Riverhead; nine of the vineyards lie within two miles of the town of Cutchogue (pronounced **kutch**-oog).

Several wineries offer full-scale tours of their facilities. Although not all places remain open to the public through the winter, October is a superb time to head out this way, not only for the spectacular fall foliage, but also for the many harvest festivals and apple-, strawberry- and pumpkin-picking opportunities.

All of the following wineries offer tastings, usually from 11am to 6pm during the summer months:

Bedell Cellars (#5; ☎ 631-734-7537; **w** www.bedellcellars.com)

Castello di Borghese/Hargrave Vineyard (#8; ☎ 631-734-5158; **w** www.castellodiborghese.com)

Duck Walk Vineyards (#17; ☎ 631-726-7555; **w** www.duckwalk.com)

Lenz Winery (#3; ☎ 631-734-6010; **w** www.lenzwine.com)

Osprey's Dominion Vineyards (#1; ☎ 631-765-6188; **w** www.ospreysdominion.com)

Palmer Vineyards (#13; ☎ 631-722-9463; **w** www.palmervineyards.com)

Paumanok Vineyards (#15; ☎ 631-722-8800; **w** www.paumanok.com)

Peconic Bay Winery (#9; ☎ 631-734-7361; **w** www.peconicbaywinery.com)

Pelligrini Vineyards (#11; ☎ 631-734-4111)

Pindar Vineyards (#4; ☎ 631-734-6200; **w** www.pindar.net)

Pugliese Vineyards (#6; ☎ 631-734-4057)

Schneider Vineyards (#16; ☎ 631-727-3334; www.schneidervineyards.com)

Wölffer Estate Sagapond Vineyards (#19; ☎ 631-537-5106; **w** www.wolffer.com)

some calf-quaking hills, but worth it for the ocean views that unfold below.

Camping and hiking are other possibilities here and there's probably no better place to stretch your legs than among the ethereal 'walking dunes' of **Hither Hills State Park**. These 80-foot high sand dunes are constantly shifting in a southeasterly direction and officials estimate they move roughly about 3½ feet per year. There are 14 miles of trails here, where you can see osprey, red tail hawks, many varieties of orchids and other flora and fauna (look for a trail map at the park entrance). Nearby Napeague Beach has good birding and beachcombing as well.

For hardcore beach action, you can't go wrong here, where the sand is soft, water clean and crowds thinner and generally better behaved than at other Long Island beaches. **Montauk Point State Park** is a terrific place to catch a free sunrise or sunset, otherwise it costs $2 to enter from 8am to 4pm, including admission to the largely unimpressive **Montauk Lighthouse Museum**. From late February to April, there are good seal-spotting opportunities south of the lighthouse. On the southern spit of coast known as **Dutch Plains**, there's excellent **surfing** at what many consider the east coast's best breaks. Most beaches charge cars to enter, but it's always free to bike or walk in.

Long Island Wineries

For more information on touring the wine trail, contact the **Long Island Wine Council** (☎ 631-369-5887; W www.liwines.com; 104 Edwards Ave, Calverton, NY, 11933). For a Winery guide, call ☎ 800-441-4601.

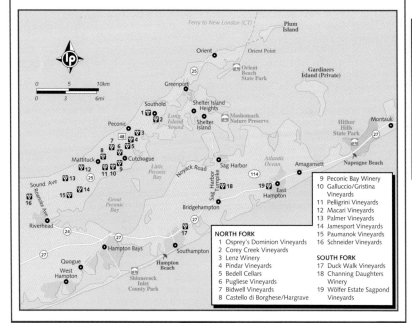

NORTH FORK
1 Osprey's Dominion Vineyards
2 Corey Creek Vineyards
3 Lenz Winery
4 Pindar Vineyards
5 Bedell Cellars
6 Pugliese Vineyards
7 Bidwell Vineyards
8 Castello di Borghese/Hargrave
9 Peconic Bay Winery
10 Galluccio/Gristina Vineyards
11 Pelligrini Vineyards
12 Macari Vineyards
13 Palmer Vineyards
14 Jamesport Vineyards
15 Paumanok Vineyards
16 Schneider Vineyards

SOUTH FORK
17 Duck Walk Vineyards
18 Channing Daughters Winery
19 Wölfer Estate Sagpond Vineyards

EXCURSIONS

N.Y.C.

Montauk retains a strong **fishing** tradition and there are many opportunities to cast a line here. You can contract charter boats at the dock for a day of fishing or jump on one of the party cruises (about $30 per person for a half-day). Captain Fred E Bird's *Flying Cloud* (☎ 631-668-2026; Viking Dock) comes highly recommended for fluke fishing May to September and sea bass, porgies and striper fishing September to November. There is also excellent **surf casting** among the slippery rocks surrounding the lighthouse point, but this is only for experienced anglers with the proper equipment. Any would-be fishermen should consult the chamber of commerce (☎ 631-668-2428) for season regulations and size and quota limits.

Montauk Downs State Park (☎ 631-668-5000) features a fine public **golf course**, which costs $33 per person per round of 18; expect long waits for tee times in the summer, however.

Places to Stay & Eat The summer season in Montauk goes from April to August, when accommodation can be hard to come by (for this reason and others, including price, crowd density and ambiance, consider coming in the fall shoulder season from September to October). While everything should be booked in advance, anything even remotely considered budget should be arranged months ahead of time, if possible. The cheaper hotels in Montauk run about $125 a night, but many are booked solid by college students working for the summer in the restaurants and resorts. Call the chamber of commerce for a list of accommodations

It's worth asking if your hotel has a BBQ: you can always pick up the catch of the day for cheap down at the docks and throw it on the coals for a fresh, hearty dinner.

Hither Hills State Park (☎ 631-668-2461, 800-456-2267; w www.nysparks.com; sites $16) is a windswept, 40-acre campground along the Old Montauk Hwy, right on the Atlantic Ocean. It's only open in the high season and is very popular. Heart-of-the-summer reservations should be made a year in advance – no joke.

Montauk Yacht Club Resort (☎ 888-692-8668; 32 Star Island Rd; suites in summer to $400) offers Montauk's toniest digs. There are no fewer than three pools here, numerous tennis courts, restaurants and a fitness center.

Gurney's Inn Resort (☎ 631-668-2345, 800-848-7639; w www.gurneys-inn.com; 290 Old Montauk Hwy; rooms/cottages from $185/350) is one of the top hotel choices, though by some accounts, it has lost a bit of its luster in recent years. It has 175 rooms and a spa, and is overpriced for what you get.

Surfside (631-668-5958; 685 Old Montauk Highway; open year-round) is a friendly, family-owned restaurant with good food, healthy portions and an economic early bird special from 4:30pm to 6pm daily. The dining room also offers beautiful ocean views.

Shagwong Restaurant (☎ 631-668-3050; Main St; open year-round) is a place serving good tavern-style meals worth the price. It's a local favorite.

The Montauket, up the hill from the train station, is a local bar with tons of divey atmosphere and local characters swirling the ice in their high balls or draining a pitcher of beer. Grab a cold one and cheer as the sun goes down over the water with the rest of the crowd.

If you're into the local bar scene, also worth checking out is **The Dock**, at the dock (duh!) on the edge of the harbor, with a good happy hour and even better policy of 'take screaming children outside.'

Getting There & Away You can take the LIRR to Montauk, ($10.25/15.25 off peak/peak one way), but it's a 10-minute walk from the train station to the center of town. Taxis are available.

Shelter Island

Nearly a third of Shelter Island is dedicated to the **Mashomack Nature Preserve**, which makes the island a largely quiet retreat that offers a true respite from the crowds in the Hamptons. The heart of the island is a small, attractive town called Shelter Island Heights where you'll find a cluster of Victorian buildings and bunches of New York City families who maintain summer getaways here.

EXCURSIONS

W Piccozzi Inc (☎ 631-749-0045; Bridge St) repairs just about anything and rents bikes for $25 a day; these are sturdy enough for a strenuous trek across the island. You can also take the bikes on the ferry to Greenport, then explore the North Fork and Orient Point. Call ahead in the summer to reserve a bike.

Places to Stay & Eat For such a small place, Shelter Island includes more than its share of B&Bs.

Azalea House (☎ 631-749-4252; 1 Thomas Ave; rooms $60-175; open year-round) has five spotless, inviting rooms; prices include continental breakfast. As a bonus, it's across from **Planet Bliss** (☎ 631-749-0053; 23 N Ferry Rd), a fabulous organic market with bistro attached.

Shelter Island B&B (☎ 631-749-0842; 7 St Mary's Rd; rooms non-holiday weekends $65-98) has four rooms in a quaint Cape Cod house. It's tough to beat the prices and atmosphere of this place.

Ram's Head Inn (☎ 631-749-0811; Ram Island Dr; rooms off-season $80, summer from $225), a large, columned place with overlooking the water, has great off-season rates and a variety of rooms (with private bathroom) to choose from.

Almost all the restaurants on Shelter Island are only open during the tourist season.

Dory (☎ 631-749-8871), near the Shelter Island Heights Bridge, is a smoky bar that serves simple fare on a waterfront patio.

Olde Country Inn (☎ 631-749-1633; 11 Stearns Point Rd; open year-round) is a fabulous place. The innovative menu has it all, from duck breast to calves liver and there's a long, creative wine list. The prix fixe winter menu ($22.50) is one of the best deals going.

Getting There & Away The **North Ferry Company** (☎ 631-749-0139) runs boats from the North Fork terminal (near the LIRR station in Greenport) to Shelter Island every 15 minutes from 6am to midnight (until 1am between Memorial Day and Labor Day). The one-way fare is $7 for a car and driver, and additional passengers cost $1; bikes cost $3/4 one way/roundtrip. The journey takes seven minutes.

South Ferry Inc (☎ 631-749-1200) leaves from a dock three miles north of Sag Harbor, with boats operating 6am to 1:45am. The cost for a car and driver is $7 and additional passengers are $1; the trip takes five minutes.

Greenport

The main town on the North Fork, Greenport used to be populated with farmers and workers from the Grumman company, but economic change in the '80s forced a downturn that Greenport is still trying to shake off. In recent years, though, weekending city dwellers have started snapping up properties in the area, changing the character of this working-class town. The realization by California and European vintners of the high-quality grapes grown on Long Island and their acquisition of wineries here are also adding new flavors to the mix. Greenport makes a fine jumping-off point for a winery tour around Long Island's forks (see the 'Long Island Wineries' boxed text).

While you're in the area, make it a point to visit the tiny hamlet of **Orient**, about three miles from the Orient Point ferry terminal; follow the signs for the 'Orient Business District' at the Civil War monument on the side of Route 25. There's not much of a business district in this 17th-century hamlet, just an old wooden post office and a general store, but Orient features a well-preserved collection of white clapboard houses and former inns. Farther out of town, you can bike past the Oyster Ponds just east of Main St and see the beach at Orient Beach State Park.

Places to Stay & Eat A large old home adorned by two huge stone lions, **White Lions Inn** (☎ 631-477-8819; 433 Main St; rooms $65-110) is the best place to stay in Greenport. It has five rooms (two with shared baths) and is only a four-block walk from the Shelter Island ferry dock and LIRR train station. There's free parking.

Seafood Barge (☎ 631-765-3010; Route 25; appetizers $6-13, pasta $17-21, seafood entrees $15-24), three miles from Greenport, is one of the best places to taste the sweet Peconic Bay scallops, a local specialty that has made a comeback after being devastated by 'brown tide' in 1994. This place also specializes in local wines, which you can savor while overlooking the Port of Egypt Marina.

Within Greenport, most restaurants are clustered around the marina.

Claudio's (☎ 631-477-0715; 111 Main St; clam bar $6.95-11.95, seafood entrees $15.95-21.95; open mid-April–Jan 1) is a landmark that gets quite noisy at the long wooden bar and that charges a bit much for its food (perhaps because it's recognized as the 'oldest same-family-owned restaurant in the US' by the National Restaurant Association?).

Aldo's (☎ 631-477-1699; 103-105 Front St) is a better option. It is also pricey, but serves sublime food and is known for its biscotti, made in the small bakery next to the restaurant. Reservations are essential.

Getting There & Away The **Cross Sound Ferry Company** (☎ 631-323-2525, 860-443-5281; W www.longislandferry.com) takes passengers and cars from Orient Point, at the tip of the North Fork, to New London, Connecticut, several times a day; reservations are recommended. Cars cost $36, including driver, and passengers are $10 one-way. The company also offers a car-free, high-speed 'sea jet' service between Orient Point and New London (with a connecting bus service to Foxwoods Casino and Resort in Connecticut). Fares are $15.50 one way, $25 same-day return; the trip takes 40 minutes.

THE HUDSON VALLEY

You'll find many charming spots just north of New York City in this region, which encompasses the villages and towns that dot the Hudson River south of Albany. Autumn is a particularly beautiful time here, and many city dwellers rent cars to see the changing colors. There are also many historic sites and stately homes up this way.

Remember that even though the towns can easily be reached by the Metro-North commuter train from Grand Central Terminal, you'll find little reliable public transportation once you get off the train. Unfortunately, you'll need to have a car for the fullest exploration of the area, though strong cyclists can design a well-rounded tour.

The regional **Hudson Valley Tourist Board** (☎ 800-232-4782; W www.pojonews.com /enjoy/index.htm) issues a guide to attractions and events. Orange County, the location of the United States Military Academy commonly known as West Point, also publishes a guide (☎ 800-762-8687; W www.orange tourism.org). Most tourist brochures can be obtained at the **New York State Information Center** (☎ 914-786-5003; exit 16 off I-87, the New York State Thruway) at Harriman.

Getting There & Around
Train While **Amtrak trains** (☎ 212-582-6875, 800-872-7245; W www.amtrak.com) run the length of the river and connect with several communities on the eastern shore, your best and cheapest bet from New York City is the **Metro-North commuter train** (☎ 212-532-4900, 800-638-7646; W www .mnr.org), which departs from Grand Central Terminal (take the 'Hudson Line').

The regular one-way fare from Grand Central to various towns in the Hudson Valley ranges from $5.50 to $9.50 (one way, off peak). On weekends, Metro-North runs special summer and autumn tourist packages that include train fare and transportation to and from specific sites such as Hyde Park and the Vanderbilt Mansion.

Boat One of the most relaxing and pleasant ways to take in several sites strung along here is by the **NY Waterway** (☎ 800-533-3779; W www.nywaterway.com), which offers ferry trips up the Hudson River. Full-day tours on offer include Washington Irving's Sunnyside home (where he penned both the *Legend of Sleepy Hollow* and *Rip Van Winkle*; $43/22 adult/child), the Rockefeller's Kykuit summer mansion ($62/57 adult/child) and Jay Gould's estate known as Lyndhurst Castle ($49/25 adult/child), among others.

Car The principal scenic river route is Route 9, which hugs the east side of the river. On the west side, the road is called Route 9W. Most towns can also be reached by taking the faster Taconic State Parkway, which runs north from Ossining and is considered one of the state's prettiest roads when the leaves turn in the autumn. The New York State Thruway runs west of the Hudson River.

Bicycle The country roads east of the Hudson River are perfect for biking. For further information, read *Ride Guide: Mountain Biking in the NY Metro Area* by Joel Sendek (Anacus Press) or *25 Mountain Bike Tours in the Hudson Valley* by Peter Kick (Backcountry Books).

West Point

Generations of American soldiers have been groomed at the United States Military Academy since its establishment in 1802, including US Grant, Douglas MacArthur and Dwight Eisenhower. Today, the cadet corps are made up of men and women who live on an impressive campus of red-brick and gray-stone Gothic- and Federal-style buildings, churches and temples.

For maps and tour information, stop in at the **West Point Visitors Center** *(☎ 914-938-2638; open 9am-4:45pm daily)*, which is actually in Highland Falls, about 100 yards south of the military academy's Thayer Gate.

By car, take the New York State Thruway to Route 9W North and look for the West Point exit, then follow the signs. It's about an hour's drive from Midtown Manhattan. You can also reach West Point by NY Waterway ferry; see the boat entry earlier.

Hyde Park

The peaceful hillsides of Hyde Park overlook the eastern edge of the Hudson and are home to three significant attractions: the Franklin D Roosevelt Home and Library, the Eleanor Roosevelt National Historic Site and the Vanderbilt Mansion National Historic Site. Work up an appetite and you can grab a bite at one of the four restaurants on the grounds of the **Culinary Institute of America** *(☎ 914-452-9600; Route 9)*; reservations are required.

The **Franklin D Roosevelt Home and Library** *(☎ 914-229-8114, 800-337-8474; Route 9, 511 Albany Post Rd; adult/senior $7/5, child free; open 9am-5pm daily Nov-Mar, 9am-6pm daily Apr-Oct)* was the first US presidential library. Roosevelt (1882–1945) made Hyde Park his summer White House during his

four terms. The museum features old photos, Roosevelt 's voice on tape (from his famous fireside chats and several speeches), a special wing in memory of Eleanor Roosevelt (1884–1962) and his famous 1936 Ford Phaeton car, with its special hand controls that enabled the wheelchair-bound president to drive. President and Mrs Roosevelt are interred in the Rose Garden on the grounds. All facilities are wheelchair accessible.

Because his mother lived at Hyde Park until her death in 1941, Eleanor Roosevelt, who did not get along with her mother-in-law (or for other reasons more personal still), stayed at her own home, which she called Val-Kill after the Dutch for 'valley stream,' after the president's death in April 1945. It's now the site of the **Eleanor Roosevelt National Historic Site** *(☎ 914-229-9115; Route 9, 519 Albany Post Rd; admission free; open daily Mar-Dec)*, two miles east of Hyde Park. The peaceful grounds are dotted with sugar maple and pine trees, and a dirt road leads to the cottage from the entrance off Route 9G.

The **Vanderbilt Mansion National Historic Site** *(☎ 914-229-9115; Route 9; adult $4, senior & child free; open 9am-5pm daily Apr-Nov, closed Tues & Wed winter)* is two miles north of Hyde Park. The spectacular 54-room beaux arts home by the venerable architectural firm of McKim, Meade and White, with many original furnishings still intact, used to be a mere weekend and summer cottage for members of the railroad dynasty. The landscaping here is phenomenal.

EXCURSIONS

ALLAN MONTAINE

Beaux-arts splendor, near Hyde Park

New Jersey

It's easy to see why the 'Garden State' is so easily mocked. Not only does it stand in the shadow of confident, popular and powerful New York City, but the refineries and factories belch nasty-smelling stuff into the air and it's the state with the most government-certified toxic Super Fund sites. Now that's attractive! To most New Yorkers, Jersey looks like a crowded corridor of tract houses, shipping docks and dirty marshland along the New Jersey Turnpike leading into New York City from Newark International Airport.

This is the New Jersey of punch lines and snickering asides and is not a bad assessment for the more disgusting sections. But in recent years, the state government has made great and largely successful efforts to emphasize the area's varied pleasures, including 127 miles of beaches, millions of acres of preserved parkland and historic sites inexorably tied to the nation's colonial history. Indeed, the tourism trade brings in $30 billion a year, largely from folks popping into Jersey for a weekend of fun in the sun or ducking into where the sun never shines – to try their luck at the casinos in Atlantic City. Those who explore New Jersey off the beaten track may find their attitude toward this much-maligned state changing fast.

LIBERTY STATE PARK

This 1200-acre park (☎ 201-915-3400; visitor center open 6am-6pm daily May-Nov, 8am-4pm winter) offers some of the best views around, as it faces the Statue of Liberty and takes in spectacular vistas of Manhattan. Ferries depart here for Ellis and Liberty Islands and are always less crowded than their counterparts operating from Battery Park (see the Things to See & Do chapter for information on the islands). Well worth a visit, Liberty State Park features a picnic area; a children's playground; paths for walking, jogging, cycling and horseback riding; and opportunities for boating, swimming and fishing.

Entering the park, you drive along State Flag Row (with the flags arranged in order of the states' induction into the Union) and

some 1750 feet ahead of you stands the Statue of Liberty. Beyond, you can also see the Brooklyn Bridge and, to the right, the bridge linking Staten Island to Brooklyn. Check out the **Liberation Monument**. 'Dedicated to America's role of preserving freedom and rescuing the oppressed,' this statue features a US soldier carrying a WWII concentration camp survivor.

Statue of Liberty Tours

Ferries (☎ 201-435-9499) travel from Liberty State Park to the Statue of Liberty and Ellis Island every day except Christmas Day. The boats tend to be less crowded than those leaving from Lower Manhattan, but the mobs on both islands mean you won't be able to take in both sites unless you depart well before noon. The trip takes just 15 minutes and costs $8/6/3 per adult/senior/child.

Liberty Science Center

This spectacular, modern, hi-tech museum (☎ 201-200-1000; W www.lsc.org; adult/senior & child $10/8; open 9:30am-5:30pm Tues-Sun), also located in the state park, bills itself as a family learning center for science, technology and nature, with three of the four floors dedicated to the theme of invention. At the interactive exhibits, you can transmit sound through a laser beam, learn how to see in 3-D or watch a million watts of electricity flow through a coil to create lightning bolts. Hands-on is the buzz word here and the Touch Tunnel, virtual reality sports and bug exhibits let your fingers do the walking. Needless to say, kids adore this place.

The museum's **shop**, Tools & Toys, sells science-related products, books and toys (also look for a branch in Newark International Airport). The **Laser Lights Cafe** offers terrific views across the Hudson to the Statue of Liberty and the Manhattan skyline, but you'll probably go mad from the noise of the school kids.

Don't miss the IMAX Dome theater out here, which is one of a kind in the tri-state area and the largest IMAX screen in the country (separate IMAX tickets cost $9/7 for adult/child or you can combine it with museum entrance and save a bundle).

HOBOKEN

Hoboken is an endearing working-class community where locals call you 'hon,' 'doll' or 'mami,' the streets are lined with row upon row of impressive brownstones, interesting alleys beckon and cool churches cry out to be photographed. What's more, it's just minutes from Downtown Manhattan by a ferry offering terrific skyline views and not much longer to Midtown by Path train. Sound too good to be true? Well, that's what all the up-and-coming young professionals thought when they started snatching up cheap properties, shepherding in a period of gentrification that shows little sign of slowing. Still, the old residents live alongside the new and Hoboken is a refreshing mix of cultures and classes that doesn't exist in similar areas such as Brooklyn Heights, which these days looks as white as a glass of milk.

Hoboken is also known as a party town and weekends get raucous with local youngsters taking full advantage of generous happy hours and folks coming from all over the tri-state area for a bit of a pub crawl. All the partying has led to some friction between law enforcement, tavern owners and residents, who have struck up a dialogue on

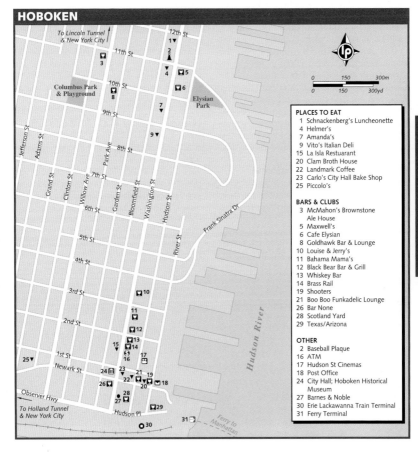

HOBOKEN

PLACES TO EAT
1 Schnackenberg's Luncheonette
4 Helmer's
7 Amanda's
9 Vito's Italian Deli
15 La Isla Restuarant
20 Clam Broth House
22 Landmark Coffee
23 Carlo's City Hall Bake Shop
25 Piccolo's

BARS & CLUBS
3 McMahon's Brownstone
 Ale House
5 Maxwell's
6 Cafe Elysian
8 Goldhawk Bar & Lounge
10 Louise & Jerry's
11 Bahama Mama's
12 Black Bear Bar & Grill
13 Whiskey Bar
14 Brass Rail
19 Shooters
21 Boo Boo Funkadelic Lounge
26 Bar None
28 Scotland Yard
29 Texas/Arizona

OTHER
2 Baseball Plaque
16 ATM
17 Hudson St Cinemas
18 Post Office
24 City Hall; Hoboken Historical
 Museum
27 Barnes & Noble
30 Erie Lackawanna Train Terminal
31 Ferry Terminal

EXCURSIONS

how to co-exist happily. As a result, if you're looking for some bottled cheer over here, you should know that you'll be required to show two forms of ID to enter a bar, there's a one-way door policy after 2am (you can leave a bar, but you can't enter one; this may be rolled back to 1am by the time you read this) and they're considering outlawing organized pub crawls. St Patrick's Day is a *big* holiday on this side of the river.

While many come only to indulge themselves, some visitors make something of a cultural-historical pilgrimage to Hoboken. It's generally agreed that the first organized baseball game was played here between the New Yorkers and the Knickerbockers, on a plain overlooking Manhattan on June 19, 1846; a memorial plaque at the corner of Washington and 11th Sts commemorates the event. Hoboken's other claim to fame is its most famous resident: Frank Sinatra. 'The Chairman of the Board' was born here in 1915 and got his start in local clubs. Hoboken also holds the sad and mournful honor of having lost the most residents of any neighborhood in the September 11 attacks: 50 people from the community died on that day.

Orientation & Information

Since it occupies little more than a square mile, Hoboken is easy to explore on foot, and a grid system makes getting around a breeze. Most of Hoboken's shops and restaurants lie within a few blocks of the ornate old Erie Lackawanna Train Terminal, where the Path trains stop, or along Washington St.

Parking in Hoboken can be a headache, especially at night and on weekends. With the parking police aggressively checking for offenders, you should consider paying to park in a lot rather than leaving your car on the street and risking a ticket. Of course, the public transportation serving Hoboken is fast and varied: Choose from a ferry, the Path or NJ Transit trains.

The city has no tourist office, but you can pick up a copy of the free weekly *Hoboken Reporter* – which covers local arts and special events – at bars and shops all around town. City Hall offers flyers on local events.

You'll find ATMs all along Washington St. The main **post office** *(#18; River St)* is between Newark and 1st Sts. The Hoboken **Barnes & Noble** *(#27; ☎ 201-653-1165; 59 Washington St)*, between Newark St and Observer Hwy, is a sprawler and carries all the reading material you'd expect; there's also the requisite café inside.

Hoboken City Hall & Museum

Built in 1881, Hoboken City Hall *(#24; ☎ 201-420-2026; 1st & Washington Sts; open 9am-4pm Mon-Fri)* qualifies as an official, yet rough-around-the-edges, State and National Historic Landmark. Inside, the Hoboken Historical Museum features a series of dusty display cases about local history, including mementos of Frank Sinatra. (Sinatra's birthplace was torn down some years ago, so this spot has become the main Frank shrine.)

New Jersey is only a hop, skip and jump from Downtown New York

Places to Eat

The quality and variety of cafés and restaurants in Hoboken are growing and glorious, making it a great spot to start off a date; you can fill up at one of the many places lining Washington St and then catch some cocktails, live music or dancing at one of many Hoboken hot spots.

Vito's Italian Deli (#9; ☎ 201-792-4944; 806 Washington St; closed Mon), between 8th and 9th Sts, makes great submarine sandwiches and sells all manner of Italian delicacies.

Landmark Coffee (#22; ☎ 201-222-8400; 88 Hudson St; open 6am-6pm Mon-Fri, 7am-3pm Sat & Sun) is a cute, friendly café with the usual coffee menu, plus scores of tea selections and hot cider.

Carlo's City Hall Bake Shop (#23; ☎ 201-659-3671; 95 Washington St; open 6:30am-8pm Mon-Sat, 6:30am-6pm Sun), between Newark and 1st Sts, has mouthwatering Italian pastries, including some of the best pignoli nut cookies around. You can take a coffee and sweets at one of the small tables overlooking the street.

Schnackenberg's Luncheonette (#1; ☎ 201-659-9836; 1110 Washington St; sandwiches $1.40-3.50), between 11th and 12th Sts, is a wonderful place upholding the grand lunch counter tradition. These folks have been serving up egg creams, cherry Cokes, sandwiches (including the classic cream cheese and jelly!) and homemade chocolates since 1931. The prices are as historic as the atmosphere: Thick, yummy milkshakes are a crazy 60¢/70¢/$1 for small/medium/large. Kids love this place.

Piccolo's (#25; ☎ 201-653-0564; 92 Clinton St), between Newark and 1st Sts, is another lunch counter place with a touch of greasy spoon ambiance; they've been serving delicious cheese steak sandwiches ($6) at this location since 1955.

La Isla Restaurant (#15; ☎ 201-659-8197; 104 Washington St; appetizers $2.50-7.95, sandwiches $3.95-4.95; entrees $10.95-15.95; open 7am-10pm Mon-Sat, 11am-4pm Sun) is so authentic, you would think you really were in Havana save for the lack of Patria o Muerte references. The food here is wholesome, the portions huge, the music hot and it's all served up with that endearing warmth that is so typically Cuban. Try the classic Ropa Vieja (shredded steak; $8.95) and wash it down with whatever alcohol you bring with you; save room for a sweet, strong cafecito.

Clam Broth House (#20; ☎ 201-659-6767; 38 Newark St; appetizers $7.95-9.95, raw bar $7.95-15.95; open 11:30am-10pm daily), near the train station, was established in 1899 and serves up such good sea tidbits it's been drawing dedicated customers from Manhattan for years. It's got that classic, upscale mafioso atmosphere replete with lots of red leather and signed celebrity photos, including Frank Sinatra's.

Helmer's (#4; ☎ 201-963-3333; 1036 Washington St at 11th St; sandwiches $6.95-9.95, wursts $10.95-15.95; open noon-10pm Mon-Thur, noon-11pm Fri & Sat) is a traditional German bar and restaurant from the 1930s, with a dizzying array of beer and scotch selections. German specialties like knockwurst sandwiches with sauerkraut and many other types of wursts (sausages) abound. Save room for dessert.

Amanda's (#7; ☎ 201-798-0101; 908 Washington St; appetizers $5.50-12, entrees $16.50-29.50) is Hoboken's contribution to the culinary arts. The menu here changes weekly, but you might savor filo-wrapped shrimp or lobster bisque to start and move on to a rack of lamb with lemon pignoli crust. The wine selection is well crafted and the atmosphere is upscale-alluring with crisp linens and fine flatware.

Entertainment

At last count, Hoboken had some 40 clubs and bars catering to all kinds; from Irish folk to indie rock, there is probably some music happening every night of the week here. Hoboken's lively music scene has even spawned a few independent record labels and is the proud launching spot of the great poetic rappers Yo La Tengo. Maxwell's is Hoboken's legendary club and the biggest groups have graced the stage here. If you're a fan of a particular band and you hear they're coming to New York, it might

EXCURSIONS

be possible to catch them twice: once in the big city and again at Maxwell's.

Hoboken also has its share of dance clubs, most of which stay open until 3am on Friday and Saturday.

Live Music The reason many people head to Hoboken is **Maxwell's** *(#5; ☎ 201-798-0406, show info: 201-653-1703; 1039 Washington St at 11th St; cover $10-20).* In the mid-'90s, Maxwell's disastrously re-created itself as a microbrewery, but regulars shunned the club and music loyalists took it over and restored the old ways. The bar's back room has been featuring acts since 1978, and visitors have included REM, Sonic Youth and Nirvana. Bruce Springsteen used Maxwell's as the setting for his 'Glory Days' video (directed by city resident John Sayles). The restaurant in front features more creative than usual pub fare.

Brass Rail *(#14; ☎ 201-659-7074; 135 Washington St)* is a bar and restaurant that offers live jazz Thursday to Saturday nights, accompanied by French food. The wine list here has to be among the best in New Jersey.

Whiskey Bar *(#13; ☎ 201-963-4300;* W *www.whiskey-bar.com; 125 Washington St)* has live rock 'n' roll Thursday to Saturday nights.

Dancing There's live bands Wednesday and Thursday at **Boo Boo Funkadelic Lounge** *(#21; ☎ 201-659-5527; 44 Newark St),* plus DJs spinning house and funk on weekends.

Bar None *(#26; ☎ 201-420-1112; 84 Washington St)* plays Top 40 music and offers 'beat the clock' drink specials on weekdays. As you'd expect, the crowd gets increasingly rowdy, befogging their beer goggles as the night progresses.

Bahama Mama's *(#11; ☎ 201-217-1642; 215 Washington St; free before 10pm)* has $1 margaritas until 11pm on Friday.

Shooters *(#19; ☎ 201-656-3889; 92 River St at Newark St)* attracts the college crowd from Hoboken's Stevens Institute of Technology. The DJs play house and drum 'n' bass.

Bars Built in 1896, **Cafe Elysian** *(#6; ☎ 201-659-9110; 1001 Washington St at 10th St)* features a beautiful old bar that transformed into a beauty salon and an ice-cream parlor to survive the Prohibition. Regulars include bikers and blues fans – catch some decent blues acts here Friday and Saturday nights.

Louise & Jerry's *(#10; ☎ 201-656-9698; 329 Washington St),* between 3rd and 4th Sts, has been pulling pints since the beginning of the 20th century. This classic basement-level hang-out has a coin-operated pool table and happy-hour specials.

Black Bear Bar & Grill *(#12; ☎ 201-656-5511; 205 Washington St)* is a sports lounge and cigar bar that attracts the Wall St crowd. You can eat pretty well here on a budget: wraps, sandwiches and burgers range from $6.95 to $8.95.

McMahon's Brownstone Ale House *(#3; ☎ 201-798-5650; 1034 Willow Ave)* is an Irish pub (with the requisite pool table and dart boards) that offers a Sunday buffet and live music on Wednesday nights.

Texas/Arizona *(#29; ☎ 201-420-0304; River St at Hudson Place),* near the train station, serves reasonably priced Tex-Mex food, but the real draw is the international beer selection. Head here during off-hours to meet some unique, local characters.

Scotland Yard *(#28; ☎ 201-222-9273; 72 Hudson St)* serves up British exports like Fullers, Bass and Double Diamond on tap in a traditional pub setting. On Friday night, people quaff gallons of ale. The happy hour (4pm to 7:30pm) has free food – a tradition more New York–area bars should embrace.

Goldhawk Bar & Lounge *(#8; ☎ 201-420-7989; 916 Park Ave at 10th St)* is a super-laidback place with mismatched velvet settees and frayed couches in the back and an energetic bar scene up front. There are often readings and live music happening here.

Getting There & Away

Train The Path train from Manhattan ($1.50) stops at the Erie Lackawanna Train Terminal in Hoboken. It runs 24 hours, though with less frequency late at night.

Car From Manhattan, take either the Holland or Lincoln Tunnels. From the New Jersey Turnpike, take exit 14C (Holland Tunnel exit), go to the bottom of the ramp and make a left at the first light, then bear right under the overpass onto Observer Hwy; Hoboken's main streets are to the left. You can also take exit 16E (Lincoln Tunnel exit), go right at the Hoboken exit and go through the first light to the bottom of the ramp; turn right onto Park Ave, then left onto 14th St. You'll find Washington St three blocks later on the right.

Boat Operating between Hoboken (connected to the Erie Lackawanna Train Terminal) and Piers A and 11 in Lower Manhattan is the **New York Waterway** (☎ *800-533-3779*). Ferries leave every six minutes during rush hours and every 10 minutes at off-peak times. The trip takes eight minutes and costs $3 each way.

ATLANTIC CITY

Since casino gambling came to Atlantic City (or AC as it's known locally) on the Jersey Shore in 1977, the town has become one of the country's most popular tourist destinations, with 33 million annual visitors spending some $4 billion at its 12 casinos and numerous restaurants. But even though the casino industry has created 45,000 jobs and experienced record profits, little of this money has benefited Atlantic City itself. Homelessness and crime are still big problems, and the four-block stretch of town from the end of the Atlantic City Expressway to the beachfront casinos is a depressing collection of empty lots, rough-looking bars and abandoned warehouses. It's really a shame because the fantastic seashore setting of Atlantic City, combined with its fascinating history, means it should be an alive and thriving place.

In the summer, the boardwalk delivers a bit of intrigue thanks to packs of feral cats, pawn shops, buskers and other fringe entertainers that pepper the beachfront, lending it a seedy and delinquent character. The beach is too popular in summer, becoming uncomfortably congested with gamblers drunk on cheap booze and even cheaper thrills.

The bottom line is that for nongamblers, there is little reason to visit Atlantic City unless you're on your way to the Cape May resort area or Philadelphia. In fact, if you're not gambling, the casinos can be downright depressing as you pass through gauntlet after gauntlet of neon-spinning, bell-ringing 'one-armed bandits' manned by glassy-eyed senior citizens. On the flipside, if you want to gamble, you can't beat Atlantic City's selection of 700 blackjack tables and nearly 30,000 slot machines. If you visit, plan on trying your luck at something – even if you wish to spend only $10 or $15 – and remember that the greatest gamblers walk away from the table winners, so 'know when to fold 'em.'

EXCURSIONS

RICHARD CUMMINS

The Trump Taj Mahal casino, Atlantic City: a combination of brashness, crassness and exotic allure

ATLANTIC CITY

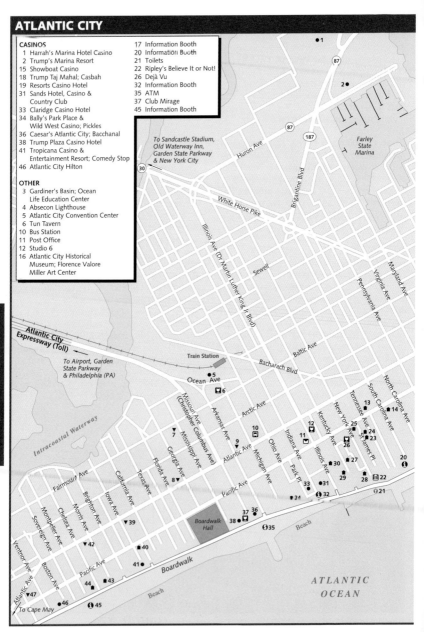

CASINOS
1 Harrah's Marina Hotel Casino
2 Trump's Marina Resort
15 Showboat Casino
18 Trump Taj Mahal; Casbah
19 Resorts Casino Hotel
31 Sands Hotel, Casino &
   Country Club
33 Claridge Casino Hotel
34 Bally's Park Place &
   Wild West Casino; Pickles
36 Caesar's Atlantic City; Bacchanal
38 Trump Plaza Casino Hotel
41 Tropicana Casino &
   Entertainment Resort; Comedy Stop
46 Atlantic City Hilton

OTHER
3 Gardiner's Basin; Ocean
  Life Education Center
4 Absecon Lighthouse
5 Atlantic City Convention Center
6 Tun Tavern
10 Bus Station
11 Post Office
12 Studio 6
16 Atlantic City Historical
   Museum; Florence Valore
   Miller Art Center

17 Information Booth
20 Information Booth
21 Toilets
22 Ripley's Believe It or Not!
26 Déjà Vu
32 Information Booth
35 ATM
37 Club Mirage
45 Information Booth

To Sandcastle Stadium,
Old Waterway Inn,
Garden State Parkway
& New York City

Farley
State
Marina

Huron Ave

Brigantine Blvd

White Horse Pike

Illinois Ave (Dr Martin Luther King Jr Blvd)

Sewell

Maryland Ave

Virginia Ave

Pennsylvania Ave

Atlantic City
Expressway (Toll)

To Airport, Garden
State Parkway
& Philadelphia (PA)

Train Station

Baltic Ave

Bacharach Blvd

Ocean Ave

Intracoastal Waterway

Falmouth Ave

California Ave

Texas Ave

Florida Ave

Georgia Ave

Mississippi Ave

Missouri Ave
(Christopher Columbus Ave)

Arkansas Ave

Arctic Ave

Atlantic Ave

Michigan Ave

Ohio Ave

Indiana Ave

Park Pl

Kentucky Ave

New York Ave

Tennessee Ave

South Carolina Ave

North Carolina Ave

St James Pl

Iowa Ave

Brighton Ave

Morris Ave

Chelsea Ave

Montpelier Ave

Sovereign Ave

Ventnor Ave

Boston Ave

Atlantic Ave

Pacific Ave

Boardwalk
Hall

Pacific Ave

Boardwalk

Beach

To Cape May

ATLANTIC
OCEAN

EXCURSIONS

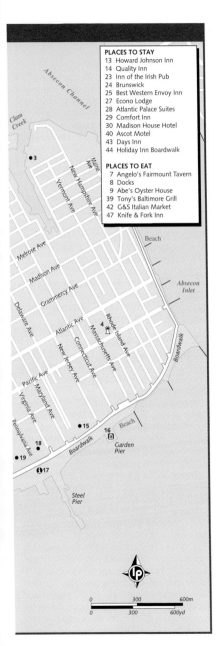

PLACES TO STAY
13 Howard Johnson Inn
14 Quality Inn
23 Inn of the Irish Pub
24 Brunswick
25 Best Western Envoy Inn
27 Econo Lodge
28 Atlantic Palace Suites
29 Comfort Inn
30 Madison House Hotel
40 Ascot Motel
43 Days Inn
44 Holiday Inn Boardwalk

PLACES TO EAT
7 Angelo's Fairmount Tavern
8 Docks
9 Abe's Oyster House
39 Tony's Baltimore Grill
42 G&S Italian Market
47 Knife & Fork Inn

Information

The **Visitors Information Center** (☎ 609-449-7130; w www.atlanticcitynj.com; Garden State Parkway; open 11am-7pm daily) is in a brand-new complex in the middle of the Parkway, 3½ miles from town. You can pick up maps, brochures and coupon books here and it makes a good spot to orient yourself before diving into the city's glitz. Four information booths are sprinkled along the Boardwalk between the Taj Mahal to the north and the Atlantic City Hilton to the south. Also, a desk inside **Boardwalk Hall** (open 10am-6pm daily) provides many brochures for local hotels.

The best of the free guides to the area is the monthly *AC Shoreline* and the weeklies *Whoot* and *At the Shore*. The last is particularly good for calendar listings and includes art, jazz and theater happenings.

Not surprisingly, you can find ATMs and ATMs near the gaming areas of all the casinos. Casinos will also do foreign-currency exchange and gladly give advances against credit cards.

Casinos

Atlantic City's casinos are obviously the major attraction here and, though high rollers all seem to have a favorite, the gaming areas tend to look alike (garish) and sound alike (loud). Bring plenty of aspirin.

Most of the casinos in AC are dedicated to gaming and, beyond the Taj Mahal, do not emphasize glitz and showmanship like their Las Vegas counterparts. This is changing, however, as big casino developers like Donald Trump and Steve Wynn vie for supremacy.

Note: You must be at least 21 years old to gamble or be on the gambling floor. If you're a fan of potent potables, you'll likely enjoy Atlantic City, as the cocktails are bottomless and free. Every casino is required to have a Casino Control Commission on the gambling floor. This is where you go if you suspect a dealer is cheating or there is some other hocus pocus going on at the tables. Serious inquiries only please.

The city's many casinos include the following. The southernmost casino, **Atlantic City Hilton** (#46; ☎ 609-340-7100; Boardwalk at Boston Ave) has over 500 hotel rooms.

EXCURSIONS

Do Not Pass Go

Gamers will notice that many of the street names here are exactly the same as in the Monopoly board game, which was modeled on Atlantic City. It's an interesting piece of AC lore that in 1904 a local teacher and Quaker named Lizzie J Magie invented a parlor game called the Landlord's Game that was enjoyed by her small circle of family and friends. Then, in 1934, an unemployed and broke family man named Charles Darrow begin reminiscing about a trip he once made to Atlantic City and dreamed up the modern-day Monopoly board game, which contained some uncannily similar characteristics to Magie's original creation; many people suspect Darrow swiped the basic idea from the Landlord's Game, which also required buying and selling utilities and properties and had a 'go to jail' space, among other aspects now associated with Monopoly. Although Parker Brothers originally rejected Monopoly for its 52 fatal board-game flaws, they finally caved in 1935 and bought the copyright after Darrow sold 5000 handmade sets. Within months of buying the rights to the game, Parker Brothers was selling 20,000 games per week! Today, the game is sold in 80 countries in 26 different languages.

N.Y.C.

Bally's Park Place & Wild West Casino (#34; ☎ 609-340-2000; *Park Place at the Boardwalk*) occupies the site of the 1860 Dennis Hotel, which is incorporated into the newer, 1200-room facility. The popular casino here takes the wild-west theme to the hilt, from the Main St faux facade to the bandanna-clad staff. It's the site of many heavyweight boxing matches (box office ☎ 800-772-7777).

Caesar's Atlantic City (#36; ☎ 609-348-4411; *Arkansas Ave at the Boardwalk*) contains 1000 rooms and Atlantic City's Planet Hollywood theme restaurant, which is just off the gaming area.

Popular with low-rolling senior citizens, the **Claridge Casino Hotel** (#33; ☎ 609-340-3400; *Indiana Ave*), between Pacific Ave and the Boardwalk, is accessible by a moving walkway that operates in one direction only – into the casino. It has 500 rooms and a three-floor, claustrophobic gaming area.

Harrah's Marina Hotel Casino (#1; ☎ 609-441-5000; *Brigantine Blvd*) contains 760 rooms in its two towers and is considered the friendliest casino in town. Newbie gamblers might try its floor, which has gracious and instructive dealers.

Resorts Casino Hotel (#19; ☎ 609-344-6000; *North Carolina Ave at the Boardwalk*) is a 670-room Victorian hotel that served as a hospital during WWII.

Near the Boardwalk, **Sands Hotel, Casino & Country Club** (#31; ☎ 609-441-4000, 800-227-2637; w *www.acsands.com; Indiana Ave*) looks like a big, black, glass box. This is Atlantic City's oldest casino.

One of the more affordable casinos in which to bunk down is **Showboat Casino** (#15; ☎ 609-343-4000; *Delaware Ave & the Boardwalk*), which has a riverboat-theme interior going on in its 700 rooms.

Tropicana Casino & Entertainment Resort (#41; ☎ 609-340-4000; *Iowa Ave at the Boardwalk*) is one of the biggest places in town, with its own indoor theme park (Tivoli Pier), a 90,000-sq-foot casino and 1020 rooms.

Trump's Marina Resort (#2; ☎ 609-441-2000; *Huron Ave*), near Brigantine Blvd, overlooks the Farley State Marina and features an art-deco theme. Away from the Boardwalk, the two casino hotels here offer a more relaxed setting.

Trump Plaza Casino Hotel (#38; ☎ 609-441-6000; *Mississippi Ave at the Boardwalk*) has 560 rooms, some with sea views.

Trump Taj Mahal (#18; ☎ 609-449-1000; *1000 Boardwalk*), a garish place that was once the most extravagant property in Atlantic City, is now being eclipsed by the newer Mirage resorts at the marina. Nine two-ton limestone elephants welcome visitors, and 70 bright minarets crown the rooftops. The German crystal chandeliers in the casino and lobby cost $15 million, but despite the garish nature of the interior, the room rates are similar to those found in more modest facilities.

EXCURSIONS

The Boardwalk

In addition to the fun stuff mentioned below, in season (late March–mid-September) you can shoot a round of miniature golf at Mississippi Ave (☎ 609-347-1661) or rent bicycles at shops dotting the Boardwalk.

Atlantic City Historical Museum On the site of the restored Garden Pier, this museum (#16; ☎ 609-347-5839; w www.acmuseum.org; New Jersey Ave at the Boardwalk; admission free; open 10am-4pm daily) provides a look at the city's colorful past, taking visitors back to AC's heyday when such stars as Benny Goodman, Frank Sinatra and Duke Ellington headlined at the casinos. The **Florence Valore Miller Arts Center** (☎ 609-347-5837), part of the same complex, features changing exhibits of regional and local art, with a strong emphasis on AC's African American community. The museum and art center share an aesthetically interesting building with loads of windows affording ocean views on the north end of the pier. It makes a nice respite from the sensory overload of the casinos.

Steel Pier This amusement pier, directly in front of the Taj Mahal casino, belongs to Donald Trump's empire. It used to be the place where the famous diving horse plunged into the Atlantic before crowds of spectators, but today it's a collection of small amusement rides, games of chance, candy stands and 'the biggest Go-Kart track in South Jersey!' Kids dig the Steel Pier, which is only open in season.

Boardwalk Hall This grand hall (☎ 609-449-2000; w www.boardwalkhall.com) was the former site of the annual Miss America pageant and was the largest auditorium in the world without interior roof posts or pillars when it opened in 1929. If there's no event in progress, see if you can take a look at the superb interior of the main hall, home to the world's largest pipe organ (with 33,000 pipes, it weighs 150 tons). This is now home to the Boardwalk Bullies amateur hockey team (see Spectator Sports, later) and the site of spectacular events like the Ringling

Brothers and Barnum & Bailey circuses, and concerts by Julio Iglesias and other superstars; see the website for event details.

Ripley's Believe It or Not! This museum (#22; ☎ 609-347-2001; New York Ave on the Boardwalk; adult/child $10.96/6.95; open 10am-10pm daily May-Aug, 11am-5pm Mon-Fri, 10am-8pm Sat & Sun Sept-Apr) offers odd and grotesque displays in a theme park–like setting. Come here to see the man with four eyes, the magical harp that plays with no strings and the shrunken heads. It's a bit of a farce, but makes a good diversion for small children.

Absecon Lighthouse

This lighthouse (#4; ☎ 609-449-1360; cnr Rhode Island & Pacific Aves; adult/child $4/1; open 11am-4pm Thur-Mon Sept-June, 11am-4pm daily July & Aug) dates from 1857 and, at 171 feet high, ranks as the tallest in New Jersey and the third-tallest in the country. It's been restored to its original specifications (including the Frensel lens) and you can climb the 228 steps to the top for phenomenal views.

Atlantic City Convention Center

A $300 million convention center (#5; ☎ 888-222-3838) opened above the train station in 1998 and houses a noncasino hotel with 12,000 rooms, plus shops, theaters and restaurants. The center, built by the company responsible for New York's successful South St Seaport complex and Baltimore's Inner Harbor, now hosts the Miss America pageant every September.

Places to Stay

Atlantic City itself offers a good **reservations service** (☎ 800-447-6667), with rooms at all price levels and package deals. The town's room rates vary considerably depending on the season. In winter, it's possible to stay in a hotel such as Resorts Casino for as little as $50 a night, but in summer the rates run much higher, especially during July 4 weekend and the week of Miss America festivities in the fall. If you plan to gamble and want a good mid-range

EXCURSIONS

hotel, book a package deal through a casino hotel or travel agent. The **AmeriRoom Reservations hotline** (☎ 800-888 5875) specializes in these mid-range packages, which usually include meals, show tickets and complimentary chips.

Budget Shoestring travelers will have a hard time in Atlantic City since the cheaper motels a few blocks off the Boardwalk tend to be pick-up spots for prostitutes.

Inn of the Irish Pub (#23; ☎ 609-344-6093; 164 St James Place; rooms $20-30, with private bath from $40) is right off the Boardwalk, but on one of the city's gamiest blocks. Still, the balcony here has plenty of rocking chairs and offers fresh breezes.

Brunswick (#24; ☎ 609-344-8098), next door to the Inn of the Irish Pub, has similar rates. Both of these places are only open in season.

Mid-Range The motels listed here are all pretty generic, but are clean, safe places to lay your head at least. Rates are always much cheaper in the winter, particularly during mid-week.

Ascot Motel (#40; ☎ 609-344-5163, 800-225-1476; Iowa at Pacific Ave; singles/doubles winter $79/89) A solid choice

Best Western Envoy Inn (#25; ☎ 609-344-7117, fax 344-5659; 1416 Pacific Ave at New York Ave; rooms from $45/125/145 Sun-Thur, Fri & Sat)

Comfort Inn (#29; ☎ 609-348-4000; 154 Kentucky Ave; rooms $69-400) Between the Boardwalk and Pacific Ave; rooms have an incredible range, depending on day and season

Days Inn (#43; ☎ 609-344-6101, 800-329-7466, fax 348-5335; the Boardwalk at Morris Ave; rooms Oct-Apr $35-440, May-Sept $50-450) Varying rates depending on the number of people in a room and if the unit is ocean facing or not

Econo Lodge (#27; ☎ 609-344-9093, 800-323-6410; W www.econolodge.com; 117 S Kentucky Ave; rooms $49-499) Between the Boardwalk and Pacific Ave; high-end prices for the best room on the 4th of July, for example

Holiday Inn Boardwalk (#44; ☎ 609-348-2200; the Boardwalk at Chelsea Ave; rooms winter/summer from $69/119)

Howard Johnson Inn (#13; ☎ 609-344-4193, fax 348-1263; Tennessee Ave at Pacific Ave; rooms $45-165)

Atlantic Palace Suites (#28; ☎ 609-344-1200, 800-527-8483, fax 347-6090; the Boardwalk at New York Ave; rooms winter $89-149, summer $129-200) Access directly to the Boardwalk

Madison House Hotel (#30; ☎ 609-345-1400; 123 Martin Luther King Jr Blvd; rooms from $55)

Quality Inn (#14; ☎ 609-345-7070; South Carolina Ave at Pacific Ave; rooms winter/summer from $55/85)

Top End Atlantic City's casino hotels (see Casinos, earlier) dominate the expensive choices. Rates run from $150 to $450 depending on the season and day of the week, usually with meals, shows, free use of the health spa, and casino chips. In the winter, rates can be as low as $50 – the trick is to walk up to the reception desk and act uncertain that you plan to stay the night. You will most likely be offered a room at a deep discount, provided you look well dressed enough to spend money in the casino.

Additionally, all the casinos have high-end dining rooms with menus posted at the entrance. Most specialize in 'surf-and-turf' items – huge steaks, big lobsters and pretty lousy wine lists.

Places to Eat & Drink

Casino towns like Atlantic City and Las Vegas are notorious for their all-you-can-eat buffets and these are usually terrific deals (expect to pay as little as $6). While it's hard to believe casinos would offer food so cheaply, it makes sense. They want you to stay within the confines of their property – which is why they never have any windows or clocks – and food is a great way to accomplish that. Wander around and you'll find myriad options on which to engorge yourself, like the Epic Buffet and Sultan's Feast. Regulars will be more than happy to share tips with you about the best ones, or simply follow that fat guy in front of you.

Irish Pub (#23; ☎ 609-344-6093; 164 St James Pl; open 24 hrs), at the Inn of the Irish Pub (see Places to Stay – Budget), has dirt cheap dinners (the most expensive item is $6.95), daily specials and decent pints. You often have to wait a moment for a table at this popular place drawing an international crowd.

Tony's Baltimore Grill (#39; ☎ 609-345-5766; 2800 Atlantic Ave at Iowa Ave) and **Angelo's Fairmount Tavern** (#7; ☎ 609-344-2439; Mississippi Ave at Fairmount Ave) are two budget Italian restaurants with entrees from around $10.

G&S Italian Market (#42; ☎ 609-345-0787; 3004 Atlantic Ave; pizza $5.50-9.50, pasta $9.50-13.50; open 10am-10pm daily) is a gregarious, family-owned place serving delicious fresh pasta (try the penne a la vodka), gorgeous pastries and huge, robust cups of coffee. You can bring your own wine.

Pickles (#34; ☎ 609-340-2000; Park Place at the Boardwalk; open 11:30am-10pm Sun-Fri, 11:30am-midnight Sat), situated in Bally's Park Place, is a local favorite for its huge portions of moderately priced, tasty fare. There are nice extras on every table like buckets of all-you-can-eat garlic-cured pickles and special-recipe mustard.

The Bacchanal (☎ 609-348-4411; #36; 7-course meal per person $45; seatings 6pm & 8:30pm Wed-Sat), at the **Caesar's Atlantic City**, offers real over-the-top entertainment. For a flat fee you'll get a meal, entertainment by 'Augustus' and possibly a higher level of service than you've ever experienced: 'Wine wenches' will pour pitchers of wine directly into your mouth.

Knife & Fork Inn (#47; ☎ 609-344-1133; w www.knifeandforkinn.com; cnr Atlantic & Pacific Aves), near Albany Ave, dates from 1927, and offers a taste of the old Atlantic City, serving seafood and steaks. You can expect to drop at least $50 on your meal, not including wine, at this place that maintains a dress code.

Two of the town's top seafood restaurants are **Docks** (#8; ☎ 609-345-0092; 2405 Atlantic Ave) and **Abe's Oyster House** (#9; ☎ 609-344-7701; Atlantic Ave at Arkansas Ave), where entrees start at $25.

Old Waterway Inn (☎ 609-347-1793; 1700 Riverside Dr; specials $12.95-18.95), in Venice Park situated away from the rest of the casinos, features a deck overlooking the

water and romantic fireplaces in the dining room.

Tun Tavern (#6; ☎ 609-347-7800; 2 Ocean Way), attached to the Sheraton, is AC's only microbrewery. The outdoor patio makes a nice spot to take in the sunset and have a pint or three.

Entertainment

Casinos Each of the casinos offers a full schedule of entertainment, ranging from ragtime and jazz bands in hotel lobbies to top-name entertainers in the casino auditoriums. Some of this stuff is way over the top, but worth it for the cheese factor alone; think sequins and feathers. Caesar's lobby extravaganza is a particularly garish display involving reams of red velvet, a litter and Cleopatra. The casino ballrooms feature top acts like James Brown and Earth, Wind & Fire; you can pay anywhere from $15 to $400 for one of these shows. The smaller lounges often provide free entertainment.

Comedy Stop (#41; ☎ 609-340-4020) in the Tropicana Casino is Atlantic City's leading comedy club.

HUGH D'ANDRADE

Clubs Atlantic City dance clubs (as opposed to the strip clubs, which are plentiful here) usually open only on weekend nights and don't get going until well after 10pm.

Studio 6 (#12; ☎ 609-347-7873; 12 South Mount Vernon), between Pacific and Atlantic Aves, attracts both a gay and straight crowd.

Casbah (#18; ☎ 609-449-5138; 1000 the Boardwalk), in the Trump Taj Mahal, is a popular place drawing crowds from Philadelphia and beyond.

Déjà Vu (#26; ☎ 609-348-4313; New York Ave & the Boardwalk) is probably the raunchiest of the bunch, featuring scantily clad cocktail waitresses.

Club Mirage (#37; The Boardwalk), near Mississippi Ave in front of Trump Plaza, is a standard disco.

Spectator Sports Checking out any of the Atlantic City minor league teams makes for a fun, affordable day out. If you've never experienced minor league sports, you're in for a treat: the 'arenas' are comfortable and cozy and the teams accessible.

Atlantic City Surf (schedules & tickets ☎ 609-344-7873) is a minor league baseball team that plays in the spanking new $15-million **Sandcastle Stadium** from May through September. There are great views from the upper decks.

Boardwalk Bullies (☎ 609-348-7825; **W** www.boardwalkbullies.com; tickets $8-20) are Atlantic City's Eastern Hockey League team. They play in the impressive Boardwalk Hall.

Atlantic City Seagulls is a basketball team that plays in less exalted confines – the **Atlantic City High School gym** (☎ 609-466-7797).

Getting There & Away

Air The **Atlantic City International Airport** (☎ 609-645-7895), off Tilton Rd in Pomona, is used by airlines servicing the city's casino industry. **Spirit Airlines** (☎ 800-772-7117) and **US Airways Express** (☎ 800-428-4322) connect the town with Boston, Cleveland, Detroit, Newark, Philadelphia and several Florida cities.

Bus NJ Transit runs buses from New York City to the depot on Atlantic Ave between Michigan and Ohio Avenues. For a better deal, check out the casino buses from New York; these cost about $20 for a roundtrip, but include food vouchers and quarters for the slots.

Academy (☎ 800-442-7272) and **Greyhound** (☎ 800-231-2222) buses depart daily for Atlantic City from the Port Authority Bus Terminal in Midtown. Fares are cheaper Monday to Thursday. **Gray Line** (☎ 212-397-2620) operates from 900 Eighth Ave between W 53rd and 54th Sts in Midtown.

Car Atlantic City is exit 38 off the Garden State Parkway. The Atlantic City Expressway runs directly to Atlantic City from Philadelphia.

Getting Around

A jitney ($1.50) tools around Atlantic City connecting the casinos to each other and several other useful points. One line runs the length of Pacific Ave from the Showboat Casino in the north to the Atlantic City Hilton in the south. Another line goes out to Gardiner's Basin and the Marina, while a third connects the casinos to the bus and train stations.

CAPE MAY

Cape May, which stands at the southern tip of the New Jersey shore, is one of the oldest seashore resorts in the USA. A quiet collection of more than 600 gingerbread Victorian homes, the entire town was designated a National Historic Landmark in 1976. In addition to its attractive architecture, accommodations (many of them B&Bs in historical homes) and restaurants, Cape May boasts a lovely beach, a famous lighthouse, craft shops, fishing and superlative bird watching. It's the only place in New Jersey where you can watch the sun both rise and set over the water.

Cape May is divided into Cape May City, with hotels, the main beach and boardwalk, and Cape May Point State Park, which includes the lighthouse, Sunset Beach and a bird refuge.

While folks will tell you Cape May is no place to go in autumn and winter, it's still worth the trip for the romantic lodgings, strolls on the deserted beach and fine dining.

Information

For comprehensive information on Cape May county attractions, stop at the **Welcome Center** (**W** www.capemayfun.com; milepost 11, Garden State Parkway). You can also get information at the Cape May website or call the **Cape May County Department of Tourism** (☎ 800-227-2297; **W** www.thejerseycape.org) for a free vacation kit.

The local **Welcome Center** (#17; ☎ 609-884-9562; 405 Lafayette St) can also help with information. This Week, a publication of the Mid-Atlantic Center for the Arts, lists all activities in town.

You can send off postcards at the **post office** (#27; 700 Washington St).

CAPE MAY

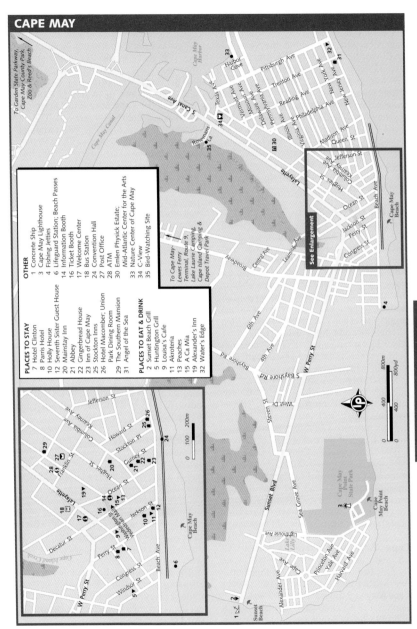

PLACES TO STAY
7 Hotel Clinton
8 Parris Hotel
10 Holly House
12 Seventh Sister Guest House
20 Mainstay Inn
21 Abbey
22 Gingerbread House
23 Inn of Cape May
25 Stockton Inns
26 Hotel Macomber; Union Park Dining Room
29 The Southern Mansion
31 Angel of the Sea

PLACES TO EAT & DRINK
2 Sunset Beach Grill
5 Huntington Grill
9 Louisa's Cafe
11 Akroteria
13 Peaches
15 A Ca Mia
19 Alexander's Inn
32 Water's Edge

OTHER
1 Concrete Ship
3 Cape May Lighthouse
4 Fishing Jetties
6 Lifeguard Station; Beach Passes
14 Information Booth
16 Ticket Booth
17 Welcome Center
18 Bus Station
24 Convention Hall
27 Post Office
28 ATM
30 Emlen Physick Estate; Mid-Atlantic Center for the Arts
33 Nature Center of Cape May
34 C-View
35 Bird-Watching Site

EXCURSIONS

Special Events

Cape May hosts a slew of festivals and special events throughout the year. The **Mid-Atlantic Center for the Arts** (☎ 800-275-4278; ⓦ www.capemaymac.org) is a clearing house for all the doings in this quaint town and is the place to call for more information about any cultural events.

The **Cape May Jazz Festival** (☎ 609-884-7277; ⓦ www.capemayjazz.com) is a twice-yearly affair held in April and November, while the **Cape May Music Festival**, held each mid-May to early June, is highlighted by outdoor jazz, classical and chamber music concerts.

Things to See & Do

The **Emlen Physick Estate** (#30; ☎ 609-884-5404; 1048 Washington St; open Sat & Sun Jan-Mar, daily Dec-Apr), an 18-room mansion built in 1879, now houses the **Mid-Atlantic Center for the Arts**. Here you can book a tour for Cape May historic homes, the lighthouse or nearby historic Cold Spring Village. They also sell Victoriana, history books and crafts at the attached shop.

The **Concrete Ship** dates from WWI, when 12 experimental concrete ships were built to compensate for a shortage of steel. *Atlantis*, with a five-inch concrete aggregate hull, began its seagoing life in 1918, but eight years later it broke free in a storm and ran aground on the western side of the Cape May Point coast. A small chunk of the hull still sits a few feet from shore on Sunset Beach at the end of Sunset Blvd.

The 18-acre **Nature Center of Cape May** (#33; ☎ 609-898-8848; 1600 Delaware Ave) is the best place to get information on the different types of fowl that pass through southern New Jersey. It features a bird-watching site with open-air observation platforms over the marshes and beaches.

Cape May Point State Park This 190-acre state park (☎ 609-884-2159; 707 E Lake Dr; open 9am-5pm daily), just off Lighthouse Ave, has two miles of trails, plus the famous **Cape May Lighthouse** (#3; ☎ 609-884-2159; admission $3.50; open 10am-5pm daily). Built in 1859, the 157-foot lighthouse recently underwent a $2 million restoration, and its completely reconstructed light is visible as far out as 25 miles out to sea. You can climb the 199 stairs to the top in the summer months.

The Cape May peninsula is a resting place for millions of migratory birds each year, and the **Cape May Bird Observatory** maintains a hotline (☎ 609-861-0700) offering information on the latest sightings. Located along the Atlantic Flyway, this is considered one of the country's 10 birding hot spots. Fall is the best time to glimpse some of the 400 species that frequent the area, including hawks, but from March through May you can see songbirds, raptors and other species. The bird observatory also offers tours of **Reed's Beach**, 12 miles north of Cape May on the Delaware Bay, where migrating shorebirds swoop down to feed on the eggs laid by thousands of horseshoe crabs each May.

There is also terrific fishing in these parts, and anglers down this way can cast for bluefish, flounder, stripers and more between March and December. Some 40 fish species swim in the saltwater wetlands and ocean over here. In addition, this area hosts more than 100 butterfly species and 75 types of dragonfly.

To get to the park, drive west from Cape May on Sunset Blvd about 2 miles to Lighthouse Ave. Make a left and drive half a mile to the lighthouse.

Cape May County Park & Zoo This zoo (☎ 609-465-5271; ⓦ www.capemaycountyzoo.com; admission free; open 10am-4:45pm daily), a few miles north of town, is one of this area's nicest attractions. The beautifully maintained, 200-acre facility features 250 different species of animals, many of which wander freely across a re-created African savanna and other natural habitats; you can observe the action from the elevated boardwalk.

The park, which is busy but not crowded even in summer, also offers nature and bike trails, a playground and a fishing pond. To get there, take the Garden State Parkway to exit 11.

Beaches The narrow **Cape May Beach** (☎ 609-884-9525; day/week passes $4/10) requires passes sold at the lifeguard station on the boardwalk at the end of Grant St. The **Cape May Point Beach** (admission free) is accessible from the parking lot at Cape May Point State Park near the lighthouse.

Sunset Beach (admission free) is at the end of Sunset Blvd and is the spot to watch the sunset with a 100% uninterrupted horizon line. This is also the place to hunt for famed Cape May Diamonds – pure quartz crystals tumbled smooth by the surf. If you're here between May and September, don't miss the pomp and ceremony of the flag lowering ceremony.

Organized Tours

Mid-Atlantic Center for the Arts (#30; ☎ 609-884-5404, 800-275-4278; **W** www .capemaymac.org; 1048 Washington St) offers a range of walking, trolley and boat tours – walking tours cost $5 and special events are under $16. You can buy tickets at the ticket booth on the western end of the Washington St Mall, just before Decatur St.

Places to Stay

Camping If you have a car and gear, there are a few camping options not too far from Cape May, though many cater to the RV pull-up and plug in crowd. You might give the following a try from May 15 through September 30:

Cape Island Campground (☎ 609-884-5777; **W** www.capeisland.com; 709 Rte 9)
Depot Travel Park (☎ 609-884-2533; 800 Broadway, West Cape May)
Lake Laurie Campground (☎ 609-884-3567; 669 Rte 9)

There are many more places; call the Cape May County Department of Tourism (☎ 800-227-2297) for a complete listing.

B&Bs Cape May is packed with expensive B&Bs and inns, and you can't walk 50 feet in the center of town without passing one. To help narrow your search, see the Cape May County Chamber of Commerce website (**W** www.capemaycountychamber.com) for a list of available accommodation. If you come during the off season, many places will be closed, but you'll have your pick of the ones remaining open and at the nice price.

A couple of old rooming houses have been converted to budget hotels. The **Hotel Clinton** (#7; ☎ 609-884-3993; 202 Perry St), near Lafayette St, and **Parris Hotel** (#8; ☎ 609-884-8015; 204 Perry St), next door, are two modest choices. Most rooms have private baths and some have TVs.

Many places in town offer rooms for less than $150 in high season.

Holly House (#10; ☎ 609-884-7365; 20 Jackson St) is an 1890 cottage run by a former mayor of Cape May. It's one of the so-called Seven Sisters, a group of seven identical homes; five of them are along Jackson St. The Holly House has six rooms, each with three windows and a shared bath.

Seventh Sister Guest House (#12; ☎ 609-884-2280; 10 Jackson St) is a few doors down from Holly House.

Hotel Macomber (#26; ☎ 609-884-3020; 727 Beach Ave; rooms $95-265), on the corner of Howard St, contains one of the best restaurants in Cape May (see Places to Eat & Drink, below).

Gingerbread House (#22; ☎ 609-884-0211; **W** www.gingerbreadinn.com; 28 Gurney St; rooms off-season $90-200, summer $110-260) is a six-room B&B. The price includes a Cape May Beach pass, continental breakfast and afternoon tea.

Stockton Inns (#25; ☎ 609-884-4036, 800-524-4283; **W** www.stocktoninns.com; 809 Beach Dr; motel rooms under $100) includes both a motel and a 'manor house.' The motel has standard motel furnishings and a pool; check into their efficiencies with cooking facilities to save some money. The manor is a converted Victorian house with 10 rooms and three suites, all with private bathroom, and these rooms are slightly more expensive.

Inn of Cape May (#23; ☎ 609-884-5555, 800-582-5933; 7 Ocean St at Beach Ave; $65-120 off-season; $115-305 summer) is a sprawling white wooden structure with

EXCURSIONS

CHARLES COOK

Tranquility in the Garden State

lavender trim. Rooms come in a wide variety of sizes and generally have high ceilings and white wicker furniture. Some have ocean views, but those without views are cheaper.

Mainstay Inn (*#20; ☎ 609-884-8690; 635 Columbia Ave; rooms off-season $115-245, summer $180-295*), built in 1872 as a men's gambling club, features rooms furnished in opulent dark woods and large beds; all have private baths and rates include breakfast.

Abbey (*#21; ☎ 609-884-4506; 34 Gurney St; rooms $100-225*), on the corner of Columbia Ave, is one of the more elegant places in town. Like the Mainstay, it features plenty of antique furniture, has high ceilings and offers a tour with tea ($5). Rates include breakfast.

Angel of the Sea (*#31; ☎ 609-884-3369, 800-848-3369; 5-7 Trenton Ave; rooms off-season $135-285, summer $175-315*) is renowned for its service. All rooms have private baths, ceiling fans and access to wraparound porches. Rates include breakfast.

The Southern Mansion (*#29; ☎ 800-381-3888; w www.southernmansion.com; 720 Washington St; rooms weekdays/weekend $185/200*) is a gorgeous property with lush rooms loaded with hard woods and bright schemes in hues of teal, orange or yellow.

Places to Eat & Drink

There are so many good places to eat here, you might want to do some of your own research before hitting town. See the Cape May Dining Out website (**w** www.capemay dine.com) for a full account of the options.

Akroteria (*#11; Beach Dr; dishes under $10*), between Jackson and Perry Sts, is a collection of small fast-food shacks.

Sunset Beach Grill (*#2; Sunset Blvd*), on Sunset Beach, overlooks the sunken *Atlantis* and the ocean. It's the perfect place to grab a sandwich and a beer, and become entranced by the sea.

A Ca Mia (*#15; ☎ 609-884-6661; 524 Washington St; lunch entrees $6.95-9.95, dinner entrees $13.95-28.95*) is a good place to dine en plein air. This popular spot has plentiful pavement tables lining the pedestrian mall where it serves up solid Italian bistro fare. It's bring your own booze here.

Louisa's Cafe (*#9; ☎ 609-884-5882; 104 Jackson St; open dinner Tues-Sat*) is an excellent small restaurant.

Huntington Grill (*#5; ☎ 609-884-5868; Grant & North Sts; buffet $15*) offers an all-you-can-eat buffet, plus fish and steaks from the grill.

Union Park Dining Room (*#26; ☎ 609-884-8811; 727 Beach Ave*), at Hotel Macomber, is one of the fine and ambitious restaurants for which Cape May is known. The menu features French fare with some Asian accents, and desserts are a house specialty. Reservations are essential in summer.

Alexander's Inn (*#19; ☎ 609-884-2555; 653 Washington St; entrees $27-40*) is another of Cape May's top-end choices with tuxedo-wearing waiters serving up the likes of Beluga caviar and filet of lobster in lush surroundings.

Water's Edge (*#32; ☎ 609-884-1717, Beach Dr at Pittsburgh Ave; full dinner & wine around $35*) looks out on the Atlantic and serves seafood with something of a Mediterranean flavor. You can also get a good steak here.

Peaches (*#13; ☎ 609-884-0202; 322 Carpenter's Lane; mains $15-25*) offers contemporary American dining at relatively high prices for this area.

EXCURSIONS

C-View *(#34;* ☎ *609-884-4712; 1380 Washington St)* is where the locals slake their thirst. This place is open year-round, has tons of friendly atmosphere and serves up cheap, filling food (nothing is over $7.95). The kitchen doesn't close until 1 am on Friday and Saturday nights.

Getting There & Away

Bus Buses to and from New York City are run by **NJ Transit** *(☎ 201-762-5100, 800-772-2222)*. The bus station is next to the Chamber of Commerce building, near the corner of Lafayette and Elmira Sts.

Car Cape May is at the southern extreme of the Garden State Parkway, which leads right into town. It takes about three hours to drive from Manhattan, and about an hour from Atlantic City.

Boat A daily **ferry** *(☎ 800-643-3779;* W *www .capemaylewesferry.com)* runs between North Cape May and the Delaware coastal town of Lewes (pronounced 'Lewis'); reservations should be made a day in advance in the high season. The price for a car/passengers is $18/4 from November to April and $20/6 May to October. The price for a car includes one driver. The 17-mile trip across the Delaware Bay takes about 70 minutes and saves some time for New York–based travelers heading south from Cape May for a visit to Washington, DC, and points south.

The **North Cape May ferry terminal** *(Route 9)* is west of the Garden State Parkway.

EXCURSIONS

N.Y.C.

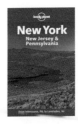

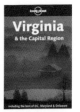

Index

Text

Bold indicates maps.

Bold indicates maps.

Places to Stay

Places to Eat

Boxed Text

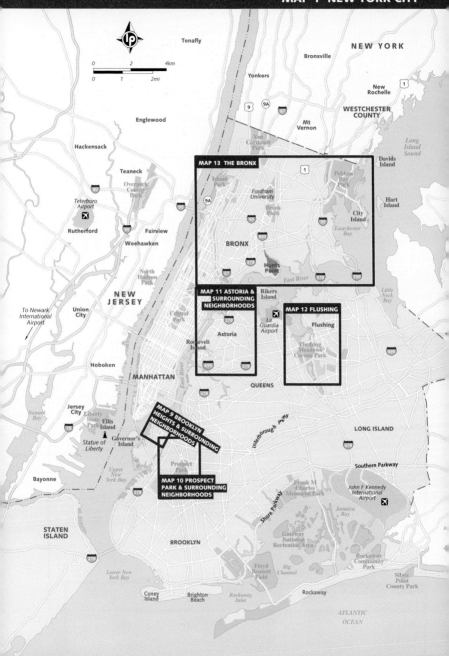

MAP 1 NEW YORK CITY

MAP 2 MANHATTAN (NORTH)

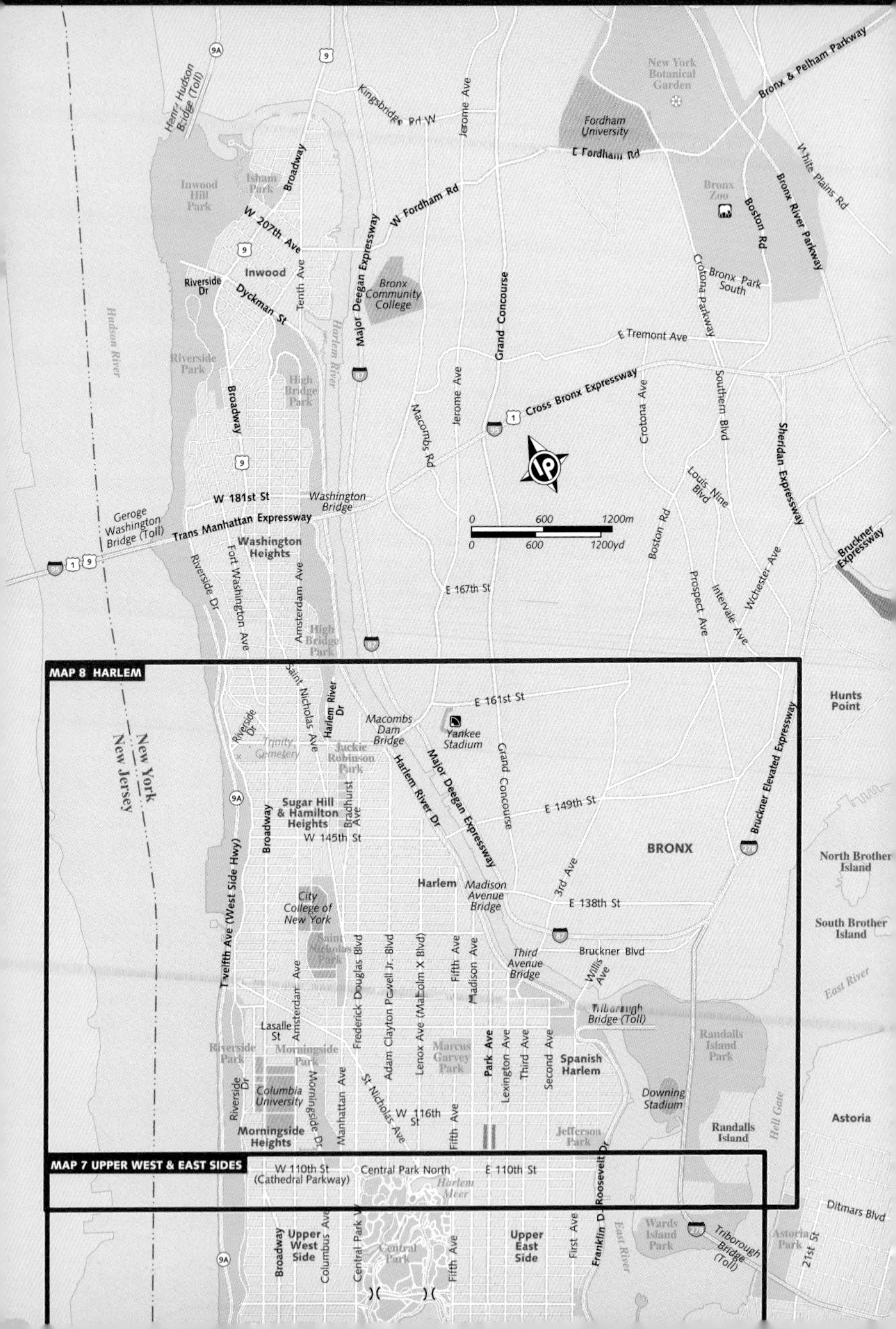

9A
9

New York
Botanical
Garden

Kingsbridge Rd W

Bronx & Pelham Parkway

White Plains Rd

Fordham
University

E Fordham Rd

Isham
Park

W Fordham Rd

Inwood
Hill
Park

Broadway

Bronx
Zoo

Boston Rd

Bronx River Parkway

W 207th Ave

Riverside
Dr

Inwood

Dyckman St

Tenth Ave

Major Deegan Expressway

Bronx
Community
College

Grand Concourse

Crotona Park
South

Crotona Parkway

Hudson River

Riverside
Park

High
Bridge
Park

Harlem River

E Tremont Ave

Broadway

Macombs Rd

Jerome Ave

1 Cross Bronx Expressway

Crotona Ave

Southern Blvd

Sheridan Expressway

VP

Louis Nine Blvd

9

W 181st St

Washington
Bridge

600   1200m

Boston Rd

Intervale Ave

Wchester Ave

Bruckner
Expressway

George
Washington
Bridge (Toll)

Trans Manhattan Expressway

600   1200yd

1 9

Riverside Dr

Washington
Heights

Prospect Ave

Fort Washington Ave

Amsterdam Ave

E 167th St

High
Bridge
Park

MAP 8 HARLEM

E 161st St

Hunts
Point

New York
New Jersey

Riverside Dr

Saint Nicholas Ave

Harlem River Dr

Macombs
Dam
Bridge

Yankee
Stadium

Trinity
Cemetery

Jackie
Robinson
Park

Major Deegan Expressway

Grand Concourse

Bruckner Elevated Expressway

North Brother
Island

9A

Sugar Hill
& Hamilton
Heights

Broadway

Bradhurst Ave

Harlem River Dr

E 149th St

South Brother
Island

W 145th St

BRONX

87

East River

City
College of
New York

Harlem

Madison
Avenue
Bridge

3rd Ave

E 138th St

Saint
Nicholas
Park

Amsterdam Ave

Frederick Douglas Blvd

Adam Clayton Pcwell Jr. Blvd

Fifth Ave

Third Ave

Willis Ave

Bruckner Blvd

Third
Avenue
Bridge

Randalls
Island
Park

Astoria

Lasalle
St

Columbia
University

Riverside
Park

Morningside
Park

Manhattan Ave

St Nicholas Ave

Lenox (Malcolm X Blvd)

Madison Ave

Marcus
Garvey
Park

Park Ave

Lexington Ave

Third Ave

Second Ave

Spanish
Harlem

Triborough
Bridge (Toll)

Downing
Stadium

Hill Gate

Morningside
Heights

Morningside Dr

W 116th St

Fifth Ave

Jefferson
Park

Randalls
Island

MAP 7 UPPER WEST & EAST SIDES

W 110th St
(Cathedral Parkway)

Central Park North

E 110th St

Franklin D. Roosevelt

Wards
Island Park

Ditmars Blvd

Harlem
Meer

Triborough
Bridge
(Toll)

Astoria Js
Park

9A

Upper
West
Side

Broadway

Columbus Ave

Central Park W

Central
Park

Fifth Ave

Upper
East
Side

First Ave

East River

Wards
Island Park

21st St

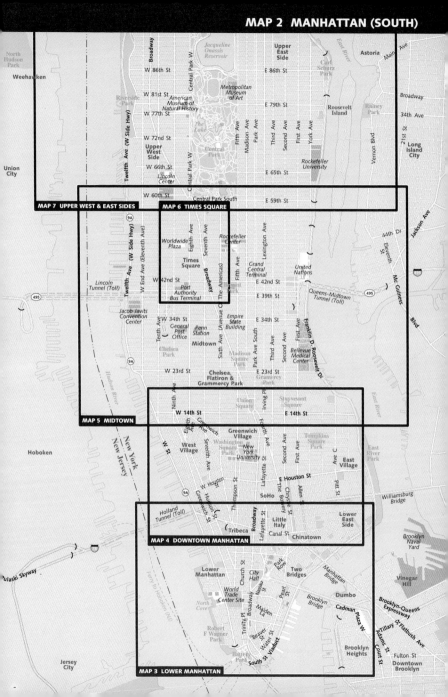

MAP 2 MANHATTAN (SOUTH)

North
Hudson
Park

Weehawken

Astoria

Broadway

W 86th St

Jacqueline
Onassis
Reservoir

Upper
East
Side

Carl
Schurz
Park

Main   Ave

Riverside
Park

W 81st St

American
Museum
of
Natural History

Central Park W

Metropolitan
Museum
of
Art

E 86th St

Broadway

34th Ave

W 77th St

E 79th St

Roosevelt
Island

Rainey
Park

W 72nd St

The
Lake

Fifth Ave
Madison Ave
Park Ave
Third Ave
Second Ave
First Ave
York Ave

Vernon Blvd

Union
City

Upper
West
Side

W 66th St

Central
Park

E 65th St

Rockefeller
University

Long
Island
City

Lincoln
Center

Twelfth Ave (W Side Hwy)

W 60th St

Central Park South

E 59th St

MAP 7 UPPER WEST & EAST SIDES   **MAP 6 TIMES SQUARE**

44th Dr

Jackson Ave

9A

Worldwide
Plaza

Rockefeller
Center

Lexington Ave

Eleventh
St

Lincoln
Tunnel (Toll)

Times
Square

Eighth Ave
Seventh Ave
Broadway
The Americas)

Fifth Ave

Grand
Central
Terminal

United
Nations

Mc Guiness

495

W 42nd St

Port
Authority
Bus Terminal

E 42nd St

E 39th St

Queens-Midtown
Tunnel (Toll)

495

Blvd

Jacob Javits
Convention
Center

Twelfth Ave (W Side Hwy)
W End Ave (Eleventh Ave)
Tenth Ave

W 34th St

General
Post
Office

Penn
Station

Empire
State
Building

Sixth Ave (Avenue of)

E 34th St

Franklin D Roosevelt Dr

Bellevue
Medical
Center

Hudson River

Chelsea
Park

Midtown

Madison
Square
Park

Park Ave South
Third Ave
Second Ave

9A

W 23rd St

Chelsea,
Flatiron &
Grammercy Park

E 23rd St

Gramercy
Park

MAP 5 MIDTOWN

Ninth Ave

W 14th St

Union
Square

Irving Pl

Stuyvesant
Square

E 14th St

East River

Eighth Ave
Greenwich Ave
Seventh Ave

Greenwich
Village

Washington
Square
Park

New
York
University

Avenue of

Second Ave
First Ave

Tompkins
Square
Park

East
River
Park

Hoboken

New York
New Jersey

W St

West
Village

Ave C

East
Village

W Houston St

Thompson St

Lafayette St

E Houston St

Allen

Pitt St

Williamsburg
Bridge

9A

Holland
Tunnel (Toll)

Greenwich St
Hudson St

Broadway
Lafayette St

SoHo

Little
Italy

The Bowery

Lower
East
Side

Brooklyn
Naval
Yard

Tribeca

Canal St

Chinatown

MAP 4 DOWNTOWN MANHATTAN

Pulaski Skyway

Lower
Manhattan

Church St

City
Hall

Nassau St

Park
Row

Two
Bridges

Manhattan
Bridge

Vinegar
Hill

North
Cove

World
Trade
Center Site

Broadway

Trinity Pl

Pearl St

Malden
Lane

Brooklyn
Bridge

Dumbo

Cadman

Plaza W

Brooklyn-Queens
Expressway

Robert
F Wagner
Park

Beaver St
Water St

South St Viaduct

Brooklyn
Heights

Tillary St
Adams St
Court St
Flatbush Ave

Jersey
City

Battery
Park

South St

Fulton St

Downtown
Brooklyn

MAP 3 LOWER MANHATTAN

Ferry to Hoboken (NJ)

MAP 3 LOWER MANHATTAN

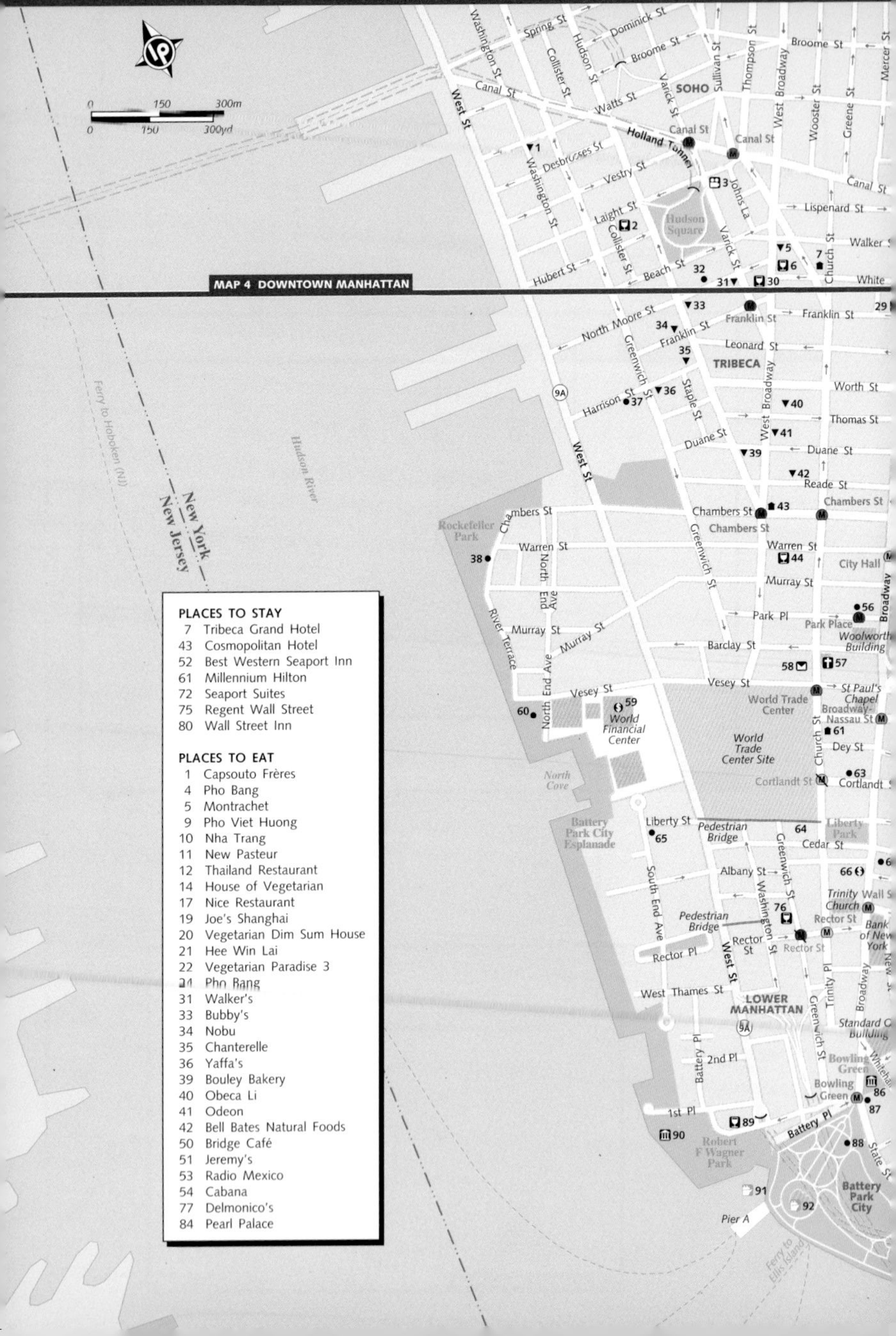

0 150 300m
0 150 300yd
MAP 4 DOWNTOWN MANHATTAN
Ferry to Hoboken (NJ)
Hudson River
New York
New Jersey
SOHO
TRIBECA
LOWER MANHATTAN
Washington St
Spring St
Dominick St
Broome St
Hudson St
Collister St
Varick St
Sullivan St
Thompson St
West Broadway
Wooster St
Greene St
Mercer St
Canal St
West St
Watts St
Holland Tunnel
Desbrosses St
Vestry St
Laight St
Hudson Square
Johns La
Lispenard St
Walker St
Hubert St
Beach St
Church St
White St
North Moore St
Franklin St
Leonard St
Greenwich St
Harrison St
Staple St
Worth St
Thomas St
Duane St
Reade St
Chambers St
Rockefeller Park
Warren St
North End Ave
City Hall
Broadway
Murray St
Park Pl
Park Place
Woolworth Building
River Terrace
Barclay St
Vesey St
St Paul's Chapel
World Trade Center
Broadway-Nassau St
World Financial Center
World Trade Center Site
Dey St
North Cove
Cortlandt St
Battery Park City Esplanade
Liberty St
Pedestrian Bridge
Liberty Park
Cedar St
Albany St
South End Ave
Trinity Church
Wall St
Rector St
Bank of New York
Rector Pl
West Thames St
Trinity Pl
Standard Oil Building
Battery Pl
2nd Pl
Bowling Green
Whitehall
1st Pl
Robert F Wagner Park
State St
Battery Park City
Pier A
Ferry to Ellis Island
9A

PLACES TO STAY

7 Tribeca Grand Hotel
43 Cosmopolitan Hotel
52 Best Western Seaport Inn
61 Millennium Hilton
72 Seaport Suites
75 Regent Wall Street
80 Wall Street Inn

PLACES TO EAT

1 Capsouto Frères
4 Pho Bang
5 Montrachet
9 Pho Viet Huong
10 Nha Trang
11 New Pasteur
12 Thailand Restaurant
14 House of Vegetarian
17 Nice Restaurant
19 Joe's Shanghai
20 Vegetarian Dim Sum House
21 Hee Win Lai
22 Vegetarian Paradise 3
24 Pho Bang
31 Walker's
33 Bubby's
34 Nobu
35 Chanterelle
36 Yaffa's
39 Bouley Bakery
40 Obeca Li
41 Odeon
42 Bell Bates Natural Foods
50 Bridge Café
51 Jeremy's
53 Radio Mexico
54 Cabana
77 Delmonico's
84 Pearl Palace

MAP 3 LOWER MANHATTAN

OTHER

2   Vinyl
3   Screening Room
6   Liquor Store Bar
8   Art in General
13 Museum of Chinese in the Americas
15 Eastern States Buddhist Temple
16 Eldridge St Synagogue
18 Confucius Statue
23 Church of the Transfiguration
25 First Shearith Israel Graveyard
26 US Courthouse
27 New York County Courthouse
28 Clocktower Gallery
29 Knitting Factory
30 Bubble Lounge
32 Fast Folk Cafe
38 Park House
44 Raccoon Lodge
45 Sun Building
46 Surrogate's Court
47 Public Toilet
48 Brooklyn Bridge Pedestrian Entrance
49 Police Headquarters
55 J&R Music & Computer World
56 Tent & Trails
57 St Peter's Church
58 Post Office
59 American Express
60 New York Mercantile Exchange
62 Servas
63 Century 21
64 World Trade Center Site Viewing Area
65 North Cove Sailing School
66 American Express
67 Equitable Building; Alliance for
    Downtown New York
68 Federal Reserve Bank
69 Chase Manhattan Bank
70 American International Building
71 Hagstrom Map & Travel Center
73 Kinko's
74 Alliance Française
76 Remy Lounge
78 India House; Bayard's
79 New York City Police Museum
81 Barclay-Rex
82 Stadt Huys
83 Fraunces Tavern Museum
85 Shakespeare & Co
86 National Museum of the American
    Indian; US Customs House
87 TKTS
88 The Sphere
89 Rise Bar & Terrace
90 Museum of Jewish Heritage
91 New York Waterway Ferry
92 Statue of Liberty Ferry Ticket Office
93 Shrine to St Elizabeth Ann Seton
94 New York Unearthed
95 Liberty Helicopter Tours
96 Staten Island Ferry Terminal

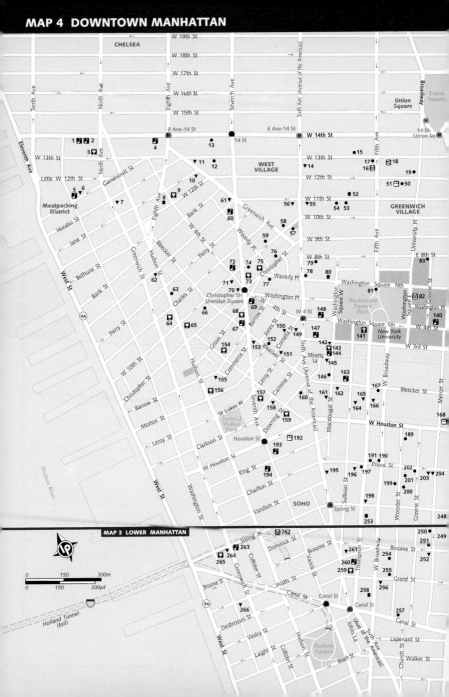

MAP 4 DOWNTOWN MANHATTAN

MAP 4 DOWNTOWN MANHATTAN

PLACES TO STAY
8 Incentra Village
52 Larchmont Hotel
80 Washington Square Hotel
92 St Marks Hotel
116 East Village B&B
170 Howard Johnson Express Inn
212 Off SoHo Suites
232 World Hotel
236 Pioneer Hotel
244 Holiday Inn Downtown
253 60 Thompson
258 SoHo Grand Hotel

PLACES TO EAT
6 Florent
7 El Faro
10 Benny's Burritos
11 Café de Bruxelles
14 Bar Six
25 Cyclo
26 Mee Noodle Shop
31 DeRobertis
32 Lanza's
33 Quintessence
35 Cafe Pick Mè Up
37 Veselka
38 Second Ave Deli
40 Sharaku
42 Hasaki
55 French Roast
56 Sammy's Noodle Shop
61 Two Boots
62 White Horse Tavern
70 Gourmet Garage
71 Chow
95 B&H Dairy
96 Stage Restaurant
100 Rose of India
101 Windows on India
104 Stromboli's Pizza
107 Yaffa
110 Benny's Burritos
111 Sidewalk Bar & Restaurant
117 Casa Adela
119 Lalita Java
120 StepMama
121 Mama's Food Shop
122 Two Boots
123 Lucky Cheng's
128 Astor Restaurant & Lounge
137 Time Cafe
142 Caffe Reggio
145 Minetta Tavern
149 Little Havana
150 Pó
151 Paticceria Bruno
153 Cones
155 Grange Hall
158 Do Hwa
161 Caffé Dante

162 Le Figaro
164 Caffe Lure
165 Rocco
166 Tomoe Sushi
171 Yonah Shimmel Bakery
174 Bereket
175 Katz's Deli
181 Kitchen Club
195 Souen
196 Raoul's
198 Ben's Famous Pizza
203 Fanelli's Café
204 Soup Kiosk
207 Balthazar
208 Spring St Natural
210 Lombardi's
216 Paladar
222 71 Clinton Fresh Foods
238 Caffe Roma
239 Benito One
240 Benito Two
242 Puglia
243 Vincent's
252 Gourmet Garage
256 Lucky Strike
261 Lupe's East LA Kitchen
264 Pão!
266 Mekong

BARS
3 The Lure
9 Corner Bistro
64 Rubyfruit
65 Blind Tiger Ale House
68 Marie's Crisis
73 55 Bar
75 Stonewall Bar
88 Joe's Pub
93 McSorley's Old Ale House
102 WCOU Radio
112 Vazac's (7B's)
113 Esperanto
114 Baraza
115 Zum Schneider
118 Plant
131 The Scratcher
132 B Bar
133 Swift's Hibernian Lounge
143 Comedy Cellar
154 Chumley's
156 Henrietta Hudson
157 Crazy Nanny's
159 Bar d'O
178 Luna Lounge
179 Orchard Bar
185 Pravda
211 Sweet & Vicious
217 Barramundi
225 Motor City Bar
227 Lolita
259 Cafe Noir

265 The Ear Inn

CLUBS
1 Baktun
2 The Cooler
4 Chicago B.L.U.E.S.
5 Hell
24 Flamingo
28 The Cock
30 Brownie's
45 Continental
60 Village Vanguard
67 Sweet Basil
69 Monster
72 Smalls
103 Tribe
125 Urge
127 CBGB
138 Fez
140 Bottom Line
144 Cafe Wha?
147 Blue Note
148 Washington Square Church
163 Back Fence
173 Sapphire
176 Mercury Lounge
177 Meow Mix
193 SOBs
194 Culture Club
214 Surf Reality
215 Arlene Grocery
231 Bowery Ballroom
237 Double Happiness
260 Naked Lunch
263 Don Hill's

SHOPS
13 Rags A Go Go
15 East-West Books
20 Virgin Megastore
21 Strand Bookstore
22 Footlight Records
23 Kiehl's
29 Rue St Denis Vintage Clothes
41 Kim's Video & Music
44 St Mark's Bookshop
63 Creative Visions/Gay
     Pleasures
66 Kim's Video & Music
74 Three Lives
76 Oscar Wilde Memorial
     Bookshop
84 Shakespeare & Co
85 Barnes & Noble
91 Norman's Sound & Vision
94 The Village Scandal
97 Fab 208
98 Tokio 7
99 Amarcord
105 Ressurection
106 Physical Graffiti

MAP 4 DOWNTOWN MANHATTAN

ANGUS OBORN

Get your workout alongside the Hudson River, a popular place for joggers and skaters

MAP 5 MIDTOWN MANHATTAN

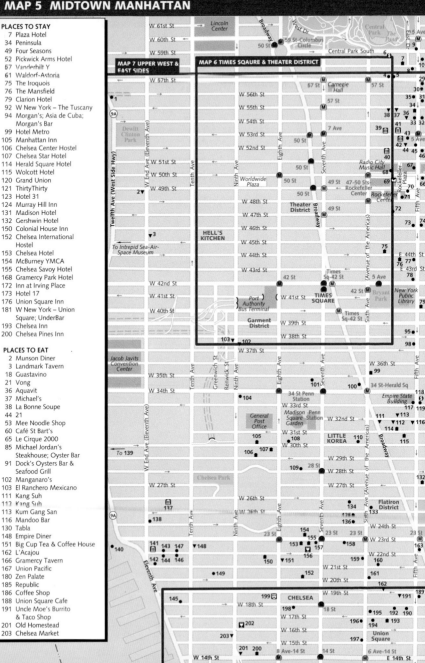

PLACES TO STAY
- 7 Plaza Hotel
- 34 Peninsula
- 49 Four Seasons
- 52 Pickwick Arms Hotel
- 57 Vanderbilt Y
- 61 Waldorf-Astoria
- 75 The Iroquois
- 76 The Mansfield
- 79 Clarion Hotel
- 92 W New York – The Tuscany
- 94 Morgan's; Asia de Cuba; Morgan's Bar
- 99 Hotel Metro
- 105 Manhattan Inn
- 106 Chelsea Center Hostel
- 107 Chelsea Star Hotel
- 114 Herald Square Hotel
- 115 Wolcott Hotel
- 120 Grand Union
- 121 ThirtyThirty
- 123 Hotel 31
- 124 Murray Hill Inn
- 131 Madison Hotel
- 132 Gershwin Hotel
- 150 Colonial House Inn
- 152 Chelsea International Hostel
- 153 Chelsea Hotel
- 154 McBurney YMCA
- 155 Chelsea Savoy Hotel
- 168 Gramercy Park Hotel
- 172 Inn at Irving Place
- 173 Hotel 17
- 176 Union Square Inn
- 181 W New York – Union Square; UnderBar
- 193 Chelsea Inn
- 200 Chelsea Pines Inn

PLACES TO EAT
- 2 Munson Diner
- 3 Landmark Tavern
- 18 Guastavino
- 21 Vong
- 36 Aquavit
- 37 Michael's
- 38 La Bonne Soupe
- 44 21
- 53 Mee Noodle Shop
- 60 Café St Bart's
- 65 Le Cirque 2000
- 85 Michael Jordan's Steakhouse; Oyster Bar
- 91 Dock's Oysters Bar & Seafood Grill
- 102 Manganaro's
- 103 El Ranchero Mexicano
- 111 Kang Suh
- 112 Kang Suh
- 113 Kum Gang San
- 130 Mandoo Bar
- 130 Tabla
- 148 Empire Diner
- 151 Big Cup Tea & Coffee House
- 162 L'Acajou
- 166 Gramercy Tavern
- 167 Union Pacific
- 180 Zen Palate
- 185 Republic
- 186 Coffee Shop
- 188 Union Square Cafe
- 191 Uncle Moe's Burrito & Taco Shop
- 201 Old Homestead
- 203 Chelsea Market

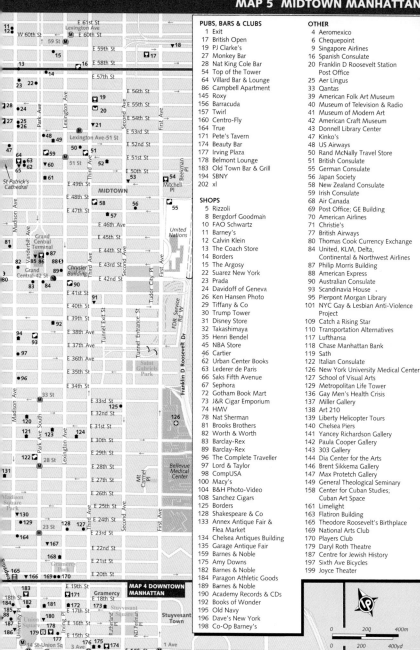

MAP 5 MIDTOWN MANHATTAN

PUBS, BARS & CLUBS
1 Exit
17 British Open
19 PJ Clarke's
27 Monkey Bar
28 Nat King Cole Bar
54 Top of the Tower
64 Villard Bar & Lounge
86 Campbell Apartment
145 Roxy
156 Barracuda
157 Twirl
160 Centro-Fly
164 True
171 Pete's Tavern
174 Beauty Bar
178 Irving Plaza
178 Belmont Lounge
183 Old Town Bar & Grill
194 SBNY
202 xl

SHOPS
5 Rizzoli
8 Bergdorf Goodman
10 FAO Schwartz
11 Barney's
12 Calvin Klein
13 The Coach Store
14 Borders
15 The Argosy
22 Suarez New York
23 Prada
24 Davidoff of Geneva
26 Ken Hansen Photo
29 Tiffany & Co
30 Trump Tower
31 Disney Store
32 Takashimaya
35 Henri Bendel
36 NBA Store
46 Cartier
62 Urban Center Books
63 Lederer de Paris
66 Saks Fifth Avenue
67 Sephora
72 Gotham Book Mart
73 J&R Cigar Emporium
74 HMV
78 Nat Sherman
81 Brooks Brothers
82 Worth & Worth
83 Barclay-Rex
89 Barclay-Rex
96 The Complete Traveller
97 Lord & Taylor
98 CompUSA
100 Macy's
104 B&H Photo-Video
108 Sanchez Cigars
125 Borders
132 Shakespeare & Co
133 Annex Antique Fair &
    Flea Market
134 Chelsea Antiques Building
135 Garage Antique Fair
159 Barnes & Noble
175 Amy Downs
182 Barnes & Noble
184 Paragon Athletic Goods
189 Barnes & Noble
190 Academy Records & CDs
192 Books of Wonder
195 Old Navy
196 Dave's New York
198 Co-Op Barney's

OTHER
4 Aeromexico
6 Chequepoint
9 Singapore Airlines
16 Spanish Consulate
20 Franklin D Roosevelt Station
   Post Office
25 Aer Lingus
33 Qantas
39 Museum of American Folk Art
40 Museum of Television & Radio
41 Museum of Modern Art
42 American Craft Museum
43 Donnell Library Center
47 Kinko's
48 US Airways
50 Rand McNally Travel Store
51 British Consulate
55 German Consulate
56 Japan Society
58 New Zealand Consulate
59 Irish Consulate
68 Air Canada
69 Post Office; GE Building
70 American Airlines
71 Christie's
77 British Airways
80 Thomas Cook Currency Exchange
84 United, KLM, Delta,
   Continental & Northwest Airlines
87 Philip Morris Building
88 American Express
90 Australian Consulate
93 Scandinavia House
95 Pierpont Morgan Library
101 NYC Gay & Lesbian Anti-Violence
    Project
109 Catch a Rising Star
110 Transportation Alternatives
117 Lufthansa
118 Chase Manhattan Bank
119 Sath
122 Italian Consulate
126 New York University Medical Center
127 School of Visual Arts
129 Metropolitan Life Tower
136 Gay Men's Health Crisis
137 Miller Gallery
138 Art 210
139 Liberty Helicopter Tours
140 Chelsea Piers
141 Yancey Richardson Gallery
142 Paula Cooper Gallery
143 303 Gallery
144 Dia Center for the Arts
146 Brent Sikkema Gallery
147 Max Protetch Gallery
149 General Theological Seminary
158 Center for Cuban Studies;
    Cuban Art Space
161 Limelight
163 Flatiron Building
165 Theodore Roosevelt's Birthplace
169 National Arts Club
170 Players Club
179 Daryl Roth Theatre
187 Centre for Jewish History
197 Sixth Ave Bicycles
199 Joyce Theater

MAP 4 DOWNTOWN
MANHATTAN

0   200   400m
0   200   400yd

MAP 6 TIMES SQUARE & THEATER DISTRICT

W 58th St — 1 2
W 57th St — 3 4 — 57 St — 5 — 57 St

Broadway

Carnegie Hall

W 56th St — 7 — W 56th St — 6 — 12

Ninth Ave
Eighth Ave
Seventh Ave
Sixth Ave (Avenue of the Americas)

8 — W 55th St — 57 St — 11 — W 55th St — 13

10 — 14

9 — W 54th St — W 54th St — 19

15 17
16 18 — 7 Ave

50 St

23 — W 53rd St — W 53rd St
24 — 21 — 20

22 — W 52nd St — W 52nd St
26 — 27 28
29

25 — W 51st St — 33 — 50 St — 30 — W 51st St

47-50 Sts-Rockefeller Center

Radio City Music Hall

Worldwide Plaza

32 — 31

W 50th St — 50 St — W 50th St

38 39
Rockefeller Center

36
34 35 37 — 49 St

43 42 — W 49th St — 50 St — W 49th St
44
41 — 47-50 Sts-Rockefeller Center

45 — W 48th St — 46 — 48 — 40 — W 48th St — 49 50

47 — 49 St — W 47th St

61 — 59 — 54 — 52
57 56
62 — 55
65 — 60 — 58 — 53 — 51
64 — 63
W 46th St
66 — 69 — 70 71 — 75 — 76 — 79
67 — 77
68 — 72 — 78 — W 45th St — 80 — 81
W 45th St
95 — 93 89 — 85 — 84
94 — 91 90
96 — 92 — 88 — 87 — 83 — 82
97 — 86
98 — 99 — W 44th St — 107

100 — 101 — 104
102 — 105 106
W 43rd St — 103 — W 43rd St
114 — 113
112 — 111 110
W 42nd St — 108 — W 42nd St — 5 Ave
115 — 109 — Times Sq-42 St
116 117 118 — 42 St — Bryant Park

Port Authority Bus Terminal — W 41st St — 119 — W 41st St — 120

Times Sq-42 St
W 40th St — W 40th St

121 — W 39th St — W 39th St

124 — 122
123

MAP 6 TIMES SQUARE

PLACES TO STAY
1 Westpark Hotel
5 Salisbury Hotel
14 Warwick
15 Ameritania Hotel
29 Novotel
44 Days Hotel Midtown
52 Portland Square Hotel
55 Doubletree Guest Suites
57 W New York – Times Square;
   UnderBar
59 Hotel Edison
60 Paramount
72 Broadway Inn
77 Marriott Marquis
81 Big Apple Hostel
82 Algonquin
94 Milford Plaza
102 Casablanca Hotel
107 Royalton
113 Hotel Carter

PLACES TO EAT
4 Hard Rock Cafe
7 Bricco
8 Soup Kitchen International
10 Carnegie Deli
13 Pan Bagnat
18 Stage Deli
23 Mee Noodle Shop
25 Island Burgers & Shakes
37 Ruby Foo's
63 Barbetta
64 Hourglass Tavern
65 Basilica
66 Zen Palate
68 Bali Nusa Indah
69 Joshua Tree
70 Joe Allen
71 Orso
122 Cupcake Cafe
123 Jam's Jamaican
124 Guido's

THEATERS
16 Ed Sullivan Theatre
21 Broadway

22 Virginia
27 Neil Simon
31 Winter Garden Theater
32 Circle in the Square
33 Gershwin
34 Ambassador
41 Walter Kerr
42 Eugene O'Neill
46 Longacre
47 Ethel Barrymore
50 Cort
54 Palace
58 Lunt-Fontanne
61 Brooks Atkinson
73 Imperial
74 Music Box
75 Richard Rodgers
76 Marquis
80 Lyceum
83 Belasco
84 Criterion Center Stage Right
86 Minskoff
87 Shubert
88 Broadhurst
89 Booth
90 Plymouth
91 Royale
92 Majestic Theater
93 John Golden
95 Martin Beck
98 St James
99 Helen Hayes
110 Ford Center Theater
111 New Victory Theater
114 Todo Con Nada Show World
118 New Amsterdam Theater
119 Nederlander

OTHER
2 Gateway Computers
3 Duane Reade
6 Mysterious Bookshop
9 Gray Line Tours
11 City Center
12 Air France
17 Gold's Gym
19 Belgian Consulate

20 NYC & Company Information
   Center; New York State
   Travel Information Center
24 Manhattan Bicycle
26 Post Office
28 Float
30 Iridium
35 Colony
36 Caroline's on Broadway
38 Canadian Consulate
39 Netherlands Consulate
40 Sam Ash Music
43 CyberCafé
45 NY Sightseeing Information
   Center; Internet
48 Thomas Cook
49 Manny's Music
51 Brazilian Consulate
53 Times Square Visitors
   Center
56 TKTS Booth
62 McHale's Bar & Cafe
67 Mercury Bar
78 Sephora
79 Virgin Megastore
85 MTV Studios
96 Film Center Cafe
97 Rudy's Bar & Grill
100 Police
101 Times Square Studios
103 Town Hall
104 American Express
105 International Center of
   Photography
106 Hagstrom Map & Travel
   Centre
108 Warner Bros Studio
   Store
109 One Times Square
112 Loews 42nd St–E Walk
   Theater
115 Post Office
116 easyEverything
117 Madame Tussaud's Wax
   Museum
120 Staples
121 Drama Bookshop

Don't try this trick yourselves folks – driving that is! Taxicabs are the only way to travel on Broadway

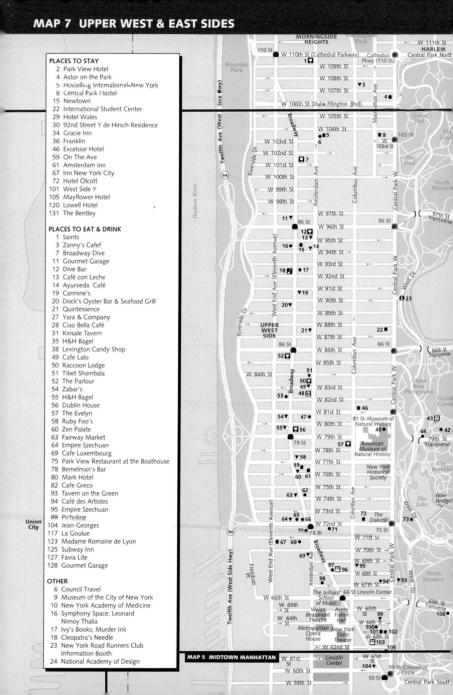

MAP 7 UPPER WEST & EAST SIDES

MAP 7 UPPER WEST & EAST SIDES

OTHER cont...

25 New York Road Runners' Club
26 Cooper-Hewitt National Design Museum
32 East River Express Ferry Terminal
33 Gracie Mansion
37 HMV
39 Czech Center
40 Ancient Playground
41 Goethe Institute
42 Belvedere Castle
43 Delacorte Theater
44 Swedishe Cottage
45 Rose Center for Earth & Space
47 NYCD
48 Children's Museum of Manhattan
53 Barnes & Noble
62 Beacon Theater
66 Gryphon Records
66 Urban Outfitters
68 Septuagesimo Uno
70 Applause Books
71 Blades West
73 Strawberry Fields
74 Bethesda Terrace
76 French Consulate
77 Bang & Olufsen
79 Vera Wang
81 Missoni Boutique
83 Sotheby's
85 Shakespeare & Co
85 Italian Cultural Institute
86 Asia Society
87 Polo/Ralph Lauren
88 Prada
89 Cartier
90 Frick Collection
91 Central Park Summerstage; Rumsey Playfield
92 Bandshell
96 Sony Theaters Lincoln Square
97 Civilized Traveler
98 Merkin Concert Hall
100 Frederick Henry Cossitt Dormitory
102 McBurney School
103 Lincoln Plaza Cinemas
106 Carousel
107 Columbus Statue
108 Dairy
109 Visitor Information
110 Central Park Wildlife Center
111 Tisch Children's Zoo
112 Temple Emanu-El
113 Giorgio Armani
114 Park Ave Armory
115 Civilized Traveler
116 Valentino
118 Givenchy
119 Waterford-Wedgwood Store
121 Horse-drawn Carriages
122 Sherry-Lehman
124 Bloomingdale's
126 Roosevelt Island Tramway Station
129 Chicago City Limits
130 Mount Vernon Hotel Museum & Garden
132 Roosevelt Island Tramway Station

MAP 8 HARLEM

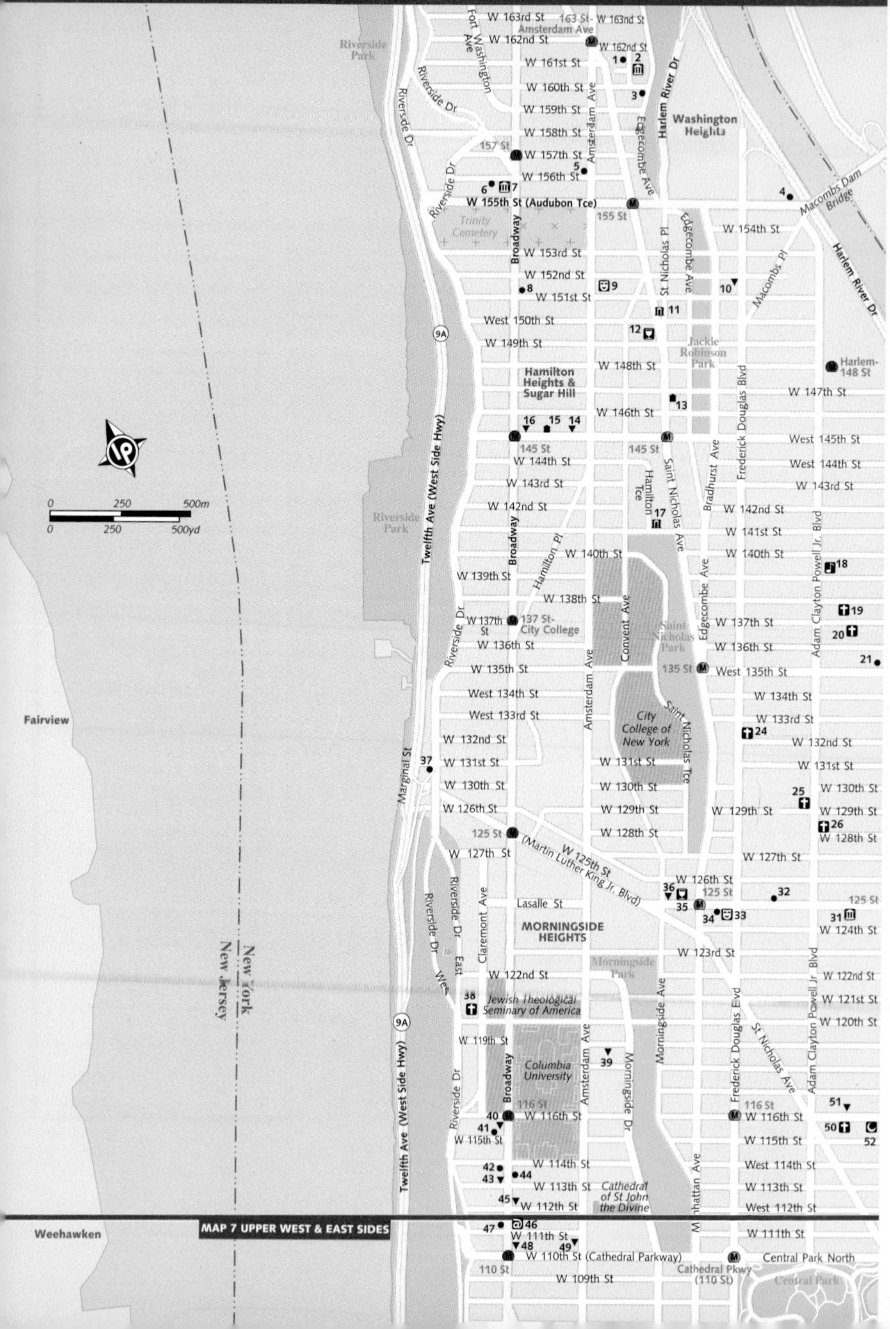

Riverside
Park

W 163rd St
W 162nd St
Amsterdam Ave
W 162nd St
W 161st St   1   2
Fort Washington Ave
W 160th St
W 159th St   3
W 158th St   Washington
Heights
157 St   W 157th St
Riverside Dr   W 156th St
6   7   W 155th St (Audubon Tce)   4
Macombs Dam Bridge

Harlem River Dr
Edgecombe Ave

Trinity Cemetery
W 153rd St   155 St
W 152nd St   St Nicholas Pl   W 154th St
8   W 151st St   9   10   Macombs Pl
West 150th St   12   11
W 149th St   Jackie Robinson Park
Hamilton Heights & Sugar Hill   W 148th St   Harlem-148 St
W 147th St
W 146th St   13
16   15   14   West 145th St
145 St   145 St   West 144th St
W 144th St   W 143rd St
W 143rd St   Saint Nicholas Ave   Bradhurst Ave   Frederick Douglas Blvd
Hamilton Tce
W 142nd St
17   W 141st St
W 140th St   W 140th St
W 139th St   Edgecombe Ave   Adam Clayton Powell Jr. Blvd   18
W 138th St   Saint Nicholas Park   W 137th St   19
137 St-City College   W 137th St   20
W 136th St   W 136th St   21
W 135th St   135 St   W 135th St
West 134th St   W 134th St
West 133rd St   City College of New York   W 133rd St
132nd St   24
W 131st St   W 131st St
W 130th St   25   W 130th St
W 129th St   W 129th St   26
W 128th St   W 128th St
W 127th St   W 127th St
125 St   W 125th St (Martin Luther King Jr. Blvd)   32   125 St
36   W 126th St   31
Lasalle St   35   125 St   33   34
MORNINGSIDE HEIGHTS   W 124th St
W 123rd St
W 122nd St   Morningside Park   W 122nd St
38   Jewish Theological Seminary of America   W 121st St
39   W 120th St
W 119th St   Columbia University   116 St   W 116th St
116 St   51
40   W 116th St   50
41   W 115th St   W 115th St   52
42   44   West 114th St
43   W 113th St   West 113th St
45   Cathedral of St John the Divine   West 112th St
47   46   W 111th St   W 111th St
48   49   W 110th St (Cathedral Parkway)   Central Park North
110 St   Cathedral Pkwy (110 St)   Central Park
W 109th St

Fairview

New Jersey   New York

Weehawken

MAP 7 UPPER WEST & EAST SIDES

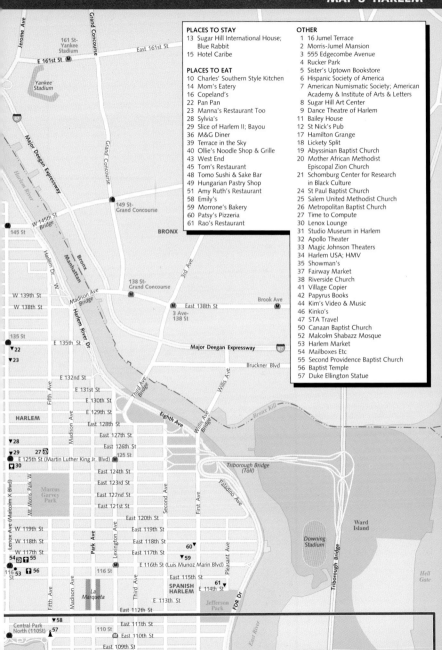

MAP 8 HARLEM

PLACES TO STAY
13 Sugar Hill International House;
   Blue Rabbit
15 Hotel Caribe

PLACES TO EAT
10 Charles' Southern Style Kitchen
14 Mom's Eatery
16 Copeland's
22 Pan Pan
23 Manna's Restaurant Too
28 Sylvia's
29 Slice of Harlem II; Bayou
36 M&G Diner
39 Terrace in the Sky
40 Ollie's Noodle Shop & Grille
43 West End
45 Tom's Restaurant
48 Tomo Sushi & Sake Bar
49 Hungarian Pastry Shop
51 Amy Ruth's Restaurant
58 Emily's
59 Morrone's Bakery
60 Patsy's Pizzeria
61 Rao's Restaurant

OTHER
1 16 Jumel Terrace
2 Morris-Jumel Mansion
3 555 Edgecombe Avenue
4 Rucker Park
5 Sister's Uptown Bookstore
6 Hispanic Society of America
7 American Numismatic Society; American
   Academy & Institute of Arts & Letters
8 Sugar Hill Art Center
9 Dance Theatre of Harlem
11 Bailey House
12 St Nick's Pub
17 Hamilton Grange
18 Lickety Split
19 Abyssinian Baptist Church
20 Mother African Methodist
   Episcopal Zion Church
21 Schomburg Center for Research
   in Black Culture
24 St Paul Baptist Church
25 Salem United Methodist Church
26 Metropolitan Baptist Church
27 Time to Compute
30 Lenox Lounge
31 Studio Museum in Harlem
32 Apollo Theater
33 Magic Johnson Theaters
34 Harlem USA; HMV
35 Showman's
37 Fairway Market
38 Riverside Church
41 Village Copier
42 Papyrus Books
46 Kim's Video & Music
47 STA Travel
50 Canaan Baptist Church
52 Malcolm Shabazz Mosque
53 Harlem Market
54 Mailboxes Etc
55 Second Providence Baptist Church
56 Baptist Temple
57 Duke Ellington Statue

MAP 9 BROOKLYN HEIGHTS & SURROUNDING NEIGHBORHOODS

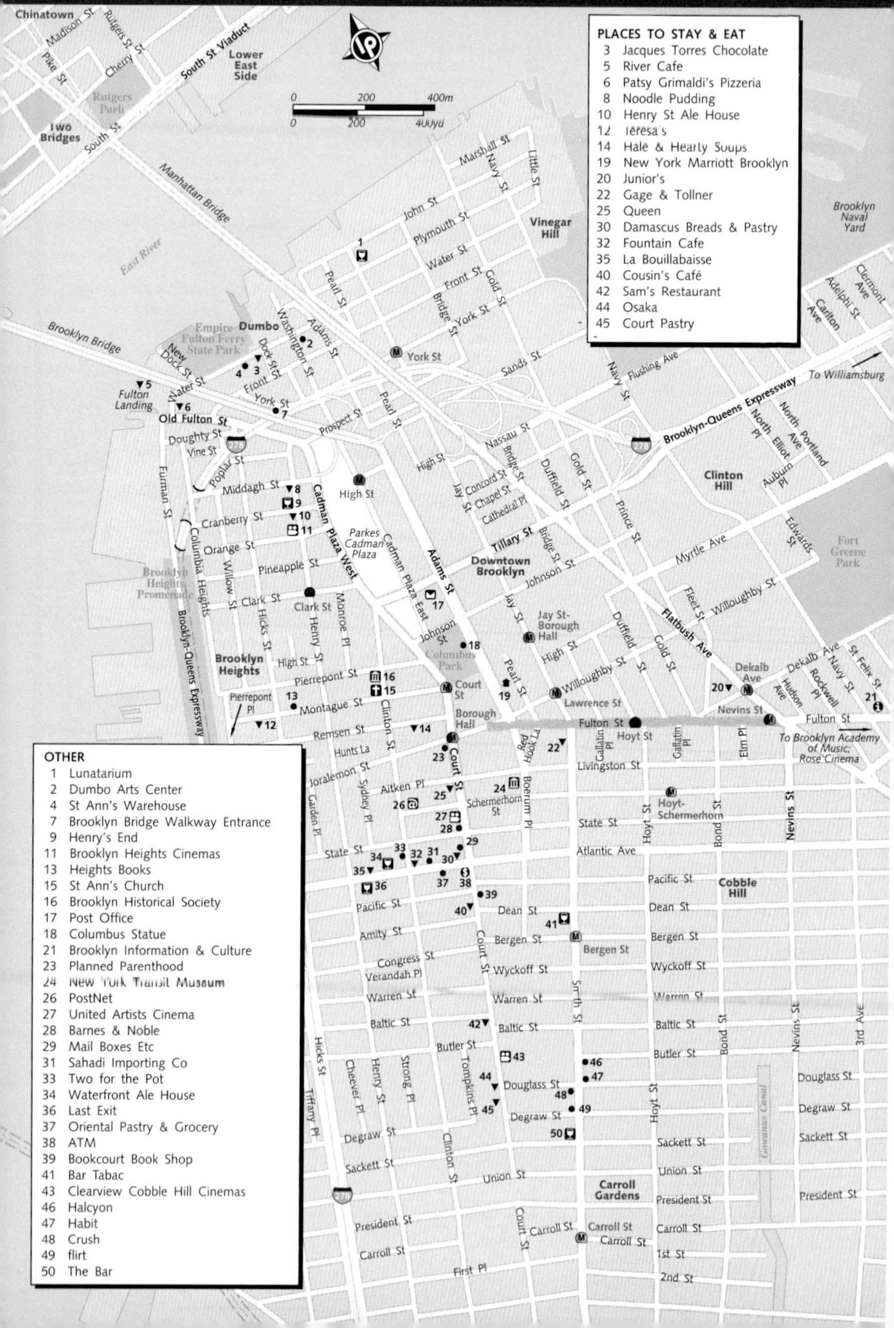

PLACES TO STAY & EAT

3 Jacques Torres Chocolate
5 River Cafe
7 Patsy Grimaldi's Pizzeria
8 Noodle Pudding
10 Henry St Ale House
12 Teresa's
14 Hale & Hearty Soups
19 New York Marriott Brooklyn
20 Junior's
22 Gage & Tollner
25 Queen
30 Damascus Breads & Pastry
32 Fountain Cafe
35 La Bouillabaisse
40 Cousin's Café
42 Sam's Restaurant
44 Osaka
45 Court Pastry

OTHER

1 Lunatarium
2 Dumbo Arts Center
4 St Ann's Warehouse
7 Brooklyn Bridge Walkway Entrance
9 Henry's End
11 Brooklyn Heights Cinemas
13 Heights Books
15 St Ann's Church
16 Brooklyn Historical Society
17 Post Office
18 Columbus Statue
21 Brooklyn Information & Culture
23 Planned Parenthood
24 New York Transit Museum
26 PostNet
27 United Artists Cinema
28 Barnes & Noble
29 Mail Boxes Etc
31 Sahadi Importing Co
33 Two for the Pot
34 Waterfront Ale House
36 Last Exit
37 Oriental Pastry & Grocery
38 ATM
39 Bookcourt Book Shop
41 Bar Tabac
43 Clearview Cobble Hill Cinemas
46 Halcyon
47 Habit
48 Crush
49 flirt
50 The Bar

MAP 10 PROSPECT PARK & SURROUNDING NEIGHBORHOODS

Cobble Hill

Clinton Hill

Carroll Gardens

Gowanus

Park Slope

Prospect Heights

Grand Army Plaza

Eastern Pkwy-Brooklyn Museum

Brooklyn Botanic Garden

Prospect Park

To Brooklyn Children's Museum

Eastern Parkway

Greenwood Cemetery

Windsor Terrace

Prospect Lake

Prospect Lefferts Gardens

Smith St, Baltic St, Butler St, Douglass St, Degraw St, Sackett St, Hoyt St, 1st St, 2nd St, Atlantic Ave, State St, Pacific St, Dean St, Bergen St, Wyckoff St, Warren St, Nevins St, Douglass St, Degraw St, Sackett St, Union St, President St, Carroll St, 3rd Ave, Union St, Third Ave, Fifth Ave, Fourth Ave, Garfield Pl, 2nd St, 3rd St, 4th St, 5th St, 6th St, 7th St, 8th St, 9th St, 10th St, 11th St, 12th St, 13th St, 14th St, 15th St, 16th St, 17th St, 18th St, 20th St, 21st St, 22nd St, 23rd St

Hanson Pl, Fort Greene Pl, South Elliot Pl, South Portland Ave, South Oxford St, Cumberland St, Carlton Ave, Adelphi St, Clermont Ave, Vanderbilt Ave, Clinton Ave, Waverly Ave, Washington Ave, St James Pl, Cambridge Pl, Grand Ave, Downing St, Irving Pl, Gates Ave, Munroe St, Madison St, Putnam Ave, Fulton St, Lefferts Pl, Atlantic Ave, Pacific St, Dean St, Bergen St, St Marks Ave, Prospect Pl, Park Pl, Sterling Pl, St Johns Pl, Grand Ave, Classon Ave, Franklin Ave, Lincoln Pl, Union St, President St, Carroll St, Crown St, Montgomery St, McKeever Pl, Empire Blvd, Sterling St, Lefferts Ave, Lincoln Rd, Maple St, Midwood St, Rutland Rd, Fenimore St, Hawthorne St, Parkside Ave, Caton Ave, Linden Blvd

Bergen St, St Marks Pl, Park Pl, 7 Ave, Sterling Pl, St Johns Pl, Lincoln Pl, Berkeley Pl, Union St, President St, Carroll St, Flatbush Ave, Plaza St West, Plaza St East, Eastern Parkway, Prospect Park, East Dr, Central Dr, West Dr, Prospect Park Southwest, Prospect Park West, Windsor Pl, Sherman St, Fuller Pl, Howard Pl, Terrace Pl, 16th St, Prospect Ave, Eighth Ave, Seventh Ave, 5th Ave-6th St, 4 Ave-9 St, Prospect Ave, Prospect Parkway, Webster Pl, Jackson Pl

South Lake Dr, East 7th St, Parkside Ave, Parade Pl, Crooke Ave, Woodruff Ave, Ocean Ave, Flatbush Ave, Coney Island Ave, Westminster Rd, Argyle Rd, Rugby Rd, Marlborough Rd, Stratford Rd, Buckingham Rd, E 17th St, E 18th St, E 19th St, E 21st St, Church Ave

Prospect Park, 15 St-Prospect Park, Prospect Park, Parkside Ave

PLACES TO STAY & EAT
2 Tom's Restaurant
4 Farmer's Market
8 Lemongrass Grill
9 Ozzie's
12 Chip Shop
13 Lopez Bakery
14 Park Slope Brewing Co
15 Two Boots Brooklyn
17 Back to the Land
21 Bed & Breakfast on the Park
23 Dizzy's
24 Tea Lounge

6 JFK Memorial
7 Hooti Couture
10 Great Lakes
11 Excelsior
16 Microchip Cafe
18 Community Bookstore
19 Brooklyn Museum of Art
20 Dongan Oak Monument
25 Grand Prospect Hall
26 Computer Café
27 Zoo
28 Lefferts Homestead Children's Historic House Museum
29 Kate Wollman Rink

OTHER
1 Freddy's
3 Brooklyn Public Library
5 Soldiers' & Sailors' Monument

0 250 500m
0 250 500yd

MAP 11 ASTORIA & SURROUNDING NEIGHBORHOODS

PLACES TO EAT
2 Angelo's Food Emporium
4 Zygo's Taverna
6 Elias Corner
9 Broadway Natural
10 Omonia Cafe
11 Kolonaki
12 Uncle George's
21 Court Square Diner

OTHER
1 Nyxterides
3 Cyber Station Café
5 Post Office
7 Lighthouse
8 Socrates Sculpture Park
13 Book Value Booksellers
14 Cafe Bar
15 Kaufman Astoria Studios
16 American Museum of the Moving Image
17 United Artist Cinema
18 Isamu Noguchi Garden Museum
19 MoMA QNS
20 NY State Supreme Court
22 PS 1 Contemporary Art Center
23 Post Office

MAP 12 FLUSHING

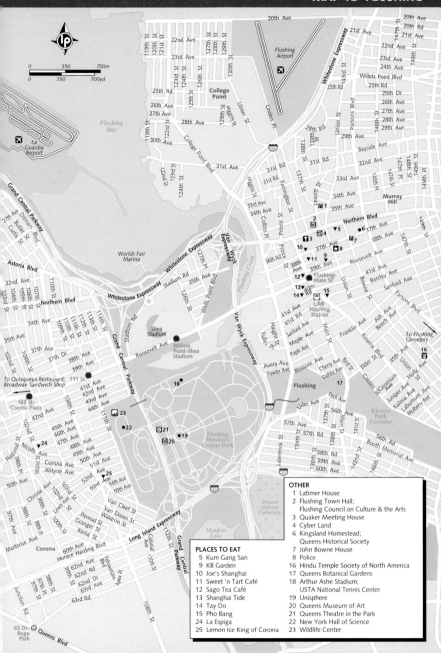

OTHER
1 Latimer House
2 Flushing Town Hall;
   Flushing Council on Culture & the Arts
3 Quaker Meeting House
4 Cyber Land
6 Kingsland Homestead;
   Queens Historical Society
7 John Bowne House
8 Police
16 Hindu Temple Society of North America
17 Queens Botanical Gardens
18 Arthur Ashe Stadium;
   USTA National Tennis Center
19 Unisphere
20 Queens Museum of Art
21 Queens Theatre in the Park
22 New York Hall of Science
23 Wildlife Center

PLACES TO EAT
5 Kum Gang San
9 KB Garden
10 Joe's Shanghai
11 Sweet 'n Tart Café
12 Sago Tea Café
13 Shanghai Tide
14 Tay Do
15 Pho Bang
24 La Espiga
25 Lemon Ice King of Corona

MAP 13 THE BRONX

New Jersey
New York

Hudson River

Riverside Park

Inwood Hill Park

Henry Hudson Parkway

Henry Hudson Bridge

Van Cortlandt Park

231 St

Woodlawn

Mosholu Parkway

Broadway

Marble Hill-225 St

W Gun Hill Rd

Mosholu Pkwy

Gun Hill Rd

Jerome Ave

Bedford Park Blvd-Lehman College

Norwood-205 St

Burke Ave

White Plains Rd

W 218th Ave

Isham Park

Tenth Ave

215 St

Bedford Park Blvd

Allerton Ave

Payson Ave
Seaman Ave
Cooper St

Inwood-207 St

Dyckman St

2 ▥

Grand Concourse

Jerome Ave

Kingsbridge Rd

W 194th St

Kingsbridge Rd

Dr The O

•3

Dr Theodore Kazimiroff Blvd

Sherman Ave

207 St

Ninth Ave

Tenth Ave

W 203rd Ave

Dyckman St

Fordham Rd

W Fordham Rd

E Fordham Rd

Fordham University

4 ✿

Bronx Park

•1

Elwood St

Hillside Ave

190 St

Bennet Ave
Broadway

191 St

Harlem River Dr

High Bridge Park

•15

183 St

Burnside Ave

Dr Martin Luther King Junior Blvd

182-183 Sts

3rd Ave
189th St
186th St
187th
Arthur

14
13
▼12
▼11

Pelham Pkwy

Bronx Park East

Washington Heights

W 184th St

181 St

★16)

181 St

Edward L Grant Highway

Jerome Ave

176 St

Tremont Ave

E Tremont Ave

Southern Blvd

Boston Rd

10 ▥

Bronx Park South

E 180 St

Bronx River Parkway

White Plains Rd

W 177th St

175 St

W 171st St

Washington Bridge

Washington Heights

176th Ave

Cross Bronx Expressway

174-175 Sts

Mt Eden Ave

Crotona Ave

Crotona Parkway

Bronx Park South

West Farms Sq-E Tremont St

174 St

168 St-Washington Heights

Fort Washington Ave

High Bridge Park

170 St

170 St

BRONX

Louis Nine Blvd

St Lawrence Ave

163 St

W 163rd St

Amsterdam Ave

Amsterdam Ave

E 167th St

167 St

167 St

Morrison-Sound Views Avs

Westchester Ave

157 St

Edgecombe Ave

Jerome Ave

Freeman St

Sheridan Expressway

Elder Ave

155 St

Sugar Hill & Hamilton Heights

Grand Concourse

17 ▥

Intervale Ave

Simpson St

Whitlock Ave

145 St-148 St

Bradhurst Ave
Frederick Douglass Blvd

Macombs Pl

Boston Rd

Hunts Point Ave

145 St

Harlem-148 St

•18

161 St-Yankee Stadium

E 161st St

Prospect Ave

Hunts Point Ave

Hunts Point Produce Market

Bronx River

W 144th St

MANHATTAN

3 Ave-149 St

Jackson Ave

Longwood Ave

W 133rd St

W 135th St

135 St

Madison Avenue Bridge

149 St-Grand Concourse

3Ave-149 St

Westchester Ave

Grand Concourse

Prospect Ave

Southern Blvd

Bruckner Elevated Expressway

Hunts Point Ave

Edgewater Halleck St

Food Center Dr

HARLEM

138 St-Grand Concourse

3 Ave-138 St

E 149th St

E 143 St-St Mary's St

E 149 St

Hunts Point

Food Center

Third Avenue Bridge

E 138th St

Brook Ave

Randall Ave

Hunts Point Meat Market

125 St

St 124th St

Marcus Garvey Park

Madison Ave

Park Ave

125 St

Willis Ave

Bruckner Blvd

Cypress Ave

North Brother Island

Food Center Dr

Major Deegan Expressway

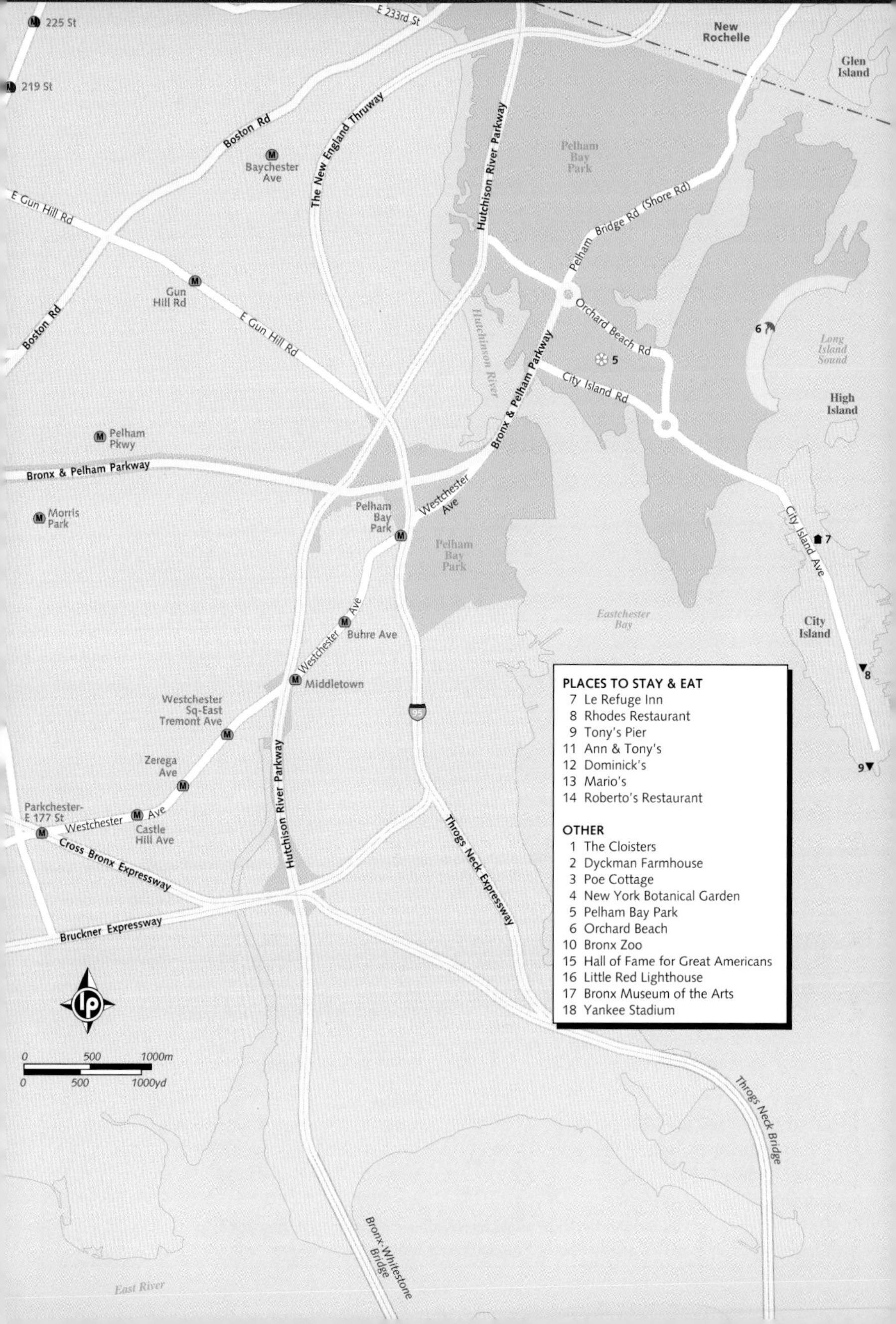

MAP 13 THE BRONX

225 St
219 St

Boston Rd
Baychester
Ave
The New England Thruway

E 233rd St

New
Rochelle

Glen
Island

E Gun Hill Rd
Boston Rd

Gun
Hill Rd
E Gun Hill Rd

Hutchison River Parkway

Pelham
Bay
Park

Pelham Bridge Rd (Shore Rd)

Hutchinson River

Orchard Beach Rd

City Island Rd

Long
Island
Sound

High
Island

Bronx & Pelham Parkway

Pelham
Pkwy

Morris
Park

Bronx & Pelham Parkway

Pelham
Bay
Park

Westchester
Ave

Pelham
Bay
Park

City Island Ave

City
Island

Eastchester
Bay

Westchester
Ave
Buhre Ave

Middletown

Westchester
Sq-East
Tremont Ave

Zerega
Ave

Parkchester-
E 177 St
Westchester Ave
Castle
Hill Ave
Cross Bronx Expressway

Hutchison River Parkway

Throgs Neck Expressway

Bruckner Expressway

PLACES TO STAY & EAT
7 Le Refuge Inn
8 Rhodes Restaurant
9 Tony's Pier
11 Ann & Tony's
12 Dominick's
13 Mario's
14 Roberto's Restaurant

OTHER
1 The Cloisters
2 Dyckman Farmhouse
3 Poe Cottage
4 New York Botanical Garden
5 Pelham Bay Park
6 Orchard Beach
10 Bronx Zoo
15 Hall of Fame for Great Americans
16 Little Red Lighthouse
17 Bronx Museum of the Arts
18 Yankee Stadium

0   500   1000m
0   500   1000yd

Throgs Neck Bridge

Bronx Whitestone Bridge

East River

MAP LEGEND

CITY ROUTES

Freeway	Freeway		On/Off Ramp
Highway	Primary Road		One Way Street
Road	Secondary Road		Pedestrian Street
Street	Street	)===	Tunnel
Lane	Lane	••••••••	Walking Tour

REGIONAL ROUTES

	Tollway, Freeway
	Primary Road
	Secondary Road
	Minor Road

SUBWAY LINES

●	Lines 1, 2, 3
Ⓜ	Lines A, C, E
Ⓜ	Lines N, Q, R, W
Ⓜ	Lines B, D, F, V
Ⓜ	Lines 4, 5, 6
Ⓜ	Lines J, M, Z
Ⓜ	Line L
●	Line 7
Ⓜ	Line G
Ⓢ	42nd St Shuttle

(see Subway map for specific line information)

HYDROGRAPHY

	River, Creek
	Canal
	Lake

BOUNDARIES

—·—·—	International
—·—··—	State
—··—··—	County

ROUTES & STATIONS

•••O••	Train
ooooooox	Underground Train
-- Ⓜ	Metro Station
----🚢	Ferry
	Path

AREA FEATURES

	Building	❄	Park, Gardens
	Cemetery		Plaza
	Market		University Campus

ROUTE SHIELDS

495	Interstate Freeway	25	New York State Highway
1	US Highway	46	County Road

POPULATION SYMBOLS

✪ CAPITAL	National Capital	● CITY	City	• Village	Village		
◉ CAPITAL	State Capital	● Town	Town		Urban Area		

MAP SYMBOLS

■	Place to Stay	▼	Place to Eat	●	Point of Interest		
⌧	Airport	⌨	Embassy, Consulate	▲	Mountain	⚓	Shipwreck
⊖	Bank	⚓	Fountain	⛩	Museum, Gallery	⛫	Stately Home
◩	Baseball Diamond	⊕	Hospital		National Park	⛩	Temple, Mahayana
↗	Beach	❶	Information		Parking	⊟	Theatre
⊟ ⊟	Bus Stop/Station	⊡	Internet Café	✚	Police Station	⊙	Toilet
⊟	Cathedral/Church	⚲	Lighthouse		Pool	⊟	Transport
⊞	Cinema	▲	Monument	◰	Post Office	⊞	Winery
⊟	Club	☾	Mosque	⊟	Pub, Bar	⊟	Zoo

Note: not all symbols displayed above appear in this book

LONELY PLANET OFFICES

Australia
Locked Bag 1, Footscray, Victoria 3011
☎ 03 8379 8000 fax 03 8379 8111
email: talk2us@lonelyplanet.com.au

USA
150 Linden St, Oakland, CA 94607
☎ 510 893 8555 TOLL FREE: 800 275 8555
fax 510 893 8572
email: info@lonelyplanet.com

UK
10a Spring Place, London NW5 3BH
☎ 020 7428 4800 fax 020 7428 4828
email: go@lonelyplanet.co.uk

France
1 rue du Dahomey, 75011 Paris
☎ 01 55 25 33 00 fax 01 55 25 33 01
email: bip@lonelyplanet.fr
www.lonelyplanet.fr

World Wide Web: www.lonelyplanet.com *or* AOL keyword: lp
Lonely Planet Images: www.lonelyplanetimages.com

Feel like a quick snack? Pushcart vendors are a NY specialty

Mobile art, a graffiti covered truck in SoHo

The Empire State Building dominates the skyline

The Brooklyn Bridge at night is a mesmerising sight with its thousands of lights

MAP 14 MANHATTAN BUS MAP

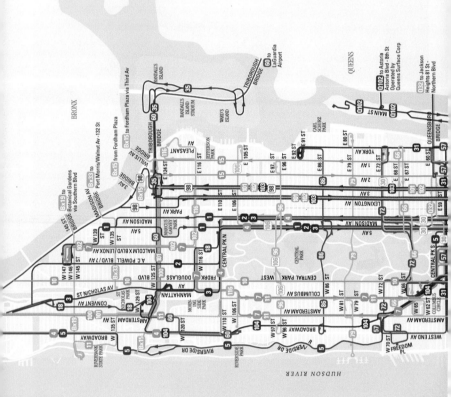

MAP 14 MANHATTAN BUS MAP

MTA New York City Transit

Manhattan Bus Map

December 2001

©2001 Metropolitan Transportation Authority Unauthorized duplication prohibited   12/5/01

Please check our website
www.mta.info often for latest
service changes.

MAP 15   MANHATTAN SUBWAY

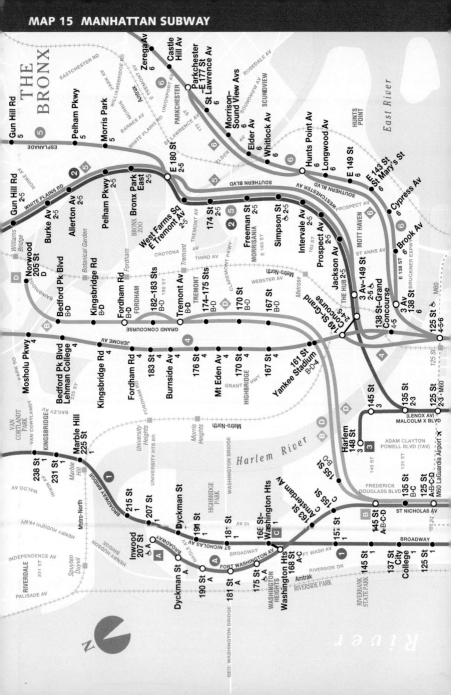

MAP 15 MANHATTAN SUBWAY

Lorimer St

L

Metropolitan Av
G

J M Z

Marcy Av
J M Z

WILLIAMSBURG

KENT AV

FLUSHING AV

FORT GREENE

Lawrence St
M·N·R

FLATBUSH AV

BERGEN AV

UNION ST

G

Smith 9 Sts
F·G

SMITH

Jay St
A·C·F

Borough Hall
M·N·R

Hoyt St
1·2

BERGEN ST

CARROLL ST

Carroll St
F·G

CARROLL
GARDENS

Bedford Av
L

N 7 ST

Court St
M·N

Borough Hall
2·3·4·5

NEW YORK
TRANSIT MUSEUM

HENRY ST

RED
HOOK

L

York St
F

NAVY
YARD

Clark St
1·2

HICKS ST

COLUMBIA ST

4·5

BROOKLYN
HEIGHTS

Fulton St
A·C

High St
A·C

FULTON ST

BROOKLYN
LANDING

Metropolitan Av

1 Avenue

3 Avenue

EAST
VILLAGE

EAST
RIVER
PARK

LOWER
EAST
SIDE

DELANCEY ST

MANHATTAN BRIDGE

Q Q W

BROOKLYN BRIDGE

A C

N R

AV D

AV C

AV B

1 AV

2 AV

AV A

East
Broadway
F·J·M·Z

RUTGERS ST

MADISON ST

SOUTH ST

1 2

M N R

WATER ST

BROOKLYN-BATTERY TUNNEL

Coast Guard Only

Delancey St
F·J·M·Z

Lower East Side
2 Avenue
F·V

Astor Pl
6

Bleecker St
6

Bowery
J·M

Grand St
B·D

Spring St
6

Canal St
J·M·N·Q

Chambers St
J·M·Z

LITTLE ITALY

CHINATOWN

J

Brooklyn Bridge–
City Hall
4·5·6

Fulton St–
Broadway Nassau
A·C·J·M·Z·2·3·4·5

Wall St
2·3

Broad St
J·M·Z

PEARL ST

8 St
NYU
N·R

W 4 St
A·C·E·F·V·S

Prince St
N·R

S

SOHO

NOHO

Canal St
A·C·E

City Hall
R·W

Chambers St
A·C

Park
Place
2·3

Wall St
4·5

Rector St
N·R

Z

Whitehall St
N·R

Broadway
City Hall

GRAND ST

BLEECKER ST

FINANCIAL
DISTRICT

NASSAU ST

LAFAYETTE ST

BOWERY

AV S

AV S·Un...
N·L·Q·R·W

SIXTH AV

23 St
F·V

14 St
F·V

18 St
1·2

14 St
1·2·3

14 St
N·R

Spring St
C·E

Canal St
1·2

Franklin St
1·2

Chambers St
1·2

World Trade
Center
E

Cortlandt St

Rector St
1

South Ferry
1

Bowling
Green
4·5

BATTERY
PARK CITY

Temporarily closed
after Sep 11, 2001

CHELSEA

14 St
1·2·3

W 4 St
F·V

8 AV

A·C·E

L

Christopher St
Sheridan Sq
1·2

PATH

GREENWICH
VILLAGE

Houston St
1·2

Canal St
1·2

TRIBECA

WORLD
TRADE
CENTER

BATTERY
PARK CITY

WEST ST

GREENWICH AV

GREENWICH ST

BLEECKER ST

BANK ST

WEST ST

CHARLTON ST

HOUSTON ST

SPRING ST

CANAL ST

VARICK ST

CHURCH ST

TRINITY PL

CORTLANDT ST

Christopher St

PATH

HOLLAND TUNNEL

PATH

Weehawken Ferry

South Ferry

Ferry

Staten
Island

MTA Metropolitan Transportation Authority

Key

Nights and
weekends
only

Local service only

All trains stop
(local and express service)

Station served by
one of two lines

Free subway transfer

Free out-of-system subway
transfer (MetroCard only)

Normal service

Special rush hour or
express service

Part time
service

Full time
service

with bus, railroad, and ferry connections

Key

Local service only

All trains stop (local or express service)

Station served by one of two lines

Free subway transfer

Free out-of-system subway transfer (MetroCard only)

Normal service

Part time service

Full time service

Special time hour or express service

Commuter rail

Nights and weekends only

Terminal

MTA New York City Transit
Subway in four boroughs, bus in five boroughs, and the MTA Staten Island Railway

The subway operates 24 hours a day, seven days a week, but not all lines operate at all times. For detailed information, consult Passenger Information Center (24 hours) at call 718-330-1234 (non-English speaking customers call 718-330-4847 (7AM to 7PM).

visit www.mta.info

© 2002 Metropolitan Transportation Authority
Design: Michael Hertz Associates, NYC

January 2002

QUEENS

MANHATTAN

Hudson River

East River

Harlem River

© 2002 Metropolitan Transportation Authority
Design: Michael Hertz Associates, NYC

January 2002

MAP 16 NEW YORK CITY SUBWAY

BROOKLYN

STATEN ISLAND